Microsoft® Windows
Security Fundamentals

Computer Security and Computer Forensic Related Book Titles:

Rittinghouse & Hancock, *Cybersecurity Operations Handbook*,
ISBN 1-55558-306-7, 1336pp, 2003.

Rittinghouse & Ransome, *Instant Messaging Security*, ISBN 1-55558-338-5, 432pp, 2005.

Rittinghouse, *Wireless Operational Security*, ISBN 1-55558-317-2, 496pp, 2004.

Ransome & Rittinghouse, *VoIP Security*, ISBN 1-55558-332-6, 450pp, 2005.

De Clercq, *Windows Server 2003 Security Infrastructures: Core Security Features*,
ISBN 1-55558-283-4, 752pp, 2004.

Erbschloe, *Implementing Homeland Security for Enterprise IT*,
ISBN 1-55558-312-1, 320pp, 2003.

Erbschloe, *Physical Security for IT*, ISBN 1-55558-327-X, 320pp, 2005.

Speed & Ellis, *Internet Security*, ISBN 1-55558-298-2, 398pp, 2003.

XYPRO, *HP NonStop Server Security*, ISBN 1-55558-314-8, 618pp, 2003.

Casey, *Handbook of Computer Crime Investigation*, ISBN 0-12-163103-6, 448pp, 2002.

Kovacich, *The Information Systems Security Officer's Guide*,
ISBN 0-7506-7656-6, 361pp, 2003.

Boyce & Jennings, *Information Assurance*, ISBN 0-7506-7327-3, 261pp, 2002.

Stefanek, *Information Security Best Practices: 205 Basic Rules*,
ISBN 0-878707-96-5, 194pp, 2002.

For more information or to order these and other Digital Press
titles, please visit our website at www.books.elsevier.com/digitalpress!
At www.books.elsevier.com/digitalpress you can:
•Join the Digital Press Email Service and have news about
our books delivered right to your desktop
•Read the latest news on titles
•Sample chapters on featured titles for free
•Question our expert authors and editors
•Download free software to accompany select texts

Microsoft® Windows Security Fundamentals

Jan De Clercq
Guido Grillenmeier

ELSEVIER
DIGITAL
PRESS

Amsterdam • Boston • Heidelberg • London • New York • Oxford
Paris • San Diego • San Francisco • Singapore • Sydney • Tokyo

Elsevier Digital Press
30 Corporate Drive, Suite 400, Burlington, MA 01803, USA
Linacre House, Jordan Hill, Oxford OX2 8DP, UK

 Recognizing the importance of preserving what has been written, Elsevier prints its books on acid-free paper whenever possible.

Library of Congress Cataloging-in-Publication Data

Application submitted.

British Library Cataloguing-in-Publication Data

A catalogue record for this book is available from the British Library.

ISBN 10: 1-55558-340-7

ISBN 13: 978-1-55558-340-8

For information on all Elsevier Digital Press publications visit our Web site at www.books.elsevier.com

Transferred to Digital Printing 2010

To my wife, Katrien, my son, Johannes, and my daughters, Elise and Heleen, for the hours I could not spend with them, and for their continuous support and loving care while I was writing this book.

—Jan De Clercq

To my wife, Sonja, my daughter, Mia, and my sons, Julian and Jonathan, for their endless love and support, and the time I could not be with them while writing this book.

—Guido Grillenmeier

Contents

Foreword by Tony Redmond   xv

Foreword by Mark Mortimore   xvii

Foreword by Steven Adler   xxi

Preface   xxiii

Acknowledgments   xxvii

Part I Introduction

1 The Challenge of Trusted Security Infrastructures   3

   1.1   Introduction   3
   1.2   Positioning Trusted Security Infrastructures   5
   1.3   The Fundamental Role of Trust   8
   1.4   Trusted Security Infrastructure Roles   8
        1.4.1 Authentication Infrastructures   9
        1.4.2 Authorization Infrastructures   11
        1.4.3 Key Management Infrastructures   15
        1.4.4 Security Management Infrastructures   18
   1.5   The Next Step: Federation   23
        1.5.1 Defining Federation   24
        1.5.2 Federation Standards   25
   1.6   Identity Management and Trusted Security Infrastructures   27
        1.6.1 Defining Identity and Identity Management   27
        1.6.2 Identity Management Infrastructure Components   29
   1.7   Microsoft and the Challenge of Trusted Security Infrastructures   31
        1.7.1 Windows Server 2003 R2 as a TSI Building Block   31
        1.7.2 Other Microsoft TSI Building Blocks   33
   1.8   Conclusion   35

2 Windows Security Authorities and Principals 37

2.1 Security Authorities 37

2.1.1 Local vs. Domain Security Authorities 38
2.1.2 The Local Security Authority 39
2.1.3 The Domain Security Authority 44

2.2 Security Principals 53

2.2.1 Principal Identifiers 54
2.2.2 Account Management 69
2.2.3 Key Windows Accounts 73
2.2.4 Password Credentials 77
2.2.5 Account Lockouts 100

3 Windows Trust Relationships 109

3.1 Defining Trust Relationships 109
3.2 Trust Properties, Types, and Features 111

3.2.1 New Trust Features 116
3.2.2 Forest Trust 118

3.3 Restricting Trusts 122

3.3.1 SID Filtering 122
3.3.2 Selective Authentication 127
3.3.3 Name Suffix Routing, and Top-Level
         Name Restrictions 132

3.4 Working with Trusts 139

3.4.1 Choosing the Correct Trust Type 139
3.4.2 Making Name Resolution Work 143
3.4.3 Creating a Trust Relationship 145
3.4.4 Assigning Permissions in a Trusted Environment 148

3.5 Trust Relationships: Under the Hood 150
3.6 Trusts and Secure Channels 154

3.6.1 Controlling Secure Channels Setup 156
3.6.2 Validating Secure Channels 156
3.6.3 Fine-Tuning Secure Channel Security Services 157
3.6.4 Trust- and Secure Channel–Related
         Management Tools 158

3.7 Trusts and Firewalls 161

4   Aspects of Windows Client Security   165

    4.1   Client Security Overview   165
    4.2   Least Privilege   166
        4.2.1   RunAs   167
        4.2.2   Fast User Switching   173
        4.2.3   Third-Party Tools   175
        4.2.4   Learn to be Least   177
    4.3   Windows XP Service Pack 2 Security Enhancements   178
        4.3.1   Windows Firewall   178
        4.3.2   Easier Security Management   183
        4.3.3   Other Important Security Changes   185
    4.4   Browser Security   186
        4.4.1   New Internet Explorer Security Functionality in
               XP Service Pack 2   187
        4.4.2   Internet Explorer Security Zones   194
    4.5   Malicious Mobile Code Protection   205
        4.5.1   Windows Defender   206
        4.5.2   Conclusion and General Spyware
               Protection Guidelines   214
    4.6   Leveraging Trusted Platform Module Security Functions 215
        4.6.1   TPM Hardware and Software Requirements   218
        4.6.2   Embedded Security for HP ProtectTools:
               Technical Implementation   219
        4.6.3   HP TPM-Enabled Applications   226
    4.7   Important Windows Vista and IE 7.0 Client Security Features   228

Part II   Authentication

5   Introducing Windows Authentication   233

    5.1   Authentication Basics   233
        5.1.1   Terminology   233
        5.1.2   Qualifying Authentication   235
    5.2   Windows Authentication Basics   238
        5.2.1   Concepts   238
        5.2.2   Authentication Architecture   242
        5.2.3   Authentication in the Machine Startup and
               User Logon Sequences   250

5.3		Logon Rights	255
	5.3.1	Managing Windows Logon Rights	259
	5.3.2	Best Practices	261
5.4		NTLM-Based Authentication	261
	5.4.1	The Protocol	261
	5.4.2	NTLM Flavors	264
	5.4.3	Controlling the NTLM Flavors	265
	5.4.4	Disabling LM Hash Storage	268
5.5		Anonymous Access	271
5.6		Credential Caching	277
5.7		Limiting Concurrent Logon Sessions	281
	5.7.1	LimitLogin Operation	282
	5.7.2	LimitLogin Architecture and Components	284
	5.7.3	Installing LimitLogin	285
	5.7.4	Configuring LimitLogin	287
5.8		General Authentication Troubleshooting	292
	5.8.1	Authentication-Related Windows Event Logging	292
	5.8.2	Netlogon Logging	298
5.9		What's in the Other Authentication Chapters?	301

6   Kerberos   303

6.1		Introducing Kerberos	303
	6.1.1	Kerberos Advantages	304
	6.1.2	Comparing Kerberos to NTLM	307
6.2		Kerberos: The Basic Protocol	307
	6.2.1	Kerberos Design Assumptions	309
	6.2.2	Step 1: Kerberos Authentication is Based on Symmetric Key Cryptography	310
	6.2.3	Step 2: A Kerberos KDC Provides Scalability	312
	6.2.4	Step 3: The Ticket Provides Secure Transport of the Session Key	314
	6.2.5	Step 4: The KDC Distributes the Session Key by Sending It to the Client	317
	6.2.6	Step 5: The Ticket Granting Ticket Limits the Use of the Master Keys	319
	6.2.7	Bringing It All Together	322
	6.2.8	Kerberos Data Confidentiality, Authentication, and Integrity Services	324

	6.2.9	User-to-User Authentication	324
	6.2.10	Key Version Numbers	326
6.3		Logging on to Windows Using Kerberos	327
	6.3.1	Logging on in Single Domain Environment	328
	6.3.2	Logging on in Multiple Domain Environment	333
	6.3.3	Multiple Forest Logon	343
6.4		Advanced Kerberos Topics	345
	6.4.1	Delegation of Authentication	345
	6.4.2	From Authentication to Authorization	361
	6.4.3	Analyzing the Kerberos Ticket and Authenticator	369
	6.4.4	Kerberos Time Sensitivity	384
	6.4.5	Kerberized Applications	387
6.5		Kerberos Configuration	390
	6.5.1	Kerberos GPO Settings	390
	6.5.2	Kerberos-Related Account Properties	392
	6.5.3	Kerberos Transport Protocols and Ports	392
6.6		Kerberos Troubleshooting	394
	6.6.1	The Event Viewer	394
	6.6.2	Troubleshooting Tools	396
6.7		Kerberos Interoperability	396
	6.7.1	Non-Microsoft Kerberos Implementations	397
	6.7.2	Comparing Windows Kerberos to Other Implementations	398
	6.7.3	Interoperability Scenarios	399

7   IIS Authentication   **409**

7.1	Secure by Default in IIS 6.0	409
7.2	Introducing IIS Authentication	411
7.3	HTTP Authentication	414
	7.3.1 Anonymous Access	416
	7.3.2 Basic Authentication	419
	7.3.3 Digest Authentication	423
7.4	Integrated Windows Authentication	426
7.5	Passport-Based Authentication	428
	7.5.1 Passport and Windows Live ID	429
	7.5.2 Passport-Enabling Web Technologies	430
	7.5.3 Passport Infrastructure	431

	7.5.4	Basic Passport Authentication Exchange	433
	7.5.5	XP and Windows Server 2003 Passport User Changes	435
	7.5.6	Passport Cookies	436
	7.5.7	Passport and Personally Identifiable Information	442
	7.5.8	Passport Integration in Windows Server 2003	443
7.6		Certificate-Based Authentication	445
	7.6.1	SSL Setup	449
	7.6.2	Web Browser SSL Support	463
	7.6.3	Certificate Validation	464
	7.6.4	Deployment Considerations	468
7.7		IIS Authentication Method Comparison	475

8   UNIX/Linux and Windows Authentication Integration   477

8.1		Comparing Windows and UNIX/Linux Authentication	478
8.2		Interoperability Enabling Technologies	479
	8.2.1	LDAP	479
	8.2.2	Kerberos	482
8.3		UNIX/Linux Security-Related Concepts	484
	8.3.1	PAM	484
	8.3.2	Naming Services	487
	8.3.3	NSS	488
	8.3.4	Local Files	491
	8.3.5	NIS	491
	8.3.6	NIS+	493
	8.3.7	NIS and LDAP Integration	494
	8.3.8	Samba	496
8.4		Windows and UNIX/Linux Account Management and Authentication Integration Approaches	498
	8.4.1	Coexistence Solutions between an NIS and an AD Infrastructure	500
	8.4.2	Solutions Providing Centralized User Management Using an AD/LDAP Repository	512
8.5		Summary	532

9   Single Sign-On   533

9.1	SSO: Pros and Cons	533
9.2	Web versus Enterprise SSO	534

9.3   SSO Architectures   535
        9.3.1   Simple SSO Architectures   535
        9.3.2   Complex SSO Architectures   538
        9.3.3   SSO Architectures: Summary   549
9.4   Extending SSO   550
        9.4.1   Extending SSO to Cover Different Organizations 551
        9.4.2   Extending SSO to Cover Different Applications   552
9.5   Microsoft SSO Technologies   553
        9.5.1   The Credential Manager   553
        9.5.2   Biztalk Server and Host Integration
                Server Enterprise SSO   559
        9.5.3   SharePoint Portal Server SSO   570
        9.5.4   Active Directory Federation Services   573
        9.5.5   Internet Authentication Service   577
9.6   Conclusion   579

Part III   Authorization

10   Windows Server 2003 Authorization   583

10.1   Authorization Basics   583
10.2   The Windows Authorization Model   584
10.3   Authorization Intermediaries   590
        10.3.1 Groups   590
        10.3.2 User Rights   622
10.4   Windows 2000 Authorization Changes   624
        10.4.1 New ACL Editor   626
        10.4.2 Fine-Grain Control over Inheritance   627
        10.4.3 Object Type-Based ACEs   635
        10.4.4 ACL Evaluation Process   651
        10.4.5 SID History   657
10.5   Windows Server 2003 Authorization Changes   659
        10.5.1 More Restrictive Authorization Settings   659
        10.5.2 Effective Permissions   660
        10.5.3 Default AD Security Descriptor Changes   661
        10.5.4 AD Link Value Replication and Group
                Membership Updates   664
        10.5.5 Quotas for AD Objects   665
        10.5.6 The Confidential Bit for AD Attributes   667

10.5.7 Hiding Data in the File System and Shares   672
10.5.8 Authorization Manager   679
10.6 Authorization Tools   690

11 Active Directory Delegation   693

11.1 Introduction   693
11.1.1 Level-of-Privilege Considerations   694
11.1.2 Multidomain Considerations   698
11.1.3 Organizational Units   701
11.2 General AD Delegation Guidelines   705
11.2.1 Honoring Least Privilege for AD Administration   706
11.2.2 Controlling Password Management   707
11.2.3 Designing Roles for AD delegation   710
11.3 Setting up Administrative Delegation   719
11.3.1 The AD Delegation Wizard   720
11.3.2 Administrative Delegation Examples   723
11.4 Hiding Objects in AD   732
11.4.1 Understanding the Challenge of
       Hiding Data in AD   733
11.4.2 Hiding Data Using "Normal" Permissions on
       AD Objects and Attributes   739
11.4.3 Enabling List Object Mode in Forest   745
11.4.4 Adjusting the Default Security of Objects in AD 754
11.4.5 Adjusting the Built-In Property Sets   758
11.4.6 Using the Confidentiality Bit   766
11.5 Third-Party AD Delegation Tools   771

Index   773

Foreword

by Tony Redmond

Over the last ten years, we have seen huge change in Microsoft technology as Windows evolved from Windows NT 3.51 running on small 32-bit servers with a restricted range of applications to Windows 2003 R2 on 64-bit platforms supporting a vastly increased range of applications and usage. At the same time, the number and variety of threats that system administrators have to protect IT infrastructures against have increased exponentially. Windows gets a lot of bad press about security, but perhaps this is due to the popularity of the platform, which makes it a huge and attractive target for attack. I am sure that attackers won't stop their activities and that the success of Windows will continue to have it in the crosshairs for new attacks.

In this context, it is absolutely critical that Windows systems administrators understand how to protect Windows infrastructures using the full range of features available in the operating system. This book is a great resource for system administrators, because it has been written from a practical perspective with the intention of telling administrators how to go about protecting their infrastructure. The advice is direct and understandable, and best of all it is based on the authors' solid experience helping some of the world's largest companies protect themselves.

Security is an evolving topic and no one book or any one person can provide all the answers to keep systems secure from every potential attack. However, books like this give you a necessary foundation that you can complement with knowledge of your own environment, a fair dose of common sense, and details of the policies and procedures that your organization mandates for the operation of IT systems to form a complete picture of what you need to do to protect your Windows systems. Use the book as a guide and make sure that you keep your knowledge up to date so that you know of improvements to software to handle new threats. It won't be a silver bullet to address all your concerns about security, but this book is a great start.

Tony Redmond
Vice President and Chief Technology Officer
HP Services

Foreword

by Mark Mortimore

Security challenges continue to command attention. We use increasingly interconnected systems to store, transfer, and process information. Technologies are getting stronger and more robust, more straightforward to use and manage, and easier to integrate with other devices and systems. But as systems add capability and we get more experienced and confident, we store and exchange information of greater value and sensitivity—so with each advance, the stakes get higher.

Industry preparation and response have undergone significant revision toward a more capable, stable, and trustworthy platform. While awareness and general preparedness have improved, the immutable laws of security remain: administrators must continue to make systems more functional for increasingly sophisticated users and easier for new users to interact with, while simultaneously improving functionality, security, and privacy.

Organizations increasingly want to allow employees to connect from work, from home, and from the road. There is also a need to collaborate more deeply with partners and customers. Businesses must have confidence that the data being transferred come from the identified sender, are complete and unaltered, and that sensitive information can be accessed only by authorized users. In a well-secured environment, a level of rigor should exist in all communications layers at the perimeter and within the local network, in systems whether domain or remotely connected, and across all relevant data storage form factors, including laptops, desktops, dedicated storage, phones, PDAs, custom devices. Including resources beyond the internal domain allows the valuable exchange of information but at the same time introduces several additional security concerns.

Start secure and remain vigilant. Getting production servers configured properly and keeping these systems well managed and up to date are fundamental to every security policy. The threat to reputations and to the bottom line is real. Being well prepared is the only way to protect sensitive information and safeguard valuable assets.

Technology alone is not sufficient to secure assets. Basic measures will tend to repel less sophisticated attacks and most automated attempts to exploit well-known vulnerabilities. To safeguard against skilled, motivated, and dedicated hackers, each aspect of the system must be safeguarded. Most attackers will choose the easiest combination of exploits that will allow the access they seek. Attacks of this type will typically include both technical exploits and social engineering techniques. The best-secured system is open if authorized users give away their passwords, or if physical access is not restricted. As technical solutions are implemented, we must also refine and drive complementary defense-in-depth measures. Every well-orchestrated security system has a balance of technical solutions and a well-articulated, well-understood, and well-executed security policy; an informed user base; and well-practiced security procedures to respond appropriately to threats or incidents.

The systems most IT professionals manage today do not consist of uniform hardware running homogeneous operating systems and a common set of applications. Some technical content delivers only procedural guidance that leads the reader step-by-step through a narrowly defined process. Understanding architectures and knowing how procedures function builds administrator insight. This insight translates into knowledge that will help administrators and consultants better secure, integrate, manage, and maximize value.

In this book, the authors have applied significant experience and deep knowledge to provide the reader with the processes needed to maximize the utility of all major Windows security features. But more important, they have provided the reader with deep insight into how these features were architected and implemented and how they can be leveraged in complex, heterogeneous, "real-world" IT environments.

Microsoft Windows Security Fundamentals is a reference guide for IT professionals who are looking for deeper and more authoritative insight than the content that can be found on the Internet or in discussion groups. Information in this book will arm the readers with the knowledge they need to go beyond executing rote processes or step-by-step procedures.

With the passion of explorers, Jan and Guido have discovered valuable insights into these technologies. With the discipline of scientists, they have comprehensively recorded and structured this information. With the artful skill of experienced authors, they have communicated these concepts and capabilities in a very clear and concise style that will be appreciated by busy professionals.

Jan De Clercq and Guido Grillenmeier have an impressive applied background and deep subject matter expertise. Together with their extended team, they have been directly engaged in architecting, designing, deploying, configuring, managing, and maintaining security solutions in many of the largest and most complex implementations in the world. This depth of experience and expertise rings through every chapter and makes this information invaluable to Windows professionals.

When we are successful in our mission to deliver trustworthy computing, we lay the foundation for future implementations. These implementations can extend our ability to develop and deliver increasingly innovative and empowering solutions. This is a noble mission that will ultimately enable future waves of innovation and capability. Be prepared, innovate, and remain vigilant.

Mark Mortimore
Technology Development Manager
Microsoft

Foreword

by Steven Adler

The release of Windows 2000 saw the introduction of Active Directory and heralded major changes to the directory and security services that were now present in a general purpose operating system.

As one of the program managers responsible for Active Directory, I quickly realized that one of the challenges that the industry faced was how to understand and adopt these new technologies. System Administrators and Developers now had to understand additional technologies, such as Kerberos, DNS, LDAP, and X.509 Public Key Infrastructures, in order to architect their Windows 2000 systems.

Fortunately many of Microsoft's partners stepped up to the challenge and developed expertise in these new technologies, enabling many customers to successfully deploy Windows 2000. During that time, Jan and Guido worked with their customers and with Microsoft on many successful projects and subsequently became acknowledged experts in their field.

Together with his colleague Micky Balladelli, Jan co-authored *Mission-Critical Active Directory: Architecting a Secure and Scalable Infrastructure* and then later, with the release of Windows Server 2003, authored *Windows Server 2003 Security Infrastructures: Core Security Features*. I have also been fortunate to co-present with Jan at many industry security conferences and have been amazed at the way he conveys complex topics to the audience.

Now that Windows Server 2003 Service Pack 1 and Windows Server 2003 R2 have been released, there is again a new set of security features available, requiring IT professionals to now understand host-based firewall services; Web browsers and servers; security configuration templates; federation; authorization; and delegation.

While this book covers all of the new security features available in Windows Server 2003 Service Pack 1 and R2, it also explains the fundamental security principles of authentication, authorization, and audit and will help both novice and experienced administrators alike improve the overall security of their infrastructure.

Steven Adler
Infrastructure Architect
Microsoft EMEA HQ

Preface

Over the last several years, Microsoft has made security a top priority. This was first illustrated by the Windows 2000 operating system (OS), which includes major security enhancements. Windows 2000 supports several open security standards (Kerberos, IPsec, and so on). These standards are critical for security interoperability with other platforms and drive the operating system's open reputation—or the fact of not just being rooted on proprietary security protocols. Windows 2000 also included an important shift in the overall security manageability of the platform: Group Policy Objects (GPOs) were a big step forward.

After the release of Windows 2000, Microsoft, its flagship OS and other MS applications were hit badly by the hacker community. They forced Microsoft into a series of strategic security announcements. The first one was the Secure Windows Initiative; its primary goal was to enhance the Windows base OS. Then came the Strategic Technology Protection Program (STTP). STTP provided a set of software tools and prescriptive guidance documents enabling customers to get secure and stay secure. In 2002, Microsoft announced the Trustworthy Computing (TWC) initiative. TWC is about four principles: secure by default, by design, by deployment, and communications. Secure by design affects the Microsoft teams directly; it means that Microsoft takes the appropriate steps to make sure the overall design of their products is secure. The goal of secure by default is to ship products that are secure out of the box. Secure in deployment means that once the software product has been installed, it is easily maintainable from a security point of view. Communications means that Microsoft has become much more talkative in the IT security community; they offer prescriptive security guidance to their customers to a maximum extent.

Windows Server 2003 is Microsoft's first enterprise OS resulting from the Trustworthy Computing initiative. The main difference with its predecessor is that Windows Server 2003 is much more hardened by default. This development continued with the release of Service Pack 1 and the R2 version of the OS. Instead of focusing on the security feature set of the OS, Microsoft now primarily stresses this default lockdown to the outside world. It is fair to say that Microsoft efforts in the security space are truly impressive.

As with any security solution, technological advances are not enough. We should never forget the important role of people and processes. Security governance has become more important, and Microsoft also delivers solutions in this space: good examples are the Microsoft Operations Framework (MOF) and security patch management initiatives.

We had the privilege to work with Windows Server 2003—or Whistler as it was codenamed back then—and the subsequent updates to it, such as Service Pack 1 and the R2 release—from a very early stage in the product's lifecycle. Hewlett-Packard was involved in the Whistler and R2 Joint Development Program (JDP). At HP, we also created a globally distributed internal test forest—codenamed QNet—starting with the beta versions of the Whistler software. Perhaps the opportunity that helped us most with gaining experience with this new Microsoft OS was the development and delivery of the Windows Server 2003 Academies and HP Microsoft Infrastructure Security Trainings. These five-day learning events consisted of both lectures and hands-on labs, and we delivered them successfully to both HP consultants and HP customers.

This book is the first part in a two-part book series featuring Windows security. The goal of these books is to provide insights into the security features and security infrastructure components of the Windows Server 2003 operating system. The books also highlight the security principles an architect should remember when designing a secure Windows Server 2003 infrastructure. Part 1 is titled *Microsoft Windows Security Fundamentals* and focuses on Windows security concepts and authentication and authorization services. Part 2 is titled *Advanced Microsoft Windows Security Services* and focuses on Windows identity management, public key infrastructure, and security management services.

The books are based on years of experience we gained with the Windows family of enterprise operating systems, both internally at HP and at customer sites. As such, the books also provide architectural guidance and best practices for the design of Windows-rooted security infrastructures.

The books do not cover the typical communications security infrastructure building blocks coming with the OS. For example, Microsoft's RADIUS solution, Internet Authentication Services (IAS), is mentioned, but is not covered in detail. Also, the books do not offer an introduction to general security and cryptographic terminology; we assume the reader is already familiar with these concepts. Finally, the book does not cover any of the security infrastructure building blocks Microsoft provides as part of their other product offerings: good examples are the security infrastructure features of Systems Management Server (SMS) and Operations Manager (MOM).

If you discover inaccuracies or if you have general comments on the structure and/or content of the book, don't hesitate to send us your feedback. Your comments are very much appreciated! You can reach us at jan.declercq@hp.com and guido.grillenmeier@hp.com.

Enjoy reading our book!

Jan De Clercq and Guido Grillenmeier
July 2006

Acknowledgments

We would like to thank the following people for helping us create this book:

The drivers on the Digital Press side: Theron R. Shreve for keeping me rolling in hard times, and Alan Rose for his incredible patience during the editing of this book.

Tony Redmond, VP and HP Services CTO, for his mentorship and leadership and for his support in bootstrapping this book project.

The following members of HP's technical community, always willing to learn and share: Ian Burgess, Olivier Blaise, Janusz Gebusia, Michael Gough, Gary Olsen, Marc Van Hooste, Els Thonnon, Marco Casassa Mont, Boris Balacheff, Erik Van Reeth, Rudy Schockaert, Herman De Vloed, Donald Livengood, Dung Hoang Khac, Aric Bernard, Joe Richards, Ken Wright, Wayne Laflamme, Scott Hebner, Patrick Salmon, Patrick Lownds, and Jeremy Pack.

The members of HP's Advanced Technology Group: Kieran McCorry, Kevin Laahs, Emer McKenna, Pierre Bijaoui, Daragh Morrissey, Veli-Matti Vanamo, and John Rhoton.

The following Microsoft people for their technical and other advice: Andreas Luther, Alain Lissoir, Martin Boller, Susan McDonald, Markus Vilcinskas, David Cross, Steven Adler, Ronny Bjones, Marie Maxwell, Tony deFreitas, Mark Rankin, Jerry Cochran, Eric Fleischmann, Khushru Irani, Olivier d'Hose, Mark Mortimore, and JK Jaganathan.

The following friends and partners for reviewing this book or otherwise supporting us: Todd Allen, Dan Coughlin, and Gil Kirkpatrick.

Jan's personal acknowledgments: I would also like to thank my parents, my wife's parents, and the whole family (especially my little nieces and nephews, Johanna, Lucas, Charlotte, Clara, Astrid, Kato, Anton, and Victor), for the time I could not spend with them, for their interest in my writing this book, and for being a great family!

Guido's personal acknowledgments: Last but not least, I would like to thank my whole family—my parents, my wife's parents, George and Michaela, Nicole and Claus, Steffi and Walter, Moni, Susan, Katherine, and all of my nieces and my nephew—for supporting me and showing so much interest in this book. You've been an enormous help!

Jan De Clercq and Guido Grillenmeier

July 2006

Part I

Introduction

The Challenge of Trusted Security Infrastructures

This chapter introduces the concept of trusted security infrastructures (TSIs). The opening sections outline the different TSI services, their components, and their interactions. All services are illustrated with a set of security product offerings. The second part of the chapter looks at what Microsoft can provide in the TSI space. This part explores both the TSI functions that are bundled with the Windows Server 2003 R2 operating system and the ones that come as part of other Microsoft software product offerings. This chapter is the introduction for both books of this two-book series on Windows Security Fundamentals.

1.1 Introduction

"Outsourcing" is a primarily economic concept that many other sciences have adopted. In information technology (IT), the outsourcing of processing functions was extremely popular during the mainframe era, but has become less common during the last two decades. With the rise of the personal computer (PC), everyone wanted more and more powerful client computing devices. Less powerful clients and the outsourcing of special functions to dedicated server machines have regained popularity only recently.

Even though specific and specialized security functions have been outsourced to trusted third-party (TTP) servers for many years in specific areas of IT security (e.g., authentication), it was only at the beginning of the 1990s that this outsourcing became accepted for a wider range of security functions (such as key management and access control). The reason this took so long was mainly because of the perception of insecurity and the feeling of losing control when security services are outsourced and centralized at a TTP. The widespread use of strong cryptographic techniques and the adoption of open security standards have been important incubators for the rise of outsourcing in the IT security space.

Recent security incidents on the Internet[1] have also shown that it will take more than just outsourcing security functions to dedicated TTP servers to make the IT world really secure. What are really needed are pervasive security services. These are security services that are omnipresent and that are implemented and used in a coherent and standardized way by different applications, platforms, and IT players. Pervasive security services require a coherent security policy enforcement mechanism, which becomes easier in a centralized TTP environment.

The next few sections provide an overview of a common trend in the outsourcing of security functionality: the creation of trusted security infrastructures (TSIs). These infrastructures provide the following core security services:

- Identification

- Authentication

- Authorization

- Auditing

- Key management

- Security-related management

In the context of TSIs, outsourcing tends to go as far as moving away all core security services from applications and making them infrastructure services, just as happened before for networking, file, print, and messaging services.

Trusted security infrastructures allow applications to focus on their core business function. Because TSIs can provide centralized security management, they can enforce security policies much more efficiently in large distributed IT environments. They also facilitate Single Sign-On (SSO) and more rapid and more secure application development. Because of their central role, trusted security infrastructures must use open standards. They also must be implemented in a platform-, application-, vendor-, and device-neutral way.

---

1.   Remember the Slammer (Sapphire) worm: see www.cs.berkeley.edu/~nweaver/sapphire/ for some interesting insights on Slammer.

1.2   Positioning Trusted Security Infrastructures

To position TSIs, we must look not only at their logical positioning as part of the security architecture but also at their physical positioning as part of the security design. A security architecture is a high-level specification of major security components and how they relate to each other. A security design specifies the physical placement of components.

From a security architecture point of view, trusted security infrastructures introduce a new layer of security services that is sometimes referred to as the access layer, a concept that was first introduced by the Burton Group. The access layer is positioned in between the resource layer and the perimeter layer (as illustrated in Figure 1.1). The resource layer contains applications and data, or, in short, the information and application assets of an organization. The perimeter layer contains all elements that make up the perimeter security infrastructure of an organization. The perimeter layer contains security devices like firewalls, access routers, intrusion detection and prevention systems (IDS and IPS), and virtual private networking (VPN) tunnel endpoints.

In the context of this chapter, we will simply refer to the access layer as the trusted security infrastructure or TSI layer. The key role of this logical layer of security services is illustrated in Figure 1.1. The TSIs are built upon and used by a set of core infrastructure services, such as directory, database, messaging, and management services. In turn, the TSIs are—like all other core infrastructure services—used by a set of commercial off-the-shelf (COTS) or custom-built applications.

Figure 1.1
The Access or TSI layer.

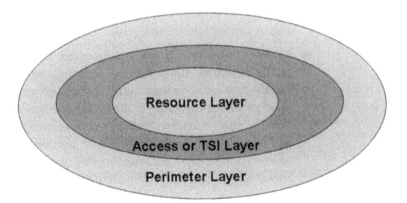

TSIs can provide a unified and universal security infrastructure for applications and services that are accessed in different environments and using different communication protocols, be it in a typical office setup, across the Web, in a remote access setup, or in a wireless environment. TSIs can serve business-to-employee (BtoE), business-to-consumer (BtoC), and business-to-business (BtoB) environments.

Looking at TSIs from a security design point of view and taking into account their critical security role, it is fair to say that they should be located in a separate security zone. This zone should be governed by a strong security policy. To shield the TSIs from the rest of the world, one will typically use a set of perimeter security devices that enforce the appropriate security policies to only let the right office, web, remote access, and wireless users in and keep the wrong ones out.

In the introduction we briefly mentioned the security services provided by TSIs. Figure 1.2 shows the key TSI components providing these services:

- Security management infrastructures are the administrative engines of a TSI. A security management infrastructure manages security identities and their attributes, including their authentication credentials, entitlements, and authorization intermediary[2] memberships. It also takes care of the security configuration management of computer systems. Two relatively recent additions to security management are compliance management and federation management.

- Authentication (Authn) infrastructures provide the entry points into a secured IT environment. They verify the identity of entities before those entities are allowed to use resources. To perform this verification, they support different authentication methods and protocols. To prove its identity, an entity provides the authentication TTP with a set of authentication credentials.

- Authorization (Authz) infrastructures are the next level of security guards following authentication infrastructures. Once an entity's identity has been verified, authorization infrastructures will decide which resources the entity is allowed to access and the level of access it has to those resources. Authorization infrastructures do not necessarily deal with the management of authorization-related objects, such as groups, roles, and entitlements; this functionality is typically provided by security management infrastructures.

---

2.   Authorization intermediaries are administrative entities that facilitate authorization administration. Examples are groups, rights, and roles.

- Key management infrastructures provide key lifecycle management services. A good example of a key management infrastructure is a public key infrastructure (PKI).

- Auditing systems are keeping track of all events (security related but also other ones) that occur in your infrastructure. Given the high degree of outsourcing in a TSI setup, auditing systems have an even more critical role.

All together, these TSI components can be referred to as the AAAA security services: Administration (or management), Authentication, Authorization, and Auditing. In the following sections, we will explore the different TSI components in greater detail. We look at how they operate and interoperate. We will also give some examples of TSI software solutions for the different TSI categories.

Availability is another service that is often referred to when talking about security services. Even though the second book of this two-book series will contain a chapter on Active Directory disaster recovery, availability is not a major focal point of these books. This doesn't mean availability is not important—quite the contrary! We decided not to pay more attention to availability mainly because it is not always perceived as being a core security service. Also, covering it in greater detail would have made these books really too large.

Figure 1.2
Positioning trusted security infrastructures.

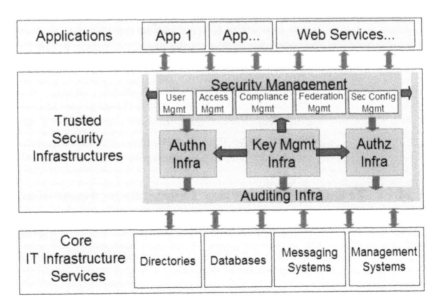

Figure 1.3
The fundamental role of trust.

Trust

Identification

Authentication   Access
                              Control

Authorization

Auditing

1.3   The Fundamental Role of Trust

All TSI services mentioned in the previous sections depend on the existence of a trust relationship between the users of the services and the service providers. As Figure 1.3 shows, all security services are built on trust. The figure also illustrates the link between access control, identification, authentication, and authorization. Access control requires three security services: identification, authentication, and authorization. Often, people use authorization and access control as synonyms.

Trust cannot be provided just by using technology solutions. A trust relationship also requires the presence of nontechnological solutions, such as security policies and administrative procedures that can provide an operational framework for the creation and maintenance of the trust relationship.

In most enterprises, it is relatively easy to create trust relationships between internal TSI users and TSI service providers. Things become much more difficult when the TSIs must provide security services to external entities, such as partners or customers. An even bigger challenge is to provide trustworthy TSI services on the World Wide Web (WWW).

1.4   Trusted Security Infrastructure Roles

The next sections focus on the four TSI roles and their supporting infrastructures: authentication, authorization, key management, and security management infrastructures.

1.4.1 Authentication Infrastructures

Authentication infrastructures are a TSI component that has been around for many years. In computing environments with high scalability requirements, it is not cost efficient from implementation and administration points of view to create a separate authentication system for every individual computer system, resource, or application server. It is much more efficient to outsource this functionality to an authentication infrastructure. Outsourcing also enhances the enforcement of a consistent authentication policy throughout the enterprise. Another major driver behind the creation of authentication infrastructures is Single Sign-On (SSO). SSO is covered in greater detail in Chapter 9.

An authentication infrastructure is made up of one or several authentication servers. Authentication security policies can be managed by the authentication TSI itself or, depending on the degree of centralization, by using tools that come with the security management infrastructure. The authentication infrastructure interacts with a repository (a database or directory) to store and validate user credentials. Authentication servers are linked to an auditing system and may have management agents from the corporate IT infrastructure management software installed.

The authentication infrastructure software products available on the market today can be categorized as follows:

- **Authentication infrastructures integrated with network operating systems.** These are typically used in enterprise environments to ease authentication for accessing internal enterprise resources.

- **Authentication infrastructures integrated with Web access management systems (WAMS).** These focus on providing authentication and authorization services for resources that can be accessed using a Web interface. Their scope goes beyond enterprise intranets and extranets—they can also be used for authentication and authorization on Internet portals. Also, these systems are not just providing authentication; most of them are integrated "authentication-authorization-security management" infrastructures.

- **Web authentication infrastructures.** These infrastructures focus on authenticating Internet users that are accessing Internet resources.

- **Federation-based authentication infrastructures.** Federation is a relatively recent set of technologies enabling the secure interchange of user data between different security infrastructures based on open federation standards. As such, it can be used for authentication and Single Sign-On (SSO) in intranet, extranet, and Web environments. Federation will be defined in more detail later in this chapter.

Table 1.1 provides a sample list of authentication TSI solutions in the different categories that were listed above. This is a nonexhaustive list: it does not give a complete overview of the authentication infrastructure products available on the market today.

Web authentication infrastructures like Microsoft Windows Live ID (formerly known as Microsoft Passport) are specifically Internet-focused. Web access management systems (WAMS) are intranet- and extranet-focused and offer SSO solutions for corporate Web portals. An important difference between both product categories is who is in control of the authentication infrastructures. In WAMS, an organization's IT depart-

Table 1.1   *Authentication Infrastructure Solutions*

Vendor	Authentication Infrastructure Product
Authentication infra integrated with network operating systems	
Microsoft	Windows 2000
	Windows Server 2003
	Windows Server 2003 R2
Novell	Netware
Authentication infra integrated with Web access management systems	
HP	HP OpenView Select Access
Computer Associates	eTrust Siteminder
RSA	ClearTrust
IBM	Tivoli Access Manager (TAM)
Web authentication infrastructures	
Microsoft	Windows Live ID (formerly known as Microsoft Passport)
Federation-based authentication infrastructures	
Microsoft	Active Directory Federation Services (ADFS)
HP	HP OpenView Select Federation
Ping Identity Corporation	PingFederate

ment controls the authentication infrastructure. In Web authentication infrastructures, control over the authentication infrastructure is outsourced to a commercial Internet authentication provider. A federation-based authentication infrastructure can cover intranet, extranet, and Web authentication and leaves control of the authentication infrastructures to the different "federated" organizations.

1.4.2   Authorization Infrastructures

Providing authorization services for employees to internal IT resources in a closed and homogeneous enterprise environment is relatively easy. Network operating systems, such as Netware, NT, Windows 2000, and Windows Server 2003, come with a set of built-in authorization management and enforcement features, such as the ability to group resources in administrative domains, object models that support access control lists, security reference monitors (SRMs) bundled with the OS to evaluate and enforce authorization settings, and groups and rights to facilitate authorization management.

Things get much more complicated if the scope of the authorization infrastructure is broadened to cover not just internal users but also external users and whether the resources can be accessed using different communication protocols and devices. Another complicating factor is that different applications are using different authorization systems. Enforcing a single coherent authorization policy throughout an organization for all IT applications and services becomes an incredibly difficult task if every application and service maintains its proper authorization settings and makes its proper authorization decisions.

An authorization infrastructure is made up of one or several authorization policy authorities. Authorization security policies can be managed by the authorization TSI itself or, depending on the degree of centralization, using tools that come with the security management infrastructure. The authorization infrastructure interacts with a repository (database or directory) to store and retrieve authorization data. Authorization infrastructure servers are linked to an auditing system and may have management agents from the corporate IT infrastructure management software installed.

Authorization Services

When discussing authorization, we must consider the following authorization services: authorization policy management, authorization decision making, and authorization enforcement.

Authorization policy management deals with the creation of entries for the resources to be protected, groups, roles, access rights, permissions, and special access rules in an authorization policy repository. Most importantly, it links users, groups, and roles with resources, access rights, and access rules. The administrator responsible for authorization policy management decides on the users' level of access to resources (e.g., can John just read a file, or can he also delete it?). The latter process is also known as the creation of permissions. TSI entities providing authorization policy management are also referred to as Policy Administration Points (PAPs).

Authorization decision making is the real-time process of deciding whether or not a user is allowed to access a resource and the level at which he or she can access the resource. The input to this process is the information that is stored in the authorization repository and governed by the PAPs. TSI entities providing authorization decision-making services are also referred to as Policy Decision Points (PDPs).

A resource manager is responsible for authorization enforcement. It ensures that the authorization decision is executed correctly; in other words, it makes sure a user is allowed or denied access to a resource. TSI entities providing authorization enforcement services are also referred to as Policy Enforcement Points (PEPs).

In the early days of distributed client/server applications, every application maintained its proper authorization database, did its proper authorization decision making, and enforced authorization accordingly. There should be no need to explain that in such an environment, creating and maintaining a coherent authorization policy was a nightmare.

The first shift toward authorization service centralization came with first generation Network Operating Systems (NOSs),[3] which centralized the definition of authorization intermediaries (objects like groups and rights) in a database. Because authorization enforcement is often very application-specific, applications kept on making their proper authorization decisions. Also, permissions remained to be stored in individual application authorization databases. Microsoft environments contain plenty of such examples. The decision whether or not a user is allowed to access a standalone XP workstation is made by the workstation's local security authority. Likewise, the decision to access a SQL Server database is made by the database server itself.

---

3.   First-generation NOSs are the operating systems that are commonly used today—they include the Windows 2000 family of enterprise operating systems.

	Authorization Administration (PAP)	Authorization Decision-making (PDP)	Authorization Enforcement (PEP)
Individual Application Resource Managers	*Decentralized*	*Decentralized*	*Decentralized*
Network Operating Systems 1st Gen (NOS)	*Centralized*	*Decentralized*	*Decentralized*
WAMS NOS Next Gen	*Centralized*	*Centralized*	*Decentralized*
WAMS	*Centralized*	*Centralized*	*Centralized*

Figure 1.4   *Shift from authorization service decentralization to centralization.*

To ease the creation of application permissions and to keep them coherent throughout an environment with many different authorization databases and resource managers, software vendors created provisioning systems. In the context of this TSI discussion, provisioning systems are considered a part of security management infrastructures and will be discussed in Section 1.4.4.

Another shift toward authorization service centralization occurred when Web access management systems (WAMS) came to the market. WAMS centralize authorization decision making. In some products they also centralize authorization enforcement. WAMS are discussed in more detail in the Section 1.4.2.

The different shifts from decentralized to more centralized authorization services are illustrated in Figure 1.4.

Web Access Management Systems

Web Access Management Systems (WAMS) are a good example of TSI solutions, where different security services are bundled in one commercial software offering. WAMS can be defined as a unified solution for Web authentication, Web SSO, authorization, and security management. WAMS were born in the Web portal world and focus on HTTP-based access to Web resources.

In the first place, WAMS are TSIs providing centralized authorization decision making and enforcement. WAMS decouple authorization decision making and/or enforcement from applications and services and centralize these services at TTPs. WAMS also include centralized security management (covering identities, credentials, and roles), can provide authentication services, and provide a set of auditing services.

WAMS are made up of a central policy engine that contains the WAMS logic for authorization, authentication, auditing, and security management services. For authentication and security management services, WAMS typically call on some external authentication or security management TSI. The WAMS policy engine also provides the intelligence for WAMS functions such as self-service management, delegation management, password synchronization, and so forth. Authorization security policies can be managed by the WAMS itself or, depending on the degree of centralization, using tools that come with the security management infrastructure. The WAMS infrastructure interacts with a repository (database or directory) to store and retrieve credentials, user identity information, attributes, and authorization data. WAMS servers are linked to an auditing system and may have management agents from the corporate IT infrastructure management software installed.

The WAMS software products available on the market today can be grouped in two categories:

- In an agent-based WAMS, clients always communicate directly with the application servers. The latter have a WAMS agent installed that validates every client request with a WAMS policy server. The WAMS policy server makes the access control decision and sends the response back to the application server. The application server's WAMS agent is responsible for the authorization enforcement and allows or denies client access accordingly.

- In a proxy-based WAMS, clients never communicate directly with the application servers. Situated between the two, a WAMS proxy intercepts every client request and enforces access control. The WAMS proxy communicates with a WAMS policy server. The latter is the access control decision maker—the proxy functions as an access control traffic filter.

Table 1.2   *Web Access Management System Vendors*

Vendor	WAMS Product
Agent-based WAMS systems	
Computer Associates	eTrust SiteMinder
Oracle	CoreID Access
HP	HP OpenView Select Access
RSA	ClearTrust
Proxy-based WAMS systems	
IBM	Tivoli Access Manager (TAM)

Table 1.2 gives a nonexhaustive list of WAMS products available on the market today.

1.4.3 Key Management Infrastructures

A key management infrastructure's primary reason for existence is, obviously, key management. Any security solution using cryptographic ciphers has to deal with cryptographic keys. When deploying these solutions in large environments, key management becomes a major issue. A scalable and easy-to-manage key management system is of critical importance, for example, for authentication infrastructures used in large environments. The latter can be corporate intranets, extranets, or even the Internet. In such environments, authentication keys would be hard to manage without a centralized key management infrastructure. The use of key management TTPs makes authentication solutions scalable to very large environments.

Key management is certainly a big issue when using symmetric key ciphers. The use of symmetric key ciphers among many different entities poses important key distribution and key update problems. The problem is alleviated when using asymmetric key ciphers—but it still remains an important issue. Let us illustrate this with an example. Setting up a symmetric key-based authentication solution between 10 people without using a TTP would require the creation and exchange of (10 * 9)/2 keys. This makes 45 keys total. When everyone trusts a TTP, only 10 keys would be needed. In the case of asymmetric keys, the amount of keys needed is (2 * 10), which makes 20 keys total. The use of asymmetric keys also has other advantages, as we will explain. See also the sidenote on "Symmetric versus Asymmetric Ciphers" for more information.

Based on the key material with which a key management infrastructure deals, we can differentiate between two different types of TTPs: key distribution centers (KDCs) and certification authorities (CAs). KDCs deal with symmetric keys—they can be linked together in multidomain or multirealm trust networks. CAs deal with asymmetric keys—they can be linked together in Public Key Infrastructures (PKIs).

A key management infrastructure is made up of one or several TTP servers (CAs or KDCs). To enroll entities, key management infrastructures may use dedicated enrollment services—in PKI terminology, registration authorities (RAs). The RAs allow for a highly decentralized administration model. To provide the widest possible range of users with access to these enrollment services, most key management infrastructures provide a set of connectors. These usually include Web, wireless, and VPN connectors. Key management security policies can be managed by the key management TSI itself or, depending on the degree of centralization, by using tools that come with the security management infrastructure. Key management servers are linked to an auditing system and may have management agents from the corporate IT infrastructure management software installed.

KDC-based key management infrastructures usually come bundled with network operating systems such as Netware, Windows 2000, or Windows Server 2003. They can also be purchased separately. A good example is CyberSafe's TrustBroker. TrustBroker is a Kerberos-based key management infrastructure product (as listed in Table 1.3).

Table 1.3   *Key Management Solutions*

Key Distribution Center-Based Key Management Solutions	
Microsoft	Windows 2000, Windows Server 2003
CyberSafe	TrustBroker
Public Key Infrastructures	
Microsoft	Windows 2000, Windows Server 2003
Entrust	Authority
Cybertrust	UniCert

Symmetric versus Asymmetric Ciphers

Symmetric ciphers are the oldest and most-used cryptographic ciphers. In a symmetric cipher, the key used to decipher the ciphertext is the same as (or can be easily derived from) the key that is used to encipher the cleartext (as Figure 1.3 illustrates). This key is called the secret key. This cipher provides secrecy by sharing the secret key only between the participants to the secure communication process. In practice, retaining this secrecy requires the key generated at one side of the communication channel to be sent to the other side of the channel using a secret channel. "Secret channel" in this context means protecting the confidentiality of the key, or keeping the key secret. The most widely used symmetric ciphers are the Data Encryption Standard (DES) and the Advanced Encryption Standard (AES).

Asymmetric ciphers are the most recent cryptographic ciphers. Contrary to a symmetric cipher, an asymmetric cipher uses two keys: one key is kept secret and is known to only one person (the private key), and another key is public and available to everyone (the public key). The two keys are mathematically interrelated, but it is impossible to derive one key from the other. An important advantage of an asymmetric cipher is that its secrecy depends not on the secrecy of the key exchanged between the communicating entities (the public key), but rather on the secrecy of the key that is never exchanged (the private key). Consequently, an asymmetric cipher does not require a secret channel for public key exchange—only an authentic channel. "Authentic channel" in this context means the recipient of the public key is assured of the origin of the key. The most widely used asymmetric cipher is RSA.

There are advantages and disadvantages to using an asymmetric cipher rather than symmetric ciphers. Here are some advantages:

- In an asymmetric cipher, no secret channel is needed for the exchange of the public key.

- Asymmetric ciphers create fewer key management problems than symmetric ciphers: Only $2n$ keys are needed for n entities to communicate securely with one another. In a system based on symmetric ciphers, we need $n(n-1)/2$ secret keys.

- Asymmetric ciphers, because of their unique mathematical background, are the only ciphers that can provide nonrepudiation services.

- Asymmetric ciphers are considered very secure. Symmetric ciphers can be cracked by a brute-force attack, in which all possible keys are tried out until the right key is found.

A disadvantage of asymmetric ciphers is that they tend to be about 1,000 times slower than symmetric ciphers—it takes about 1,000 times more CPU time to process an asymmetric encryption or decryption than to process a symmetric encryption or decryption.

Because of all these characteristics, asymmetric ciphers are typically used for data authentication (through digital signatures), the distribution of a symmetric bulk encryption key, nonrepudiation services, and key agreement. Symmetric ciphers are used for the bulk encryption of data.

CA-based key management infrastructures are sometimes available as an add-on to a network operating system (e.g., Windows 2000, Windows Server 2003, and R2), or can be purchased as separate products. Big names in the PKI product space are Entrust and Cybertrust PKI (as listed in Table 1.3).

1.4.4   Security Management Infrastructures

Security management infrastructures deal with user, access control, compliance, federation, and security configuration management:

- **User management** provides IT administrators with a centralized infrastructure for managing user profile and preference information.

- **Access control management** provides IT administrators with a centralized infrastructure for managing user authentication and authorization data.

- **Compliance management** translates company, industry, or governmental regulations or standards into IT security controls. These controls can then be used to assess and demonstrate compliance of the IT infrastructure. Privacy management can be considered a part of compliance management: it ensures that privacy and data protection policies are respected in an IT infrastructure.

- **Federation management** enables the establishment of trusted relationships between distributed TSIs and the secure exchange of identity data between them.

- **Security configuration management** ensures that computer systems are configured following a predefined secure configuration and that they run the latest software and security patches. The latter is also referred to as security patch management.

Security management infrastructures are governed and driven by policy controls. The latter may cause events to be audited or even the subject of an identity to be notified when information is accessed. Common policy controls in use today are listed below—Table 1.4 gives some sample content for each policy control:

- **Identity policies** control the format and lifetime of an identity and its attributes.

- **Authentication policies** control the characteristics and quality requirements of authentication credentials.

- **Authorization policies** determine how information is manipulated, what resources are allocated to which identity, and how the resources are allocated and deallocated.

- **Privacy and data protection policies** govern how information may be disclosed.

- **Federation policies** control what data can be shared between organizations.

- **Security configuration policies** dictate the security controls that must be set and the security patches that must be installed on a computer system.

A security management infrastructure leverages a repository, typically a database or a directory, to store its security configuration data. To provide more granular management capabilities, a security management infrastructure may also provide self-service and delegated management facilities. Security management infrastructures also guarantee that these critical data remain highly available and synchronized among the different repositories and applications of an IT infrastructure.

Security management infrastructures often come integrated with other TSI solutions, such as authentication or authorization infrastructures. Examples are NOSs, such as Windows NT (or greater) or Novell NetWare, or WAMS such as CA eTrust Siteminder or HP OpenView Select Access. Security management services are also provided by enterprise management

Table 1.4 *Security Policy Control Examples*

Policy Control	Sample Content
Identity policy	Account expiry date.
Authentication policy	Password complexity rules.
Authorization policy	Resource access is controlled by group or role membership.
Privacy and data protection policy	Access to Personally Identifiable Information (PII) is controlled by group or role membership.
Federation policy	A predefined set of user attributes can be shared with other organizations.
Security configuration policy	All systems must have a predefined set of security patches installed.

systems such as HP Openview, CA Unicenter, and BMC Patrol. Relatively recently several specialized compliance, security configuration, and federation management solutions have popped up in the security management space. Examples are Bindview (Symantec) Compliance Manager (compliance management), Symantec Enterprise Security Manager (security configuration management), HP OpenView Server Configuration Management (security configuration management), and Ping Identity PingFederate (federation management).[4] Table 1.5 provides a nonexhaustive list of security management solutions.

Two technologies that play a critical supporting role in today's security management infrastructures are directories (and related solutions) and provisioning systems. They are discussed next.

Table 1.5   *Security Management Solutions*

Security Management Solutions integrated with NOS	
Microsoft	Windows 2000, Windows Server 2003
Novell	Netware
Security Management Solutions integrated with WAMS	
Computer Associates	eTrust SiteMinder
HP	HP OpenView Select Access
Enterprise Management Systems	
HP	HP OpenView
CA	Unicenter
Compliance Management Solutions	
Bindview (Symantec)	Compliance Center
Security Configuration Management Solutions	
Symantec	Enterprise Security Manager
HP	HP OpenView Configuration Management
Federation Management Solutions	
Ping Identity	PingFederate

---

4.   Federation management is discussed in more detail in Section 1.5.

Directories and Related Solutions

Directories are commonly used as the central repository for security-related information. This information includes security identities; authorization intermediaries (groups and roles); entitlements (what a security identity is allowed to do) and other security identity attributes; and security policy information. Lately, directories have been promoted as the cornerstone for identity management systems.

Different directory-related solutions can occur in the context of TSIs: enterprise directories, directory synchronization utilities, meta-directories, and virtual directories. Table 1.6 gives a sample list of directory-related solutions.

Enterprise directories are typically the single authoritative source for identity information throughout an enterprise. All users and directory-enabled applications rely on the identities stored in the enterprise directory.

Directory synchronization utilities are intelligent Lightweight Directory Access Protocol (LDAP)-based engines capable of synchronizing data between different directories and other repositories.

Table 1.6   *Directory-Related Solutions*

Vendor	Directory Product
Enterprise Directory	
Novell	eDirectory
Microsoft	Active Directory
Sun	Sun One Directory Server
Meta-Directory	
CriticalPath	Metadirectory Server
Siemens	DirX
Directory Synchronization	
Microsoft	Microsoft Identity Integration Server (MIIS)
HP	LDAP Directory Synchronizer (LDSU)*
Virtual Directory	
Radiant Logic	Radiant One Virtual Directory Server

* More info on LDSU can be found at http://h20219.www2.hp.com/services/cache/11212-0-0-225-121.html.

A meta-directory provides a consolidated view on data that are stored in different directories and repositories. It links the data together in a central repository and keeps them synchronized between different repositories.

Unlike a meta-directory, a virtual directory does not build a central repository—instead, it acts as a proxy between a client and various other directories. It relies on directory server and client functions to access the data, and provides different views on the data stored in different repositories.

Provisioning Systems

Provisioning systems allow companies to centralize and automate the process of supplying, or provisioning, internal and external entities with access to the company's resources. In the mainframe era, identity and resource provisioning was relatively easy—everything could be done on a single machine. The rise of the PC and the growing importance of distributed client/server applications have made provisioning an administrative nightmare. Provisioning systems extend the simplicity of mainframe provisioning to today's distributed PC networks.

Provisioning systems extend the ease of management available in NOS environments, such as Windows Server 2003 and NetWare, to cover other applications and platforms. They provide a centralized management layer on top of the NOS's decentralized authorization enforcement. This makes them very different from Web Access Management Systems (WAMS). In WAMS, both authorization management and enforcement are centralized. Like a NOS, most provisioning systems can use directory-based repositories to store identity, authentication, and authorization information.

The ultimate goal of a provisioning system is to provide a highly automated management system. For example, the deletion of an identity in the HR database will make the provisioning system automatically trigger the deletion process for all other occurrences of this identity in all authorization

Table 1.7   *Provisioning Solutions*

Vendor	Provisioning Product
HP	HP OpenView Select Identity
IBM	Tivoli Identity Manager (TIM)
Sun	Sun Java System Identity Manager

databases in your organization. This can—if managed properly—significantly enhance the overall security quality of your IT systems. Used the other way around—to speed up the creation of new identities and authorization settings—it can enable new employees to become productive much faster. Obviously, centralized provisioning and a highly automated management also make identity and authorization management more consistent and easier to audit.

Most provisioning solutions are made up of the following services and components:

- **A self-service management facility** to let users maintain their proper credential and profile information

- **A delegated management facility** to delegate part of the management of a subset of the accounts and/or resources maintained in the provisioning system to other administrators; this may be a much-needed option in organizations with decentralized management models or in the context of Internet or application service providers (ISPs or ASPs)

- **A password synchronization service** to synchronize passwords between the different credential databases of an organization; this functionality may overlap with features offered by an authentication infrastructure providing SSO capabilities

- **A workflow engine** to automate the processes behind account and resource provisioning (for example, in many organizations the creation of a corporate account requires approval by multiple instances before the account is allowed access to the company's knowledge base)

- **A set of agents or connectors** to link up the provisioning system with applications and other TSI components

Table 1.7 gives a sample list of provisioning solutions available on the market today.

1.5   The Next Step: Federation

Federation is one of the trendiest topics in the IT industry. It represents an important next step in the creation of trusted security infrastructures. As will be explained next, federation is about linking different TSIs together to enable them to securely exchange identity data.

1.5.1   Defining Federation

The goal of federation is to make it easier for organizations to share data with authorized external users. These can be users in partner organizations or simply an organization's customers. For example, a manufacturing company may want to make its supply-tracking database accessible to supplier organizations. Another example is an industry analysis company that wants to open its publication repository to customer organizations. The key requirement in these examples is that access to the data is secured and restricted to authorized users. Two commonly used solutions to provide these services are Web access management systems (WAMS) and identity brokers.

To build WAMS organizations typically leverage commercial software packages. Examples of WAMS were given earlier in this chapter. Classical WAMS control access to an organization's resources by defining individual accounts for external users. This approach does not scale very well, may become an administrative burden, and is not easy to use. This is certainly the case if users must deal with the Web access management systems of different organizations. Users are then forced to maintain different accounts and credentials, and they may quickly end up with a user account nightmare. This problem is also referred to as the shadow account problem.

A better alternative is to give users a single account they can use to access the resources in different organizations. This also makes it trivial to provide Single Sign-On (SSO) services. This is exactly the goal of another solution category for our problem: identity brokers. A good Microsoft identity broker example is the Microsoft Passport system (now called Windows Live ID). Identity brokers are not perfect either. A key problem with identity brokers is that only few organizations trust the outsourcing of their account management to an external entity. The use of a central repository for storing the accounts also makes identity brokers a central point of attack and single point of failure.

Federation is the third solution to our problem, and it does not have any of the problems of the previous solutions. Identity federation allows users to

Table 1.8   *Federation Solutions*

Vendor	Federation Product
Hewlett-Packard	HP OpenView Select Federation
PingIdentity	PingFederate
Microsoft	Windows Server 2003 R2 Active Directory Federation Services (ADFS)

use a single account. It provides SSO services and allows organizations to maintain control over their proper accounts. Also, identity federation does not create central points of attack or single points of failure. On the other hand, current identity federation solutions lack some of the features that can be found in, for example, Web access management solutions, such as easy application integration and advanced auditing and reporting.

In federation-speak, an organization can be an identity provider, a resource provider, or a combination of both.

- An identity provider is an organization that issues and manages identities. A classical Microsoft-rooted example is a Windows domain controller: a domain controller issues and manages domain identities.

- A resource provider provides and controls access to resources. A Windows file server is an example of a resource provider: it controls access to files and folders.

Most organizations are a combination of both: they provide resources to their partner organizations and issue and manage the accounts for their proper employees.

From the above Windows example, you shouldn't conclude that federation is simply about setting up a trust between a Windows account and resource domain. Federation goes far beyond Windows domains: it can link heterogeneous identity and resource providers—for example, a Windows domain identity provider and a UNIX resource provider.

In summary, identity federation solutions link several identity and resource islands. These islands certainly exist between organizations but can also exist in a single organization. A common misconception is that identity federation is only about enabling and securing interorganizational data exchanges. Organizations often have internal islands created for security or political reasons that may benefit from federation as well. Good examples of identity islands are separate Windows Active Directory forests that may exist within a single enterprise or in different organizations. Table 1.8 shows a sample list of federation solutions.

1.5.2   Federation Standards

The approach of linking several authorities in a loosely coupled fashion and using distributed authentication and authorization services makes federation a unique security-enabling technology. It breaks with earlier approaches that tried to integrate resources and identities by bringing them together in the kingdom of a single security authority.

At the same time, loosely coupling security authorities makes federation an interesting technological challenge. Kingdoms typically have their own habits and ways of doing things. Security authorities use customized identity naming standards, mechanisms to verify identities (authentication) and control access to resources (authorization). This is why federation standards are so important. They can provide a lingua franca (common language) that expresses identity, authentication, and authorization data in a format that is understood by different identity and resource providers.

There are three main federation standard threads in the IT industry today:

- The **Security Assertion Markup Language (SAML)** thread is driven by OASIS (more info at www.oasis-open.org/committees/tc_home. php?wg_abbrev=security). SAML provides an XML dialect to embed identity data in an XML message. The SAML versions currently used in federation deployments are 1.2 and 2.0. SAML 2.0 can be considered the convergence of the SAML 1.2 and Liberty ID-FF 1.1 (explained below) specifications.

- The **Liberty Identity Federation Framework** (ID-FF 1.1 and 1.2) and **Liberty Identity Web Services Framework** (ID-WSF 1.1) threads are driven by the Liberty Alliance (more info at www.project-liberty.org/). The Liberty Alliance is an industry consortium of more than 150 companies and organizations focused on standardizing identity federation. The Liberty ID-FF 1.1 specification is built on the SAML 1.1 specification.

- The **WS-Federation** thread (more info at http://schemas.xml-soap.org/ws/2003/07/secext/) is driven by IBM, Microsoft, and Verisign. WS-Federation is a portion of a larger set of specifications that focuses on developing standards for Web services. WS-Federation has been a relatively independent thread that overlaps with the work that is done by the Liberty Alliance. In 2005, Sun and Microsoft announced specifications that allow interoperability between the WS-Federation and Liberty ID-FF standards for Web Single Sign-On (see http://xml.coverpages.org/WebSSO-InteropProfile200505.pdf for more detail).

Organizations that want to set up a federation should preferably use the same federation standard, but this isn't a necessity. Some federation solutions (such as HP OpenView Select Federation and IBM Tivoli Federated Identity Manager) can deal with different federation standards or translate one standard format to another.

For a more detailed overview of these federation standard threads, we refer to the HP white paper titled "Making sense of the federation protocol landscape" (http://devresource.hp.com/drc/resources/fed_land/index.jsp) or to Ping Identity's paper titled "Federation Standards Overview" (www.ping-identity.com/resources/showResource. action?id=7).

1.6 Identity Management and Trusted Security Infrastructures

After reading the previous sections you may conclude that the notion of Trusted Security Infrastructures (TSIs) that is introduced in this book is very similar to what is referred to as "identity management." This is true to a very large extent. Identity management, however, is an even broader concept than TSIs. For example, identity management infrastructures not only deal with security-related identity data, but also with all other identity attributes, including things like profile and personalization data.

The Identity management services offered by Microsoft in a Windows Server 2003 R2 environment will be covered in greater detail in the second book of this two-book series. In this introduction, we will define the concepts of an identity and identity management. We will also explain the technical components of what is generally referred to as identity management infrastructure.

1.6.1 Defining Identity and Identity Management

Identity is a complicated concept with many nuances, ranging from philosophical to practical. In the context of this book, we define the identity of an individual as the set of information known about that person. In the digital world, a person's identity is typically referred to as their digital identity. A person can have multiple digital identities.

Even though digital identities are still predominantly associated with humans, they are not an exclusive quality of humans and they will increasingly be associated with nonhuman entities, such as services, systems, and devices that could be used to act on behalf of people. Examples are trusted platforms, next generation mobile phones, Digital Rights Management (DRM)-based devices, etc.

The content of an identity is illustrated in Figure 1.5. It consists of a person's unique identifiers; authentication and authorization data; and profile data. All of these can be linked to different contexts (company, Web, application) and the role the person has in that context.

For example, a person's identity can be made up of a set of names, addresses, driver's licenses, passports, field of employment, etc. This information can be used for identification, authentication, and authorization purposes:

- A name can be used as an identifier—it allows us to refer to the identity without enumerating all of the items.

- A passport can be used as an authenticator—it is issued by a relevant authority and allows us determine the legitimacy of someone's claim to the identity.

- A driver's license can be used as a privilege—it establishes the permission to operate a motor vehicle.

In different contexts, different unique identifiers can be used. For example, in the above example, the driving license could be a relevant unique identifier for interacting with the Department of Motor Vehicles; name-surname-address is the unique identifier for the post office or a delivery service, etc. Often data associated with an identity are used improperly. For example, the use of a birth certificate as an authenticator represents a particularly poor choice, for there is generally nothing about the birth certificate

Figure 1.5
Identity definition.

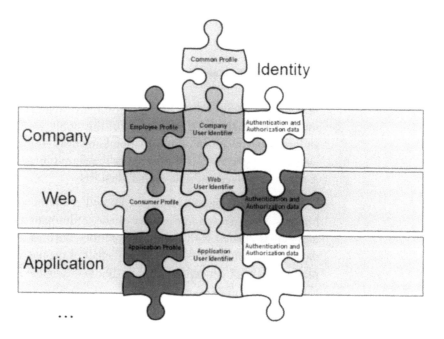

that allows an individual to be correlated to the claims on the certificate. Far better choices would be a passport that includes an individual's photograph, or a smart card storing an individual's thumbprint.

Identity management can be defined as the set of processes, tools, and social contracts surrounding the creation, maintenance, utilization, and termination of a digital identity for people or, more generally, for systems and services to enable secure access to an expanding set of systems and applications.

1.6.2 Identity Management Infrastructure Components

Figure 1.6 shows the identity management infrastructure components as they are defined in HP's technical identity management taxonomy. The components are grouped in four horizontal layers and one vertical layer.

Data Repository Components

Data repositories deal with the representation, storage, and management of identity and profiling information and provide standard APIs and protocols for their access.

Figure 1.6
Identity management infrastructures: technical components.

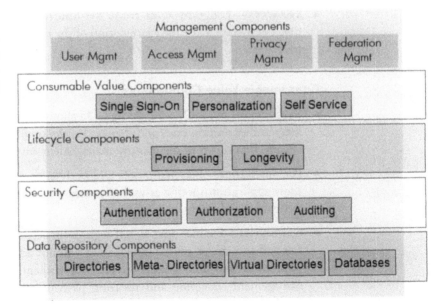

Security Components

- **Authentication Providers**—The authentication provider, sometimes referred to as the identity provider, is responsible for performing primary authentication of an individual, which will link him/her to a given identity.

- **Authorization Providers**—An authorization provider enforces access control when an entity accesses an IT resource. Authorization providers allow applications to make authorization and other policy decisions based on privilege and policy information stored in the repository.

- **Auditing Providers**—Secure auditing provides the mechanism to track how information in the repository is created, modified, and used.

Lifecycle Components

- **Provisioning**—Provisioning is the automation of all the procedures and tools to manage the lifecycle of an identity: creation of the identifier for the identity; linkage to the authentication providers; setting and changing attributes and privileges; and decommissioning the identity.

- **Longevity**—Longevity tools create the historical record of an identity. These tools allow the examination of the evolution of an identity over time.

Consumable Value Components

- **Single Sign-On (SSO)**—Single Sign-On allows a user to perform primary authentication once and then access the set of applications and systems that is part of the identity management environment.

- **Personalization**—Personalization and preference management tools allow application-specific as well as generic information to be associated with an identity.

- **Self-Service**—Enables users to self-register for access to business services and to manage profile information without administrator intervention. It also allows users to perform authentication credential management: assigning and resetting passwords, requesting X.509 certificates, etc.

Management Components

- **User Management**—Provides IT administrators with a centralized infrastructure for managing user profile and preference information.

- **Access Control Management**—Provides IT administrators with a centralized infrastructure for managing user authentication and authorization.

- **Privacy Management**—Ensures privacy and data protection policies are respected in identity management solutions.

- **Federation Management**—Enables the establishment of trusted relationships between distributed identity providers.

1.7   Microsoft and the Challenge of Trusted Security Infrastructures

This book focuses on how Microsoft has provided built-in support for TSIs in the latest versions of its enterprise server operating system Windows Server 2003 R2. These built-in TSI features are introduced in Section 1.7.1. We will also very briefly look at other Microsoft products that are not bundled with Windows Server 2003 R2 and that can provide TSI services. These other Microsoft products will not be covered in detail in this book.

1.7.1   Windows Server 2003 R2 as a TSI Building Block

Table 1.9 shows the TSI building blocks that come bundled with the Windows Server 2003 R2 server operating system, and the book part and chapter in which these building blocks will be covered in more detail.

In the context of this section, it is worth mentioning that Windows Server 2003 Service Pack 1 (SP1)—the Service Pack Microsoft released right before R2—obtained Common Criteria (CC) EAL4+ certification in December 2005.[5] This certification is the result of an evaluation process, led by the US federal government, that judges the security of computer systems using a predefined set of criteria. The CC EAL4+ certification for Windows Server 2003 SP1 applies to the Standard (32-bit), Enterprise

---

5.   More information is available at: www.microsoft.com/technet/security/prodtech/windowsserver2003/ccc/default.mspx and http://niap.nist.gov/cc-scheme/st/ST_VID4025.html.

Table 1.9   *Microsoft TSI Services Built in Windows Server 2003 R2*

Windows Feature	TSI Service	Discussed in Part/Chapter
Kerberos authentication infrastructure	Authentication infrastructure	Part 1/Chapter 6
IIS Web server authentication infrastructure	Authentication infrastructure	Part 1/Chapter 7
Services for UNIX (SFU)	Authentication infrastructure	Part 1/Chapter 8
Microsoft Windows Live ID authentication infrastructure (formerly known as Microsoft Passport)	Authentication infrastructure	Part 1/Chapter 9
Authorization Manager and Framework	Authorization infrastructure	Part 1/Chapter 10
Active Directory Authorization	Authorization infrastructure	Part 1/Chapters 10 and 11
Malicious Mobile Code Protection	Authorization and security management infrastructure	Part 1/Chapter 5 Part 2/Chapter 1
Active Directory Federation Services (ADFS)	Authentication infrastructure	Part 2/Chapter 5
Public Key Infrastructure	Key management infrastructure	Part 2/Chapters 6-10
Built-In Auditing System	Auditing infrastructure	Part 2/Chapter 13
Built-In Security Policy Enforcement (using Group Policy Objects)	Security Management infrastructure	Part 2/Chapter 11
Security Patch Management	Security Management infrastructure	Part 2/Chapter 12

(32- and 64-bit), and Datacenter (32- and 64-bit) versions of the operating system[6] and also includes the Windows Server 2003 Certificate Server.

Linked to this Windows Server 2003 SP1 Common Criteria certification is a set of collaterals that can guide customers in the deployment and operation of the Windows Server 2003 SP1 operating system in a highly secure networked environment. You can download this collateral from the following URLs:

■ Windows Server 2003 Common Criteria Configuration Guide: http://download.microsoft.com/download/4/6/4/46402d2a-45ce-4c1e-98d2-51cb7c9a1556/WS03_Common_Criteria_Configuration_Guide.zip.

---

6.   At the same time, Microsoft obtained CC EAL4+ certification for Windows XP Service Pack 2 (SP2) Professional and Embedded.

- Windows Server 2003 Common Criteria Administrator's Guide: http://download.microsoft.com/download/0/b/4/0b45ffb0-0fe4-43b1-b71b-fb4c5745d4a2/WS03_Common_Criteria_Admin_Guide.zip.

1.7.2 Other Microsoft TSI Building Blocks

Table 1.10 provides an overview of other Microsoft software products that can be used to provide TSI services. The Microsoft Operations Manager (MOM) and the Microsoft Systems Management Server (SMS) will be briefly discussed in the following sections: Windows Rights Management Service (RMS) will be covered in Chapter 2 of the second book, and Microsoft Identity Integration Server (MIIS) will be covered in Chapter 4 of the second book.

Microsoft Operations Manager

Microsoft Operations Manager (MOM) is Microsoft's solution for enterprisewide event and performance management. In the context of trusted security infrastructures, MOM can be used to build a centralized auditing infrastructure. Microsoft licensed MOM's core engine from NetIQ and rebranded it. MOM's highly flexible and distributed architecture is illustrated in Figure 1.7. The latest MOM version (at the time of writing) is MOM 2005. The next MOM release—planned for 2007—will be called Microsoft System Center Operations Manager 2007.

Out-of-the-box MOM includes agents for the following platforms, applications, and services (as part of the base management pack): Windows

Table 1.10 *Other Microsoft Software Providing TSI Services*

Microsoft Software	TSI Service	More Information at
Microsoft Identity Integration Server (MIIS)	Provisioning solution—security management infrastructure	www.microsoft.com/miis Discussed in Part 2/Chapter 4
Microsoft Operations Manager (MOM)	Security management and auditing infrastructure	www.microsoft.com/mom
Microsoft Systems Management Server (SMS)	Security management and auditing infrastructure	www.microsoft.com/sms
Windows Rights Management Services (RMS)	Authorization infrastructure	www.microsoft.com/rms Discussed in Part 2/Chapter 2

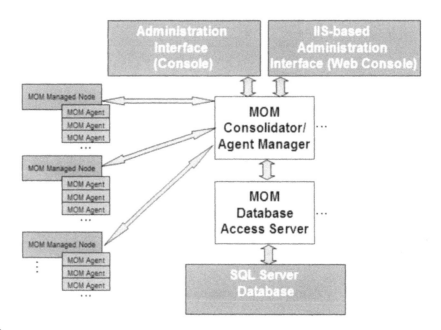

Figure 1.7   *MOM architecture.*

2000, Windows Server 2003, Active Directory, Internet Information Server, Terminal Server, Distributed Transaction Coordinator, WINS, DHCP, RRAS, Transaction Server, Message Queue Server, DNS, MOM, and SMS. MS also provides optional agents (as part of application management packs) for the following MS applications: Exchange, SNA Server, ISA Server, Proxy Server, SQL Server, Commerce Server, Site Server, and Biztalk Server. Other agents covering many more applications and platforms (including non-Microsoft platforms and applications) are available from third-party software vendors.

Microsoft Systems Management Server

The functionality of Microsoft's Systems Management Server (SMS) is sometimes confused with the functionality of Microsoft's MOM. Although there are some small overlaps, both products have very different focus areas. Whereas MOM is focused on performance monitoring and log consolidation, SMS's key strengths are in the areas of software distribution, hardware and software inventories, and helpdesk functions.

The latest SMS release is SMS 2003, which Microsoft released in late 2003. The next SMS release—planned for 2007—will be called Microsoft System Center Configuration Manager 2007. At the time of writing this

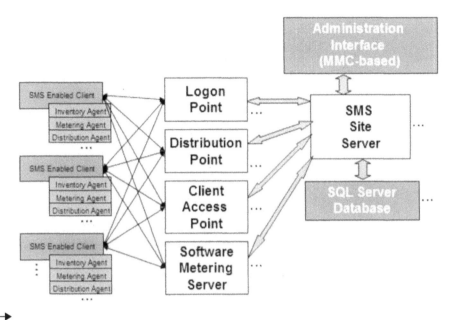

Figure 1.8   *SMS architecture.*

book, many enterprises are still using SMS 2.0 and are gradually upgrading to the new version, especially for its improved support for mobile clients and Active Directory integration. In 2003, Microsoft released an interesting add-on called the Software Update Services (SUS) Feature Pack, which specifically extends SMS 2.0's capabilities in the security patch management space for Windows OSs and MS Office applications. The SUS Feature Pack functionality is included out of the box in SMS 2003.

Figure 1.8 gives an overview of the SMS architecture. As for MOM, this architecture is highly flexible and distributed. Figure 1.8 does not show SMS's hierarchical site capabilities, consisting of primary and secondary sites.

1.8   Conclusion

This chapter introduced the Trusted Security Infrastructure (TSI) services and showed how Microsoft can help in this space. It introduced the Microsoft TSI product offerings and shed some light on the TSI features that come bundled with the Windows Server 2003 R2 Operating System, which are explored in much more detail in the rest of this book and its follow-up.

Windows Security Authorities and Principals

This chapter focuses on two building blocks of Windows Server 2003 and Windows Server 2003 R2 operating system security: security authorities and security principals. Among the concepts discussed in this chapter are security principal, domain, security identifier, domain controller, logon name, LSA, and LSA policy.

2.1 Security Authorities

To illustrate the fundamental role of trust in the Windows Server 2003 R2 operating system and to make the link with Chapter 1 on trusted security infrastructures (TSIs), we will first discuss the concept of Windows OS security authorities. In an OS, trust is embodied and materialized by security authorities.

A security authority reigns over a kingdom of shared resources (things like files, printers, applications…) and uses a database to store the security-related information that is needed to allow or deny access to the resources. OS users trust security authorities because they believe they can adequately secure the access to shared resources. Bringing multiple resources together in a kingdom ruled by a security authority facilitates security policy enforcement and provides ease of use to both the users and administrators of an OS.

A security authority's kingdom is represented by the ellipse in Figure 2.1. We will reuse these representations as other Windows security concepts are introduced throughout this chapter.

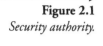
Figure 2.1
Security authority.

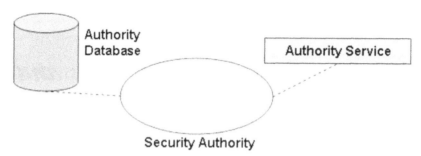

2.1.1   Local vs. Domain Security Authorities

In the Windows OS, we have to deal with two types of security authorities: the local security authority (LSA) and the domain security authority.

- A Windows **domain security authority** reigns over a kingdom of resources called a domain. A domain's security authority is called a domain controller (DC).

- A Windows **local security authority** (LSA) reigns over a Windows machine's local resources. An LSA is available on every domain-joined and standalone (or nondomain-joined) machine. Even domain controllers have an LSA, which is only activated when DCs boot in the directory services restore mode for disaster recovery operations.

When using Windows, you should always leverage Windows domain authorities: even if you have only a single file server, you should incorporate it in a domain. Domains ease security administration and close possible security holes. These advantages are illustrated in the following example. In environments where the same user needs to get access to multiple file or application servers, the inclusion of these servers in a domain means you must define the user once—in the domain database—instead having to define it on each server (a thing you would need to do in case you were not using a domain). Also, you reduce the attack surface of your Windows servers (or the chances that your environment and its resources are accessed by unauthorized users) when you build your security infrastructure on a single security database (the domain database) instead of relying on multiple databases—one for each file or application server—in a standalone server setup.

This doesn't mean the LSA and its database shouldn't be managed after machines join a Windows domain. All Windows machines—with the exception of domain controllers—have an active LSA. One of the tasks of the local LSA is to validate local user logons when users choose to log on locally instead of logging on to a domain.

2.1.2 The Local Security Authority

The local security authority (LSA) plays a crucial role in the authentication and authorization security processes. Among their tasks are security principal authentication, credential validation, and access token generation. The LSA also enforces the local security policy, including the auditing policy, memory quotas, user logon rights, and privileges.

Physically, the LSA is an OS subsystem running in OS user mode. The LSA process is visible in the Windows task manager as lsass.exe. The lsass process hosts a set of other important security processes implemented as dynamic link libraries (dlls) that are illustrated in Figure 2.2: the LSA authority process (lsasrv.dll), the SAM process (samsrv.dll), the AD process (ntdsa.dll), the Netlogon process (netlogon.dll), the Kerberos Key Distribution Center (KDC) service (kdcsvc.dll), and a set of authentication packages (the NTLM authentication package (msv1_0.dll) and the Kerberos authentication package (Kerberos.dll)).

The Netlogon process is only available on Windows domain controllers. The AD process and KDC service are only available on Windows 2000 and later domain controllers. The Kerberos authentication package is only available on Windows 2000, Windows XP, Windows Server 2003, and R2 platforms. Both the Netlogon and Kerberos processes are covered in greater detail in Chapters 5 and 6 of this book.

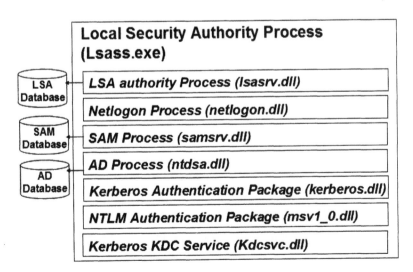

Figure 2.2
SA process and subprocesses available on Windows domain controllers.

The LSA has its proper database, which is referred to as the LSA database. It holds system-specific security policy information. The information stored in the LSA database is known as the LSA policy. The objects stored in the LSA policy are known as policy objects. Physically, the LSA security policy database is a secured part of the system registry.

The Security Accounts Manager (SAM) and Active Directory (AD) LSA subprocesses govern access to the local and domain credential databases. The SAM is available on all Windows versions to store local security principal information. On NT4 and earlier versions, it is also used to store domain security principal information. From Windows 2000 onwards, the AD is used to store domain security principal information. The concepts of domain and security principal will be explained in greater detail later in this chapter.

The LSA Database

The LSA security policy database holds different types of policy objects: policy, trusteddomain, account, and private data objects.

- A **policy object** determines who can access the LSA database. It also contains global system information such as system memory quota and auditing settings. Every system has a single policy object.

- A **trusteddomain object** stores information about a domain's trust relationship with another domain. This information includes the name and SID of the trusted domain, as well as the SID and password of the account used to submit authentication requests to the trusted domain.

- An **account object** contains information specific to a user or group (e.g., special user logon rights, privileges, and quotas).

- A **private data object** is used to store confidential information, such as system or service account passwords. LSA private data objects are also known as LSA secrets. LSA secrets are encrypted using the system key (syskey, explained in Section 2.1.2) and stored in the registry on the system's disk. When the system boots, the LSA secrets are retrieved from disk, decrypted, and made available to the LSA—which from that point onwards keeps the secrets in its memory space.

LSA secrets can also be used by applications to store secret data on their behalf. To store data in an LSA secret, the account in which security context the application is executed must be a member of the local administrators group. The APIs for dealing with LSA secrets are called LsaStorePrivateData and LsaRetrievePrivateData.

There is a limit on the number of LSA secrets that can be stored in the LSA database. In Windows Server 2003, this limit is 4,096, of which 2,048 are reserved for the operating system; the rest can be used by applications. LSA secrets are encrypted using a system-specific key and stored in the HKEY_LOCAL_MACHINE\security container of the system registry.

LSA secrets can be one of the following types: local, global, machine, or private.

- **Local** LSA secrets can only be read locally from the machine that stores them. Local LSA secrets have a name that starts with L$.

- **Global** LSA secrets are replicated between domain controllers. Global LSA secrets have a name that starts with G$.

- **Machine** LSA secrets can only be accessed by the operating system. Machine LSA secrets have a name that starts with M$.

- **Private** LSA secrets are not replicated, and can be accessed locally or remotely. They don't use special naming conventions. For example, service account password private LSA secrets start with an _SC_ prefix.

You can use the registry editor (regedt32) to see how and where LSA secrets are stored: the LSA secrets are stored in the HKEY_LOCAL_ MACHINE\Security registry container. There's one small problem, though: by default, the security settings on this container prevent access from any account other than the system account. You could change the permissions on the Security registry key and all its subkeys so that your account has full control access. A better idea is to start the registry editor in the security context of the system account. You can do this using the SysInternals psexec utility, which can be downloaded from the following URL: www.sysinternals.com/utilities/psexec.html. To start the registry editor in the system account's security context from your current logon session, type the following at the command line:

```
psexec -s -i -d c:\windows\regedit.exe
```

You should never use this tool on a production system—always use a test system. Once you have system-level access to the HKEY_LOCAL_ MACHINE\Security registry key, it will reveal a new list of registry subkeys, including the Policy key and, one level deeper, the Secrets subkey. In the Secrets subkey, you can find a list of LSA secrets.

To look at your Windows NT, Windows 2000, Windows XP, Windows Server 2003, or R2 machine's LSA secrets, you can also use the Cain tool. This GUI tool is bundled with another tool called Abel in a single executable that can be downloaded from www.oxid.it/cain.html. Cain's brother can dump the LSA secrets of a remote machine. A tool that can be used to look at an NT4.0 or Windows 2000 machine's LSA secrets from the command line is lsadump2. At the time of writing, lsadump2 did not work on Windows XP and Windows Server 2003. Lsadump2 can be downloaded from www.bindview.com/Services/RAZOR/Utilities/Windows/lsadump2_readme.cfm.

Do not run any of these tools on your production systems—use a test system. Also, you should only use them after you get the proper authorization from your IT security department. Remember, LSA secrets are critical NT system data that you do not want to distribute to everyone.

The System Key

The system key (also known as syskey) security feature adds an extra level of encryption protection for the LSA secrets stored in the LSA database. Syskey only protects the LSA secrets when the OS is not running. When the OS boots, the syskey "system key" is loaded into memory so it can be used to unlock the LSA secrets. Syskey is enabled by default on Windows 2000, Windows Server 2003, Windows Server 2003 R2, and Windows XP systems.

Besides the LSA secrets, syskey also protects the following important system data:

- Master keys that are used to protect private keys

- Protection keys for user account passwords stored in the SAM

- Protection keys for user account passwords stored in AD

- The protection key for the administrator account password used for system recovery startup in safe mode

Out of the box, the syskey is stored in the system registry of the local system. This location is not the best one for systems that require a very high level of security. That is why you may consider letting syskey prompt the user for a system key password at system startup. To set this up, type "syskey" at the command prompt, choose update, and select the "password startup" option. The syskey password length can be between 1 and 128 characters. As with passwords, we recommend at least nine characters.

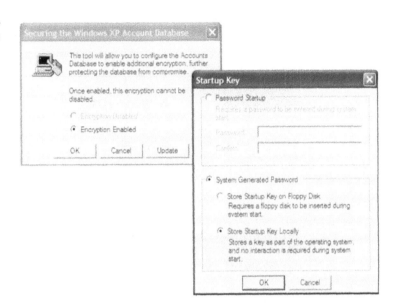

Figure 2.3
Configuring syskey.

Syskey also offers the possibility of storing the startup key on a floppy disk (as illustrated in Figure 2.3). In that case, you must provide the floppy each time the system boots. Both the password startup and floppy disk options require the user or administrator to be physically present when the system boots up: no pain, no gain! But read on…

Some hardware vendors have remote access capabilities for servers that can enter the Windows syskey password remotely or use a virtual syskey floppy disk during the Windows boot sequence. Both solutions allow the system key to be handled securely with less pain. An example of such solution is the HP ILO (integrated Lights-Out) for HP Integrity and Proliant Servers.

Table 2.1 summarizes the different syskey options, which are also referred to as syskey levels.

The easiest way to find out whether an NT machine has syskey enabled is to type "syskey" at the command prompt. This command brings up the Securing the Windows Account Database dialog box (shown in Figure 2.3), which indicates whether syskey encryption is enabled.

Alternately, you can check for the registry value HKEY_LOCAL_MACHINE\SYSTEM\CurrentControlSet\Control\Lsa\Secureboot. If the Secureboot value (of type REG_DWORD) exists and is set to a value of 0x1, 0x2, or 0x3, syskey is enabled on the system.

Table 2.1   *Syskey Levels and Their Meanings*

	Syskey Level 1	Syskey Level 2	Syskey Level 3
System key is…	Random key generated by the Windows OS	Random key generated by the Windows OS	Derived from a password chosen by the administrator
System key storage	System registry of local system	Floppy disk	System key not stored anywhere
Requires physical administrator presence to boot system	No	Yes	Yes
Important notes	Default on Windows 2000, Windows Server 2003, R2, and Windows XP systems	Floppy disk must be stored in a secure place	

More details on syskey are also available from the following Microsoft article: www.microsoft.com/resources/documentation/windows/xp/all/reskit/en-us/prnb_efs_zbxr.Asp.

2.1.3   The Domain Security Authority

As explained in Chapter 1, bringing multiple resources together in a kingdom ruled by a trusted third party facilitates security policy enforcement and provides ease of use to both users and administrators. In Windows Server 2003, the kingdom is called a *domain* and the trusted third party is called a *domain controller* (DC).

The Domain Concept

A Windows domain defines in the first place a management boundary. It is an administrative grouping of users, machines, and resources that can be managed by the same domain administrators.

From Windows 2000 onwards, a domain is also an Active Directory (AD) namespace and a replication partition. AD is the LDAP- and X.500-based directory Microsoft introduced in Windows 2000. An AD namespace defines the subset of the data stored in AD that is replicated and kept synchronized between AD copies on different domain controllers. The most important AD replication partition types are forestwide replication and domain-only replication; the difference between the two is illustrated in Figure 2.4.

Figure 2.4
*Domain-only vs.
forest-wide AD
replication.*

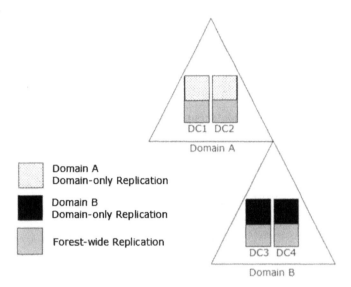

- **Domain-only replication** means that a subset of the AD objects (for example, user accounts and their password hashes) is replicated only between the domain controllers that are part of the same domain.

- **Forestwide replication** means that the AD data (for example, site configuration data and the AD schema) are replicated to all the domain controllers from any domain in the AD forest.

In an AD forest, different domains are linked together using trust relationships and DNS names. A forest can be made up of one or more domains and one or more domain trees. In a domain tree, domains are linked together using parent-child domain trust relationships, and all domains have contiguous DNS namespace. When a forest is made up of multiple domain trees, the trees are linked together using peer-to-peer trust relationships set up between the top-level domains of the domain trees and the trees have a noncontiguous DNS namespace. These concepts are illustrated in Figure 2.5, which shows an AD forest made up of several AD domain trees: hp.com, compaq.com, and tandem.com. In every AD tree there are multiple hierarchical parent-child domain relationships. Within the different domain trees in Figure 2.5, the DNS namespace is contiguous. Between domain trees, there's a noncontiguous DNS namespace.

Even though the concept of Windows Server 2003 domains, trees, and forests is completely different from the concept of a DNS domain, both concepts are closely intertwined in the context of an AD infrastructure. AD uses DNS to name and locate AD domains and services, and every Win-

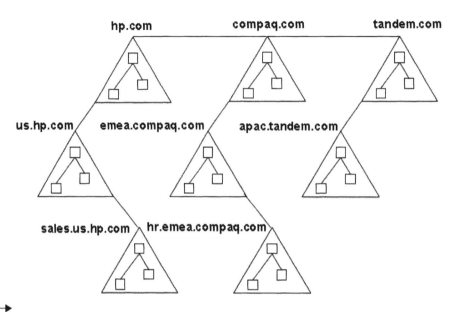

Figure 2.5   *Windows Server 2003 AD domains, trees, and an AD forest.*

dows Server 2003 domain is identified by its DNS domain name. In fact, the AD namespace is contained within the DNS namespace. Every AD domain tree can be mapped to a DNS domain hierarchy, and every AD domain corresponds to a DNS domain.

In Windows NT4 and earlier Windows versions, the domain was also a security boundary. The introduction of the forest concept in Windows 2000 changed the Windows security boundaries as they existed in earlier Windows versions. From Windows 2000 on, the notion of referring to a domain as a security boundary was no longer valid: now, the true security boundary is the forest. The forest enterprise administrators must always have a certain level of trust in the domain administrators of any domain in the forest, and vice versa. As previously mentioned, all DCs from any domain in a forest store both domain-only and forestwide data. And because any domain administrator has access to the AD database on his/her DCs, he/she also have the potential power to add, delete, or change any object anywhere in the AD forest.

Domain Functional Levels

The most important property of a Windows 2000 domain was its mode. The most important property of a Windows Server 2003 domain is its functional level.

A Windows 2000 domain can be in one of the following states: mixed or native mode.

- A mixed-mode Windows 2000 domain provides backward compatibility with Windows NT4 or earlier DCs. A mixed-mode domain can contain both NT4 and Windows 2000 DCs.

- A native-mode Windows 2000 domain provides additional AD functions. In a native-mode domain, all DCs are Windows 2000 DCs.

In Windows Server 2003, Microsoft provides a new set of AD functions that are only available if all the DCs are Windows Server 2003 DCs. This forced Microsoft to introduce more domain modes in order to link the correct AD function to a domain and its homogeneous or heterogeneous DC population. The Windows Server 2003 domain modes must be capable of differentiating between domains that hold only Windows Server 2003 DCs and domains that contain a mixture of Windows Server 2003, Windows 2000, and NT4 DCs.

To deal with the domain-mode problem in Windows Server 2003 once and for all, Microsoft introduced the concept of functional levels. "Functional levels" is just another name for a portable version management system that can be used in current and future versions of the Windows OS. Windows Server 2003 functional levels not only apply to DCs and domains, but also to forests. Domain and forest functional levels can be increased to a higher level if all DCs in the domain or forest have reached the appropriate level. Similar to an AD schema change, the switch to a higher domain or forest functional level cannot be undone. The switch activates new features that are incompatible with older versions of Windows DCs.

Tables 2.2 and 2.3 give an overview of the Windows Server 2003 domain and forest functional levels and their features. The tables also show what kind of DCs can be contained in a domain or forest with a certain functional level. Table 2.4 lists new Windows Server 2003 AD features and their domain or forest functional level requirements.

Domain Controllers

A domain controller (DC) is a domain's security authority. It hosts the domain security database and authenticates security principals that want to access the resources that are part of the domain.

Security principals are entities that want to use the resources (e.g., files, printers), applications, or services hosted on a Windows computer or Windows domain. The entity can be a user, a computer, a service, or an application. The concept of a security principal will be explained in more detail later.

A domain can have multiple DCs. All DCs host a copy of the same domain security database. This security database contains identifiers and authentication credentials of domain security principals. In simpler terms, it contains user names (identifiers), secured copies of user passwords (authentication credentials), group definitions, etc.

The domain security database of Windows 2000 and Windows Server 2003 is the AD domain naming context (or partition). It replaces the SAM database that is used in Windows NT 4.0. In Windows 2000 and Windows Server 2003, every domain controller contains a read-write copy of the domain directory database. This is also referred to as a multimaster DC

Table 2.2   *Domain Functional Levels*

Reference Name	Windows 2000 Domain Mode Windows Server 2003 Domain Functional Level	Possible Domain Controllers	Available Features
Windows 2000 mixed domain	Mixed Level 0	Windows NT Windows 2000 Windows Server 2003	■ Ability to replicate to Windows NT BDCs ■ Windows 2000 feature set
Windows 2000 native domain	Native Level 0	Windows 2000 Windows Server 2003	■ No ability to replicate to Windows NT BDCs ■ Windows 2000 feature set
Windows Server 2003 interim domain	— Level 1	Windows NT Windows Server 2003	■ Ability to replicate to Windows NT BDCs ■ Windows 2000 DCs cannot join domain ■ Windows 2000 feature set
Windows Server 2003 domain	— Level 2	Windows Server 2003	■ No ability to replicate to Windows NT BDCs ■ Windows 2000 DCs cannot join domain ■ Windows 2000 feature set ■ Application directory partitions ■ DC rename ■ DNS stub zones in application naming contexts ■ Kerberos KDC key version numbers

model, and is different from Windows NT4 where the primary domain controller (PDC) was the only one to host a read-write copy. All other Windows NT4 domain controllers held a read-only copy of the domain database and served as backup domain controllers (BDCs).

Table 2.3 *Forest Functional Levels*

Reference Name	Forest Functional Level	Possible Domain Controllers	Available Features
Windows 2000 forest	Level 0	Windows NT Windows 2000 Windows Server 2003	■ Level 0 mixed mode domains can exist with Windows NT, Windows 2000, and Windows Server 2003 DCs ■ Level 0 Windows 2000 native mode domains can exist with Windows 2000 and Windows Server 2003 DCs ■ Level 1 Windows Server 2003 interim mixed mode domains can exist with only Windows NT and Windows Server 2003 DCs ■ Level 2 Windows Server 2003 mode domains can exist with only Windows Server 2003 DCs ■ Windows 2000 feature set
Windows Server 2003 Interim forest	Level 1	Windows NT Windows Server 2003	■ Level 1 Windows Server 2003 interim mixed mode domains can exist with only Windows NT and Windows Server 2003 DCs ■ Level 2 Windows Server 2003 mode domains can exist with only Windows Server 2003 DCs ■ Windows 2000 feature set ■ Link Value Replication among Windows Server 2003 DCs ■ Prevent Windows 2000 Domain Controller from joining the forest ■ New ISTG (KCC) algorithm among Windows Server 2003 DCs
Windows Server 2003 forest	Level 2	Windows Server 2003	■ Level 2 Windows Server 2003 mode domains can exist with only Windows Server 2003 DCs ■ Domain rename ■ Dynamic auxiliary classes ■ Schema deletions ■ Transitive forest trusts

Table 2.4   *Domain or Forest Functional Level Requirements for Windows Server 2003 Features*

Feature	Functional Level Requirement
Global Catalog not required for logon	Domain Functional Level = 0
Install from media	Domain Functional Level = 0
Application directory partitions	Domain Functional Level = 2
Domain controller rename	Domain Functional Level = 2
DNS stub zones in application directory partitions	Domain Functional Level = 2
Kerberos key version numbers	Domain Functional Level = 2
Application directory partitions	Forest Functional Level = 0
Install from media	Forest Functional Level = 0
Universal group membership caching	Forest Functional Level = 0
Domain rename	Forest Functional Level = 2
Schema classes and attributes can be deactivated	Forest Functional Level = 2
Forest trusts	Forest Functional Level = 2
Link value replication	Forest Functional Level = 2
New ISTG (KCC) algorithm for AD replication	Forest Functional Level = 2
Dynamic auxiliary classes	Forest Functional Level = 2
New attribute replication only to global catalogs (no GC rebuild for schema extensions and inclusion into the GC)	Forest Functional Level = 2

Windows 2000 also introduced the notion of special-purpose DCs: the global catalog (GC) DCs. These are DCs that not only host a read-write copy of the domain directory database, but also a read-only copy of a subset of the other AD forest domains' security databases. This subset contains all objects of all other domains in the forest, only with a smaller set of attributes. This subset is referred to as the partial attribute set (PAS) and does not include application partitions. The PAS content can be adjusted by authorized administrators. Here are some examples of what data are in a GC and what is not:

■ A GC holds users' samAccountName attributes but not their password hash attributes.

- A GC includes the group memberships of universal groups but not the group memberships of global and domain local groups.

- GCs can be used to query objects throughout the forest and can be accessed using a separate LDAP port: port 3268 (a normal DC uses port 389). GCs are also required for authentication in a multidomain environment unless you have enabled GCless logon.[1]

Domain Controller Operations Master Roles

Just like Windows 2000 DCs, Windows Server 2003 and R2 DCs can have special roles in a Windows Server 2003 domain or forest. These roles are called Operations Master roles (in Windows 2000 they were referred to as flexible single master of operations (FSMO) roles). Operations Master roles exist because some of the AD services must operate in a single-master mode—even though the bulk of the AD services are built on a multimaster model. Table 2.5 gives an overview of the different FSMO roles. The PDC emulator, RID master, and infrastructure master Operations Master roles are security related. A good tool to manage and control Operations Master roles on Windows DCs (for example, to transfer and seize roles between different DCs) is the ntdsutil.exe command line tool.

Table 2.5 *Overview of Domain Controller Operations Master Roles*

DC Operations Master Role (Uniqueness)	Comments
Schema Master (one for every AD forest)	The Schema Master is unique in the entire AD forest. AD schema extensions (new object classes or attributes) can only be created on the Schema Master DC. The Schema Master is also required for forest functional level increases. It can be hosted on either a DC or a GC.
Domain Naming Master (one for every AD forest)	The Domain Naming Master manages the names of every naming context in the forest. The Domain Naming Master must be available to add and remove domains or application partitions in an AD forest. This avoids naming conflicts. In Windows 2000, the Domain Naming Master must be hosted on a GC. In Windows Server 2003 and R2 forests, the Domain Naming Master can be hosted on either a DC or a GC.

1.   GCless logon can only be enabled in Windows Server 2003. It is explained in more detail in Chapter 6.

Table 2.5   *Overview of Domain Controller Operations Master Roles (continued)*

DC Operations Master Role (Uniqueness)	Comments
PDC Emulator (one for every domain)	The PDC Emulator provides various features, the most obvious one being backward compatibility for downlevel clients and servers in the following ways: ■ Provides downlevel client support for password updates ■ Performs replication to downlevel BDCs (NT 4.0) ■ Acts as the Master Domain Browser, if the Windows NT 4.0 Browser service is enabled It also plays an important role regarding its peer Windows Server 2003 DCs. Windows Server 2003 DCs attempt to replicate password changes to the PDC emulator first. Each time a DC fails to authenticate a password, it contacts the PDC emulator to see whether the password can be authenticated there, perhaps as a result of a change that has not yet been replicated down to the particular DC. Furthermore, the PDC Emulator is also used for the following: ■ Domain functional level increases ■ Time synchronization ■ Distributed account lockout ■ Maintenance and coordination of shared secrets between trusted and trusting domains ■ Preferred DC for Group Policy updates ■ Default DC for updates of domain-based DFS metadata The PDC Emulator role can be hosted on either a DC or a GC.
RID Master (one for every domain)	When a security principal is created, it receives a domainwide *Security ID* (SID). A part of the SID is a domainwide unique *Relative ID* (RID). The RID master allocates a pool of RIDs for each of the DCs and keeps track of the sets of allocated RIDs. The RID master can be hosted on either a DC or a GC.
Infrastructure Master (one for every domain)	When an AD object from another domain in the same AD forest is referenced (for example, by making a user from one domain a member of a domain local group in another domain), DCs that are not GCs create a phantom object in the domain database to allow this reference to occur in the AD database tables. The reference contains the GUID, the SID, and the DN of the object. If the referenced object moves the following will happen: ■ The object GUID does not change. ■ The object SID changes if the move is cross-domain. ■ The object DN always changes. A DC holding the infrastructure master role is responsible for updating the SIDs and DNs in cross-domain object references for objects in the domain. It should be located on a DC (i.e., a nonglobal catalog server). However, if all DCs in a domain are GCs, it does not matter which DC holds the infrastructure master role, as there will be no phantom objects that need updating (since every GC will hold a real reference to all objects in the forest in its AD database).

2.2 Security Principals

In Windows, any entity that can be uniquely identified and that needs to have access to resources governed by a security authority is called a security principal. The concept of security principals is illustrated in Figure 2.6. Unique identification allows security principals to be distinguished from one another and allows administrators to give them different levels of access to resources. Users and computers are examples of security principals. Security principals can be used in the context of both a local and a domain security authority. A security principal's entry in a local or domain security authority's security database (the SAM or AD) is referred to as an account. Local accounts can be used to secure access to a machine's local resources: things like files, folders, printers, applications, and services. Domain accounts can be used to secure access to resources on any computer in the account's domain or trusting domain.

From Windows 2000 onward, machine security principals are true security principals: they can identify themselves to any other principal. This was not the case in NT4 and earlier Windows versions. A machine's account name always ends in a dollar sign ($).

The unique identifiers that Windows uses to refer to security principals are logon names and security identifiers (SIDs). These will be explained in the following sections.

Figure 2.6
Security authority and security principals.

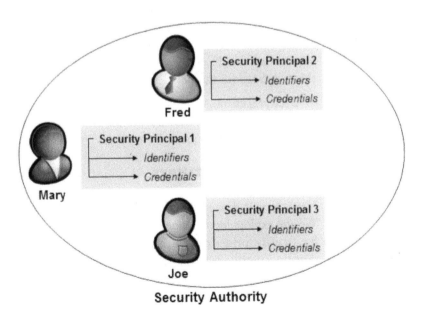

To verify a security principal's claimed identity, Windows can use different authentication credentials. These credentials can be based on different authentication methods: passwords, smart cards, biometric data, and so forth. The main difference between these methods is the use of different credentials or things that uniquely identify an entity. Out-of-the-box Windows Server 2003 supports password-based and smart card–based authentication. Other authentication methods can be supported by using third-party software. Next, we will provide more details on the Windows security principal identifiers and the default Windows credentials: passwords. Authentication methods are discussed extensively in Chapter 5.

So what's the use, besides identification and authentication, of being a security principal? Every "security principal" can be used in other Windows security-related processes such as authorization, delegation, and auditing. A security principal can be granted access to resources (this process is known as authorization). It can also be granted administrative permissions (this process is known as delegation) and can be uniquely referred to in security logs (creating and maintaining security logs is the task of the auditing process). Authorization, delegation, and auditing will again be covered in later chapters.

Windows Server 2003 supports a new type of security principal: the iNetOrgPerson security principal. The enabler of this new principal type is the iNetOrgPerson AD object class. Contrary to the AD user object class (which is used to define plain user accounts), the iNetOrgPerson object class complies with an Internet standard: RFC 2798. Microsoft implemented this class to achieve compatibility with legacy applications that leverage an LDAP database for their object storage and assume that a user account has the iNetOrgPerson class. Starting with Windows Server 2003, these applications can now leverage AD for their LDAP queries.

iNetOrgPerson AD objects are true Windows security principals. Like any other user object, they can be used to define authorization settings or administrative delegation.

2.2.1 Principal Identifiers

Next we will discuss Windows Server 2003 security principal identifiers. We will explore logon names and security identifiers. Logon names are used by security principals when they authenticate themselves to a local or domain security authority. They are real names and thus user-friendly. Security identifiers are of no use to normal users: they are used to refer to security principals by the built-in Windows security processes. Security identifiers are alphanumerical strings and are not user-friendly.

Logon Names

In a Windows Server 2003 environment, security principals can use different logon names. They can use their downlevel name or their user or service principal name (UPN or SPN).

A downlevel name has the format "domainname\username." It was a security principal's unique identifier in Windows versions before Windows 2000. Downlevel names can be used to refer to security principals in the kingdoms of both local and domain security authorities.

As mentioned earlier, Windows 2000 introduced the concept of a forest as an administrative and security boundary. The forest concept required the creation of a new type of unique security principal identifier. This is why Windows 2000 introduced the concepts of User Principal Names (UPNs) and Service Principal Names (SPNs).

User Principal Names

A UPN has the following format: username@company.com. It consists of a username, the @ symbol, and a DNS domain name. The format of a UPN is defined in RFC 822. The UPN is stored in the userprincipalname attribute of a Windows 2000, Windows Server 2003, and R2 AD account object. UPNs can only be used to refer to users in the context of a domain security authority; they are not used by local security authorities in a standalone setup.

A UPN is an AD user account's unique forest identifier. The uniqueness of a UPN is validated every time a new user account object and UPN are created. This is done first by searching the local AD domain naming context, then by searching the global catalog (GC). Even though AD validates UPN uniqueness when a new user account object is created, AD has no means to enforce this uniqueness, especially when bulk updates occur on multiple DCs in an AD forest. In those cases, it is the responsibility of the administrators to ensure that no duplicate UPN entries are added to an AD forest.

In Windows 2000 and Windows Server 2003 there is no need for the DNS domain name portion of a UPN to correspond to the DNS domain name of the domain that contains the user account's definition. The DNS domain name portion can also be the DNS domain name of the forest root domain,[2] or an alternate DNS domain name that is listed in the UPN suffixes attribute of the AD partitions container (which is a part of the AD Configuration container). The sidenote on "Defining UPN Suffixes" explains how you can define UPN suffixes from the Windows graphical user interface (GUI).

UPN suffixes can, for example, enable users to log on with their e-mail address. The latter may be risky from a security point of view: a hacker sniffing SMTP traffic can immediately catch half of the user's credentials.

Defining UPN Suffixes

UPN suffixes can be set from the Windows Server 2003 GUI by using the properties of the Active Directory Domains and Trusts container in the Active Directory Domains and Trusts MMC snap-in, as illustrated in Figure 2.7. To add a UPN suffix, type the name of the suffix in the Alternative UPN suffix entry box, then click the Add button.

You can set a user account's UPN from the AD Users and Computers (ADUC) MMC snap-in: simply use the User logon name drop-down list in the Account tab of the user account's properties (as illustrated in Figure 2.8). The drop-down list shows the DNS suffixes of the user account's definition domain, of the forest's root domain (if the account's definition domain belongs to the forest root domain's domain tree), and also all UPN suffixes manually defined in the properties of the AD Partitions container.

A nice thing about using a UPN for authenticating to a Windows Server 2003 domain security authority is that it takes away the requirement for a user to choose or enter a domain name in the logon dialog box. When a user types his UPN, the "Log On To…" drop-down list will be automatically disabled. More importantly, the UPN allows users to authenticate across a forest trust relationship, which will be explained in more detail in Chapter 3.

A UPN also stays the same, independent of what happens with a user's account object after it was created. The following administrative actions do not affect a user's UPN (this does not mean an administrator cannot change UPNs manually, as was explained earlier):

- Moving a user to another domain in the forest

- Renaming a user's downlevel name (<domainname>\<username>)

---

2.   This is only true for a child domain that is in the same domain tree as the forest root domain. If the child domain is another domain tree, by default only the child domain's proper DNS domain name will show up in the UPN list.

Figure 2.7
Defining UPN suffixes.

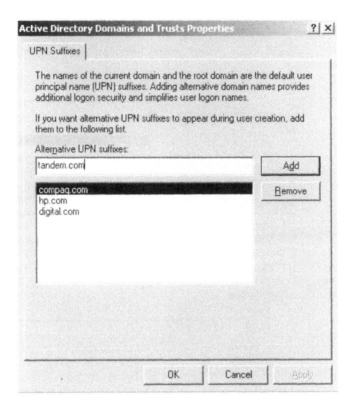

Service Principal Names

A service principal name (SPN) is a unique identifier for the security identity that is used by a Windows 2000 (or later) service. Like any other piece of code executing on a Windows machine, a Windows service must run in the security context of a particular security identity.

SPNs were introduced in Windows 2000 to uniquely identify a service during the Kerberos authentication sequence. When a user sends a Kerberos ticket request for a particular service to the Windows Server 2003 Kerberos Key Distribution Center (KDC), the ticket specifies the service the user wants to connect to using its SPN. The SPN will also be specified in the ticket that is generated by the KDC. The user can use the ticket only to authenticate to the service that is identified by that particular SPN.

An SPN is very similar to the concept of a user principal name (UPN)—the unique identifier for a user in a Windows forest. Like a UPN, an SPN must be unique in the Windows forest.

Figure 2.8
Defining a user's UPN from the ADUC MMC snap-in.

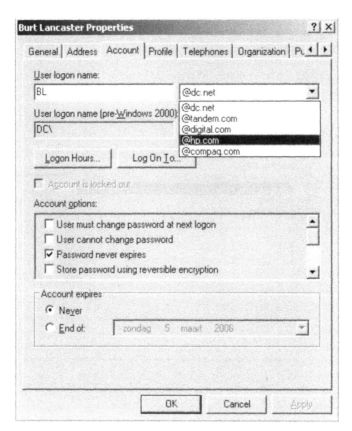

An SPN is stored in a security principal's AD object: in the Service-PrincipalName attribute. Because many Windows services run in the security context of a machine account, you often find their SPNs in the ServicePrincipalName attribute of a machine's AD object.

To look at the SPNs associated with a particular machine account, you can use the adsiedit or the setspn tools. Both come with the Windows Server 2003 Support tools. Adsiedit is a generic MMC-based tool that allows you to retrieve all kinds of AD information. Setspn is a command-line tool that specifically deals with SPN information. As opposed to UPNs, you cannot set SPNs from the ADUC MCC snap-in.

Typing "setspn –L test1" at the command prompt will list all the SPNs that are linked to the machine called test1 (as illustrated in Figure 2.9). To add an SPN, use setspn with the -A switch. To delete one, use the -D switch.

Figure 2.9   *Using setspn to display the SPNs linked to a machine.*

SPNs can only be manipulated (created and deleted) by an administrator, with the exception of a system account that can manipulate the SPN of its proper computer account.

To enable the user of a Windows service to construct the service's SPN without completely knowing it, SPNs have a fixed format. In most cases, the Kerberos software just gets an LDAP or HTPP URL from the user. To deal with the conversion from, for example, a URL to an SPN, Windows includes a special OS function called "DsCrackNames."

An SPN has the following format:

```
<ServiceClass>/<Host>:<Port>/<ServiceName>
```

The different SPN parts have the following meaning:

- **<ServiceClass>** is a string identifying the service. Examples are "www" for a Web service and "ldap" for a directory service.

- **<Host>** is the name of the computer on which the service is running. This can be a NetBIOS or a DNS name.

- **<Port>** is an optional parameter for the service port number. It enables differentiation between multiple instances of the same service running on the same machine and using a different TCP/IP port number.

- **<ServiceName>** is an optional parameter used to identify the data or services provided by a service or to identify the domain served by a service.

Below is a sample SPN that uniquely identifies the AD LDAP service of a domain controller called test1 in the hr.hewlettpackardtest.net domain:

```
ldap/test1.hr.hewlettpackardtest.net/HR
```

Security Identifiers

Every Windows security principal has a security identifier (SID), which is a unique alphanumeric identifier. Unlike logon names, SIDs are not user- and administrator-friendly. They are used by Windows security-related processes, such as authorization, delegation, and auditing, to uniquely identify security principals.

The SID for a domain account is created by a domain's security authority. The SID for a local account is created by a local security authority. The SID of a domain account is stored in the objectSid attribute of the account's AD object. The SID of a local account is stored in the SAM.

An important property of a SID is its uniqueness in time and space. A SID is unique in the environment where it was created (in a domain or on a local computer). It is also unique in time. If you create an object "Paul," delete it, and recreate it with the same name, the new object will never have the same SID as the original object. The format of SIDs for local and domain authorities will be outlined next.

SID Layout

Let's have a look at what a SID looks like. The string representation of a SID and its different components together with an example are shown in Table 2.6.

Table 2.7 shows the predefined Windows SID layouts. In this table, the following conventions are used:

- **TA** represents the identifier for the top-level authority (as shown in Table 2.8).

- **X and Y** represent two 32-bit fields that are used to uniquely identify a logon session.

- **WM1, WM2, and WM3** represent three 32-bit fields used to uniquely identify a workstation or member server.

Table 2.6 *SID Structure*

Field	Example: S-1-5-21-4064627337-2434140041-2375368561-1036
Character S identifying the object as a SID	S
The revision level of the SID structure (currently always 1)	1
An identifier for the top-level authority that issued the SID. The six possible values are listed in Table 2.7.	5 (SECURITY_NT_AUTHORITY)
A variable number of identifiers for subauthorities.	21 (This is a normal SID for some account in some domain or on some machine)
A domain subauthority identifier is always made up of three 32-bit numbers.	4064627337-2434140041-2375368561 (three 32-bit numbers referring to a domain)
A relative ID (RID) to uniquely identify the security object relative to the authority issuing the SID. Predefined users and groups (e.g., administrator, domain admins, etc.) always have a SID lower than 1,000. Newly created users and groups have a SID equal to or higher than 1,000.	1,036 (a user account in the domain)

Table 2.7 *Predefined SID Layouts*

SID Type	Comments	SID Layout						
Special Groups		S	1	TA	WID			
Built-In Groups	Refers to the Built-In Domain	S	1	5	32	WID		
Logon Sessions		S	1	5	5	X	Y	
Local Well Known SIDs	On Workstations and Member Servers	S	1	5	21	WM1	WM2	WM3	WID
Local Incremental SIDs	On Workstations and Member Servers	S	1	5	21	WM1	WM2	WM3	RID
Shared Well Known SIDs	On the Domain Level	S	1	5	21	D1	D2	D3	WID
Shared Incremental SIDs	On the Domain Level	S	1	5	21	D1	D2	D3	RID

- **D1, D2, and D3** represent three 32-bit fields used to uniquely identify a Windows domain.

- **RID** represents a relative identifier. This is a value above 1,000 that is maintained in an incremental way by the OS.

- **WID** represents a well known identifier or a RID with a predefined meaning.

  From the SID layouts in Table 2.8 we can learn the following:

- The built-in domain accounts' SIDs always start with S-1-5-32. The built-in domain contains a set of important predefined groups—e.g., users, guests, backup operators, etc.

- A normal user account's SID always starts with S-1-5-21. This is true both for local and domain user accounts.

- For local accounts, SIDs are based on the SID of the machine where the account is defined. A RID is appended to the machine SID to obtain the local account's SID. For example, if S-1-5-21-1449803782-4062493886-24154685 is a machine SID, then the local administrator account on that machine will have SID S-1-5-21-1449803782-4062493886-24154685-500 (this is the machine account SID with RID 500 appended to it).

Table 2.8 *SID Top-Level Authorities*

Top-Level Authority Value	Meaning
0	SID_IDENTIFIER_AUTHORITY
1	SECURITY_WORLD_SID_AUTHORITY Contains the Everyone group (S-1-1-0)
2	SECURITY_LOCAL_SID_AUTHORITY
3	SECURITY_CREATOR_SID_AUTHORITY Contains Creator Owner, Creator Group, Creator Owner Server, and Creator Group Server groups (S-1-3-0 through S-1-3-5)
4	SECURITY_NON_UNIQUE_AUTHORITY
5	SECURITY_NT_AUTHORITY Contains all other well-known security principals (S-1-5-x), users, groups, etc.
9	SECURITY_RESOURCE_MANAGER_AUTHORITY

- For domain accounts, SIDs are based on the SID of the domain where the account is defined. A RID is appended to the domain SID to obtain the domain account's SID. For example, if S-1-5-21-4064627337-2434140041-2375368561 is a domain SID, then the domain administrator account will have SID S-1-5-21-4064627337-2434140041-2375368561-500 (this is the domain SID with RID 500 appended to it).

Well Known SIDs

Well known SIDs represent special entities that are predefined and controlled by the Windows security subsystem. Popular examples are the Everyone, Authenticated Users, Local System, Self, and Creator Owner security principals. Unlike normal security principals, well known security principals cannot be renamed or deleted. Also, you cannot create your own well known security principals; they are the same on every Windows system, although the list of available well known security principals slightly varies by OS version.

A list of well known SIDs and their meanings is shown in Table 2.9. The exact function of these well known SIDs is not explained in this chapter but in the chapters on authorization later in this book.

Table 2.9 *Well Known SIDs*

SID	Meaning
S-1-0	Null Authority SID (identifier authority)
S-1-0-0	Nobody
S-1-1	World Authority SID (identifier authority)
S-1-1-0	Everyone group SID
S-1-2	Local Authority SID (identifier authority)
S-1-3	Creator Authority SID (identifier authority)
S-1-3-0	Creator Owner SID
S-1-3-1	Creator Group SID

Table 2.9   *Well Known SIDs (continued)*

SID	Meaning
S-1-3-2	Creator Owner Server SID (not used in Windows 2000)
S-1-3-3	Creator Group Server SID (not used in Windows 2000)
S-1-4	Non-unique Authority SID (identifier authority)
S-1-5	NT Authority SID (identifier authority)
S-1-5-1	Dial-up SID
S-1-5-2	Network logon SID
S-1-5-3	Batch logon SID
S-1-5-4	Interactive logon SID
S-1-5-5-X-Y	Session logon ID (X and Y values are different for each logon session)
S-1-5-6	Service logon SID
S-1-5-7	Anonymous logon SID
S-1-5-8	Proxy SID (not used in Windows 2000)
S-1-5-9	Enterprise Domain Controllers SID
S-1-5-10	Principal Self SID
S-1-5-11	Authenticated Users SID
S-1-5-12	Restricted Code SID (Windows XP SP2, Windows Server 2003, and R2 only)
S-1-5-13	Terminal Server Users SID
S-1-5-14	Remote Interactive Logon SID (Windows XP SP2, Windows Server 2003, and R2 only)
S-1-5-15	This Organization SID (Windows Server 2003 and R2 only)
S-1-5-18	Local System SID

Table 2.9 *Well Known SIDs (continued)*

SID	Meaning
S-1-5-19	Local Service SID (Windows XP SP2, Windows Server 2003, and R2 only)
S-1-5-20	Network Service SID (Windows XP SP2, Windows Server 2003, and R2 only)
S-1-5-XXX-500	Administrator Account SID (XXX is domain-specific identifier)
S-1-5-XXX-501	Guest Account SID (XXX is domain-specific identifier)
S-1-5-XXX-502	Krbtgt Account SID (XXX is domain-specific identifier)
S-1-5-XXX-512	Domain Admins SID (XXX is domain-specific identifier)
S-1-5-XXX-513	Domain Users SID (XXX is domain-specific identifier)
S-1-5-XXX-514	Domain Guests SID (XXX is domain-specific identifier)
S-1-5-XXX-515	Domain Computers SID (XXX is domain-specific identifier)
S-1-5-XXX-516	Domain Controllers SID (XXX is domain-specific identifier)
S-1-5-XXX-517	Certificate Publishers SID (XXX is domain-specific identifier)
S-1-5-XXX-518	Schema Admins SID (XXX is domain-specific identifier)
S-1-5-XXX-519	Enterprise Admins SID (XXX is domain-specific identifier)
S-1-5-XXX-520	Group Policy Creator Owners SID (XXX is domain-specific identifier)
S-1-5-XXX-533	RAS and IAS servers SID (XXX is domain-specific identifier)

Table 2.9   *Well Known SIDs (continued)*

SID	Meaning
S-1-5-32-544	Administrators SID
S-1-5-32-545	Users SID
S-1-5-32-546	Guests SID
S-1-5-32-547	Power Users SID
S-1-5-32-548	Account Operators SID
S-1-5-32-549	Server Operators SID
S-1-5-32-550	Print Operators SID
S-1-5-32-551	Backup Operators SID
S-1-5-32-552	Replicators SID
S-1-5-32-554	Pre-Windows 2000 Compatible Access SID
S-1-5-32-555	Remote Desktop Users SID
S-1-5-32-556	Network Configuration Operators SID
S-1-5-32-557	Incoming Forest Trust Builders SID
S-1-5-32-558	Performance Monitor Users SID
S-1-5-32-559	Performance Log Users SID
S-1-5-32-560	Windows Authorization Access Group SID
S-1-5-32-561	Windows Terminal Server License Servers SID
S-1-5-64-10	NTLM Authentication SID (Windows Server 2003 and R2 only)
S-1-5-64-14	SChannel Authentication SID (Windows Server 2003 and R2 only)
S-1-5-64-21	Digest Authentication SID (Windows Server 2003 and R2 only)
S-1-5-1000	Other Organization SID (Windows Server 2003 and R2 only)

SID-Related Utilities

A set of interesting free utilities that can translate user account names to SIDs and the other way around are available on the Internet. On the Web site of ntbugtraq, you can find a copy of user2sid and sid2user (http://www.ntbugtraq.com). On the LCPsoft Web site (www.lcpsoft.com), you can find SID&User (SAU). SID&User adds a nice GUI (illustrated in Figure 2.10) to the user2sid and sid2user programs. SAU, user2sid, and sid2user can all deal both with user and machine accounts and SIDs. Another tool you can use to retrieve an account's SID is the Support Tools getsid tool. Even though getsid is a SID comparison tool, you can use it to translate user names to SIDs. For example, you can use getsid as follows to retrieve the administrator SID of the server named "JansServer":

```
Getsid \\JansServer Administrator \\JansServer
Administrator
```

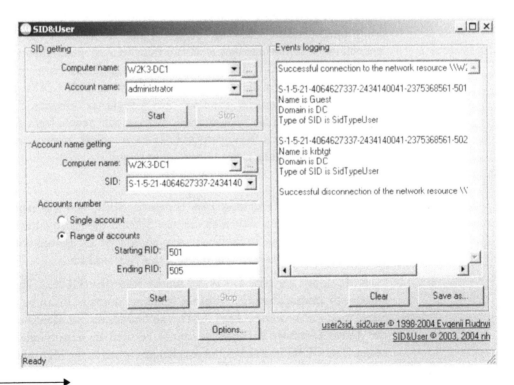

Figure 2.10   *Using SID&User.*

To identify the SID that is associated with your security principal, type the following at the command line:

```
whoami /logonid
```

The whoami tool comes both with the Windows Server 2003 operating system and the Windows 2000 Resource Kit. When using the Windows 2000 Resource Kit whoami version, you must use the following syntax to obtain your SID:

```
whoami /user /sid
```

Sysinternals provides a utility called newsid to generate new machine SIDs. This utility can be very useful when dealing with machine cloning technology that doesn't automatically generate a new SID for every cloned machine. A good example is the copying of VMWare images to create new virtual machines; the original VMWare image was not prepared for cloning with a tool like sysprep from the Windows resource kit. Although it is not a problem to give copied machines a new name and IP address, when you bring these identical VMWare images together in the same AD domain, you will receive error messages at startup time because the machines all have identical machine SIDs. You may even run into similar issues when migrating previously imaged clients from an NT4 domain to AD. NT4 does not treat computers as security principals and a duplicate computer SID does not cause an issue in an NT4 domain. You can run newsid from the command line or from the Windows GUI. To automatically reset a computer's SID, type the following at the command prompt:

```
newsid /a
```

In addition to generating new computer SIDs, newSID replaces all occurrences of the old SIDs with the new SIDs in the registry, in the registry objects' ACLs, and in the file-system objects' ACLs. newsid is available for free from www.sysinternals.com/Utilities/NewSid.html.

A SID is not the same as a global unique identifier (GUID). The SID is an object's unique identifier within a Windows domain. It can be used for security-related processes. The GUID is an object's unique identifier within the Active Directory database. It cannot be used in security-related processes. The GUID of an object never changes, whereas the SID can change. For example, when a user object is moved between two domains, it will receive a new SID—but the GUID will remain identical.

2.2.2 Account Management

Both domain and local Windows accounts can be created, deleted, and modified using different tools that will be discussed in more detail below.

Domain Account Management

To deal with domain accounts from a Windows XP, Windows 2000, or Windows Server 2003 machine, you can use the tools outlined below.

- Use the "Active Directory Users and Computers" (ADUC) MMC snap-in. On Windows XP and Windows 2000 Professional, the ADUC MMC snap-in is only available if you have the Administrative Tools installed. The ADUC is the most advanced account administration tool Microsoft makes available as part of its base OS. The ADUC provides support for features such as template accounts (that can be used to rapidly generate new accounts based on a predefined account template), saving previous AD queries, etc.

- Use the command line and the ds* commands. These commands include the dsadd (to add AD objects), dsmod (to modify AD objects), dsget (to list AD objects), dsquery (to query AD), dsrm (to remove AD objects), and dsmove (to move AD objects). For example, type the following dsadd command to add user Joe to the organizational unit (OU) Brussels in an AD domain called HP.net:

```
dsadd user "cn=Joe,ou=Brussels,DC=HP,DC=Net"
```

- Use the command line and the "net user" command. For example, type the following net user command to add user Joe to your domain database:

```
net user Joe /add /domain
```

  When dealing with AD domain accounts from the command line, we recommend you to use the ds* commands instead of the net user commands. The net commands use the NT4 APIs and connect to the AD PDC emulator DC to make AD changes. Also, they cannot deal with all AD object properties. The ds* commands use the AD APIs and can thus connect to any DC in a distributed environment. They are also much more powerful and can deal with many more (but also not all) AD object properties. The net command is still a valid tool to manage local accounts, though.

Local Account Management

If you do take the option to use standalone machines instead of domain-joined machines (again, we don't recommend that you take this option unless there is a need for complete administrative isolation of a machine) you can administer the machine's local accounts using the tools outlined below. They all manipulate user account data stored in the local security database or SAM. Table 2.10 compared the administrative features of the different local account management tools. Also—remember from above—you'll need these tools on domain-joined machines as well, to manage their local accounts.

- **The Local Users and Groups (LUG) MMC snap-in** (illustrated in Figure 2.11) can be accessed by opening the Microsoft Management Console (MMC—this can be done by typing mmc in the Run... dialog box) and then adding the LUG MMC snap-in. The LUG MMC snap-in can also be accessed by clicking Advanced in the Advanced tab of the User Accounts dialog box.

  In Windows Server 2003 you can also access the LUG MMC snap-in by typing the following command:

  ```
  control userpasswords
  ```

Table 2.10 *Administrative Features of Local Account Management Tools*

Task	Users and Passwords (User Accounts in XP)	Local Users and Groups	User Accounts	Net User Commands
Create user account	Yes	Yes	Yes	Yes
Delete user account	Yes	Yes	Yes	Yes
Place account in a security group	Yes, but you can add an account to only one group	Yes	Yes, but you can add an account only to the Administrators group or the Users group	Yes
Change user name	Yes	Yes	No	No
Change full name	Yes	Yes	Yes	Yes
Change description	Yes	Yes	No	Yes
Change picture	No	No	Yes	No

Table 2.10 *Administrative Features of Local Account Management Tools (continued)*

Task	Users and Passwords (User Accounts in XP)	Local Users and Groups	User Accounts	Net User Commands
Set a password	Yes, but only for a local account other than the one with which you're currently logged on	Yes	Yes	Yes
Set a password hint	No	No	Yes	No
Set password restrictions	No	Yes	No	Yes
Set logon hours	No	No	No	Yes
Enable or disable account	No	Yes	Yes, but only the Guest account	Yes
Unlock account	No	Yes	No	Yes
Set account expiration date	No	No	No	Yes
Specify profile and logon script	No	Yes	No	Yes
Link account to Microsoft .NET Passport (Windows XP only)	Yes	No	Yes	No

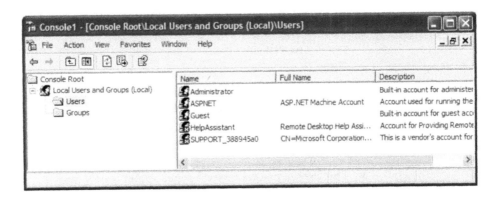

Figure 2.11 *Local Users and Groups MMC snap-in.*

The LUG snap-in is also integrated with the Computer Management (CM) MMC snap-in. You can get to the CM snap-in by right-clicking "My Computer" in the Windows Explorer and selecting "Manage," or by right-clicking a computer object in the AD Users and Computers (ADUC) MMC snap-in andselecting "Manage."

- **The User Accounts (Windows XP Professional) or Users and Passwords (Windows 2000 and Windows Server 2003) dialog box** (illustrated in Figure 2.12) can be accessed from the Users and Passwords control panel applet on a Windows 2000 or Windows Server 2003 standalone machine. In Windows XP Home Edition, this interface is also available, but it is useless: it doesn't allow you to do anything.

  In Windows XP and Windows Server 2003, the User Accounts or User and Passwords dialog boxes can also be accessed by running the following command:

  ```
  control userpasswords2
  ```

- **The User Accounts control panel applet** is only available on nondomain-joined Windows XP clients and is illustrated in Figure 2.13. This control panel applet can also be accessed by typing the following command:

  ```
  control userpasswords
  ```

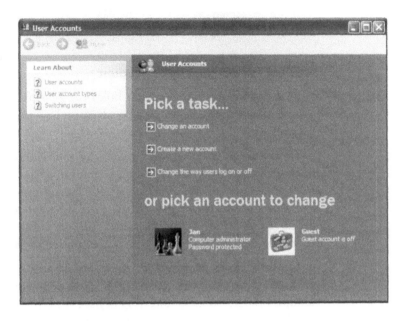

Figure 2.13
*User Accounts
control panel
applet.*

- Use one of the following command-line commands:
  - net accounts: to manage account and password policies
  - net localgroup: to create, delete, and manage local groups and their memberships
  - net user: to create, delete, and manage local users

2.2.3 Key Windows Accounts

Every Windows installation has a set of predefined accounts that are automatically generated when the OS is installed. The most important predefined accounts are the administrator and guest account.

The administrator account is the most privileged account on a Windows system and in a Windows domain. In the context of a local machine, the administrator has full control over local resources and has the permission to create, modify, or delete other local accounts. The same is true for a domain administrator for domain resources and domain accounts.

The guest account is a low-privilege Windows account that exists on every Windows system. It is for users who don't have an account defined and need occasional access to a Windows system. Users logging on using the guest account can access local data and applications, but cannot install software or hardware. By default, the guest account is disabled and is not password protected. It also has the "User cannot change password" and "Password never expires" account properties set.

Securing the Administrator Account

Because the administrator account holds the keys to the kingdom, it is a favorite hacker target. Below is some advice on how to secure administrator accounts.

Do not use an administrator account as your everyday account. A normal system user should always use an account that has fewer privileges. Failure to do so may result in malicious code executing on the local machine with administrator privileges. When users do want to perform security-related maintenance or administrative tasks, they can easily switch to the security context of an administrator account using tools like runas.exe.

Choose a strong password for the administrator account. Consult the password section in this chapter for password complexity guidelines. Administrator accounts should also not have the LM hash of their password stored in AD or the SAM—guidelines on how to avoid LM hash storage will be given in Chapter 5 of this book.

Do not reuse the same administrator password on different systems. Practical guidance on how to bulk change the administrator password on different systems is given in the section on bulk password change tools later in this chapter.

Rename the administrator account. This can be done from the User Accounts dialog box (as illustrated in Figure 2.14): select the Administrator account, click Properties, and edit its username property. The administrator rename can also be handled from the Group Policy Object (GPO) or Local Security Policy settings: use the "Accounts: Rename the Administrator Account" option. Renaming the administrator account is really only a cosmetic protection measure; it doesn't make the account less recognizable, because you can always recognize it from its SID (which always ends in 500). On systems where anonymous enumeration[3] is not allowed, renaming the administrator account forces hackers to guess both the administrator account's name and password.

Implement and use a strong authentication mechanism for your domain administrator accounts. For key accounts like administrators, you should implement a stronger authentication mechanism than the standard

---

3.   Using, for example, the user2sid tool—see also the section on SID-related utilities.

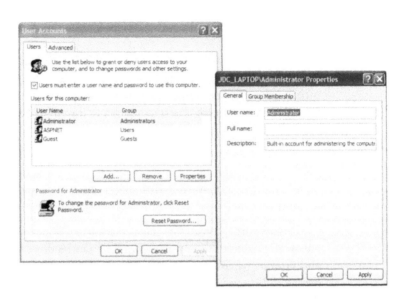

Figure 2.14
Renaming the administrator account.

password-based Windows authentication. From Windows 2000 onward, Windows includes smart card logon support—a multifactor authentication mechanism based on the possession of a smart card and the knowledge of an associated PIN code. The use of a smart card for administrator logon can also be enforced in the account properties. In Windows Server 2003, Microsoft has smart card–enabled additional administrative utilities, such as dcpromo, the net command, terminal services, and the runas command.

Disable the administrator account, if possible. If you have another account with administrative privileges on your Windows XP or Windows Server 2003 system, you can disable the administrator account. The administrator account cannot be disabled in Windows 2000. In that case, you should prevent it from logging on by giving it the "Deny Logon Locally" user right.

Securing the Guest Account

You must also secure the guest account. Even though it has a limited set of privileges, a guest account can be used by malicious anonymous users to access system resources. Below is some advice on how to secure the guest account.

Disable the guest account if you don't use it. The guest account is disabled by default, but it may be worthwhile to double-check this. When you enable the guest account occasionally, make sure that you disable it when it is not used anymore.

Rename the guest account. Although this is security by obscurity (the guest SID always ends in 501), it can be a simple but effective measure to protect the guest account. On systems where anonymous enumeration is not allowed, renaming the guest account forces hackers to guess both the guest account's name and password.

Password protect the guest account. Windows XP and Windows Server 2003 include important restrictions to limit what anonymous users can do on a Windows system, so it also makes sense to password protect the guest account.

To password protect the guest account in Windows XP, you must first password enable the guest account. This can be done from the Local Users and Groups MMC snap-in. On standalone Windows 2000 and Windows Server 2003 standalone machines, the guest account is password enabled by default, but has a blank password. The same is true for Windows 2000 and Windows Server 2003 domain environments. On standalone Windows 2000 and Windows Server 2003 platforms, you can assign the guest account a password from the Local User and Groups MMC snap-in. In domain environments, you must use the AD Users and Computers (ADUC) MMC snap-in.

You must also make sure that you assign the guest account a strong password that is updated regularly—so you may want to remove the "Password never expires" default property of the guest account. You do not need to enable the guest account to password enable it or set its password.

Prevent guest account network logon. Make sure that the guest account is given the "Deny access to this computer from the network" user right.

Prevent a guest account from shutting down the system. By default, the guest account is prohibited from doing this, but to make sure you can double-check the following:

- The guest account is not given the "Shut down the system" user right.

- Systems must prohibit system shutdown without logging on. This can be controlled using the following security option in the local security policy or GPO settings: "Shutdown: Allow System To Be Shut Down Without Having To Log On."

Prevent a guest account from accessing the system logs. To prevent this, open the HKEY_LOCAL_MACHINE\System\CurrentControlSet\Services\

Eventlog registry key and check each of the Application and System subkeys. Make sure that each of them contains a DWORD value named RestrictGuestAccess that is set to value 1. You don't need to make this change for the security log; the guest account is prohibited from accessing this log by default.

You should make these changes even if the guest account is disabled. Even though hackers with administrator access can easily enable the guest account, it will make their lives and attacks more difficult if they need to change multiple security settings. Also remember the most fundamental security principle: "defense in depth." This means you should not rely on a single security solution but rather a combination of different security solutions.

2.2.4 Password Credentials

Security authorities use credentials to verify a security principal's claimed identity. Although password credentials are not the best way to identify security principals, they are certainly the most widely used credentials. Passwords are also the default Windows credentials.

In this section, we will explore how passwords can be used and configured in Windows 2000, Windows XP, Windows Server 2003, and R2. Chapter 5 contains more information on other credential types. In the following sections, we will also explain how password quality can be enhanced and how you can audit password quality.

Password Configuration

Password-related properties can be configured in the properties of local and domain accounts and using GPO settings (including the domain password policy). They are discussed below, as well as a set of password-related reporting tools.

Password-Related Account Properties

Table 2.11 lists all password-related account properties as they can be set in the Active Directory Users and Computers MMC snap-in (for domain accounts) and the Local Users and Groups MMC snap-in (for local accounts).

An interesting password-related account property is the "password required" property. When this property is disabled, the affected user account is not required to have a password—in other words, this property

Table 2.11   *Account Password-Related Properties*

Account Property	Applies to	Description
Account is locked out	Domain and local accounts	This property is set automatically based on the account lockout policy. If a user tries to log on with a wrong password too many times, the account is locked (see also the section on account lockout later in this chapter).
User must change password at next logon	Domain and local accounts	It's a best practice to set this property after the administrator has assigned a password to a user. The next time the user logs on with the new password, he or she will be prompted to change it.
User cannot change password	Domain and local accounts	This property can be set for users who share a single account. It prevents them from changing the account's password.
Password never expires	Domain and local accounts	Normally, users are forced to change their passwords periodically, as specified in the password policy. You can exempt accounts from this policy by setting this property. This can be a good option for service accounts.
Store password using reversible encryption	Domain accounts only	This property must be set if a user is using a Macintosh workstation or if he/she wants to use HTTP digest authentication against an IIS Web server.
Password required	Domain and local accounts	When this property is disabled the user account is not required to have a password set.

takes away the authentication requirement for that account.[4] While it is clear that this should be avoided in corporate environments, it may be required for kiosk or lab environments or similar situations.

The password required property is not exposed in the Local Users and Groups (LUG—for local accounts) or AD Users and Computers (ADUC—for domain accounts) MMC snap-ins; it can only be set from the command line using the net user command. Chapter 11 explains how you can delegate permissions in AD to disable the ability to set this property on domain accounts.

To disable the password requirement for a user named Jan from the command line, you would type the following:

```
Net user Jan /passwordreq: no
```

---

4.   This feature should not be confused with automatic logon. Automatic logon automates the Windows logon process by storing a predefined username and password in the system registry. Automatic logon is available on Windows 2000, Windows XP, Windows Server 2003, and R2. It is mainly used to facilitate unattended setups.

To see all password-related account properties for user Jan from the command line, type:

```
Net user Jan
```

Password Policy Settings

Table 2.12 gives an overview of the Windows password policy settings. It also gives a recommended value for each setting. The preferred methods to set password policies in a Windows Server 2003 domain environment is via Group Policy Objects (GPOs). GPOs are important Windows administration tools that can be used by administrators to centrally control the system configuration settings of Windows workstations and servers in a domain environment. The table does not include the machine account password-related settings: they will be discussed in a later section.

Table 2.12 *Windows Server 2003 Password Policy GPO Settings*

Setting	Comments
Password Policy (in Computer Configuration\Windows Settings\Security Settings\Account Policies GPO Container)	
Enforce password history	Value: 0-24 (default:* 24)
	Sets the number of passwords Windows will remember and forces users to choose a password different from the one in the history.
	Recommended value: 24
Maximum password age	Value: 0-999 (default: 42)
	Specifies number of days a password remains valid. Value 0 means that the password never expires. This setting can be overridden by setting "Password never expires" in the account properties.
	Recommended value: as short as feasible for the organization.
Minimum password age	Value: 0-999 (default: 1)
	Specifies number of days before a user is allowed to change his password. "0" means that the user can always change his password.
	Recommended value: 1
Minimum password length	Value: 0-14 (default: 7)
	Specifies the minimum password length. Value 0 means that the user is allowed to have no password at all. Like Windows 2000, Windows Server 2003 supports a maximum password length of 127 characters. In NT4 the password length was limited to 14 characters.
	Recommended value: at least 9

Table 2.12   *Windows Server 2003 Password Policy GPO Settings (continued)*

Setting	Comments
Password must meet complexity requirements	Value: enabled-disabled (default: enabled)
	Enabling this setting requires that passwords:
	■ Are at least six characters long.
	■ Contains characters from three of the following categories: uppercase characters (A through Z), lowercase characters (a through z), numbers (0 through 9), and nonalphabetic characters (for example: *, ?, !).
	■ Do not contain the username or any part of the user's full name.
	Recommended value: enabled
Store passwords using reversible encryption for all users in the domain	Value: enabled-disabled (default: disabled)
	When this setting is enabled, passwords will not be stored in a hashed format in the SAM or AD. This setting is used to support the HTTP-based Digest authentication protocol.
	Recommended value: disabled

* All default values in this table are the values of the Windows Server 2003 AD Default Domain Policy.

For domain accounts, the password policy can only be set from GPOs that are linked to the domain. You cannot, for example, enforce a specific password policy only for the users that are contained in a particular organizational unit (OU). For domain accounts this is true for all account policy settings: not only the password policy, but also the account lockout and Kerberos policies. See also the sidenote on "Setting Security Policy Settings for AD Domain Accounts."

The password policy settings set in GPOs that are applied to AD computer objects (workstations or member servers—not domain controllers!) will apply to the local accounts defined on those computers. For local accounts you can also set the password policies in the Local Security Policy. The Local Security Policy can also be administered from the GPO MMC snap-in by selecting the Local Computer GPO.

Other Password-Related Configuration Settings

Table 2.12 lists other password-related configuration settings that can be configured using GPOs in a Windows Server 2003 domain environment. These settings can be defined in GPOs that are linked to different AD objects (domain, OU...): the domain limitation for password policies does

---

Setting Security Policy Settings for AD Domain Accounts

The following security policy settings can only be applied to domain accounts using GPOs that are linked to the domain:

For both Windows 2000 and Windows Server 2003 AD: all settings contained in the Computer Configuration/Windows Settings/Security Settings/Account Policies GPO container:

- Password policy

- Account lockout policy

- Kerberos policy

Only for Windows 2000 AD: the following settings contained in the Computer Configuration/Windows Settings/Security Settings/Local Policies/Security Options GPO container:

- Automatically log off users when logon time expires

- Rename administrator account

- Rename guest account

Only for Windows Server 2003 AD: the following settings contained in the Computer Configuration/Windows Settings/Security Settings/Local Policies/Security Options GPO container:

- Accounts: Administrator account status

- Accounts: Guest account status

- Accounts: Rename administrator account

- Accounts: Rename guest account

- Network security: Force logoff when logon hours expire

---

not apply here. All settings in Table 2.13 apply to local accounts or to local security logic, so it makes sense that you can configure them from different AD locations—for example, for different Organizational Units.

The default domain policy does not have values defined for these settings. On a standalone Windows XP SP2 workstation, the Password Expiry Warning setting defaults to 14 days, the "limit local use of blank passwords to console logon only" setting defaults to enabled, and the "Do not store LAN Manager hash value on next password change" defaults to disabled.

Table 2.13   *Other Windows Server 2003 Password-Related GPO Configuration Settings*

Security Options (in Computer Configuration\Windows Settings\Security Settings\Local Policies GPO Container)

Accounts: Limit local account use of blank passwords to console logon only	Value: enabled-disabled (default:* not defined)
	Enabling this setting will make it impossible for users who have blank passwords defined to perform a network or a remote desktop logon. Only local logons will be allowed. The difference between local and network logon is explained in Chapter 5.
	Recommended value: enabled
	Even though this policy setting limits the risks related to blank passwords on local accounts, it is much preferred not to have blank passwords at all. You can use the minimum password length setting in the password policy to block the use of blank passwords.
Network Security: Do not store LAN Manager hash value on next password change	Value: enabled-disabled (default: not defined)
	When this setting is enabled, no LAN Manager password hashes will be stored in the SAM or AD.†
	Recommended value: enabled
Interactive Logon: Prompt user to change password before expiration	Value: 0-999 days (default: not defined)
	Specifies number of days before password expiration that the user is presented with a password change notification.
	Recommended value: 14

* All default values in this table are the values of the Windows Server 2003 AD Default Domain Policy.

† More details on the differences between the LAN Manager hash of a password and the more secure NT hash of a password will be provided in Chapter 4 of this book.

Password-Related Reporting Tools

As a domain or system administrator, you may be interested to regularly learn about the password-related account properties of the accounts on your system or in your domain and see those data in a nice report format. Typical points of interests are the password ages and expiration dates of local or domain user accounts.

Aloinfo.exe, a tool that comes with the Microsoft Account Lockout and Management toolset,[5] is a command-line tool that can be used to display a list of the user accounts stored in AD and the amount of days that are left before their passwords expire. To retrieve this information, type the following aloinfo command at the command line:

```
Aloinfo /expires /server:<servername>
```

---

5.   These tools are discussed in more detail in the account lockout section of this chapter and can be downloaded from www.microsoft.com/downloads/thankyou.aspx?familyId=7af2e69c-91f3-4e63-8629-b999adde0b9e.

Two freeware tools that can also help here are SomarSoft's Dumpsec (dumpsec.exe, available from www.systemtools.com/somarsoft/index.html) and the Network Password Age tool (netpwage.exe, available from www.systemtools.com/free.htm).

Enhancing Password Quality

Three important recommendations to enhance password quality in a Windows environment are to use the built-in Windows password policies, to provide your users with guidelines for choosing high-quality passwords, and to regularly audit the password quality. We strongly advise you to implement these guidelines—they are your first (or your last) line of defense against hackers and malicious users trying to exploit the inherent weaknesses of passwords. These three guidelines will be explored in more detail in the following sections.

Microsoft highlights the importance of good password quality in law five of their ten immutable laws of security:

> "Weak passwords trump strong security."

User Password Guidelines

Enforcing a minimum password length and setting the password complexity requirement can really enhance the quality of the passwords used in your Windows environment. But you must also teach your users how to choose good passwords and how to use them in a secure way. Below are several golden rules.

Use passwords. In Windows XP the use of passwords is an option. We recommend that you always use a password, not only at work but also on your personal and home computers.

Never share a password with anyone. Social engineering attacks on passwords are not uncommon. It also happens that colleagues share passwords. Password sharing cannot be allowed, because it circumvents the primary reason of existence of a personal account with a password and could eventually lead to misleading audit-trails.

Be careful when saving passwords. Naturally, it is best not to save or write down passwords at all. But when you do save your password in a file because it is too difficult to remember, make sure that only you can access the password. On Windows XP and later systems, you could use the Encrypting File System (EFS) to encrypt the file holding your password. If you store your password on a USB token, make sure that access to the token is password protected or that the technology you use to store your password supports encryption or a special access control mechanism. A bad example is writing passwords on sticky notes and sticking them to your computer screen or to your keyboard.

Windows also includes tools users can use to cache their password credentials so they don't have to type them again when they're accessing the same resource. These tools are the credential manager and Internet Explorer (IE)-level password caching. Of the two, the credential manager is the more secure password caching mechanism—it will be covered in more detail in Chapter 9 of this book. Never use IE-level password caching. Passwords cached in IE are stored in the temporary Internet files folder and are not secured. Tools exist on the Internet that can dump the credentials cached in your IE cache. An example is the passview tool available from www.nirsoft.net/utils/pspv.html.

Use longer passwords. The longer a password is, the better. Windows 2000, Windows XP, and Windows Server 2003 all support 127 character passwords, so why not use this feature to your advantage?

Usually people are bad at remembering long passwords. To help your users remember longer passwords, you can teach them to use pass phrases. A pass phrase is a phrase of normal words that is easy to remember for the user using it. For example, a movie fan could use the following pass phrase: "What a great idea to go watch the new King Kong movie."

Use stronger passwords. Strong in the password context means more random passwords, or passwords that are not or are less linked to the commonalities of life (e.g., your pet's name, name of the city where you live, names of relatives, etc.).

An easy trick to strengthen the quality of common passwords is to use substitution. In this context, substitution means that you replace common characters with less common or simply different characters. For example, replace all occurrences of "a" with "@", or "o" with "0" (zero), "u" with "y", "e" with "3", and so on. In this case, the password "coffeecup" would result in "c0ff33cyp", which is much more random than the original one.

To get even better passwords, teach your users to combine pass phrases and substitution. This will make user passwords both longer and more random. Granted, pass phrases combined with substitution would preferably be shorter than the pass phrase example mentioned above (to avoid typos), but the following example would still be a good compromise: "Wh@t @ gr3@t m0vi3!"

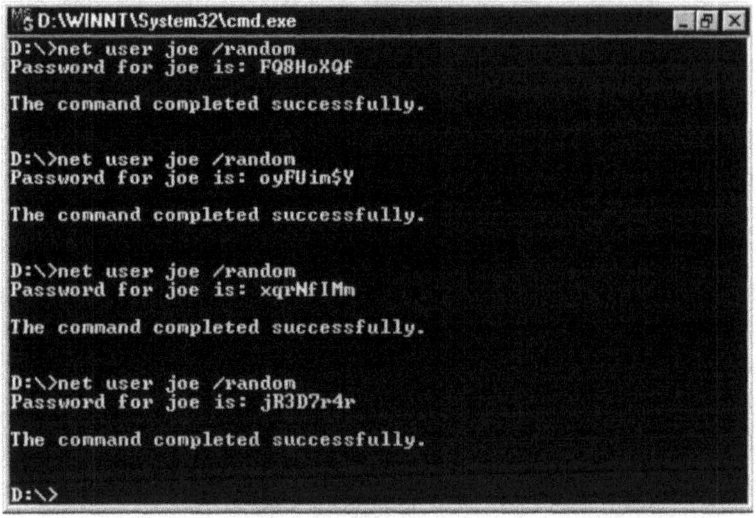

Figure 2.15
*Using net user
with the /random
switch.*

```
D:\WINNT\System32\cmd.exe                                  _ 8 X
D:\>net user joe /random
Password for joe is: FQ8HoXQf

The command completed successfully.

D:\>net user joe /random
Password for joe is: oyFUim$Y

The command completed successfully.

D:\>net user joe /random
Password for joe is: xqrNfIMm

The command completed successfully.

D:\>net user joe /random
Password for joe is: jR3D7r4r

The command completed successfully.

D:\>
```

Administrators, helpdesk operators, and users can also use software tools to help them generate more random passwords.

An easy solution for administrators and helpdesk operators who have reset password permissions[6] is to use the built-in Windows net user command with the /random switch (as Figure 2.15 shows for user joe). The command automatically generates a strong random password and assigns it to the user account. This works for both local and domain accounts, and the generated passwords adhere to the Windows 2000 and Windows Server 2003 password complexity rules.

To help your users generate random passwords, you can provide them with special password generation programs or even online password generation services. These tools must be handled with care, however (certainly the online password generation services). The users may keep the passwords they generate for later attacks against the accounts of the users that requested the passwords. In corporate environments, the password generation programs should only be used if they have been approved by your IT security department.

An example of an online password generation service is available from www.winguides.com/security/password.php. An example of an offline password generation program can be found at www.mark.vcn.com/password/.

---

6.   Normal users cannot use this command because it requires reset password permission. Users have only change password
      permission. See also the sidenote on "Reset Password vs. Change Password Permission."

Reset Password vs. Change Password Permission

Even though resetting a password and changing a password have the same effect, they are two different actions. The difference between the two is not always well understood.

A password change is a user action during which a user chooses a new password for his proper account. Windows authenticates a user before he is allowed to change his password: a user must always first enter his old password. A user must also have the Change Password permission on his local or domain account object to be allowed to change his password.

In Windows XP, a user can change his password from the User Accounts Control Panel applet. In Windows 2000 and Windows Server 2003, a user can use the Change Password... option in the Logon dialog box (which pops up after pushing CTRL-ALT-DEL).

A password reset is an administrator action during which an administrator or an account that has the reset password permission on a user's account object resets a user's password. A password reset does not require knowledge of the old password. Any account that has the Reset Password permission on a user's local or domain account object can do a password reset. Password resets can be launched from one of the account management tools that were explained in Section 2.2.2 of this chapter.

Starting with Windows Server 2003, Windows logs events with different event IDs for a password change and password reset event:

- Event ID 627 is logged for a password change attempt.
- Event ID 628 is logged for a password reset event.

Windows 2000 only logs event ID 627 and uses it for both password change and password reset events.

An Internet search for "password generator" will reveal similar tools. These password generation tools typically generate a random password of a length and complexity specified by the user—they also let you generate multiple random passwords in a single run. The online password generation services are generally accessible for free. Some of the standalone programs have to be purchased.

Checking Password Quality

To perform basic password quality tests for local accounts,[7] you can use the Microsoft Baseline Security Analyzer (MBSA). MBSA is a freeware tool available for download from the Microsoft Web site, at

---

7.   MBSA does not test the passwords of global domain accounts when it is run on a domain controller.

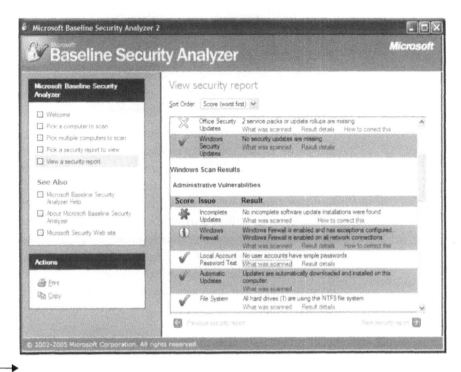

Figure 2.16 *Using the MBSA tool to audit password quality.*

www.microsoft.com/downloads/details.aspx?FamilyID=4b4aba06-b5f9-4dad-be9d-7b51ec2e5ac9&DisplayLang=en.

The MBSA version 2 tool (illustrated in Figure 2.16) can check for the following password conditions:

- Password is blank.
- Password is the same as the user account name.
- Password is the same as the machine name.
- Password uses the word "password."
- Password uses the word "admin" or "administrator."

MBSA also includes a command-line version (mbsacli.exe) that can perform the same checks, which is more applicable for automation tasks.

For advanced password quality tests of local and domain accounts, we recommend you to look at a set of third-party tools that attempt to crack the password hashes Windows stores in its security database (the SAM or Active Directory). These tools are not just hacking tools. They are excellent tools to run regular password quality audits for the user accounts of your Windows domains. Next, we will discuss three such tools: LCP, John the Ripper (JtR), and a relatively recent tool called RainbowCrack. Other tools that have similar capabilities but are not discussed in this book are the Elcomsoft Proactive Password Auditor (more information at www.elcomsoft.com/ppa.html), Ophcrack2 (more information at http://ophcrack.sourceforge.net), and Cain & Abel (more information at www.oxid.it/cain.html).

The password cracking tools outlined below can be used by malicious persons to mount offline password cracking attacks against the passwords stored in AD or the SAM. "Offline" means that these tools circumvent the Windows security authority by accessing the hashes in the AD or SAM databases directly or by sniffing them from the wire traffic between Windows machines. Offline password cracking attacks are fundamentally different from password guessing attacks, during which attackers guess passwords in real time using different user logon attempts with different password credentials. The Windows password policies and account lockout policies (explained earlier in this chapter) are good tools to protect against password guessing attacks.

LCP   The LCP password cracking tool is distributed by LCPsoft. You can download a free copy of the latest LCP version (at the time of writing, it was version 5.04) from www.lcpsoft.com/english/index.htm.

Figure 2.17 shows the LCP GUI. Note that LCP displays both the LM and NT password hashes. In Chapter 5, we will explain in more detail how the Windows security authorities use these hashes to authenticate users.

LCP can obtain password hashes from different sources:

■ **From a SAM file.** The SAM file cannot be accessed while the Windows is running. You can access it by booting the machine using another OS, by retrieving it from a backup file, or from an emergency repair disk (ERD).

New to version 5.04 of the LCP program is that this method also works if syskey protection has been enabled. For more information on syskey, see the sidenote entitled "System Key Protection of SAM Security Data." Depending on where the system key is stored, you will need different things to retrieve the password hashes from the syskey-protected SAM file:

— If the system key is stored in the system registry (which is the default), you will also need a copy of the system file (like the SAM file, this file can be found in %systemroot%\system32\config).

— If the system key is stored on a floppy disk, you will need a copy of the *.key file on the floppy.

— If the system key is based on a startup password, you must know this startup password.

- **From a local or remote registry, or local or remote system memory.** This method requires administrator-level access to the system. This method supports both password hash retrievals from the SAM security database and from the AD domain security database.

- **From the output file (*.txt) of the pwdump2 tool.** This tool uses a technique called DLL injection to retrieve a list of password hashes from the Windows SAM or AD. It can do this independently of whether syskey is enabled. To use pwdump2, you must have administrator-level access to the system: pwdump2 requires the Windows "Debug programs" user right (seDebugPrivilege), which by default is only given to the built-in Administrator account and Administrators group. Pwdump2 can be downloaded from the following URL: www.bindview.com/Services/razor/Utilities/Windows/pwdump2_readme.cfm.

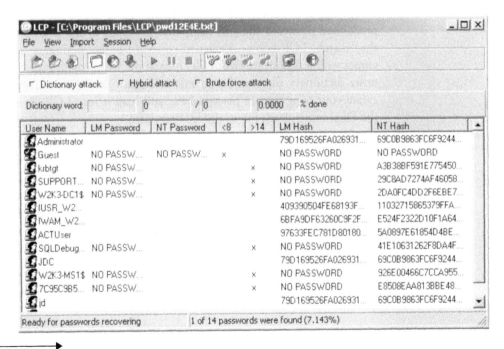

Figure 2.17   *LCP GUI.*

- **From the output file (*.txt) of certain network sniffers.** These sniffers can scan network traffic for NTLM version 1 (NTLM) authentication-related challenge-response exchanges and derive LM and NT password hashes from these exchanges. A good example is the ScoopLM sniffer, which can be downloaded from www.security-friday.com/tools/ScoopLM.html.[8] At the time of writing there was no publicly available tool[9] that could do the same thing with NTLM version 2 (NTLMv2) authentication-related challenge-response exchanges. Chapter 5 of this book contains more information on the difference between NTLM and NTLMv2.

- **From the hash files (*.lc or *.lcs) of older L0phtcrack (an older cracking tool similar to LCP) and LCP versions (versions 2.0, 2.5, 3.0, 4.0 or 5.0).**

LCP supports different methods for cracking Windows password hashes: dictionary, hybrid, and bruteforce cracks. When starting a cracking session, L0phtcrack runs the three methods in the following order: first dictionary, then hybrid, and finally brute force. You can disable or enable the different cracking methods from the Session\Options... menu item.

During a dictionary crack, LCP hashes all of the passwords listed in a predefined password file and compares the result to the password hash. If they match, LCP knows the actual password is the dictionary word. LCP comes with a default password file, named the words-english.dic file. Many other dictionary files can be downloaded from the Internet. You can also create your own custom password file and load it into LCP. To do so, use the Dictionary attack tab in the LCP options.

During a hybrid crack, LCP extends the dictionary crack by adding simple number and symbol patterns to the word list in the password file. For example, as well as trying out the word "Galileo", L0phtcrack will also try "Galileo24", "13Galileo", "?Galileo", and so on. The number of characters in the pattern (added to the left or right) can be specified in the Hybrid attack tab of the LCP options. The default number of characters is two (added to the right).

When performing a brute-force crack, LCP tries every possible combination of characters. The characters LCP uses can be defined in a character

8.   LC5 (the L0phtcrack version prior to LCP) had similar sniffing capabilities (this was referred to as SMB Packet Capture), but this feature is not available in LCP 5.0.4.

9.   See www.blackhat.com/html/win-usa-02/win-usa-02-spkrs.html#Urity for an interesting story on cracking NTLMv2 authentication traffic.

Figure 2.18 *Pwdump2 output.*

set. This set can be specified in the Brute Force Attack tab of the LCP Options. The default character set is A–Z.

John the Ripper John the Ripper (JtR) is a command-line password cracking tool. You can download the tool from www.openwall.com/john (at the time of writing, the latest version was 1.6). Be sure that you download the Win32 binaries.

Unlike LCP, JtR does not include tools to retrieve the password hashes from the NT SAM or Active Directory or to sniff the network for password hashes.[10] To retrieve the hashes, you need a tool like pwdump2.exe (which can be downloaded from www.bindview.com/Services/razor/Utilities/Windows/pwdump2_readme.cfm). The following pwdump2 command dumps all password hashes to a file called passwd.lanman:

```
Pwdump2 >passwd.lanman
```

If you use Notepad to open the passwd.lanman file, you will see output similar to that in Figure 2.18. Note that the file contains one line for every user account in the SAM. A set of colon-separated alphanumeric values that represent the password hash follow each user account name.

Next, switch from the directory that contains pwdump2.exe to the directory that contains the JtR executable called john.exe, which by default is in the \john-16\run directory. Before starting the password cracking process, test whether JtR is operating properly on your system. To do so, type the following at the command line:

```
john -test
```

This command starts a JtR benchmarking test that checks the JtR cracking speed for different password hashing formats. You will notice that in

---

10.   A special JtR version can also crack the NT hashes that the cachedump utility retrieves from the Windows 2000, Windows XP, and Windows Server 2003 credential cache. See Chapter 5, Section 6 on credential caching for more info.

addition to cracking NT password hashes, JtR can crack the password hashes on FreeBSD, OpenBSD, and other UNIX systems.

When the benchmark terminates successfully, you can start the password cracking process. JtR can do both dictionary-based and brute-force–based password cracking. By default, JtR performs a dictionary-based password crack. To start this cracking process on the password hashes in the passwd.lanman file, you would type the following at the command prompt (illustrated in Figure 2.19):

```
john passwd.lanman
```

To start a brute-force–based password cracking process, use the -incremental switch:

```
john -incremental:all passwd.lanman
```

When you use the -incremental switch, you must include an incremental option (e.g., "all" in this example), which specifies the brute-force cracking scheme used. For details about all the incremental options and how to configure them, see the documentation that accompanies the JtR tool.

JtR saves its results in the john.pot file. To see an overview of the cracked passwords for the passwd.lanman file, type the following at the command prompt, as Figure 2.19 shows:

```
john -show passwd.lanman
```

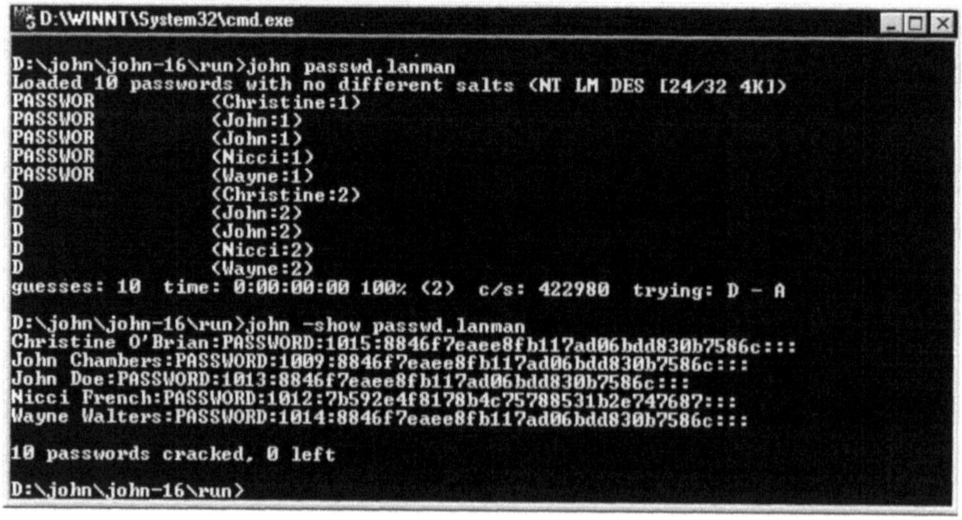

Figure 2.19   *Running John the Ripper.*

RainbowCrack RainbowCrack uses a relatively recent password hash cracking method called the Rainbow attack. The Rainbow attack method is an implementation of the Faster Cryptanalytic Time-Memory Trade-Off method developed by Dr Philippe Oechslin.[11] The main idea behind this method is to generate password hash tables in advance. This significantly reduces the cracking time, because the only thing that must be done during the cracking process is look up the hash in the precomputed hash tables.

The Rainbow attack method has also two important disadvantages: calculating the hash tables takes a considerable amount of time and processing power, and the resulting hash tables can also get fairly large (meaning hundreds of gigabytes).

Version 1.2 of RainbowCrack can be downloaded from the following Web site: http://www.antsight.com/zsl/rainbowcrack/. The Rainbow attack method is also supported by Elcomsoft's Proactive Password Auditor (more information is available at www.elcomsoft.com/ppa.html).

RainbowCrack comes with three tools:

- Rtgen.exe: to compute and generate the hash tables

- Rtsort.exe: to sort newly generated hash tables—sorting the tables speeds up the cracking process

- Rtcrack.exe: to do the actual cracking of the password hashes; to retrieve the hashes from the SAM or AD, use the pwdump2 utility

If you don't want to spend the time and resources for computing and sorting your own hash tables, you can buy them online from www.rainbowcrack-online.

Bulk Password Change Tools

In the section on the administrator account, we mentioned that you must use different administrator passwords for each Windows system. This is especially important for the local administrator password on the workstations and member servers in your Windows domains. Windows GPOs unfortunately don't include an option to bulk change the administrator passwords yet (even though you can use them to bulk rename and disable the administrator account). This section lists and explains tools that can be used to perform administrator password changes on multiple target machines in a single run.

---

11.   More info on the Rainbow attack can be found in the following paper: http://lasecwww.epfl.ch/~oechslin/publications/crypto03.pdf.

It is relatively easy to find solutions to bulk change the administrator password on different systems. You can use a scripting solution or one of the special tools you can find on the Internet.

If you search the Internet, you will find plenty of scripting tools to bulk change the local administrator password. Sample scripts can be found at www.spoogenet.com/index.php?module=article&view=13 or at www.scripting-answers.com/Community/DiscussionForums/tabid/154/forumid/6/postid/6488/view/topic/Default.aspx.

If you have implemented Microsoft Systems Management Server (SMS) or a similar desktop management tool in your environment, an even simpler solution is to create the following one-line installer script and execute it on the machines where you want to change the administrator passwords:

```
Execute %systemdrive%\net user administrator <password>
```

Two bulk administrator password changing tools are available from Danish Company (DC PasswordChanger: www.danish-company.com/dcwcm/page/{4D40EC77-0788-48E7-9FB6-B81A51F70CD2}.html) and ZenSoft (Batch User Manager: www.zensoft.com/download_bum.html). These tools, in particular, have nice graphical user interfaces.

Utilities that can bulk change administrator passwords and assign a different password to each administrator account are much more difficult to find.

One of the tools that can help here is Foghorn Security's Local Account Password Manager (LAPM—at the time of writing, the latest version is 2.5): it gives every workstation a unique administrator password and centralizes the administration related to this operation. You can download a fully functional, nonexpiring demo version of LAPM from www.foghorn-security.com/lapm/download. The demo version has a built-in host limit of 35 machines.

LAPM works by grouping workstations and member servers into logical groups called LAPM security groups. LAPM assigns all machines that belong to a LAPM security group the same knowledge key, which is a simple passphrase that an administrator sets. To generate a unique administrator password for every machine, LAPM uses an undocumented combination of the machine's NetBIOS name and the knowledge key of the LAPM security group to which the machine belongs.

Two interesting features that were added in version 2.5 of LAPM are Auto Populate and Auto Remove. Auto Populate allows administrators to automatically assign new machines to LAPM groups at configurable intervals using a predefined set of rules. The rules can be based on OU, machine name patterns, and OS version. Auto Remove means that LAPM will, at regular intervals, automatically remove the machines that are no longer in the domain.

Installing LAPM is as simple as extracting to a folder all files bundled in the LAPM.zip file. To make LAPM work in a Windows NT, Windows 2000, or Windows Server 2003 domain environment, you must create a global account called the "RunAs" account and add it to a global group. Then, on every machine whose administrator account's password you want to manage, you add the global group to the local Administrators group. The RunAs account needs the Logon as a service user right on the machine from which you'll be running LAPM. Administrators using LAPM need the following user rights on the machine running the tool: Act as part of the operating system, Bypass traverse checking, and Replace a process level token.

Password Reset Tools

Local and domain Windows administrators can always reset other users' passwords using the standard Windows account management tools mentioned earlier in this chapter. For example, a domain administrator can reset a user password from the AD Users and Computers MMC snap-in, simply by right-clicking the account object and selecting "reset password…"

Two less trivial password reset scenarios are when users forget the password they use to log on to their standalone machines and when administrators forget the password of their single almighty administrator account on standalone servers or in domain environments.

Administrator Password Reset Tools

Losing access to your system's administrator password is bad and can be disastrous if you don't have a functioning and up-to-date backup. Often, the need to regain these passwords is caused by administrators leaving a company and taking this knowledge along. Luckily, there are utilities available on the Internet that can help you reset your local administrator password. Like for password cracking tools employees should never use these tools on corporate machines unless they got explicit authorization from the IT security department.

Most of these administrator password reset tools are based on a Linux boot medium that has NTFS drivers, and that includes software that's intelligent enough to read and write to the Windows registry. If they can edit the registry, they can also change the administrator password. Table 2.14 gives a short (nonexhaustive) list of tools that can help in resetting your administrator password.

Most of the tools mentioned in Table 2.14 can only overwrite the passwords of administrator accounts stored in the SAM, not those stored in an Active Directory. An interesting method of resetting the administrator password on Windows Server 2003 AD, using AD Directory Services Restore Mode (DSRM) and the srvany.exe and instsrv.exe Resource Kit tools, is described at the following URL: www.petri.co.il/reset_domain_admin_ password_in_windows_server_2003_ad.htm. As this solution requires you to know the Restore Mode password, which is basically the administrator's password stored in an AD DCs SAM database that becomes active when booted to DSRM, you may still need the tools in Table 2.14 if you also do not know the Restore Mode password.

Password Reset Disk

A Password Reset Disk (PRD) offers a solution to the problem of a forgotten password for a local user account. If users create password reset disks for their local accounts before they forget their passwords, they can easily reset their passwords at any point later in time—on the condition that they still have access to the PRD floppy disk. The PRD should always be kept in a secure place, so that no one except the authorized user can get to it.

A PRD can only be used to reset the password of a local account. PRDs are only supported on Windows XP, Windows Server 2003 Service Pack 1 (SP1), and Windows Server 2003 R2. A PRD is linked to a single machine and cannot be used on different machines.

Table 2.14   *Administrator Password Reset Tools*

Tool	URL
Offline NT password and registry editor	http://home.eunet.no/~pnordahl/ntpasswd
Winternals' ERD Commander	www.winternals.com/Products/ErdCommander
Login recovery	www.loginrecovery.com
Password-reset	www.password-reset.com
NTAccess	www.mirider.com/ntaccess.html
Windows XP/2000/NT Key	www.lostpassword.com/windows-xp-2000-nt.htm

On a standalone Windows XP machine, a PRD can be created from the user account properties in the control panel User Accounts applet. To start the PRD Forgotten Password Wizard, you must click Prevent a forgotten password (as illustrated in Figure 2.20). The wizard then guides you through the rest of the PRD generation process.

On domain-joined Windows XP, and domain-joined or standalone Windows Server 2003 SP1 or R2 machines, a PRD can be created as follows:

- Press CTRL+ALT+DEL and click Change Password.

- In the username field, type the name of the account you want to create a PRD for.

- In the Log on to field, select the name of the local computer.

- Click Backup to start the PRD Forgotten Password Wizard.

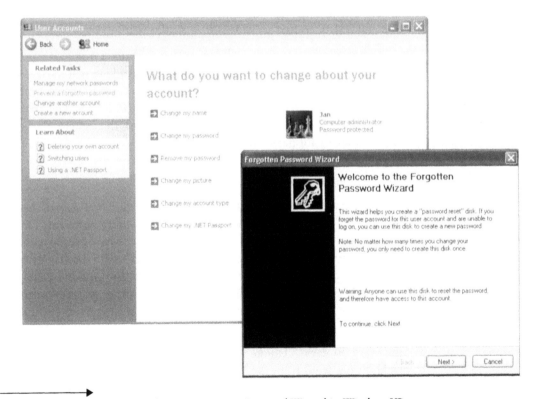

Figure 2.20   *Calling the PRD Forgotten Password Wizard in Windows XP.*

When a PRD is created, Windows creates a public-private key pair and a self-signed certificate. The PRD logic encrypts the user's actual password using the public key and stores the result of this encryption in the HKEY_ LOCAL_MACHINE\Security\Recovery\<user SID> registry key. The PRD logic then exports the private key to a floppy disk and deletes it from the local system.

When you enter a wrong password on the logon screen of a standalone Windows XP machine, XP will prompt you "Did you forget your password? You can use your password reset disk." Clicking this phrase will start up the Password Reset wizard. This particular XP prompt will only appear for users who have created a PRD.

On domain-joined Windows XP, and domain-joined or standalone Windows Server 2003 SP1 or R2 machines, you can call the password reset wizard from the Logon Failed dialog box, by clicking the Reset button. The Logon Failed dialog box only appears after users have typed a wrong password and if they created a PRD.

The password reset wizard will request you to enter a new password and supply the PRD floppy disk. Behind the scenes, Windows will retrieve your PRD private key from the PRD floppy disk and use it to decrypt the encrypted copy of your password on the local machine. The fact that you have supplied the correct PRD floppy proves to the system that your request to reset your password is authentic.

Machine Passwords

In a Windows domain environment, machine security principals have— just like user security principals—a password. Machine passwords are one of those little-known Windows security facts of life. Many people ignore it, mainly because a machine's password cannot be dealt with directly from the Windows GUI. Another reason is that most of the machine password-related maintenance tasks occur automatically without any administrator intervention.

A Windows client OS initiates a machine password change automatically every 30 days.[12] Unlike user passwords, you cannot manually reset a machine's password from the Windows XP or Windows Server 2003 GUI. You must use the command prompt tool netdom with the /resetpwd switch

---

12.   This is for all Windows 2000, Windows XP, Windows Server 2003, and R2 platforms. An NT4.0 requests machine password changes every 7 days.

to manually force a machine password change. Netdom comes with the Windows Server 2003 Support Tools. When you do so, netdom will write a copy of the new machine password to the local LSA database and to the Active Directory. The complete netdom command is the following—you must execute this command from the machine whose password you want to reset:

```
netdom resetpwd /s:<domaincontroller> /ud:<accountname>
/pd:*
```

In this command <domaincontroller> is the name of the domain controller to which you want to send the machine password reset request—it must be in the same domain as the machine whose password you want to reset. <accountname> is the name of the administrative account that is used to connect to the DC mentioned in the /s: parameter and perform the password reset. This accountname must have the format <domainname>\<username>. /pd: followed by a star means that you want to be prompted to enter the password of the administrative account. Instead of using a star, you can also enter the administrative account's password right away.

Windows Server 2003 includes a set of GPO settings to change the machine password update behavior. The GPO settings together with their corresponding registry hacks are listed in Table 2.16. All registry keys are located in the HKEY_LOCAL_MACHINE\system\currentcontrolset\services\netlogon\parameters registry container.

Two of the registry settings in Table 2.15 allow you to disable machine password changes. The RefusePasswordChange (that can be set on domain controllers) will make a DC reject all incoming machine password change requests. If, in addition, you want your workstations and member servers to stop requesting machine password changes, then you must also enable the DisablePasswordChange key on them. At first sight this sounds like a bad idea, because always relying on the same machine password makes machines more vulnerable to hacker attacks. There are, however, a couple of scenarios where this could be a welcome registry change:

- To reduce the replication traffic of automatic machine password changes in environments with many clients and where bandwidth is limited

- For dual-boot configurations, where both Windows instances are using the same machine account in the same domain

Table 2.15 *Machine Password Update Registry Hacks*

Can Be Applied to...	Parameter (Type) *(Corresponding GPO Security Options Setting)*	Values	Meaning
Workstations, member servers	DisablePasswordChange (REG_DWORD) *("Domain member: disable machine account password changes")*	0	Workstation automatically changes machine account password
		1	Workstation never changes machine account password (this value does not prevent manual change)
	MaximumPasswordAge (REG_DWORD) *("Domain member: maximum machine account password age")*	1–1,000,000 days	Interval for automatic machine password change (only used if DisablePasswordChange is disabled)
Domain Controllers	RefusePasswordChange (REG_DWORD) *("Domain controller: refuse machine account password changes")*	0	Domain controller accepts machine password changes
		1	Domain controller rejects machine password changes

2.2.5 Account Lockouts

From its early versions, Windows has come with a feature known as account lockout. Account lockout ensures that user accounts automatically become unusable when a user has entered a certain amount of bad passwords. The bad password threshold is defined by an administrator in the account lockout security policy. If this threshold is set to zero, the account lockout feature is disabled. The default Windows administrator account is not subjected to the account lockout policy.

Account lockout protects your Windows systems against account hijacking when attackers try to guess account passwords. On the other hand, account lockout can also be looked at as a great denial-of-service (DOS) attack tool: hackers could lock out all your Windows accounts, making it impossible for anyone except the default administrator account to log on the Windows infrastructure. This is why many security experts argue that you should not use account lockout. They also argue the increased support costs due to accounts being locked out and users calling the help desk. We believe account lockout is a useful feature in small to medium business environments, where it can be used as a free and basic intrusion detection system. We also agree that account lockout should not necessarily be used in large enterprise environments for the DOS and financial reasons that were mentioned earlier.

If large companies still prefer to activate this feature, it is critical that they prepare themselves for appropriate countermeasures in case of a mass lockout of many hundreds or even many thousands of accounts. This could be the result of a successful DOS attack; it could also be the result of a badly executed internal password audit, using tools that guess and check the account passwords by performing logon attempts to an AD domain. If you do not have a way to quickly unlock all of your accidentally locked accounts, you might be in trouble.

A far better protection against account hijacking is to make sure that your users use good passwords, combined with enabling auditing of logon events and monitoring the security event logs to ensure that you notice password guess attempts. See the section on passwords for some guidelines on good passwords.

Nevertheless, we will explore the account lockout feature in more detail in the following text.

When an account is locked out, only an administrator can unlock it. To do so, the administrator must uncheck the "account is locked out" checkbox in the account tab of the account properties using the AD Users and Computers (ADUC) MMC snap-in. Although Windows Server 2003 has added the multi-edit feature in the ADUC MMC snap-in to perform the same changes on a selection of users, unchecking the "account is locked out" checkbox is not an option with this feature. Other tools, such as unlock.exe from www.joeware.net, can help with unlocking different accounts in a single administrative action.

Account lockout should not be confused with disabling an account, which is the consequence of an explicit action performed by the administrator. Disabling an account does not occur automatically following, for example, a set of security policy settings.

Account Lockout Process

Figure 2.21 illustrates the Windows 2000 and Windows Server 2003 account lockout process. In this process the domain's PDC emulator domain controller plays the key role.

The following list describes what happens when a user provides a wrong password when authenticating to a Windows domain.

1. A user attempts to log on to a Windows domain using a wrong password.

2. The authenticating DC detects the password is wrong. To make sure that the user really entered a wrong password—and that the problem is not caused by, for example, AD replication latency— the authenticating DC double-checks with the domain's PDC emulator.

3. The PDC emulator checks the password and detects that it is really wrong. The PDC emulator increments the BadPwdCount attribute in the user account object's properties by 1.

4. The PDC emulator informs the authenticating DC that the user's password was really wrong.

5. The authenticating DC updates the BadPwdCount attribute in his local AD copy of the user account object.

6. The user is informed about the fact that he provided a wrong password.

If the user's BadPwdCount property exceeds the value defined in the Account Lockout Threshold of the domain's lockout policy (this policy is explained later), the user's account will be marked as locked out. The Bad-PwdCount property is automatically reset to 0 when the user enters a correct password following a set of bad password entries.

Windows Server 2003 domain controllers always perform a password history check before a user's BadPwdCount attribute is incremented. The password provided by the user is checked against the two last passwords in

Figure 2.21
Account lockout process.

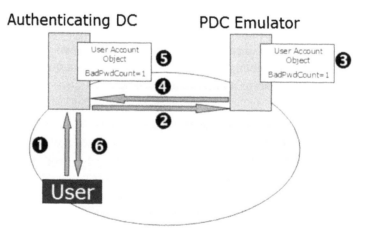

the user object's password history (that is stored in the NtPwdHistory AD user object attribute). If the password is the same as one of the last two entries in the password history, the BadPwdCount is not incremented, but the user is still informed that he entered a wrong password. This feature reduces the number of lockouts that occur because of user errors.

Besides the BadPwdCount property, every Windows Server 2003 account object also has the following account lockout–related property: the BadPasswordTime property. The BadPasswordTime property contains the last time the user, machine, or service submitted a bad password to the authenticating DC. Both the BadPwdCount and the BadPasswordTime property are not replicated between DCs. The authenticating DC only informs the PDC emulator DC of the domain. If multiple logon attempts with bad passwords are performed against different DCs in the domain, the PDC emulator's role will also be to ensure that the BadPwdCount value is updated appropriately across all DCs that are involved in the logon attempts.

Account Lockout Policy

Windows 2000 and later domains' account lockout policy settings are set from the account lockout portion of a domain-level group policy object (GPO). They are located in the Computer Configuration\Windows Settings\Security Settings\Account Policies GPO container. Like all other account policies (password and Kerberos policies), account lockout settings will only be applied to domain accounts if they are defined on the Windows domain level, for example, using a GPO that is linked to the default Domain Controllers OU.

Table 2.16 shows a set of recommended values for the account lockout policy settings.

If you are setting the account lockout policies for the first time, Windows Server 2003 will automatically suggest recommended settings for the "account lockout duration" and "reset account lockout counter after" account lockout policy settings. This is illustrated in Figure 2.22.

To make sure that the Windows account policies (including the account lockout policies) are also applied when a user unlocks his desktop, we advise you to activate the "Interactive logon: require domain controller authentication to unlock workstation" GPO setting (also known as the forceunlocklogon registry setting). This is explained in more detail in the sidenote on "Making Sure That Account Security Policies Are Enforced When a User Unlocks the Windows Console."

Table 2.16   *Account Lockout Policy Settings*

Account Lockout Policy Setting	Value/Meaning
Account lockout duration (ObservationWindow)	0-9,999 minutes (Defaults to 30) Recommended value: 30 Specifies the amount of time after which an account's bad-PwdCount attribute is reset.
Account lockout threshold (LockoutThreshold)	0-999 invalid logon attempts (Defaults to 0) Recommended value: 0 for large enterprises, 10 for small environments (see also discussion at the beginning of the account lockout session). Specifies the number of times a user can send a bad password to the authentication service before the account is locked out. An "account lockout threshold" with value 0 means that account lockouts are disabled in the domain.
Reset account lockout after (LockoutDuration)	0-99,999 minutes (Defaults to 30) Recommended value: 30 (for environments with normal security requirements) and 0 (for environments with high security requirements). Specifies the amount of time that lockout is enforced on an account that has exceeded the Account lockout threshold value. If "reset account lockout after" is set to 0, it means that a locked-out account remains locked out forever or until it is manually unlocked by an administrator.

Figure 2.22
OS suggested account lockout policy settings.

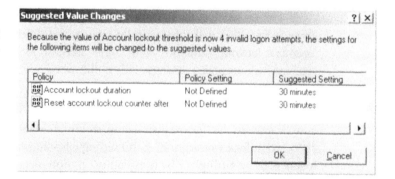

Account Lockout-Related Management Tools

In early 2003 Microsoft added some interesting new account lockout–related tools to their management tool portfolio. Some of these tools are made available with the Windows Server 2003 Resource Kit. All of them are also available in a software package that is downloadable for free from the Microsoft Web site at the following URL: www.microsoft.com/downloads/details.aspx?FamilyID=7af2e69c-91f3-4e63-8629-b999adde0b9e&DisplayLang=en. Table 2.17 gives an overview of these tools.

The acctinfo.dll adds a new property tab to an AD user account's properties (as illustrated in Figure 2.23). The new tab holds different types of account logon feature–related information. A very interesting feature of the tool is its capability to reset a user's password on a specific DC in the domain. This can be done by clicking the "Set PW on Site DC" push button at the bottom of the "Additional Account Info" tab. To add the tab to your AD account properties, register the acctinfo.dll on every machine from which you're using the AD Users and Computers MMC snap-in. To register a dll, use the regsvr32.exe command-line tool.

The alockout.dll helps with identifying the program or service that is causing an account lockout or—in other words—the entity that is sending the wrong credentials. In the altools.exe file, it comes in two versions: one for Windows 2000 or Windows Server 2003, and one for Windows XP. To

Table 2.17   *Account Lockout–Related Management Tools*

Tool Name (Available From)	Usage
AcctInfo.dll (Resource Kit and altools.exe)	Adds a new property page to the AD account properties (illustrated in Figure 2.23) that can help isolate and troubleshoot account lockouts. The tool can also be used to change a user's password on a domain controller in a particular site.
ALockout.dll (altools.exe)	Client-side tool that helps with identifying the process or application that is sending wrong credentials.
ALoInfo.exe (altools.exe)	Command line tool for displaying all user account names and the age of their passwords.
LockoutStatus.exe (Resource Kit and altools.exe)	GUI tool (illustrated in Figure 2.24) that can query all domain controllers in a domain for user account lockout-related information.

Making Sure That Account Security Policies Are Enforced When a User Unlocks the Windows Console

When a user unlocks his desktop (also referred to as "Windows console"), his password will be validated against a set of cached credentials. This means that the domain-level account security policies (including the account policies) are not enforced—which is a potential security hole.

To make sure that the account security policies are enforced when a user unlocks his desktop, you must change the following GPO setting: "Interactive logon: require domain controller authentication to unlock workstation." This setting is located in the Machine Configuration\ Windows Settings\Security Settings\Local Policies\Security Options GPO container.

Under the hood, this GPO setting changes the forceunlockLogon registry key located in HKEY_LOCAL_MACHINE\Software\Microsoft\Windows NT\CurrentVersion\Winlogon\. If you set this key to value 1, the user's password will be validated against a domain controller (DC) and the domain account policies will be enforced. As a consequence, the user won't be able to unlock the desktop when no DC is available.

Below are some more details that will help you better understand desktop locking and unlocking. When a user logs on to a computer, the Winlogon service stores a hash of the user password for future unlock attempts. When the user attempts to unlock the workstation, this stored copy of the password is verified. If the password entered in the unlock dialog box and the stored hash match, the workstation is unlocked. If they don't match, the workstation will attempt to validate the password against a domain controller by performing a logon. If the logon succeeds, the local hash is updated with the new password. If the logon is unsuccessful, the unlock process is unsuccessful. When you enable forceunlocklogon the workstation will always perform a logon against the DC when a user unlocks his desktop.

The password hash used to unlock a user's desktop is different from the cached credentials that will be explained in the "Credential Caching" section of Chapter 5. The latter are used to allow an interactive domain logon in the absence of a domain controller.

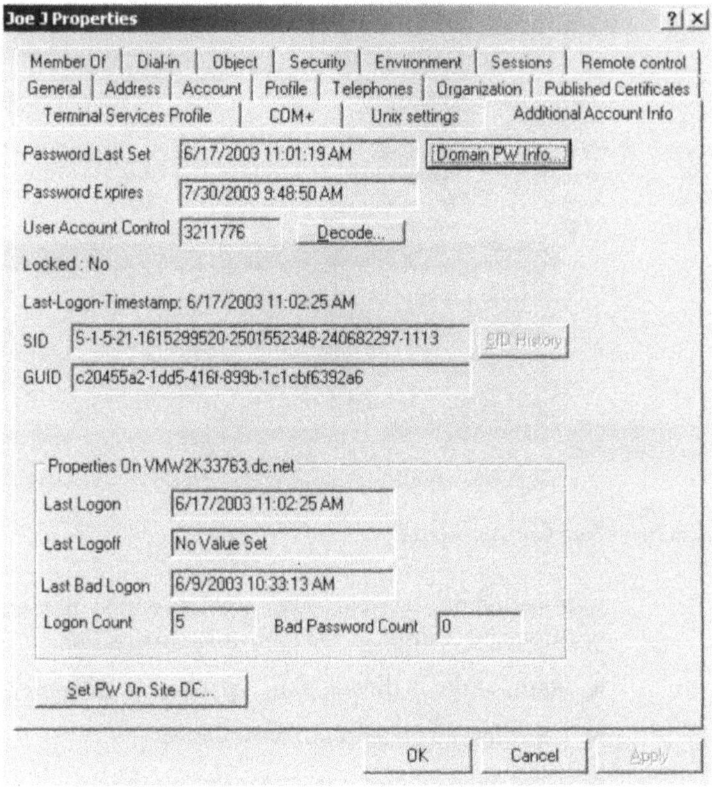

Figure 2.23
Additional Account
Info tab.

install the tool, use the appinit.reg registry file that comes with the tool. When the dll is installed and an account lockout occurs, alockout.dll generates an entry in the alockout.txt file—which is stored in the %windir%\ debug folder. Microsoft does not recommend using this tool on servers running important network services or applications (such as Microsoft Exchange).

Aloinfo.exe is a command-line tool that can be used to display a list of the user accounts stored in AD and the amount of days that are left before their passwords expire. To retrieve this information, type the following aloinfo command at the command line:

```
Aloinfo /expires /server:<servername>
```

Another interesting tool is lockoutstatus.exe, a GUI tool (illustrated in Figure 2.24) that can be used to query for the account lockout–related

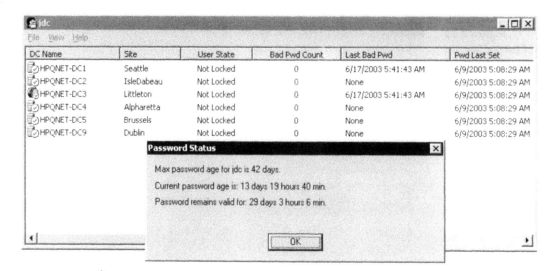

Figure 2.24 *Lockoutstatus.exe tool.*

information of a particular user account on the different domain controllers of a domain. It displays the following information:

- Status of the BadPwdCount attribute on different domain controllers

- Last time a bad password was entered

- Time the password was set for the last time

- Time when the account was locked out

- Name of the domain controller that locked the account (in the "originating lock" field): This is the domain controller that wrote to the Lockouttime attribute of the user account.

Under the hood, LockoutStatus.exe uses the NLParse.exe tool to parse the Netlogon logs for specific Netlogon return status codes. The tool's output can be saved to a comma-separated text file.

3

Windows Trust Relationships

The previous chapter introduced Windows security authorities and security principals. In this chapter, we will look at how we can establish security relationships between Windows domain security authorities using trust relationships. Note that this chapter will only concentrate on the standard Windows AD trust features in Windows Server 2003 and R2. The new Active Directory Federation Services (ADFS) introduced with Windows Server 2003 R2 will be discussed in greater detail in Chapter 5 *of the second book of this two-book series.* ADFS can be used to set up trust relationships between Windows security authorities and between Windows and other security authorities.

3.1 Defining Trust Relationships

Trust relationships define an administrative and security link between two Windows domains or forests. They enable a user to access resources located in a domain or forest that's different from the user's proper domain or forest. The creation of a trust between domains or forests does not automatically grant users general access to resources in the trusting domains or forests; the domain or forest administrator still has to assign access rights to the users for the appropriate resources. However, the creation of a trust does typically extend the reach of the Authenticated Users' well known security principal,[1] which every user of a domain is a member of, after successfull logon to his proper domain. Permissions granted to Authenticated Users will also be valid for users from trusted domains. We will discuss what this means for the planning and configuration of trusts later on in this chapter.

In the context of a Windows domain or forest, a trust basically means that one domain trusts the authentication authorities of another domain,

---

1. Well known security principals will be discussed in more detail in Chapter 10, "Active Directory Authorization."

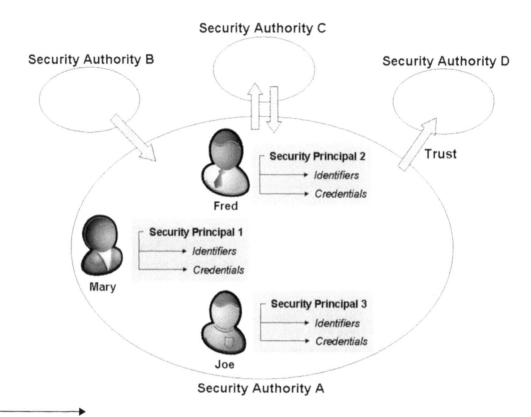

Figure 3.1   *Security authorities and trust relationships.*

or, in other words, it creates cross-domain visibility and usability of security principals. When security authority A has authenticated a user, Joe, and security authority B trusts security authority A (as illustrated in Figure 3.1), B will not start another authentication process to verify user Joe's identity. In Windows domain speak, the fact that a domain controller (DC) in domain A has authenticated user Joe and the existence of a trust between domains A and B are enough for the DCs in domain B to trust user Joe's identity.

When a trust relationship is set up between two domains, there's always a *trusted* and a *trusting* domain. The trusting domain is the one that initiates the setup of a trust relationship. The trusted domain is the subject of the trust definition. If domain compaq.com sets up a trust with the hp.com domain (as illustrated in Figure 3.2), with hp.com as the trusted domain and compaq.com as the trusting domain, all accounts defined in hp.com will be trusted by compaq.com. This means that all hp.com accounts and groups can be used to set access control settings on resources in the com-

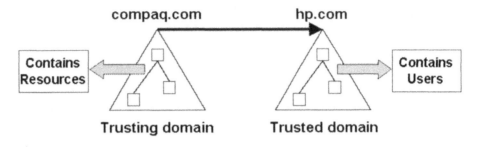

Figure 3.2   *Trust relationships—trusting versus trusted domain.*

paq.com domain. This is typically done by adding them to existing domain local groups or server local groups, which grant the actual permissions on resources in the compaq.com domain.

The users from the trusted domain, hp.com, can thus access authorized resources in the trusting domain, compaq.com—for example, a project-related file share on a member server in compaq.com. The opposite is not true, unless another trust is defined going from hp.com to compaq.com; in that case compaq.com is the trusted domain and hp.com domain the trusting domain. The latter case is referred to as a two-way trust relationship. The first case is referred to as a one-way trust relationship.

In the following sections, we will discuss the Windows Server 2003 trust properties and types, ways to create trusts, and how trust relationships work behind the scenes. We will pay special attention to an important new Windows Server 2003 trust type: forest trust.

3.2   Trust Properties, Types, and Features

Trust relationships in a Windows environment can be classified based on the following properties: the way they are created (implicitly or explicitly), whether they are one- or two-way trust relationships, and whether they are transitive or not. The different trust types and their properties are listed in Table 3.1. They are illustrated in Figure 3.3.

Which trust should be used for which situation will be discussed in Section 3.4. But first, let's cover some of the basics to understand how trusts work and what options we have to control them.

A Windows Server 2003 administrator can view trust relationships and their properties through each domain object's properties in the "Active Directory Domains and Trusts" MMC snap-in, or by using the netdom.exe or nltest.exe command prompt utilities (these utilities will be explained in

Table 3.1   *Trust Types and Default Properties*

Trust Type	Default Properties
Tree-Root Trust	Implicitly created, transitive, two-way
Parent-Child Trust	Implicitly created, transitive, two-way
Shortcut Trust	Explicitly created, transitive, one- or two-way
Forest Trust	Explicitly created, transitive, one- or two-way
External Trust	Explicitly created, non-transitive, one- or two-way
Non-Windows Trust (to UNIX or DCE Kerberos realm)	Explicitly created, non-transitive or transitive, one- or two-way

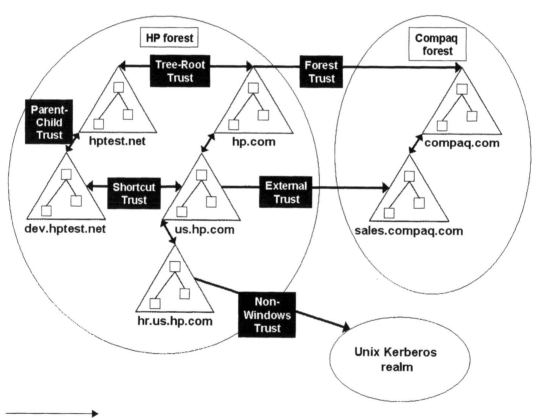

Figure 3.3   *Windows trust types.*

Figure 3.4
Trusts tab.

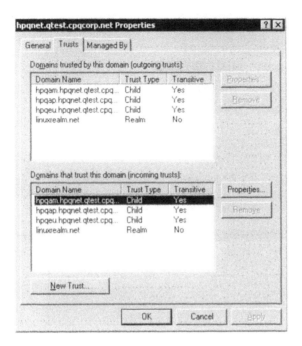

Section 3.6.4). Figure 3.4 shows the Trusts tab in the properties of a domain as you can see it from the AD Domains and Trusts MMC snap-in. If you open the properties of a particular trust relationship, you get more detailed information on that particular trust relationship (as shown in Figure 3.5).

In Windows Server 2003 (and beginning with Windows 2000), Microsoft simplified trust creation and management by creating trusts within the same AD forest automatically, as part of the domain hierarchy building process, and by making these trusts transitive. Before, in NT4 and earlier Windows versions, all trust relationships had to be created manually and were nontransitive.

Implicitly created trust relationships are created as part of the dcpromo process. Dcpromo—the process that installs an AD instance and promotes a standalone or member server to a domain controller—can automatically create trust relationships between AD parent and child domains and between the top-level domains of an AD tree and the root domain of the forest. All the other trust relationship types are created explicitly and manually by domain administrators.

All implicitly created AD trust relationships are two-way trust relationships. In other words, running dcpromo automatically defines two-way

Figure 3.5
Trust properties.

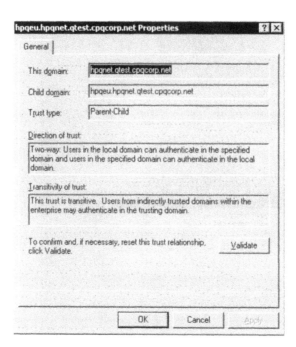

trust relationships. In this case each domain is both a trusting and a trusted domain. All explicitly created AD trust relationships can be either one- or two-way trust relationships, depending on the requirements and the administrators' decisions.

Transitive means that the trust extends beyond the directly trusted and the trusting domain to any other transitively trusted domain. For example, if both the europe.hp.com and us.hp.com domains trust the hp.com domain, then the europe.hp.com domain implicitly trusts the us.hp.com domain. Transitive trust reduces the number of trusts that are needed for authentication interoperability between different domains. In Figure 3.6, only three trusts are needed (between each parent and child domain in the same AD forest) to obtain authentication interoperability between all four domains. In an NT4 setup, we would have needed six trust relationships to do the same thing.

Users working from Windows 2000 or later workstations can see the effect of transitive trusts when they log on. They can choose every domain with which their domain has a direct trust or an indirect trust (through trust transitivity). An NT 4.0 end user sees only the direct trusts of his or her domain.

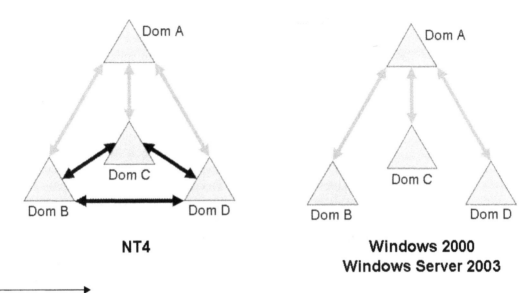

Figure 3.6   *Number of trust relationships required in Windows Server 2003 and in NT4.*

Transitive trust is only a logical concept—there's no shared secret between the domain controllers of the domains that share a transitive trust. This means that for authentication to occur between two domains on opposite ends of two or more transitive trusts—for example, domain B and domain D of Figure 3.6, both of which trust domain A in the same AD forest—the authentication process will not flow directly between the two domains but along a path that is known as the trust path. Basically, this means that all other domains that link the two domains together by means of a transitive trust will participate in the authentication process. So in this example, domain A will participate when a user from domain B tries to access resources in domain D. This also means that if domain A is unavailable, a user in domain B cannot access the resources in domain D.

This is why Microsoft allows administrators to create shortcut trusts for not directly trusted domains in a forest—these will remove the dependency on other domains in a scenario such as the one described above. Shortcut trusts can make sense if cross-domain resource access happens frequently and if the network link to DCs of other domains along the trust path is not sufficiently stable or is fairly slow. The concept of the trust path and how it works behind the scenes will be illustrated extensively in Chapter 6 of this book, on Kerberos.

3.2.1   **New Trust Features**

Windows Server 2003 includes a set of important enhancements that facilitate the setup and administration of trust relationships:

- A new trust type, "Forest Trust," enables the creation of a transitive trust between all domains of two forests using a single trust relationship. How this works will be described in great detail in the next section. An important requirement for creating Windows Server 2003 forest trust is that both forests need to be at Windows Server 2003 functional level 2. This forest functional level is only available if all domains are at functional level 2, and the latter is only possible if all the domain controllers in a domain are running the Windows Server 2003 operating system.

- Trust relationships can be defined in a very granular way. Windows Server 2003 supports three ways to restrict trusts: SID filtering (which is also available for NT4 and Windows 2000), selective authentication and Top-Level Name restrictions. The latter applies only to forest trusts. These options are a great enhancement over Windows 2000, where trust definitions are very coarse-grain: when you set up a trust between domains in a Windows 2000 environment, you either trust everyone or don't trust anyone. The three trust-restriction concepts will be explained in greater detail later.

- Windows Server 2003 includes a new trust wizard (accessible from the Active Directory Domains and Trusts MMC snap-in) that guides you through the different trust configuration options (illustrated in Figure 3.7). This wizard can be used for the setup of a forest trust and all other trust types (shortcut, external, and realm trusts). When the wizard detects the trusted domain is a forest root domain, you can choose to set up either a forest trust or an external trust (the difference between the two is explained below). When setting up a forest trust the wizard guides you through the following steps:

    1. Specification of the DNS or NetBIOS name of the target domain

    2. Specification of whether the trust will be bidirectional, one-way incoming, or one-way outgoing

    3. Specification of whether you want to create the trust in both domains or just in your proper domain

    4. Specification of whether selective authentication must be enabled

5. Specification of which DNS name suffixes should be enabled for cross-forest name suffix routing

6. Confirmation of the creation of the trust

■ Processing of GPOs, logon scripts, and profiles has been improved for cross-forest trusts. During a user's interactive logon on a computer in an externally trusted Windows Server 2003 domain, the logon process must determine whether the user's group policies should be applied on the computer in the trusted domain. In Windows 2000, the user policies used to be applied automatically to the target machine, independent of the machine's domain affiliation. This caused interesting challenges for administrators, when, for example, a user's group policy was used to deploy software to a computer. In Windows Server 2003, you can influence the execution of logon scripts, the roaming profiles, and the user portions of the GPOs in the user's logon domain by modifying the "Allow Cross-Forest User Policy and Roaming User Profiles" GPO setting in the following GPO container:

```
Computer Configuration\Administrative Templates
   \System\Group Policy\
```

This new policy has also been backported to Windows 2000 with SP4.

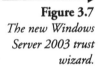

Figure 3.7
The new Windows Server 2003 trust wizard.

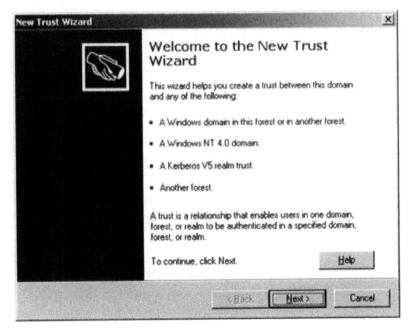

3.2.2 **Forest Trust**

Windows 2000 introduced the concept of a forest as a logical and administrative grouping of several Windows domains that are linked together using trust relationships. A forest provides ease of use and administration for resources that must be available to the users of different domains. It also facilitates the deployment, administration, and use of enterprise applications, such an Exchange-based mail infrastructure.

As the knowledge of the forest concept matured, it became clear that it takes away some of the domain boundaries available in earlier Windows versions. In Windows 2000 and Windows Server 2003, the domain cannot be considered a true security boundary any more: it is merely a replication boundary and, to a certain extent, an administrative boundary as well. However, the real security boundary is the forest, as Section 3.3.1 on SID filtering explains in more detail. As a consequence, a certain amount of personal trust is required between the different domains in a forest and their administrators.

A lot of organizations cannot live with these personal trust requirements for political, legal, or purely administrative reasons and have as a result deployed multiple Windows forests. Other organizations have built multiple forests because of a company merger or a set of company acquisitions. Another example is the requirement to build two forests for perimeter security reasons: one forest for the intranet and another one for the demilitarized zone (DMZ).

A major problem in Windows 2000 is the definition of a true forest trust, where all domains in both forests should have a specific level of trust to each other. From a security administration point of view, the creation of such a "full trust model" between two AD forests with multiple child domains is an administrative nightmare that basically puts your Windows 2000 environment back in the NT4 era (remember the spaghetti model of trust). A general shortcoming of Windows 2000 trust relationships is that, just like their predecessors, they can only define trust in a very coarse-grained way. This characteristic 'is not particularly useful in a cross-forest environment, where you may want to restrict what's exchanged and accessed between forests.

It is clear that Windows 2000 was not made to easily support multiple forests. In Windows Server 2003 Microsoft resolved most of the Windows 2000 multiple forest and cross-forest trust problems and shortcomings through the introduction of a new trust type: the "forest" trust.

Windows Server 2003 forest trust relationships allow administrators to securely federate two AD forests using a single trust relationship. The forest trust features can provide a seamless, AD object-browsing, user authentication and access control experience between different forests. Windows Server 2003 also offers new powerful tools to define fine-grain trust security policies, some of which have been introduced specifically for forest trusts. In the next sections, we will explore more in detail how the trust-restriction features work.

Key features of forest trust relationships are:

- *Forest trust relationships are transitive between two forests.* In Windows Server 2003, it is enough to have a single trust between the two root domains of two different forests to enable interforest authentication between all domains in the two forests. This is illustrated in Figure 3.8 for domain C in the compaq.com forest: because of the transitive forest trust between compaq.com and hp.com, domain C will automatically have a transitive trust relationship with domains D, E, and F in the hp.com forest (the same is true for the other domains). Transitive trusts greatly simplify forest trust administration and provide transparent Single Sign-On between all domains in two multidomain forests. In Windows 2000, the same level of functionality required the definition of a trust relationship between every other domain in the two forests. Transitive forest trusts do not allow for transparent object browsing (for example, when setting access control settings) between all domains in the two forests: this is only possible between the root domains of the two forests. However, objects of the other domains in the forest can be searched for by name.

Forest trusts are not transitive between multiple forests (as illustrated in Figure 3.9 for the digital.com, compaq.com, and hp.com

Figure 3.8
Cross-forest trust transitivity between two forests.

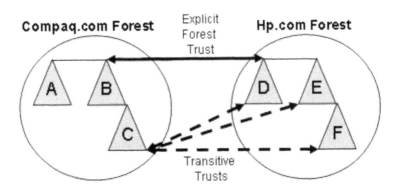

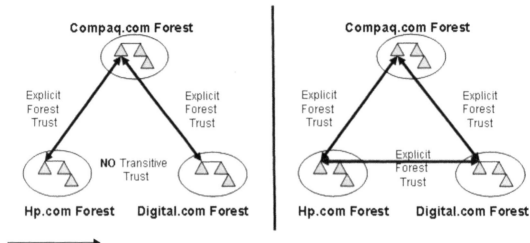

Figure 3.9 *Cross-forest trust between multiple forests.*

forests). If forest trusts exist between the digital.com and the compaq.com forest and between the compaq.com and the hp.com forest, then there won't automatically be a transitive trust between digital.com and hp.com (as illustrated in the left picture of Figure 3.9). If a transparent SSO experience is required between the hp.com and the digital.com forests, an explicit forest trust relationship would be required between those two forests (as illustrated in the right picture of Figure 3.9).

■ Forest trust relationships enable the use of different authentication protocols and methods for cross-forest resource access. When performing a cross-forest network logon, both Kerberos and NTLM are supported. Interactive cross-forest logon users can use either a Kerberos PKINIT-based smart card logon or a user principal name (UPN)–based logon (the latter supports both the Kerberos and the NTLM authentication protocols). Using the SAM account name (the pre-Windows 2000 logon name) is also supported; however, it bears some restrictions as described in the sidenote "Limitations for Using the SAM Account Name for Interactive Logon in a Forest Trust Setup."

So Windows Server 2003 now supports two ways to link forests together: using either a forest or an external trust. The latter was the only way to link forests together in Windows 2000. The key difference between a forest trust and an external trust is that a forest trust contains information about all domains in the remote forest. As a consequence, it can support

---

Limitations for Using the SAM Account Name for Interactive Logon in a Forest Trust Setup

Just like the UPN logon, the interactive logon between two Windows Server 2003 forests via the SAM account name supports both the Kerberos and the NTLM authentication protocols. However, it is preferred to use the UPN for logon in these scenarios, since the logon via the SAM account name bears various restrictions:

- If users enter the SAM name in the logon dialog box, only the root domain of the user's proper forest can be selected; thus, they will not be able to logon using this method if their account is located in a child domain.

- Users could choose to use the domain\username syntax in the dialog box; however, this only works with Windows XP and Windows Server 2003 clients, not with Windows 2000 clients.

- Users are often unaware of the domain that they need to choose during the logon procedure, so that there is a high likelihood that logon attempts will fail simply by trying to logon to the wrong domain. Once users have been trained to use their UPN to logon, the knowledge about their own domain becomes unnecessary.

---

transitivity, Kerberos-based authentication, UPN-based logon, and object lookups between any of the domains in the two forests. Figure 3.10 shows how two other forests, "cpqtest.net" and "digitaltest.net," are displayed in the Windows object picker (used for setting access control settings) after two forest trust relationships have been defined: one between hewlettpackardtest.net and cpqtest.net, and another between hewlettpackardtest.net and digitaltest.net. Note that you do not see the child domains of either trusted forest; the child domains are also trusted transitively. As such, you cannot browse through the OUs of the not-directly trusted domains; it is, however, no problem to search for objects in either domain of the trusted forests by name.

The cross-forest trust features are a fundamental building block for Microsoft's federation strategy. Windows Server 2003 cross-forest trust primarily focuses on federation between different Microsoft AD environments, mainly to link together two forests within the same company or a larger corporation. Nevertheless, the need for federating identities beyond the realm of Microsoft AD environments continued to evolve, especially to allow seamless access to Web resources between different organizations. For these scenarios, the creation of a Windows trust is often inappropriate or impossible. With the release of Windows Server 2003 R2, Microsoft has introduced the new Active Directory Federation Service (ADFS), which

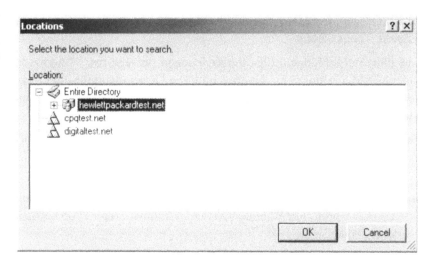

Figure 3.10
*Display of other
forest, "hptest.net,"
in object picker.*

enables the creation of external federation between Windows forests and other organizations' trusted third parties (TTPs) that are not necessarily rooted on MS AD technology. ADFS will be discussed in greater detail *in Chapter 5 in the second book of this series.*

3.3   Restricting Trusts

Windows Server 2003 includes several ways to restrict a trust: SID filtering, selective authentication, name suffix routing, and top level name restrictions. While SID filtering is not a new concept, it is critical to understand how it works and the impact it has on the new forest trust type. Selective authentication was called the ""authentication firewall"" during the development phase of Windows Server 2003, because it acts just like a firewall: it only allows authorized authentication requests to come through to a domain or forest. The last two options, name suffix routing and top level name restrictions, belong together and are only applicable for the new forest trust type.

3.3.1   SID Filtering

Security Identifier (SID) filtering was first introduced in Windows 2000 Service Pack 2 and is still an important security feature in Windows Server 2003 and R2. It does not require any special domain or forest functional level.

The idea behind SID filtering is that security identifiers for which the domain controllers in a forest are not authoritative should not be included in the access control information that is sent to other external domains or forests. When a user tries to authenticate to the DC of another forest, the user's authorization data (e.g., group memberships) are sent along with the authentication request. To make sure that only authorization data from the home forest are stored in the user's security token, the DC of the remote forest validating the authentication request will filter out all SIDs that do not originate from the user's home forest.

SID filtering protects against attempts to add foreign SIDs to authorization data in order to elevate a user's privileges (these threats are also known as elevation of privilege attacks). For example, if a user succeeded in adding the SID of the Enterprise Administrators group of the other forest to its access control data, the user could gain enterprise administrator-level access to the other forest.

Figure 3.11 shows the effect of SID filtering between two forests (the Compaq forest and the HP forest). In this example a user who is defined in and logged into the Compaq forest wants to access a resource in the HP

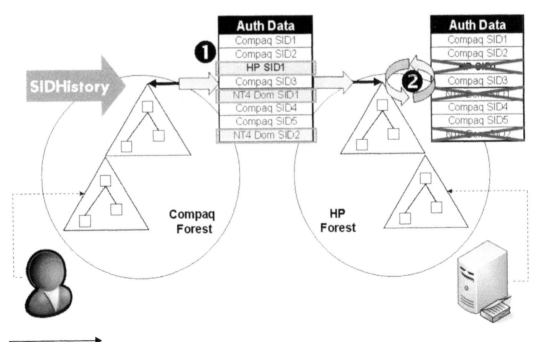

Figure 3.11 *SID filtering between two forests.*

forest. In the first step, his authorization data are sent along with his authentication request to a DC in the HP forest. In the second step, the DC in the HP forest filters out all SIDs that are not linked to the user's definition forest (which is the Compaq forest). In the example, the HP DC automatically removes all SIDs referring to the HP forest and another external domain called NT4 Dom.

Realize that when you use SID filtering across a Windows Server 2003 forest trust with multidomain forests, this security feature does have some caveats. SID filtering will also filter any SIDs associated with a user's membership in universal groups of his proper forest, if these universal groups do not belong to the user's proper account domain. So if, for example, a universal group of the child domain in the Compaq forest above is used to grant access to a resource in the HP forest, a user from the root domain in the Compaq forest would not be able to access the resource although his account is a member of the correct universal group. As such, although SID filtering is enabled by default at creation time for other external trusts, this feature is disabled by default on forest trusts between two Windows Server 2003 forests in order not to disrupt the transitive nature of this trust relationship. Enabling SID filtering between multidomain forests basically makes the forest trust relationships half-transitive (not transitive on the trusted side). However, if both forests are single-domain forests and there are no other reasons to leave SID filtering disabled, it can be enabled using the following command with the netdom.exe tool, which is part of the Windows Server 2003 support tools:

```
Netdom trust <trusting_domain_name>
/domain:<trusted_domain_name> /Quarantine: yes
```

As a counterexample, it is not uncommon to have SIDs from foreign domains or forests cloned to the SIDHistory attribute of group- and user-accounts via scripts or migration tools, during a migration scenario coming from a legacy NT4 domain, or between two AD forests after a merger or acquisition of a company. These scripts and tools leverage a special API (clonePrincipal) that Microsoft provided in AD to allow for an easier migration of accounts from one domain to another. The goal of this API was to ensure seamless and secure access for migrated users to resources that are still using the old SIDs of the source domain in their access control lists (ACLs). So for the migration phase of a company, the SIDHistory feature is typically a useful thing, as the SIDs from the source domain are added to user's authorization data after the user authenticates to a DC in his new domain. This gives the administrator some additional time to clean up the ACLs on all resources to leverage the new domain's SIDs. If, in this case,

SID filtering is enabled and the resources with the old ACLs that are accessed by the user are still located in the trusted source domain, SID filtering would prevent the migrated user to access data that he is actually allowed to access. SID filtering and SIDHistory are basically mutually exclusive mechanisms. To allow SIDHistory to work across trusts for the migration phase of a project, SID filtering may need to be disabled by the netdom.exe tool:

```
Netdom trust <trusting_domain_name>
/domain:<trusted_domain_name> /Quarantine: no
```

It is important to note that SID filtering should only be disabled across a trust to a domain whose administrators are fully trusted in person, as SIDHistory does bear the risk of being misused for an elevation of privilege attack, as mentioned above. This risk is explained in more detail in the side-note "Elevation of Privilege Using the SIDHistory Attribute."

At last, SID filtering should not be applied to trust relationships between domains in the same forest. Doing so breaks AD and Global Catalog replication. Combined with the knowledge of what was previously

---

Elevation of Privilege Using the SIDHistory Attribute

Scripts or tools leveraging the clonePrincipal API must meet various requirements to ensure that only authorized administrators can read a SID from an existing object in a source domain and apply it to the SIDHistory attribute of a security principal in the target domain. These requirements include supplying an account with administrative privileges to the source domain during the process.

Usually, these measures ensure that it is not possible for someone who doesn't already have administrative access to a trusted (source) domain to gain this access by adding the SID of a highly privileged account or group from the source domain to his account. However, if a rogue administrator could find a way to inject a SID to his SIDHistory attribute without using the clonePrincipal API, he would not have to fulfill these constraints. He could thus add the SID of a remote forest's enterprise administrator group to his own account, which would elevate his privileges, giving him permissions he previously did not have. For example, this can be achieved by editing the AD database on a DC while it is booted into Directory Services Restore Mode, where the AD database file (NTDS.dit) is offline and unlocked.

While it is not the goal of this book to give you a guideline on how to attack an AD forest, you should be aware that tools to perform this offline edit of SIDHistory are readily available for free download in the Internet (e.g., www.tbiro.com/projects/SHEdit/index.htm), and that this is not some theoretical scenario that only a genius could perform.

Setting Trust Properties from the Command Line

Most trust restrictions explained in this chapter can be set from the command line. To do so, you must use the netdom.exe utility: the most important trust-related switches are explained below.

General netdom command:

```
Netdom trust <trusting_domain_name> /domain:<trusted_domain_name>
```

Specific netdom command switches:

/NameSuffixes

Lists the routed name suffixes for trust_name on the domain named by trusting_domain_name.

/ToggleSuffix

Use with /NameSuffixes to change the status of a name suffix.

/SelectiveAUTH

Specifying "yes" enables selective authentication across this trust. Specifying "no" disables selective authentication across this trust. Specifying /SelectiveAUTH without yes or no will display the current state of this trust attribute.

/AddTLN

Adds the specified Top Level Name to the Forest Trust Info for the specified trust.

/AddTLNEX

Adds the specified Top Level Name Exclusion to the Forest Trust Info for the specified trust.

/RemoveTLN

Removes the specified Top Level Name from the Forest Trust Info from the specified trust.

/RemoveTLNEX

Removes the specified Top Level Name Exclusion from the Forest Trust Info from the specified trust.

/Quarantine

Enables or disables SID filtering across trusts.

explained, you should understand that any administrator of a child domain in a multidomain forest could also leverage SIDHistory as a means to elevate his or her own privileges to that of the forest's enterprise administrator. This attack won't be stopped by SID filtering, which basically means that any child-domain administrator needs to be trusted in person in the same way as an enterprise administrator. It also undermines the statement that not a domain, but a forest is the security boundary in an Active Directory infrastructure.

3.3.2 Selective Authentication

When the selective authentication feature of a trust relationship is enabled, foreign users from externally trusted domains or forests, accessing the local trusting domain's resources, will not be allowed to authenticate to a domain controller or resource server (file and print server, database servers, and so forth) in the local domain unless they are explicitly allowed to do so. As this feature requires special logic on all DCs in the trusting domain, it requires the domain to run at Windows Server 2003 domain functional level. The

---

The Scope of Authenticated Users in Trusted Domains or Forests

When setting up a trust between two external domains or forests, the reach of the well known security principal "Authenticated Users" is instantly expanded to include the trusting domain(s). By default, users from the trusted domain(s) have access to any servers and data in the trusting domain authorized for authenticated users, including read access to most objects in the foreign AD.

Authenticated Users can be viewed as a dynamic group that users are added to after they've successfully authenticated themselves to their home domain. However, the SID of Authenticated Users (SID: S-1-5-11) in the access token of the foreign user is honored in the trusting domain when they cross the trust, which explains the expansion of the scope. Naturally, the type of trust will influence this scope, as is shown in the three examples in Figure 3.12.

In examples 1 and 2, a legacy external trust has been configured between the root domains of forests A and B. As there are no other trusts to domains in forest B, the scope of Authenticated Users was merely extended for domain 1 in forest A to include users (and computers) from the root domain of forest B. Due to the transitive nature of a Windows Server 2003 forest trust (as used in example 3), the Authenticated Users' scope has been extended for any domain in forest A to include users from any domain in forest B.

Enabling selective authentication for a trust in a Windows Server 2003 AD helps to control this expanded reach for Authenticated Users.

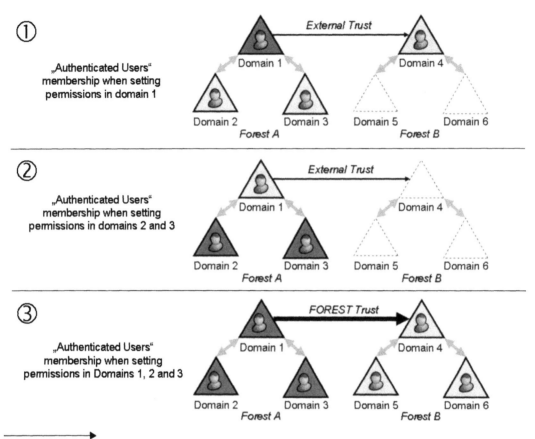

Figure 3.12   *Scope of Authenticated Users across trusts.*

trusted domain on the other side of the trust does not have to meet any specific requirements—it can even be a legacy NT4 or mixed-mode Windows 2000 domain or forest.

The reason Microsoft added the feature was to enable a more granular trust definition. Without selective authentication enabled, all users from the foreign domain or forest become almost perfect peers of the local domain users from an access control point of view. See the sidenote, "The Scope of Authenticated Users in Trusted Domains or Forests," for examples of what this means.

Even though foreign domain users will still be members of the Authenticated Users groups when the selective authentication option is enabled, they will only be allowed to authenticate to the trusting domain or forest after they pass an additional access control check (that will be explained next). Note that selective authentication is always configured on the outgoing side of a trust relationship, i.e., it must be configured on the domain that is trusting another domain.

A trust relationship's selective authentication function can be enabled from the trust wizard or from the properties of the trust relationship. To enable it from the trust properties, select the authentication tab and select the "allow authentication only for selected resources in the local domain…" (as illustrated in Figure 3.13). This setting activates a firewall-like behavior for authenticating trusted users to the domain and its resources, which is why this feature was called Authentication Firewall during its early stages of development.

Let's have a look at how enabling this feature would notify the foreign users, if you have not yet assigned the correct permissions in the trusting domain to grant the user access to the resources they require. When you try to access a resource in a domain for which selective authentication has been enabled from a machine in a trusted domain, the following error will be displayed: "Logon Failure: The machine you are logging onto is protected by an authentication firewall. The specified account is not allowed to authenti-

Figure 3.13
Enabling the selective authentication feature of a trust relationship.

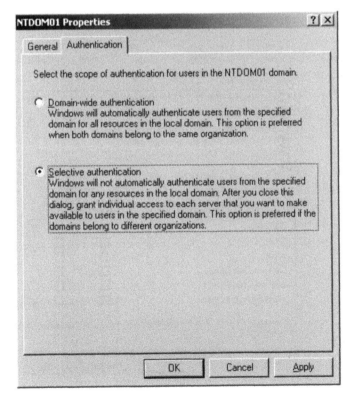

cate to the machine." When a foreign domain's user tries to interactively log on to a computer in the protected domain, the warning message is not as descriptive: "Unable to log you on because of an account restriction." The same warning messages would appear if foreign users simply tried to browse around in the trusting domain and access servers to which they are not granted access. Naturally, the user would not notice any difference if he was only accessing the resources he was authorized to access.

The good thing about selective authentication is that administrators of the trusting domain can centrally and separately configure every computer object in their domain to grant the rights for authenticating foreign users or to revoke them. This includes the computer objects for domain controllers of the trusting domain: administrators can choose not to grant permissions to authenticate to their AD DCs, which will limit the capabilities of the users in any trusted domain to read the AD data.

For example: to enable users to authenticate to file servers across trusts that have the selective authentication option enabled, the administrator of the trusting domain or forest must change the access control settings of the

Figure 3.14
Setting the "Allowed to Authenticate" permission for a foreign security principal.

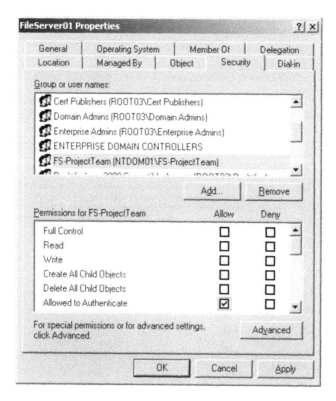

file server computer objects. To do so, use the Advanced Features view of the Active Directory Users and Computers MMC snap-in, open the properties of the appropriate computer object and give the appropriate group the "Allowed to Authenticate" permission (as illustrated in Figure 3.14). This can be a group from the foreign domain or forest, as used in the example, or a local group in the trusting domain, which contains users or groups from the foreign domain. There are different reasons for assigning the permissions either way, which will be discussed in greater detail in Section 3.4.4.

If foreign users should be granted permissions to authenticate to all computer objects (clients and servers alike) in a specific OU, this can be done by using the advanced permission options for that OU. Doing so allows you to choose the type of objects to which specific permissions will be applied. In this case, you would choose the option to "Apply onto" computer objects, as shown in Figure 3.15, and grant the "Allowed to Authenticate" permission, just as you would for a single computer object. Furthermore, there is another benefit that selective authentication gives you, which we will discuss next.

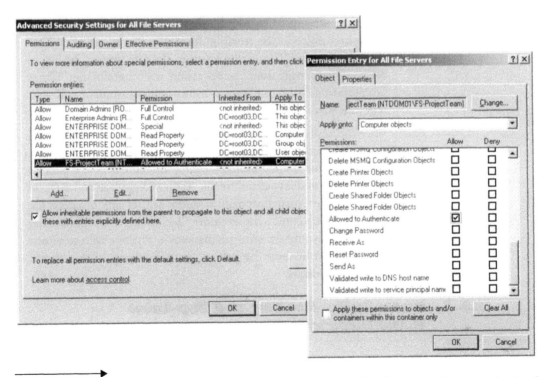

Figure 3.15   *Setting the "Allowed to Authenticate" permission for all computers in an organizational unit.*

Besides the additional access control check for the "Allowed to Authenticate" permission, selective authentication also adds a special security identity to the access token of local users and foreign users, which allows administrators to keep the two apart when assigning more general permissions to resources. Remember that all users are "Authenticated Users," so permissions applied to this ID are valid for all local and all foreign users. To differentiate the two, the DCs of the trusting domain add the "This Organization" ID (SID Value S-1-5-15) to their own users and the "Other Organization" ID (SID Value S-1-5-1000) to users who have been authenticated across a trust for which selective authentication is enabled. Like Authenticated Users, these IDs are well known security principals that can be viewed as a dynamic group to which a user is added after he or she has successfully authenticated him- or herself. You can check for the presence of these IDs in a user's access token by using the whoami command line tool and the /groups switch.

This additional SID allows administrators to granularly control access for trusted accounts at two stages, prior to allowing a foreign user to access local resources:

1. A foreign user must first be allowed to authenticate to the target computer object in the trusting domain or forest, which will be checked by the DCs of the trusting domain (step 1 in Figure 3.15). The foreign users' access token will contain the "Other Organization" SID, while users from the local domain will contain the "This Organization" SID.

2. After successful authentication to the resource, for example, a file server, the server itself will analyze the permissions (ACL) on its shares, file, and folder resources (step 2 in Figure 3.16). If permissions are set to deny access for the "Other Organization" SID, no user from any trusted domain or forest will be able to access the resource. This could, for example, be leveraged to grant users from their own forest write permissions to a public data store and read-only permissions for remote users from any of the trusted domains or forests.

3.3.3 **Name Suffix Routing and Top-Level Name Restrictions**

Windows Server 2003 uses a mechanism called name suffix routing to provide name resolution between forests linked together using a forest trust. As

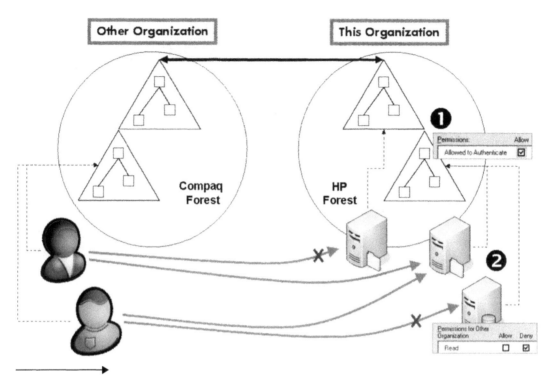

Figure 3.16 *Selective authentication between two forests.*

this feature is only available for forest trusts, it requires the forest to run at Windows Server 2003 Forest Functional Level. As previously explained, name resolution is needed to route cross-forest authentication and object query requests. The Windows Server 2003 cross-forest routing mechanism is rooted on a list of DNS domain suffixes stored in the AD Trusted Domain Object (TDO) of the root domain of a forest. The suffixes can be disabled, enabled, or excluded to modify the cross-forest routing behavior. How to do this will be explained in the following text.

In the example in Figure 3.17, a one-way forest trust has been defined between the cpqtest.net and the hewlettpackardtest.net Windows forests. The hewlettpackardtest.net domain is the root domain of the forest with the same name. The hewlettpackardtest.net forest is made up of a second domain tree called hp.com. In this scenario, cpqtest.net is the trusting domain containing the resources, and hewlettpackardtest.net is the trusted domain containing the users. The administrator in the cpqtest.net domain decides that he or she doesn't want to trust the authentication requests or object query requests that are coming in from accounts in the hp.com

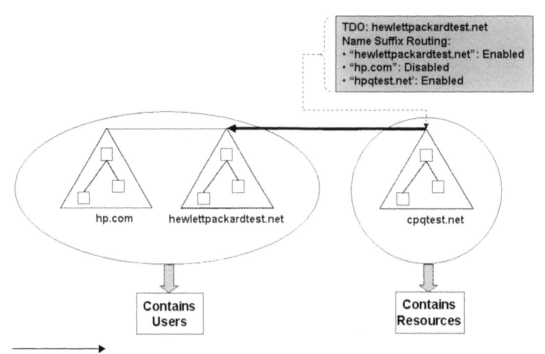

Figure 3.17   *TLN restrictions example: disabling DNS namespaces.*

domain. To do so he or she can disable the hp.com namespace in the msDS-TrustForestTrustInfo attribute of the TDO for the hewlettpack-ardtest.net domain in the cpqtest.net AD.

DNS namespaces can be disabled when running the new Windows Server 2003 Trust Wizard. The page where this is done is illustrated in Figure 3.18. The wizard displays all the DNS suffixes of the top-level domains in a forest (with the exception of the DNS suffix of the root domain itself) and all UPN suffixes that have been defined on the forest level. In the example of Figure 3.18, there's one additional top-level DNS suffix, hp.com, and one UPN suffix has been defined, hptest.net. To disable the routing of all incoming requests with a *.hp.com suffix in the cpqtest.net forest, simply uncheck the box—as illustrated in Figure 3.18. To enable routing (in the example, routing is enabled for *.hptest.net), simply leave the checkbox checked.

UPN suffixes in a forest are officially defined via the AD Domains and Trusts MMC snap-in. To add or delete additional UPN suffixes, right-click the Active Directory Domains and Trusts container and select Prop-erties. Realize that any UPN suffix can be added to a user object program-matically or that you could even leverage UPN suffixes at the OU level

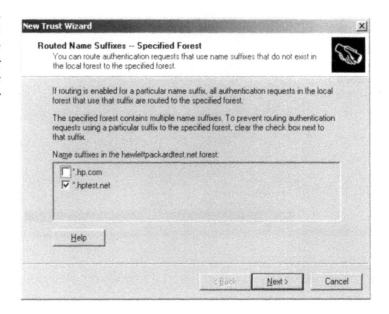

Figure 3.18
*TLN restrictions
example: disabling
DNS namespaces
when running the
trust wizard.*

(using the UPNSuffixes attribute of an OU object). However, the TLN name restrictions only allow using the "officially registered" forest UPN suffixes, which are entered via the AD Domains and Trusts MMC. The other suffixes can neither be used for TLN filtering nor for cross-forest logon, as the trusting forest has no information on these suffixes in its TDO.

DNS namespaces can also be disabled from the Name Suffix Routing tab in the properties of a trust object (available from the AD Domains and Trusts MMC snap-in). This is illustrated in Figure 3.19 for the hp.com suffix in the properties of the hewlettpackardtest.net trust object. To disable or enable suffixes, select them and click the Enable or Disable pushbuttons, as needed. Note that the dialog box also shows another DNS suffix called hewlettpackard.net that is set to disabled and marked as New. This is a UPN suffix that was added to the hewlettpackardtest.net forest after the trust wizard was run. By default, Windows Server 2003 disables these newly added suffixes.

Disabling a namespace in the properties of a forest trust relationship fully disables the routing of requests to that namespace and all its subordinate namespaces. For example: disabling the hp.com namespace will disable the routing from all subordinate namespaces, including emea.hp.com, americas.hp.com, and asiapac.hp.com. Top-Level Name (TLN) restrictions also allow you to exclude the routing of only certain subordinate

Figure 3.19
TLN restrictions example: disabling DNS namespaces from the trust properties.

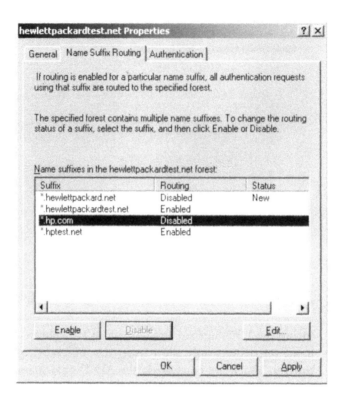

namespaces. For example, if routing from the hp.com namespace was enabled, you could exclude just the routing from the emea.hp.com subordinate namespace.

TLN restrictions can also be used to avoid DNS namespace collisions during the routing of cross-forest authentication requests. A DNS namespace collision occurs when the Windows security software can follow two or more different DNS paths to get to a target domain or forest.

In the example in Figure 3.20, a bidirectional forest trust relationship has been set up between the hewlettpackardtest.net and hr.hewlettpackardtest.net forests. A one-way forest trust relationship exists both between the cpqtest.net and the hewlettpackardtest.net forests and between the cpqtest.net and the hr.hewlettpackardtest.net forests. Both the hewlettpackardtest.net and hr.hewlettpackardtest.net forests contain users; the cpqtest.net forest contains resources.

By default, the forest trust between cpqtest.net and hewlettpackardtest.net routes all authentication traffic for the *.hewlettpackardtest.net DNS suffix to the hewlettpackardtest.net forest. *.hewlettpackardtest.net

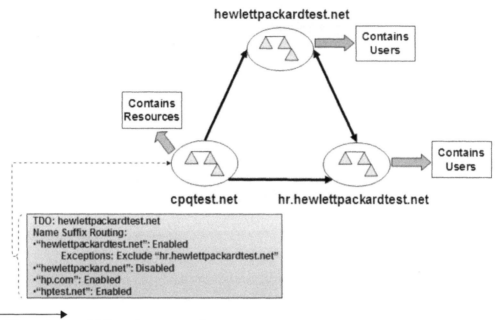

hewlettpackardtest.net

Contains
Users

Contains
Resources

cpqtest.net   hr.hewlettpackardtest.net

Contains
Users

TDO: hewlettpackardtest.net
Name Suffix Routing:
•"hewlettpackardtest.net": Enabled
        Exceptions: Exclude "hr.hewlettpackardtest.net"
•"hewlettpackard.net": Disabled
•"hp.com": Enabled
•"hptest.net": Enabled

Figure 3.20   *TLN restrictions example.*

includes both hewlettpackardtest.net and hr.hewlettpackardtest.net DNS domains. Because of the lack of trust transitivity between multiple forests, this may lead to problems. An authentication request coming from the cpqtest.net forest for a service in hr.hewlettpackardtest.net—that is, routed to hewlettpackardtest.net—cannot be forwarded by the DCs in the hewlettpackardtest.net forest to the hr.hewlettpackardtest.net forest.

To avoid these DNS namespace collisions a TLN restriction should be set in the cpqtest.net forest to exclude the hr.hewlettpackardtest.net namespace from the forest trust with hewlettpackardtest.net.

TLN restrictions that exclude DNS namespaces are also defined on the Name Suffix Routing tab of the properties of a trust object (available from the AD Domains and Trusts MMC snap-in). This is illustrated in Figure 3.21 and Figure 3.22 for the TLN restriction for the hr.hewlettpackard-test.net domain on the hewlettpackardtest.net trust. Note that the status of the *.hr.hewlettpackardtest.net suffix in the name suffix routing tab says "Exceptions" (Figure 3.21). Switching to the Edit view (after selecting the *.hr.hewlettpackardtest.net entry in Figure 3.21) allows you to define the TLN restrictions (Figure 3.22). Contrary to the disabling and enabling of DNS namespaces, TLN restrictions cannot be set from the new Windows Server 2003 trust wizard.

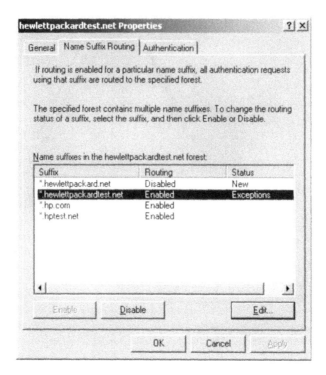

3.4   Working with Trusts

Before we delve a little deeper into how trusts work under the hood, this section will give you some guidelines on how to work with trusts. These include understanding which trusts to choose when, how to set them up, and how to manage permissions on resources for users from trusted domains.

3.4.1   Choosing the Correct Trust Type

With all the options Windows Server 2003 offers for trusts and related features, it can be difficult to choose the correct type for a given situation. As the previous sections described, the existing domain or forest functional levels of an AD forest will limit the options that an administrator can choose from. These dependencies are summarized in Table 3.2.

However, meeting a specific functional level isn't everything—simply because an AD forest is operating at Windows Server 2003 Forest Func-

Table 3.2   *Minimal Domain or Forest Functional Levels for Trust Types and Features*

Trust Type	Minimal Domain Functional Level	Minimal Forest Functional Level
Tree-Root Trust	Windows 2000 Mixed Mode	Windows 2000
Parent-Child Trust	Windows 2000 Mixed Mode	Windows 2000
Shortcut Trust	Windows 2000 Mixed Mode	Windows 2000
Forest Trust	Windows Server 2003	Windows Server 2003
External Trust	Windows 2000 Mixed Mode	Windows 2000
Non-Windows Trust (to UNIX or DCE Kerberos realm)	Windows 2000 Mixed Mode	Windows 2000
Trust Feature		
SID Filtering	Windows 2000 Mixed Mode	Windows 2000
Selective Authentication	Windows Server 2003	Windows 2000
Name Suffix Routing and Top-Level Name Restrictions	Windows Server 2003	Windows Server 2003

tional level doesn't mean that an administrator should always create a forest trust.

To begin with, trusts should only be set up between AD infrastructures where there is also a respectable level of personal trust between the two parties operating the AD domains or forests. If, additionally, there is a valid requirement to disable SID Filtering across the trust (e.g., during a migration phase of a company), both sides of the trusted AD infrastructure should be administered by the same team of people who have a very high level of personal trust with each other. If the latter cannot be guaranteed, it is inappropriate to disable SID Filtering. This will directly influence the migration strategy to use, since leveraging SIDHistory during the phase of the migration is no longer an option.

If the goal, for example, is to migrate specific users from one company's forest to another company's forest (e.g., after an acquisition of a specific business unit, not the whole company), creating any type of trust between the forests of the two companies is highly unlikely. In this case, consider the creation of an interim forest with a trust only to company1, solely to allow migration of the business unit's users and resources into a separate entity, similar to phase I shown in Figure 3.23. After completion of the migration, the trust to the forest of company1 can be removed, and management of the interim forest is handed over to company2. This company can now create a new trust to their own forest, so that the acquired business unit can be integrated into the target forest, as shown in phase II of Figure 3.23. This

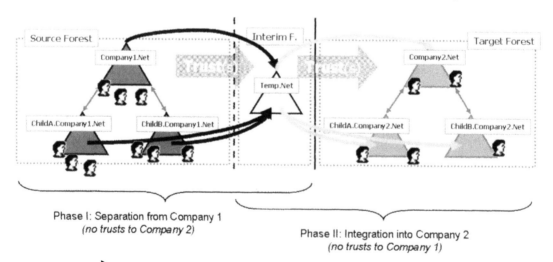

Figure 3.23   *Using an interims forest to migrate users between companies.*

way, a direct trust between the forests of the two companies is not required at any time. While the interim forest may seem like an excessive burden, it will ensure that the security of both companies cannot be compromised at any time by untrusted people via the Windows trust.

The general goal should always be to create a trust with the smallest scope possible to meet the requirements for resource sharing. For example, let's take the scenario where you have a multidomain production forest, with two child domains and a separate single-domain development forest both running at Windows Server 2003 Forest Functional Level. Users from the development forest are not to access any resources in the production forest. However, there is a database server in the development forest that needs to be accessed by a particular business unit from the production forest, whose users are all contained in a specific OU of the second child domain. If the situation is as straightforward as this, there is not necessarily a need to set up a forest trust between the two forests. The smallest scope in terms of trusts would be to set up a one-way external trust from the development forest trusting the child2 domain of the production forest. As

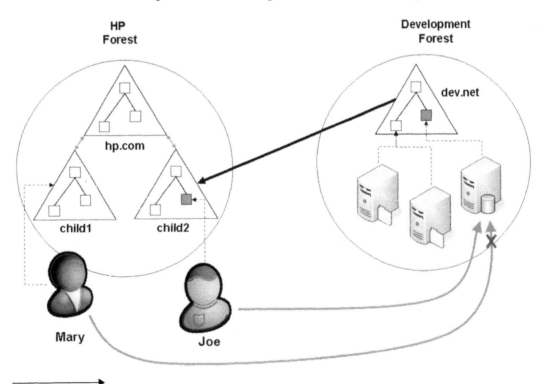

Figure 3.24 *Minimizing the scope of a trust between two forests.*

shown in Figure 3.24, users such as Joe from the child2 domain are able to access the SQL server via the trust. Users from other domains in the production forest, such as Mary from the child1 domain, cannot access any resources in the development forest.

The scope of Joe's access could further be refined by leveraging the Selective Authentication feature in the dev forest, so that Joe and any other users from his business unit are allowed to authenticate only to the SQL Server and to no other resource, such as the file-servers hosted in the same forest. Note that the external trust will only support NTLM authentication, so if there is a need to use Kerberos authentication to access a resource in another forest, then a forest trust is the only choice. To set up the forest trust with the same scope as the external trust described above, you would then have to leverage the Top Level Name Restrictions feature to filter the child1 domain from accessing resources across the trust.

There is another reason that a forest trust is the only choice to enable trusts between the child domains of different forests: if the child domains have the same NetBIOS domain name. Although it is no longer considered a best practice today, it was not uncommon in the early days of Active Directory for global companies to deploy multidomain AD forests made up of an empty forest root domain and regional domains to control replication traffic between DCs of the different regions. Often a three-region model was chosen, which split the world into "Americas," "EMEA," and "Asia-Pacific"—and the child domains were named accordingly. Due to the ongoing mergers and acquisitions in our industry today, chances are actually quite likely that one company will buy another company that has the same or a similar child-domain structure with overlapping NetBIOS names. This would hinder the creation of normal trusts between the domains of the forests—an external trust between any two equally named domains is not possible, as shown in Figure 3.25. However, as long as the root domains are not named the same way, a forest trust can resolve the issue of equally named child domains, as the transitive nature of the forest trust will not require a direct trust between the child domains.

At last, here is an example where the usage of shortcut trusts may make sense. Shortcut trusts can only be leveraged between domains in the same forest, not to an external domain or forest. So let's again assume a company has deployed a multi-domain forest with three child domains (Americas, EMEA, and AsiaPacific) and an empty forest root domain, just like that described in the previous example. The DCs for the respective regions would be distributed in the various locations within their region and thus be highly available. However, as the forest root domain does not really con-

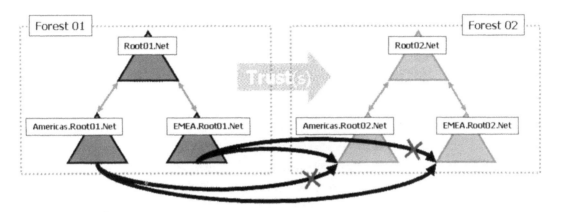

Figure 3.25   *Direct trusts between domains with equal DNS or NetBIOS names are not possible.*

tain any normal users, there are only two DCs for the root domain, and these have been located in two different sites in the United States. If a user from the AsiaPacific domain needs to access resources from the EMEA domain, the user's authentication process would have to follow the trust path that is built automatically due to the transitive trusts between the domains in the forest.

As there is no direct trust to the EMEA domain, the authentication process would follow the trust path and first be referred to a DC of the root domain, which can only be reached via a rather expensive WAN link to the US. In a second step, it is then referred to a DC in the EMEA domain to complete the authentication process and allow direct access to the resource in EMEA. More details about the trust path and how it works behind the scenes will be illustrated extensively in Chapter 6 of this book. However, this simple example shows that even if IP connectivity is given between the user's client in the AsiaPacific domain and the resource in the EMEA domain, the AsiaPacific user would not be able to authenticate to the EMEA resource without availability of the root DCs. If WAN-link outages to the locations hosting the root DCs are a frequent occurrence, or if there is extensive resource sharing going on between the different regions, a short-cut trust between the child domains should be considered.

3.4.2   Making Name Resolution Work

Before you start creating trust relationships between Windows domains, you must make sure that name resolution works between the two domain environments. Following are some hints and tips on how to set up name resolution to function correctly.

Windows Server 2003 ⇔ Windows NT4

If a trust needs to be set up to an NT4 domain (external trust), NETBIOS name resolution is a must. This is typically achieved by configuring WINS and ensuring that the PDC of the NT4 domain, as well as the PDC emulator of the AD domain, registers its NETBIOS records with the WINS server. If the two domains are not leveraging the same WINS infrastructure, you'll either have to set up LMHosts files, or enter the appropriate records as static records in WINS, as listed in Table 3.3.

Note that WINS servers running on Windows 2000 or later don't allow manual entry of the 1Bh record via the WINS MMC snap-in. Instead you must use the NetSh command as follows:

```
NetSh wins server>add name Name=<domain> EndChar=1b _
  RecType=0 Group=4 IP={<IP-Address-of-PDC>}
```

Enter all as one command without the "_".

Windows Server 2003 ⇔ Windows 2000

Although NetBIOS is supported as a name resolution mechanism to set up an external trust between Active Directory domains, DNS is clearly preferred. As such, the configuration for enabling DNS name resolution between a Windows Server 2003 domain and a Windows 2000 domain strongly depends on how DNS has been implemented in a given infrastructure. The goal is that the DNS servers used by either domain's DCs can resolve the DC names and service records of the other domain.

Let's assume that the DCs of both AD domains are also used as DNS servers, which is a common practice for most companies. In Windows 2000, the main options to ensure that another domain's DNS zone is resolved correctly by the Windows 2000 DCs are either to configure DNS forwarding or to add a copy of the whole target DNS zone as a secondary zone on the Windows 2000 DCs. Note that when leveraging the forwarding option, any unknown names are forwarded to the configured DNS

Table 3.3   *WINS Records Required for Trust Creation*

WINS Records	IPAddress of
[00h], [03h], [20h]	PDC (or PDC emulator)
[1Bh], [1Ch], [1Eh]	Domain (any DC)

servers of the target AD domain; this can create limitations when setting up trusts to multiple AD domains in different forests.

Windows Server 2003 and R2 offer two new options that make the DNS configuration even easier: conditional forwarding and stub zones. As the name implies, conditional forwarding allows administrators to configure multiple target DNS servers that would each only be contacted if a name of the respective DNS zone is unknown to the local DNS server. For example, records for us.hp.com could be forwarded to DNS server A, while records for emea.hp.com could be forwarded to DNS server B. Stub zones are similar to secondary zones, as they provide a local read-only copy of another DNS server's zone. However, different from secondary zones, stub zones don't contain a full copy of the zone and thus don't need to be updated as frequently. Instead, they only copy the SOA and NS records for the defined zones—all other requests for the respective zones are forwarded to the originating name servers. The feature that makes stub zones really interesting is that they are replicated between AD DCs (domain- or forest-wide), so that the knowledge of the stub zone is available on all DCs hosting the DNS service.

Windows Server 2003 ⇔ Windows Server 2003

Just as in Windows 2000, it is possible to create a normal external trust between two Windows Server 2003 AD domains. In this case, name resolution again requires either NetBIOS/WINS or DNS, as described above. More interesting, though, is the creation of a forest trust, which has a firm requirement of DNS name resolution to be configured between the forests. How to do so has been explained above.

3.4.3 Creating a Trust Relationship

In Windows Server 2003, the implicit trust relationships within a forest are created automatically, while trusts to other external domains have to be created manually. The trust-creation wizard in Windows Server 2003 has been vastly improved over that in Windows 2000. The whole process of creating a trust is less confusing. There have been no changes to this wizard in R2.

By default, only domain administrators can create trusts for their respective domains. However, Windows Server 2003 and R2 have added a new built-in group called "Incoming Forest Trust Builders." This domain local group is only available in the root domain of a forest and allows members to create incoming, one-way trusts to the AD forest. As such, the creation of

Locating DCs during Cross-Forest Authentication

When a client wants to authenticate to a resource in a different forest across a Windows Server 2003 trust, it leverages DNS to locate a DC in the target forest. In the example shown in Figure 3.26, a client from *compaq.com* wants to access a fileserver in *hp.com*. As will be explained in detail in Chapter 6, on Kerberos (Section 6.3.3), the client must receive a referral ticket from a DC in his forest to authenticate to a DC in the trusted forest before the client can access the resource. This side-note explains how a client locates the DC in the resource forest. The example leverages two single domain forests, but DC lookups for child-domains in the resource forest work the same way. The DNS interactions work as follows (the location of the DNS zones will dictate which DNS server is contacted by the client; here, the hp.com forest's DNS zones are hosted on a DNS server in the hp.com forest):

1. Client queries for *_kerberos._tcp.<ClientSiteName>._sites.dc._ msdcs.<ResourceForestFQDN>*. In our example this would be: *_kerberos._tcp.SiteA._sites.dc._msdcs.hp.com*.

2. If the sites are not synchronized between the forests, so that the **compaq** client's site (Site A) does not exist in the **hp** forest, the query fails (Name does not exist). Otherwise, the client would receive an ordered response with site-specific KDCs in the resource forest hp.com and would continue with step 5.

3. Client requests any KDC in resource forest by querying *_kerberos._tcp.dc._msdcs.hp.com*.

4. Client will receive a response for all KDCs registered in *_kerberos._tcp.dc._msdcs.hp.com* for the resource forest.

5. Client attempts to contact KDC based on the ordered response returned from DNS. If the attempt fails, the client will attempt to contact the next KDC from the ordered response returned from DNS.

6. Client accesses resource in trusted forest.

The response with the list of KDCs in the resource forest is ordered by priority configured for the respective SRV records. To ensure that clients will contact the most appropriate KDC in the resource forest, consider either tweaking the DNS record priority or synchronizing site names between the forests.

SITE A in Compaq Forest   **SITE B in HP Forest**

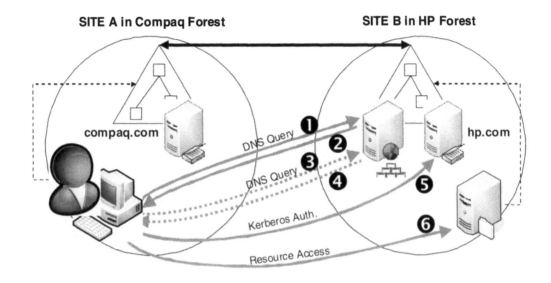

Figure 3.26 *DC lookup for cross-forest authentication.*

incoming forest trusts can be delegated to non-domain admins, if this should be required.

Trusts can be created in a variety of ways:

- The implicit Windows 2000/2003 trust relationships within the same forest are created automatically as part of the dcpromo process—for example, when adding an additional domain to the forest. The dcpromo process builds an AD instance on a Windows server and makes the server a Domain Controller of an existing or a new domain. In the latter case, it also automatically creates a transitive trust to its parent domain in the forest.

- To create a trust manually via the UI, use the Active Directory Domains and Trusts MMC snap-in. During manual trust setup, you will be prompted to enter a trust password. For the implicit trusts, this trust password is generated and exchanged without administrator intervention.

- To create a trust manually via the command line, use the netdom command (part of the Windows Server 2003 support tools):

```
netdom trust <trusting_domainname> _
/domain:<trusted_domainname> /add _
/UserD:<admin account from trusted domain> /PasswordD:* _
/UserO:<admin account from trusting domain> /PasswordO:*
```

Enter all as one command without the "_"; specifying "*" as the password will request entering the real password at runtime. There are further netdom options to define other trust details, such as two-way, one-way, realm, and transitive. The realm option is only valid for a non-Windows trust to a UNIX Kerberos realm. Creation of cross-realm trusts between UNIX and Windows is described in detail in Chapter 6 on Kerberos, Section 6.7.3.

Realize that in addition to meeting the required domain or forest functional level for a specific type of trust, some other limitations for creating trusts between two domains must also be taken into consideration when planning for trusts. First of all, as mentioned in the previous section, you cannot create a trust relationship if either the NetBIOS or the DNS domain names of the two domains are identical. In the example of Figure 2.2, the NetBIOS name of the trusting domain is compaq, while that of the trusted domain is hp. However, even if the trusted and trusting domains kept their DNS names as they are, if both had the same NetBIOS domain name "root," creating a trust between the two would fail. Similarly, you cannot create a trust between two domains if either domain already has a trust established to another domain with the same NetBIOS or DNS name.

3.4.4   Assigning Permissions in a Trusted Environment

Once trusts have been established between domains or forests, administrators are faced with correctly granting permissions for users from the trusted authority to access resources in their own environment. While this can be achieved in a variety of ways with no single "right" way of assigning permissions, this section should give you some guidelines as to how to proceed.

In general, cross-trust permissions can be set up by adding security principals (user accounts, global, or universal groups) from the trusted account domain to domain local groups or server local groups in the trusting resource domain. The domain local groups or server local groups would then be leveraged to assign the correct permissions to the resource—for example, a shared folder on a file server. Naturally, it is also possible to grant permissions to the resource directly for the security principals from the trusted account domain, however this should be avoided as it will make long-term management of the resource permissions extremely difficult. The different group types are explained in more detail in Chapter 10 on AD Authorization.

So how do you grant a user from the trusted account domain permissions to access a share on a file server in the trusting resource domain? Do you first add him to a global group in this domain, then add that global group to a universal group in the forest which is then nested to a domain local group in the resource domain? Or do you add the user directly to the domain local group in the resource domain? The correct answer depends on various parameters, which are discussed next.

Naturally, there are a couple of technical things to consider, such as:

- What type of trust was set up?

- Is SID Filtering enabled?

- Have other restrictions been configured, such as Selective Authentication?

If a forest trust has been configured, the trusting resource forest will by default trust all domains in the trusted account forest, which basically means that any universal group from the trusted account forest could be used to grant permissions in the resource forest, as SID Filtering is disabled by default between forest trusts. Naturally, if you enable SID Filtering, you are limited to groups of the same domain that the user resides in, just as you would if you have only configured a direct external trust between two domains. As such, if groups from the account forest are to be leveraged at all, it is usually appropriate to concentrate on leveraging global groups from the respective domains. Furthermore, if restrictions such as Selective Authentication have been configured, a trusted domain's user must also be added to the group that grants the permission to authenticate to the computer account of the resource server.

On the other hand, there are a couple of security-related issues to consider, such as:

- Who is managing the domains in the trusted forest?

- How sensitive are the data that are being granted access to?

- Who is responsible for the data?

If the two trusting AD infrastructures are managed by two different teams who do not completely trust each other in person, it is questionable whether any group from the trusted account domain should be leveraged at all for assigning permissions in the resource domain. This includes nesting a global group from the account domain into a domain local group of the resource domain. Even though the domain local group is used to grant the actual permission on the resource, for example, the shared folder on the file server, the administrators of the account forest are the ones that manage the global group and determine its membership. In the end, this also means that the administrators of the account forest determine who is being granted access to the resource.

If it is all right that administrators of the trusted domain control access to your resources in the trusting domain (e.g., to control access to public shares) then the global/local group nesting is a valid aproach. However, if you need to ensure that only specific users are granted access to the resource and that this access must be controlled by the resource owners, then you would want to add the users from the trusted account domain directly to your domain local groups or server local groups in the resource domain. This is typically done in security-sensitive environments, where controlling correct access is more important than distributing the workload of group administration to different parties, especially across trusts.

Information on setting permissions in Active Directory itself—for example, how to grant delegated administration capabilities to users that are not members of the domain administrators group—is explained in detail in Chapter 12 on AD delegation.

3.5   Trust Relationships: Under the Hood

Let's look at what is behind a trust relationship and what happens when you manually set up a one-way trust relationship in Windows Server 2003.

In the example in Figure 3.27, the domain administrator of domain South.net decides to trust another domain, North.net. In this case, South.net is the trusting domain and North.net is the trusted domain. When the administrator sets up the trust, Windows will create a Trusted Domain Object (TDO) for the North.net domain in the AD domain naming context of domain South.net (this is on the outgoing side of the trust). This object is a security principal, similar to a user account, which will be named after the DNS domain name of the domain that the trust is being configured for (if the other domain is an NT4 domain, the NetBIOS name will be used). In the South.net domain, the TDO account is thus called North.net.

Just as for any other AD account, there will be a security principal password linked to this object, which is stored in a hashed format in the TDO account's password attribute. This password is sometimes also referred to as the interdomain secret. When you set up a trust relationship manually, the OS will actually prompt you for this password.

When the administrator in the South.net domain or the administrator in the North.net domain creates the other side of the trust in the North.net

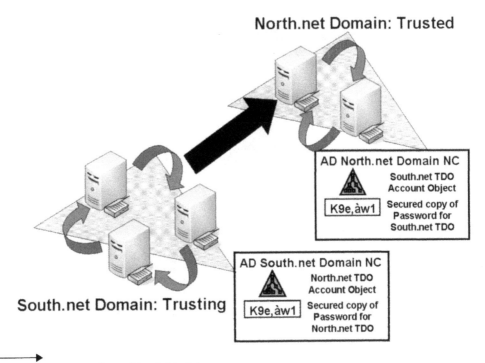

Figure 3.27 *Trust relationships, behind the scenes.*

domain (the incoming side), another TDO account called South.net will be created in the AD domain naming context of domain North.net.

You can look at the TDO account objects using the AD Users and Computers MMC snap-in or using ADSIedit. The TDOs are located in the domain naming context directly underneath the system container (as illustrated in Figure 3.28). Table 3.4 shows the most important trust-related attributes of a TDO object.

The South.net TDO account is replicated among the DCs in the North.net domain via the normal AD replication of the domain naming context. The same is true for the North.net TDO account in the South.net domain. The TDOs and some of their attributes are also replicated to the global catalog (GC). This makes them available to all entities in a Windows forest. The latter enables the routing of cross-domain and cross-forest authentication requests and object browsing.

What are these TDOs and their password (the interdomain secrets) used for? One of the things they are used for is the setup of a secure channel between the domains North.net and South.net. A secure channel is set up when the first domain controller of domain South.net boots up, on the

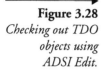

Figure 3.28
Checking out TDO objects using ADSI Edit.

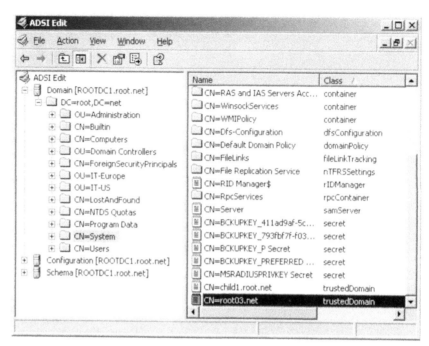

Table 3.4   *Key AD TDO Object Attributes*

TDO Attribute	Meaning/Values
flatName	The NetBIOS name of the domain with which a trust exists.
TrustAttributes	Trust properties.
	Values:*
	1: trust is nontransitive
	2: trust valid only for Windows 2000 and later computers
	4: quarantine domain (SID filtering enabled)
	8: trust is forest transitive
	16: cross organization trust
	32: trust within forest
	64: treat as external trust
	A trust can have multiple properties from this list; their values are simply added together. For example, a forest trust with SID filtering is enabled equals 8 + 4 = 12. A normal parent-child domain trust in a forest has a TrustAttributes value of 32.

Table 3.4 *Key AD TDO Object Attributes (continued)*

TDO Attribute	Meaning/Values
TrustDirection	The direction of a trust. Values: 0: disabled 1: incoming trust 2: outgoing trust 3: two-way trust
TrustPartner	The name of the domain with which a trust exists. For Windows 2000 and later, this is a DNS name. For Windows NT, this is a NetBIOS name.
TrustType	The type of trust. Values: 1: downlevel trust (to a Windows NT domain) 2: uplevel Windows 2000/2003 trust (with an AD domain) 3: MIT trust (with MIT Kerberos v5 realm) 4: DCE trust (with DCE realm)
TrustAuthIncoming	Authentication information for the incoming portion of a trust.
TrustAuthOutgoing	Authentication information for the outgoing portion of a trust.
msDS-TrustForestTrustInfo	Only valid for forest trusts. Contains a binary blob that stores information about the trusted forest, including its domain names and trust restrictions, and is used to route authentication requests and object lookups between forests.

* *Source:* http://msdn.microsoft.com/library/default.asp?url=/library/en-us/secmgmt/security/
trusted_domain_information_ex.asp.

condition that a domain controller of domain North.net is available. A secure channel is used to secure the authentication traffic between the trusting and the trusted domain. As other domain controllers become available, they will set up their proper secure channels. The way to fine-tune secure channels is described in Section 3.6.3.

The basic enabler behind forest trust is a new trusteddomain Active Directory object (TDO) type called "forest." TDOs of type forest contain a new attribute called msDS-TrustForestTrustInfo that is used to store information about the domains in the trusted forest. This is basically security and NetBIOS and DNS naming information of the root domain of the

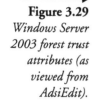

Figure 3.29
*Windows Server
2003 forest trust
attributes (as
viewed from
AdsiEdit).*

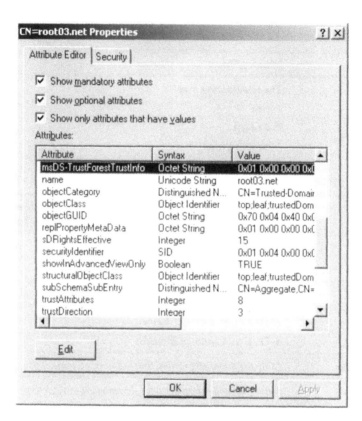

trusted forest and any Top-Level Name (TLN) restrictions (explained in the following text) related to the other domains in the trusted forest. The information stored in the msDS-TrustForestTrustInfo object is used to route authentication requests and object lookups between forests.

Remember that the TDOs and their attributes are replicated to the Global Catalog (GC). As a consequence, any machine in the forest can look up forest trust TDO objects and use their content. To take a look at a TDO's attributes, you can use the ADSIedit tool that comes with the Windows Server 2003 support tools (as illustrated in Figure 3.29 for the root03.net TDO).

3.6 Trusts and Secure Channels

A secure channel is created between two Windows domain controllers each time a trust relationship between the domains hosting the DCs is used. For example, a secure channel will be set up when a cross-domain resource access occurs. Many different secure channels can be created between the

DCs of trusted domains. The DCs that are actually involved in a secure channel setup depend on factors like the authenticating DC (on the trusting side of the trust) and DC name resolution (on the trusted side of the trust). In summary, trusts are defined between domains, secure channels are set up between DCs.

In a Windows environment, secure channels are not only set up between domain controllers, they also provide a secure communication path between the security principals listed below.

- Between a workstation or member server and a domain controller located in the same domain

- Between domain controllers located in the same domain

- And, as mentioned earlier, between domain controllers located in different domains

"Secure" in this context means providing authentication of the requestor and also confidentiality, integrity, and data authentication services for the data sent across the secure channel. The service responsible for the setup of the secure channel is a Windows machine's NetLogon service.

A secure channel enables the secure replication of Active Directory data between domain controllers in the same and different domains. Also, the exchange of the challenge-response messages and pass-through authentication in an NTLM authentication sequence takes place across a secure channel.

You can look at a secure channel as the enabler of secure communication between machines and their trusted authority in the same domain and between the trusted authorities of different domains. The security services offered by a secure channel are based on machine account passwords (within a domain) and on trusteddomain (TDO) account passwords (between domains).

To authenticate the requestor of the secure channel, different accounts are used depending on where the secure channel is set up:

- Between a workstation or member server and a domain controller located in the same domain, the workstation or member server's machine account is used.

- Between domain controllers located in the same domain, the domain controller's machine account is used.

- Between domain controllers located in different domains, the trusteddomain (TDO) account is used.

3.6.1   Controlling Secure Channels Setup

In Windows Server 2003, there are two ways to control secure channel setup: using an entry in the LMHosts file and using the nltest.exe utility (in NT 4.0, there was a third way: using the setprfdc.exe utility). "Control secure channel setup" means: making sure that the secure channel is set up to a particular domain controller (DC). This may be an interesting option for cross-domain authentication traffic when domains are spanning different physical AD sites.

- **Using the LMHosts file**—you can use the LMHosts file to preload DC entries for a particular domain in the NetBIOS name resolution cache. The following LMHosts entry will preload DC1 for domain HP in the client's NetBIOS cache:

  ```
  10.0.0.1     DC1      #PRE  #DOM:HP
  ```

- **Using the nltest.exe utility**—to set the secure channel to a domain "HP" to a DC called "DC1", use the following nltest command:

  ```
  Nltest /sc_reset:HP\DC1
  ```

3.6.2   Validating Secure Channels

In Windows Server 2003 and R2, you can use different methods for validating the secure channels that are set up between the domain controllers of two domains linked using a trust relationship. You can do so from the GUI or from the command line.

To validate a secure channel from the Windows GUI follow these steps:

- Start the Domains and Trusts MMC snap-in.

- Open the properties of the domain whose secure channel you want to validate and go to the trusts tab.

- Open the properties of the trust relationship whose secure channel you want to validate.

- In the properties, click the Validate button.

If the secure channel is all right, the system will pop up a dialog box similar to the one illustrated in Figure 3.30. If the secure channel is not all right, the system will prompt you to reset the trusteddomain object (TDO) password. If you agree, the system will perform a password reset and inform you about the outcome of the reset.

Figure 3.30
*Validating a secure
channel from the
GUI.*

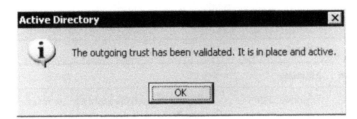

To validate a secure channel from the command line, you can use the nltest.exe, netdom.exe, or dcdiag.exe command-line tool. The exact syntax needed to do this is explained in the section on secure channel– and trust-related management tools.

3.6.3 Fine-Tuning Secure Channel Security Services

Besides authentication of the requestor, a secure channel also provides confidentiality, integrity, and data authentication services for the data sent across the channel. These security services can be tuned using the registry settings shown in Table 3.5 (located in the HKLM\System\Current-ControlSet\Services\Netlogon\Parameters registry folder).

Table 3.5 *Secure Channel Security Registry Settings*

Registry Parameter	GPO Setting	
	Meaning	
Requiresignorseal	Windows 2000	Secure channel: Digitally encrypt or sign secure channel data (always)
	Windows Server 2003	Domain member: Digitally encrypt or sign secure channel data (always)
	If set 1 (Enabled), secure channel traffic must be either signed or sealed. If this cannot be done, the system refuses to set up a secure channel. If set to 0, the use of signing and sealing will depend on the outcome of the negotiation between the two entities.	
Sealsecurechannel	Windows 2000	Secure channel: Digitally encrypt secure channel data (when it is possible)
	Windows Server 2003	Domain member: Digitally encrypt secure channel data (when it is possible)
	Encrypt secure channel traffic, if set to 1 (Enabled)	

Table 3.5   *Secure Channel Security Registry Settings (continued)*

Registry Parameter	GPO Setting	Meaning
Signsecurechannel	Windows 2000	Secure channel: Digitally sign secure channel data (when it is possible)
	Windows Server 2003	Domain member: Digitally sign secure channel data (when it is possible)
	Sign secure channel traffic, if set to 1 (Enabled).	
	If Sealsecurechannel is enabled, this setting is superseded, as encryption is more secure than signing.	
RequireStrongKey	Windows 2000	Secure channel: Require strong (Windows 2000 or later) session key
	Windows Server 2003	Domain member: Require strong (Windows 2000 or later) session key
	If set to 1 (Enabled), enforces the use of a strong 128-bit key for securing the channel. 128-bit key encryption will only be used if both sides of the channel support 128-bit encryption (this setting requires the high-encryption pack on NT4 domain controllers. Windows 2000 and newer DCs support 128-bit encryption by default).	

The secure channel security settings can also be controlled using the Windows 2000 and Windows Server 2003 Group Policy Object settings located in the Computer Configuration\Windows Settings\Security Settings\Local Policies\Security Options GPO container. By default, every Windows 2000, Windows XP, and Windows Server 2003 workstation and server has the Sealsecurechannel and Signsecurechannel parameters enabled.

The secure channel security configuration parameters (explained in Knowledge Base article Q183859) should not be confused with the "SMB signing and sealing" configuration parameters (explained in Knowledge Base article Q161372).

3.6.4   Trust- and Secure Channel–Related Management Tools

Table 3.6 lists some tools you can use to monitor, test, and troubleshoot your Windows trust relationships and their associated secure channels. It also shows where you can find the tools. The last tool in the list—the setprfdc.exe tool—can be used to influence the Windows secure channel setup behavior.

Monitoring Trust Relationships Using Windows Management Instrumentation (WMI)

To monitor trust relationships using WMI, you can use one of the following three WMI classes. All three are part of the Root\Microsoft-ActiveDirectory namespace:

- Microsoft_LocalDomainInfo: This class provides information about the domain on which the instance of the trust monitor is running.

- Microsoft_DomainTrustStatus: Instances of this class provide information about the domains that have a trust relationship with the local domain.

- Microsoft_TrustProvider: The properties of this class parameterize the operation of the trust monitor.

Below is a sample WMI Query Language (WQL) event query you can use to monitor a trust:

```
Select * From __InstanceModificationEvent Within 10
Where TargetInstance ISA 'Microsoft_DomainTrustStatus'
And TargetInstance.TrustIsOk = "False"
```

Table 3.6   *Trust and Secure Channel Troubleshooting Tools*

Tool (Available from)	Function
netdom.exe (Support Tools)	Command prompt tool enabling an administrator to manage trusts and secure channels, check their status, and reset them.
	Sample netdom commands: ■ To query the trusts defined: *netdom query trust* ■ To verify the status of a trust (secure channel) to a particular domain: *netdom trust <trusting_domainname> /domain:<trusted_domainname /verify* ■ To reset a trust (secure channel) to a particular domain: *netdom trust <trusting_domainname> /domain:<trusted_domainname /reset* ■ To create a trust from one domain to another: *netdom trust <trusting_domainname> /domain:<trusted_domainname> /add*

Table 3.6   *Trust and Secure Channel Troubleshooting Tools (continued)*

Tool (Available from)	Function
nltest.exe (Support Tools)	Command prompt tool enabling an administrator to check the status of a trust and to reset it.
	Sample nltest commands:
	■ To list the trust relationships existing from a particular domain controller: *nltest /trusted_domains /server:<dcname>*
	■ To verify the status of a trust: *nltest /sc_query:<domainname>*
	■ To reset a trust (secure channel) from a particular domain controller to a particular domain: *nltest /server:<dcname> /sc_reset:<domainname>*
	■ To force a secure channel password change for a particular machine and a particular domain: *nltest /server:<machinename> /sc_change_pwd:<domainname>*
	■ To reset a trust (secure channel) for a particular domain to a particular domain controller: *nltest /sc_reset:<domainname>\<dcname>*
	■ To identify all domain controllers in a domain *nltest /dclist:<domainname>*
dcdiag (Support Tools)	Command prompt tool to test domain controllers.
	Sample dcdiag command:
	■ To test the secure channels originating from a particular domain controller to a particular domain: *Dcdiag /s:<dcname> /test:outboundsecurechannels /testdomain:<domainname>*
netdiag (Resource Kit)	Command prompt tool that can be used to validate and test secure channels.
	Sample netdiag command:
	■ To test and validate secure channels: *Netdiag /test:Trust*
setprfdc.exe (NT4 SP4)	Enables the specification of a preferred list of domain controllers for secure channel setup.

3.7   Trusts and Firewalls

Many enterprise environments require Windows trust relationships to be set up between domains or forests that are crossing firewalls. Because the true security boundary is the forest in Windows 2000 and later, this practice has become common between different Windows forests. Some organizations, for example, maintain a separate internal and an external Windows forest, separated by a firewall. Table 3.7 gives an overview of common multiforest enterprise scenarios and their trust-related firewall requirements, both for inbound and outbound traffic.

Table 3.7   *Firewall Port Configuration for Multiforest Scenarios*

Scenario	Inbound Ports		Outbound Ports	
Trust setup on both sides from an internal forest (two-way trust)	LDAP	389 UDP and TCP		
	MS DS	445 TCP		
	Kerberos	88 UDP		
Trust validation from an internal forest domain controller to an external forest domain controller (outgoing trust only)	LDAP	389 UDP and TCP		
	MS DS	445 TCP		
	DCE endpoint resolution— Portmapper	135 TCP		
	Netlogon	fixed port		
Using object picker on an external forest to add objects in an internal forest to groups and ACLs			LDAP	389 UDP and TCP
			LSA	fixed port
			Netlogon	fixed port
			Kerberos	88 UDP
			DCE endpoint resolution— Portmapper	135 TCP
Set up a trust on the external forest from the external forest			LDAP	389 UDP and TCP
			MS DS	445 TCP
			Kerberos	88 UDP

Table 3.7   *Firewall Port Configuration for Multiforest Scenarios (continued)*

Scenario	Inbound Ports		Outbound Ports	
Network logon from an internal forest domain controller to an external forest domain controller with Kerberos authentication	MS DS	445 TCP		
	Kerberos	88 UDP		
Network logon from an internal forest domain controller to an external forest domain controller with NTLM authentication			DCE Endpoint resolution—Portmapper	135 TCP
			Netlogon	fixed port

Remote Procedure Calls (RPCs) and Dynamic Service-Port Mappings

An important goal behind the development of the remote procedure call (RPC) protocol was to build a solution for the limited number of service ports available in the TCP and UDP protocols. In both TCP and UDP, ports are defined in a 2-byte field, which limits the number of ports to 65,536.

Instead of using static service-port mappings, RPC provides a dynamic service-port mapping function. In RPC, incoming RPC calls are mapped to a variable port in the 1,024 to 65,535 range. Although RPC uses variable service ports, it needs a unique way to identify services. The RPC protocol resolves this need by using a special service identifier and a dedicated Portmapper service. The unique RPC identifier is called the RPC service number. Service numbers are defined in a 4-byte field, which provides up to 4,294,967,296 possible service numbers. The Portmapper service listens on a static port (TCP or UDP port 135). The service exists primarily to map the unique RPC service number on a variable TCP/UDP port. Thus, RPC can provide both a unique way to identify RPC services and a way to dynamically allocate the scarce number of TCP/UDP service ports.

Figure 3.31 illustrates how this dynamic port allocation works. In Step 1, the RPC server starts and registers with the RPC Portmapper service. The RPC Portmapper maps the RPC service number to a port in the range 1,024 to 65,535. In Step 2, the Portmapper returns the port to the RPC server. The first two steps are known as the RPC registration steps. The RPC client then tries to connect to the RPC server. To find out the exact port on which the server is listening, the RPC client contacts the Portmapper (Step 3). The Portmapper then maps the RPC service number it received from the client to the server's port and returns the number to the client (Step 4). Finally, the RPC client connects to the server (Step 5), and the server replies to the client (Step 6).

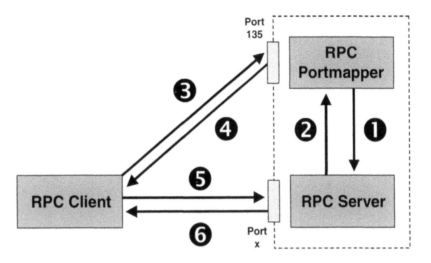

Figure 3.31
RPC operation.

Windows trust setup and maintenance heavily relies on remote procedure calls (RPCs). One of the key problems with RPCs in a firewall environment is their use of dynamic port allocations (see also the sidenote "Remote Procedure Calls (RPCs) and Dynamic Service-Port Mappings"). To limit the amount of firewall ports that must be opened to enable trust-related RPC traffic to pass through the firewall, Windows Server 2003 includes the following registry keys:

- The LSA RPC port, which is used for trust creation and access to the LSA Policy database, can be defined using the TCP/IP Port entry in HKEY_LOCAL_MACHINE\System\CurrentControlSet\Services\ NTDS\Parameters.

- The Netlogon RPC port, which is used for NTLM and secure channel setup, can be defined using the DCTcpipPort entry in HKEY_ LOCAL_MACHINE\System\CurrentControlSet\Services\Netlogon\Parameters.

4

Aspects of Windows Client Security

This chapter focuses on important client security aspects that are not covered in the other chapters of these books. It covers least privilege, Internet Explorer (IE) security, security changes in XP Service Pack 2, spyware protection, and the Trusted Platform Module (TPM). At the end of the chapter, we will also have a look at what client security features are coming up in Internet Explorer 7.0 and Windows Vista.

4.1 Client Security Overview

Figure 4.1 gives an overview of client security aspects. Table 4.1 shows which book chapters address what client-side security aspects. Note that not all client security aspects are covered in these books. For example, we will not discuss virus protection and physical access.

Figure 4.1
Client security aspects.

Table 4.1 *Overview of Client Security Aspects Coverage in This Book Series*

Client Security Aspect	Covered In ...
Browser Security	■ This chapter (XP SP2 browser security changes and security zones) ■ Chapter 7 (browser authentication)
Client Authentication	■ Chapters 5 (NTLM, strong authentication) ■ Chapter 6 (Kerberos) ■ Chapter 7 (browser authentication) ■ Chapter 10 (smart card-based authentication) in *Advanced Microsoft Windows Security Services* (part 2 of this series)
Client Security Policy Management	■ This chapter (XP SP2 security feature configuration) ■ Chapter 11 in *Advanced Microsoft Windows Security Services* (part 2 of this series)
Credential Caching	■ Chapter 5
Least Privilege	■ This chapter
Malicious Mobile Code Protection	■ This chapter (overview) ■ Chapter 1 (Software Restriction Policies [SRPs]) in *Advanced Microsoft Windows Security Services* (part 2 of this series)
Patch Management	■ Chapter 12 in *Advanced Microsoft Windows Security Services* (part 2 of this series)
Personal Firewall	■ This chapter
Physical Access	■ Not covered in these books
Secure Client-Side Storage	■ This chapter (Trusted Platform Module) ■ Chapter 2 (Rights Management Services) and Chapter 10 (Encrypting File System and S/MIME) in *Advanced Microsoft Windows Security Services* (part 2 of this series)
Spyware Protection	■ This chapter
Strong Authentication	■ Chapter 5
Virus Protection	■ This chapter (overview of Microsoft virus protection technologies)

4.2   Least Privilege

Too many users run Windows in the security context of the administrator account or an account that's a member of the local Administrators or Domain Admins group. Logging on to Windows with administrator privileges creates significant security threats. For example, malicious code accidentally downloaded by users while surfing the Web can do a lot of harm, because it can execute in the security context of a highly privileged account. The same problem arises with Windows developers who are writing code that requires administrator privileges to work properly. Highly privileged processes can do much more harm than lower privileged processes. This is certainly the case when these highly privileged processes are compromised, or if they are simply buggy. These are dangerous practices; even more so when you consider that most applications don't really need administrator-level privileges to function properly.

All of the above examples are violations of one of security's most fundamental principles: the principle of least privilege. This principle means that you should give a user or a piece of code only the privileges it needs to do the job—nothing less, and certainly nothing more. For administrators, this basically means that they should have two accounts in an AD domain—one low-privilege account that they use to log on to their client to perform their everyday nonadministrative work (writing e-mails, browsing the Web, etc.), and another one that is only used for performing administrative tasks which do require the use of a highly privileged account.

Least privilege is a principle that is well respected in the UNIX world. UNIX users and administrators consider least privilege a given they have to live and work with. Also, most UNIX operating systems have, from the start, included tools that can make it easier for users and administrators to comply with least privilege.

Microsoft only started taking this principle seriously with the release of Windows 2000 and Windows XP. And even in these OSs it must be said that there's lot of work to be done. The support for a Least Privileged User Account (LUA) is one of the key security themes of the next wave of Windows client and server operating systems: the Windows Vista client OS and the next Windows server edition, code-named "Longhorn." Microsoft also refers to these upcoming LUA features as User Account Protection (UAP). See also the sidenote on "Least Privilege Support in Windows Vista" for more information.

The following sections explain what tools administrators and users can use today in Windows 2000, Windows Server 2003, R2, and Windows XP to honor least privilege, or in other words to run Windows processes and applications with a nonadministrator account.

4.2.1 RunAs

If you're logged on with a lower privileged account on a domain-joined machine, the easiest way to start a secondary logon session with other credentials is by using the runas.exe command line utility. On standalone machines you would use Fast User Switching (FUS), which will be explained later.

To start the Microsoft Management Console (MMC) in the security context of the administrator of the R2Accounts domain for example, you would type the following RunAs command at the command line:

```
RunAs /user:r2accounts\administrator mmc
```

After typing this command, RunAs will prompt you for the administrator's password (as illustrated in Figure 4.2). If the password is correct it will start an instance of the MMC.

Least Privilege Support in Windows Vista

Microsoft plans to release its new client operating system Windows Vista in early 2007. One of the most fundamental security changes in Windows Vista is the addition of new least privilege support features, referred to as User Account Control (UAC). In earlier Vista Beta releases, UAC was called Least Privileged User Account (LUA).

A fundamental change in Vista is that Microsoft redefined what a limited user account can and cannot do on a Vista system. For example, Vista allows a limited user to change the system's time and time zone settings, change display properties, install additional fonts, and change power management options. This change takes away the reason for the existence of the Power Users group, which is not around anymore in Vista. Examples of Vista tasks that still require a privileged account are the installation of software and the repartitioning of disks.

Also in Vista, every account—even the built-in administrator account and other privileged accounts with administrator-level privileges—initially only has limited user privileges. During their logon sessions, users can elevate their privileges to the administrator level whenever needed. Starting with Vista Beta 2—the latest version available at the time of writing—this is standard Vista behavior, because UAC is enabled by default.

Administrator accounts with initially limited user privileges is possible thanks to a change that Microsoft has made in Vista—specifically, the process of creating access tokens for privileged-account users. An access token contains a user's privileges and is attached to a user logon session. When a privileged-account user logs on to Vista, the OS creates a filtered token that contains only the user's limited-account privileges and is the user's default token during his logon session. Vista can temporarily expand the filtered token to a full token when the user needs to perform an administrative task or launch an application that requires privileged user access. The full token contains all the user's privileged-account privileges.

Figure 4.2   *Using RunAs from the command line.*

In the context of honoring least privilege, it is a good practice to create a shortcut to an "administrator" command prompt window on the desktop of your normal user account. To draw your attention continuously to the fact that you're running in a highly privileged environment when you double-click this shortcut, you may want to change the appearance of the administrator command prompt window. For example, you can change the window's appearance by changing the shortcut's target configuration as follows:

```
C:\WINDOWS\system32\runas.exe /u:r2accounts\
administrator "%windir%\System32\cmd.exe /k cd c:\ &&
color fc && title !!!!! Administrator console!!!!!"
```

RunAs can also be started from the Windows Explorer. To do so, right click an executable's or shortcut's icon and select "Run as..." (as illustrated in Figure 4.3). This will bring up the Run As dialog box, which allows you to select alternate credentials. For icons where the RunAs option does not automatically show up in the context menu (this is the case for Control Panel applets), hold down the Shift key while right-clicking the icon.

You can make RunAs the default action for a particular .exe or shortcut by opening its Properties, clicking Advanced, and checking the "Run with different credentials" box (as illustrated in Figure 4.4).

The RunAs utility is rooted on the Secondary Logon Service (SLS) service. SLS allows users to start logon sessions with other credentials within their current logon session. Before Windows 2000, Microsoft provided a special utility to provide this functionality. This utility came with the Windows NT4 Resource kit and was called su.exe. Su required the installation of the su service on NT4 clients (yes, the name is stolen from UNIX's switch-user utility). Today, the SLS service is installed by default on Windows XP, Windows 2000, Windows Server 2003, and R2 systems and starts automatically when the system boots.

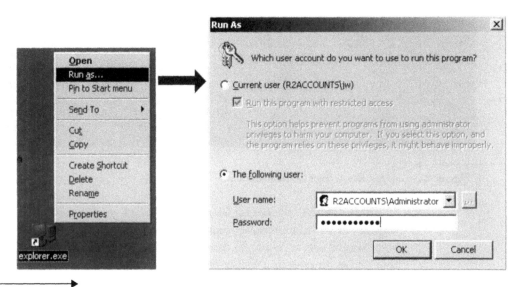

Figure 4.3   *Using RunAs from the Windows Explorer.*

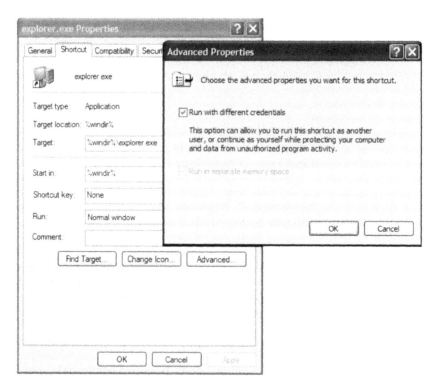

Figure 4.4   *Making RunAs the default action for a shortcut.*

If you try to run the above RunAs command to start a new instance of Windows Explorer, you may have experienced that nothing actually happens—even though you provided the correct credentials. This is because, by default, RunAs will first check whether an instance of Explorer already runs on the current user desktop. If there is one running—which is always the case—it will pass the request to the existing Explorer process instead of starting a new one.[1]

You can resolve this issue by checking the "Launch folder windows in a separate process" option in the View tab of the Explorer's Folder Options (that are accessible from the Explorer Tools menu option). To set this setting directly in the registry, you can also navigate to HKEY_CURRENT_USER\Software\Microsoft\Windows\CurrentVersion\Explorer\Advanced and change the SeparateProcess REG_DWORD value to 1. This is a user setting that must be set for the account in which security context you want to start the new Explorer instance (and NOT in the security context of your current account!). To set this flag in the security context of the other account from your current account's logon session, you can do two things:

- Start Internet Explorer (IE) in the security context of the other account, enter a local address in the address bar to change the menus to those of Windows Explorer, and then choose the Tools / Folder Options / View menu option. In this dialog box check the "Launch folder windows in a separate process" box.

- Run regedit or regedt32 in the security context of the other account and navigate to the HKEY_CURRENT_USER\Software\Microsoft\Windows\CurrentVersion\Explorer\Advanced registry container; change the SeparateProcess DWORD registry value to 1.

You may have noticed in the RunAs dialog box in Figure 4.4 that instead of selecting another user account, in Windows XP, Windows Server 2003, and R2 you can also select the current user and the "Protect my computer and data from unauthorized program activity" option (which is grayed out in Figure 4.2). When you select this option, the application will be started in the security context of the current user account and with a restricted access token. "Restricted access token" in this context means that the new process will be denied several privileges:

- If the current user is a member of the Administrators, Power Users, Domain Admins, or Enterprise Admins groups, these group memberships will be removed from the application's access token.

---

1. You may also encounter this problem when you try to start another instance of Microsoft Office Word using RunAs.

- The application will have read-only access to the registry. The application will have no access to the HKEY_CURRENT_USER\Software\Policies registry container.

- The application cannot access the user's profile directory or any of its subdirectories.

- The application has no system-wide privileges with the exception of the "Bypass traverse checking" user right.

The above list makes this option a very powerful security feature that you can use, for example, to block certain Web sites from writing data to your local system. More information on this interesting RunAs option is also available from http://blogs.msdn.com/aaron_margosis/archive/2004/09/10/227727.aspx.

Table 4.2 gives an overview of the most important RunAs command line switches. A little-known detail is that you can also use RunAs to start the complete Windows shell in an alternate security context. This can be interesting when you want to use drive mappings in your secondary logon session. A drive that is mapped from the command line in a secondary logon session will not be accessible from your Windows Explorer. It will be accessible if you start the complete Windows shell in the alternate security context. To do so, kill the explorer.exe process from the Task Manager. Then,

Table 4.2 *RunAs Switches*

RunAs Switch	Meaning
/env	Instructs RunAs to use the environment variables of the currently logged-on user rather than the ones of the alternate user specified in the RunAs command.
/noprofile	Instructs RunAs to use the default user profile instead of the profile of the alternate user specified in the RunAs command.
/savecred	Instructs RunAs to use logon credentials previously saved by the user (in the credential manager). As a consequence, the user will not be prompted for the password of the alternate user specified in the RunAs command.
/smartcard	Instructs RunAs to use smart card logon for the secondary logon.
/netonly	Instructs RunAs to use the credentials you provide only for remote resource access: for example, when connecting to a remote share or printer. Local resources are accessed in the security context of the current logon session. When using the /netonly switch, RunAs will neither create cached credentials nor a local user profile for the account that is specified in the RunAs command.

using the Task Manager's File\Run menu option, start the secondary logon by typing, for example, "RunAs /u:Joe explorer.exe".

Multiple RunAs commands can be nested into a single command. As an example, let's say that you want to install software on your machine, and the software image is located on a network drive. Access to the network drive will typically require a different set of local or domain credentials. In this example, you can nest RunAs commands as follows:

```
RunAs /u:%COMPUTERNAME%\Administrator "runas /netonly /
u:%USERDOMAIN%\%USERNAME% cmd.exe"
```

The above command line will prompt you for credentials twice: first for your local Administrator credentials, second for your domain credentials. The result will be a command window that runs in the security context of the local Administrator account (this means you also use the local Administrator's profile) but uses your domain credentials to access the remote resources.

4.2.2 Fast User Switching

Fast User Switching (FUS) is a Windows XP Home and Professional Edition feature that allows for multiple and simultaneous interactive logon sessions on a single Windows computer. It allows users to switch easily between different logon sessions without logging off and/or closing their running applications. FUS is only available if all of the following conditions are met:

■ The machine must have at least 64 Mb RAM.

■ The machine must a member of a workgroup. FUS is not available on domain-joined machines.

■ The machine must have the Welcome screen (to log on to Windows) enabled.

■ The machine may not have any GINA (Graphical Identification and Authentication module) replacement (e.g., a custom GINA enabling biometric authentication or another strong authentication method) installed.

■ The user may not have Offline Files support enabled.

The following Microsoft Knowledge Base article also contains interesting FUS details: http://support.microsoft.com/default.aspx?scid=kb;en-us;279765&sd=tech.

Figure 4.5
*Changing the way
users log on or off
in Windows XP.*

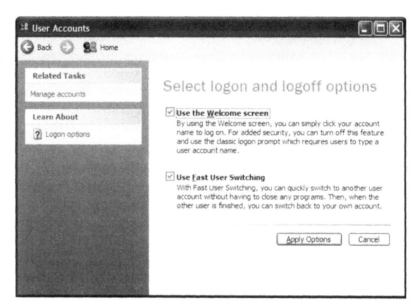

To enable or disable the Welcome screen to log on to Windows, open the Control Panel, double-click the User Accounts applet, then click "Change the way users log on or off." FUS can be enabled/disabled from the same dialog box (as illustrated in Figure 4.5). The advantages and disadvantages of using the Welcome Screen to log on to Windows are explained in Chapter 5, "Introducing Windows Authentication."

When using FUS, switching to another logon session can be done in different ways:

- By clicking Start, Log off, and then Switch User

- By opening the Task Manager (press CTRL+ALT+DELETE), and then clicking Switch User in the Shut Down menu

- By holding down the Windows key, and then pressing the L key

To see which user sessions are active on your computer, open the Task Manager and switch to the Users tab. If you have administrator privileges, you can also use this screen to log users off, to disconnect users, or to send them a message. This is comparable to how you can handle Terminal Server sessions in Windows Server 2003 and R2.

A short description on how you should use FUS to better honor least privilege follows:

- Create an account that has computer administrator privileges. Windows XP gives you the option to assign a password to an administrator account or leave its password blank. We recommend you assign it a password. Even though, starting with Windows XP, Microsoft has locked down what an account with a blank password is allowed to do,[2] we recommend you to assign a password to all accounts, even those that have limited privileges.

- Create a user account that has limited privileges. Again, Windows XP gives you the option to assign the user account a password or leave its password blank. We recommend you to assign it a password.

- Use the user account to do your day-to-day work, such as surfing the Web, using e-mail, using Instant Messaging (IM), and so on. Switch to the security context of the administrator account if you need to install programs or run programs that require administrator privileges. When you're done with a job that requires administrator privileges, log off the administrator account and switch back to your normal user account. Since your normal user account has very reduced privileges, you shouldn't necessarily log it off each time you leave your computer; simply locking the screen is enough.

    For a good overview of programs that require administrator privileges, have a look at Microsoft Knowledge Base article 307091 (available from http://support.microsoft.com/default.aspx?scid=kb;en-us;307091) or at the following URL: http://nonadmin.editme.com/KnownProblems.

Using FUS improperly can create additional security risks. For example, you don't want to leave the administrator logon session up and running on your system all the time. This is one of the reasons why enterprises where security is high on the priority list should disable FUS on their nondomain-joined machines. The least they should do is clearly instruct their users to always log off the administrator session when they are done with the work that requires administrator privileges.

4.2.3 Third-Party Tools

This section explains two third-party tools—dropmyrights and the privilege bar—that both provide good least privilege–related functionality.

---

2.   Starting with Windows XP, accounts that have a blank password are by default not allowed to log on remotely to a system. This feature can be controlled using the "Accounts: Limit local account use of blank passwords to console logon only" Group Policy Object (GPO) option.

DropMyRights

Michael Howard created a program called DropMyRights that can be used to launch a new process in the context of a nonadministrator account with reduced privileges. It takes the user's current security token, removes various privileges and Security Identifiers (SIDs) from the token, and then uses the token to start a new process.

This tool is meant for scenarios in which the user must be logged on with a highly privileged account (for example, as an administrator on a server) and needs to run an application that is potentially dangerous (for example, Internet Explorer). In this scenario, to run IE in the context of a nonadministrator account, you would type the following DropMyRights command at the command line:

```
DropMyRights iexplore.exe
```

DropMyRights supports three different nonadministrator accounts: Normal user (which is the default), Constrained user, and Untrusted user. You specify which account you want to use by appending an N, C, or U to the DropMyRights command.

The privileges DropMyRights gives to the Normal, Constrained, and Untrusted user accounts are described in detail at the following URL: http://msdn.microsoft.com/security/securecode/columns/default.aspx?pull=/library/en-us/dncode/html/secure11152004.asp. The DropMyRights executable can be downloaded from the same URL.

Privilege Bar

The Privilege Bar (which is illustrated in Figure 4.6) is a Windows Explorer and Internet Explorer add-on toolbar that was developed by Aaron Margosis, a well-known Windows least privilege guru. It shows the privilege level of the current Windows or Internet Explorer window. The circle on the Privilege Bar will be red if you are a member of the Administrators group, yellow if you are a Power User, and green otherwise. If you click the circle, the Privilege Bar will pop up a window that displays detailed group and privilege information of your current logon account (this information is basically the content of your access token).

Even though this tool doesn't offer functionality to switch to the context of a LUA account, it is a great awareness tool that underlines the dangers of surfing the Web and browsing local and network resources using highly privileged accounts. You can download the Privilege Bar code from

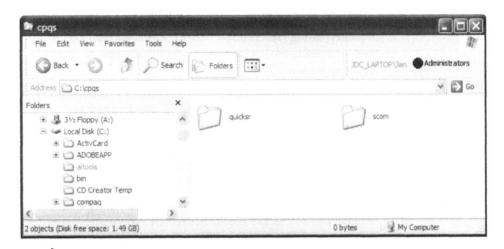

Figure 4.6 *The Privilege Bar in Windows Explorer.*

http://blogs.msdn.com/aaron_margosis/archive/2004/07/24/195350.aspx.
The Privilege Bar installation is manual and is explained at the above URL.

4.2.4 Learn to Be Least

This section outlined some straightforward solutions to let users and administrators better honor the principle of least privilege.

The list of solutions provided in this section is certainly not complete. Other solutions include using virtualization software (like VMWare or Microsoft Virtual PC or Virtual Server) to isolate security contexts, strictly restricting the programs that can run on the user desktop (using, for example, Microsoft Software Restriction Policies[3]), using Remote Desktop (RDP) connections, etc. There are also third-party products that can help better honoring least privilege on Windows XP. Good examples are the Winternals Protection Manager (more info at www.winternals.com/Products/ProtectionManager/Default.aspx) and the AppSense Desktop Security software (more info at www.appsense.com/content/products/desktop_security/desktop/desktop_security_suite.asp).

As with any security problem, technological solutions aren't enough. Certainly, in the context of least privilege, it is paramount to address user awareness and training.

---

3. These are also known as SAFER and are explained in more detail in Chapter 1 of the second part of this book series.

We also recommend you to have a look at the following Microsoft document explaining how you can better honor least privilege in Windows XP: www.microsoft.com/technet/prodtechnol/winxppro/maintain/ luawinxp.mspx.

4.3   Windows XP Service Pack 2 Security Enhancements

Since its 2001 release, Windows XP—Microsoft's predominant client operating system— has been a favorite hacker target. Windows XP Service Pack 1 (SP1) contained critical software and security patches but didn't bring fundamental changes to the client security experience. Since SP1, Microsoft has optimized its security patching process through better patch distribution and installation automation. Optimizing the patching process is nice, but it doesn't improve your security unless you apply the patches. XP Service Pack 2 adds important security features for clients who have a lax attitude towards security and security patching. It provides intelligent and automated security configuration, locks down the platform by default, and thus better protects even unpatched systems against hacker attacks.

Windows XP Service Pack 2 includes critical security enhancements for both users and developers. Most important is the fact that XP SP2 offers more security resilience: it increases the level of security and protection even on systems that don't have the latest security patches installed. It is Microsoft's first step in offering more proactive (instead of reactive) security protection for their platforms and applications.

This section discusses SP2's key security changes in the areas of the Windows firewall, networking security, and security management. The security changes SP2 included for Internet Explorer (IE) are explained in the IE section of this chapter. Most security changes introduced in Windows XP SP2 are also available in Windows Server 2003 Service Pack 1, as explained in the side note "Windows XP SP2 Security Changes Available in Windows Server 2003 SP1."

4.3.1   Windows Firewall

In Windows XP, Microsoft introduced a built-in personal firewall: the Internet Connection Firewall (ICF). In SP2, Microsoft renamed the ICF to Windows Firewall (WF), extended its configuration features and enabled it by default for every network connection (the ICF was disabled by default). The latter change applies to both IPv4- and IPv6-based connections and to

---

Windows XP SP2 Security Changes Available in Windows Server 2003 SP1

Windows Server 2003 SP1 was released after the Windows XP SP2 release and incorporates most of the Windows XP SP2 security changes.

Windows Server 2003 SP1 includes the following key Windows XP SP2 security features (this list does not list ALL XP SP2 security features that are also included in Windows Server 2003 SP1):

- Internet Explorer (IE) security enhancements: see section 4.4.1 for more info

- Outlook Express (OE) security enhancements: see section 4.3.3 for more info

- Data Execution Prevention (DEP): see section 4.3.3 for more info

- RPC security enhancements: see section 4.3.3 for more info

- Windows Firewall (WF): see section 4.3.1 for more info

Windows Server 2003 SP1 does not include the following Windows XP SP2 security feature:

- Security Center: see section 4.3.2 for more info

As opposed to the Windows XP SP2 WF, the Windows Server 2003 SP1 WF is not enabled by default. It is only enabled when you upgrade a Windows Server 2003 system where Internet Connection Sharing (ICS) or the Internet Connection Firewall (ICF) was previously enabled. WF is also enabled on brand new installations that use a bundled Windows Server 2003/Service Pack 1 installation package (this is also referred to as a slip-streamed installation package).

---

connections that are available at installation time and added after the installation. WF is enabled by default even if other personal firewall software is installed and enabled on your XP system.

WF is a stateful firewall. This means that it automatically matches inbound traffic with outgoing requests. WF only restricts unsolicited inbound traffic—"unsolicited" meaning "traffic that was not requested by a local application." WF does not filter outbound network traffic. Outbound traffic filtering can, however, be provided by IPsec (that's available on all Windows clients, starting with Windows 2000). In Windows Vista—the next Windows client OS version—the management of the WF and IPsec settings will be integrated into a single MMC snap-in, and WF will also support outbound filtering.

The WF has a special boot-time policy that is enabled and applied before XP's networking stack is up and running. The ICF had a gap here that allowed attacks to take place before ICF was operational. The WF boot-time policy cannot be configured and does not interfere with basic DHCP and DNS system boot-up communication traffic.

Changes that will immediately catch your eye are the new WF configuration options. The ICF could only be configured from the Advanced tab in the properties of every network connection. That is still possible for the WF; in addition, Microsoft added a Control Panel applet for configuring WF, intelligent WF configuration guidance, command line configuration support (using the netsh command), unattended setup, and Group Policy Object (GPO)-based configuration. SP2 also supports a global WF firewall policy allowing you to configure global firewall rules that span the different network interface WF policies. The global policy is in addition to the individual network interface firewall policies already supported by the ICF. If you want to change the WF configuration using any of the tools listed above, you must have administrative rights.

Figure 4.7 shows the WF global configuration interface as it is available from the new WF Control Panel applet. Note that in Windows XP SP2, the WF is enabled by default. From the Advanced tab of this dialog box, you can access the WF configurations of the different network interfaces. An interesting new option in the Advanced tab is the Restore Defaults pushbutton: it allows you to easily restore the WF configuration settings to the default configuration.

Figure 4.7
Windows Firewall global configuration interface.

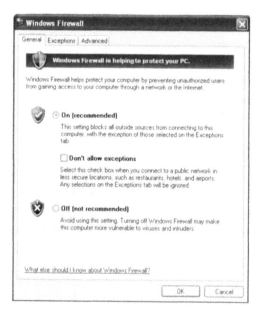

When WF detects the startup of a new application that must communicate with other network entities, it will pop-up a dialog box that asks the user whether that particular application should be allowed to receive network requests. This is illustrated in Figure 4.8 for Windows Messenger and the Microsoft Management Console. If the user chooses to allow the application to connect with the network, WF will add an exception entry to the global WF configuration. When an exception is added, WF will automatically open the necessary inbound network ports for the external network to communicate properly with the application. Exceptions for a particular application or network port can also be added manually. WF exception configuration is accessible from the Exceptions tab in the WF Control Panel applet. WF comes with several preconfigured exceptions such as file and print sharing, remote assistance, and so on.

In Windows XP SP2, the netsh command-line configuration utility has been extended to include WF configuration switches. Using netsh, you can display, add, delete, dump, and reset (to the defaults) WF configuration options. In domain environments, the local configuration of WF settings using netsh may be overridden by the WF settings that are enforced through the Group Policy Objects (GPOs)—the GPO WF configuration is explained below.

Below are some netsh WF configuration examples. To enable the WF and to disable the definition and application of global policy exceptions, type the following command at the command line:

```
Netsh firewall set opmode mode = ENABLE exceptions =
DISABLE
```

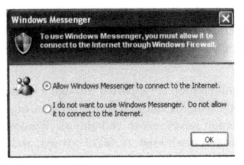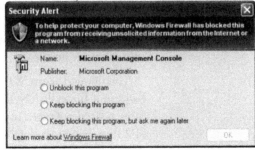

Figure 4.8 *Windows Firewall dialog box for Windows Messenger and the Microsoft Management Console.*

To enable WF to let TCP traffic pass on port 80 (HTTP), type:

`Netsh firewall set portopening TCP 80`

To get a complete overview of the netsh WF-related switches type:

`Netsh firewall ?`

The WF can also be configured as part of a Windows XP unattended setup, and its configuration can be forced through a set of new GPO settings. Earlier Windows versions had a single ICF-related GPO entry: "Prohibit Use of Internet Connection Firewall on your DNS domain." In SP2, ALL global WF configuration parameters can be set using GPO. The WF settings are contained in the following GPO container: Computer Configuration\Administrative Templates\Network\Network Connections\Windows Firewall. To update your existing GPOs with the new WF administrative template settings, it's sufficient to log on to a Windows XP SP2 machine using an account that's a member of the Domain Administrators, Enterprise Administrators, or Group Policy Creator Owners security group and open each of the GPOs.

WF supports two different configuration profiles for machines that belong to a Windows domain. Microsoft refers to this feature as multiple profile support. Both profiles can be configured from the WF-related GPO settings. This feature enables XP machines that are joined to a domain to have a different WF configuration depending on whether they are connected to a Windows domain or connected to a network in standalone mode. This can be quite useful for companies that need to ensure remote accessibility to their notebook clients when they are in the office (for example, by opening up the firewall to allow inbound connections from certain sources), but want to lock down the same clients when they are traveling and are connecting to public networks. This multiple profile feature does not apply to machines that are part of a workgroup; they have a single WF configuration profile.

Unattended setup WF configuration is supported through a special initialization file called Netfw.inf. The file must be stored on your organization's central software installation server, which contains all Windows XP SP2 files. For more details on WF netsh support, GPO settings, and unattended setup, refer to the following Microsoft white paper: "Deploying Windows Firewall Settings for Microsoft Windows XP with Service Pack 2" (available from www.microsoft.com/technet/prodtechnol/winxppro/deploy/depfwset/wfsp2sum.mspx).

Two final WF features worth mentioning are the enhanced Remote Procedure Call (RPC) support and authenticated IPsec bypass feature. Thanks to the authenticated IPsec bypass feature, WF can allow inbound traffic through the firewall for systems that successfully authenticated with IPSec.

One of the key problems with RPC is its use of variable ports, which basically punches holes in your firewall if you allow RPC to pass through it. WF's enhanced RPC support includes the following important changes:

- WF can be configured to automatically open and close inbound RPC ports for local services that must communicate with external applications over RPC. This works only if the service runs in the security context of the Local System, Network Service, or Local Service account. The main goal behind this feature is to protect the system from applications that run in a user security context and that require inbound RPC connectivity. An application that runs in the security context of another account can still be allowed to receive inbound RPC connections by configuring a WF exception for it.

- WF can be easily configured to make RPC work for remote administration. RPC is often required for remote administration using scripts, WMI, or one of the built-in MMC-based administration tools. You can enable remote administration through WF by enabling the following GPO setting: Computer Configuration\Administrative Templates\Network\Network Connections\Windows Firewall\Allow Remote Administration Exception. When this setting is enabled, WF will automatically define exceptions for the RPC Endpoint Mapper (TCP 135), SMB over TCP (TCP 445), and ICMP echo requests.

4.3.2 Easier Security Management

The main enabler of SP2's easier security management is the new Security Center component. Security Center is a new Control Panel applet that enables easy configuration of a Windows firewall, virus protection, and automatic updates settings. It is also an engine that continuously checks the configuration status of the above security services and informs the user about his or her status in an intelligent way. The service's status is checked against the configuration settings specified in the Security Center dialogs. Security Center checks whether the Windows Firewall and automatic updates are enabled and whether virus protection is configured as specified by participating anti-virus software vendors. The latter typically includes checks that verify whether real-time virus scanning is enabled and whether

Figure 4.9
*Security Center
notification.*

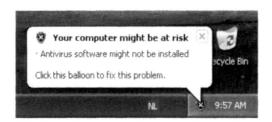

the virus protection signature files are up to date. For an overview of support by anti-virus software vendors, have a look at the following URL: www.microsoft.com/security/partners/antivirus.asp.

If the Security Center finds a setting that is not compliant with the setting specified in its configuration, it informs the user by displaying a red icon in the user's taskbar (as illustrated in Figure 4.9 for the virus protection settings) and by providing an alert message at logon. Figure 4.10 shows the Security Center configuration interface. Security Center is enabled by default on computers that are not joined to a domain. For domain-joined machines, administrators can enable this through the "Turn on Security Center (computers in Windows domain only)" GPO setting, located in the Administrative Templates\System\Security Center GPO container.

An important new feature that affects the overall Windows patch management experience is the inclusion of the latest Windows Installer technol-

Figure 4.10
*Security Center
configuration
interface.*

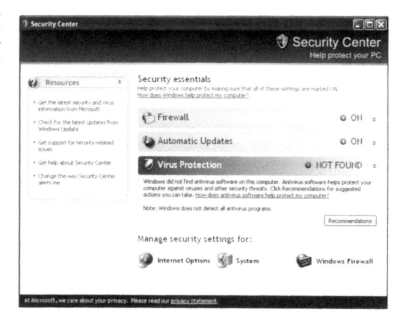

ogy (version 3.0) in Windows XP SP2. The new installer provides more efficient and faster patch installation—especially when combined with Windows Update Services (WUS) (previously called Software Update Services) on the back end. Patch authors using Windows Installer 3.0 can take advantage of Microsoft's delta compression technology, which significantly reduces the patch payload. It also allows authors to add patch installation sequencing instructions to packages, installing multiple patches in a single run.

SP2 also comes with built-in support for the Microsoft Update service. Microsoft Update (MU) is Microsoft's follow-up service to Windows Update (WU). In the long run, MU will enable centralized software updating for all Microsoft software components and applications, WU-only supported components, and applications that were installed together with the base Windows OS. Among the first applications that Microsoft is planning to MU-enable are MS SQL Server, Exchange, and Office.

4.3.3 Other Important Security Changes

XP SP2 includes a new Attachment Manager (AM) and API for handling attachments that are downloaded in Internet Explorer, Windows Messenger, and Outlook Express. The AM blocks or allows attachments based on their file type and security zone classification. AM uses a consistent interface for warning and informing users about the dangers of downloading, executing, or saving attachments and for asking users whether they want to block or allow the attachment. AM also saves attachments' security zone classifications when they are stored on the local system (in the zone.identifier NTFS alternate data stream (ADS)). For more information on the SP2 Attachment Manager, consult the following Microsoft knowledge base article: http://support.microsoft.com/kb/883260.

XP SP2 includes important security enhancements for Outlook Express (OE), Microsoft's built-in Internet mail client. OE supports the advanced attachment handling that was mentioned above: OE will block the transfer of potentially unsafe files (such as *.zip files) and will display a dialog box similar to the one used by IE when it attempts to download and open a mail attachment that has been generated by an unknown publisher.

You can also restrict OE from downloading external HTML links. External HTML links are links that are classified in the Internet or Restricted Sites IE security zones. The latter are often exploited by Web bugs. Both options can be set from the OE Security Options. Finally, OE supports plain text mode, a feature that forces all mail messages to be read in plain text rather than HTML. This stops malicious code from being delivered through HTML headers. This option can be set from the OE Read Options.

SP2 includes a number of important changes in the Remote Procedure Call (RPC) service that significantly reduce the attack surface of Windows XP. The new RestrictRemoteClients registry key will, by default, block remote anonymous access to RPC interfaces on the system. If the Enable-AuthEpResolution key is set, the RPC client will be forced to use NTLM for RPC endpoint mapper (port 135/TCP) authentication. Both registry keys offer an efficient defense against worms that initiate buffer overruns through anonymous RPC connections. The keys are both located in the HKEY_LOCAL_MACHINE\Software\Policies\Microsoft\Windows NT\ RPC registry container.

Beginning with XP SP2, both the XP 32- and 64-bit versions can utilize the no-execute page-protection (NX) processor feature as defined by processor manufacturers AMD and Intel. In XP SP2 documentation, this feature is also referred to as Data Execution Protection (DEP). DEP is a memory protection feature that can protect against buffer overflow attacks. At the time of writing, DEP was only supported on the AMD Opteron processor for 32-bit and 64-bit Windows. In the future, DEP will also be supported on the Intel Xeon processors for 32-bit and 64-bit Windows. DEP marks all memory locations as nonexecutable unless it explicitly contains executable code. By doing so, it blocks attacks that try to insert and execute code from nonexecutable memory locations. DEP relies on the processor hardware to mark memory locations with a special attribute that indicates that code should not be executed from that particular location. DEP can be configured from the Performance Options in the Advanced tab of a Windows XP SP2 system's properties.

4.4 Browser Security

A computer's browser has become users' most important window to the world beyond their computer. Often it is also a gate through which malicious code can enter a computer and confidential information can leave a computer. Today, browser security is not an option, it is a must.

In this section we will cover two IE-security related topics: the new Internet Explorer (IE) security features that were introduced in Windows XP Service Pack 2, and IE Security Zones—a fundamental IE security feature.

4.4.1 New Internet Explorer Security Functionality in XP Service Pack 2

The IE version coming with Windows XP SP2 includes important security enhancements. The headlines are the inclusion of an add-on manager and a pop-up blocking mechanism, better untrusted publisher mitigation, and IE Local Machine security zone lockdown.

Intelligent Add-on Management

Browser add-ons include ActiveX controls, browser helper objects, and browser and toolbar extensions that users install intentionally or unintentionally. Users can install them while running an executable, but add-ons can also be installed unnoticed while viewing Web pages. The latter can create security risks: a user might, for example, accidentally install an add-on that records all user credentials and sends them to a server on the Internet. The SP2 IE add-on manager allows users to view, enable, disable and update ALL IE add-ons. Updating means that the add-on manager allows a user to connect to the add-on publisher's Web site and download the latest version to his/her browser. The add-on manager also comes with add-on crash detection. When IE crashes occur due to an add-on, IE will prompt the user to disable the add-on.

The new add-on manager is illustrated in Figure 4.11. Users can access the add-on manager from:

- The Tools\Manage Add-ons… IE menu item

- The Tools\Internet Options IE menu item (click "Manage Add-ons" in the Programs tab)

- From the Control Panel Internet Options applet (click "Manage Add-ons" in the Programs tab).

In the add-on manager, the Show drop-down box allows the browser user to control what add-ons are displayed: only the add-ons currently loaded in IE ("Add-ons currently loaded in Internet Explorer" option) or all add-ons ("Add-ons that have been used by Internet Explorer" option). To enable/disable an add-on, select it, and then click the enable/disable radiobutton. To update an ActiveX add-on, click the Update ActiveX button.

Administrators can centrally control the add-on manager's behavior and users' access to its configuration features through a set of registry settings. For example, to disable users' capability to manage add-ons, administrators must

Figure 4.11
*Internet Explorer
add-on manager.*

set the following registry key to value 0: HKEY_LOCAL_MACHINE or HKEY_CURRENT_USER\Software\Policies\Microsoft\Internet Explorer\ Restrictions\NoExtensionManagement (REG_DWORD). Administrators can also create explicit denied and allowed add-on lists using the AllowList and DenyList registry keys. When using the AllowList key, IE denies all add-ons except for the ones specified in the AllowList key. When using the DenyList key, IE allows all add-ons except for the ones specified in the DenyList key. In the AllowList and DenyList keys, add-ons are uniquely identified using their class identifier (CLSID). All the add-on manager-related registry settings are listed in Table 4.3.

You can use Group Policy Object (GPO) settings to centrally control the Table 4.4 registry settings. The GPO settings are in the User Configuration\Administrative Templates\Windows Components\Internet Explorer GPO container. To update your existing GPOs in a Windows 2000 or later AD environment with the new inetres.adm administrative template settings, log on to an XP SP2 machine by using an account that's a member of

Table 4.3 *Internet Explorer Add-on Management Registry Hacks*

Setting Name	Registry Location*	Values
Disable add-on crash detection	HKLM or HKCU\Software\Policies\Microsoft\Internet Explorer\Restrictions\NoCrashDetection (REG_DWORD)	0=Off 1=On
Disable add-on extension management	HKLM or HKCU\Software\Policies\Microsoft\Internet Explorer\Restrictions\NoExtensionManagement (REG_DWORD)	0=Off 1=On
Add-on management mode	HKLM or HKCU\Software\Microsoft\Windows\CurrentVersion\Policies\Ext\ManagementMode (REG_DWORD)	0=Normal 1=AllowList 2=DenyList
Add-on allow list	HKLM or HKCU\Software\Microsoft\Windows\CurrentVersion\Policies\Ext\AllowList (REG_SZ)	GUID subkeys (CLSIDs)
Add-on deny list	HKLM or HKCU\Software\Microsoft\Windows\CurrentVersion\Policies\Ext\DenyList (REG_SZ)	GUID subkeys (CLSIDs)

* The registry keys mentioned in this table can be applied both to HKEY_CURRENT_USER for user-specific settings and HKEY_LOCAL_MACHINE for global machine settings (applying to all machine users).

the Domain Administrators, Enterprise Administrators, or Group Policy Creator Owners security group, then open each of the existing GPOs in the Group Policy Editor (GPE). From the GPE, right-click the administrative templates container and select add/remove templates: in the add/remove templates dialog box select the new XP SP2 inetres.adm file to load it into your existing GPOs.

In SP2, Microsoft also enhanced the IE add-on installation and download prompt dialog boxes. They are more informative in the sense that they inform the user about the risks of installing IE add-ons. Figure 4.12 gives some examples: the dialog box in the left portion of Figure 4.12 pops up when a user downloads a file from the Web; the dialog box in the right portion of Figure 4.12 pops up when the user accesses a Web site that tries to install add-ons (like ActiveX controls) from untrusted publishers.

Untrusted publishers are Web content providers whose content contains an invalid digital signature. By default, IE will refuse to run untrusted content. This behavior is controlled by the following registry key: HKEY_LOCAL_MACHINE or HKEY_CURRENT_USER\Software\Microsoft\Internet Explorer\Download\RunInvalidSignatures (default value is 0, which means: don't run untrusted content).

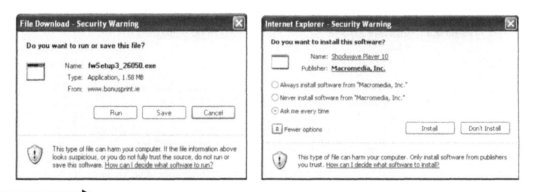

Figure 4.12   *Enhanced IE add-on download and installation prompt dialog boxes.*

Pop-Up Blocking

Browser pop-ups—windows that automatically appear when you're browsing the Web and that typically advertise something—are a major annoyance and potential risk for today's Internet users. Before XP SP2, IE users had to install additional software to provide IE add-on blocking. An example of such software is the Google toolbar (which can be downloaded for free from http://toolbar.google.com).

XP SP2 comes with built-in IE pop-up blocking support. Pop-up blocking can be enabled in different ways. You can use the prompt that appears when the first pop-up window is about to be displayed. You can enable and configure it from the IE Tools\Pop-up Blocker menu item. You can also enable and configure it from the Tools\Internet Options IE menu item or Control Panel applet by going to the Privacy tab (as illustrated in Figure 4.13) and clicking the Settings… pushbutton in the Pop-up blocker section.

The pop-up blocker configuration options allow you to exclude Web sites from pop-up blocking (in the example in Figure 4.13: www.compaq.com, www.hp.com, and so on) and configure IE pop-up blocking behavior. The latter includes playing a sound and/or displaying the pop-up information bar when a pop-up is blocked. The configuration options also allow you to set a pop-up blocking filter level. There are three filter levels: High (block all pop-ups), Medium (block most automatic pop-ups) and Low (allow pop-ups from secure sites). If you want to see a blocked pop-up when the filter level is set to High, hold down the CTRL key while opening the pop-up window. To exclude a Web site from pop-up blocking, type its URL in the address field, then click the Add pushbutton. This action will add the Web site's URL to the IE pop-up allow list. The pop-up allow list is

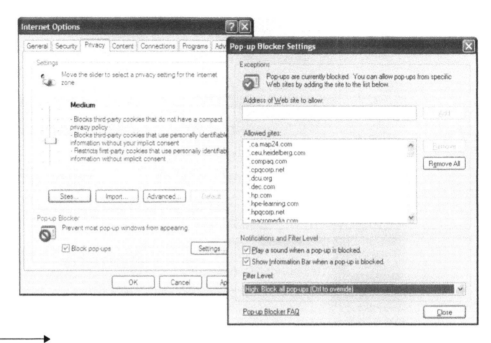

Figure 4.13 *IE pop-up blocking configuration.*

stored in the following registry key: HKEY_CURRENT_USER\Software\ Microsoft\Internet Explorer\New Windows\Allow.

Although the new inetres.adm template file doesn't include the Allow registry subkey, you can use the template to centrally enable and disable pop-up management on your users' desktops. To do so, use the "Disable pop-up management and its UI" setting in the User Configuration\Administrative Templates\Windows Components\Internet Explorer container. This setting affects the HKEY_CURRENT_USER\Software\Policies\ Microsoft\Internet Explorer\Restrictions\NoPopupManagement registry subkey.

When IE detects a pop-up, it will automatically display the pop-up information bar at the top of the browser and a pop-up notification icon in the IE status bar at the bottom of the browser (which is illustrated in Figure 4.14). If you click the notification icon, you have the following options: show the blocked pop-up window, allow pop-up windows from this site (which adds the site's URL to the pop-up allow list), block pop-up windows, or open the pop-up management window (pop-up window options).

By default, IE does not block pop-ups from Web sites included in the Trusted Sites and Local Intranet IE security zones. The sites classified in

Figure 4.14   *IE pop-up blocking behavior.*

these security zones can be controlled from the Security tab in the IE Internet Options dialog box (this dialog box is available from the Tools menu). Also, if you want you can turn on pop-up blocking for these zones from the same IE configuration dialog box: on the Security tab, select the appropriate security zone, then click Custom Level…, and enable "Use Pop-up blocker" in the Miscellaneous section.

Hidden IE Security Changes

Under the hood, XP SP2's IE includes more interesting security features. Most important here are more secure object caching, Window restrictions, zone elevation blocking, and Local Machine security zone lockdown.

IE provides more secure object caching in SP2 because it disallows Web pages to access Web content cached by Web pages in other domains (in this context, a domain is a Fully Qualified Domain Name (FQDN)). This feature can, for example, block Web pages containing scripts that monitor events such as browser users entering credit card numbers on Web pages that are part of other domains. This feature is enabled by default for IE processes and can be controlled through the following registry key:

HKEY_LOCAL_MACHINE\Software \Microsoft \Internet Explorer\Main \FeatureControl \FEATURE_OBJECT_CACHING\Iexplore.exe (value 1 means: feature enabled). You can centrally control this feature by using the GPO settings in the User Configuration\Administrative Templates\Windows Components\Internet Explorer\Security Features\Object Caching Protection container.

IE Windows restrictions will restrict a script's capabilities to programmatically open new windows, resize existing windows, or turn off a window's title or status bar. This feature effectively blocks windows that try to spoof desktop objects or overlay the IE address bar. It also ensures that IE users can always see a Web page's security zone. This feature is enabled by default for IE processes and can be controlled through the following registry key: HKEY_LOCAL_MACHINE\Software \Microsoft \Internet Explorer\Main \FeatureControl \FEATURE_WINDOWS_RESTRICTIONS\Iexplore.exe (value 1 means: feature enabled). You can centrally control this feature by using the GPO settings in the User Configuration\Administrative Templates\Windows Components\Internet Explorer\Security Features\Scripted Window Security Restrictions.

Zone elevation blocking means IE will prevent Web pages from calling pages that are part of a less-restrictive IE security zone. Malicious Web pages may attempt to do so in order to elevate their privileges on the local machine. In this context, the IE security zones are ranked as follows: (from the highest security context to the lowest): Restricted Sites zone, Internet zone, Local Intranet zone, Trusted Sites zone, and Local Machine zone. Remember that the security zone of a Web page is determined by its location. For example, Internet pages are automatically assigned to the Internet security zone.

In previous IE versions, the Local Machine security zone allowed Web content to run with relatively few restrictions. Web content is automatically assigned to the Local Machine security zone if it is stored on the local file system; this includes Web content that is cached locally by IE. Hackers exploited this feature to elevate privileges and compromise computers. In SP2, this becomes more difficult because the Local Machine security zone was locked down, which means that the Web content assigned to it has fewer privileges. In SP2, the Local Machine security zone is even more restrictive than the Internet security zone. Every time Web content attempts a restricted Local Machine security zone action, the following text will appear in the IE information bar: "This page has been restricted from running active content that might be able to access your computer. If you trust this page, click here to allow it to access your computer." This feature is enabled by default for IE processes and can be controlled through the following registry key: HKEY_LOCAL_MACHINE\Software \Microsoft \ Internet Explorer\Main \FeatureControl \FEATURE_LOCALMACHINE_ LOCKDOWN\Iexplore.exe (value 1 means: feature enabled). You can centrally control this feature by using the settings in the User Configuration\ Administrative Templates\Windows Components\Internet Explorer\Security Features\Local Machine Zone Lockdown Security container.

4.4.2   **Internet Explorer Security Zones**

Internet Explorer (IE) security zones are a powerful and often neglected security feature of Microsoft's Internet browser. Microsoft first introduced them in IE version 4.01. This section provides an overview of IE security zones and focuses on advanced IE security zone administration topics: it explains how to centrally control security zone settings using Group Policy Objects (GPOs) and the Internet Explorer Administration Kit (IEAK), how to customize the security settings of the Local Computer IE security zone, and so on.

IE security zones are a fairly complex security feature of Microsoft's Web browser. Proper configuration requires a detailed knowledge of Web security risks and an organization's network architecture. That is why it is strongly recommended to centrally configure and enforce IE security zone configuration settings using one of the tools outlined in this section.

Defining Security Zones

IE security zones offer a convenient way for grouping Web sites and giving them specific IE security settings. IE users and administrators can use them to assign different trust levels to Web sites. When you visit a Web site, IE will automatically categorize it in one of the predefined security zones (explained below) and apply and enforce the corresponding security settings. You can find out the result of the IE Web site security zone classification process by checking the right corner of the IE status bar (as illustrated in Figure 4.15).

IE includes the following predefined security zones (as illustrated in Figure 4.16):

- **Local Intranet zone.** This zone includes all Web sites that are located on an organization's internal network and/or Web sites that should only be accessible to internal users.

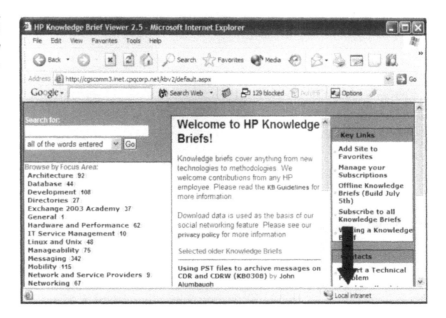

Figure 4.15
*IE Web site security
zone indication.*

- **Trusted Sites zone.** This zone includes Web sites that are located on the Internet and that the IE user or computer administrator consider trustworthy.

- **Restricted Sites zone.** This zone includes Web sites that are located on the Internet and that the IE user or computer administrator do not consider trustworthy.

- **Internet zone.** This zone includes all other Web sites on the Internet that are not part of the Trusted Sites or the Restricted Sites zones.

- **Local Computer zone.** This zone includes all data that are stored on the local computer and that can be accessed from IE. This zone does not include locally cached temporary Internet files.

Web site security zone classification is done by the urlmon.dll IE dynamic link library (DLL). Security zone configuration information is stored in the following user and machine portions of the system registry: HKEY_CURRENT_USER\Software\Microsoft\Windows\CurrentVersion\Internet Settings\Zones and HKEY_LOCAL_MACHINE\Software\Microsoft\Windows\CurrentVersion\Internet Settings\Zones.

Users can configure security zones and their properties from the Security tab in the Internet Options dialog box, which can be accessed from the IE Tools/Internet Options menu item from the Control Panel/Internet Options applet (illustrated in Figure 4.17) or by double-clicking the security

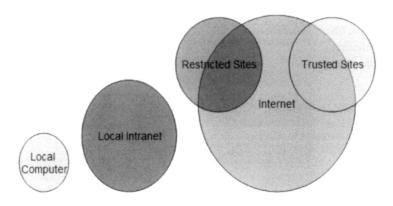

Figure 4.16   *IE security zones.*

zone label in the IE status bar (illustrated in Figure 4.15). By default, users cannot modify the properties of the Local Computer zone.

To ease IE security zone administration, Microsoft has predefined a set of security levels. These levels can be used to raise or lower all security zone settings for a particular zone in a single administrative action. The predefined levels are high, medium, medium-low, and low. To assign a security level to a security zone, raise or lower the "Security Level for This Zone"

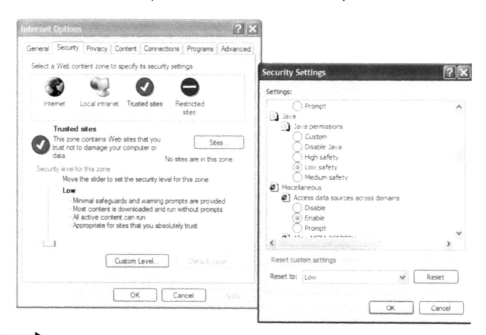

Figure 4.17   *IE Internet Options security configuration interface.*

Table 4.4 *Default IE Security Zone Security Levels*

Security Zone	Default Security Level
Internet zone	Medium
Local Intranet zone	Medium-low
Restricted Sites zone	High
Trusted Sites zone	Low
Local Computer zone	Medium

button in the Security tab of the Internet Options dialog box. Table 4.4 below shows the default security levels for the built-in IE Security Zones.

You can also define custom security settings for a security zone. To define custom security settings for a security zone and to override the predefined settings linked to the security levels mentioned above, click the "Custom Level..." pushbutton. This action will bring up the Security Settings dialog box, which is illustrated on the right side of Figure 4.17. Table 4.5 gives an overview of the browser security settings that can be controlled using security zones and their default values for the different security levels. For more information on the different security settings, see Chapter 4 of the IE Resource Kit, which is available online at www.microsoft.com/resources/documentation/ie/6/all/reskit/en-us/part2/c04ie6rk.mspx.

Administrators can centrally configure IE security zone settings using the Internet Explorer Administration Kit (IEAK) and/or Group Policy

Table 4.5 *Security Zone Security Option Default Values for Different Security Levels*

	Low	Medium-Low	Medium	High
ActiveX Controls				
Download signed ActiveX controls	Enable	Prompt	Prompt	Disable
Download unsigned ActiveX controls	Prompt	Disable	Disable	Disable
Initialize and script ActiveX controls not marked as safe	Prompt	Disable	Disable	Disable
Run ActiveX controls and plug-ins	Enable	Enable	Enable	Disable
Script ActiveX controls marked safe for scripting	Enable	Enable	Enable	Disable

Table 4.5   *Security Zone Security Option Default Values for Different Security Levels (continued)*

	Low	Medium-Low	Medium	High
ActiveX Controls				
Downloads				
File download	Enable	Enable	Enable	Disable
Font download	Enable	Enable	Enable	Prompt
Miscellaneous				
Access data sources across domains	Enable	Prompt	Disable	Disable
Allow META REFRESH	Enable	Enable	Enable	Disable
Display mixed content	Prompt	Prompt	Prompt	Prompt
Don't prompt for client certificate selection when no certificates exist or only one certificate exists	Enable	Enable	Disable	Disable
Drag and drop or copy and paste files	Enable	Enable	Enable	Prompt
Installation of desktop items	Enable	Prompt	Prompt	Disable
Launching programs and files in an IFRAME	Enable	Prompt	Prompt	Disable
Navigate subframes across different domains	Enable	Enable	Enable	Disable
Software channel permissions	Low safety	Medium safety	Medium safety	High safety
Submit nonencrypted form data	Enable	Enable	Prompt	Prompt
Userdata persistence	Enable	Enable	Enable	Disable
Scripting				
Active Scripting	Enable	Enable	Enable	Disable
Allow paste operations via script	Enable	Enable	Enable	Disable
Scripting of Java applets	Enable	Enable	Enable	Disable
User authentication				
Logon	Automatic logon with current username and password	Automatic logon only in Intranet zone	Automatic logon only in Intranet zone	Prompt for username and password

Object (GPO) settings. Both tools and how they can be used for IE security zone administration are explained in more detail in the sections below.

Security Zone Web Site Identification

The IE security settings applied to a Web site are dependent on that Web site's security zone classification. This explains the importance of uniquely identifying Web sites. Even more secure is the authentication of Web sites, which is possible when using the Secure Sockets Layer (SSL) protocol. As will be explained below, the Trusted Sites, the Local Intranet and the Local Computer security zones—the zones with the highest security privileges (and thus the lowest security level)—can be configured to require SSL-based Web site authentication.

In a security zone, a Web site is identified using its HTTP or FTP Uniform Resource Locator (URL). Sites can be added manually to all security zones except the Internet and Local Computer zones. Remember from above that a site is automatically added to the Internet zone when it does not match any of the other Security Zones; the Local Computer zone applies to all content stored on local machine drives. To add a Web site to a security zone, select the appropriate security zone in the Security tab of the Internet Options dialog box, then click the Sites... button.

When explicitly adding Web site URLs to the Restricted Sites or Trusted Sites Security Zones, keep in mind that in a browser, Web sites can be accessed using both DNS names and plain IP addresses. If you only add Web sites' DNS names to the Restricted Sites or Trusted Sites security zones, the site will be classified as part of the Internet security zone when it is addressed using its IP address. So make sure that you add both a Web site's DNS name and its IP address when classifying it as either member of the Restricted Sites or Trusted Sites security zones.

Wildcards can be used to add different Web sites in a single administrative action. Adding *.hp.com to Trusted Sites, for example, will classify all sites ending in hp.com (hr.hp.com, emea.hp.com...) to the Trusted Sites security zone.

The right dialog box in Figure 4.18 shows how the Local Intranet security zone can be configured to require SSL-based authentication for all Web sites categorized within it. The same option is available for the Trusted Sites and the Local Computer security zones. Since these are the three most privileged security zones, strong server-side authentication is a welcome security addition. For the Trusted Sites security zone, strong SSL-based authentication is a must.

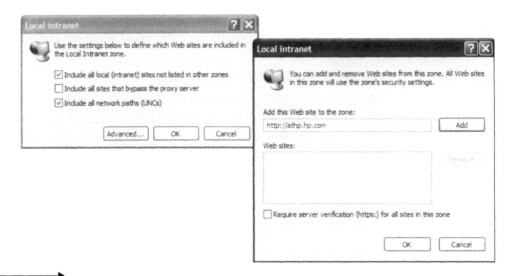

Figure 4.18   *Explicitly adding URLs to the Local Intranet security zone.*

The configuration of the Local Intranet zone deserves some more attention. For the Local Intranet zone, users and administrators are presented with the following membership configuration options (as illustrated in the left dialog box in Figure 4.18):

- Include all local (intranet) sites not listed in other zones. When this option is checked, all URLs that do not include dots will be added to the Local Intranet zone. This is the case for intranet sites on which Web content is addressed using plain hostnames—for example, http://intraweb. Addressing a Web site using a hostname is possible because the Windows networking logic includes a feature called DNS Domain Suffix Search Order that allows for the construction the Fully Qualified Domain Name (FQDN) given the hostname.

This rule also applies when addressing a Web site using the number-version URL of its IP address; a number also doesn't include dots and thus, by default, the Web site will be classified as Local Intranet content. For example, a Web site with the URL http://15.29.34.4 can also be addressed using http://253567492. To obtain this number from the site's IP address, use the following formula:

$$15(256^3) + 29(256^2) + 34(256) + 4$$

In short: when the "Include all local (intranet) sites not listed in other zones" option is checked, and users use URLs without dots to access

Internet content, you must make sure these URLs are also added explicitly to the Trusted Sites or Restricted Sites security zones.

- Include all sites that bypass the proxy server. Intranet architectures typically use a proxy server to access Internet content. Checking this box automatically categorizes Web content that is accessed while bypassing the proxy server in the Local Intranet zone. Web content that can be accessed while bypassing the proxy server is defined in the Connections tab of the Internet Options configuration dialog box.

  If you also use proxy servers to access intranet content, you should clear this box and explicitly define the intranet URLs as being part of the Local Intranet zone. To do so, click the Advanced... pushbutton and then explicitly add the intranet URLs (as illustrated in Figure 4.18).

- Include all network paths (UNCs). Network paths using Universal Naming Convention (UNC) names are typically used to reference intranet content. An example is \\webserver\webshare\report.doc. Checking this box automatically categorizes all UNC-addressed content in the Local Intranet zone. Clear this box if you also use UNCs to access Internet-based Web content.

- Manually add Web site URLs to the Local Intranet zone. This is done using the Advanced... pushbutton in the Local Intranet zone dialog box (as illustrated in Figure 4.18).

From the above, it becomes clear that in order to configure the Local Intranet zone properly the user must have a detailed knowledge of the organization's network configuration, including proxy servers and firewalls. Since very few users have this knowledge, it is recommended to use one of the centralized IE security zone configuration options (GPO or IEAK) that are outlined below.

Customizing and Administering the Local Computer Security Zone

By default the Local Computer zone doesn't appear on the Security tab of the Internet Options dialog box. In other words, by default, if you want to modify the Local Computer security zone properties, you must edit the system registry directly. Locking down the security settings of the Local Computer security zone is recommended on pre-Windows XP SP2 systems. On these systems, the default security settings of the Local Computer security zone are at a very low security level. Windows XP SP2 comes with a new feature called Local Computer security zone lockdown that mitigates the risks related to this zone.

Here's an example of how malicious code could exploit the insecure security settings of the Local Computer security zone. An IE user may be browsing a Web site that's classified in the Restricted Sites Security Zone. On one of the pages of the site, there could be a piece of malicious code that looks for and transmits user password files to a malicious Web site. As a restricted site, the script is part of the downloaded Web page, so it won't be able to do any harm due to the Restricted Sites security restrictions that are in place. Things change if the employee decides to save the page to his/her computer's hard disk. Later, when the employee opens the page from the hard drive, it will be classified as being part of the Local Computer security zone. Because the security level for this zone is low, the malicious code could then execute and still cause damage by silently transmitting data.

A little-known detail is that IE users can make Local Computer security zone show up on the Internet Options Security tab (illustrated in Figure 4.19) by modifying a registry setting. Doing so, they can easily modify the Local Computer Security Zone's configuration settings—just as they can do for the other four security zones.

To see the Local Computer security zone on pre-Windows XP SP2 systems, set the "Flags" (REG_DWORD) registry key to value 47 (hex) (default value is 21). The "Flags" key is located in the following registry container on pre-Windows XP SP2 systems: HKEY_CURRENT_USER\Software\ Microsoft\Windows\CurrentVersion\Internet Settings\Zones\0, which is the container where IE stores all configuration information related to the Local Computer security zone. On Windows XP SP2 systems, the "Flags" key is in the following registry container: HKEY_CURRENT_USER\Software\ Microsoft\Windows\CurrentVersion\Internet Settings\Lockdown_Zones\0.

For more information on the different security zone-related registry keys and their values, we refer to the following Knowledge Base article: http:// support.microsoft.com/default.aspx?scid=kb;en-us;182569.

Using Machine-Level-Only Security Zone Configuration Settings

As mentioned above, security zone settings are stored in the user and machine portions of the system registry (HKEY_CURRENT_USER and HKEY_LOCAL_MACHINE). The zone settings that are stored in machine portion of the registry apply to all users that are using a particular machine.

Figure 4.19
IE Internet options security configuration interface with My Computer security zone.

You can enforce that only the machine-level security zone settings are applied independent of the user-level security zone settings; this means that all users of a particular machine will get the same security zone settings.[4] To do so, enable the "Security Zones: Use only machine settings" GPO entry (which is located in the Computer Configuration\Administrative Templates\Windows Components\Internet Explorer GPO container), or add the Security_HKLM_only (REG_DWORD) and set it to 1 in the following registry container: HKEY_LOCAL_MACHINE\Software\Policies\Microsoft\Windows\CurrentVersion\Internet Settings.

Controlling Security Zone Configuration Settings

To centrally control the IE security zone configuration settings, you can either use Group Policy Object (GPO) settings or the Internet Explorer Administration Kit.

Using GPOs to Centrally Administer Security Zones

Table 4.6 provides an overview of the different GPO settings that can be used to control Security Zone-related IE settings.

---

4. By default, the machine-level GPO settings are first applied and then merged with the user-level GPO settings. This behavior can also be controlled using the GPO loopback processing feature, as explained in http://support.microsoft.com/default.aspx?scid=kb;en-us;231287.

Table 4.6   *GPO Security Zone-Related Configuration Options*

Setting	Location	Remarks
Security Zones: Use only machine settings	Computer Configuration\Administrative Templates\ Windows Components\Internet Explorer	
Security Zones: Do not allow users to change policies		
Security Zones: Do not allow users to add/delete sites		
Security Zones and Content Ratings	User Configuration\Windows Settings\ Internet Explorer Maintenance\Security	Imports GPO administrator's current IE Security Zone settings
Disable Security Page	User Configuration\Administrative Templates\ Windows Components\Internet Explorer\Internet Control Panel	
Zone Templates	User Configuration\Administrative Templates\ Windows Components\Internet Explorer\ Internet Control Panel\Security	Works only from IE 6.0 SP2 onwards
Internet		Does not import a GPO administrator's current IE Security Zone settings
Intranet		
Trusted Sites		
Restricted Sites		
Local Machine Zone		
Local Machine Zone Lockdown		
Local Machine Zone Lockdown	User Configuration\Administrative Templates\ Windows Components\Internet Explorer\ Security Features\Local Machine Zone Lockdown Security	Only XP SP2

Using the IEAK to Centrally Administer Security Zones

The Microsoft Internet Explorer Administration Kit (IEAK) allows administrators to easily customize, deploy, and manage IE software running on their users' desktops. The latest version of the IEAK, version 6 Service Pack 1 (SP1), can be downloaded from the following URL: www.microsoft.com/ windows/ieak/downloads/ieak6/ieak6sp1.mspx.

The IEAK consists of two programs: the Internet Explorer Customization Wizard and the IEAK Profile Manager. The first program allows administrators to create custom IE installation packages. The second allows administrators to customize previously created IE installation packages and to centrally configure IE settings using the IE auto-configuration feature.

In the IEAK Internet Explorer Customization Wizard, the IE security zone-related parameters are configured in Stage 4 (Import current security zone settings) and Stage 5 (IE security page configuration).

In the IEAK Profile Manager, the IE security zone-related settings can be configured from the "Wizard Settings\Security Zones and Content Ratings" and the "Policies and Restrictions\Corporate Restrictions\Security Page" containers.

4.5 Malicious Mobile Code Protection

Malicious mobile code (MMC) has become one of the most annoying security and privacy problems browser users have to deal with. Common MMC annoyances are viruses, spyware, and rootkits. In this section, we will focus on one of the Microsoft spyware protection solutions for consumers: Windows Defender. As Table 4.7 shows, Windows Defender is not the only Microsoft MMC protection solution.

These MMC protection solutions clearly illustrate Microsoft's efforts to provide their customers with secure software right out of the box. Microsoft's active participation in the Anti-Spyware Coalition (www.anti-spywarecoalition.org) also shows that Microsoft wants to align its solutions with industry-wide security efforts.

More information on the Microsoft MMC protection solutions listed in Table 4.7 can be found at the following URLs:

- Windows Defender: http://safety.live.com/site/en-US/default.htm.

- Windows Live Safety Center: http://safety.live.com/site/en-US/default.htm.

- Windows OneCare Live: www.windowsonecare.com.

- Malicious Software Removal Tool: www.microsoft.com/security/malwareremove/default.mspx.

- Microsoft Forefront Client Security: www.microsoft.com/forefront/clientsecurity/default.mspx.

Table 4.7   *Overview of Microsoft Malicious Mobile Code Protection Solutions*

Microsoft MMC Protection Solution	Focus: Business User/ Consumer	Provides Virus Protection	Provides Spyware Protection	Provided at No Additional Cost
Windows Defender	Consumer	No	Yes	Yes
Windows Live Safety Center	Consumer	Yes	Yes	Yes
Windows OneCare Live	Consumer	Yes	Yes	No
Malicious Software Removal Tool	Consumer / Business User	Yes	No	Yes
Microsoft Forefront Client Security*	Consumer / Business User	Yes	Yes	No

* This was previously referred to as Microsoft Client Protection.

4.5.1   Windows Defender

Spyware can be defined as software that installs without a user's knowledge or consent, monitors certain aspects of a user's activities, and then uses an Internet connection to transmit the collected information to a third party. A well known type of spyware is adware—spyware that specializes in displaying advertisements and collecting consumer information. Despite all the security enhancements Microsoft provides in XP Service Pack 2 (SP2), Internet Explorer users are not relieved from the spyware burden.

Popular spyware protection solutions that run on Windows XP and that can be used to search and delete or quarantine spyware code are Lavasoft Ad-Aware Personal (more info at www.lavasoft.de/ms/index.htm) and Spybot Search&Destroy (S&D) (more info at www.safer-networking.org/microsoft.en.html). But Microsoft itself could not leave this customer call for help unanswered.

In early January 2005, Microsoft released the beta 1 version of its Anti-Spyware solution—the rebranded version of the Giant AntiSpyware solution. Microsoft acquired Giant (http://www.giantcompany.com) in December 2004. In January 2006, Microsoft released the beta 2 version of AntiSpyware, renamed as Windows Defender. Windows Defender will be bundled with Windows Vista (the next client OS version) and Longhorn (the next server OS version) and will be made available at no additional cost as an add-on for Windows XP, Windows 2000, and Windows Server 2003 users. Compared to the AntiSpyware Beta 1 version, Windows Defender includes the following changes:

- Redesign of the user interface

- Spyware protection features for all users, independently of whether they have administrator-level privileges

- Spyware definition updates are delivered through Automatic Updates; antiSpyware beta 1 used a special auto-updater service for downloading definition updates

- Windows Defender now runs as a service—the "Windows Defender Service"—which is started automatically and continuously protects your system, even when no one is logged on

This section provides an overview of the Windows Defender spyware protection solution, its strengths, and its weaknesses. It is based on the beta 2 version of the Windows Defender software.

Overview and Installation

You can install the Windows Defender software by running the Windows-defender.msi installation program, which you can download from www.microsoft.com/downloads/details.aspx?FamilyID=435bfce7-da2b-4a6a-afa4-f7f14e605a0d&displaylang=en&Hash=DXDFYCC. To run the Windows Defender software, your operating system must be Windows 2000 SP4, Windows XP SP2, Windows Server 2003 SP1, or any later version.

Before running the Windows Defender installation program, Microsoft recommends uninstalling any other spyware protection software running on your system and restarting your machine. We don't necessarily agree with relying on a single spyware protection solution for protecting your desktops: as with any security solution, you should honor one of security's most fundamental principles: defense in depth. On our personal Windows XP installation, for example, we are running both Ad-Aware and the Windows Defender solution. The spyware holes left by Ad-Aware may be filled by the feature set of the Windows Defender solution (and the other way around).

During the Windows Defender installation you will be asked whether you want to automatically install spyware definition updates and whether you want to join Microsoft SpyNet. At the end of the installation, Windows Defender also gives you the option to run a first spyware scan on your system. As opposed to the AntiSpyware Beta 1 version, the Windows Defender installation program enables real-time protection by default. Spynet participation, real-time protection and definition updates can also be configured after installation from the General Settings dialog box in the Windows

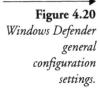

Figure 4.20
*Windows Defender
general
configuration
settings.*

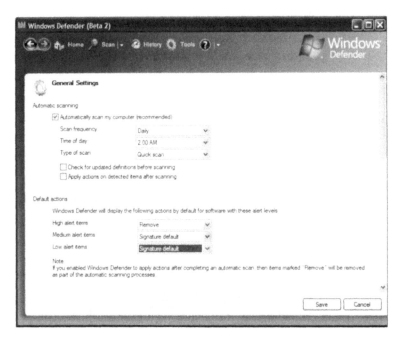

Defender GUI (which is illustrated in Figure 4.20); this dialog box is accessible through the Tools menu item. Successful installation of the Windows Defender software adds a Windows Defender entry in your Start menu and an icon in your system tray.

Windows Defender real-time protection is built on a set of security agents that monitor different Windows system and software configuration change attempts on your computer. For example, when software tries to write data to the registry or register an Internet Explorer (IE) add-on, you will be warned using a pop-up dialog box in the system tray. Figure 4.21 illustrates the Windows Defender dialog box that pops up when an installation program tries to register an IE Browser Helper Object (BHO). This dialog box gives you the option to either allow or block the BHO registration. Real-time protection will be explained in more detail below.

SpyNet (www.spynet.com) is the trademarked name Microsoft uses for its spyware discovery and reporting network. Spyware threats detected by the Windows Defender security agents can be sent to SpyNet servers on the Internet. The SpyNet servers analyze the spyware threats, catalogue them, and possibly include them in the Windows Defender spyware definition updates. Spynet might become an important differentiator for Microsoft's spyware protection solutions and could make a real difference in the fight

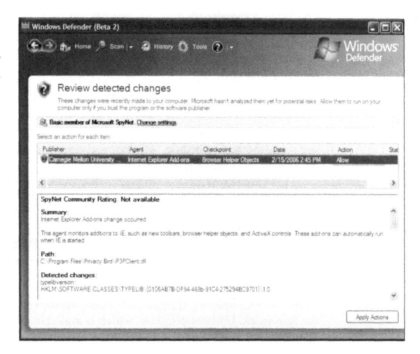

Figure 4.21
*Windows Defender
"Review detected
changes" dialog
box.*

against spyware. Its greatest potential lies in the fact that it can automate the process of reporting potential spyware. Windows Defender users can control whether and how they want to connect to the SpyNet network from the Setup Assistant or from the Microsoft SpyNet settings dialog box which can be accessed through the Tools menu item. To make sure that Windows Defender can communicate with SpyNet when firewalls are involved, the Windows Defender process (msascui.exe) must be allowed to access TCP port 80. For an interesting case related to Microsoft SpyNet and Microsoft's spyware classification system, see www.eweek.com/article2/ 0,1759,1749409,00.asp?kc=EWRSS03129TX1K0000614.

In Windows Defender, users can select one of the following SpyNet participation levels: do not participate, basic member, or advanced member. Basic membership means that Windows Defender only sends basic information about suspected files and does not alert the user when unclassified software is detected. Advanced membership means Windows Defender captures details like the memory used by the suspect process, its file system path, etc. This additional information is only sent to SpyNet if the user agrees. Advanced membership also means that Defender will alert the user when it detects unclassified software. Microsoft included these different user participation levels to make sure that users can keep complete control over their personally identifiable information (PII) that is sent to the Spy-Net servers.

Getting Started

The first screen that comes up when you start Windows Defender (msascui.exe) is the Summary screen (Figure 4.22). It shows information on when your system was scanned for the last time, what the results were of the last scan, the scan schedule, whether real-time protection is enabled, and the version of the spyware definition files.

A Windows Defender scan can be run with different scan options: you can run a quick scan (which is the default), a full scan, or a custom scan (where Defender only scans selected drives). All scan options are available from the dropdown arrow beside the Scan menu item (see Figure 4.22). You can also start a Defender scan from the command line using the mpcmdrun.exe utility (use the "scan" switch).

Windows Defender spyware definition updates are downloaded using the Automatic Updates program, which is available on all Windows 2000, Windows XP, and Windows Server 2003 versions. Automatic Updates can be enabled and configured from the Control Panel Automatic Updates applet. You can also manually force a Defender spyware definition update:

- Using the mpcmdrun.exe command line utility and the SignatureUpdate switch

- From the Windows Defender menu: click the arrow next to the Help menu item (the question mark symbol—see Figure 4.22), then click About Windows Defender; in the Windows Defender dialog box, click "Check for Updates"

The results of a Windows Defender scan are displayed in the Scan Results screen, which is illustrated in Figure 4.23. For each spyware threat, you can take different actions: allow, remove, or always allow. For each threat, the Scan Results screen shows the threat category (for example: Trojan), description, advice on what action you should take, and a list of the affected system resources.

When you quarantine a spyware threat, it is isolated in the Windows Defender quarantine file. Any threat that is quarantined can also be removed from the quarantine using the Quarantined Items screen, which can be accessed from the Tools option in the Defender menu.

In the beta version of the AntiSpyware software, you may have noticed that even though the tool showed "cookies scanned" and "cookies infected"

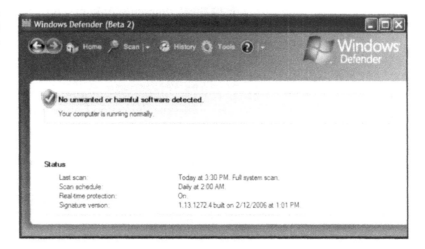

Figure 4.22
*Windows Defender
summary screen.*

during a scan run, it never detected infected cookies. Cookie scanning was available in the original Giant product, was disabled in the AntiSpyware beta, and is not available in Windows Defender beta 2. Microsoft considers cookies, as opposed to spyware, to be innocuous files that cannot compromise a computer. If you really want to scan your cookies for spyware threats,

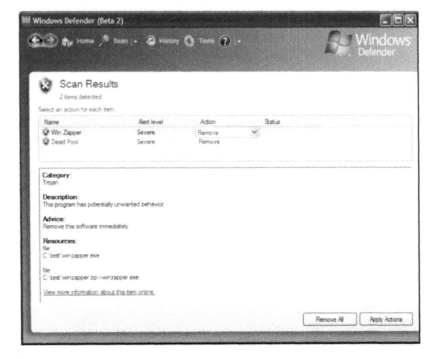

Figure 4.23
*Windows Defender
scan results screen.*

you must use one of the competing products—for example, Lavasoft's Ad-Aware (more information on this product is available at www.lavasoft.de/ms/index.htm).

Configuring Real-Time Protection

Windows Defender's Real-time Protection feature is rooted on a set of security agents that will block unknown events before they can do harm to your machine and its resources. When new software is installed or a configuration change is made to your system, the security agents react. They analyze the change and will allow it if they know the change is safe, block it if they know the change is initiated by spyware, or prompt the user for additional input if they don't have enough information. When Defender prompts the user, a warning window similar to the one illustrated in Figure 4.24 pops up. From this window, the user can remove the spyware threat from the system or ignore it. Another example is the Defender screen illustrated in Figure 4.21, which pops up when a system change is detected—in this example, it followed the installation of new software. Note in Figure 4.21 the SpyNet Community Rating, which informs the user about the Spynet threat level rating of a particular piece of code. Defender retrieves the rating in real-time each time a system change or a spyware threat is detected.

Pop ups to allow or block software events are nice, but worthless if users don't read them and simply click through them. Here is another reason for educating your users: you must teach them about the risks of just clicking "ignore" without understanding the potential consequences of doing so.

Windows Defender real-time protection includes the following security agents that continuously monitor your system: Auto Start, System Configuration (settings), Internet Explorer Add-ons, Internet Explorer Configurations

Figure 4.24
*Windows Defender
alert.*

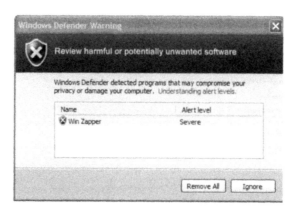

(settings), Internet Explorer Downloads, Services and Drivers, Application Execution, Application Registration, and Windows Add-ons. You can activate or deactivate real-time protection and individual security agents from the Defender General Settings configuration screen. Extensive information about the agents' role and functionality can be found in the Windows Defender Help file.

Windows Defender uses its proper history log to keep track of all blocked and allowed spyware threats and system change events. The history log can be accessed from Defender's History menu item.

Extra Tools

Windows Defender also includes a Software Explorer tool (illustrated in Figure 4.25) that allows you to view detailed information about software currently running on your machine. The software is categorized in startup programs, currently running programs, network-connected programs, and winsock service providers. From the Software Explorer, you can block, terminate, disable, or remove programs running on your computer. The Software Explorer can be accessed from the Tools menu item.

The AntiSpyware beta 1 version of Windows Defender included two other nice tools that didn't make it into beta 2: a browser hijack restore and the tracks eraser tool. The browser hijack restore feature allowed a user to easily restore IE configuration settings (like homepage, default search

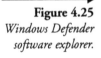

Figure 4.25
Windows Defender
software explorer.

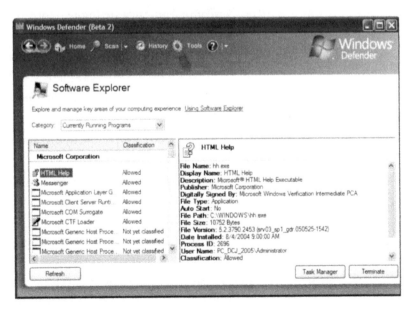

page...) after they were reset or "hijacked" by spyware code. The tracks eraser feature was a privacy feature that allowed a user to easily remove Windows and application history logs and activity trails.

4.5.2 Conclusion and General Spyware Protection Guidelines

Windows Defender is a consumer-oriented tool that has an easy-to-use and straightforward user interface and that is well integrated with the Windows OS. Two great Windows Defender features are real-time protection and the system explorer. They can make the difference when users have to choose between Windows Defender and one of its alternatives. Alternatives such as Lavasoft Ad-Aware Plus and Professional edition (www.lavasoft.de/ms/index.htm) have similar real-time protection support (called Ad-Watch), but they don't have a system explorer feature. If you do an Internet search, you will discover more freeware tools that can provide the features that Microsoft bundles in Windows Defender in a single product.

Until Microsoft releases their enterprise malicious mobile code protection solution, "Microsoft Client Protection," enterprise customers can consider the following alternatives:

- McAfee Anti-Spyware Enterprise (more information at www.mcafee.com/us/products/mcafee/anti_spyware/anti_spyware.htm)

- CA eTrust PestPatrol Anti-Spyware (more information at www.ca.com/products/pestpatrol)

- Sunbelt Software CounterSpy Enterprise (more information at www.sunbeltsoftware.com/CounterSpyEnterprise.cfm)

- Trend Micro Anti-Spyware Enterprise Edition (more information at www.trendmicro.com/products/anti-spyware)

- Webroot Spy Sweeper Enterprise (more information at www.webroot.com/enterprise/products)

Three final pieces of advice to better protect your systems against spyware:

- Fighting spyware is not always a question of making choices: remember "defense in depth," and install and use two solutions on your system.

- A very efficient tactic to protect against spyware (from the start) is to honor least privilege. Don't run your browser in the security context of a high-privileged account—use RunAs or su to switch to a less-privileged account when logged on as an administrator and surfing the Web, or log on with lower privileges in the first place.

- Last but not least: educate your users. Teach them about the dangers of spyware and, if they are using a spyware scanner, make sure they know how to use the tool properly.

4.6 Leveraging Trusted Platform Module Security Functions

A Trusted Platform Module (TPM) is a specialized security hardware module that is integrated with a computer's motherboard. It can provide tamper-proof security services to a computer and its users. These security services include protected storage for cryptographic keys and data, platform integrity verification and strong device and user authentication.

The most important security services a TPM can provide are the wrapping and sealing of cryptographic keys:

- A TPM can create and encrypt cryptographic keys so that they can only be decrypted by that particular TPM. This process is referred to as wrapping or binding a cryptographic key.

- A TPM can create cryptographic keys that are tied to certain computer platform measurements. This means that the cryptographic key can only be unwrapped when those platform measurements have the same values that they had when the key was created. This process is referred to as sealing a cryptographic key to the TPM.

Using the TPM for cryptographic key wrapping and sealing has the following advantages:

- A TPM is more resistant to attack. Computer hardware components are generally more resistant to attack than their software counterparts. A TPM basically protects itself. If someone tries to physically tamper with it, the TPM content is damaged and/or deleted.

- Cryptographic keys can be configured to not leave the TPM and kept separate from computer memory that is controlled by the operating system.

- Cryptographic keys can be sealed by a TPM. This means that certain assurances about the trustworthiness of a computer system can be made before the TPM releases the keys to the OS and its applications.

- A TPM uses its own internal firmware and logical circuits for processing instructions. A TPM does not rely on the operating system which is subjected to external software vulnerabilities and attacks.

TPMs are a critical technology for the client security space: they can provide strong data protection services, strong user and device authentication, and client software integrity checking services. The Windows platform may play an important role in the widespread adoption of the TPM: Microsoft plans to make TPM-enabled security features available in the Windows Vista client and Longhorn Server operating systems. See also the sidenote on "How Microsoft Leverages the Trusted Platform Module in Windows Vista."

A TPM is sometimes referred to as an embedded smart card. Although it has important smart card similarities, it also has important differences. Both host microprocessors that provide cryptographic and data protection services. A TPM, however, is bound to a computer platform. A smart card can roam between different computers, provided the computers are equipped with a smart card reader. A TPM, on the other hand, is better suited to protect access to sensitive information stored on a computer system.

The TPM is built according to the specifications of the Trusted Computing Group or the TCG (https://www.trustedcomputinggroup.org/home). The TCG evolved from what was once the Trusted Computing Platform Alliance (TCPA). TCG is an industry consortium that defines the specifications for trusted computing platforms and networking architectures. The five founders of TCPA/TCG were IBM, Intel, Microsoft, HP and Compaq. The latest TCG TPM specifications are at version 1.2. The TPM functionality discussed in this book is that of version 1.1b.

Today's leading computer vendors (Dell, HP, and IBM) all sell computers with a TPM option. All of them also provide special software that you can use to provide TPM-based security services to Windows users. For example, the HP TPM-based software solution is called Embedded Security for HP ProtectTools; the IBM solution is called ThinkVantage Technologies. For a good overview of computer hardware that currently includes a TPM chip and applications supporting the TPM functionality now, have a look at the TPM matrix available from the following URL: www.tonymcfadden.net/tpmvendors.html.

This section provides an introduction to Embedded Security for HP ProtectTools[5]—the HP TPM-based software solution. It explains the technical

---

5.   More information is available at http://h18004.www1.hp.com/products/security/embedded_security.html.

How Microsoft Leverages the Trusted Platform Module in Windows Vista

In Windows Vista, Microsoft will include volume-level encryption services to better protect Windows clients from offline data attacks. This feature is referred to as BitLocker Drive Encryption (BDE). BitLocker will not be available in all Vista versions: it will only be supported in the Windows Vista Enterprise and Windows Vista Ultimate Editions. BDE-protection for a volume is not enabled by default and needs to be turned on manually. Also, in the initial Vista release only the system boot partition can be BDE-protected. Rumor says that Microsoft will support BDE-protection of multiple volumes in Vista Service Pack 1 (SP1) and Longhorn.

BitLocker not only protects (encrypts) the data stored on a Windows system, it also makes the OS itself more resilient from attacks. BDE includes a file integrity checking feature that automatically checks the status of boot files such as the BIOS, Master Boot Records (MBRs), and so on when the system boots and prior to the start of the OS. If a hacker inserted malicious code in one of the boot files or modified them, BDE will detect it and block the OS from starting. Microsoft refers to this feature as the static root of trust measurement for early boot components.

BitLocker can also offer pre-OS multifactor authentication. Before the Windows OS starts, BDE can prompt the user to authenticate himself by providing a secret that is stored on a USB token and/or entering a PIN code. Preboot authentication protects the Windows OS from attacks that attempt to bypass OS-level access checks and get to the data on a Windows OS-protected volume by booting from a Linux CD or floppy disk.

Finally, BitLocker can also speed up the recycling process of decommissioned computers. Enterprises often invest considerable time and effort in zeroing the computers' hard disks to assure that the data the disks carry become unreadable and thus worthless to an attacker. Recycling a system's hard disk becomes very easy when using BDE: only the BDE decryption keys must be erased to make the data on a BDE-protected volume completely useless.

BitLocker can optionally leverage a Trusted Platform Module (TPM) for hardware-based encryption key protection (in TPM terminology, "encryption key sealing"). BitLocker requires a version 1.2 TPM and a Trusted Computing Group (TCG)-compliant computer BIOS.

BitLocker supports two authentication modes that are leveraging the TPM:

- **TPM-only**. In this mode, the TPM protects the BitLocker encryption key. If a system's TPM is missing or changed, BitLocker enters recovery mode, in which case the user needs a recovery key or password to regain access to the data stored on the system.

- **TPM and Startup key**. In this case the user needs a startup key to log on to the computer. The startup key can be either a USB token with a machine-readable key written to it or a personal PIN set by the user.

BitLocker can also be used on systems that do not have a TPM installed. In that case it can leverage a USB token to store the BitLocker encryption key.

See also the following URL for more information on Windows Vista BitLocker:

www.microsoft.com/technet/windowsvista/library/c61f2a12-8ae6-4957-b031-97b 4d762cf31.mspx.

implementation of the HP TPM solution and how Windows XP, Windows Server 2003, and R2 users can leverage the TPM security services using the Embedded Security for HP ProtectTools software. The TPM functionality Embedded Security for HP ProtectTools provided (at the time of writing) was based on version 1.1b of the TCG TPM specifications. HP will release an updated version of Embedded Security for HP ProtectTools that will work with Windows Vista and 1.2 TPMs; this will probably occur around the time that Microsoft ships Windows Vista.

More information on the TPM and Embedded Security for HP Protect-Tools is also available from the HP Business PC Security Solutions Web site (http://psgwebdev02.americas.cpqcorp.net:84/products/security/) and from the TCG Web site (https://www.trustedcomputinggroup.org/home). A very good introduction to the TCG specifications is available in the book *Trusted Computing Platforms—TCPA Technology in Context*[6] (ISBN 0-13-009920-7).

4.6.1   TPM Hardware and Software Requirements

To take advantage of the TPM security features, you must have a TPM-enabled computer. On the HP side, the TPM chip is available on the HP Compaq dc7100 Business PCs; xw4200, xw6200, and xw8200 workstations; and nc4010, nc4200, tc4200, nc6000, nc6200, nc8000, nc8200, nw8000, and nw8200 business notebooks.[7] To check from the Windows interface whether your HP system is equipped with a TPM chip, open the Device Manager and expand the System Devices container: if your system has a TPM installed, this container must hold an "Infineon Trusted Platform Module" entry.

To take advantage of the TPM functionality in Windows XP, Windows Server 2003, and R2 you also must have the following HP software installed: the "HP ProtectTools Embedded Security Module and Infineon TPM Driver" and the "HP ProtectTools Security Manager" software. Both software packages can be downloaded from the HP "Software & Driver Downloads" public Web pages, at www.hp.com/country/us/en/support.html?pageDisplay=drivers. Select the "Software—Security" option for your computer type.

The HP ProtectTools Security Manager (illustrated in Figure 4.26) is a Windows Control Panel applet that can be used to configure system security-

---

6.   See also www.hp.com/hpbooks/prentice/ptr_0130092207.html.
7.   For an up-to-date list of HP TPM-enabled machines check the HP Web site at www.hp.com.

Figure 4.26
*HP ProtectTools
Security Manager.*

related parameters: these include the TPM configuration as well as BIOS settings (like the BIOS password), smart card and USB token configuration, and credential manager settings (this is an HP client-side credential caching-based SSO solution).

4.6.2   Embedded Security for HP ProtectTools: Technical Implementation

The following sections explain the TPM administrative concepts and key hierarchy as they are implemented in the Embedded Security for HP ProtectTools software.

TPM Administrative Concepts

Key to understanding how a TPM works and is secured in the context of Embedded Security for HP ProtectTools are the administrative concepts (or the way users and administrators interact with and use or manage the TPM) and the corresponding Key Hierarchy (that is linked to those users and administrators and the platform the TPM is associated with). Both the administrative concepts and key hierarchy explain how the TPM and

Embedded Security for HP ProtectTools can support hardware-based separation of administrative roles, also known as separation of duty (SOD)— another very important TPM and Embedded Security strength.

The next paragraphs explain the roles related to usage and administration of the TPM and associated Embedded Security for HP ProtectTools software. They also describe responsibilities and privileges associated to these roles. The section following that will explain the key hierarchy. All roles and their responsibilities and privileges are summarized in Table 4.8.

TPM Owner

The most important TPM user role is the TPM owner. The owner can permanently disable/enable the TPM, initialize it, and allow the migration of secrets stored on the TPM to another TPM (or another platform). Access to the owner role is secured using the TPM owner password. For each TPM, there can be only one owner (and thus, only one owner password). In a typical enterprise scenario, the TPM owner role could be given to an IT

Table 4.8   *TPM Administrative Roles and Their Responsibilities and Privileges*

TPM Administrative Role	Responsibilities and Privileges
TPM owner	■ Permanently disabling the TPM ■ Changing the TPM owner password and recovery token password ■ Authorizing migration for TPM users ■ TPM must be a member of the local Windows Administrators group and has thus all privileges of the Windows administrator account
TPM user	■ Change the TPM user password ■ Can use the TPM to securely store its personal secrets, and/or use the chip for Secure Email or Secure Web access (SSL/TLS-based) ■ Can use a TPM-protected personal secure drive (PSD) ■ Can temporarily disable the TPM within the current Windows logon session ■ Can migrate its TPM-based user keys to another TPM-enabled platform (if authorized by the TPM owner)
TPM recovery agent	■ Must have Windows Administrator privileges ■ Knows the recovery token password (can only change it if he/she is also the TPM owner) ■ Has access to the recovery token ■ Can recover user keys from the recovery archive
Windows administrator	■ Can change Embedded Security software security policy settings ■ Has all Windows privileges
BIOS administrator	■ Change the BIOS administrator password ■ Enable the TPM and change the TPM BIOS configuration settings

administrator. Since enabling/disabling the TPM requires knowledge of the BIOS administrator password (explained in more detail below), the TPM owner must also know this password.

TPM User(s)

Although there can be only a single TPM owner per TPM, multiple users can be enabled for each TPM. On a TPM-enabled PC, these could be users who are logging on to the system and who want to use the TPM to protect access to their secrets and data. Each user's TPM-protected secrets are fully isolated, meaning that one TPM user's secrets cannot be accessed by another TPM user.

TPM Recovery Agent

The TPM owner and user(s) are the only administrative roles defined in the TCG TPM specifications. The HP Embedded Security administrative model builds on top of the TCG specification and additionally defines and enables the role of a TPM recovery agent.

In the HP Embedded Security administrative model, the recovery agent is an administrator that has the permission to recover user TPM keys from the TPM recovery archive. For many enterprises, the key recovery agent is a must-have role. It can serve in the scenario where an employee leaves the company without disclosing his or her TPM password and the administrator must recover company-sensitive documents stored on the employee's former PC and protected by the TPM.

The recovery agent role requires Windows administrator privileges, administrator access to the recovery archive and token, and knowledge of the recovery password (recovery concepts are explained in more detail below). The recovery agent's role is typically assigned to the TPM owner, although it may also be delegated by the TPM owner to any Windows administrator (together with the recovery token and password).

The process of enabling a TPM recovery agent is exactly the same as enabling a recovery agent for the Windows encrypting file system (EFS).[8] In fact, on a TPM-enabled Windows platform that has the Embedded Security software installed, the roles of TPM recovery agent and EFS recovery agent are identical. Besides recovering TPM-protected EFS keys, a TPM recovery agent can also recover the keys that are used by the Embedded Security personal secure drive (PSD) application. PSD is an HP

---

8.   The process of enabling a recovery agent for EFS will be explained in Chapter 10 in *Advanced Microsoft Windows Security Services* (part 2 of this series).

ProtectTools-specific solution for the secure (encrypted) storage of files and folders—similar to the functionality offered by EFS in Windows 2000 and later Microsoft operating systems.

Windows Administrator

The Windows administrator is the built-in Windows account with the highest level of Windows operating system privileges. He or she can do basically anything on a Windows installation. The Windows administrator can change certain software configuration settings of the Embedded Security software (either locally or centrally using group policy objects (GPOs)): examples are temporarily disabling the TPM, enabling the caching of the basic user key (BUK) password, defining the location for the emergency recovery archive, etc. The Windows administrator cannot control any of the TPM services themselves, as this would require that he/she is also the TPM owner.

Even though the TPM owner must be a member of the local Administrators group, each Windows administrator is not necessarily a TPM owner. Because there can be multiple Windows administrators on a single system, there must be a separation mechanism to differentiate between the one administrator who is also the owner and all the other administrators. This separation mechanism is based on the fact that the TPM owner must know the TPM owner password.

BIOS Administrator

On HP Embedded Security-enabled systems, the BIOS administrator can also be considered a separate TPM administrative role. Only the BIOS administrator has access to the BIOS TPM administrative features. Also, before the TPM can be enabled in BIOS, a BIOS administrator password must be defined. This enables an IT administrator to establish a BIOS administrator password and prevents users from enabling the TPMs on their systems until the IT organization is ready to enable, deploy, and manage TPMs throughout the whole organization.

TPM Key Hierarchy

The TPM key hierarchy (Figure 4.27) shows and explains how the data protected by the TPM and Embedded Security for HP ProtectTools are secured. In this context, "protected data" means keys that are used to cryptographically protect (encrypt or sign) user data, such as e-mail messages or user files and folders. The keys must be integrity-protected to protect them from unauthorized and undetected changes, and they must be kept confidential: only a single user should have access to them. Hence, the importance of using a key hierarchy or protecting keys using other keys.

The TPM key hierarchy shows how the TPM can provide an unlimited volume of data protection. Instead of storing the protected data (which can be quite voluminous) and all the keys, the TPM only stores a limited set of keys internally in TPM secured storage. The TPM key hierarchy outlined below is used to protect both keys and data stored in system memory or simply on disk. Access to these protected data and keys—including the keys that are not stored inside the TPM secured storage—always requires TPM intervention.

More detailed information on the TPM key hierarchy can be found in the TPM Architecture Overview. This document can be downloaded from the TCG Web site at https://www.trustedcomputinggroup.org/downloads/Main_TCG_Architecture_v1_1b.zip.

Endorsement Key and Storage Root Key

At the top of the TPM key hierarchy are the Endorsement Key (EK) and the Storage Root Key (SRK). Both keys are stored in TPM-protected storage and are thus protected by the tamper resistance of the TPM chip. Both keys cannot be migrated to another TPM platform.

- The EK is uniquely bound to a particular TPM platform. It is used to identify a TPM as a unique and genuine device. It is embedded in the TPM chip by the TPM manufacturer. Note that the Endorsement Key is not used in the HP Embedded Security software version that is discussed in this section. It will however become an important element in future versions.

- The SRK is used to protect TPM user keys and data. It is generated when the TPM is initialized by the TPM owner. It is at the root of the TPM key hierarchy that will be explained below.

User Storage Keys

The next level in the TPM key hierarchy is made up of the user storage keys (USKs). For each user that is using a TPM-enabled machine, a USK key pair (2048-bit private and public key) is generated as part of the user initialization process. USKs are not stored on the TPM itself, but in the user profile (%userprofile%\Documents and Settings\<username>\Application Data\Infineon\TPM Software\UserKeyData\TSPps.xml). USKs are stored securely in the user profile: they are encrypted using the SRK (a process that

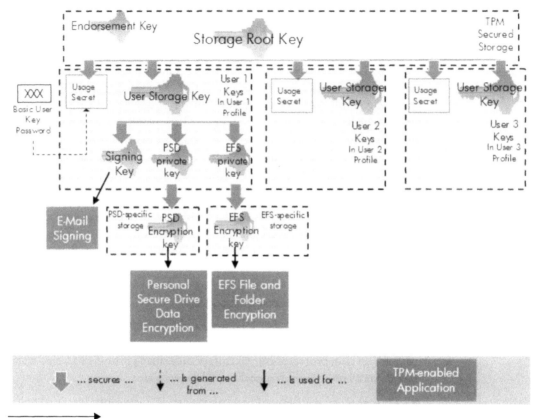

Figure 4.27   *The TPM key hierarchy.*

is also referred to as wrapping) and access to them is secured using a password: the basic user key (BUK) password. A BUK password can be between 6 and 255 characters long. The BUK password is a separate password that is independent of the user's Windows local or domain logon password and that must be entered when the TPM software loads.

As opposed to the EK and the SRK, USKs and all the keys in the TPM key hierarchy below the USKs can be migrated to another TPM. This means that they can be protected by another USK that is secured by another TPM.

To access the encrypted USK in the user profile, a user must always first prove knowledge of the associated BUK password to the TPM. This access control mechanism is based on the secured storage of another secret: the usage secret in the user profile. Again, the usage secret is stored securely, meaning encrypted by the SRK. The usage secret is the result of a SHA1 hash operation on the BUK password. Each time a user accesses data or keys that are protected by the USK, he/she will be prompted for the BUK password. The TPM will then check the user's knowledge of the correct password by comparing the usage secret to the hash value resulting from the hash calculation using the BUK password. In practice, the software stack managing these keys might allow the caching of the BUK password for a timed session (say a Windows reboot, logoff, or x number of minutes, etc) whereby the sequential access to keys that require BUK password verification can be silently accommodated by the software stack.

Signing and Storage Keys

The next level of secured key material stored in the user profile can be either signing keys or storage keys:

- Signing keys are used for user and data authentication, data integrity protection, and nonrepudiation services. A good example is a private key used for S/MIME-based e-mail signing.

- Storage keys are used to provide integrity and confidentiality protection for other keys. They are asymmetric keys. Good examples are the storage key that is used to securely store a user's Encrypting File System (EFS) private key or the storage key that is used for the Personal Secure Drive (PSD) application.

Application-Specific Keys

Applications that are using the above keys for providing data encryption services are using another level of symmetric key material in the key hierarchy. These symmetric keys are not stored in the user profile but in application-specific storage. Examples are EFS and the Personal Secure Drive (PSD) TPM-enabled applications.

- The EFS symmetric encryption key is securely stored (meaning: encrypted by the EFS private key) in an NTFS file stream that is attached to EFS-encrypted files.

- The PSD symmetric encryption key is securely stored (meaning: encrypted by the PSD private key) in the PSD storage volume.

Both EFS and PSD also encrypt a copy of their symmetric encryption key with a recovery private key (which sits at the "signing and storage key" level in the TPM key hierarchy), as illustrated in Figure 4.28 for an administrator that has EFS and PSD recovery privileges. Both EFS and PSD have a key archival and recovery mechanism. In the context of the TPM and the

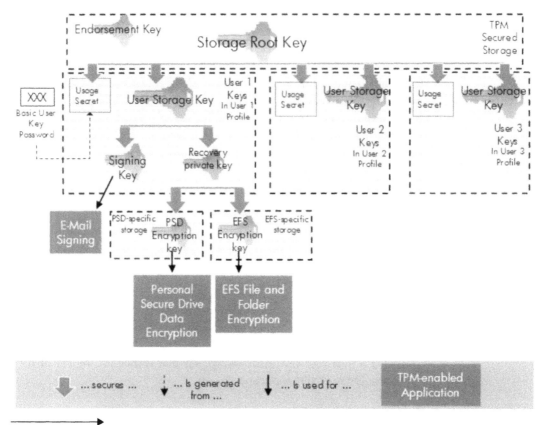

Figure 4.28   *The TPM Key hierarchy, including the EFS and PSD recovery key for an administrator that has EFS and PSD recovery privileges.*

Embedded Security software, EFS and PSD use the same recovery private key and rely on the same TPM-rooted mechanism to protect this key. The TPM-secured EFS recovery private key is stored in the user profile of the administrator who has EFS and PSD key recovery privileges. Again, for EFS the encrypted copy of the EFS symmetric key is stored in an NTFS file stream. For PSD the encrypted copy of the PSD symmetric key is stored in the PSD storage volume.

4.6.3   HP TPM-Enabled Applications

Table 4.9 gives an overview of the HP applications that can take advantage of the security services offered by the TPM. You can use these applications on the Windows XP, Windows Server 2003, and R2 platforms.

Table 4.9   *Overview of TPM-Enabled Applications*

TPM-Enabled Application	How Does It Take Advantage of the TPM?
Microsoft Encrypting File System (EFS) for file and folder encryption using 56-bit DESX, 128-bit 3DES, or 256-bit AES	Access to the EFS private key and EFS symmetric key is secured using the TPM-based user storage key. By default, each time a user encrypts a file or accesses an encrypted file he/she will be prompted for its TPM basic user key (BUK) password. Optionally, the BUK password can also be cached for the duration of the user logon session.
Embedded Security for HP ProtectTools "Personal Secure Drive" (PSD) for file and folder encryption using 192-bit AES	Access to the PSD private and PSD symmetric key is secured using a TPM key. Each time a user accesses the PSD, he/she will be prompted for the TPM BUK password (if the BUK password is not cached).
Secure e-mail using S/MIME: e-mail signing and encryption	Access to the S/MIME private decryption and signing keys is secured using a TPM key. Each time a user signs or decrypts a message, he/she will be prompted for the TPM BUK password (if the BUK password is not cached).
Wireless LAN 802.1x EAP-TLS-based strong two-factor-based user authentication	The 802.1x authentication is based on two factors: knowledge of the TPM BUK password and possession of a particular TPM-enabled machine. Access to the user's 802.1x authentication credentials (public-private key pair) can be secured using a TPM key. Each time an 802.1x authentication sequence takes place, the user will be prompted for the TPM BUK password (if the BUK password is not cached).
Enhanced SecurID authentication	Combining SecurID with the TPM provides two-factor authentication based on the possession of a particular TPM-enabled machine and the knowledge of the SecurID software token PIN and the TPM BUK password. Access to the SecurID seed is secured using a TPM key. Each time a SecurID authentication sequence takes place, the user will be prompted for its TPM BUK password and SecurID PIN (if the BUK password is not cached).
HP ProtectTools Credential Manager	Credential Manager provides a SSO solution based on client-side credential caching. Access to the credentials cached in the Credential Manager vault is secured using the USK. Each user stores, retrieves, or changes credentials in the Credential Manager vault, he/she will be prompted for its TPM BUK password (if the BUK password is not cached). This HP ProtectTools credential caching feature is totally separate from the built-in Windows XP, Windows Server 2003, and R2 Credential Manager (which is discussed in more detail in Chapter 9).

Table 4.9   *Overview of TPM-Enabled Applications (continued)*

TPM-Enabled Application	How Does It Take Advantage of the TPM?
User preboot authentication (on HP notebooks only)	User preboot authentication uses a user's TPM keyblob and BUK password to authenticate the user in the machine preboot phase (before OS software is loaded).
DriveLock (on HP notebooks only)	DriveLock blocks access to a machine's hard disks. A DriveLock password is automatically and randomly generated by the BIOS, and protected via a TPM. This solution ties a system's hard disks to a TPM (and thus a platform) because only a particular TPM will be able to unlock the random DriveLock password.
Any CryptoAPI or PKCS#11 enabled application	All CryptoAPI and PKCS#11 enabled applications can secure their secrets using the TPM. Embedded Security for HP ProtectTools comes with CryptoAPI cryptographic service providers (CSPs) and PKCS#11 modules that can be leveraged by these applications.

4.7   Important Windows Vista and IE 7.0 Client Security Features

At the time of writing, Microsoft had released the Beta 1 version of Windows Vista (the next version of the Windows client OS) and the Beta 2 version of Internet Explorer 7.0[9] to the public. Table 4.10 summarizes the major new security features Microsoft will introduce in these two new software releases.

---

9.   IE 7.0 will come in two versions: a reduced-feature and upgrade version for IE 6.0 on Windows XP SP2, and a full-feature version that will be part of Windows Vista.

Table 4.10 *Windows Vista and IE 7.0 Security Features*

Security Feature	Comment
IE 7.0	
Phishing filter	Detection feature for known and suspected phishing sites.
Protected Mode IE (on Windows Vista only)	Low-rights IE, linked to UAP in Windows Vista.
Security zone enhancements	Further lockdown and extended configuration features.
SSL enhancements	SSL 2.0 disabled and TLS 1.0 enabled by default. Per-site security report. More and better information about certificate problems.
PKI: OCSP support	OCSP is the Online Certificate Status Protocol, a PKI certificate revocation checking mechanism
Windows Vista	
User Account Protection (UAP)	Also referred to as LUA (Least Privileged User Account): Windows Vista's new least privilege feature.
BitLocker Drive Encryption (previously referred to as Secure Startup)	Provides a Windows system code integrity protection and a hard disk–level encryption and signing solution. BitLocker can leverage a version 1.2 Trusted Platform Module (TPM).
New logon interface architecture	Replaces GINA. Provides richer logon experience and supports different authentication devices (including better biometrics support).
Integrated anti-malware protection	Automatically detects, removes, and blocks malware (worms, viruses, spyware, rootkits, etc.). This functionality includes the Windows Defender spyware protection logic and the Malicious Software Removal Tool (MSRT).
Network Access Protection (NAP) client	Network edge-protection system that checks the security status of connecting systems prior to admitting them. NAP is the next version of the Windows Server 2003 VPN Quarantine system. Requires the Longhorn NAP server.
CardSpace client (formerly known as InfoCard)	Client identity management service for the selection and maintenance of different user identities.
Enhanced Windows Firewall	Includes combined Windows Firewall and IPsec management, outbound filtering support, more intelligent firewall rules (specification of AD users and groups, security and encryption requirements, etc.).
Better control over device driver installation	Controls unwanted USB device installation.

Table 4.10 *Windows Vista and IE 7.0 Security Features (continued)*

Security Feature	Comment
Credential roaming support for domain clients	Supports AD-based roaming of PKI credentials for domain-joined machines (also known as DIMS: Digital Identity Management System).
Enhanced smart card support	Smart cards can be leveraged by Rights Management Services (RMS) and Encrypting File System (EFS).
Service hardening	Reduces Windows service attack surface. Provides Security Identifiers (SIDs) for individual Windows services.
Improved Auditing	Support for many more auditing subcategories: logon, logoff, file system access, registry access, use of administrative privilege, etc. Easier to filter out noise in logs and find the event you are looking for.
Encrypting File System (EFS) enhancements	Support for smart cards, client-side encryption, and decryption for EFS-based file sharing, better EFS group policy, re-key wizard, key backup notification.
Built-In Rights Management Services (RMS) client	RMS can be used for enterprise rights management-based protection of Microsoft Office documents.
Restart Manager	Intelligent restart mechanism for restarts caused by system updates.
IE 7.0 Security Enhancements	See above.

Part I

Authentication

5

Introducing Windows Authentication

This and the following four chapters focus on the most fundamental security service of the Windows operating system: authentication. Before an entity is given access to a resource, the operating system must validate the entity's identity. The primary purpose of authentication is to prove and validate an entity's identity. Authentication answers the question: with whom or what is the system dealing?

5.1 Authentication Basics

The two following sections paragraphs discuss general non-Windows specific authentication and authentication infrastructure terminology and explain the importance of qualifying authentication solutions.

5.1.1 Terminology

Authentication builds on the following key concepts:

- **Authentication Infrastructure** refers to a set of authentication servers and authentication authorities, providing authentication services.

- **Authentication Servers** are the physical machines providing and performing the authentication functions.

- **Authentication Authorities** are a logical trust-related concept. They are the entities trusted by users to perform reliable authentication functions. Physically, an authentication authority is represented by one or more authentication servers. In Windows-speak, a domain is an authentication authority, and the authentication servers are the domain's domain controllers (DCs).

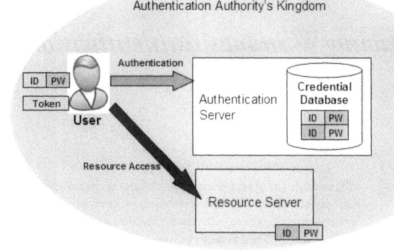

Figure 5.1   *Authentication terminology.*

Figure 5.1 illustrates these three key concepts together with other authentication terminology:

- **Authentication Credentials**, for example an identifier (ID) and password (PW), are shared with the authentication authority by the user. Depending on the type of credentials, the user can simply remember the credentials (for example, a user ID and password) or safeguard the credentials in some other way (for example, by storing them on a smart card). Biometric credentials are based upon one of the user's physical or behavioral traits.

   All entities that are members of or participate in an authentication authority's kingdom share a set of credentials with the authentication authority. This is also true for resource servers that are joined to the authentication authority's kingdom. In Figure 5.1, the resource server shares an ID and password with the authentication authority.

- **Credential Database** is where an authentication authority stores a secured copy of user and machine credentials. An authentication authority needs a credential database to validate the credentials that are provided by users and machines during the authentication process. Popular credential databases are LDAP-accessible directories.

- **Authentication Token** is a proof of authentication used during subsequent accesses to other resources in an authentication authority's kingdom. An authentication token is issued by an authentication authority to a user or machine after successful authentication.

During a typical authentication process (like the one illustrated in Figure 5.1), a user submits his or her credentials (for example, a user ID and a password) or the result of a cryptographic operation involving his or her credentials to the authentication authority. The authentication authority then validates the credentials using the data stored in its credential database. If the credentials supplied by the user and the ones stored in the database match, or if the result of a cryptographic operation on the credentials stored in the database equals the information supplied by the user, the user's identity is considered authentic. Consequently, the user is given or denied access to the authentication authority's kingdom. To prove that the user has been authenticated, the authentication authority will issue a cryptographic authentication token to the user. This authentication token is used as proof of authentication in subsequent accesses to other resources in the authentication authority's kingdom, for example a file server.

5.1.2 Qualifying Authentication

The security quality of an authentication infrastructure largely depends on the following two factors: the authentication protocol and the authentication method.

From an authentication protocol point of view, it is always better to use a proven authentication protocol based on an open security standard instead of a proprietary authentication protocol. Open standards tend to be better tested—tested by a larger community of vendor-neutral people. Open standards are typically also supported on different platforms. Proprietary protocols are mostly bound to a single platform.

A well known example of a proven open authentication protocol is the Kerberos protocol. An example of a proprietary protocol is Microsoft's NTLM (NT LAN Manager) authentication protocol. Table 5.1 gives an overview of common authentication protocols used in IT today. This list is not exhaustive.

The quality of the authentication method mainly depends on the number of factors (or credentials) it considers when authenticating a user. One of the most used authentication methods—user ID and password—is a

Table 5.1   *Common I.T. Authentication Protocols*

Authentication Protocol	Comment and References
Basic Authentication	Basic authentication is the authentication protocol defined in the HTTP standard. It uses a base64 user ID-password authentication exchange.
Digest Authentication	Digest authentication is another HTTP-based authentication protocol. Digest uses a challenge-response–based protocol. As with basic authentication, the credentials are user ID-password based. Unlike basic authentication, the credentials are not sent across the network.
SSL/TLS	SSL stands for Secure Sockets Layer; TLS stands for Transport Layer Security. TLS is the follow-up protocol to SSL that has been standardized by the IETF. SSL/TLS operates on the OSI Transport layer and uses certificates to authenticate both the client- and server-sides. It can be used to add strong authentication to SMTP, HTTP, NNTP, and other application-level protocols.
Kerberos	Defined in RFC 1510. Kerberos is the default authentication protocol of Microsoft Windows 2000, Windows Server 2003, and R2.
NTLM	Proprietary authentication protocol developed by Microsoft. NTLM is the default authentication protocol of Microsoft Windows NT4.

one-factor authentication method. It uses a single factor—knowledge—to authenticate a user.

Multifactor authentication methods authenticate a user based on multiple factors. That is why they offer higher security quality than single-factor authentication methods. A good example of a multifactor authentication system is a smart card: It combines possession (of the card) and knowledge (of the card's PIN, or personal identification number). Table 5.2 gives an overview of different authentication methods and the number of authentication factors they support.

In Chapter 2 of this book, we discussed password-based credentials as a means to authenticate users against a Windows authentication authority. You can also provide stronger authentication methods to your Windows users. Table 5.3 shows some of the stronger and/or multifactor authentication solutions available for Windows (this is a nonexhaustive list).

The number of authentication factors is not the only quality-related element of an authentication method. Much also depends on how the authentication method is implemented and how applications are using the authentication method. For example, a fingerprint-based authentication

Table 5.2   *Overview of Authentication Methods and their Authentication Factors*

Authentication Factor	Authentication Method						
	Password	PIN	Smart Card	Token	Biometrics	Biometrics and Smart Card	Dial-Back
Knowledge	X	X	X	X		X	
Possession			X	X		X	
Biometric Data					X	X	
Location							X

Table 5.3   *Strong and Multifactor Authentication Options for Windows*

Smart card (Knowledge and possession)

    Built-in support with Windows 2000 and later OSs

    (More details are available in Chapter 6 of this book and Chapter 10 in *Advanced Microsoft Windows Security Services* (part 2 of this series)

    HP Smart Card Security for HP ProtectTools

    (http://h18004.www1.hp.com/products/security/protecttools_smartcard.html)

Security token (Knowledge and possession)

    RSA Security SecurID

    (www.rsasecurity.com/node.asp?id=1157)

Fingerprint (Biometric data)

    Identix Biologon

    (www.identix.com/products/pro_info_biologon.html)

Iris scan (Biometric data)

    Iridian Technologies Iris Recognition

    (www.iridiantechnologies.com)

Facial Scan (Biometric data)

    Biovisec Nemesis

    (www.biovisec.com)

solution will not bring much extra security if the fingerprint image is sent in the clear to an authentication server after it has been recorded by a biometric device on the client.

Many IT environments require that the authentication infrastructure support multiple authentication methods and protocols. This requirement may be necessary because the environment supports internal and external users who are using a variety of methods and protocols to access resources. Another reason why different authentication methods and protocols may be needed is because resources have different business value or contain more sensitive information. Access to confidential information, for example, may require a stronger authentication method than access to information published on the corporate Internet Web site. In some authentication infrastructures, this feature is known as graded authentication. This means that the resources and information a user is allowed to access will vary depending on the strength of the authentication protocol and method the user used to authenticate. An example of a product providing this kind of functionality is Novell's Modular Authentication Service (NMAS; see more information at www.novell.com/products/nmas/overview.html).

5.2   Windows Authentication Basics

In the two following sections we will discuss the basics of Windows authentication. These include Windows authentication concepts and an overview of the Windows authentication architecture.

Windows does not always require user authentication before giving a user or process access to Windows resources:

- Remember from Chapter 2 (section 2.4) that Windows user accounts can be configured to not require a password.

- Even though anonymous access to Windows resources has been locked down considerably in Windows Server 2003, it is still possible to allow it for certain resources. Anonymous access will be discussed in more detail in Section 5.5 of this chapter.

5.2.1   Concepts

The following paragraphs discuss common Windows authentication concepts: interactive and noninteractive logon, Windows security principals, authentication authorities, and protocols.

Interactive and Noninteractive Logon

In Windows a user can start an interactive authentication or logon process in different ways:

- By pressing the CTRL+ALT+DEL key sequence. This key sequence is known as the Secure Attention Sequence (SAS), and this method of starting an authentication process is also referred to by Microsoft as "secure logon" or "classic logon." The SAS guarantees that the authentic Windows logon dialog box appears. It ensures that a user entering his password is communicating with the OS by means of a trusted path and not with a program that mimics a logon prompt to retrieve password information. This interactive logon option is available on both standalone and domain-joined machines.

- By entering a user account and password in the classic logon dialog box if the CTRL+ALT+DEL key sequence is not required for calling the classic logon dialog box. CTRL+ALT+DEL can be disabled for calling the classic logon dialog box both on domain-joined and standalone machines. For domain-joined machines you must enable the "Interactive Logon: Do not require CTRL+ALT+DEL" GPO security option or create the following registry key and set it to value 1:

  HKEY_LOCAL_MACHINE\Software\Microsoft\Windows NT\ CurrentVersion\Winlogon\DisableCAD (REG_DWORD)

  This registry key can also be used on standalone machines. We don't recommend that you disable CTRL+ALT+DEL in enterprise environments for the reason mentioned in the previous bullet.

- By clicking a user account on the Welcome screen. This option is only available on Windows XP and can only be used to log on locally. For more information on the advantages and disadvantages of using the Welcome Screen for logging on to Windows, read the sidenote titled "Evaluating the Welcome Screen for Logging on to Windows?" or, if you want the brief version, we recommend not using the Welcome screen for logging on to standalone Windows XP machines in enterprise environments.

- By requesting a secondary logon session using the RunAs command line utility, or by using Fast User Switching (FUS).

- By starting a connection to another machine using Terminal Services or Remote Desktop. Microsoft refers to these two logon types as "remote" interactive logon.

All of the above actions tell Windows that a user wants to authenticate either to a local machine or to a domain. Following these actions, Windows will prompt the user for a set of authentication credentials. Because of this interaction between the OS (requesting credentials) and the user (providing credentials), Microsoft calls this method of starting an authentication process "interactive" logon. Interactive logon is also referred to as "local logon." A successful interactive logon results in a logon session.

There are interactive logon scenarios where the interaction between the user and the authentication server remains hidden. For example, you can save the username and password that you use to connect to a remote desktop computer object so you don't have to retype it. Also, Windows allows you to automate the logon process at system startup by storing a username and password in the registry. This feature is known as autologon. In Windows XP, autologon can be enabled from the GUI: simply select the "Users must enter a user name and password to use this computer" checkbox in the Windows XP User Accounts dialog box. To call the Windows XP User Accounts dialog box from the command line, type: control userpasswords2. See the following URL to learn how you can enable autologon in the system registry: http://support.microsoft.com/?id=324737.

If, during a logon session, a user wants to access a resource located on another machine (for example, a shared folder on a member server in a domain), another authentication process will be started. If this process can leverage previously established credentials, this authentication process is referred to as a "noninteractive logon" or "network logon". A valid noninteractive logon results in a network logon session. This authentication process is called noninteractive because it does not require interaction between the user and the OS. The client OS will automatically supply previously established credentials to the authenticating server. Examples of previously established credentials that can be leveraged for noninteractive authentication are cached credentials (that Windows caches on the client-side after a successful interactive domain logon) and Kerberos tickets (that Windows caches on the client-side after a successful Kerberos authentication sequence).

Windows Security Principals, Authentication Authorities, and Protocols

Entities that authenticate to a Windows system are referred to as security principals. A Windows security principal is uniquely identified by its security identifier (SID). Typical Windows security principals are users and

Evaluating the Welcome Screen for Logging on to Windows?

The Welcome screen allows users to start a Windows logon process simply by clicking their user account on the Welcome screen. The Welcome screen is only available on standalone Windows XP machines. In enterprise environments, we recommend that you disable the Welcome screen for logging on to Windows—even on standalone machines. The main security objection against using the Welcome screen to log on to Windows is that it enables users to start a logon process without using the Secure Attention Sequence (CTRL+ALT+DEL). Remember that the SAS guarantees that the authentic Windows logon dialog box appears. It ensures that a user is communicating with the OS by means of a trusted path when entering his password and not with a program that mimics a logon prompt to retrieve password information. Note that a user can always evoke the classic Windows logon dialog box from the Welcome Screen by pressing CTRL+ALT+DEL twice.

Two other security disadvantages of using the Welcome screen are that it can display user account names and give password hints. But these two problems can be remedied: you can hide user accounts from the welcome screen, and you can not use password hints. All of the above issues are good examples of how ease of use can result in bad security.

There are two ways to hide accounts from the Windows XP Welcome screen:

- Disable the account: you can do this in the account properties that are accessible from the Local Users and Groups (LUG) MMC snap-in

- Make the following registry change: open the HKEY_LOCAL_MACHINE\Software\ Microsoft\Windows NT\CurrentVersion\Winlogon\SpecialAccounts\UserList registry folder, create a new REG_DWORD value, set its name to the username of the account you want to hide and leave its value to 0.

There are two ways to enforce the use of secure logon (CTRL+ALT+DEL) for logging on to Windows on standalone Windows XP machines:

- Using the "Change the way users log on or off" option in the Windows XP User Accounts Control Panel applet: uncheck the "Use the Welcome screen" option.

- By creating the LogonType registry key and setting it to value 0. This key is located in the HKEY_LOCAL_MACHINE\Software\Microsoft\Windows\CurrentVersion\ Policies\System registry container.

The best solution is joining the standalone machines to a Windows domain. On domain-joined machines users must by default always use CTRL+ALT+DEL and the classic Windows logon dialog box to log on interactively to the domain. In that case, we also recommend that you do not give your users local accounts, but only domain accounts (see also Chapter 2 for a discussion on this).

computers. For more information on the security principal and SID concepts, I refer to Chapter 2 of this book. In what follows, we will use the terms "user" and "computer" to refer to a security principal.

To prove his identity during the authentication process, a user provides credentials to a Windows authentication authority. Examples of credentials are a user's account name and password. If the operating system accepts password-based credentials for authenticating a user, the simple fact that this user knows his account name and associated password is regarded by the operating system as a proof of the user's identity. Password credentials and how to use them were explained in Chapter 2.

The authentication authority used during a Windows authentication sequence differs depending on what a Windows user is logging on to. If a user logs on locally to a machine, the authentication authority is the Local Security Authority (LSA) on the machine itself. If a user logs on to a domain, authentication is performed against the LSA of a domain controller. To validate a user's identity, the authentication authority needs a secure copy of a user's credentials. The latter are stored in the authentication authority's credential database. Once more, for more information on local and domain security authorities and their security databases, I refer to Chapter 2.

In Windows 2000-, Windows Server 2003-, R2-, and Windows XP-centric environments, the authentication process can use different authentication protocols—for example, the different flavors of the NTLM (NT LAN Manager) protocol, or Kerberos. The following sections explain how these authentication protocols fit in the Windows authentication architecture.

5.2.2 Authentication Architecture

From its early days, one of the most important design principles of NT has been modularity. NT's authentication architecture is an excellent example of a modular architecture that is built on different abstraction layers.

In Windows Server 2003 and R2, the authentication architecture is basically the same as the one used in Windows 2000. Ninety percent of the changes that Microsoft incorporated in Windows Server 2003 can be described as plugging in supplementary security modules.

The following sections discuss the authentication architectures for interactive (local) and noninteractive (network) logon.

Architecture for Interactive Authentication

The architecture for interactive authentication is illustrated in Figure 5.2. In this section, we will use the most commonly used and most secure way of logging on interactively to Windows—using the CTRL-ALT-DEL key sequence—to explain the interactive authentication architecture. In that case, an interactive logon sequence starts whenever a user initiates a SAS key sequence to log on to the local machine or to a domain. The SAS sequence makes the Winlogon service call the GINA module. Winlogon is the OS component that manages security-related user interactions, including interactive authentication. GINA (Graphical Identification and Authentication) is the component responsible for displaying the logon interface, extracting the user's credentials, and passing them to the Local Security Authority (LSA). The sidenote on "Controlling Interactive Logon using Group Policy Object Settings" contains some guidelines on how you can control interactive logon in an Active Directory (AD) environment.

The LSA is an OS user mode component that acts as the local authentication authority. As explained in Chapter 2, the LSA also has other security functions. To verify user credentials, the LSA interacts with authentication

Figure 5.2
*Interactive
authentication
architecture.*

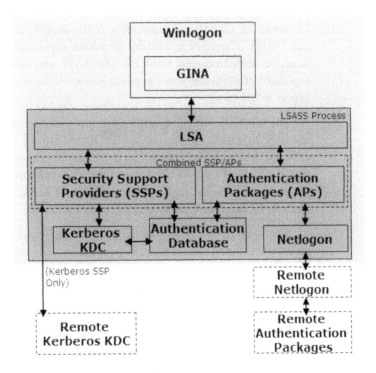

packages (APs) and security support providers (SSPs). The APs and SSPs, in their turn, call on authentication databases for credential verification. The difference between APs and SSPs will be explained below. The LSA, SSPs, APs, authentication database, and a set of related processes (Kerberos KDC, authentication databases (SAM or AD), Netlogon) are all hosted inside the lsass.exe process (as Figure 5.2 shows).

The authentication database stores secured copies of the credentials that are needed during the authentication process.

- NT4 machines, Windows XP, and Windows 2000 Professional work-stations, and Windows 2000, Windows Server 2003, and R2 member servers store credentials in the SAM database. The SAM database contains local user accounts that can be used to log on locally to a machine.

- A Windows 2000, Windows Server 2003, and R2 domain controller stores credentials in the Active Directory. The AD database contains domain user accounts that can be used to log on to a Windows domain.

Both authentication packages (APs) and security support providers (SSPs) are software packages that implement an authentication protocol. Unlike an AP, an SSP can interface with the security support provider inter-face (SSPI). The SSPI is used by Windows applications to provide nonin-teractive authentication services. The SSPI and the available SSPs are explained in more detail in the next section on the noninteractive authenti-cation architecture.

You can find out what authentication packages are available on your machine by checking the content of the following registry key: HKEY_ LOCAL_MACHINE\System\CurrentControlSet\Control\Lsa\Authentica-tion Packages. To get an overview of the SSPs supported on your machine, go to the following registry key: HKEY_LOCAL_MACHINE\System\ Current-ControlSet\Control\Lsa\Security Packages.

Windows 2000, Windows XP, Windows Server 2003, and R2 also include combined authentication package/security support provider pack-ages; these are referred to as SSP/AP packages. In Figure 5.2, a combined SSP/AP package is indicated using the dashed line. These combined pack-ages can be used both for interactive and noninteractive logon. In other words, the LSA can leverage them for interactive logon, while applications can leverage them for noninteractive logon.

The Windows Kerberos and MSV1_0 packages are examples of com-bined SSP/AP packages. The MSV1_0 package supports the NTLM version

1 and 2 authentication protocols; the different NTLM flavors will be discussed in more detail later in this chapter. The MSV1_0 authentication package also includes the logic for NTLM pass-through authentication. NTLM pass-through authentication occurs if there is no domain authentication database available locally to validate a user's NTLM credentials.

To ease the reading we will refer to APs, SSPs, and combined SSP/AP packages as "authentication packages" for the rest of this section.

The MSV1_0 authentication package is available on NT4, Windows 2000, Windows XP, Windows Server 2003, and R2 installations. The MSV1_0 logic can support the following interactive logon types:

- Local logon on standalone machines

- Local logon on domain-joined workstations or member servers

- Domain logon using cached credentials on pre-Windows 2000 computers; this feature, discussed in more detail in Section 5.6, allows users to log on with their domain credentials when no domain controller is available

- Domain logon using the NTLM authentication protocol

The Kerberos authentication package is available on Windows 2000, Windows XP, Windows Server 2003, and R2 installations. The Kerberos authentication package contains the logic to support the following interactive logon types:

- Domain logon using cached credentials on Windows 2000 and later computers

- Domain logon using the Kerberos authentication protocol

The entities the MSV1_0 and Kerberos authentication packages interact with to verify user credentials differ depending on the logon type (local versus domain logon). The easiest case is when a user logs on locally to a standalone machine, or a domain-joined workstation or member server. In that case, the MSV1_0 authentication package will always validate the user credentials against the local SAM authentication database independently of the Windows version used.

Domain logon is a bit more complicated:

- When a user logs on to a domain from an NT4 or earlier DC, the MSV1_0 authentication package will verify the user's credentials against the local SAM.

- When a user logs on to the domain from an NT4 or earlier workstation or member server, the local MSV1_0 authentication package will call on the local Netlogon service. This one will set up a secure channel with the Netlogon service of a DC. The DC's Netlogon service will then call on the DC's MSV1_0 authentication package to verify the user credentials against the DC's AD or SAM authentication database. The Netlogon service is the service responsible for setting up secure channels between Windows workstations, member servers, and DCs—secure channels were covered in Chapter 2.

- When a user logs on to the domain from a Windows 2000 or later DC, the local Kerberos authentication package will call on the local KDC service (each Windows 2000 or later DC hosts a KDC service) that will validate the user credentials against the local AD authentication database.

- When a user logs on to the domain from a Windows 2000 or later workstation or member server, the local Kerberos authentication package will call on a DC's KDC service. The KDC service will then validate the user credentials against the DC's AD authentication database.

Table 5.4 lists the GPO settings you can use to control interactive logon in a Windows AD environment and their recommended values. All settings are located in the Computer Configuration\Windows Settings\Security Settings\Local Policies\Security Options GPO container.

Table 5.4   *Interactive Logon-Related GPO Settings*

GPO Setting	Recommended Value	Meaning
Interactive logon: Do not display last user name	Enabled	Hides last username used for logon from the logon dialog box.
Interactive logon: Do not require CTRL+ALT+DEL	Disabled	Disables the use of CTRL+ALT+DEL for calling the classic Windows logon dialog box.
Interactive logon: Message text for users attempting to log on	Enter a custom message for your environment	Used to set message in dialog box that Windows displays when users use the SAS sequence.
Interactive logon: Message title for users attempting to log on	Enter a custom title for your environment	Used to set title of dialog box that Windows displays when users use the SAS sequence.

───────▶

Table 5.4   *Interactive Logon-Related GPO Settings (continued)*

GPO Setting	Recommended Value	Meaning
Interactive logon: Number of previous logons to cache (in case domain controller is not available)	Enable on laptops and desktops, disable on machines that don't need it (DCs, member servers)	Enables credential caching and sets number of credentials to cache; see also Section 5.6.
Interactive logon: Prompt user to change password before expiration	Enable—14 days	Informs user that his/her password is about to expire and must be changed; allows user to set the number of days before the actual password expiry when he/she will be informed.
Interactive logon: Require Domain Controller authentication to unlock workstation	Enable	Can be used to ensure that user credentials are validated against a DC when user unlocks Windows desktop. See also Section 2.2.5 (Chapter 2).
Interactive logon: Require smart card	Depends on organization's security requirements	Enforces use of smart card for Windows logon. See also Chapter 6 of this book.
Interactive logon: Smart card removal behavior	Depends on organization's security requirements	Determines smart card removal from smart card reader behavior. Possible settings are No action, Lock workstation, and Force Logoff. See also Chapter 6.

Architecture for Noninteractive Authentication

Figure 5.3 provides a simplified overview of the noninteractive authentication architecture as it is used in distributed Windows application environments consisting of a client and a server component. Good examples of distributed applications are an Outlook mail client accessing a mailbox on an Exchange messaging server, or simply a Windows client accessing a shared folder on a Windows file server.

A noninteractive logon can only occur after a successful interactive logon sequence. As opposed to an interactive logon, a noninteractive logon is invoked by an application—not by the Winlogon process. Also, a noninteractive logon does not prompt the user for credentials but instead leverages previously established Windows credentials.

The architecture for Windows noninteractive authentication introduces two new concepts: the security support provider interface (SSPI) and security support providers (SSPs).

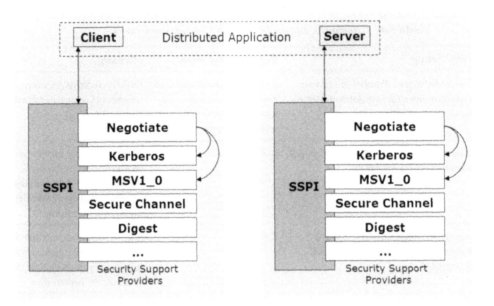

Figure 5.3   *Noninteractive authentication architecture.*

The SSPI is an application programming interface (API) that sits between applications and authentication protocols. It has two important functions:

1.   Its primary function is to abstract the commonalities of different authentication protocols and to hide their implementation details. For example, Kerberos and NTLM both use the concept of a master key. NTLM, however, uses a challenge-response mechanism, while Kerberos relies on a ticketing system to authenticate users.

2.   Abstract applications from authentication protocols. Every authentication protocol should be available to each application. Also, the implementation of an authentication protocol should not contain any application–specific code.

The SSPI is the Microsoft implementation of the generic security service application programming interface (GSS-API), which is defined in Request For Comments (RFCs) 2743 and 2744.

As was explained earlier, an SSP is a software module that implements an authentication protocol. SSPs can be plugged into the SSPI. Out-of-the-box Windows Server 2003 includes the following SSPs (as illustrated in Figure 5.3): Negotiate, MSV1_0 (supporting NTLM versions 1 and 2),

Kerberos, SChannel (supporting the SSL and TLS protocols), and Digest Authentication.[1] Software vendors can also implement their own SSPs to support other authentication protocols. To get an overview of the SSPs supported on your machine, see the following registry key: HKEY_LOCAL_ MACHINE\System\Current-ControlSet\Control\Lsa\Security Packages.

NTLM is the default authentication protocol of NT4; it is explained in more detail later in this chapter. Kerberos is explained in Chapter 6. Digest Authentication and the SSL/TLS protocols, two Web authentication protocols, are explained in more detail in Chapter 7.

The Negotiate SSP is a special SSP; it does not implement authentication protocol logic, but rather logic that enables distributed applications to use the strongest authentication protocol. When an application calls the Negotiate SSP, it basically instructs it to select the strongest authentication protocol possible. Depending on the authentication parameters provided by the application, the Negotiate SSP can either select the MSV1_0 (implementing NTLM version 1 and 2) or Kerberos SSP. The Negotiate SSP's first choice for noninteractive authentication is always the Kerberos protocol. It will fall back to NTLM if no service principal name (SPN), user principal name (UPN), or NetBIOS name is provided as the identifier for the target application of the non-interactive logon.

The Negotiate package is a Microsoft implementation of the SPNEGO (Simple and Protected GSS-API Negotiation Mechanism) mechanism, as specified in RFC 2478.

A detail that Figure 5.3 does not show is that most SSPs rely on cryptographic service providers (CSPs). CSPs are modules that provide basic cryptographic functions. For example: encryption using the data encryption standard (DES), signing using RSA, or hashing using Message Digest 4 (MD4). SSPs can call on different CSPs thanks to another abstraction layer that Microsoft introduced in NT4: the CryptoAPI (or CAPI). We will return to CAPI in Chapter 6 in *Advanced Microsoft Windows Security Services* (part 2 of this series).

An excellent tool to get a deeper understanding of how the SSPI works is the SSPI workbench tool, illustrated in Figure 5.4. SSPI workbench is written by Keith Brown and can be downloaded for free from www.develop.com/technology/default.aspx.

---

1. The Digest SSP was not available in Windows 2000. In Windows 2000, support for Digest authentication was provided using a special IIS-level software package.

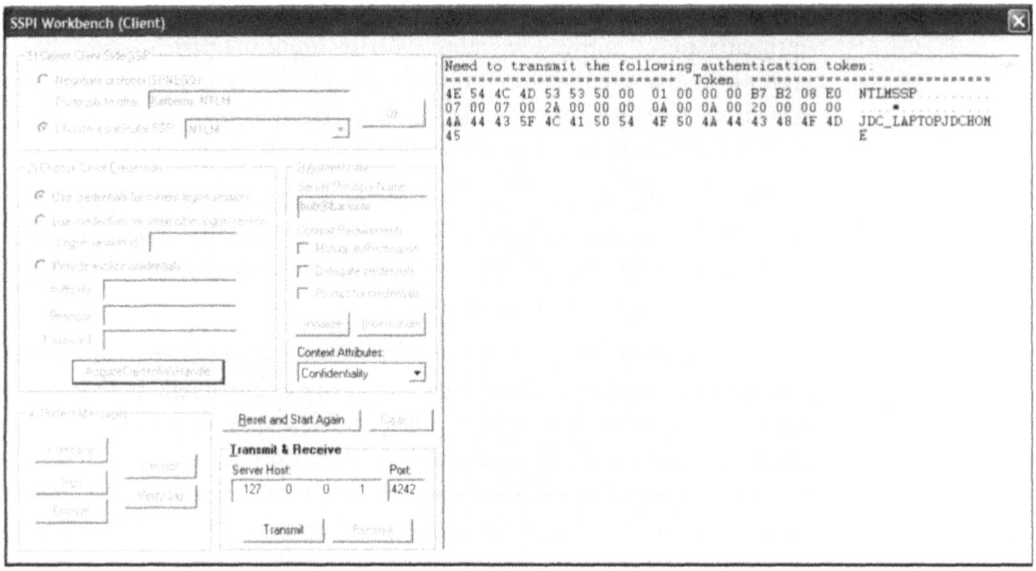

Figure 5.4   *Using SSPI workbench.*

5.2.3   Authentication in the Machine Startup and User Logon Sequences

The following sections examine authentication's place in the Windows machine startup and user logon sequences. The following sections show that authentication is performed more than once during machine startup. Also, they discuss what else happens during machine startup and user logon besides user and machine authentication.

Machine Startup

Figure 5.5 shows the different processes that occur during a Windows machine startup. The machine runs Windows XP and is a member of a Windows 2000, Windows Server 2003, or R2 domain. The different processes are listed below:

1. **Network Interface Initialization:** The Windows client starts up and the network interface is initialized. If the machine is not configured with static IP configuration information, the machine will run through the Dynamic Host Configuration Protocol (DHCP) configuration process to obtain its IP configuration.

Figure 5.5
Machine startup.

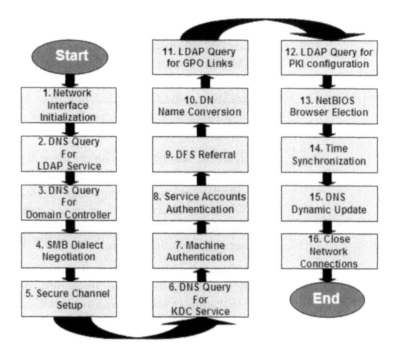

2.   **DNS Query for LDAP Service:** Once the client's network inter-
     face has been configured and the network protocol stack initial-
     ized, the machine will perform a site discovery process to find a
     DC in an AD site that is as close as possible to the machine.[2] This
     AD site discovery process first launches a generic DNS query for
     an LDAP service (read domain controller) to one of the machine's
     configured DNS servers. The DNS query will look for an _ldap._
     tcp. dc._msdcs.<domain> service (SRV) record. This query will
     return a list of IP addresses of all DCs in the domain. The client
     then pings these DCs. The first DC to reply will use the client's
     IP address and check it against its subnet configuration in AD.
     This enables the DC to determine the name of the closest site for
     the client. The DC can then inform the client about its AD site.
     The client safeguards the site information for subsequent queries
     in the following registry location: HKEY_LOCAL_MACHINE\
     System\CurrentControlSet\Services\NetLogon\Parameters\
     DynamicSiteName.

---

2.   This assumes that the machine has not yet cached its AD site information; in that case, the machine would directly request
     a DC in its AD site.

3.   **DNS Query for Domain Controller**: When a generic LDAP service (read domain controller) has been located and the machine's AD site is known, the client will launch a DNS query for a domain controller belonging to the machine's site and definition domain.[3] The DNS query will now look for an _ldap._tcp.<sitename>._sites.dc._msdcs.<domain> SRV record. This query returns a DC in the machine's site that will be used for the rest of the authentication process.

4.   **SMB Dialect Negotiation**: The client will then negotiate an SMB dialect with the domain controller. The Server Message Block (SMB) protocol is an important file-sharing protocol used in all Windows versions. Later on in the startup, the client will use SMB to download configuration information (including GPO settings) from the domain controller.

5.   **Secure Channel Setup**: Next, the client will set up a secure channel with the domain controller. To do this, the client's Netlogon service will connect to the domain controller's Netlogon service. The secure channel is needed to securely send confidential information, such as authentication data, from the client to the domain controller. Secure channels were discussed in Chapter 3.

6.   **DNS Query for KDC Service**: Once the secure channel has been set up, the client will launch another DNS query to its DNS server to find an authentication server (in Windows 2000 and later, this is a domain controller running a KDC service). The DNS query will look for a _kerberos._tcp.<sitename>._sites.dc._msdcs.<domain> SRV record. The AD site name used in this SRV record depends on the one that was registered on the machine, as determined in step 2.

7.   **Machine Authentication**: The machine authenticates to the DC using the Kerberos authentication protocol.

8.   **Service Accounts Authentication**: Kerberos authentication takes place for all services that are not running in the security contexts of the local system, network service or local service accounts.

9.   **DFS Referral**: To prepare the processing of group policy objects (GPOs), the client must now determine the location of the domain's SYSVOL share. This share stores the various group policy templates in the SYSVOL folder of each DC. The

---

3.   The machine's definition domain is the domain where the machine account is defined.

domain's SYSVOL share is implemented as a domain-based distributed file system (DFS) root that can be accessed using the following share name: \\<domain-dns-name>\SYSVOL. When connecting to this DFS root, the DFS referral process will return a list of DCs that host the SYSVOL share to the client using the SMB protocol. This list contains all DCs in the domain, and the DCs of the client's proper AD site are listed at the top of the list. In Windows 2000, any DCs outside the client's site are listed in a random order. In Windows Server 2003, the DCs from other sites are ordered by their site-link costs relative to the client's site. The client will use the first DC on this list to connect to the SYSVOL share and read group policy related data. This is typically the DC that the client used for authentication.

10.   **DN Name Conversion**: The client launches an RPC call to the domain controller to convert its name into a distinguished name (DN).

11.   **LDAP Query for GPO Links**: Using the DN, the client performs an LDAP query against its DC to find out the group policies applicable to the client. The group policy information is downloaded from the DC determined in step 9 using the SMB protocol.

12.   **LDAP Query for PKI Configuration**: The client then launches another LDAP query to the domain controller to find out public key infrastructure (PKI) configuration information (for example, what are the Enterprise CAs available in the forest?).

13.   **NetBIOS Browser Election**: If NetBIOS is enabled, the client will start a NetBIOS browser election process.

14.   **Time Synchronization**: The client performs time synchronization with its domain controller using the simple network time protocol (SNTP).

15.   **DNS Dynamic Update**: Finally—if dynamic DNS updates are allowed—the client will launch a DNS query for a start of authority (SOA) DNS server of its DNS domain. The client will then perform a dynamic update of its DNS records on the DNS server returned in the SOA query.

16.   **Close Network Connections**: The client startup is completed by closing down the connections with the domain controller.

User Logon

Once a machine has been started, a user can log on to it interactively. Figure 5.6 shows the different processes that occur during a regular Windows 2000, Windows Server 2003, or R2 domain user logon process from a Windows XP workstation. The different processes are listed below:

1.   **CTRL-ALT-DEL**: The user presses CTRL-ALT-DEL, fills in a set of credentials (for example: a user account and password), and clicks OK or Enter.

2.   **DNS Query for Domain Controller**: The logon process launches a DNS query for a domain controller belonging to the user's definition domain. If the user account and the machine account of the machine the user logs on to are defined in different domains (a typical multidomain scenario) the discovery of a DC in the user's definition domain can be a time-consuming process.

3.   **User Authentication**: The user authenticates to the DC in the user's definition domain using the Kerberos authentication protocol.

4.   **DN Name Conversion**: The machine launches an RPC call to the domain controller to convert the user name to a DN.

5.   **LDAP Query for GPO Links**: Using the DN of the user, the logon process performs an LDAP query against its DC to find out the group policies applicable to the user. The user group policy information is downloaded using the SMB protocol.

6.   **Close Network Connections**: The user logon is completed by closing down the connections with the domain controller.

Figure 5.6
User logon.

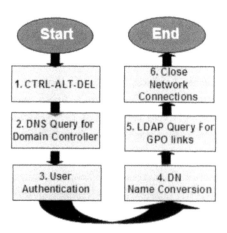

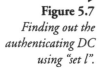

Figure 5.7
Finding out the authenticating DC using "set l".

An Easy Way to Find a User's Authenticating Domain Controller

The easiest way to find out the authenticating DC is to check the content of the environment variables available in a user's logon session. To do so, open a command prompt window, then type "set l". This brings up all environment variables starting with an l (as illustrated in Figure 5.7). The user's authenticating DC is listed on the LOGONSERVER= line.

5.3 Logon Rights

The Windows access control subsystem—the system that determines which user can access which resources and how they can access these resources—is rooted on the concepts of permissions and user rights. Permissions are related to objects: examples include permission to print a file, permission to create folders, permission to add a user object to Active Directory, and so on. User rights are related to a Windows system as a whole: examples are the user right to log on to a Windows system or the user right to change the system clock. Permissions will be explained in more detail in Chapters 10 and 11.

Windows user rights can also be split in two categories: logon rights and user privileges. Logon rights control which user accounts can log on to a Windows computer and how a user account can log on to a system. User privileges are used to control access to system resources and system-related operations. Examples of user privileges are "Change the System Time" and "Shut down the System." User privileges are covered in more detail in Chapters 10 and 11; logon rights are explained below.

In Windows XP and Windows Server 2003, Microsoft defined ten different logon rights. They can be used to control different types of local- and domain-level user authentication attempts to Windows systems. Logon rights also cover user authentication actions like logging on to a Windows-rooted FTP service. To enable a user account to logon to a Windows-rooted FTP service, you must give it the "Log On Locally" right on the Windows machine that is hosting the FTP service.

The deny logon rights were introduced in Windows 2000 and are thus not available in NT4 and earlier OS versions. The Terminal Services-related logon rights are supported in Windows Server 2003, Windows XP, and Windows 2000 Service Pack 2 and later OS versions.

The Windows logon rights are explained in the next paragraphs and listed in Table 5.5. The table also shows the corresponding API name for each logon right and identifies the built-in groups for which the logon rights are assigned by default on a domain controller, a member server, and

Table 5.5   *Windows Logon Rights and Default Assignments*

Logon Right (Internal System Name)	Default on Standalone Machines and Member Servers (XP & Windows Server 2003)	Default on Domain Controllers (Windows Server 2003)
Log on locally (SeInteractiveLogonRight)	Administrators, Power Users, Backup Operators, Users, Guest	Administrators, Server Operators, Account Operators, Print Operators, Backup Operators
Access this computer from the network (SeNetworkLogonRight)	Administrators, Power Users, Backup Operators, Users, Everyone	Administrators, Authenticated Users, Everyone
Log on as a batch job (SeBatchLogonRight)	Support_xxxxx	—
Log on as a service (SeServiceLogonRight)	Network Service	Network Service
Allow logon through Terminal Services (SeRemoteInteractiveLogonRight)	Administrators, Remote Desktop Users	—
Deny logon locally (SeDenyInteractiveLogonRight)	Guest, Support_xxxxx	—
Deny access to this computer from the network (SeDenyNetworkLogonRight)	Support_xxxxx	—
Deny logon as a batch job (SeDenyBatchLogonRight)	—	—
Deny logon as a service (SeDenyServiceLogonRight)	—	—
Deny logon through Terminal Services (SeDenyRemoteInteractiveLogonRight)	—	—

a standalone machine. The API names are the internal names Windows uses to refer to logon rights. You may need them when using some of the command line tools that will be outlined in the section on configuring user logon rights.

- The "Log on locally" logon right allows a user to log on to Windows from a computer's keyboard by using CTRL+ALT+DEL or the Welcome screen, or by starting a secondary logon session using, for example, the RunAs command line utility. In Windows, this way of logging on is referred to as local or interactive logon. In Windows 2000, this logon right was also required to log on using Terminal Services or Remote Desktop. Another very efficient mechanism to restrict a user's interactive logon rights is to restrict the machines to which a user can log on interactively—how to set this up is explained in the sidenote on "Restricting Interactive Logon to Windows Machines."

- The "Access this computer from the network" logon right allows a user to connect to a computer over the network. All users who want to remotely connect to a system in order to access a file, folder, application, or any other resource must have this right. In Windows, this way of logging on is referred to as network or noninteractive logon.

- The "Log on as a batch job" logon right allows a user to log on using a batch-queue facility. The Windows Scheduled Tasks service and certain other services use this right for logging on users. Scheduled Tasks automatically grants this right as needed—this is, when a scheduled task is about to be executed.

- The "Log on as a service" logon right allows a user to log on as a service. This right allows services to run on Windows systems in the background. On all Windows XP and Windows Server 2003 machines, this right is granted by default to the network service account. If you're using another special account to run a service, you must assign it this right explicitly. The computer management MMC will grant this right automatically if the service account is configured via the UI.

- The "Allow logon through Terminal Services" logon right controls which users have the right to log on using a Terminal Services or Remote Desktop.

- "Deny log on locally" denies a user the ability to log on at the computer's console using CTRL+ALT+DEL or the Welcome screen or by starting a secondary logon session. It has precedence over the "Log on locally" right.

- "Deny access to this computer from the network" denies a user the ability to connect to the computer over the network. It has precedence over the "Access this computer from the network" right.

- "Deny log on as a service" denies a user the ability to log on as a service to establish a security context. It has precedence over the "Log on as a service" right.

- "Deny log on as a batch job" denies a user the ability to log on using a batch-queue facility. It has precedence over the "Log on as a batch job" right.

- "Deny Logon through Terminal Services" denies a user the ability to log on using Terminal Services or Remote Desktop. It has precedence over the "Log on through Terminal Services" right.

Restricting Interactive Logon to Windows Machines

AD Administrators can restrict to which domain machines a domain user can logon interactively using the AD "Log On To…" user account property. This property can be accessed from the Account tab of the user's account properties (as illustrated in Figure 5.8) in the AD Users and Computers (ADUC) MMC snap-in. To restrict the machines a user can log on to interactively, select "The following computers" radio button. You can then add machines by typing their NetBIOS name in the Computer Name field and clicking Add. AD stores these data as a comma-separated list in the user workstations user account AD attribute. The "Log On To…" domain user account property does not impact a user's capability to log on locally to a machine using a local account.

The Account tab in the ADUC's user account properties contains another feature that can be used to restrict a user's logon behavior: the Logon Hours… pushbutton allows an AD administrator to restrict the hours a user can log on to the domain. These time restrictions apply to all logon types (interactive, network, etc.) and do not impact a user's capability to logon locally to a machine using a local account.

These two domain user account restrictions also apply when a user starts a secondary logon session using, for example, the RunAs utility, or when a user logs on using a Terminal Services or Remote Desktop connection.

The Deny logon rights can be very handy in large Windows setups. For example, assume you want to give everyone, with the exception of a couple of specific accounts, the right to "Access this computer from the network." In that case, it is much easier to grant the Authenticated Users group the "Access this computer from the network" right and assign the specific accounts the "Deny access this computer from the network" right, instead of figuring out all the accounts that should have access, putting them in a special group and then giving this group "Access this computer from the network" right.

5.3.1   Managing Windows Logon Rights

Windows logon rights can be assigned and managed from the Local Security Policy tool for standalone machines and from the group policy object (GPO) MMC snap-in for both standalone and domain-joined machines. The Windows Server 2003 and Windows 2000 Resource Kits also contain

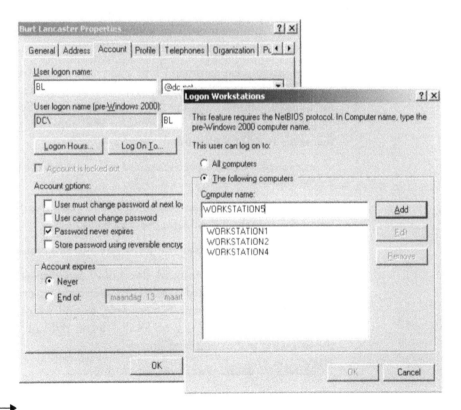

Figure 5.8   *Configuring Log On To... restrictions for an AD account.*

two command line tools that can help with managing logon rights: ntrights.exe and showpriv.exe.

You can access the Local Security Policy tool from the Administrative Tools in your Start menu. In the Local Security Policy interface, logon rights can be assigned from the Security Settings\Local Policies\User Rights Assignments container.

To access the GPO MMC snap-in, start the MMC, then load the GPO snap-in.

- For managing logon rights on standalone machines, select the Local Computer GPO object.

- For managing logon rights on domain-joined machines, select the Default Domain GPO.

- For managing logon rights on domain controllers, select the Default Domain Controllers GPO.[4]

In the GPO MMC snap-in, the logon rights can be assigned from the Computer Configuration\Windows Settings\Security Settings\Local Policies\User Rights Assignments container.

The ntrights.exe command line utility can be used to grant or revoke Windows user rights (both logon rights and privileges) to users and groups on a local or remote computer. For example, to grant ServiceAccount1 the "Logon as a service" right on computer MyComputer, you must type the following ntrights command:

```
ntrights +r SeServiceLogonRight -u ServiceAccount1 -m \\
MyComputer
```

To revoke the Everyone group's right to "Access this computer from the network," type the following at the command line:

```
ntrights -r SeNetworkLogonRight -u Everyone
```

The showpriv.exe command line utility can display which users and groups have been assigned a particular user right. It can only be used to interrogate the local system. For example, to find which users and groups have been assigned the "Log on locally" logon right on your system, type the following at the command line:

```
Showpriv SeInteractiveLogonRight
```

---

4.   We recommend that you not edit the default GPOs (such as the Default Domain and Default Domain Controllers GPOs); instead, you should add a new GPO and link it to the same AD object, then change the values in this new GPO.

5.3.2 Best Practices

To facilitate Windows access control administration, Windows supports the concept of groups. Instead of assigning permissions and rights to many individual users, it is much easier to organize these users into groups and then assign the permission and rights to the groups. The same is true for logon rights.

Another best practice is to assign user rights to domain accounts and not to local accounts. Local accounts can be used to bypass the central security policy enforced on the Windows domain level. Remember that you should always try to use a Windows domain setup, no matter how small your IT environment is.

Looking at the default logon rights assignments that are listed in Table 5.5, you may also find these assignments are not restrictive enough. We advise you to lock down the logon rights assignments as follows:

- Take away the "Log on locally" right for the Users, Power Users, and Guest groups on member servers.

- Take away the "Access this computer from the network" right for the Everyone group on both member servers and domain controllers.

5.4 NTLM-based Authentication

NTLM is a challenge/response-based authentication protocol. It is the default authentication protocol of NT 4.0 and earlier NT versions. For backward compatibility reasons, NTLM is still supported in Windows 2000, Windows XP, Windows Server 2003, and R2.

5.4.1 The Protocol

This section explains the basic operation of the NTLM version 1 authentication protocol, which is commonly referred to as NTLM. To ease the explanation, we will use the example of a user who is using Outlook XP to access his or her mailbox on an Exchange server. The Exchange server is running Exchange 2000 and is installed on a Windows 2000 member server. All machines involved are members of a Windows Server 2003 domain.

The reason we use an Outlook XP–Exchange 2000 example is because starting with Outlook 2003 and Exchange 2003, Microsoft embedded support for the Kerberos authentication protocol in its mail clients and servers.

In this example, the client, the Exchange server, and the domain controller will run through the following six authentication steps (as illustrated in Figure 5.9):

1.   The client tells the Exchange server the user wants to access his mailbox.

2.   The Exchange server sends an NTLM challenge (this is a random string) to the client.

3.   The client will then send back two authentication responses to the Exchange server:

     a. A LAN Manager (LM) response, consisting of the NTLM challenge, and the NTLM challenge DES-encrypted using a key that's derived from the LM hash of the user password

     b. An NTLM response consisting of the NTLM challenge, and the NTLM challenge DES-encrypted using a key that's derived from the NT hash of the user password

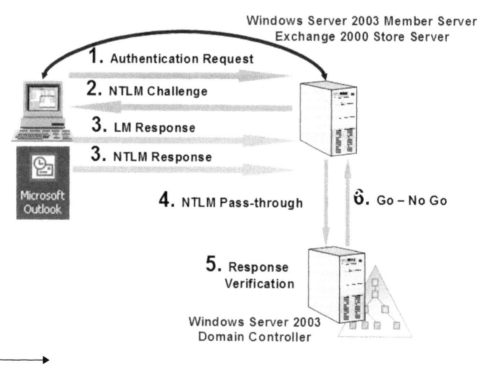

Figure 5.9   *NTLM authentication flow.*

4. Because the Exchange server is not a domain controller and does not have access to a copy of the LM and NT hashes of the user password, it will forward the LM and NTLM responses (together with the NTLM challenge) to a domain controller. The latter process is known as NTLM pass-through authentication.

5. The domain controller will then first validate the NTLM response by encrypting the NTLM challenge using a key derived from its local copy of the NT hash of the user password. If the NTLM response matches the outcome of the domain controller's calculation, the user is authenticated. If they don't match, the domain controller will validate the LM response by encrypting the LM challenge using a key derived from its local copy of the LM hash of the user password. If the LM response matches the outcome of the domain controller's calculation, the user is authenticated. If they don't match, user authentication fails.

6. The domain controller finally informs the Exchange server about the success or failure of the user authentication process.

The above exchange shows (in step 3) that the NTLM authentication protocol actually consists of two subprotocols: the NTLM and LM protocols. In the response to the server's NTLM challenge, the client replies with two messages: an NTLM and an LM response.

The NTLM exchange also shows the following NTLM weaknesses:

- The NTLM responses in step 3 are calculated using the DES symmetric cipher, which at the time of writing is no longer considered cryptographically secure. As we explained in Chapter 2, there are also tools available on the Internet (for example: ScoopLM[5]) that can sniff the NTLM challenge and response messages and extract the LM and NT hashes. The hashes can then be fed to cracking tools like LCP or John the Ripper to derive the original password.

- Another weakness is that in the NTLM authentication exchange (see mainly steps 2 and 3 above), the only real secrets are the LM and NT hashes. The NTLM challenge is not a secret: sniffers can relatively easily retrieve it from the NTLM exchange. This means that if tools like the ones referred to above can sniff the NTLM exchanges and extract the hashes, and if in addition there are also tools that can generate an NTLM response given the NTLM challenge and the

---

5.   More info at www.securityfriday.com/tools/ScoopLM.html.

password hashes, there is no real need to crack the password hashes anymore. Put another way: if a bad guy can generate an NTLM response given the hash and NTLM challenge, he can authenticate to a remote server—even without cracking and knowing a user's password. This attack is known as the pass-the-hash attack. One of the tools that can generate an NTLM response, given the NTLM challenge and the password hashes, is the smbproxy tool, which can be downloaded from www.cqure.net/wp/?page_id=11. The pass-the-hash attack also explains why the password hashes stored in AD and the SAM cannot be accessed unless you have system or administrator privileges.

Given the above weaknesses, the NTLM authentication protocol cannot be considered a secure authentication algorithm. The good news is that starting with Windows NT 4.0 Service Pack 4 (SP4), Microsoft embeds NTLM version 2 (NTLMv2) support in its operating systems, which remedies the weaknesses that were outlined above. NTLMv2 will be explained in more detail in the next section.

5.4.2 NTLM Flavors

From the above NTLM protocol exchange we learned that NTLM includes two authentication protocols: the LM and NTLM protocols. Microsoft also offers an enhanced version of NTLM, called NTLMv2, from NT4 SP4 onwards. As we will explain in more detail later in this chapter, the LM protocol is less secure than the NTLM protocol, which is less secure than the NTLMv2 protocol.

NT 3.x, NT4.0, Windows 2000, Windows XP, Windows Server 2003, and R2 all support the NTLM protocol. On NT 3.x and NT 4.0, NTLM is also the default authentication protocol. Because the standard NTLM authentication exchange includes both the LM and NTLM responses, these platforms can also authenticate against platforms that only support LM authentication, and the other way round. Win9x, Windows 3.x, DOS, and OS/2 platforms by default only support LM authentication.

NTLM support can be added to 9x machines by installing the Directory Services Client (dsclient.exe). This client can be downloaded from the following URL: http://download.microsoft.com/download/0/0/a/00a7161e-8da8-4c44-b74e-469d769ce96e/dsclient9x.msi.

LM authentication is also used when authenticating against Windows 9x machines using share-level passwords. If the Win9x machines can pass through the authentication request to a domain controller, NTLM will be used.

The NTLMv2 logic is available on any NT machine running SP4 or later, Windows 2000, Windows XP, Windows Server 2003, and R2. Microsoft also provides NTLMv2 support for Win9x with the Directory Services Client. NTLMv2 is never enabled by default. To turn it on, you must change the value of the LMCompatibilityLevel registry key, as explained in Section 5.4.3.

NTLMv2 includes important new security features that remedy the NTLM security issues outlined in the previous section:

- NTLMv2 only uses the NT hash, and not the LM hash. The way Windows generates the LM hashes contains weaknesses that can significantly speed up the password cracking process. For more information, see also the sidenote on "The LM Hash vs. the NT Hash".

- NTLMv2 supports session security negotiation. Administrators can configure the NTLM authentication package (MSV1_0)[6] to require a certain level of session security quality when applications call it for NTLM-based authentication. These session security settings can be configured using GPO settings, as we will explain in Section 5.4.3.

- NTLMv2 includes important cryptographic changes. Unlike NTLM, NTLMv2 does not use DES for generating the response but the HMAC-MD5 algorithm. Also, NTLMv2 not only uses a challenge generated by the server (as NTLM does), but also uses an additional client-side generated challenge for the calculation of the NTLMv2 response (this protects against chosen-plaintext attacks).

5.4.3 Controlling the NTLM Flavors

Before NT4 Service Pack 4 (SP4), there was no easy way to disable the LM portion of the NTLM authentication protocol or enforce the use of the NTLMv2 protocol. In all later Windows versions, administrators can control the NTLM subprotocols that Windows clients and servers send and accept to tighten the overall security of their infrastructure.

To control the NTLM subprotocols, you can use a GPO setting or the corresponding registry key. The GPO setting is called "Network Security:

---

6.   To be completely correct, we should say the NTLM Security Support Provider (SSP) package, because in this context we refer to the MSV1_0 portion that is used for noninteractive authentications initiated by applications.

LAN Manager Authentication Level" and is located in Computer Configuration\Windows Settings\Security Settings\Local Policies\Security Options. The corresponding registry key is called LMCompatibilityLevel (REG_DWORD) and is located in HKEY_LOCAL_MACHINE\SYSTEM\CurrentControlSet\Control\Lsa.

Table 5.6 shows the LMCompatibilityLevel settings, the corresponding GPO settings, and their meanings. The LMCompatibilityLevel is also documented in the following Microsoft Knowledge Base article: http://support.microsoft.com/default.aspx?scid=kb;en-us;147706.

The default LMCompatibilityLevel value for Windows Server 2003 is 2, meaning "Send NTLM response only." In all other Windows versions, the default value is 0 meaning "Send LM and NTLM responses." In other words, there is no Windows version that will send NTLMv2 by default, and all will accept LM, NTLM, and NTLMv2.

In environments that are only made up of Windows 2000, Windows XP, Windows Server 2003, and R2 systems, we recommend that you set the LMCompatibilityLevel setting to at least level 4 ("Send NTLMv2 response only\refuse LM").

When applications use NTLMv2 for noninteractive authentication, administrators can also influence the NTLM session security quality using the following GPO settings; both settings are located in the Windows Settings\Security Settings\Local Policies\Security Options GPO container:

- Setting affecting the client-side of the distributed application: "Network Security: Minimum session security for NTLM SSP-based (including secure RPC) clients." This GPO setting sets the HKEY_LOCAL_MACHINE\ System\CurrentControlSet\control\ LSA\MSV1_0\NtlmMinClientSec registry key (REG_DWORD).

- Setting affecting the server-side of the distributed application: "Network Security: Minimum session security for NTLM SSP-based (including secure RPC) servers." This GPO setting sets the HKEY_LOCAL_MACHINE\ System\CurrentControlSet\control\ LSA\MSV1_0\NtlmMinServerSec registry key (REG_DWORD).

The NtlmMinClientSec and NtlmMinServerSec registry keys can have one of the values specified in Table 5.7. The individual settings can be combined both in the GPOs and in the registry. For example, you can require both message integrity and confidentiality protection by checking the corresponding boxes in the GPO editor (as illustrated in Figure 5.10). In the registry, you can obtain the same effect by adding the corresponding

------>

Table 5.6 *LMCompatibilityLevel Settings*

LMCompatibilityLevel Setting	GPO Setting	Meaning	
		Sends	Accepts
0	Send LM & NTLM responses	LM, NTLM	LM, NTLM, NTLMv2
1	Send LM & NTLM responses—use NTLMv2 session security if negotiated	LM, NTLM, Session Security	LM, NTLM, NTLMv2
2	Send NTLM response only	NTLM, Session Security	LM, NTLM, NTLMv2
3	Send NTLMv2 response only	NTLMv2, Session Security	LM, NTLM, NTLMv2
4	Send NTLMv2 response only/refuse LM	NTLMv2, Session Security	NTLM, NTLMv2
5	Send NTLMv2 response only/refuse LM & NTLM	NTLMv2, Session Security	NTLMv2

registry values: in the above example, you would add the 0x00000030 value to the NtlmMinClientSec or NtlmMinServerSec registry keys.

In environments where all Windows platforms support NTLMv2 we recommend you to set both registry keys to 0x00080000 (Require NTLMv2 session security). When you change these settings, you must be sure that they match on the client and server side of a distributed application: failing to do so will break your distributed application. For

------>

Table 5.7 *Possible NtlmMinClientSec and NltmMinServerSec Values*

Registry Value	Corresponding GPO Setting
0x00000000	GPO setting not configured: this is the default in Windows XP, Windows Server 2003, and R2. This means there are no specific NTLM session security requirements.
0x00000010	Require message integrity
0x00000020	Require message confidentiality
0x00080000	Require NTLMv2 session security
0x20000000	Require 128-bit encryption

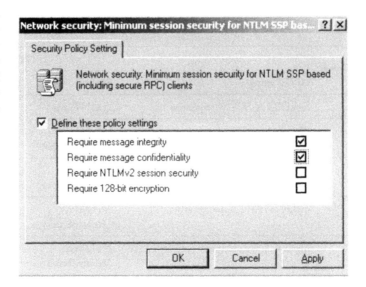

Figure 5.10
Setting the
NtlmMinClientSec
and
NltmMinServerSec
values from the
GPOs.

information on the NtlmMinClientSec and NtlmMinServerSec registry keys, we refer to the following Microsoft Knowledge Base article: https://premier.microsoft.com/default.aspx?scid=kb;en-us;239869.

5.4.4 Disabling LM Hash Storage

Windows stores passwords in a hashed format in its security database (AD or SAM). Password hashes allow Windows to authenticate users without requiring a plaintext copy of each user password in the security database. The NTLM flavors discussed in the previous sections leverage different password hashes. This explains why the security database contains both an LM hash (used by the LM subprotocol) and an NT hash[7] (used by the NTLM and NTLMv2 protocols) of every user's password.

In Active Directory (AD), the LM hash is stored in the DbcsPwd account property. The LM hash history is stored in the LmPwdHistory account property. The NT hash is stored in the UnicodePwd account property. The NT hash history is stored in the NtPwdHistory account property.

As is explained in the sidenote on "The LM Hash versus the NT Hash," the LM hash is weak compared to the NT hash and can be cracked relatively easily using brute-force attacks. To perform brute-force attacks on password hashes, you can use one of the tools explained in Chapter 2.

---

7.   The NT hash is also known as the Unicode hash.

It is a security best practice to disable LM hash storage or make sure that the LM hash is not generated when a new password is set. How to do this is explained below. The LM hash weaknesses do not mean that the NT hash is unbreakable; they simply mean that it will take more time to break an NT hash.

Besides disabling LM hash storage, you can also ensure that your Windows users are using the stronger NTLMv2 authentication protocol to

---

The LM Hash versus the NT Hash

Windows' method of generating LM hashes contains weaknesses that can significantly speed up the password-cracking process. One of the weaknesses of the LM hash is that it actually doesn't use a hash function, but rather a symmetric cipher to generate the hash. As such, it isn't a true hash function, but rather a simple one-way function. Figure 5.11 shows how the LM hash is generated for a user password "hpinvent1".

During the LM hash generation process the password is first converted to uppercase; in this example, this operation results in "HPINVENT1". Next the uppercase password is split into two seven-character strings; in the example, the resulting strings are "HPINVEN" and "T1*****". The second string is padded with null characters to make it a seven-character string. The two strings are then used as the encryption keys for the encryption of a constant using the DES (digital encryption standard) symmetric cipher. Finally, the resulting DES-encrypted blobs are concatenated to create the LM hash. Figure 5.11 also shows three other LM hash weaknesses:

- The limited character set—passwords are made case insensitive because they are converted to uppercase during the LM hash calculation

- The limited password length—passwords cannot be longer than 14 characters

- The LM hash is not salted—salting appends a different string to the password each time a password hash is generated, and prevents two identical passwords resulting in identical password hashes

The NT Hash is a true hash, calculated by taking the plaintext password and generating an MD4 hash from it. The NT hash is much more resistant to brute-force attacks than the LM hash.

Figure 5.11
*LM hash
calculation.*

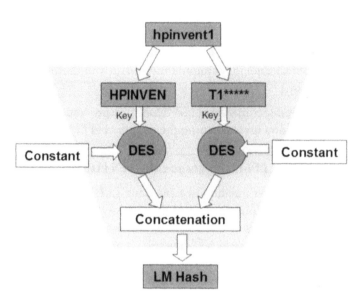

mitigate the risks associated to the LM hash: NTLMV2 only uses the NT hash. How to do this was explained in previous section.

In Windows 2000 Service Pack 2 (SP2) and later SPs, Windows XP, Windows Server 2003, and R2, Microsoft offers the possibility to disable LM hash storage in the AD or SAM credential databases. To do this, you must use the NoLMHash registry key or the corresponding "Network security: Do not store LAN Manager hash value on next password change" GPO setting. The NoLMHash (REG_DWORD) registry hack is located in the HKEY_LOCAL_MACHINE\SYSTEM\CurrentControlSet\Control\ Lsa registry key and should be set to 1 to disable LM hash storage. The GPO setting is located in Computer Configuration\Windows Settings\ Security Settings\Local Policies\Security Options.

When you disable LM hash storage using the NoLMHash registry key, no more LM hashes will be stored in the credential database at and after the next user password change. Enabling the NoLMHash setting does not clear the LM hash history entries in a Windows 2000 security database. They are cleared in Windows XP and Windows Server 2003. If you enable the NoLMHash setting in a domain environment, you must enable it on all domain controllers of the domain.

Two other less-known methods will not generate an LM hash when a user enters a new password:

■ Using a password that is longer than 14 characters

Table 5.8 *ALT Character Codes That Do Not Generate an LM Hash*

0128-0159	0306-0307	0312	0319-0320	0329-0331
0383	0385-0406	0408-0409	0411-0414	0418-0424
0426	0428-0429	0433-0437	0439-0447	0449-0450
0452-0460	0477	0480-0483	0494-0495	0497-0608
0610-0631	0633-0696	0699	0701-0707	0709
0711	0716	0718-0729	0731	0733-0767
0773-0775	0777	0779-0781	0783-0806	0808-0816
0819-0893	0895-0912	0914	0918-0919	0921-0927
0929-0930	0933	0935-0936	0938-0944	0947
0950-0955	0957-0959	0961-0962	0965	0967-1024

- Using certain ALT characters in your password (ALT characters can be entered by holding down the ALT key and then typing a four-digit numeric code; the ALT characters that do not generate an LM hash are listed in Table 5.8)

Because the LM protocol is still used for authenticating Windows 9x (or older) Windows clients, you cannot use these settings when you have these client platforms in your Windows 2000, Windows Server 2003, or R2 environment. Doing so would make it impossible for these clients to authenticate. This problem does not exist if your 9x clients have the Directory Services Client software installed (which adds NTLM support).

Also, if you enable NoLMHash in a clustered Windows 2000 or Windows Server 2003 environment, you must make sure that the cluster service account password is at least 15 characters long. If you don't do this, you will experience problems using the cluster administrator tool. See also the following Microsoft article for more information on this issue: http://support.microsoft.com/default.aspx?scid=kb;en-us;828861.

5.5   Anonymous Access

Anonymous access means that a user can access a Windows system or one of its resources without authenticating to a Windows security authority. A session that is established without authenticating the user on the other end is also referred to as a null session. Microsoft introduced anonymous access to allow users without Windows credentials to also access Windows-hosted resources.

In the early days, Microsoft opened too many gates for anonymous users—giving way to many (in)famous security exploits. On NT4 and Windows 2000, for example, it is trivial for anonymous users to enumerate all accounts defined on a system and to retrieve the names and security identifiers of key accounts, such as the default administrator account. In Windows XP, Windows Server 2003, and R2, Microsoft more effectively restricts what can be done to a Windows system and its resources when they are accessed anonymously. To further lock down anonymous access, Microsoft added a couple of new registry keys and locked down certain configuration settings that before were wide open.

A key security enhancement in Windows Server 2003 is that the privileges of the Everyone group no longer automatically apply to anonymous users. In earlier Windows versions, the Everyone group was automatically added to the access token of the anonymous user account—hence, anonymous users automatically received all privileges of the Everyone group. This behavior can be controlled using the following GPO setting: "Network access: Let Everyone permissions apply to anonymous users." This setting is located in the Computer Configuration\Windows Settings\Security Settings\Local Policies\Security Options GPO container. It corresponds to the following registry key: HKEY_LOCAL_MACHINE\System\CurrentControlSet\Control\LSA\everyoneincludesanonymous.

All anonymous access–related GPO security options, the corresponding registry keys, their default and recommended settings, and their meanings are listed in Table 5.9. All settings can be found in the Computer Configuration\Windows Settings\Security Settings\Local Policies\Security Options GPO container. Table 5.9 only lists the anonymous access-related GPO security options for Windows 2000, Windows XP, Windows Server 2003, and R2; NT4 and earlier Windows versions are not covered.

In Windows XP, Windows Server 2003, and R2 most of these settings are enabled by default. The only anonymous access-related GPO settings we recommend you to change are:

- On Windows Server 2003 and R2 domain controllers: "Network access: Allow anonymous SID/Name translation." On Windows Server 2003 and R2 DCs, this setting is enabled by default. When it

Table 5.9 *Anonymous Access-Related Security Options in the GPO Settings*

GPO Setting *Corresponding Registry Key* (Available on…)	Recommended Setting (Default Setting)	Meaning
Network Access: Allow anonymous SID/Name translation (Windows XP, Windows Server 2003, R2 only)	Disabled: disables anonymous SID/name translation (Disabled by default on Windows XP workstations, and Windows Server 2003 and R2 member servers; enabled by default on Windows Server 2003 and R2 domain controllers)	Determines whether an anonymous user can request the SID attributes of another user. It restricts whether anonymous users can call the LookupAccountSid API.
Additional Restrictions for Anonymous Connections Windows 2000: *RestrictAnonymous** (Windows 2000)	Enabled: No access without explicit anonymous permissions† (registry value 2)‡ (Disabled (value 0) by default)	Determines whether anonymous users are allowed to enumerate the names of accounts and network shares. It restricts whether anonymous users can call the NetUserEnum, NetShareEnum and LookupAccountSid APIs. It also determines whether the Everyone group SID is included in the access token of the anonymous user.
Network Access: Do not allow anonymous enumeration of SAM accounts Windows XP, Windows Server 2003, R2: *RestrictAnonymousSAM*** (Windows XP, Windows Server 2003, R2)	Enabled: disables anonymous enumeration of SAM accounts (registry value 1) (Enabled (value 1) by default on Windows XP, Windows Server 2003, and R2)	Determines whether anonymous users are allowed to enumerate the names of SAM accounts. It restricts whether anonymous users can call the NetUserEnum API. This setting only impacts standalone machines. It has no impact on domain controllers.
Network Access: Do not allow anonymous enumeration of SAM accounts and shares *RestrictAnonymous*†† (Windows XP, Windows Server 2003, R2)	Enabled: disables anonymous enumeration of SAM accounts and shares (registry value 1) (Disabled (value 0) by default on Windows XP, Windows Server 2003, R2)	Determines whether anonymous users are allowed to enumerate the names of accounts and network shares. It restricts whether anonymous users can call the NetUserEnum, NetShareEnum APIs.

Table 5.9 *Anonymous Access-Related Security Options in the GPO Settings (continued)*

GPO Setting *Corresponding Registry Key* (Available on…)	Recommended Setting (Default Setting)	Meaning
Network Access: Let Everyone permissions apply to anonymous users *Everyoneincludesanonymous*‡‡ (Windows XP, Windows Server 2003, R2 only)	Disabled: disables the application of everyone permissions to anonymous users (registry value 0) (Disabled (value 0) by default on Windows XP, Windows Server 2003, R2)	Determines whether the Everyone group SID is in the access token of the anonymous user. It determines whether everyone permissions apply to anonymous users.***
Network Access: Restrict anonymous access to Named Pipes and Shares *RestrictNullSessAccess*††† (Windows Server 2003 and R2)	Enabled: restricts anonymous access to named pipes and shares (registry value 1) (Enabled by default on Windows Server 2003 and R2, even though the key is missing from the registry)	Determines whether named pipes and shares can be accessed anonymously. This is a systemwide setting, meaning that it applies to all named pipes and shares on a Windows system. On Windows 2000, this setting is not available in the GPOs: to restrict anonymous access to named pipes and shares the RestrictNullSessAccess key must be created manually in the registry and set to value 1 to enable it. On Windows XP, this setting is not available in the GPOs but enabled by default.
Network Access: Named pipes that can be accessed anonymously *NullSessionPipes*‡‡‡ (Windows 2000, Windows XP, Windows Server 2003, and R2)	Restrict anonymous access to named pipes (Default list on Windows Server 2003 and R2: COMNAP, COMNODE, SQL\QUERY, SPOOLSS, netlogon, lsarpc, samr, browser) (Default list on Windows XP: COMNAP, COMNODE, SQL\QUERY, SPOOLSS, llsrpc, browser)	Determines which named pipes will allow anonymous access. This setting defines exceptions to the systemwide rule set using the RestrictNullSessAccess key (see above). If RestrictNullSessAccess is enabled, the NullSessionPipes key will hold the names of the named pipes that can be accessed anonymously.
Network Access: Shares that can be accessed anonymously NullSessionShares**** (Windows 2000, Windows XP, Windows Server 2003, R2)	Restrict anonymous access to shares (Default list on Windows XP, Windows Server 2003, and R2: COMCFG, DFS$)	Determines which network shares can be accessed by anonymous users. This setting defines exceptions to the systemwide rule set using the RestrictNullSessAccess key (see above). If RestrictNullSessAccess is enabled, the NullSessionShares key will hold the names of the shares that can be accessed anonymously.

Table 5.9   *Anonymous Access-Related Security Options in the GPO Settings (continued)*

GPO Setting *Corresponding Registry Key* (Available on...)	Recommended Setting (Default Setting)	Meaning
Network Access: Remotely accessible registry paths Windows 2000, Windows XP: *AllowedPaths*†††† Windows Server 2003, R2: *AllowedExactPaths*‡‡‡‡ (Windows 2000, Windows XP, Windows Server 2003, and R2)	Restrict anonymous access to registry paths (Default list was too long to include in this table)	Determines which registry paths can be accessed by anonymous users. These keys control exceptions to the ACL settings of the winreg***** registry key. Winreg controls who can access the registry remotely. In Windows 2000 and Windows XP, these exceptions apply to the entire registry tree underneath the key. In Windows Server 2003, these exceptions apply only to the key itself.
Network Access: Remotely accessible registry paths and sub-paths AllowedPaths††††† (Windows Server 2003 and R2)	Restrict anonymous access to registry paths (Default list was too long to include in this table)	Determines which registry paths can be accessed by anonymous users. These keys control exceptions to the ACL settings of the winreg registry key. Winreg controls who can access the registry remotely. These exceptions apply to the entire registry tree underneath the key.

*	Key is located in HKEY_LOCAL_MACHINE\System\CurrentControlSet\Control\LSA.
†	See also http://support.microsoft.com/default.aspx?scid=kb;en-us;246261 for more information on this setting in Windows 2000.
‡	In Windows 2000, the possible values for this key are: 0 (GPO: None. Rely on default permissions), 1 (GPO: Does not allow enumeration of SAM accounts and names), or 2 (No access without explicit anonymous permissions).
**	Same registry key as footnote †.
††	Same registry key as footnote †.
‡‡	Same registry key as footnote †.
***	Even though this setting is not available in Windows 2000, you can obtain the same effect in Windows 2000 by setting the RestrictAnonymous registry key to value 2—see also previous discussion of RestrictAnonymous in Windows 2000.
†††	Key is located in HKEY_LOCAL_MACHINE\System\CurrentControlSet\Services\LanManServer.
‡‡‡	Key is located in HKEY_LOCAL_MACHINE\System\CurrentControlSet\Services\LanManServer\Parameters.
****	Same registry key as footnote †††.
††††	Key is located in HKEY_LOCAL_MACHINE\System\CurrentControlSet\Control\SecurePipeServers\winreg.
‡‡‡‡	Same registry key as footnote ††††.
*****	Key is located in HKEY_LOCAL_MACHINE\System\CurrentControlSet\Control\SecurePipeServers.
†††††	Same registry key as footnote ††††.

is enabled, attackers can still use anonymous access-based enumeration tools like sid2user, user2sid (see Chapter 2), userdump,[8] etc. To block these tools, we recommend that you disable the "Network access: Allow anonymous SID/Name translation" setting on Windows Server 2003 and R2 DCs. This GPO setting does not have a corresponding registry key.

■ On all Windows XP, Windows Server 2003, and R2 machines: "Do not allow anonymous enumeration of SAM accounts and shares." This setting is, by default, disabled. We recommend that you enable it to provide your systems with an additional layer of protection against anonymous access-based enumeration. Enabling this GPO setting corresponds to setting the restrictanonymous registry key to value 1.

Changing some of these settings can have interesting side effects. Use these settings with extreme care, and make sure that you apply changes first in a test environment before using them in your production network. For an overview of things that may not work anymore if you change some of the settings listed in Table 5.9, have a look at the following Microsoft Knowledge Base article: http://support.microsoft.com/kb/823659. Most of the potential problems are related to the operation of machines running older Windows versions.

A last recommendation we want to give in the context of this discussion on restricting anonymous access is related to the built-in "Pre-Windows 2000 Compatible Access" Active Directory (AD) domain local group. If, during AD installation (dcpromo), you select "Permissions compatible with pre-Windows 2000 server operating systems" (as Figure 5.12 illustrates), this group will include the anonymous logon security principal. By default, the Pre-Windows 2000 Compatible Access group has the permissions to see all AD objects and all properties of AD user and group objects. In other words, thanks to the default memberships of this group, anonymous users can perform AD data enumeration. That is why in Windows Server 2003 environments where you don't need this group for compatibility with NT servers,[9] we recommend that you remove the anonymous logon account from the Pre-Windows 2000 Compatible Access group. You can do this by changing the group's membership

---

8.   See http://www.joeware.net/win/free/tools/userdump.htm.
9.   The NT RAS server is an example of a server that requires anonymous access to AD and, thus, anonymous membership of the "Pre-Windows 2000 Compatible Access" group. See the following Microsoft Knowledge Base article for more information: http://support.microsoft.com/kb/325363/en-us.

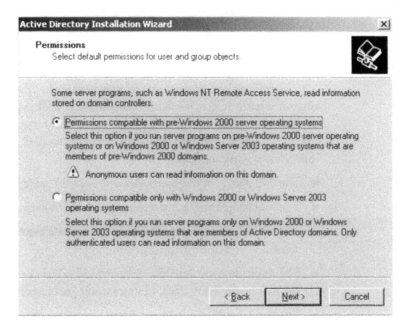

Figure 5.12
Selecting
"Permissions
compatible with
pre-Windows 2000
server operating
systems" during
dcpromo.

from the AD Users and Computers (ADUC) MMC snap-in or from the command line as follows:

```
Net localgroup "Pre-Windows 2000 Compatible Access"
"Anonymous Logon" /delete
```

5.6 Credential Caching

Each time you log on interactively to a Windows domain, your Windows system securely caches your domain credentials, i.e., your username and password. The same thing happens during secondary interactive logons that are initiated using, for example, the RunAs utility,[10] and during remote interactive logons over a Terminal Services or Remote Desktop connection.

Thanks to this "credential caching" feature, you can log on to a Windows domain using your domain credentials when no DCs are available or when your machine is disconnected from the network. Logging on with cached domain credentials gives you only access to local machine resources, not to resources hosted on other domain members.

---

10. RunAs does not create cached credentials if you use it with the /netonly; this switch can be used when the credentials specified in the RunAs command are for remote access only. In this case, RunAs also does not create a local profile for the user specified in the RunAs command.

Domain logon using credential caching is a nice solution for enterprises that have lots of disconnected road warriors and that don't want to give their users a local account on their computers. As opposed to local accounts, domain accounts can be centrally controlled and configured.

"Secure" caching in this context means that the LSA stores an encrypted copy of a hash of the NT hash in the HKEY_LOCAL_MACHINE\Security\Cache registry key following each successful interactive domain logon. Figure 5.13 illustrates how the LSA generates cached credentials. In short, this process works as follows:

- The NT hash[11] of the user password is salted using the username.

- The resulting string is hashed using the MD4 hashing algorithm.

- The MD4 hash is concatenated with the username and the domainname.

- The resulting concatenation is encrypted using the RC4 cipher and a key that is the MD5 hash of a randomly generated LSA key.[12]

- The resulting RC4-encrypted string represents the cached credentials.

In early 2005, a tool named cachedump was released that can retrieve a list of usernames and their hashed NT hash from the cached credentials store in the system registry. Figure 5.14 illustrates the operation of the cachedump tool. The creators of the tool also provide an update of the John the Ripper cracking tool (discussed in Chapter 2) that can crack the cachedump output and reveal the user passwords. Both cachedump and the John the Ripper update can be downloaded from the following URL: www.off-by-one.net/misc/cachedump.html. When you use these tools, you will experience that cracking a hash of a hash using the updated John the Ripper version takes considerably more time than cracking a simple password hash (which is, as explained in Chapter 2, what you normally use John the Ripper for).

The cachedump tool can be used against Windows 2000, Windows XP, and Windows Server 2003 and R2 systems; at the time of writing, it did not work on NT4. To successfully use the tool, you must have administrator-level privileges. Cachedump dumps all cached credentials of all users that logged on interactively to a particular machine: the cachedump results are not restricted to the cached credentials of the administrator account you use

11.   Remember from the section on NTLM that the NT hash is an MD4-generated hash derived from the user password.
12.   This LSA key is different for each cached credential and stored together with the cached credential in the system registry.

NT Hash
Username
MD4
Salting
MD4 Hash
Username
Domainname
Concatenation
LSA Key
MD5
RC4
Cached Credentials

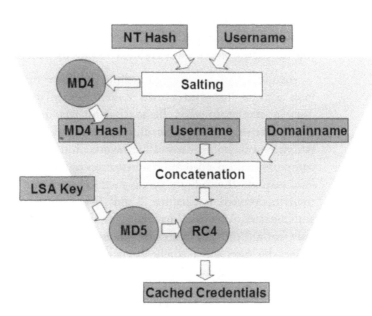

Figure 5.13 *Cached credentials generation process.*

to log on to the machine. Also, if an administrator account logs on locally to a domain-joined machine, he still can use cachedump to dump the cached credentials of previous interactive domain logons. The latter is a dangerous use of the tool, because a local administrator could use it to elevate his privileges to domain administrator. There's another good reason for not using local accounts but only domain accounts!

Using credential caching also creates the following security risk: users could intentionally disconnect their machine from the network and log on to the domain using cached credentials, to get around the fact that the administrator disabled their domain account. Even though this does not give them any access to live and up-to-date domain data, these users can still access local data—which could contain copies of domain data or simply cached domain data.

Command Prompt
C:\>cachedump
jdc:A658526EB855EB83CCD421A07A93D57F:dc:dc.net
administrator:0ACB7BEED30F301485DA8AFBBD6AF058:dc:dc.net
bl:8A2083B0DB6AA70D238B70D1C83B96AF:dc:dc.net
pp:C644A945763F36DB6DB420C41B8C2EE3:dc:dc.net
jj:CC68D25B2C9CB28918AAB6E83ADD8195:dc:dc.net
C:\>

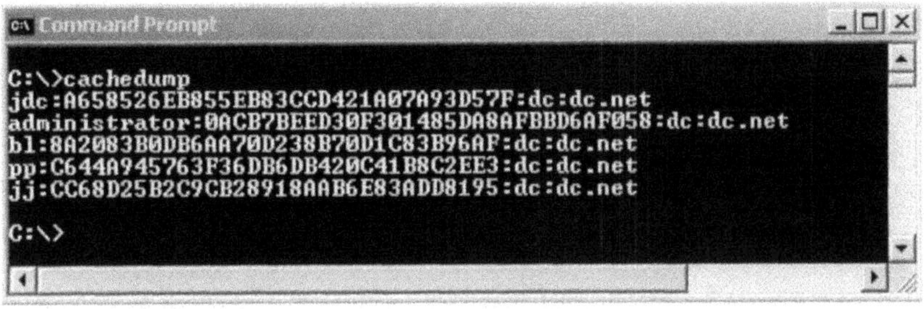

Figure 5.14 *Dumping cached credentials using cachedump.*

Still, for most organizations, the benefits of using credential caching and domain accounts instead of local accounts outweigh the risks associated with the cachedump tool and the ability to bypass domain account lockouts.

An alternative to credential caching would be the use of two accounts: a local account for when a user is disconnected from the domain, and a domain account for when the user is connected to the domain. When users must maintain passwords for different accounts, there's a fair risk that certain users will choose identical passwords. In that case, if a user's laptop was compromised and a bad guy gained access to the password hash of the user's local account, the bad guy could crack the password hash using one of the tools mentioned in Chapter 2 and then use the password not only to authenticate to the local machine, but also to the domain (remember, this only works if the passwords of both accounts are identical). In the scenario where the user has a single domain account and credential caching is enabled on his laptop, if the laptop is compromised, the bad guy can still only use the cached credentials to access local resources. Uncracked cached credentials can only be used to authenticate to the local Windows system where they were generated. If the bad guy wants to leverage cached credentials to access other domain resources, he must crack them. Again, the latter is difficult and takes considerably more time given the fact that cached credentials are a hash of a password hash.

You can disable interactive domain logon using cached credentials and force a user's machine to contact a domain controller before the user can log on interactively to the domain. To do so, you must use the following registry or GPO setting:

- To disable domain logons using cached credentials using a registry setting, create the CachedLogonsCount registry entry of type REG_SZ and set it to value 0 in the HKEY_LOCAL_MACHINE\SOFTWARE\Microsoft\Windows NT\CurrentVersion\Winlogon registry subkey.

- To do the same thing using a GPO setting, enable the "Interactive logon: number of previous logons to cache (in case domain controller is not available)" setting. This setting is located in the Computer Configuration\Windows Settings\Security Settings\Local Policies\ Security Options GPO container.

You must restart your computer for the cachedlogonscount changes to apply. For example, if you disable credential caching by setting cachedlogonscount to 0, Windows will keep on caching credentials until you restart your machine. Although the cachedlogonscount key doesn't appear in the registry, Windows automatically caches a set of 10 domain credentials. The maximum value for CachedLogonsCount is 50.

The credential caching discussed in this section should not be confused with the Windows XP and Windows Server 2003 capability to store user credentials in the user's profile. The latter feature is known as the credential manager and is discussed in more detail in Chapter 9. This credential caching mechanism is also different from the caching mechanisms offered by certain authentication protocols. Kerberos, for example, offers client-side ticket credential caching. Kerberos will be discussed in more detail in Chapter 6. Also, this credential caching mechanism is different from application-level credential caching mechanisms such as the one offered by Internet Explorer (IE). Finally, the cached credentials referred to in this section are different from the cached password hash that is used to unlock a user's desktop.[13]

We recommend using credential caching on mobile users' laptops. This allows them to log on with their domain credentials when they are away from the office. We also recommend disabling credential caching (as described above) on machines that don't need this feature: member servers, domain controllers, and even user desktops.

5.7 Limiting Concurrent Logon Sessions

Organizations deploying operating system software often have a requirement for a feature or tool that allows for the definition and enforcement of a limited number of concurrent logon sessions of a particular account. Often, this is a must-have feature for highly privileged accounts like administrators. Most organizations even want to block concurrent administrator logon sessions completely. If administrators are logged on at multiple locations, it becomes much more likely that they will leave one of these sessions open, which creates additional security risks. Even though such a feature has been supported natively in operating systems like Novell NetWare for many years, it is still missing in the Windows OS today.

In late 2004, Microsoft released a new add-on tool for Windows that administrators could use to limit concurrent logon sessions to the Windows OS. The tool is called LimitLogin and can be downloaded from http://download.microsoft.com/download/f/d/0/fd05def7-68a1-4f71-8546-25c359cc0842/LimitLogin.exe. LimitLogin was developed by a team of Microsoft Consulting Services (MCS) consultants.

---

13.   This was explained in the account lockout section of Chapter 2; read the sidenote on "Making sure that account security policies are enforced when a user unlocks the Windows console" for more information.

LimitLogin requires a Windows Server 2003 AD and an IIS 6.0 Web server with ASP.NET support enabled. LimitLogin runs on the following Windows client platforms: Windows 2000 Professional Service Pack 4 and above, Windows 2000 Server Service Pack 4 and above, Windows XP Professional Service Pack 1 and above, and Windows Server 2003. A very important detail is that—just as is the case for other Windows add-on and Resource Kit tools—Microsoft Product Support Services (PSS) does not provide official support for LimitLogin.

LimitLogin is a revamped version of the Cconnect tool that Microsoft made available as part of the Windows Server 2000 Resource Kit. Cconnect provides basic functionality to limit concurrent logon sessions in Windows 2000 and NT 4.0 environments. LimitLogin provides better integration with the Active Directory (AD) and AD administration tools. LimitLogin leverages AD for storing the connection limit data; Cconnect required a SQL Server database. Like Cconnect, LimitLogin can only restrict interactive logon sessions. Interactive logon sessions are the ones users and administrators initiate from the Windows console (for example using CTRL+ALT+DEL or the XP Welcome screen; see Section 5.2 for more information).

LimitLogin is a must-have tool for enterprise-level AD deployments where administrators want to securely control Windows logon sessions. Besides controling concurrent logon sessions, LimitLogin can also report on open logon sessions in a Windows domain. Organizations that only need a logon reporting tool don't necessarily need to deploy LimitLogin. Reporting on logons can easily be done using simpler tools: for example, by dumping a simple machinename.username text file to a hidden shared folder at logon time via the logon script.

The following sections explain the LimitLogin architecture and components and look at how to set it up, configure, and use it.

5.7.1 LimitLogin Operation

Figure 5.15 illustrates the LimitLogin components and operation when a user logs on interactively to a LimitLogin-enabled Windows domain. In this example the following events will occur:

1.   The user initiates an interactive logon sequence from a Windows client. The LimitLogin logon script (llogin.vbs) executes.

2. The LimitLogin logon script sends the user and computer data to the LimitLogin Web service. The data are sent in an XML format using SOAP and include the username, computername, IP address, session ID, and authenticating domain controller (DC).

3. The LimitLogin Web service checks whether the user has been enabled for LimitLogin and, if it is enabled, identifies the user's logon quota (or concurrent logon limit). These data are stored in the AD LimitLogin application partition.

4. AD replies with the requested information.

5. If the user has not been enabled for LimitLogin, the LimitLogin Web service notifies the logon script that it should continue to log the user in normally. If the user has been enabled for Limit-Login and does have a logon quota defined, the LimitLogin Web service counts the number of logons that have been registered for the user in the LimitLogin application directory partition. From here there are two possibilities:

   - If the user's logon quota is less than the actual number of logons registered in AD, the Web service updates the user's logon information in the LimitLogin application directory partition and notifies the logon script to continue the logon process normally.

   - If the user's logon quota is equal to or exceeds the number of logons registered in AD, the Web service notifies the logon script to log off the current session. LimitLogin can optionally be configured to inform the user about its other logon locations before the user is actually logged off.

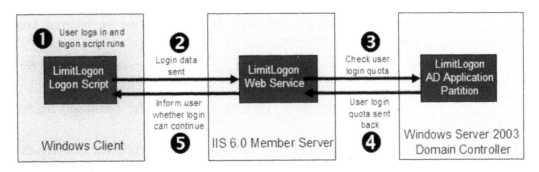

Figure 5.15   *LimitLogin operation.*

5.7.2 LimitLogin Architecture and Components

LimitLogin requires configuration changes and special components on the Windows clients, the IIS 6.0 Web server, and the AD domain controllers. Most of these changes and components are created automatically when the LimitLogin software is installed. The logon and logoff scripts that Limit-Login uses (llogin.vbs and llogoff.vbs) come with the LimitLogin software but must be copied manually to a share that is accessible by all Windows clients. Typically, the NetLogon share of a DC or (preferably) the scripts folder of the GPO are used to trigger the LimitLogon scripts. Also, the user Logon/Logoff script group policy object (GPO) settings must be changed manually to reference these scripts.

The client-side LimitLogin components consist of the SOAP runtime and a set of LimitLogin-specific DLLs and executables. On the Web server, LimitLogin installs the LimitLogin Web service in the WSLimitLogin virtual directory. By default, WSLimitLogin is created in the Default Web site, and the Web service can be accessed on port 80. Even though the Limit-Login client does not submit user credentials to the Web service, it is recommended that organizations with higher security requirements manually configure SSL for the WSLimitLogin virtual directory. LimitLogin does not automatically provide this SSL protection.

LimitLogin extends the AD schema and builds an application partition to host the LimitLogin configuration data; this is the reason LimitLogin requires a Windows Server 2003 AD. Figure 5.16 shows the LimitLogin AD application partition as viewed from the ADSI Edit tool (which comes with the Windows Server 2003 Support Tools).

The AD application partition LimitLogin uses is named DC=limit-login,dc=*<domainname>*. The new object type LimitLogin uses to store a user's logon quota is called msLimitLoginUser. It has the following Limit-Login-specific attributes:

- msLimitLoginDenyLoginOnQuotaExceed. A user is enabled for LimitLogin if this attribute is set to true.

- msLimitLoginQuota. This attribute holds the LimitLogin logon quota.

- msLimitLoginInfo. This attribute holds the logons that are currently registered in AD. The data in this attribute are compared to the quota set in the previous attribute to decide upon whether a user can get another logon session.

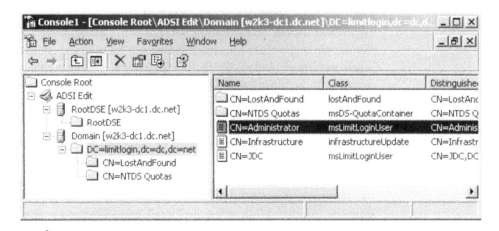

Figure 5.16   *LimitLogin AD application partition.*

- msLimitLoginUsername. This attribute holds the user's account name.

All above AD objects and attributes can be configured using the Limit-Login AD Users and Computers (ADUC) MMC snap-in extensions and the LimitLogin command line utilities, which will be explained in Section 5.74.

5.7.3   Installing LimitLogin

Installing LimitLogin is relatively straightforward. The LimitLogin code comes with three installation executables: one for installing the Web server components (LimitLoginIISSetup.msi), one for installing the AD domain controller components (LimitLoginADSetup.msi), and another one to install the client-side components (LimitLoginClientSetup.msi). It is important that you run these installation programs in a particular order: first the Web server installation, then the AD installation, and only then the client-side installation.

The Web server installation allows for the definition of a custom virtual directory name and port for the LimitLogin Web service. Running the LimitLogin Web server installation requires administrator rights on the Web server.

Remember from above that the LimitLogin installation program does not take care of the LimitLogin SSL configuration. When you configure SSL for the LimitLogin Web service, you must only make changes on the server side. You must install a server-side SSL certificate and link it to the Limit-Login Web service. You also must edit the limitlogin.wsdl file located in the LimitLogin logon share (described below; this share contains the LimitLogin logon and logoff scripts). In the limitlogin.wsdl you must change all URLs referring to the LimitLogin Web service: instead of HTTP, they should use HTTPS. All the URLs that must be changed are located in the `<wsdl:service name="LimitLogin">` section of the limitlogin.wsdl file.

The LimitLogin AD setup is split in three parts: preparation of the AD forest, preparation of the AD domain, and installation of the LimitLogin extensions for the AD Users and Computers (ADUC) MMC snap-in. The AD forest and domain LimitLogin installation parts can be run separately from the command line using the LimitLoginADSetup.exe executable and the /ForestPrep and /DomainPrep switches.

To run the first two parts of the LimitLogin AD setup, your account must have schema administrator privileges in the root domain of the forest. Also, you must run the tool on the forest DC that has the "Domain Naming Master" operations master role (for creating the LimitLogin Application Partition). The last part of the setup (ADUC extensions installation) can be run with domain administrator privileges on any DC in your forest, or with administrator privileges on a Windows workstation—in case you're using the Administrative Tools to manage AD from a workstation.

The forest preparation extends the AD schema and modifies the AD configuration context. The domain preparation creates the LimitLogin AD application partition and the LimitLogin logon/logoff scripts. During the domain preparation portion, the DC where the LimitLogin application partition will be created can be specified.

For high availability or disaster recovery reasons, you may want to create multiple replicas of the LimitLogin application partition on different DCs. How to do this is described in the "Advanced Configuration Options" section of the LimitLogin help file.

At the end of the AD setup, you must manually copy the LimitLogin logon and logoff scripts to a share, and reference them in your domain GPO settings. The LimitLogin setup program reminds you to do so at the end of the LimitLogin AD installation (as illustrated in Figure 5.17).

The AD installation portion of LimitLogin creates detailed log files in the %systemdrive%/program files/LimitLogin (limitloginadsetup.log) and %systemdrive%/windows/system32 (ldif.log) file system folders.

The LimitLogin client setup program can be run manually, but most organizations may want to run it in an automated way. Automated

Figure 5.17
AD LimitLogin installation.

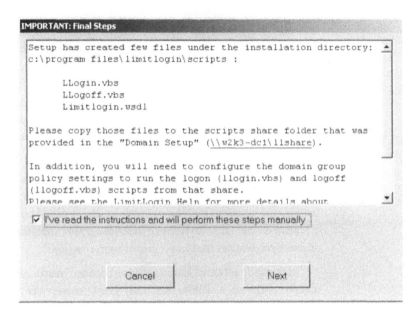

Microsoft-centric installation options include SMS, GPOs, and logon scripts. To run the client installation from the command line in quiet mode (requires no user interaction), use the /qn switch. Because the client setup installs the SOAP client, it requires administrator rights.

If the LimitLogin Web service is running on a different machine than the domain controller hosting the LimitLogin application partition, you must make sure that you trust the Web server's computer account for delegation to the LimitLogin DC. How to do this is described in the Limit-Login help file in the LimitLogin Active Directory Setup section. For more information on Kerberos delegation and how to configure it, see Chapter 6.

5.7.4 Configuring LimitLogin

Your best friend when configuring concurrent logon settings on AD user objects is the AD Users and Computers (ADUC) MMC snap-in. The LimitLogin AD installation program adds several ADUC LimitLogin configuration options. The "LimitLogin Tasks…" menu option can be accessed from the context menu of user, computer and Organizational Unit (OU) objects.

Figure 5.18 shows the configuration dialog box that pops up when you select the LimitLogin Tasks… option for a user account object—in this example, the Administrator account. This dialog box in the first place shows the machines where the selected account is currently logged on interactively. It can also be used to log off selected logon sessions and delete them from the AD LimitLogin application partition, to save the logon overview in a comma-separated or XML-formatted report, and most importantly to configure concurrent logon quota for the selected user account. The latter can be done by clicking "Configure." This brings up the dialog box illustrated in Figure 5.19. In this example, the administrator account is only allowed to be logged in interactively to a single machine at once.

The LimitLogin software also comes with a Visual Basic script sample that automates concurrent logon setting configuration for all users in a particular OU or domain. The script is called Bulk_LimitUserLogins.vbs and is located in the %systemdrive%\program files\Limitlogin folder on domain controllers that have LimitLogin installed.

Selecting the LimitLogin Tasks... context menu option on a computer object brings up a dialog box that gives an overview of all users currently logged on interactively to that particular machine. The dialog box also allows you to delete and optionally log off selected logon sessions, ping the remote machine, and save the list of interactive logon sessions into a comma-separated or XML-formatted report. If you select a logon session, then click Delete/Logoff Selected Sessions, LimitLogin will by default delete the logon session from the AD application partition and log off the remote session without prompting the administrator for confirmation. The LimitLogin delete/logoff behavior can be configured by clicking "Click Here to Set Logoff Options" in the same dialog box (as illustrated in Figure 5.20).

Figure 5.18
LimitLogin user object configuration dialog box.

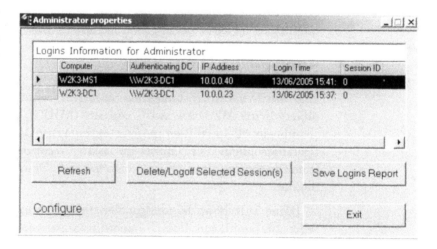

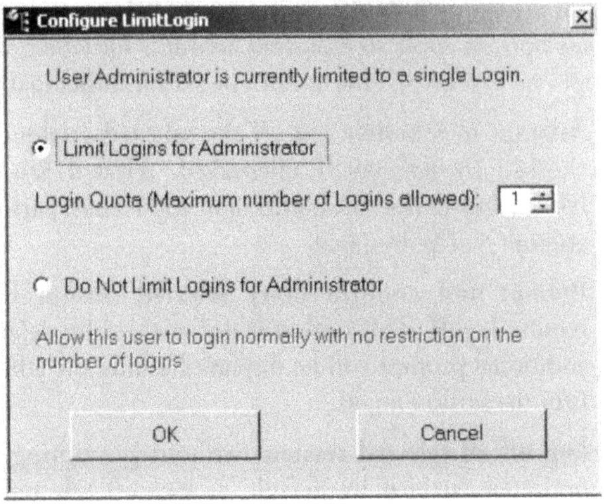

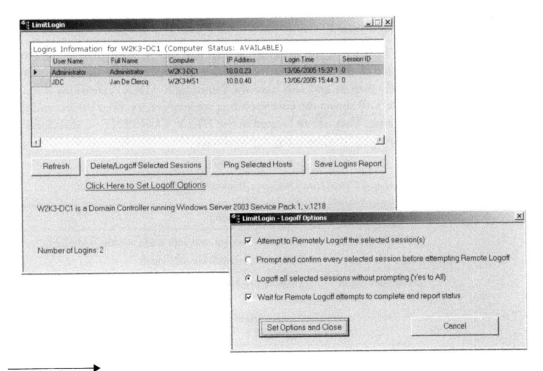

Figure 5.19 *LimitLogin user object configuration dialog box.*

Figure 5.20 *Setting logoff options.*

LimitLogin offers the delete/logoff behavior options outlined below. These options apply to ALL user accounts for which the LimitLogin logon scripts are executed. They cannot be set for individual user accounts.

- **Attempt to remotely log off the selected session(s).** This option is checked by default. If unchecked, selected sessions will only be removed from the AD LimitLogin application partition and no logoff attempt will be initiated.

- **Prompt and confirm every selected session before attempting remote logoff.** This option is not enabled by default. If enabled, an additional prompt will be displayed asking the administrator to confirm the session logoff.

- **Log off all selected sessions without prompting (yes to all).** This option is enabled by default. It logs off selected sessions without prompting the administrator.

- **Wait for remote logoff attempts to complete and report status.** This option is checked by default. When enabled, LimitLogin will wait for a status notification to come back from the remote host after a logoff was initiated.

The delete/logoff behavior settings can also be configured in the system registry of the administrative machine on which you're using the ADUC MMC snap-in and also have the LimitLogin ADUC extensions installed. Table 5.10 shows the corresponding registry entries, their values, and their meaning. They are all located in the HKEY_CURRENT_USER\Software\Microsoft\LimitLogin registry container.

Table 5.10   *LimitLogin Delete/Logoff Behavior Registry Configuration Settings*

Registry Key	Values and Meaning
EnableLogoff	1 means LimitLogin will both delete and logoff (default)
	0 means LimitLogin will only logoff
PromptForLogoff	1 means LimitLogin will prompt for confirmation before logging off
	0 means LimitLogin will not prompt for confirmation before logging off
WaitAndReport	1 means LimitLogin will wait for a status notification (default)
	0 means LimitLogin will not wait for a status notification

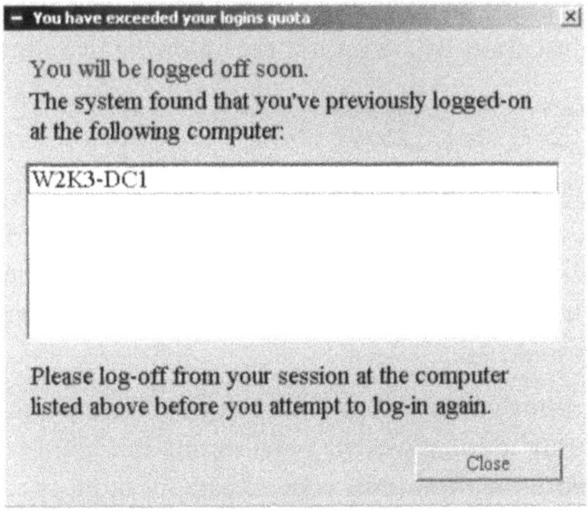

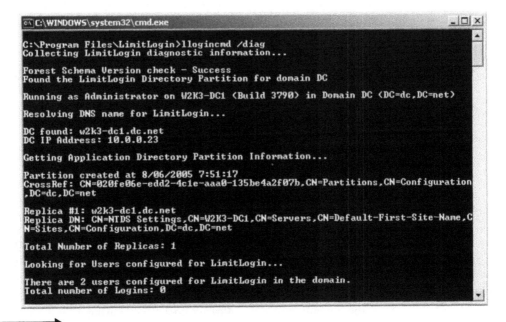

Figure 5.21   *LimitLogin delete/logoff behavior registry configuration settings.*

Finally, the LimitLogin Tasks… context menu option on an OU object can be used to set concurrent logon quota for all user objects in the selected OU at once.

To inform the user about its other logon locations before the user is actually logged off (as illustrated in Figure 5.21), you must make the fol-

Figure 5.22   *LimitLogin diagnostics using llogincmd.*

lowing manual change in the LimitLogin logon script (llogin.vbs): simply remove the comment mark from the following two lines:

```
wshShell.run "lloginsessions" & loginok
wscript.sleep 10000
```

The above configuration guidelines show that LimitLogin can also be used as a logon reporting tool; from the ADUC interface, you can generate XML- or CSV-formatted files. To generate logon reports that cover entire domains, you can use the llogincmd.exe command line utility with the /report switch.

The same command line utility can be used to run a LimitLogin diagnostics (use the /diag switch, as illustrated in Figure 5.22) and to perform maintenance on the LimitLogin AD application partition. To remove all logon information from the LimitLogin AD partition, use the /ClearLogins switch. To synchronize user accounts and their naming information in the LimitLogin AD partition with their corresponding AD entries, use the /Update switch.

5.8   General Authentication Troubleshooting

This section gives an overview of general authentication troubleshooting tools. The tools discussed here are not related to specific Windows authentication protocols. We will discuss authentication-related Windows event logging and netlogon service logging.

5.8.1   Authentication-Related Windows Event Logging

This section only provides a short introduction to authentication-related event logging. We will come back to Windows auditing in more detail in Chapter 13 in *Advanced Microsoft Windows Security Services* (part 2 of this series).

The Windows auditing and event logging system includes two authentication-related audit categories. The difference between the two categories is very subtle and lies in the place where logon events are recorded.

- **Audit logon events (Success, Failure).** Logon events are recorded in the event log of the system where the logon or logoff takes place. For example, when a user logs on to the domain, a logon event will be recorded on the domain member where the logon takes place, not on the domain controller. When a user logs on using a local account, a logon event will be recorded on the local machine. Logon events can be generated for both interactive and noninteractive logons. When a user connects to a remote system for example, a logon event will be recorded in the event log of the remote system.

- **Audit account logon events (Success, Failure).** Account logon events are recorded in a system's event log when a user logs on or off using an account that is defined on the system. For example, when a user logs on to the domain, an account logon event will be recorded on the domain controller that authenticates the user.[14] When a user logs on using a local account, an account logon event will be recorded on the local machine.

These two audit categories include both user and computer account logon and logoff events.

Enabling auditing for the above event categories can be of great use for forensic research or simply when troubleshooting Windows authentication problems. In Windows Server 2003 and R2 domains, auditing for successful logon and account logon events is enabled by default.

When auditing is enabled for logon events, your event logs will contain entries similar to the ones shown in Figures 5.23 and 5.24. Figure 5.23 shows the event details for a successful logon event. Figure 5.24 shows the event details for a failed account logon event.

Table 5.11 shows all the event detail fields that can be found in Windows authentication-related events. Table 5.12 shows the most important event IDs generated for logon events and their meaning. Table 5.13 shows the most important event IDs generated for account logon events and their meaning.

Table 5.14 shows the values of the Logon Type field and their meaning. The most frequently occurring Logon Type values are 2 and 3. When you see a Logon Type 2 in the Event Viewer logs, you know that somebody has logged on interactively to your machine. When you see a Logon Type 3, you know that somebody has tried to access a resource on your computer from the network.

The Logon ID field uniquely identifies a logon session on a particular machine. Because both a logon session's logon and logoff events refer to

---

14. A very important detail is that an account logon event is not recorded in the security event logs of all domain controllers of a domain, but only on the authenticating DC. That's why you must consolidate the security event logs of all DCs in a user's definition domain when troubleshooting authentication problems or tracing logon/logoff behavior. The same is true for the storage of the user's last logon time in AD. See also the sidenote on "Where Is a User's Last Logon Time Stored in Active Directory?" for more information.

Figure 5.23
*Successful logon
event.*

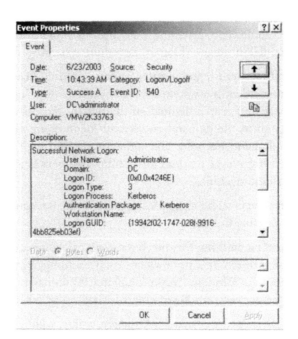

Figure 5.24
*Failed account
logon event.*

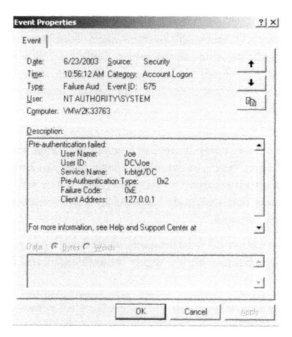

the same Logon ID, you can use the Logon ID to find the logoff event that corresponds to a particular logon event. A logon event has event ID 528 and a logoff event has event ID 538. Event ID 538 (logoff event) is, however, rarely logged to the event log: Microsoft says this behavior is by design, and occurs because during the shutdown process, the Windows service that writes to the security event log is already stopped when the last token for the user who logs off is released. It is documented in the following Microsoft Knowledge Base article: https://premier.microsoft.com/default.aspx?scid=kb;en-us;828857.

Table 5.11   *Event Detail Fields for Logon Events*

Event Detail Field Name	Description
Date	The date on which the event occurred.
Time	The time at which the event occurred.
User	The user account performing the logon.
Computer	The account name of the computer on which the event occurred.
Event ID	The identifier for the event. Tables 5.12 and 5.13 list the most important event IDs for logon and account logon events.
Source	The source of the event.
Type	The type of event: successful (Success Audit) or failure (Failure Audit).
Category	The category of the event.
Description	A short description of the event. This field can hold the following user authentication–related information.
Reason	An explanation of why the authentication failed (applies only to authentication failures).
User Name	The name of the user account that tried to log on.
Domain	The NT domain of the user account that tried to log on.
Logon ID	The unique identifier for a logon session.
Logon Type	A numeric value that indicates the NT logon type. The possible values are listed in Table 5.13.
Logon Process	The name of the process that performed the logon. The possible values are listed in Table 5.14.
Authentication Package	The name of the authentication package used for the logon.
Workstation Name	The account name of the workstation that the user account used for logon.

Table 5.12 *Event IDs for Logon Events*

Event ID	Meaning
528	Successful logon to a computer.
529	Logon Failure: Unknown user name or bad password.
530	Logon Failure / Possible Account Misuse: Account logon time restriction violation.
531	Logon Failure / Possible Account Misuse: Account currently disabled.
532	Logon Failure / Possible Account Misuse: The specified user account has expired.
533	Logon Failure / Possible Account Misuse: User not allowed to log on at this computer.
534	Logon Failure: The user has not been granted the requested logon type at this machine.
535	Logon Failure: The account's password has expired.
536	Logon Failure: The NetLogon service is not active.
537	Logon Failure: An unexpected error occurred during logon.
538	User Logoff.
539	Logon Failure: Account locked out.
540	Successful network logon.
548	Logon Failure: The SID from a trusted domain does not match the account domain SID of the client.
549	Logon Failure: All SIDs corresponding to untrusted namespaces were filtered out during an authentication across forests.
551	A user initiated the logoff process.
552	A user successfully logged on to a computer using explicit credentials while already logged on as a different user.
682	Possible Terminal Services attack: A user has reconnected to a disconnected Terminal Services session.
683	Possible Terminal Services attack: A user disconnected a Terminal Services session without logging off.

Table 5.13   *Event IDs for Account Logon Events*

Event ID	Meaning
672	An authentication service (AS) ticket was successfully issued and validated.
673	A ticket granting service (TGS) ticket was granted.
674	A security principal renewed an AS ticket or TGS ticket.
675	Preauthentication failed.
676	Authentication ticket request failed.
677	A TGS ticket was not granted
678	An account was successfully mapped to a domain account.
680	Identifies the account used for the successful logon attempt and the authentication package used to authenticate the account.
681	A domain account logon was attempted.
682	A user has reconnected to a disconnected Terminal Services session.
683	A user disconnected a Terminal Services session without logging off.

Table 5.14   *Logon-Type Field Values*

Logon Type	Meaning
2	Interactive logon
3	Network logon
4	Batch logon
5	Service logon
6	Proxy logon
7	Unlock workstation
8	Network cleartext logon
10	Remote desktop (RDP) or Terminal Services logon
11	Logon using cached credentials

Table 5.15   *Logon Process Field Values*

Logon Process Field Entry	Description
User32 or WinLogon\MSGina	A typical NT logon process occurred. Winlogon.exe and msgina.dll are files used by the NT authentication UI.
SCMgr	The NT Service Control Manager (SCM) logged on and started a service.
Advapi	An application called the LogonUser function to initiate a logon process.
MS.RADIU	The Remote Authentication Dial-In User Service (RADIUS) initiated a logon.
Kerberos	The Kerberos SSP initiated the logon.
Ntlmssp	The NT LAN Manager (NTLM) SSP initiated the logon.
IIS	Microsoft IIS initiated the logon (this occurs for IIS anonymous access or basic authentication).

The Logon Process field shows the name of the process that initiated the logon session. Table 5.15 shows some of the possible values for this field and their meanings.

5.8.2   Netlogon Logging

The Netlogon service is one of the key LSA processes that run on every Windows domain controller (see Chapter 2 for more information on the LSA). It plays a critical role during interactive and noninteractive logon. When troubleshooting authentication problems, it can be very useful to turn on Netlogon service logging. The Netlogon service stores its log data in a special log file called netlogon.log, which is stored in the %Windir%/debug folder.

The Netlogon log files can also be very helpful when troubleshooting DNS registration failures. The Netlogon service also dynamically registers a domain controller's service records in DNS.

To turn on Netlogon logging,[15] type the following nltest command—nltest is included in the Windows 2000 and Windows Server 2003 Support Tools:

```
nltest /dbflag:2080ffff
```

---

15.   See also the following Microsoft Knowledge Base article: http://support.microsoft.com/?id=109626.

Where Is a User's Last Logon Time Stored in Active Directory?

Active Directory (AD) stores a user's last logon time in the LastLogon AD user object attribute. As is the case for the logging of account logon events, the last logon time is only updated in the AD instance of the DC that authenticated the user. That is why you must query all DCs in a user's definition domain to find out the user's last logon time.

In Windows Server 2003, Microsoft included a new AD user object attribute called LastLogonTimeStamp that resolves the LastLogon problem outlined above, to a certain extent… LastLogonTimeStamp stores the "approximate" value of the last logon of a user to other DCs. The value is approximate because AD replicates it only once every 14 days to avoid replication overhead. So even though LastLogonTime-Stamp does not resolve the LastLogon problem completely, at least it gives administrators a way to discover inactive accounts that have not logged on in the last few weeks. The LastLogonTimeStamp attribute is only activated when the domain is switched to the Windows Server 2003 domain functional level. See also the following Microsoft Technet reference for more information: www.microsoft.com/technet/script-center/topics/win2003/lastlogon.mspx.

Enabling or disabling Netlogon logging requires a Netlogon service restart. You can do this using the net stop netlogon and net start netlogon commands.

To disable netlogon logging type:

```
nltest /dbflag:0
```

Great tools to query the Netlogon log files are the nlparse.exe and the findstr.exe tools.

- The nlparse.exe is a GUI tool that comes with the Microsoft account lockout and management tools (altools.exe), which can be down-loaded from the Microsoft website at http://go.microsoft.com/fwlink/?linkid=16174.

  Figure 5.25 shows the nlparse GUI: It contains the most common Netlogon error codes and their meanings. Nlparse stores the output of its queries in two files (that are both stored in the %Windir%\debug folder)—the netlogon.log-out.scv and the netlogon.log-summaryout.txt.

- Findstr.exe is a command-line tool that is included in the default Windows 2000, Windows XP, Windows Server 2003, and R2 installations.

You can use findstr to query a single or multiple Netlogon log files (or any other textfile) for occurrences of a particular user account or error codes. The following command queries the netlogon log file for occurrences of user JoeJ and stores the results of the query in the output.txt file.

```
Findstr "JoeJ" netlogon.log >c:\output.txt
```

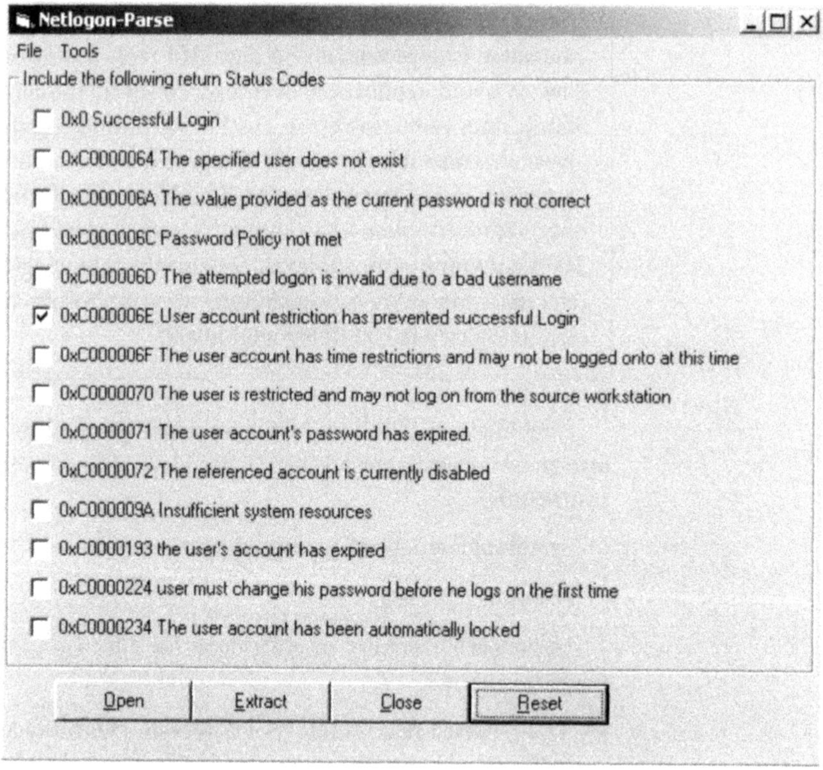

Figure 5.25   *Using the nlparse.exe tool.*

5.9 What's in the Other Authentication Chapters?

The following four chapters will cover different Windows Server 2003 authentication aspects in more detail:

- Chapter 6 focuses on the Kerberos authentication protocol.

- Chapter 7 explains the authentication features of Internet Information Server 6.0, the Web server included in Windows Server 2003 and R2.

- Chapter 8 focuses on Windows and UNIX authentication integration.

- Chapter 9 gives an overview of different SSO architectures and solutions available for a Windows environment

6

Kerberos

This chapter focuses on the Kerberos authentication protocol, the default authentication protocol of Windows 2000, Windows XP, Windows Server 2003, and R2. The chapter looks at how the protocol works, how Microsoft implemented it, and some advanced Kerberos topics. This chapter pays special attention to the new Kerberos features introduced in Windows Server 2003:

- Constrained delegation and protocol transition
- KDC key version numbers
- User-to-User authentication

6.1   Introducing Kerberos

In Greek mythology, Kerberos is a three-headed dog guarding the entrance to the underworld. In the context of this book, Kerberos refers to the authentication protocol developed as part of the MIT Athena project.[1]

Microsoft introduced Kerberos as the new default authentication protocol in Windows 2000. Every Windows 2000, Windows XP, Windows Server 2003, and R2 OS platform includes a client Kerberos authentication provider. Neither Windows 2000, Windows Server 2003, nor R2 includes Kerberos support for other legacy Microsoft platforms. Your NT4, Windows 95, or Windows 98 clients will not be able to authenticate using Kerberos—you'll need to upgrade these workstations to either Windows 2000 Professional or Windows XP. In the early days of Windows 2000, Microsoft promised to include Kerberos support for Windows 95 and 98 in the

---

1.   More historical information on the MIT Athena project is available from the following URL: http://www-tech.mit.edu/V119/N19/history_of_athe.19f.html.

Figure 6.1
The three heads of
Kerberos.

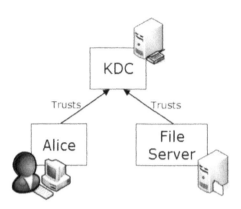

Directory Services Client (dsclient.exe), an add-on for Windows 95 and 98 that can be downloaded from http://download.microsoft.com/download/0/ 0/a/00a7161e-8da8-4c44-b74e-469d769ce96e/dsclient9x.msi, but the Kerberos support never made it into this client.

A little more about the dog's three heads: they stand for authentication, authorization, and auditing. The basic Kerberos protocol (Version 5, as defined in Request for Comments (RFC) 1510) only deals with authentication. Microsoft's implementation of the protocol also includes extensions for authorization. So far, no Kerberos implementation covers auditing. Kerberos can also offer more than the three As. Later in this chapter, we will explain how one of the secret keys exchanged during the Kerberos authentication sequence can be used for packet authentication, integrity, and confidentiality services.

Another analogy to the dog's three heads is the number of basic entities the Kerberos protocol is dealing with. There are always three: two entities that want to authenticate to one another (for example, a user and a resource server, or simply Alice and a file server) and an entity that mediates between the two, a trusted third party, or, in Kerberos terminology, the Key Distribution Center (KDC). This is illustrated in Figure 6.1.

6.1.1   **Kerberos Advantages**

In this section, we will explain the key differences between the NTLM and the Kerberos authentication protocols and the advantages that Kerberos brings to the Windows 2000, Windows XP, Windows Server 2003, and R2 operating systems and their users. Many of the terms used in this section will be explained in more detail later in this chapter.

Faster Authentication

The Kerberos protocol uses a unique ticketing system that provides faster authentication:

- Every authenticated domain entity can request tickets from its local Kerberos KDC to access other domain resources.

- The tickets are considered as access permits by the resource servers.

- The ticket can be used more than once and can be cached on the client side.

When a resource server or the KDC gets a Kerberos ticket and authenticator[2] from the client, the server has enough information to authenticate the client. This differs from the NTLM authentication protocol, which requires resource servers that are not domain controllers to contact a domain controller in order to validate a user's authentication request—this process is known as pass-through authentication. Thanks to its ticketing system, Kerberos does not need pass-through authentication. This is why Kerberos accelerates the authentication process. A downside to the ticketing system is that it puts a greater workload on the client. On the other hand, it offloads the resource servers: they don't have to spend time using pass-through authentication anymore.

Mutual Authentication

Kerberos can support mutual authentication. Mutual authentication means that not only the client authenticates to the service, but also the service authenticates to the client. Mutual authentication is a Kerberos option that can be requested by the client. The support for mutual authentication is a key difference between Kerberos and NTLM. The NTLM challenge-response mechanism only provides client authentication. In the NTLM authentication exchange, the server generates an NTLM challenge for the client, the client calculates an NTLM response, and the server validates that response (as was explained in more detail in Chapter 2). Using NTLM, users might provide their credentials to a bogus server.

Kerberos Is an Open Standard

Microsoft based its Kerberos implementation on the standard defined in RFC 4120. RFC 4120 defines version 5 of the Kerberos protocol. Because

---

2.   An authenticator is the Kerberos object that is providing the actual authentication information, such as the name of the user trying to access a resource—this concept is explained in detail in Section 6.4.3.

Kerberos is defined in an open standard, it can provide SSO between Windows and other Operating Systems supporting an RFC 4120–based Kerberos implementation. RFC 4120 can be downloaded from the Internet Engineering Task Force (IETF) at http://www.ietf.org.

Over the past years, Microsoft has been actively involved in the Kerberos standardization process. Microsoft software engineers participated in the creation of several Kerberos-related Internet drafts, some of which are listed in Table 6.1.

Support for Authentication Delegation

Authentication delegation can be looked at as the next step after impersonation. Thanks to impersonation, a service can access local resources on behalf of a user. Thanks to delegation, a service can access remote resources

Table 6.1   *Kerberos IETF Standards and Drafts*

IETF Drafts	Available from
Public Key Cryptography for Initial Authentication in Kerberos (PKINIT)	www.ietf.org/internet-drafts/draft-ietf-cat-kerberos-pk-init-32.txt
OCSP Support for PKINIT	www.ietf.org/internet-drafts/draft-ietf-krb-wg-ocsp-for-pkinit-06.txt
ECC Support for PKINIT	www.ietf.org/internet-drafts/draft-zhu-pkinit-ecc-00.txt
Kerberos Cryptosystem Negotiation Extension	www.ietf.org/internet-drafts/draft-zhu-kerb-enctype-nego-04.txt
Generating KDC Referrals to Locate Kerberos Realms	www.ietf.org/internet-drafts/draft-ietf-krb-wg-kerberos-referrals-06.txt
Kerberos Set/Change Password: Version 2	www.ietf.org/internet-drafts/draft-ietf-krb-wg-kerberos-set-passwd-04.txt
IETF Standards	**Available from**
AES Encryption for Kerberos 5 (RFC 3962)	www.ietf.org/rfc/rfc3962.txt
Encryption and Checksum Specifications for Kerberos 5 (RFC 3961)	www.ietf.org/rfc/rfc3961.txt
The Kerberos Network Authentication Service V5 (RFC4120)	www.ietf.org/rfc/rfc4120.txt RFC4120 was published in July 2005 and obsoletes RFC 1510.
The Kerberos Version 5 Generic Security Service Application Program Interface (GSS-API) Mechanism: Version 2	www.ietf.org/rfc/rfc4121.txt

on behalf of a user. What delegation really means is that user A can give rights to an intermediary machine B to authenticate to an application server C as if machine B was user A. This means that application server C will base its authorization decisions on user A's identity, rather than on machine B's account. Delegation is also known as authentication forwarding. In Kerberos terminology this basically means that user A forwards a ticket to intermediary machine B, and that machine B then uses user A's ticket to authenticate to application server C.

You can use delegation for authentication in multitier applications. An example is database access using a Web-based front-end application. In a multitier application, authentication happens on different tiers. In such a setup, if you want to set authorization on the database using the user's identity, you should be capable of using the user's identity for authentication both on the Web server and the database server. This is impossible if you use NTLM for authentication on every link, simply because NTLM does not support delegation. We will come back to delegation in more detail later in this chapter.

Support for Smart Card Logon

Through the Kerberos PKINIT extension, Windows 2000, Windows XP, Windows Server 2003, and R2 include support for the smart card logon security feature. Smart card logon provides much stronger authentication than password logon because it relies on a two-factor authentication. To log on, a user needs to possess a smart card and know its PIN code. Smart card logon also offers other security advantages. For example, it can block Trojan horse attacks that try to grab a user's password from the system memory.

6.1.2 Comparing Kerberos to NTLM

Table 6.2 compares Kerberos, the default authentication protocol of Windows 2000, Windows XP, Windows Server 2003, and R2, to NTLM, the default authentication protocol of NT4 and earlier Windows versions.

6.2 Kerberos: The Basic Protocol

The following sections explain the basic Kerberos protocol as it is defined in RFC4120. Those not familiar with Kerberos may be bewildered by the need for numerous keys to be transmitted around the network. To break down the complexity of the protocol, we will approach it in five steps:

1. Kerberos authentication is based on symmetric key cryptography.

2. The Kerberos KDC provides scalability.

3. A Kerberos ticket provides secure transport of a session key.

4. The Kerberos KDC distributes the session key by sending it to the client.

5. The Kerberos Ticket Granting Ticket limits the use of the entities' master keys.

Before starting to explore how Kerberos works, we must explain the notations that will be used in the illustrations (see also Figure 6.2); note

Table 6.2 *Kerberos-NTLM Comparison*

	NTLM	Kerberos
Cryptographic Technology	Symmetric Cryptography	Basic Kerberos: ■ Symmetric Cryptography Kerberos PKINIT: ■ Symmetric and Asymmetric Cryptography
Trusted Third Party	Domain Controller	Basic Kerberos: ■ Domain Controller with KDC service Kerberos PKINIT: ■ Domain Controller with KDC service and Windows Enterprise CA
Microsoft-Supported Platforms	Windows 95, Windows 98, Windows ME, Windows NT4, Windows 2000, Windows XP, Windows Server 2003, and R2, Windows Vista, and Windows codename "Longhorn"	Windows 2000, Windows XP, Windows Server 2003, and R2, Windows Vista, and Windows codename "Longhorn"
Features	Slower authentication because of pass-through authentication	Faster authentication because of unique ticketing system
	No mutual authentication	Optional mutual authentication
	No support for delegation of authentication	Support for delegation of authentication
	No native protocol support for smart card logon	Native protocol support for smart card logon
	Proprietary Microsoft authentication protocol	Open standard

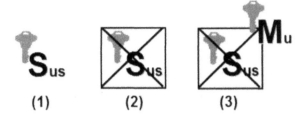

Figure 6.2
Session keys and encrypted session keys.

that characters with different capitalization (upper- and lowercase) have a different meaning:

- The u stands for user, s stands for resource server, and k stands for KDC.

- S stands for session key. Sus means the session key shared between the user and the resource server.

- M stands for master key. Mu is the master key of the user.

- Drawing (1) in Figure 6.2 represents the session key shared between the user and resource server.

- Drawing (2) represents the same session key, but this time encrypted.

- Drawing (3) represents the same session key, encrypted using the master key of the user.

To ease reading we will talk about a client Alice and a resource server that authenticate using Kerberos. The identities used in this Kerberos authentication exchange are Alice's security identifier (SID) and the SID of the service account used by the application or the service responsible for the resource. To be fully correct, we should talk about the service account of the service, but this would not promote ease of reading. Also, when we talk about Alice, we really mean the Local Security Authority (LSA) on Alice's machine, which is acting on her behalf. In the rest of this chapter, the following words are synonyms: principal, security principal, and entity, as well as domain and realm.

6.2.1 Kerberos Design Assumptions

Before diving into the nuts and bolts of the protocol, let's have a quick look at some of the design assumptions the Kerberos designers at MIT took. It is very important to keep these assumptions in mind as we run through the Kerberos internals.

- Kerberos always deals with three entities: users, servers, and a set of security servers that mediate between the users and the servers for authentication. Remember the three heads of Kerberos.

- Time must be reliable and trustworthy. Kerberos uses timestamps to protect against replay attacks.

- User workstations must be trustworthy. This is because Kerberos caches authentication tokens on the client side.

- The security server must be online all the time. Kerberos requires the availability of the security server to generate new Kerberos security tokens.

- The security servers are stateless. Kerberos limits the amount of security-principal–related information that is kept on the server side.

- User password time on the workstation must be minimized. Kerberos considers a password a weak secret that must be protected in the best possible way. One solution is to limit the password time on the user workstation. Another one is to use a key hierarchy. Standard Kerberos leverages both solutions. As we will explain in this chapter Windows Kerberos leverages a key hierarchy, but stores a secured copy of the user password on the workstation.

6.2.2   Step 1: Kerberos Authentication Is Based on Symmetric Key Cryptography

To authenticate entities, Kerberos uses symmetric key cryptography.[3] In symmetric key cryptography, the communicating entities use the same key for both encryption and decryption. The basic mathematical formula behind this process is the following:

$DK(EK(M)) = M$

This formula means that if the encryption (E) and decryption (D) processes are both using the same key K, the decryption of the encrypted text $EK(M)$ results in the readable text M.

The steps below outline how Alice can authenticate to a resource server using a symmetric key cipher (the process is also illustrated in Figure 6.3):

- Alice encrypts her name and the current timestamp using a symmetric key.

---

3.   When the Kerberos design was started, public key cryptography was still patented (by RSA). This explains why the default Kerberos protocol (as defined in RFC 1510) relies on symmetric key cryptography.

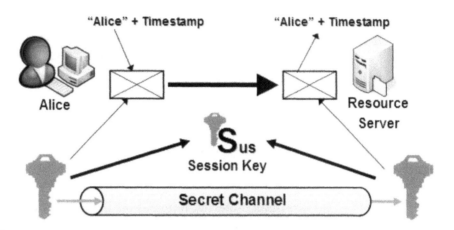

Figure 6.3 *Kerberos authentication is based on symmetric key cryptography.*

- Alice sends the encrypted message and name to the resource server.

- The resource server decrypts the message using the same symmetric key.

- The resource server checks Alice's name and the timestamp (this is the result of the decryption process). If these data are OK, Alice has authenticated to the server.

Why does this process authenticate Alice to the resource server? If the resource server can successfully decrypt the message, this means that, if the decryption process results in Alice's name and an acceptable timestamp, the resource server knows that only Alice could have encrypted this information, because she is the only one, besides the resource server, who also knows the "secret" symmetric key. In this context, "acceptable timestamp" means the following: upon receipt of Alice's encrypted packet, the resource server will compare the timestamp in Alice's packet against the local time. If the time skew between these two timestamps is too big,[4] the resource server will reject the authentication attempt, because a hacker could have replayed Alice's original authentication packet.

In this explanation, you may have noticed similarities with the NTLM authentication protocol. Both Kerberos and NTLM use symmetric cryptography for authentication: "If you can prove you know your secret key, I believe you are who you say you are." In NTLM the knowledge of the secret key is proven using a challenge-response mechanism. Kerberos uses a symmetric encryption of the timestamp and the username to do the same thing.

---

4. The default allowed time skew in Windows is five minutes.

The encrypted packet containing Alice's name and the timestamp is known as the Kerberos authenticator, and the symmetric key is called a session key. A session key exists between all Kerberos principals, such as Active Directory users and computers, that want to authenticate to one another.

A critical element in this exchange is the timestamp; it provides authenticator uniqueness and protects against replay attacks. Without the authenticator, a hacker could grab a ticket off the network and use it to impersonate Alice to a resource server. The timestamp explains the time sensitivity of the Kerberos protocol and of Windows 2000 and Windows Server 2003.

Remember from the introduction that Kerberos can provide mutual authentication. To provide this, the Kerberos protocol includes an additional exchange that authenticates the server to the client. In this example, it means that, in turn, the server will encrypt its name and the timestamp it received from Alice using the symmetric key it shares with Alice and send the result back to Alice. If Alice can successfully decrypt the response from the server and find the timestamp she originally sent, the server is authenticated.

A big problem when using a symmetric protocol is the secure distribution of the secret key. The secret key is generated at one side of the communication channel and should be sent to the other side of the communication channel in a secure way. Secure means that the confidentiality and integrity of the key should be protected. If anybody could read the secret key when it is sent across the network, the whole authentication system becomes worthless: the secrecy of the secret key is a vital part of a symmetric cipher.

Steps 2, 3, and 4 explain how the Kerberos developers have resolved the problem of secure session key distribution.

6.2.3   Step 2: A Kerberos KDC Provides Scalability

The Kerberos protocol always deals with three entities: two entities that want to authenticate to one another and one entity that mediates between these two entities for authentication: the key distribution center (KDC). Why do we need a KDC?

If Alice is a member of a workgroup consisting of five people who all want to authenticate to each other using symmetric key cryptography, every workgroup member must share a secret key with every other member, and a total of 10 keys are needed. (See Figure 6.4.) The mathematical formula behind this is $n\,(n-1)/2$.

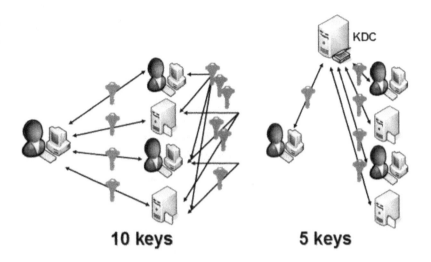

Figure 6.4
A KDC provides scalability.

10 keys   **5 keys**

In a 50,000-employee company, 1.25×10^9 (1.25 billion) keys are needed. This setup not only requires the management of an enormous amount of keys, it also means that there are a large amount of small authentication databases. There would be an authentication database on every client, containing all the secret keys of the employees a particular user wants to authenticate with. This solution clearly does not scale in a large environment. Imagine using this solution on the Internet...

To make Kerberos and the management of the keys Kerberos uses more scalable, the Kerberos developers introduced the concept of a Key Distribution Center (KDC). A KDC is a trusted third party with which every user shares a secret key. This secret key is called the user's master key. All users trust the KDC to mediate in their mutual authentication. The KDC also maintains a centralized authentication database containing a copy of every user's master key.

In Windows 2000, Windows Server 2003, and R2, the KDC[5] service is installed on every domain controller (DC) during the dcpromo Active Directory installation process. Every Windows 2000, Windows Server 2003, and R2 DC also hosts an instance of the central authentication database: the Active Directory (AD) Directory Information Tree (DIT) database, called NTDS.DIT. That is why a Windows domain made up of

---

5.   The KDC itself is made of two subservices: the Authentication Service (AS) and the Ticket Granting Service (TGS). In other Kerberos implementations, these two subservices can run on different machines. Spreading the two services on different machines is not possible in Windows 2000, Windows Server 2003, and R2.

multiple DCs provides fault tolerance for the authentication process and the authentication database. If one DC is down, another one can automatically take over. The AD authentication database is replicated between the domain controllers using a multimaster replication model: all DCs host a read-write copy of the domain portion of the AD database.[6]

The concept of a master key is not new to Windows 2000, Windows Server 2003, R2, and Kerberos. This concept already existed in NT4 and earlier Windows versions. In Windows, the master key is derived from a security principal's password.

The password is a secret key that is shared between each security principal and the central authentication authority. Both the security principal and the KDC must know the master key before the actual Kerberos authentication process can take place. For obvious security reasons, the AD never stores the plain password; it stores a hashed version.[7]

An entity's master key is generated as part of the domain enrollment process: for example, when an administrator creates a user account and enters a password. A machine's master key is derived from the machine password that is automatically generated when an administrator joins the machine to a domain.

6.2.4 Step 3: The Ticket Provides Secure Transport of the Session Key

Figure 6.5 shows the three Kerberos entities: a user (for example, Alice), a resource server, and a KDC. Figure 6.5 also shows the master keys that are shared between the user, the resource server, and the KDC.

In the first step, we talked about the problem of distributing the secret key (the Kerberos session key) when dealing with symmetric key ciphers. This section explains how Kerberos resolves this problem. It makes the link between the session key and the master key that was introduced in step 2.

In step 2, we explained that every entity shares a master key with the KDC. We also mentioned that all entities trust the KDC to mediate in their mutual authentication. Trust in this context means that every entity trusts the KDC to generate session keys. In the scenario shown in Figure 6.5, the

6.   A standard Kerberos domain is made up of a master KDC and one or more slave KDCs. The master KDC is collocated with a read-write copy of the authentication database. Standard Kerberos uses a single-master authentication database model.

7.   See Chapter 5 for more information on Windows password hash functions.

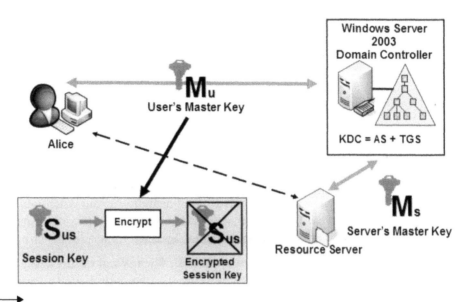

Figure 6.5 *Kerberos entities and master key concept.*

resource server would never directly trust Alice to generate session keys, because Alice has not authenticated to the resource server (and the other way around would not work, either).

To authenticate to the resource server, Alice will request a session key from the KDC. The KDC will generate the session key and distribute it to both Alice and the resource server. To secure the transport of the session key to an entity, Kerberos encrypts the session key with the master key of that particular entity.

Because there are two entities, Alice and the resource server, the KDC must generate two encrypted copies of the session key:

- One copy is encrypted with Alice's master key

- The other copy is encrypted with the resource server's master key

In Kerberos terminology, the session key encrypted with the resource server's master key is referred to as a ticket. A Kerberos ticket provides a secure mechanism to transport a Kerberos session key. Only the resource server and the KDC can decrypt it, because only they have access to the resource server's master key.

By securing the transport of the session key using the master key, Kerberos creates what is known as a key hierarchy. Figure 6.6 shows the Windows Kerberos key hierarchy. It consists of three key layers:

- **Layer 1: the session key (or short-term key)**. A session key is a secret key shared between two Kerberos entities for authentication purposes. The session key is generated by the KDC. Because the session key is a critical part of the Kerberos authentication protocol, it is never sent in the clear over a communication channel: it is encrypted using a master key.

- **Layer 2: the master key (or long-term key)**. The master key is a secret key shared between each entity and the KDC. It must be known to both the entity and the KDC before the actual Kerberos protocol communication can take place. The master key is generated as part of the domain enrollment process and is derived from a user, a machine, or a service's password. The transport of the master key over a communication channel is secured using a secure channel.

- **Layer 3: the secure channel**. When Windows uses a secure channel, it uses a master key to secure the transport of another master key. The following example illustrates the secure channel concept. When an administrator creates a new user account from his administrator workstation, the user's password will be sent to the domain controller using a secure channel. In this example, the secure channel consists of the master key shared between the administrator workstation and the domain controller. This master key is derived from the administrator workstation's machine account password. The concept of a secure channel was also explained in Chapter 2.

In this key hierarchy the following are true:

- Higher-level keys protect lower-level keys.

- Higher-level keying material has a longer lifetime than lower-level keying material.

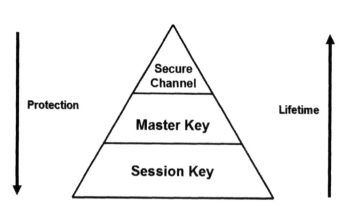

Figure 6.6
Windows Server 2003 key hierarchy.

- Lower-level keying material is used more frequently for sending encrypted packets. As a consequence, there is a higher risk for (brute-force or dictionary) attacks against these packets. To better protect them, the associated lower-level keys should be changed more often or should have a shorter lifetime.

As we will explain in Section 6.5.1, a Windows administrator can influence the lifetimes of the lower-level keys by changing the user and service ticket lifetimes in the Group Policy Objects (GPOs) Kerberos settings. Chapter 2 explained how you can fine-tune the lifetimes of higher-level keys (user and machine passwords).

6.2.5   Step 4: The KDC Distributes the Session Key by Sending It to the Client

The KDC could theoretically distribute the encrypted session keys to Alice and the resource server in two ways:

1.   Method 1: The KDC could send each encrypted session key directly to Alice and the resource server (illustrated in Figure 6.7).

2.   Method 2: The KDC could send both encrypted session keys to Alice. Alice could then send the resource server's encrypted session key at a later point in time during the Kerberos authentication sequence (as shown in Figure 6.8).

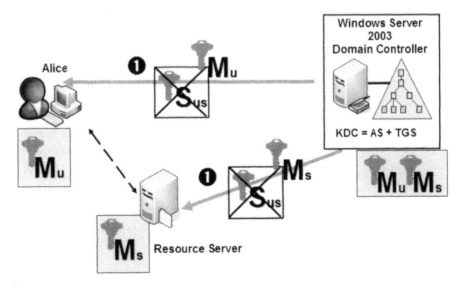

Figure 6.7   *Kerberos ticket distribution, method 1.*

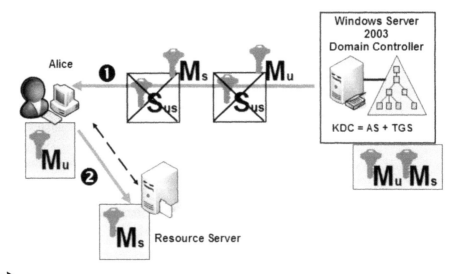

Figure 6.8   *Kerberos ticket distribution, method 2.*

The first encrypted session key distribution method has the following disadvantages:

- The resource server must cache all session keys. It must cache one session key for each client that wants to access a resource on the server. This would create a significant security risk on the resource server side.

- Synchronization problems could occur. The client could already be using the session key before the resource server received its copy.

Because of the disadvantages associated with method 1, Kerberos uses the alternative explained next as method 2 (illustrated in Figure 6.8):

- Both encrypted session keys are sent to Alice.

- Alice can decrypt the packet encrypted with her master key and retrieve her copy of the session key. Alice's system can then cache both Alice's copy of the session key and the server's copy of the encrypted session key (the ticket).

- When Alice needs to authenticate to the resource server, Alice can bundle the server's copy of the encrypted session key with her authentication request.

The key advantage of method 2 lies in its unique caching architecture. Alice's machine can cache tickets and reuse them. On the Windows 2000, Windows XP, Windows Server 2003, and R2 client side, tickets are kept in a special volatile system memory area protected by the LSA. The ticket cache is purged when the principal's logon session ends. The cache is preserved and written to disk when a system goes into hibernation mode. The reuse of the cached tickets is also limited because of a ticket's limited lifetime (by default, 10 hours) and renewal time (both concepts are explained in more detail below).

Method 2 also takes away the need for the resource server to cache tickets. The resource server will receive tickets from the Kerberos clients as needed. This makes Kerberos stateless on the resource server side, which has obvious advantages if some load-balancing or redundancy technology must be implemented on the resource server side. The fact that no caching is required also positively impacts performance: the resource server doesn't need to look up a user's key each time a user requests access to the resource.

6.2.6   Step 5: The Ticket-Granting Ticket Limits the Use of the Master Keys

There is another important weakness in the above protocol exchanges that we have not addressed so far: the session key that is sent back from the KDC to Alice is encrypted using Alice's master key (as illustrated in Figure 6.9[8]). This encrypted packet is sent over the network every time Alice needs a session key to authenticate to a resource server. This also means that every time, there is an opportunity for hackers to intercept the encrypted packet and to perform an offline brute-force or dictionary attack[9] against the packet to derive the user's master key.

There is a clear need here for a strong[10] secret to replace Alice's master key. This will be the role of the session key shared between each Kerberos entity and the KDC. This session key will replace Alice's password, and it will be used to authenticate Alice to the KDC after the initial authentication.

Although it has an identical function (authenticating a Kerberos user), the session key introduced in this step is not the same as the one that was

---

8.   To simplify things, Figure 6.9 only shows a part of the Kerberos exchanges that are shown in Figure 6.8: Figure 6.8 does not include the exchange between Alice and the resource server.

9.   The difference between these attacks was explained in Chapter 2. This chapter also explained some of the tools that can be used to ease these attacks.

10.   In this context, strong means less susceptible to brute-force and dictionary attacks. To better resist these attacks, there are two possibilities: (1) Use longer keys—longer keys create bigger key spaces and make it more difficult to guess the right key; and (2) change the keys more often; if you change a key more often, by the time a hacker has guessed the key, it may not be valid anymore. The Kerberos developers have chosen the latter solution.

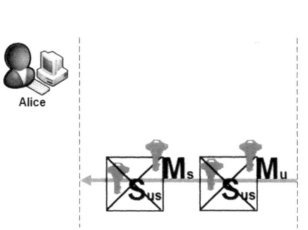

Figure 6.9   *The use of the master key.*

used in the previous steps. The session key introduced here is shared
between Alice and the KDC. The session key used in previous steps was
shared between Alice and the resource server.

As was the case for Alice's master key, both Alice and the KDC must
know this session key. To securely transport this session key, Kerberos uses
the same mechanism as the one described in steps 3 and 4 for the other session key:

- Step 3: Kerberos uses a ticket to provide secure transport of the session key. The special ticket used here is known as the ticket-granting
  ticket (TGT).

- Step 4: Kerberos distributes the session key by sending it to the client.
  The KDC sends the TGT to Alice. Alice caches the TGT and can
  send it to the KDC whenever needed. Again, there is no need for the
  KDC to cache the TGTs of every client. This makes the Kerberos
  protocol stateless on the KDC side. If you do not consider this state-
  lessness argument, it may sound silly that the KDC first generates the
  session key, then sends it out to the client, and then gets it back from
  the client at a later point in time.

Figure 6.10 shows how this new session key (Sku) and the associated
TGT are used in the Kerberos authentication protocol exchange:

- In Step 1, Alice sends a logon message to the domain controller. This message is secured using Alice's master key Mu, which is derived from Alice's password.[11]

- In Step 2 the KDC sends the encrypted copies of the session key Sku to be used for authentication between Alice and the KDC for the rest of Alice's logon session. The copy of the session key that is encrypted with the KDC's master key Mk is called the TGT.

- The session key and the TGT are cached in Alice's local Kerberos ticket cache.

- Alice wants to access a resource on the resource server, and in Step 3 Alice sends a service ticket request to the KDC using the locally cached TGT. This request is secured using the session key Sku and contains an authenticator that authenticates Alice to the KDC.

- In Step 4, the KDC sends a service ticket and a new session key Sus to Alice. Notice that the new session key is not encrypted using Alice's master key Mu, but using the newly created session key Sku. This clearly shows how the session key Sku replaces Alice's master key Mu (compare Figures 6.9 and 6.10).

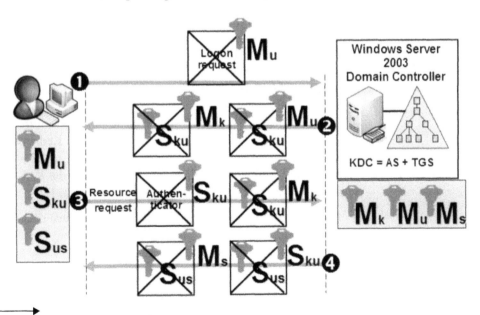

Figure 6.10   *The role of the Kerberos TGT.*

---

11.   The encryption of this request is not a part of the basic Kerberos protocol as defined in RFC 1510; it is based on a Kerberos extension known as Kerberos preauthentication. It will be explained later on in this chapter.

This sequence shows how in the basic Kerberos exchange:

- The TGT can be reused to request new service tickets for other application or resource servers. The reuse of the TGT is limited by its lifetime (see Section 6.5.1 for more information on how to fine-tune the TGT lifetime in Windows using GPO settings).

- Service ticket requests do not require further use of the client's master key.[12] During the logon session, a weak secret (the master key derived from a client's password) is exchanged for a strong secret (the session key contained in the TGT). In other words, at logon time and at each TGT renewal, the user will authenticate to the KDC with his or her master key. In subsequent service ticket requests, the user will authenticate using his or her session key.

- The newly created session key doesn't need to be cached on the KDC; the KDC gets it from the client in the TGT each time the client requests a new service ticket. In the TGT, the session key is encrypted using the KDC's master key[13] so only the KDC can access it. This feature makes Kerberos stateless on the KDC side, which has (as for the resource server side) obvious advantages if some load-balancing or redundancy technology must be implemented on the KDC side. The fact that no caching is required also positively impacts performance: the KDC doesn't need to look up a user's key each time the user requests a new service ticket.

6.2.7 Bringing It All Together

This section brings together all the elements that were introduced in the previous five steps. Figure 6.11 shows the complete Kerberos protocol: it consists of three subprotocols (or phases), each made up of two steps. The cryptic names between parentheses are the names of the Kerberos protocol messages as they are referred to in the Kerberos standards.

- Phase 1: Authentication Service Exchange (occurs once for every logon session)

---

12.   This also means that once you have a session key, in a standard Kerberos implementation there's no more need to cache the master key on the client, which is very nice from a security point of view. Microsoft Windows 2000, Windows XP, Windows Server 2003, and R2 still cache the master key for the duration of a user logon session, because they need it to perform NTLM authentication to down-level clients and to automatically renew the user's Kerberos TGT.

13.   In Kerberos realms made up of different KDCs, a single KDC master key is shared between the KDCs. This allows all KDCs to decrypt the TGT and retrieve the session key. In Windows-speak, this means that the KDC master key is shared between all domain controllers of a domain. The KDC master key is derived from the password of the krbtgt AD account.

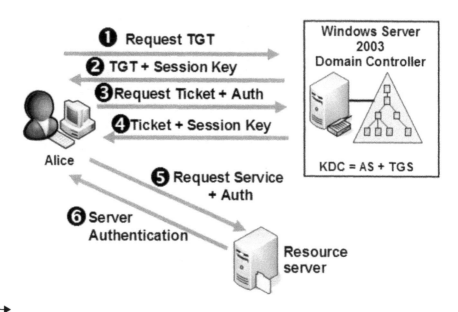

Figure 6.11 *The complete Kerberos protocol.*

- — Step 1: Authentication Server Request (KRB_AS_REQ). Alice logs onto the domain from her local machine. A TGT request is sent to a Windows KDC.

- — Step 2: Authentication Server Reply (KRB_AS_REP). The Windows KDC returns a TGT and a session key to Alice.

- ■ Phase 2: Ticket-Granting Service Exchange (occurs once for every resource server)

- — Step 3: TGS Request (KRB_TGS_REQ). Alice wants to access a resource. A ticket request for the resource server is sent to the Windows KDC. This request consists of Alice's TGT and an authenticator.

- — Step 4: TGS Reply (KRB_TGS_REP). The Windows KDC returns a ticket and a session key to Alice.

- ■ Phase 3: Client-Server Authentication Exchange (occurs once for every server session)

- — Step 5: Application Server[14] Request (KRB_AP_REQ). The ticket is sent to the resource server. Upon receiving the ticket and the authenticator, the server can authenticate Alice.

---

14. Kerberos documentation typically talks about application servers; we refer to application servers as resource servers.

— Step 6: Optional Application Server Reply (KRB_AP_REP). This is the optional Kerberos mutual authentication step that can be requested by the client in the KRB_AP_REQ message. In the KRB_AP_REP message the server replies to Alice with another authenticator. On receiving this authenticator, Alice can authenticate the server.

The KRB_AP_REP message consists of the timestamp the server received from Alice encrypted with the session key. Validating it on Alice's side consists of decrypting using the session key and then checking the timestamp.

During these exchanges the following Kerberos keys and tickets are cached on Alice's computer: the TGT, the ticket used to authenticate to the resource server, and two session keys—one to authenticate to the KDC and one to authenticate to the resource server.

6.2.8 Kerberos Data Confidentiality, Authentication, and Integrity Services

Windows 2000, Windows XP, Windows Server 2003, and R2 all include the Kerberos extensions that can be used to provide data confidentiality, authentication, and integrity for messages that are sent after the initial Kerberos authentication exchange. These extensions are known as the KRB_PRIV (providing data confidentiality) and the KRB_SAFE (providing data authentication and integrity) Kerberos extensions.

Both extensions leverage the session key that exists between two entities at the end of a Kerberos authentication protocol exchange:

■ The session key can be used to sign a message. A hash, which is the result of applying a hash function to a message, can be encrypted using the session key. A hash encrypted with a session key is also referred to as a message authentication code (MAC).

■ The session key can be used to seal a message by encrypting the message using the session key.

6.2.9 User-to-User Authentication

User-to-user (U2U) authentication is a Kerberos version 5 extension that Microsoft added in Windows Server 2003. User-to-user authentication avoids encrypting service tickets using a master key. As such it limits master key network exposure and the risk of a dictionary or brute-force attack being mounted against packets encrypted with a master key.

Instead of a master key, U2U authentication uses a session key to encrypt Kerberos service tickets. Session keys are randomly generated by the Kerberos KDC. Master keys are often less random because they are derived from a user or administrator chosen password. Also, the session key has a shorter lifetime than the master key. This makes the possible damage resulting out of an attack against the session key smaller than the possible damage resulting out of an attack against the master key.

Kerberos U2U authentication allows applications running on a Kerberos user's client machine (for example: a Kerberized FTP or Telnet service) to use the user's identity and its associated session key—without leveraging the user's master key. This also means there is no need to configure a special master key for the service and to cache the service's master key on the client machine. For more background information on the U2U extension, see the following Web site: www.faqs.org/faqs/kerberos-faq/general/section-27.html.

In Windows Server 2003, Kerberos uses U2U authentication for services that don't have a service principal name (SPN) registered in the AD. When a user requests a service ticket for such service, the KDC will return a KRB_ERR_MUST_USE_USER2USER error message. Windows Server 2003 Kerberos also uses U2U authentication when the destination service requests it. This is illustrated in the example in Figure 6.12, in which Alice tries to obtain a service ticket for a service running on Alice's machine using Alice's identity. In this example the destination service requests U2U because it doesn't have access to Alice's master key.

Figure 6.12 illustrates the Kerberos exchange that is used in a U2U authentication scenario. In this example, Alice needs a service ticket to access a service that is running on her machine using her identity:

- In Step 1, Alice requests a service ticket for the service to the KDC

- The KDC generates a service ticket. In this example, the service's SPN is associated with Alice's AD account. That is why the KDC encrypts the service ticket with Alice's master key. In Step 2, the KDC returns the service ticket to Alice.

- In Step 3, Alice sends the service ticket to the service.

- The service tries to decrypt the service ticket to retrieve the session key, but fails because the service does not have access to Alice's master key. The service generates an error message and forwards it in Step 4,

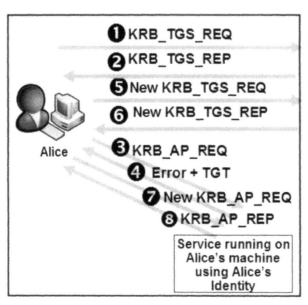

Figure 6.12   *Kerberos user-to-user authentication.*

along with its TGT and a request for a service ticket encrypted using the service's proper session key to Alice.

- In Step 5 Alice requests a new service ticket to the KDC. This request includes the service's TGT and a special flag notifying the KDC that the new service ticket should be encrypted using the service's session key.

- The KDC generates a new session key and service ticket—this time the service ticket is encrypted with the service's session key—and forwards it in Step 6 to Alice. This exchange also includes an encrypted copy of the session key for Alice.

- In Step 7, Alice retries authentication to the service using the new service ticket.

- Step 8 is the optional mutual authentication step.

A similar Kerberos authentication exchange would take place when another user accesses the service on Alice's machine.

6.2.10   Key Version Numbers

Key version numbers is another Kerberos feature that Microsoft introduced in Windows Server 2003. In the Kerberos version 5 specification (defined in RFC4120), key version numbers are an optional feature. They allow security principals to select the correct master key for decrypting a Kerberos TGT or ticket based on the key version information stored in the TGT and ticket headers.

Windows security principals keep a copy of their old master key after they switch to a new password. This enables them to decrypt Kerberos TGTs and tickets that were encrypted using old master keys. To get to the correct master, a security principal could try out all master keys. With a long list of master keys, though, this becomes a time- and resource-wasting process. It is much more efficient to select the correct master key based on a serial number that's included in the Kerberos' ticket header information and also attached to the archived master keys. That's exactly the goal of the Kerberos key version numbering system.

The Windows Server 2003 AD schema includes a new security principal AD object attribute called ms-DS-KeyVersionNumber to store key version information. Windows Server 2003 KDCs will only start using and updating this attribute when the domain is switched to the Windows Server 2003 domain functional level. Ms-DS-KeyVersionNumber is a read-only attribute that is incremented by one each time a principal's[15] password is changed.

Windows Server 2003 KDCs reflect a security principal's latest key version number in the principal's TGTs and tickets. Windows 2000 KDCs always issue Kerberos TGTs and tickets with a key version number equal to 1.

6.3 Logging on to Windows Using Kerberos

Now that we have explained the basic Kerberos protocol, we can discuss some real-world Windows Kerberos logon examples. In this section we will look in detail at both interactive (local) and noninteractive (network) Kerberos-based logon in single and multiple domain environments and in a multiple forest scenario.

Remember from Chapter 4 that in Windows 2000, Windows XP, Windows Server 2003, and R2, Kerberos is always the first choice for authentication. If Kerberos authentication cannot succeed for one or the other reason, Windows will automatically fall back to NTLM authentication.

A scenario that also calls on the Windows Kerberos Security Support Provider (SSP) but that is not discussed below is local logon with a local

---

15.   This applies to all security principals: user, computer, and domain trust security principals.

account. In this scenario, the LSA will first pass the authentication request to the Kerberos SSP. The Kerberos SSP will check whether the logon target is the same as the local machine name. If that is the case, it will send an error request to the SSPI telling it that no logon server is available. The SSPI will then call on the NTLM SPP for authentication.

6.3.1   Logging on in a Single Domain Environment

Typical Kerberos logon examples in a single domain environment are:

- **Interactive (local) logon**: Alice is logging on from a machine that is a member of the domain where Alice's user account has been defined.

- **Noninteractive (network) logon**: Alice accesses a resource located on a machine that is a member of Alice's logon domain.

Interactive Logon

Figure 6.13 shows what happens during an interactive logon process in a single domain environment.

Everything starts when Alice presses CTRL+ALT+DEL on her client to log on to the domain.

1.   The client-side Kerberos logic will first try to locate a KDC service for the domain. To do so, it queries the DNS service.[16] The Kerberos package will retry up to three times to contact a KDC. At first, it waits 10 seconds for a reply; on each retry it waits an additional 10 seconds. In most cases, a KDC service for the domain is already known. The discovery of a domain controller is also a part of the secure channel setup that occurs when the machine account logs on to the domain. Secure channel setup is explained in Section 5.2.3 on "Authentication in the Machine Startup and User Logon Sequences."

2.   When a DC is found, Alice sends a Kerberos authentication request to the DC. This message (KRB _AS_REQ) contains a TGT request.

3.   The Authentication Service authenticates Alice, generates a TGT, and sends it back to Alice (KRB _AS_REP).

16.   Windows 2000, Windows Server 2003, and R2 publish two Kerberos-specific SRV records to DNS: _kerberos and _kpasswd. The list of all published SRV records can be found on a domain controller in the "%windir%\system32\config\ netlogon.dns" file. The SRV DNS records are created automatically during the domain controller setup (as part of the dcpromo process).

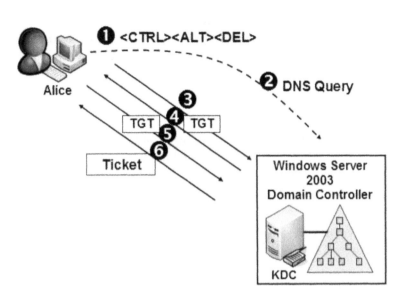

Figure 6.13
Interactive logon in a single domain environment.

4.   The local machine where Alice logged on is—just like any other resource—a resource for which Alice needs a ticket. Alice sends a ticket request to the DC using her TGT (together with an authenticator) (KRB_TGS_REQ).

5.   The TGS of the DC checks the TGT and the authenticator, generates a ticket for the local machine, and sends it back to Alice (KRB_TGS_REP).

6.   On Alice's machine, the ticket is presented to the local security authority, which will create an access token for Alice. From then on, any process acting on Alice's behalf can access the local machine's resources (provided Alice has the proper permissions).

If Alice's TGT expired during Alice's logon session, it would be automatically renewed. Automatic TGT renewal is possible because Windows 2000, Windows XP, Windows Server 2003, and R2 cache the user's master key on the workstation for the duration of a user's logon session. Windows 2000, Windows XP, Windows Server 2003, and R2 use slightly different mechanisms to trigger automatic TGT renewal:

■ On Windows 2000 and Windows XP, TGT renewal is triggered when it is used within five minutes of its expiration.

■ On Windows Server 2003 and R2, TGT renewal is triggered periodically by the system.

During TGT renewal, the KDC checks whether the user account has not been disabled, and the KDC also refreshes the authorization data contained in the TGT using a brand new group expansion process (this process is explained in more detail in Section 6.4.2).

Noninteractive Logon

When Alice is already logged on to a domain and wants to access a resource located on a server located in the same domain, a noninteractive (network) logon process will occur. In this case, the logon sequence is as follows (as illustrated in Figure 6.14):

1. Alice sends a server ticket request to the DC using her TGT (together with an authenticator) (KRB_TGS_REQ).

2. The TGS of the DC checks the authenticator, generates a server ticket, and sends it back to Alice (KRB_TGS_REP).

3. Alice sends the ticket (together with an authenticator) to the resource server (KRB_AP_REQ).

4. The resource server verifies the ticket with the authenticator and optionally sends back its authenticator to Alice for mutual authentication of the server (KRB_AP_REP, as requested by Alice in the KR_AP_REQ exchange).

Once the connection to the resource server is established, it will not be interrupted if the service ticket expires. The connection to the resource server can be deleted explicitly by Alice (using, for example, a net use command) or when she logs off and closes the logon session.

If Alice initiates a connection request using an expired service ticket, the resource server will return an error message. This message will automatically trigger Alice's client-side Kerberos software to request a new service ticket to the KDC.

Disabling Kerberos in Migration Scenarios

In certain migration scenarios (like the one given in the example below), it may be necessary to disable the Kerberos authentication protocol on your Windows domain controllers. Remember from Chapter 5 that for Windows 2000 Professional and later clients, the first authentication protocol of choice is always Kerberos.

Imagine the following migration scenario. You have migrated all your client platforms to Windows XP and want to perform an in-place upgrade

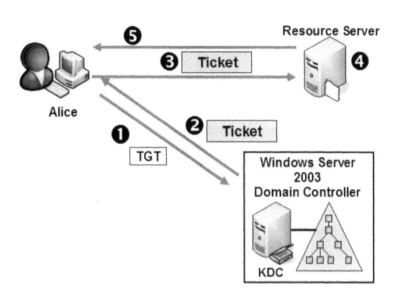

Figure 6.14
*Noninteractive
logon in a single
domain
environment.*

of your Windows NT4 domain to Active Directory. The very first step in this scenario is to upgrade your Windows NT 4.0 PDC to Windows Server 2003—all the remaining DCs are still on NT 4.0. In this scenario, this one and only Windows Server 2003 DC may become overloaded by Kerberos authentication traffic. This is because all Windows XP clients will try to authenticate to it. This is a typical scenario in which you may want to temporarily disable the Kerberos authentication protocol on the Windows Server 2003 DC.

To disable Kerberos, Microsoft provides a registry setting that is available from Windows 2000 Service Pack 2 onward only. The setting is called NT4Emulator (REG_DWORD) and should be added to the HKEY_LOCAL_MACHINE/System/CurrentControlSet/Services/Netlogon/ Parameters registry key of a Windows 2000 SP2 or later DC and set to value 1. This setting only takes effect after a system reboot.

The creation of this key on a Windows 2000 SP2 or later DC also creates the following problems:

- It makes it impossible to manage the AD using any of the MMC-based AD management tools from a domain member client or server (problem 1).

- It will not allow you to promote machines to new domain controllers in the domain of the domain controller that has NT4Emulator enabled (problem 2).

- It will not allow the application of group policies to Windows 2000 and newer clients and thus hinders leveraging the full potential of AD for these clients (problem 3).

To get around these problems, you must make the following registry change on the clients from which you want to use the AD management tools (for problem 1), on the machines that are about to be promoted to domain controllers (for problem 2), and on the clients that you want to use to test group policies in your new AD domain (for problem 3): add the NeutralizeNT4Emulator registry value (REG_DWORD) in the HKEY_LOCAL_MACHINE/System/CurrentControlSet/Services/Netlogon/Parameters registry key and set it to value 1. As is the case for NT4Emulator, this setting only takes effect after a system reboot.

In general, disabling the Kerberos protocol via the NT4Emulator key should be seen as a short-term workaround until sufficient AD DCs are available in the upgraded domain to handle the Kerberos authentication workload.

The Role of SPNs

One of the key features of the Kerberos protocol is its ability to support mutual authentication. Two important enabling technologies for mutual authentication are user principal names (UPNs) and service principal names (SPNs). The UPN and SPN concepts were introduced in Chapter 2. In the following paragraphs we will explain how SPNs are used during the Kerberos authentication exchanges.

Let's consider the example of a noninteractive logon process. A user decides to access a file located on another machine during his or her logon session. In this example, the following SPN-related events will occur during the Kerberos authentication exchanges:

- The Kerberos software on the client side constructs a Kerberos KRB_TGS_REQ message, containing the user's TGT and the SPN of the service hosting the file the user wants to access. This message is sent to the user's domain controller. A Kerberos client can always construct a service's SPN—how this works was explained in Chapter 2.

- The KDC queries the AD[17] to find an account that has a matching SPN—this process is also known as SPN name resolution. Note that

---

17.   In the first place, the KDC will query the local domain Naming Context of the user's authentication DC. If this is unsuccessful, the KDC will query the AD global catalog (GC).

a service's SPN must be unique in the AD. If more than a single account is found with a matching SPN, the authentication will fail.

- Given the service account that has a matching SPN in its AD attributes, and the service account's master key, the KDC can construct a service ticket and send it to the client. This is the KRB_TGS_REP message.

- In the next step, the client sends a KRB_AP_REQ message to the file server. This message includes the service ticket and a Kerberos authenticator.

- Optionally, the service will then authenticate to the client (as requested by the client in the KRB_AP_REQ message). This happens in the KRB_AP_REP message.

6.3.2 Logging on in Multiple Domain Environment

Typical Kerberos logon examples in a multiple domain environment are:

- Interactive (local) logon: Alice logs on from a machine that is a member of a different domain than the one where Alice's account is defined.

- Noninteractive (network) logon: Bob accesses a resource that is located on a machine that is a member of a different domain than the one Bob initially logged on to.

In the following examples, we will frequently use the concepts "referral ticket" and "interrealm key." Both concepts enable cross-domain Kerberos authentication and will be explained in more detail in Section 6.3.2.

Interactive Logon

Figure 6.15 shows a typical multidomain environment, consisting of a parent domain, hp.com, and two child domains, North America (NA) and Europe. In our interactive logon example, Alice's account is defined in the Europe domain and Alice logs on from a workstation defined in the NA domain.

The interactive logon process illustrated in Figure 6.15 can be broken down into the following four steps:

- Step 1: Authentication Service (AS) exchanges (KRB_AS_REQ and KRB_AS_REP):

— When Alice logs on, a TGT request is sent to a KDC in Europe.hp.com.

— If authentication is successful, the selected KDC replies with a TGT and session key. Note that only a KDC of Alice's account domain can authenticate Alice. Windows credentials are never replicated between the domain controllers of different domains. To locate a KDC for the Europe.hp.com domain the NA workstation will perform DNS queries (see also Section 5.2.3).

■ Steps 2, 3, and 4: Ticket Granting Service (TGS) exchanges (KRB_TGS_REQ and KRB_TGS_REP):

— Step 2: To request a ticket for Alice to work on the NA workstation, a TGS request is sent from the workstation to the KDC of Europe.hp.com. The KDC of Europe.hp.com cannot issue a ticket for Alice's NA workstation. Only a KDC of NA can return such a ticket.[18] Therefore, the TGS reply contains a referral ticket to the domain closest to NA.hp.com (from a DNS point of view) and with which NA.hp.com has a real (nontransitive) Kerberos trust relationship. In this example, this is the hp.com domain.

Figure 6.15
Interactive logon in a multiple domain environment.

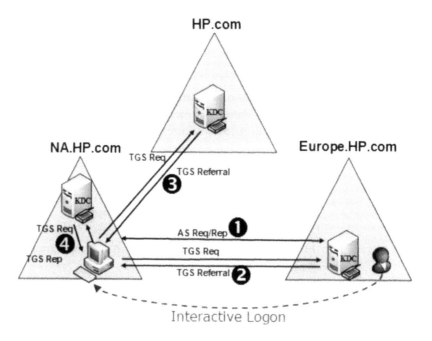

---

18.   This is because only a KDC of NA knows the NA workstation's master key.

— Step 3: On receiving the referral ticket, Alice locates a KDC of the intermediary domain hp.com and sends a TGS request including the referral ticket to the hp.com KDC. The hp.com KDC decrypts the referral ticket using an interdomain key that is shared between Europe.hp.com and hp.com. The KDC detects that the referral ticket contains a ticket request for a ticket for a resource located in NA. The KDC checks on the domain that is closest to NA.hp.com from hp.com's point of view and sends Alice a referral ticket to this domain—which is, in this case, the NA.hp.com domain itself.

— Step 4: Alice asks a KDC of NA.hp.com for a ticket for the NA workstation. The KDC of NA.hp.com will send Alice a TGS reply with a valid ticket for the NA workstation.

The amount of interdomain authentication traffic occurring in the above scenario should not be overestimated for several reasons:

- The size of Kerberos tickets is relatively small.

- Tickets have a lifetime and are cached on the client side.

- The referral traffic does not occur for every resource access. It occurs only when a service ticket for the resource is requested.

An interesting sidenote is to look at what happens if, at some point in this exchange, the administrator of the Europe domain decides to disable Alice's account. The answer to this question is relatively straightforward. The KDC of NA will continue to issue tickets as long as the original TGT is valid. The disabled account will only be detected when Alice tries to get a new TGT, either after expiry of the TGS (default 10 hours) or when Alice logs on locally (interactively) to a different machine in NA. This scenario is further explained in the sidenote, "Kerberos and Disabled Accounts."

Noninteractive Logon

Let's look at what happens during a noninteractive (network) logon process in a multidomain environment. Again, we use the example of a parent domain and two child domains. In this example, Bob is logged on to the NA domain: both Bob's and the computer accounts are defined in the NA domain. Bob wants to access a resource that is hosted on a server in the Europe domain.

The noninteractive logon process illustrated in Figure 6.16 can be split into the following four steps:

- Steps 1, 2, and 3: TGS exchanges:

— Step 1: Before Bob can contact the KDC in the Europe.hp.com domain, he must have a valid ticket to talk to the KDC of that domain. Because there is no direct trust between Europe.hp.com and NA.hp.com, Bob must request the ticket via an intermediary domain. Bob first tries to request a ticket for the KDC of the domain closest to the Europe.hp.com domain: in the example, this is hp.com. Because there is a direct trust between NA.hp.com and hp.com, Bob can request this ticket to his proper KDC. The KDC will return a referral ticket encrypted with the interdomain key shared between NA.hp.com and hp.com.

— Step 2: Armed with this referral ticket, Bob can request a ticket for the KDC of the Europe.hp.com domain to the KDC of the hp.com domain. Because there is a direct trust between hp.com and Europe.hp.com, the KDC of hp.com can answer this request. The returned referral ticket will be encrypted with the interdomain key shared between hp.com and Europe.hp.com.

— Step 3: With this referral ticket, Bob can finally request a ticket for the resource server to a KDC of the Europe.hp.com domain.

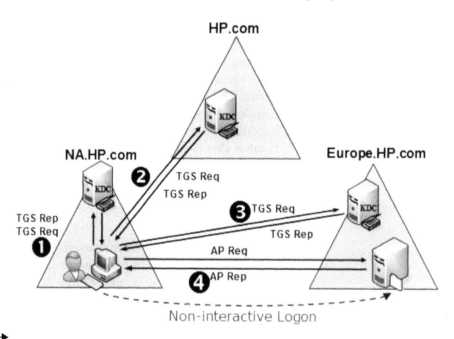

Figure 6.16   *Noninteractive logon in a multiple domain environment.*

Kerberos and Disabled Accounts

The following example illustrates how the fact that Kerberos Ticket-Granting Tickets (TGTs) are reusable as long as they are valid, together with the disabling of a Windows user account, can lead to security holes in a Windows multidomain environment. The AD environment illustrated in Figure 6.17 consists of a forest with a single domain tree. A user and machine account are defined in the NA domain, a file server is hosted in the Europe domain.

When the user logs on to the NA domain, he will receive a TGT for the NA domain. When the user accesses the file server in Europe, he will in addition receive a TGT for the Europe domain. When—during the user's logon session—the administrator disables the user account in the NA domain, he won't be able to get new service tickets for resources hosted in NA. The user will, however, still be able to get new service tickets for resources hosted in the Europe domain. This will be possible as long as the user's TGT for Europe is valid. The reason for this is that the DCs in the Europe domain don't check the user's account status in the NA domain when they issue new service tickets. Section 6.5.1 explains how the TGT lifetime can be adjusted using a Group Policy Object (GPO) setting.

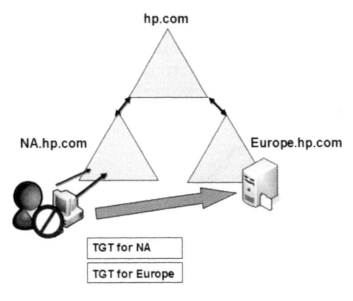

Figure 6.17   *Kerberos disabled account example.*

- Step 4: Application Server Exchange:

    — With the ticket he received from the KDC in the Europe.hp.com domain, Bob can send an authentication request to the resource server.
    — During the optional last step, the resource server will authenticate to Bob (mutual authentication).

The Effect of Shortcut Trusts on Multiple Domain Logon Traffic

A typical scenario in which you would create a shortcut trust is a Windows Server 2003 domain tree with a considerable amount of authentication traffic between two domains that are logically linked together using a transitive trust (see Chapter 3 for more details on the various trust types). The example illustrated in Figure 6.18 shows how the number of referrals is reduced and how the trust path used during authentication is shortened thanks to the creation of a shortcut trust. Note that the KDC in the user domain can detect the existence of shortcut trust when querying AD. The KDC has enough intelligence to leverage the shortcut trust and refer the user directly to the KDC in the resource domain.

In the example that was illustrated in Figure 6.16, Bob goes through the following steps to access the resource in the Europe domain when a shortcut trust is defined between the Europe and the NA domains:

- Step 1: Bob uses his TGT to request to the KDC in the NA domain a ticket for the resource server in the Europe domain. The KDC in the

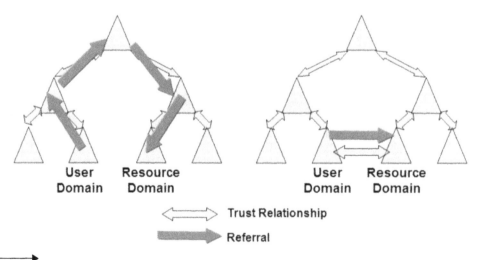

Figure 6.18   *Effect of a shortcut trust on multiple domain logon traffic.*

NA domain is not an authoritative KDC for the Europe domain, and must refer Bob to the domain closest to the target domain with which it has a Kerberos trust relationship. Due to the shortcut trust, this is now the Europe domain.

- Step 2: The KDC in the Europe domain can generate a ticket for Bob.

- Step 3: Bob uses the ticket to access the resource server.

Figure 6.19 shows two more examples of the effect of the creation of a shortcut trust on the interdomain Kerberos authentication referral traffic. In example A, a shortcut trust is created between two child domains of the user and the resource domain. This shortcut trust will not reduce the referral traffic between the user and the resource domain because the shortcut trust is not on the referral path between the user and the resource domain. In example B, the shortcut trust will have an effect on the referral traffic, because the shortcut trust is on the referral path.

Multiple Domain Logon: Under the Hood

In this section we will explain some of the concepts behind the multiple domain logon process: referral tickets and the KDC's Authentication Service (AS) and Ticket Granting Service (TGS). To fully understand the multiple

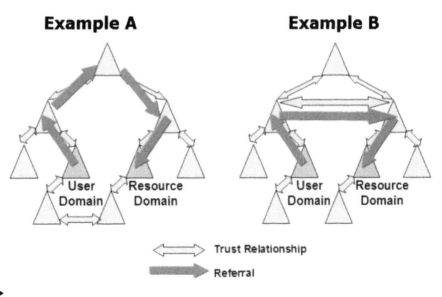

Figure 6.19   *More shortcut trust examples.*

domain logon process, we will also introduce a special Kerberos security principal: the krbtgt security principal.

We will not return to the concepts of trusteddomain object (TDO) and interdomain secret that were explained in detail in Chapter 3. To enable interdomain authentication, every domain that is trusted by another domain is registered in the domain's AD domain naming context as a security principal. These principals are also known as TDOs. The TDO's master key is referred to as an interdomain secret.

The referral tickets used during interdomain authentication traffic are secured using the master and session keys of the TDO principals. As with any other principal and its associated account, a trusteddomain account's master key is derived from its password. The creation of the TDOs and their master keys can happen automatically during the dcpromo domain controller promotion process or manually when an administrator explicitly defines a trust relationship.

To explain the use of the krbtgt account, we must first explain why the Kerberos KDC is made up of two subservices: the Authentication Service (AS) and the Ticket-Granting Service (TGS). Both subservices have a set of different tasks:

- The Authentication Service authenticates accounts defined in the domain where the AS is running and issues TGTs for these accounts.

- The Ticket-Granting Service issues service tickets for resources defined in the domain where the TGS is running. As such, it leverages the TGTs previously created by the AS.

The AS and TGS share a secret derived from the password of the krbtgt security principal. The krbtgt principal's master key is used to encrypt the TGTs that are issued by the KDC. If the Windows domain consists of multiple domain controllers—which, of course, it should—the krbtgt principal's master key is made available to the KDCs on all domain controllers.

The krbtgt account is created automatically when a Windows 2000, Windows Server 2003, or R2 domain is created. It cannot be deleted or renamed. As with any other account, its password is changed automatically at regular intervals. In the Windows 2000, Windows Server 2003, and R2 AD Users and Computers MMC snap-in, this account is always shown as disabled.

Now that we have explained the TDO, interdomain secret, and krbtgt concepts, let us revisit how the multiple domain logon process works. A basic rule in Kerberos is that a user needs a ticket when accessing a

---

Transitive Trusts in Domains Containing Different Domain Controller Versions

Be careful when relying on transitive trust in domains containing a mix of Windows 2000, Windows Server 2003, R2, and/or NT4 DCs. Because NT4 domain controllers do not support Kerberos, transitive trust will only work if a user is authenticated by a Windows 2000 or later DC.

Consider the network logon example illustrated in Figure 6.20. A user defined in NA logs on from a Windows 2000 workstation in NA and accesses a resource in the Belgium domain (Belgium.Europe.hp.com). There is a transitive trust between the NA and Europe and between the NA and Belgium domains. In this scenario, Kerberos authentication will fail if the DC authenticating the user in the Belgium domain is an NT4 DC. Because of this failure, authentication will fall back to NTLM. NTLM, however, does not understand the notion of transitive trust and requires a real trust relationship.

What does this mean? When the NT4 domain controller receives the authentication request from the user in NA, it cannot create a trust path back to the Belgium domain because NT4 and NTLM can only deal with single-hop trust relationships. You could make NTLM work in this scenario by defining an explicit shortcut trust relationship between the NA and Belgium domains.

Figure 6.20
Transitive trusts in mixed mode domains.

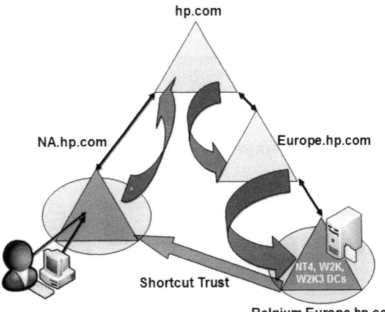

resource. How can Alice get a ticket for a resource hosted in a domain different from Alice's definition domain? Let's once more take the example of Alice, who is defined and logged on in domain na.hp.com, and who decides to access a resource in europe.hp.com—this example is illustrated in Figure 6.21.

In this scenario, the KDC of na.hp.com will issue a referral ticket to Alice to access hp.com. What exactly is a referral ticket? A referral ticket is a TGT that Alice can use in domain hp.com to get a ticket for a resource in that domain. The KDC of na.hp.com can issue such TGTs because hp.com has an account in the na.hp.com domain. To be more precise, hp.com has a TDO—Trusted Domain Object—account in na.hp.com.

How can the KDC of hp.com trust a TGT that was issued not by itself, but by the KDC of na.hp.com? To retrieve the session key the KDC of hp.com will decrypt the TGT with the interdomain secret of its TDO account in na.hp.com. It will then use this session key to validate the associated Kerberos authenticator. If the authenticator is valid, the KDC will consider the TGT trustworthy. Similar steps will occur when hp.com issues a referral ticket for Alice to authenticate to a domain controller in europe.hp.com.

Figure 6.21
Multiple domain logon, revisited.

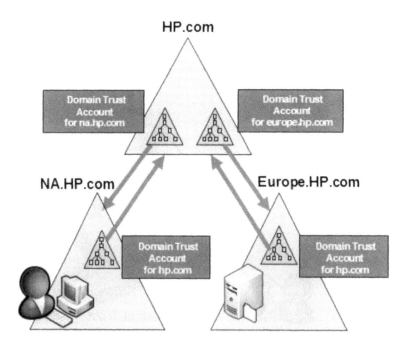

Figure 6.22
Multiple domain logon: under the hood.

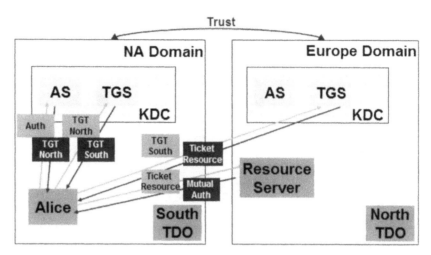

The referral process we just explained relies heavily on the AD and more particularly on the global catalog (GC). First, it uses the GC to find out—given the SPN—in which domain the resource is located, and which domain controller is capable of issuing a resource ticket. Then it uses the AD to find out the domain closest to the target domain to which Alice should be referred.

Figure 6.22 illustrates the process outlined in the previous sections: it shows the interdomain Kerberos authentication exchanges that occur between the NA and the Europe domains when Alice wants to access a resource in the Europe domain. Figure 6.22 shows that there is a TDO account for Europe in the NA domain, and vice versa.

6.3.3 Multiple Forest Logon

Starting with Windows Server 2003, Microsoft adds additional information in the TDO account objects to enable interforest authentication traffic. Figure 6.23 gives an example that shows how Windows Server 2003 and R2 domain controllers use the extra information stored in the TDO to route Kerberos authentication requests during a cross-forest resource access between two forests that are linked together using a forest trust. See Chapter 3 for more information on forest trust relationships.

In the example, a user who is logged on to the emea.compaq.com domain (both the user and machine accounts are defined in emea.compaq.com) wants to access a resource located on a server in the us.hp.com

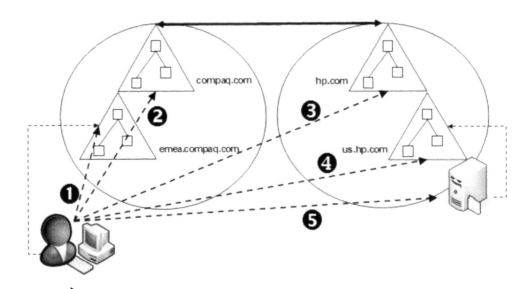

Figure 6.23 *Forest trust authentication flow.*

domain. Both forests are at Windows Server 2003 functional level 2, and a bidirectional forest trust relationship has been set up between them. The remote resource is identified using an SPN that has the following format: <servicename>/us.hp.com.

In this example, the Kerberos authentication requests will be routed as follows:

1. The user's machine contacts the local DC to request a Kerberos service ticket for the resource in the us.hp.com domain. The DC in emea.compaq.com cannot find an entry for the remote service in its local domain database and asks a Global Catalog (GC) server[19] for help. The GC suspects (based on the resource SPN DNS suffix) that the service is located in the hp.com forest, and forwards this routing hint to the DC. The DC refers the user to a DC in the compaq.com root domain, since a direct trust only exists between the root domains of both forests.

2. The user's machine contacts a DC in the compaq.com root domain. This DC refers the user to a DC in the hp.com root domain of the other forest.

3. The user's machine contacts a DC in the hp.com root domain. The hp.com DC will first double-check with its local GC

19. The TDO routing extensions added in Windows Server 2003 are replicated to the GC domain controllers.

whether the requested resource is really in its proper forest. If that's the case, the DC of the hp.com domain refers the user to a DC in the us.hp.com domain.

4.   The user's machine contacts a DC in the us.hp.com domain. This DC can issue a service ticket to the user.

5.   The user uses the service ticket to authenticate to the resource server in the us.hp.com domain.

In the above Kerberos exchange, the client must perform various DNS lookups to follow the referrals to the DCs in the respective domains. If you are operating trusts across firewalls or merely need to optimize the authentication traffic, knowing which DC a client will likely connect to in the target forest becomes a critical thing to understand. See the sidenote on "Locating DCs during Cross-Forest Authentication" in Chapter 3.

6.4   Advanced Kerberos Topics

In this section we will focus on advanced Kerberos topics, such as delegation of authentication, the link between authentication and authorization, the content of Kerberos tickets and authenticators, the details behind a Kerberos-based smart card logon process, the Kerberos transport protocols, and port usage.

6.4.1   Delegation of Authentication

Delegation refers to the ability of a service to impersonate a user and to authenticate to remote services using the user's identity. To the remote services, it will look as if they are communicating directly with the user, whereas in reality a service located on another machine sits between them and the user.

A classical example demonstrating delegation's usefulness is a Web-based multitier application. Examples are Web sites launching user queries against a database located on some back-end server, or a user accessing his mailbox from a Web interface (a good example is Microsoft's Outlook Web Access (OWA)). In the future, when Web services become widespread, the need for authentication delegation support will only become bigger. Web services are rooted on highly distributed architectures that can make data and other resources available to a wide range of users. They require multitier application designs and the ability to reuse the user identity end to end.

The ability to refer to a user's identity end to end in a multitier application scenario is one of the key advantages of the Kerberos delegation sup-

346 Advanced Kerberos Topics

port. It means that administrators can enforce authorization settings at the different tiers using a single user identity. This not only simplifies management, but also facilitates user tracking and auditing on the different levels of a multitier application.

Delegation also brings other security advantages. Because of its ability to transparently authenticate a user on multiple tiers, delegation also provides SSO support. Finally, when delegation is used, the middle-tier servers have no privileges on the back-end servers. This means that if the middle-tier server's identity is compromised, it is more difficult to compromise the data on the back-end servers.

Figure 6.24 illustrates the benefits of using delegation in a multitier application. In the "with delegation" example, the user's identity can be referred to end to end: on Server 1, as well as on Server 2. In the "no delegation" example, Server 1 talks to Server 2 using its proper identity. This means that on Server 2, authorizations can only be set using Server 1's identity. In the "with delegation" example, you can use the user's identity for setting permissions on Server 2 resources, which also benefits auditing.

A disadvantage of using delegation is that you cannot take advantage of connection pooling between Server 1 and Server 2. Connection pooling provides faster connection setup times, because existing connections can be reused instead of setting up brand new ones. This is because a connection pool between two resources can only be linked to a single identity. When using delegation, you use a different identity for each connection.

Figure 6.24
Delegation benefits in a multitier application.

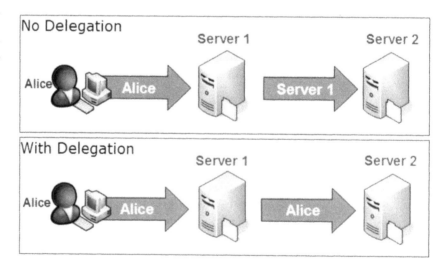

Kerberos' ability to support delegation is a consequence of its unique ticketing mechanism. When sending a ticket to a server, the Kerberos client can add additional information to it so the server can reuse it or even request other tickets on the user's behalf to the Kerberos KDC.

Delegation: Behind the Scenes

Kerberos delegation uses special flags that can be set in a Kerberos ticket. The Kerberos standard (RFC 4120) defines four flags that are listed and explained in Table 6.3.

Notice in Table 6.3 that forwardable, forwarded tickets are much more powerful and flexible concepts than proxiable, proxy tickets:

- A forwardable ticket can be used to request a new TGT, a proxiable ticket can only be used to request a new service ticket. Remember from the introduction that a ticket can be used to access a single resource, and a TGT can be used to access multiple resources.

- When requesting a proxy ticket, the requestor must know the name of the back-end server for which it is requesting the ticket. This is not the case when requesting a forwarded ticket.

Because of the power behind forwardable tickets, Windows 2000, Windows Server 2003, and R2 AD provide a user object property to control which user objects are issued forwardable tickets. The property is called "Account is sensitive and cannot be delegated" and is located on the Account tab of an AD user object's properties. If this setting is enabled, the associated user account will be issued nonforwardable tickets. It is a security

Table 6.3   *Kerberos Ticket Delegation Flags*

Flag	Meaning
Proxiable	Tells the TGS that a new service ticket with a different network address may be issued based on this ticket
Proxy	Indicates that the ticket is a proxy ticket
Forwardable	Tells the TGS that a new TGT with a different network address may be issued based on this TGT
Forwarded	Indicates that this ticket has been forwarded or was issued based on an authentication using a forwarded TGT

best practice to enable the "Account is sensitive and cannot be delegated" property on highly privileged AD accounts (for example, your administrator accounts). Enabling this setting will make it impossible for these accounts to use multitier Web-based applications—for example, Web-based AD administration.

Figures 6.25 and 6.26 detail the Kerberos delegation exchanges in a multitier application environment for proxy (Figure 6.25) and forwarded (Figure 6.26) tickets.

In a Kerberos delegation setup that uses proxy tickets, the following messages are exchanged (as illustrated in Figure 6.25):

- Step 1: Alice checks whether the middle-tier server (Server 1) is trusted for delegation (she checks for the ok-as-delegate flag in a Server 1 ticket)

- Step 2: Alice checks whether she has a proxiable TGT.

- Step 3 (KRB_TGS_REQ and KRB_TGS_REP): Using her proxiable TGT, Alice requests a service ticket for Server 2 that has the proxy flag set (this exchange also includes Alice's authenticator).

- The KDC validates the request and returns a proxy ticket for Server 2. The KDC also returns a new session key for the session between Server 1 and Server 2.

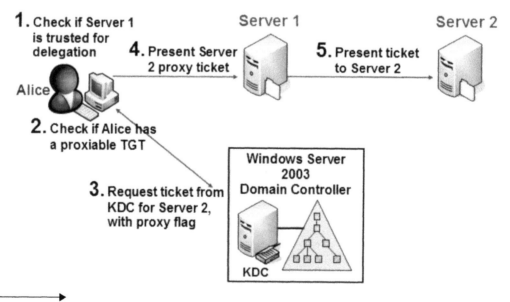

Figure 6.25   *Kerberos delegation exchange for proxy tickets.*

- Step 4 (KRB_CRED): Alice forwards the proxy ticket for Server 2 and the session key to Server 1.

- Step 5 (KRB_AP_REQ): Server 1 authenticates to Server 2 on Alice's behalf and using the proxy ticket.

Note in the above exchange the KRB_CRED Kerberos message type. KRB_CRED messages allow Kerberos entities to forward their tickets and session keys to other Kerberos entities in a secure way.

In a Kerberos delegation setup that uses forwarded tickets, the following messages are exchanged (as illustrated in Figure 6.26):

- Step 1: Alice checks whether the middle-tier server (Server 1) is trusted for delegation (she checks for the ok-as-delegate flag in a Server 1 ticket).

- Step 2: Alice checks whether she has a forwardable TGT.

- Step 3 (KRB_TGS_REQ and KRB_TGS_REP): Using her forwardable TGT, Alice requests a service ticket for Server 1 that has the forwarded flag set (This exchange also includes Alice's authenticator).

The KDC validates the request and returns a forwarded ticket for Server 1. The KDC also returns a new session key for the session between Alice and Server 1.

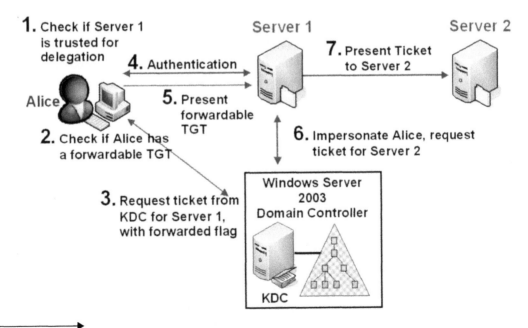

Figure 6.26   *Kerberos delegation exchange for forwarded tickets.*

- Step 4 (KRB_AP_REQ and KRB_AP_REP): Alice authenticates to Server 1 using the forwarded ticket and her authenticator and requests mutual authentication.

  Server 1 authenticates to Alice using the Server 1 authenticator.

- Step 5 (KRB_CRED): Alice forwards her forwardable TGT and associated session key to Server 1. This session key can be used by Server 1 to authenticate to the KDC on Alice's behalf.

- Step 6 (KRB_TGS_REQ and KRB_TGS_REP): Using Alice's forwardable TGT and session key Server 1 requests a service ticket for Server 2 to the KDC.

  The KDC validates the TGT and authenticator and returns a service ticket for Server 2.

- Step 7 (KRB_AP_REQ): Server 1 authenticates to Server 2 using the service ticket and associated authenticator.

In this scenario, Alice did not need to know that the final destination for the data that she needs to access would be Server 2. It is very likely that Server 1 made this decision dynamically, based on its proper application configuration and other dependencies such as performance utilization.

What's Missing in Windows 2000 Kerberos Delegation?

One of the possible reasons Kerberos delegation in Windows 2000 is rarely used is because few people really know and understand it. Another reason is that the Windows 2000 implementation lacks some important security-related configuration options.

In Windows 2000, when a computer is trusted for delegation, it can impersonate a user to any other service on any other computer in the Windows 2000 domain. When a Windows 2000 administrator trusts a computer for delegation, the delegation is almost complete—the only constraint is the time constraint on the Kerberos ticket. Windows 2000 does not provide configuration options to constrain the delegation in space, that is, to restrict the delegation to a set of predefined services.

Another obstacle is that Kerberos delegation in a Windows 2000 Web scenario only works if the user has authenticated to the Web server using Kerberos or Basic authentication. There is no way to use Kerberos delegation when you prefer to use the more secure digest authentication protocol to authenticate your users to the Web server. This is because Windows 2000 requires the user credentials to make Kerberos delegation work on the

Web server. We also have to keep in mind that the use of Kerberos between a browser and a Web server is only possible when the browser supports Kerberos and the Kerberos KDC is accessible from the browser. The latter is a real problem in Internet scenarios. Few companies are willing to expose their KDC to Internet users. Also, on the Internet, not every user has a Kerberos-enabled Web browser. Microsoft's Internet Explorer is Kerberos-enabled from version 5.0 onwards. A Kerberos plug-in for Mozilla-based Web browsers can be downloaded from http://negotiateauth.mozdev.org/.

In Windows Server 2003 and R2, Microsoft embedded a set of Kerberos protocol extensions to remedy these problems. These extensions are referred to as the Service-for-User (S4U) Kerberos extensions. There are two new extensions: the Service-for-User-to-Proxy extension (S4U2Proxy) and the Service-for-User-to-Self extension (S4U2Self). S4U2Proxy is also referred to as constrained delegation. The combined operation of S4U2Proxy and S4U2Self enables a new Kerberos feature that is referred to as protocol transition.

The new Kerberos extensions are only available if your Windows Server 2003 or R2 domain is at Functional Level 2 (this is the native Windows Server 2003 functional level).

Kerberos Constrained Delegation

When using the Kerberos forwardable flag, a user can forward his/her TGT to another service. A TGT is a very powerful security token. It is a digital piece of evidence that proves that the Kerberos KDC has validated a user's identity. A service can use a TGT to get other service tickets on the user's behalf. This is why in Windows 2000, Kerberos delegation is considered unconstrained (or complete).

Kerberos delegation using a proxy ticket—as explained in Section 6.4.1—could be considered a constrained delegation feature, but only to a certain extent. In a proxy ticket-based delegation scenario, the client must explicitly request a server ticket for another server. It doesn't provide administrator control over what service tickets a server can request on behalf of the user. The constrained delegation feature explained in this section offers AD-based administrator control over what service tickets can be requested.

The Windows Server 2003 and R2 S4U2Proxy or constrained delegation Kerberos extension offer the following delegation benefits:

■ A service can reuse a user's service ticket to request a new service ticket to the KDC on the user's behalf. In other words, there is no

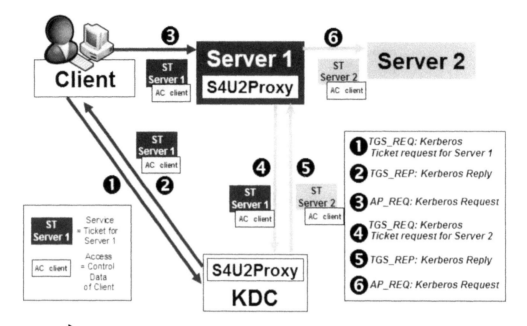

Figure 6.27 *Service-for-User-to-Proxy (S4U2Proxy) operation.*

need to forward a user's TGT to the service[20]—which would allow requesting any service ticket on behalf of the user.

- If a service would be allowed to access any other service on the user's behalf, the ticket feature outlined in the first bullet would create a security hole. This is why Microsoft added a fine-grain delegation configuration feature in Windows Server 2003 and R2. It allows an administrator to constrain delegation in space: in AD the administrator can configure which services a service is allowed to access on a user's behalf.[21]

The Kerberos exchanges occurring in a constrained delegation scenario are illustrated in Figure 6.27.

In Figure 6.27, steps 1 through 3 illustrate the Kerberos exchanges related to a user authenticating to Server 1.

- Step 1: The user requests a service ticket for Server 1 to the KDC (Kerberos TGS_REQ message).

---

20.   This is the case for forwardable ticket-based delegation, as explained in Section 6.4.1.

21.   This is very different from proxy ticket-based delegation (which was explained in Section 6.4.1). When using proxy-based delegation, there is no administrator control over what services delegation is allowed for.

- Step 2: The KDC returns a service ticket for Server 1 to the user (Kerberos TGS_REP message).

- Step 3: The user presents the service ticket for Server 1 to Server 1 (Kerberos AP_REQ message).

Server 1 then needs to access a resource on Server 2 on the user's behalf. Server 1 is running Windows Server 2003, and thus supports the S4U2Proxy extension.

- Step 4: The S4U2Proxy extension on Server 1 requests a service ticket for Server 2 to the KDC on the user's behalf. To prove the user's identity to the KDC, Server 1 presents the user's service ticket for Server 1 (Kerberos TGS_REQ message).

- Step 5: The KDC returns a service ticket for Server 2 to Server 1. Even though this new ticket is passed to Server 1, it contains the user's authorization data (Kerberos TGS_REP message).

- Step 6: Server 1 presents the service ticket for Server 2 to Server 2 (Kerberos AP_REQ message).

Configuring Constrained Delegation

When you open the properties of a machine or a service account in the Windows Server 2003 or R2 AD Users and Computers (ADUC) MMC snap-in, you will notice the new Delegation tab. This tab is not available in the properties of a plain user account. It only shows up if the account has an associated SPN. To make the new delegation tab show up for an account, you can explicitly associate an SPN to it—you can do this using the setspn utility discussed in Chapter 2. You would, for example, need to do this when you created a custom service account for one of your Web-based applications that is involved in a multitier setup where you want to constrain delegation.

From the Delegation tab, you can configure delegation in three different ways (as illustrated in Figure 6.28):

- **Disallowed**: This is done by checking the "Do not trust this computer for delegation" option. This option is also available in Windows 2000.

- **Allowed for all services**: This can be done by checking the "Trust this computer for delegation to any service (Kerberos only)" option. This is the default option and is also available in Windows 2000. In Windows 2000, you would check the "Trust computer for delegation"

Figure 6.28
Configuring
delegation in
Windows Server
2003.

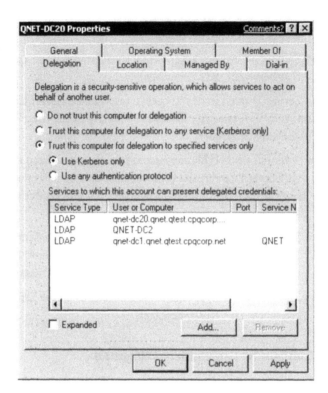

checkbox in the account properties (illustrated in Figure 6.29) to enable delegation for all services.

■ **Only allowed for a limited set of services**: This can be done by checking the "Trust this computer for delegation to specified services only" option. This option refers the new constrained delegation feature coming with Windows Server 2003.

If you allow delegation for an AD account using the "allowed for all services" option, all tickets the KDC issues for that account will contain the ok-as-delegate flag. This flag will not be set if you use the "only allowed for a limited set of services" option.

When selecting the constrained delegation option, you can select the SPNs of the services for which the delegation is allowed by using the "Add…" pushbutton. Clicking this button will bring up the "Add Services" dialog box. Initially, the available services list in this dialog box appears empty. To fill the list, press the "User or Computers…" pushbutton. The latter will bring up the AD object picker dialog box, which will allow you to select the appropriate SPNs. You can only select the SPNs of machines that are a member of the machine's domain.

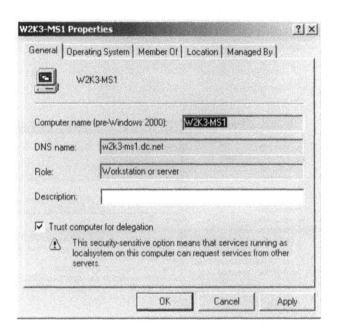

Figure 6.29
*Configuring
delegation in
Windows 2000.*

The SPNs of the services for which an account can use delegation are stored in a new AD account object attribute called msDS-AllowedToDelegateTo. You can examine the content of this multivalued attribute using the Support Tools AdsiEdit tool (as illustrated in Figure 6.30). When the Kerberos KDC receives a service ticket request from an account that has been configured for constrained delegation, it will compare the SPNs listed in the ticket request against the ones listed in the computer or service account's msDS-AllowedToDelegateTo attribute. If there are no matches, the delegation request will be denied.

In the scenario illustrated in Figure 6.27, you would set up constrained delegation in the account properties of Server 1. And you would only trust Server 1 for delegation to the SPN of Server 2.

The S4U2Self Kerberos Extension

The Windows Server 2003 and R2 Service-for-User-to-Self extension (S4U2Self) Kerberos extension allows a server to request a service ticket on a user's behalf without knowing the user's credentials.

If S4U2Self appears to be a dangerous password-less logon process, keep in mind that before a server can request a service ticket on a user's behalf, the server must be authenticated by the KDC and hold a valid TGT. The real security goal behind the S4U2Self extension was not to enable pass-

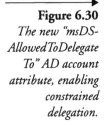

Figure 6.30
The new "msDS-AllowedToDelegate To" AD account attribute, enabling constrained delegation.

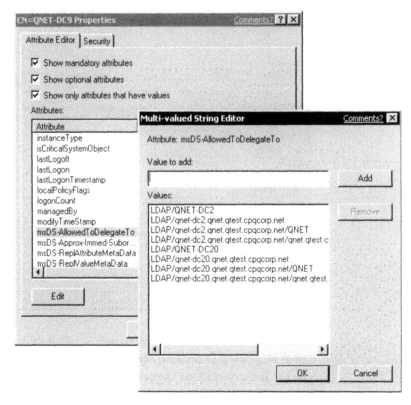

word-less logon, but to enable a server to use Kerberos when authenticating on any user's behalf WITHOUT storing a local copy of the user credentials on the server.

A service that wants to use S4U2Self to obtain a ticket on behalf of another user must also satisfy the following requirements:

- The service's service account must have the "act as a part of operating system" user right on the server hosting the service.

- The service's service account must be able to enumerate the group membership of AD user objects. You can give a service account this permission by adding it to the built-in "Windows Authorization Access Group" AD group. This enables the service account to read the Token-Groups-Global-And-Universal attribute of an AD user object. See also the following Microsoft Knowledge Base article for more information on this: Q331951.

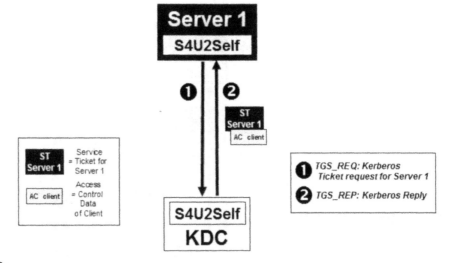

Figure 6.31 *Service-for-User-to-Self extension (S4U2Self) operation.*

The operation of the S4U2Self Kerberos extension is illustrated in Figure 6.31.

- Step 1: The S4U2Proxy extension on Server 1 requests a service ticket for Server 1 to the KDC on the user's behalf (Kerberos TGS_REQ message). Thanks to the S4U2Proxy logic, Server 1 can do this even without knowing the user credentials.

- Step 2: The KDC returns a service ticket for Server 1. Even though this new ticket is passed to Server 1, it contains the user's authorization data (Kerberos TGS_REP message).

Kerberos Protocol Transition

An important issue when using Kerberos delegation in a Web-based multi-tier Windows 2000 application environment is that it can only be used when the client uses Kerberos or basic authentication to authenticate to the Web server. The Web servers that ship with Windows 2000, Windows Server 2003, and R2 come with many other interesting authentication options, such as digest- or certificate-based authentication.

In Windows Server 2003 and R2, you can use any Web authentication protocol on the front end while using Kerberos authentication and delegation on the back end. This is thanks to the combination of the S4U2Proxy

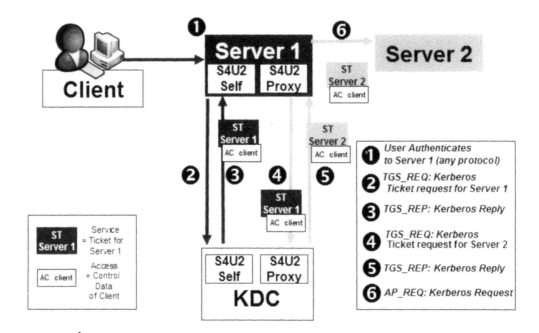

Figure 6.32   *Combined S4U2Self and S4U2Proxy operation.*

and S4U2Self Kerberos extensions. The service provided by the combined operation of S4U2Self and S4U2Proxy is known as protocol transition.

This combined S4U2Self and S4U2Proxy operation is shown in Figure 6.32.

- The figure nicely illustrates the authentication protocol transition: a user who first authenticates to Server 1 using, for example, the digest authentication protocol, later authenticates to Server 2 using the Kerberos protocol.

- Once the user has authenticated to Server 1 and the KDC has issued a service ticket for Server 1, Server 1 can reuse this ticket to request a ticket for Server 2 on the user's behalf. When Server 1 requests the ticket for Server 2, the KDC can enforce constrained delegation: it can check whether Server 1 is allowed to request tickets for Server 2 on a user's behalf.

Configuring Protocol Transition

Configuring protocol transition is relatively easy. It can be configured using the "Use Kerberos only" and "Use any authentication protocol" configuration options on the Delegation tab of an AD account's properties (illustrated in Figure 6.28). If you select "Use any authentication protocol," protocol transition can be used. If you select the other option, you cannot use protocol transition.

In the scenario illustrated in Figure 6.32, you would set up protocol transition in the account properties of Server 1. If, in this scenario, the service impersonating the user is the IIS service, you would give the special S4U2Self permissions that were explained in the S4U2Self section to the IIS service account.

A Delegation Test Scenario

You can test the new Kerberos services in a lab environment like the one illustrated in Figure 6.33. It consists of a simple Web application that queries an SQL Server database on the back end. The database query is defined in a .NET application running on the Web server. The query is called from an ASP.NET page. The Web server and SQL server are members of the same domain. The client machine should not necessarily be a domain member.

The goal of this test scenario from an authentication point of view is to let the user use any authentication protocol (with the exception of Kerberos) to authenticate to the Web server. On the back end, to authenticate to the SQL Server database, we want to use Kerberos and Kerberos delegation. This can only be set up if the new Windows Server 2003 and R2

Figure 6.33
Sample scenario.

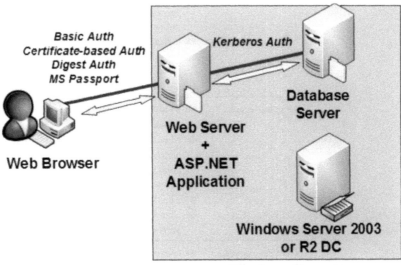

Kerberos delegation extensions (S4U2Proxy and S4U2Self) are available both on the Web server and the domain controller. Table 6.4 summarizes the software requirements and configuration options you must keep in mind when setting this up.

For more information on Kerberos constrained delegation and protocol transition we refer to the Microsoft white paper titled "Kerberos Protocol Transition and Constrained Delegation" that can be downloaded from www.microsoft.com/downloads/details.aspx?familyid=F856A492-AD87-4362-96D9-CBDF843E6634&displaylang=en.

Table 6.4   *Configuration of Different Components in Sample Delegation Scenario*

Component	Software Requirements and/or Configuration Settings
Web Browser	■ Support for basic authentication, digest authentication or certificate-based authentication (SSL), or MS Passport–based authentication. ■ The browser user uses an account defined in the Windows domain.
Web Server	■ Web application is set to support basic authentication, digest authentication, certificate-based authentication (SSL), or MS Passport–based authentication. ■ The user has the appropriate access permissions to the Web site. ■ The Web server is a member of the domain. ■ Web server is running Windows Server 2003 or R2. ■ The Web application's service account must have the "act as part of the operating system" user right and must be a member of the "Windows Authorization Access Group" AD group. ■ Delegation settings for the Web application's service account: — Trust this computer for delegation to specified services only. — Use any authentication protocol. — Add the SPN of the SQL service on the database server (A).
Database Server	■ The SQL Server is configured to support Windows Integrated authentication. ■ The SQL Server service has a registered SPN that is the one referred to in the Web server's computer account delegation settings [see (A) above]. ■ The user has the appropriate access permissions to the database. ■ The database server is a member of the domain. ■ The database server is running Windows 2000, Windows Server 2003 or R2, and SQL Server 2000 or SQL Server 2005.
Domain Controller	■ Are running Windows Server 2003 or R2. ■ Domain is at Windows Server 2003 Functional Level (Level 2).

6.4.2 From Authentication to Authorization

This section explains the link between authentication and authorization in the context of a Kerberos authentication exchange in a Windows AD environment. We will look at how Windows gets from the Kerberos ticket (an important authentication element) to the access token (an important authorization element) and how it completes the list of a user's authorization data along the way.

An important element in this process is the Kerberos Privilege Attribute Certificate (PAC). Microsoft uses the PAC to include a user's authorization data in his/her Kerberos tickets. These user authorization data include a user's group memberships and user rights.[22]

Single Domain Environment

Figure 6.34 shows a typical Windows single domain setup consisting of a user (Alice), her workstation, a resource server, and a set of domain controllers (that are hosting Kerberos KDCs). The domain is at the Windows Server 2003 Functional Level (Level 2).

The following paragraphs explain how Windows constructs the list of Alice's authorization data (group memberships and user rights) when she logs on to the domain and accesses a resource on a member server. All the steps of this process are illustrated in Figure 6.34. The process of finding out a user's group memberships and user rights is also referred to as group and user right expansion.

When Alice has successfully authenticated to her domain controller (DC—this is the DC of the domain where Alice's account is defined), the DC's KDC constructs a Kerberos TGT. To enable the KDC to populate the TGT's PAC with Alice's authorization data, the DC completes the following steps:

- In step 1, the DC queries the local AD domain partition to find out Alice's global group memberships. These not only include Alice's global group memberships that were assigned to her directly, but also the global group memberships that were assigned to one of the global groups Alice belongs to.[23]

---

22. Both Windows groups and user rights will be explained in more detail in Chapters 10 and 11 of this book.
23. In Windows 2000 and Windows Server 2003 domains that do not include NT4 or earlier DCs, groups can be nested. In other words, group nesting is only available if your domains are at domain Functional Level 0 (Windows 2000 native) or 2 (Windows Server 2003). See Chapter 10 for more information.

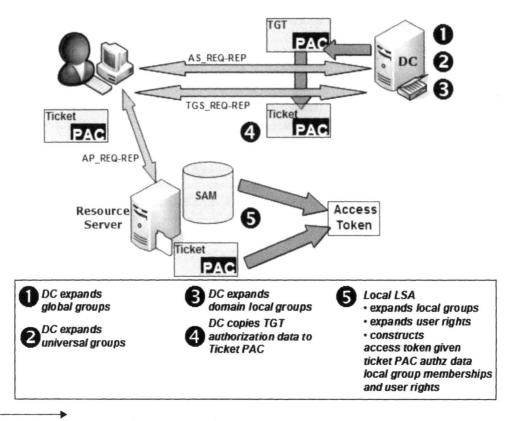

Figure 6.34 *From authentication to authorization in a single domain environment.*

- In step 2, the DC queries the local AD domain partition to find out Alice's universal group memberships. These not only include Alice's universal group memberships that were assigned to her directly, but also the universal group memberships that were assigned to one of the universal or global groups Alice belongs to.

- In step 3, the DC queries the local AD domain partition to find out Alice's domain local group memberships. These not only include Alice's domain local group memberships that were assigned to her directly, but also the domain local group memberships that were assigned to one of the domain local, universal, or global groups Alice belongs to.

The KDC then stores the authorization data in Alice's TGT and forwards the TGT to Alice. Alice's workstation automatically caches the TGT in Alice's local Kerberos ticket cache.

To enable Alice to access a resource located on a member server, the Kerberos logic on Alice's workstation will use Alice's cached TGT to request a service ticket for the resource.

If the ticket request is valid, the KDC will generate a service ticket. To populate the new service ticket's PAC, the KDC simply copies the authorization data from the PAC of Alice's TGT. The KDC then sends the service ticket to Alice. Again, Alice's workstation automatically caches the service ticket in Alice's local Kerberos ticket cache.

When Alice wants to access the resource on the member server, her workstation's Kerberos logic will use Alice's cached service ticket to authenticate Alice to the member server.

In step 5, the LSA on the resource server generates Alice's access token. The LSA embeds the following authorization data in Alice's access token:

- All authorization data found in the PAC of Alice's service ticket. These include Alice's global, universal, and domain local group memberships that were assigned either to her directly or to one of the groups she belongs to.[24]

- Alice's authorization data stored in the local security database (SAM) of the resource server. These include:

   — Alice's local group memberships that were assigned either to her directly or to one of the groups she belongs to
   — And also: Alice's user rights that were assigned either to her directly or to one of the groups she belongs to

From this section, you must remember the following:

- Within a logon session, the PAC data are copied from a user's TGT to the new service ticket. The DC does not refresh the PAC data when a new service ticket is requested.[25] This means that if a user's group memberships change during the user's logon session, the user must do one of the following to force the addition of the new authorization data to his/her Kerberos credentials:

   — Log off, and then log on
   — Wait for an automatic TGT renewal

---

24. Windows groups can be nested, as will be explained in detail in Chapters 10 and 11.
25. Even though Windows does not refresh a user's authorization data, it does check whether the user account hasn't been disabled before it actually allows the generation of a new service ticket. Read also the sidenote on "Kerberos and Disabled Accounts" for an interesting case study on the effect of disabling accounts on service ticket requests in a multidomain environment.

— Purge the Kerberos ticket cache using the klist or kerbtray utilities (which are both explained later in this chapter) and then reauthenticate to the DC—Kerberos reauthentication happens automatically when a Kerberized application is used

- Unlike group expansion, user rights expansion always occurs on the local machine where the access token is created.

Multiple Domain Environment

Earlier sections in this chapter showed how logging on in a multiple domain environment complicates the logon process. This section explains how Windows completes the list of a user's authorization data in a simple multiple domain setup. The example in Figure 6.35 consists of a root domain and two child domains. The user—Alice—defined in the account domain logs on to the account domain from a machine in the same domain (this is an interactive (local) logon). Then Alice decides to access a resource that is located on a server in the resource domain (this triggers a noninteractive (network) logon).

In this example Windows will perform Alice's group and user rights expansion as follows (see Figure 6.35):

- In step 1, Alice authenticates to a local DC in the account domain using the Kerberos protocol. During this step, the DC gathers the following authorization data and adds them to Alice's Ticket-Granting Ticket (TGT):

  — Alice's global group memberships—these can be found in the DC's local AD domain naming context. These global group memberships not only include the global group memberships that were assigned to Alice directly, but also the global group memberships that were assigned to one of the global groups Alice belongs to.

  — Alice's universal group memberships—these can be found on a Global Catalog (GC) DC or if GCless logon is enabled in a DC's local AD domain naming context. These universal group memberships not only include the universal group memberships that were assigned to Alice directly, but also the universal group memberships that were assigned to one of the universal or global groups Alice belongs to. For more information on GCless logon see the sidenote "Understanding GCless Logon."

  — Alice's domain local group memberships—these can be found in the DC's local AD domain naming context. These not only

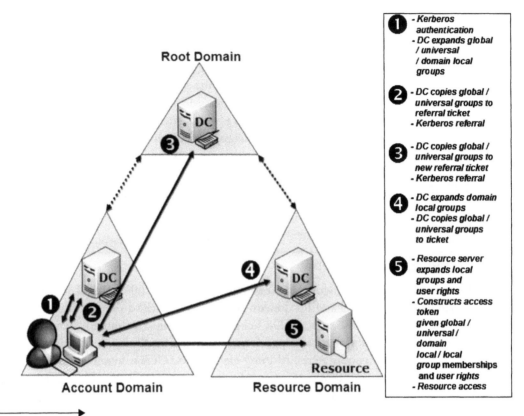

Figure 6.35 *From authentication to authorization in a multiple domain environment.*

include the domain local group memberships that were assigned to Alice directly, but also the domain local group memberships that were assigned to one of the domain local, universal, or global groups Alice belongs to.

- In step 2, Alice tries to get a service ticket for the resource from her authenticating DC. The DC of the account domain cannot issue such a ticket, and refers Alice to a DC in the root domain using a Kerberos referral message. This message contains a Kerberos referral TGT, which has Alice's global and universal group memberships embedded in it. Alice's domain local group memberships in the account domain are filtered out, because they don't make sense beyond the account domain.

- In step 3, the DC of the root domain copies the authorization data in the referral TGT to a new referral TGT. The DC then refers Alice to a DC in the resource domain.

- In step 4, the DC of the resource domain constructs a service ticket for Alice. During this step the DC expands Alice's domain local group memberships in the resource domain and adds them, together with Alice's global and universal group memberships (which can be found in the referral TGT), to the newly constructed service ticket. The service ticket is then forwarded to Alice. The domain local groups expanded in this step not only include the domain local group memberships that were assigned to Alice directly, but also the domain local group memberships that were assigned to one of the domain local, universal, or global groups Alice belongs to.

- In step 5, Alice uses the service ticket to access the resource. The LSA will then construct an access token for Alice given Alice's service

---

Understanding GCless Logon

Global Catalog-less (GCless) logon is a new Windows Server 2003 and R2 feature that enables Windows Server 2003 and R2 domain controllers to cache a user's universal group memberships. To do so, it uses the msDS-Cached-Membership attribute of the user's AD user object. Universal group memberships are cached in this attribute the first time a user logs on. They are automatically refreshed every eight hours. GCless logon can be enabled from the NTDS Site Settings Properties of an AD site object—as illustrated in Figure 6.36.

This new Windows Server 2003 feature does not completely take away the need to put a GC in every site—or at least to have one reachable GC for every site. Although GCs are no longer needed to find out about a user's universal group memberships, you still need them to resolve UPNs when your users log on using a UPN.

A Windows 2000 DC requires a GC DC to retrieve a user's universal group membership. This means that, by default, if no GC is available, a user cannot log on. Luckily, Microsoft also provides a workaround for this Windows 2000 logon requirement. You can instruct a Windows 2000 DC to ignore GC failures. A GC failure occurs when at logon no GC can be contacted to find out a user's universal group memberships. This Windows 2000 workaround is based on the IgnoreGCFailures registry key (located in the HKEY_LOCAL_MACHINE\System\CurrentControlSet\Control\Lsa registry folder). If the Windows 2000 domain consists of multiple DCs, this setting must be set on all DCs.

An annoying side effect is that this registry change can create security risks when universal groups are used to set permissions in a Window 2000 forest. For example, if a user's universal group memberships are not expanded, a user could potentially access data on which a universal group he belongs to was given deny permissions. (This is also documented in Microsoft Knowledge Base article Q241789.)

ticket and authorization data in the local SAM. Alice's final access token holds the following data:

— Alice's global group membership from Alice's definition domain (the account domain), universal group memberships from any domain in the forest, and domain local group memberships from the resource domain (these are all embedded in the service ticket)
— Alice's local group memberships and user rights (the LSA retrieves these from the local SAM on the resource server)

How Does This Work for NTLM?

So far, we only discussed group and user rights expansion in Kerberos-based logon examples. It is also worthwhile to explain how the group and user right expansion process works in an NTLM-based logon.

Figure 6.37 illustrates this process in a simple multiforest environment that consists of an account domain in forest A and a resource domain in forest B. Both forests are linked using a two-way external trust relationship. In the example, Alice is logged on to the account domain and initiates a noninteractive (network) logon to access a resource in the resource domain.

Figure 6.36
From authentication to authorization in a multiple domain environment: NTLM example.

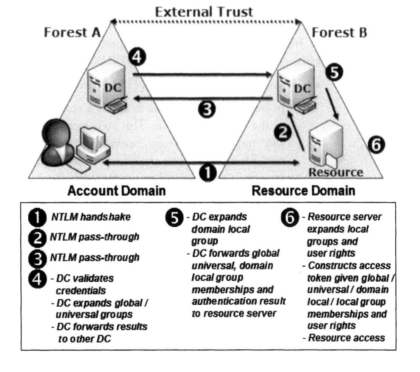

Figure 6.37
*Enabling GCless
logon.*

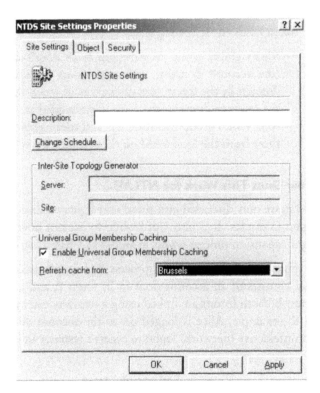

In this example Windows will perform Alice's group and user rights expansion as follows (see Figure 6.37):

- Steps 1 through 3 shows the NTLM handshake:

    — In step 1, Alice attempts to access a resource on a resource server in the resource domain. This step includes an NTLM challenge and response exchange between Alice's workstation and the resource server (as was explained in more detail in Chapter 5).

    — In step 2, the resource server forwards the NTLM response to a DC of the resource domain for validation (remember the notion of pass-through authentication).

    — In step 3, the DC of the resource domain forwards the NTLM response to a DC in the account domain. This is because only DCs in Alice's account domain have a copy of Alice's password hash, and thus only they can validate the NTLM response.

- In step 4, the DC of the account domain validates Alice's NTLM response. If the response is valid, Alice is authenticated. The DC will then expand Alice's global and universal group memberships and forward them together with the authentication result to the DC in the resource domain.

- In step 5, the DC of the resource domain expands Alice's domain local group memberships in the resource domain. It then forwards the authentication result together with Alice's global and universal groups from the account domain and domain local group memberships from the resource domain to the resource server.

- In step 6, the LSA of the resource server constructs an access token for Alice, given the authorization information it got back from the local DC and the authorization data it finds in the local SAM. Alice's final access token holds the following data:

  — Alice's global and universal groups from the account domain and domain local group memberships from the resource domain (these were forwarded by the local DC)
  — Alice's local group memberships and user rights (the LSA retrieves these from the local SAM on the resource server)

6.4.3 Analyzing the Kerberos Ticket and Authenticator

This section provides more detailed information on the Kerberos ticket and authenticator content. The concepts of a ticket and an authenticator and how they are related are illustrated in Figure 6.38.

The primary purpose of a ticket is to securely transport the session key (Sus in Figure 6.38) used for authenticating two Kerberos entities. A ticket can only be decrypted by a KDC and the destination resource server; this is because only they have access to the resource server's master key (Ms in Fig-

Figure 6.38
Relationship between Kerberos ticket and authenticator.

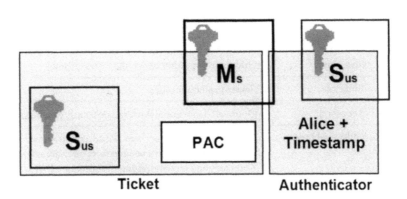

ure 6.38). As a consequence, a Kerberos client cannot decrypt the ticket and change its proper authorization data (this information is kept in a ticket's PAC field).

An authenticator is the Kerberos object that provides the actual authentication. An authenticator can be checked by anyone that has access to the correct session key (Sus in Figure 6.38).

Ticket Content

Table 6.5 shows the ticket fields, their meaning, and whether they are sent in an encrypted format across the network. This format applies to both ticket granting tickets (TGTs) and service tickets.

Table 6.5 *Kerberos Ticket Content*

Encrypted?	Name	Meaning
No	Protocol version	Version number of the Kerberos ticket format. In Windows, this defaults to 5.
No	Realm	Name of the realm (domain) to which the KDC that issued the ticket belongs.
No	Server name	Name of the server.
Yes	Key	Session key.
Yes	Flags	Ticket options. These are explained in more detail in Section 6.4.3 on "TGT and ticket flags."
Yes	Client realm	Name of the realm where the client is defined.
Yes	Client name	Name of the client that requested the ticket.
Yes	Authentication time	Time the ticket was issued. The KDC places a timestamp in this field when it issues a TGT. When it issues tickets based on a TGT, the KDC copies the authentication time content of the TGT to the authentication time field of the ticket.
Yes	Start time	(Optional) Time after which the ticket is valid.
Yes	End time	Ticket's expiration time.
Yes	Renew till	(Optional) Time until which the ticket can be renewed.
Yes	Client addresses	(Optional) One or more client IP addresses from which the ticket can be used. If omitted, the ticket can be used from any address. See also the sidenote on "Kerberos and Network Address Translation (NAT)."
Yes	Authorization data	(Optional) Privilege attributes for the client. Microsoft calls this part the Privilege Attribute Certificate (PAC).

Kerberos and Network Address Translation (NAT)

A Kerberos ticket has an optional field called "client addresses" that can contain the IP addresses of the Kerberos client that is authorized to use the ticket. The Kerberos KDC can use this field to check whether the ticket was sent from the client that initially requested the ticket. As such, the KDC can detect ticket replay attacks in which an impostor tries to impersonate a client by intercepting the client's ticket and then sending it to the KDC.

If the KDC checks and validates client addresses, Kerberos authentication will fail when Network Address Translation (NAT) is used on the communication link between the Kerberos client and the KDC. Authentication will also fail if the Kerberos client has received a new IP address from a DHCP server while its old address is still in its Kerberos ticket. In these scenarios, you may want to disable the inclusion of client IP addresses in Kerberos client TGT requests or disable the checking of these IP addresses on the KDC. The following paragraphs explain how you can control this behavior in Windows XP, Windows 2000, and Windows Server 2003.

Windows 2000, Windows XP, and Windows Server 2003 Kerberos clients do not automatically send their client addresses and do not automatically request their client addresses to be included when they request a TGT from a KDC. When a ticket does not include client addresses, it can be used from all addresses.

This Kerberos client behavior can be controlled using the ClientIPAddresses (REG_DWORD) registry key, which is located in the HKEY_LOCAL_MACHINE\System\CurrentControlSet\Control\Lsa\Kerberos\Parameters registry folder. If this key does not exist or is set to 0, the Kerberos client will not include its client addresses in a TGT request (which is the default). On a Linux or UNIX Kerberos client, you can request addressless tickets using kinit and the -a switch.

For non-Windows KDCs that do require client addresses, you can selectively require the inclusion of client addresses for a particular Kerberos realm. You can do this using the ksetup Support Tools utility. The following ksetup will make a registry change on a Windows client that will tell it to send its client addresses when it requests a TGT from a KDC in a realm named Unixrealm:

```
ksetup /setrealmflags Unixrealm sendaddress
```

In Windows Server 2003, Microsoft also added new registry keys to control KDC behavior for client address checking and client address propagation. Both Windows 2000 and a Windows Server 2003 KDC will, by default, check client addresses if they are present, and will not propagate them to the new tickets (TGTs or service tickets) they generate. To reverse this default behavior in Windows Server 2003, you must use the KdcUseClientAddresses and KdcDontCheckAddresses registry keys (both REG_DWORD), which are located in the HKEY_LOCAL_MACHINE\System\CurrentControlSet\Services\Kdc registry folder. Setting both keys to value 1 will disable client address checking and will enable client address propagation to newly generated tickets. If the KdcDontCheckAddresses key does not exist or is set to 0, the KDC will check client addresses. If the KdcUseClientAddresses key does not exist or is set to 0, the KDC will not propagate client IP addresses to tickets.

Kerberos Encryption Types

Windows 2000, Windows XP, Windows Server 2003, and R2 Kerberos support the following Kerberos encryption types: RC4-HMAC, DES-CBC-CRC, and DES-CBC-MD5. The default Windows Kerberos encryption algorithm is RC4-HMAC. The Kerberos version 5 standard (RFC4120) specifies that a Kerberos implementation must always support DES-CBC-MD5.

In Windows, all three encryption types use special encryption keys derived from a user's password, and stored in the SupplementalCredentials attribute of the user's AD account object. The encryption key used by RC4-HMAC is referred to as the RC4 key. The encryption key used by DES-CBC-CRC and DES-CBC-MD5 is referred to as the DES key.

By default, AD always stores both an RC4 and DES key for each AD account. There are two exceptions to this rule:

- Accounts that are members of a domain that is upgraded from NT4 to Windows 2000 or Windows Server 2003 only have an RC4 key.

- When a new Windows AD domain is created, an administrator account is automatically added. This administrator account only has an RC4 key.

In both cases you can add a DES key for the account by changing its password. Each time an account's password changes, the KDC generates both the RC4 and DES keys.

There are two reasons Microsoft did not use DES-CBC-MD5 or DES-CBC-CRC as the default Kerberos encryption algorithm:

- Ease of upgrading from NT4 to Windows 2000 or Windows Server 2003. The RC4 cipher is also used in NT4 and the RC4 encryption key is available in NT4 user account objects.

- Export law restrictions.[26] In the early stages of the Windows 2000 development, 56-bit DES could not be exported outside the United States. Because Microsoft wanted to use the same Kerberos encryption technology in both the domestic and export versions of the Windows 2000 operating system, it selected the 128-bit RC4-HMAC alternative. At that point in time, RC4-HMAC was already exportable.

---

26.   For a great overview of existing and proposed laws and regulations on cryptography (including the export restrictions in the United States) have a look at the following URL: http://rechten.uvt.nl/koops/cryptolaw/.

Table 6.6   *Kerberos Encryption Types: Key Lengths in Bits*

Algorithm	Key Length
RC4-HMAC (default)	128
	(56 on Windows 2000 without High Encryption Pack)
DES-CBC-CRC	56
DES-CBC-MD5	56

Table 6.6 shows the Windows Kerberos encryption algorithms and their supported key lengths. RC4-HMAC with 128-bit keys is the default for Windows XP, Windows Server 2003, and R2. On Windows 2000, RC4-HMAC uses 56-bit keys by default. Installing the High Encryption Pack on Windows 2000[27] enables RC4-HMAC to use 128-bit keys.

The algorithm a Windows KDC uses to generate a ticket can be checked using the klist or kerbtray resource kit utilities. Both utilities are explained in more detail later in this chapter.

The default encryption type a Windows KDC uses to generate an account's tickets can be changed to DES-CBC-MD5 using the "Use DES encryption types for this account" AD account property. This property can be set in the account options, which are available from the account tab in the account properties. Enabling this property is often required for UNIX and Windows Kerberos interoperability.[28]

A Kerberos client can also request a particular encryption type to the KDC during the Kerberos authentication exchanges. A Windows 2000 KDC always encrypts the Kerberos tickets using the algorithm requested by the client. A Windows Server 2003 KDC, however, always selects the RC4-HMAC algorithm—independent of the encryption type requested by the client. If the client doesn't support RC4-HMAC (this can happen with UNIX clients), the ticket it gets back from the Windows Server 2003 KDC is unusable.

You can force a Windows Server 2003 KDC to respect the Kerberos encryption type requested by the client by installing the hotfix mentioned in Microsoft Knowledge Base article 833708 and by adding the KdcUseRequestedEtypesForTickets (REG_DWORD) registry key, and setting it to

---

27.   The High Encryption Pack for Windows 2000 can be downloaded from www.microsoft.com/windows2000/downloads/recommended/encryption/default.mspx.
28.   There are UNIX Kerberos implementations that support RC4-HMAC: an example is Heimdal Kerberos.

value 1 at the following registry location: HKEY_LOCAL_
MACHINE\SYSTEM\CurrentControlSet\Services\Kdc. A simpler solution is to install Windows Server 2003 Service Pack 1 (SP1), which also
fixes this problem.

The Privilege Attribute Certificate

In this section, we define the Kerberos Privilege Attribute Certificate (PAC)
and explain a related Denial-of-Service (DOS) attack.

Definition   The Privilege Attribute Certificate (PAC) enables the Kerberos protocol to transport authorization data inside Kerberos tickets. In
Windows, these data include a user's group memberships. The PAC and its
content were also discussed in Section 6.4.2. Table 6.7 gives an overview of
the Windows user account data that are stored in the PAC; the data marked
with a * are also stored in the token used during an NTLM authentication
exchange.

Shortly after the release of Windows 2000, Microsoft received negative
press attention because of the proprietary way Microsoft uses the PAC in a
Kerberos ticket. This forced Microsoft to release the PAC specifications.
This specification document can be downloaded from www.microsoft.com/
downloads/details.aspx?displaylang=en&familyid=BF61D972-5086-49FB-
A79C-53A5FD27A092. It can be used only for informational purposes and
explicitly forbids the creation of software that implements the PAC as
described in the specifications. A summary of the specifications can also be
found at http://msdn.microsoft.com/library/default.asp?url=/library/en-us/
dnkerb/html/MSDN_PAC.asp. Microsoft submitted its PAC definition as

Table 6.7   *Windows User Account Data Stored in the PAC*

LogonTime	LogoffTime	KickOffTime	PasswordLastSet
PasswordCanChange	PasswordMustChange	EffectiveName (samAccountName)	FullName
LogonScript	ProfilePath	HomeDirectory	HomeDirectoryDrive
LogonCount	BadPasswordCount	UserId*	PrimaryGroupId
GroupCount*	GroupIds*	UserFlags*	LogonServer
LogonDomainName	LogonDomainId*	UserAccountControl	SidCount*
ExtraSids*	ResourceGroupDomainSid*	ResourceGroupCount*	ResourceGroupIds*

an Internet Draft to the IETF; the draft is called draft-brezak-win2K-krb-authz-01.txt. More information on this draft is available from https://datatracker.ietf.org/public/idindex.cgi?command=id_detail&id=8361.

Most non-Microsoft Kerberos implementations ignore the PAC field and its content. Interoperability issues may arise if a user is a member of a large amount of Windows groups. In that case, the PAC size may become too large to be transported in a single UDP packet. If this happens, a Windows KDC requests the client to switch to TCP. This switch cannot be done by some of the early non-Windows Kerberos implementations, and they will fail. This is also explained in Section 6.5.3 on Kerberos Transport Protocols and Ports later in this chapter.

An important PAC security detail is that the Windows KDC signs the PAC's content. Thanks to this feature, unauthorized changes to the PAC's authorization data by malicious users or services can be detected. The Kerberos PAC content is signed twice:

- Once with the master key of the KDC. This signature prevents malicious resource server-side services from changing authorization data. This signature must always be validated before the PAC data can be used for authorization on the resource server.

- Once with the master key of the resource server's service account. This signature prevents a malicious user from modifying the PAC content and adding its proper authorization data. The validation of this signature is optional.

Denial-of-Service Attack Based on the PAC Content and the MaxToken-Size Property This section explains a denial-of-service attack against Windows domain accounts. The attack is based on the PAC content and the MaxTokenSize property.

The Kerberos ticket has a fixed size, which indirectly also limits the PAC size. Because of this limit, if a user is a member of a large number of groups (100 or more),[29] the Kerberos ticket size might be exceeded. If this is the case, the Kerberos authentication will fail and a client's logon process will by default fall back to NTLM authentication. Even if the NTLM authentication still succeeds, group policy processing will fail. Users with Active Directory (AD) permission to create and modify groups could exploit this

---

29. Remember from Section 6.4.2 that a user's group memberships not only include the groups that are directly assigned to the user account, but also the groups that are assigned to groups the user is a member of—Windows groups can be nested!

weakness to mount a denial-of-service (DoS) attack against user accounts. Such an attack could prevent any user account, including administrator accounts, from logging on to the network.

To prevent this attack, you must start by being extremely careful when delegating AD administrative permissions for group management. You must especially restrict the permission to manage an administrator's account group membership. This restriction is difficult to achieve with the default permissions in AD, because delegated administrators don't need any special rights to add any user account in the forest to the groups they are allowed to manage. As long as a delegated administrator has been granted the permission to write to the member attribute of a group, he does not need any special permissions on a user object to add the user to the group or to nest another group into it. Naturally, any administrator needs to honor the group types when adding users or nesting groups, but, for example, when adding members to domain local and universal groups, the users could be located in any domain in the forest.

So, as a precautionary measure, you should place highly privileged administrator accounts and any groups they belong to (such as Enterprise Administrators, Domain Administrators, and even Domain Users) in special organizational units (OUs) without read permissions for delegated administrators. Although this measure cannot fully prevent this attack, it does hinder the delegated administrators to find the highly privileged accounts and groups in the object picker when adding users to groups via the GUI.

In addition, you can adjust the maximum size of a Kerberos ticket by using the HKEY_LOCAL_MACHINE\SYSTEM\CurrentControl-Set\Control\Lsa\Kerberos\Parameters\MaxTokenSize registry subkey. The MaxTokenSize subkey is documented in the Microsoft article "New resolution for problems that occur when users belong to many groups" at http://support.microsoft.com/?kbid=327825.

The MaxTokenSize subkey (REG_DWORD) should be adjusted on all Windows machines from which users use Kerberos to log on to a domain. In the RTM version of Windows 2000, the default MaxTokenSize value is 8,000 bytes. In Windows 2000 Service Pack 2 (SP2) and later and in Windows Server 2003, the default value is 12,000 bytes.

To further increase the number of group-memberships data in the PAC, Microsoft also implemented a new method to store authorization data in the PAC in Windows 2000 Service Pack 4 (SP4). The new PAC authorization data storage method can be summarized as follows:

- If the groups are local groups or are from other domains (for example, groups added via SIDHistory, or when a user is a member of a universal group in another domain), the entire SID of the group (for example, S-1-5-21-1275210071-789336058-1957994488-3140) is stored in the PAC.

- If the global and universal groups a user belongs to are local to the domain where the user is defined, then only the Relative Identifier (RID) of the group (for example, 3140) is stored.

Microsoft provides a special process on the client and server side to explode RIDs back to the SID format during the Windows authorization process. Note that even on platforms where this new PAC authorization data storage method is available, you might still need to adjust the MaxTokenSize or reduce the number of group memberships for a user.

To avoid wasting space in a Kerberos ticket's PAC field, you should also remove the SIDhistory attribute from your AD accounts when your migration from the NT 4.0 domain to the Windows Server 2003 or Windows 2000 domain is done by following the instructions in the Microsoft article "How To Use Visual Basic Script to Clear SIDhistory" at http://support.microsoft.com/?kbid=295758.

Setting the Kerberos MaxTokenSize value to its maximum value of 64k would technically allow a user to be a member of more than 1,500 domain local groups (or universal groups of other domains) or more than 8,000 global groups (or universal groups of the same domain). The large variance in numbers by group type is related to how SIDs are stored in the Kerberos token, as explained above.

However, the logon process will run into other issues before it would ever reach the technical limits of a Kerberos ticket. There is another more important limit to remember regarding the number of security identifiers (SIDs) a user can collect at logon, before AD will have an issue: 1,024. This is a hard-coded restriction in Active Directory; if any user belongs to more than 1,024 groups (either directly or through group nesting), he can no longer authenticate against AD. This limit is equally applicable to the Kerberos and the NTLM protocol and can directly impact any user account, regardless of the user's administrative privileges in AD. Even if an affected Domain or Enterprise Administrator logs on locally to a domain controller, the logon attempt will fail.

The more accurate maximum value of SIDs (e.g., group-memberships for a user) that can be administratively affected in AD before causing logon issues is 1,015. This is due to nine well known SIDs such as S-1-5-11

(Authenticated Users) or S-1-1-0 (Everyone) and the account's primary group, which are always present for any domain account. Adding users to more groups than AD can handle is referred to as the TokenBloat attack. Administrators need to be prepared to quickly recover from such a DoS attack, which is described in the sidenote "Recovering from a TokenBloat Attack." As a general recommendation, it is a good practice to continuously monitor the number of groups of which a user is a member.

Microsoft implemented the tokensz tool to troubleshoot problems related to the Kerberos token size. You can download the tool from http://www.microsoft.com/downloads/details.aspx?familyid=4a303fa5-cf20-43fb-9483-0f0b0dae265c&displaylang=en. The following tokensz command lists the current system value for MaxTokenSize and the size of the current token:

```
tokensz /compute_tokensize
  /package:negotiate
  /use_delegation
  /target_server:<MachineName>
```

The following tokensz command can be leveraged on a Windows Server 2003 server against a Windows Server 2003 KDC to evaluate the number of groups any AD account is a member of, including all the account's memberships that are due to group nesting:

```
tokensz /calc_groups <samAccountName or UPN>
```

You can find more details about how to use tokensz in the Microsoft white paper, "Troubleshooting Kerberos Errors," at www.microsoft.com/downloads/details.aspx?familyid=7dfeb015-6043-47db-8238-dc7af89c93f1&displaylang=en.

Kerberos Preauthentication Data

In this section, we define the Kerberos preauthentication data and explain a related password-cracking attack.

Definition   Preauthentication was introduced in Kerberos version 5. With preauthentication data, a client can prove the knowledge of its password to the KDC before the KDC issues a TGT. In Kerberos version 4, anyone, including malicious persons, could send an authentication request to the KDC. The security Kerberos version 4 offers is relatively weak: it is completely based on the client's ability to decrypt the packet that is returned from the KDC using its master key.

Recovering from a TokenBloat Attack

What do you do if your AD forest has been attacked and nobody, including the default administrator account, can log on to the domain?

Restoring AD from backup is actually not a good option, assuming the attack is performed with new groups that were created to perform the attack. This is due to the fact that even if an authoritative restore of the whole domain were to be performed on one DC, the new group objects and their links to the users would NOT be removed on the other DCs in the domain and thus would replicate back to the restored DC, causing the same issues as prior to the restore. This is true for any new objects added to AD after a backup was performed—an authoritative restore can neither remove new objects nor can it remove newly added attributes from existing objects (such as attributes that were empty and were then filled with data via a script or via another method). The only way to successfully remove new objects from AD via a restore operation is by restoring all DCs in the domain at the same time (or by taking all DCs offline, then restoring a single DC and re-installing and re-promoting all other DCs).

But there is a much easier method to recover from this attack: you simply have to boot one DC into Safe Mode—not into Directory Services Recovery Mode (DSRM). As with DSRM, you enter this mode by pressing F8 during the boot-sequence of a DC: from the list of boot options you then either choose Safe Mode or Safe Mode with Networking. (See Figure 6.39.)

In contrast to the DSRM mode, which boots the DC in a mode without Active Directory running, this mode will boot the DC with AD running and thus allows you to log on to Active Directory directly (i.e., it does not require the "Restore Password" used to log on to a DC booted to DSRM). More importantly, this mode has special capabilities to recover from a TokenBloat attack: the domain's default Administrator account is capable of logging on successfully to AD, even if the account is disabled and is a member of too many groups!

Once logged on, the default administrator can remove the new groups and thus repair the issues caused by the TokenBloat attack. If just the Safe Boot option (without Networking) was chosen, the changes performed by the administrator would not replicate out to the other DCs until this DC was booted back into normal mode.

Figure 6.39   *Logging on to domain on DC in safe mode.*

Preauthentication lowers the probability of an offline password-guessing attack. Without preauthentication data, it is easy for a hacker to do an offline password-guessing attack[30] on the encrypted packets that are returned from the KDC. A hacker can send out dummy requests for authentication: each time he or she will get back another encrypted packet, which means he or she gets another chance to do a brute-force or dictionary attack on the encrypted packet and guess the user's master key. When pre-authentication is used, a hacker must contact the KDC each time he or she tries a new password.

In a standard Kerberos authentication sequence, the preauthentication data consist of an encrypted timestamp. When logging on using the smart card–based Kerberos extensions, the preauthentication data consist of a

---

30.   During an offline password-guessing attack, a hacker intercepts an encrypted packet, takes it offline, and tries to break it using different passwords.

signed timestamp and the user's public key certificate. The smart card–based Kerberos extensions are covered in more detail later in this chapter.

In Windows 2000, Windows XP, Windows Server 2003, and R2, preauthentication is enabled by default. An administrator can turn it off using the "Do not require Kerberos preauthentication" checkbox in the properties of a domain account (you can find this checkbox on the Account tab). Turning preauthentication off might be required for compatibility with other implementations of the Kerberos protocol.

Password Cracking Based on Preauthentication Data   For a long time, we assumed that when we used the default Kerberos authentication provider on Windows Server 2003, Windows XP, or Windows 2000 machines to protect our passwords, brute-force password cracking attacks such as the ones outlined in Chapter 2 couldn't be successful. But in late 2002—two years after the release of Win2K—a tool named kerbcrack appeared on the Internet. Kerbcrack—which is made up of two tools, kerbsniff and kerbcrack—can perform brute-force cracking attacks on Kerberos packets. Kerbsniff captures Kerberos packets from the network, and kerbcrack performs the actual brute-force cracking on the output of the first tool. Both tools can be downloaded from www.ntsecurity.nu/toolbox/kerbcrack. A paper outlining a similar attack but using different tools is available from www.hut.fi/~autikkan/kerberos/docs/phase1/pdf/LATEST_password_attack.pdf.

Kerbcrack targets the encrypted timestamp embedded in the Kerberos preauthentication data. The timestamp is encrypted using a key based on the user's password (or, in Kerberos-speak, based on the user's master key).

There are two ways to protect against Kerberos preauthentication attacks: use Windows smart card logon, or encrypt the network traffic between the Kerberos client and the DC by using IPsec. Windows smart card logon uses a Kerberos extension called PKINIT, which doesn't encrypt the packet by using the user's master key but rather uses the user's private key. At this point in time, it's impossible to perform a brute-force attack on packets that are secured by using public-private key cryptography. For more information about PKINIT, see the section on smart card logon later in this chapter.

Authenticator Content

Table 6.8 shows the Kerberos authenticator fields, their meaning, and whether they are sent in encrypted format across the network.

Table 6.8   *Kerberos Authenticator Content*

Encrypted?	Name	Meaning
Yes	Authenticator version number	Version number of the authenticator format. In Windows, this defaults to 5.
Yes	Client realm	Name of the realm where the client is defined.
Yes	Client name	Name of the client that requested the ticket.
Yes	Checksum	(Optional) Checksum of the application data in the KRB_AP_REQ Kerberos message.
Yes	Current seconds (Cusec)	Microsecond part of the client's timestamp.
Yes	Current time (Ctime)	Current time on the client's machine.
Yes	Subkey	(Optional) Client's choice for an encryption key to be used to protect an application session. If this field is empty, the session key from the ticket is used.
Yes	Sequence number	(Optional) Initial sequence number to be used by the KRB_PRIV or KRB_SAFE messages (to protect against replay attacks).
Yes	Authorization data	(Optional) Privilege attributes for the client. Microsoft calls this part the Privilege Attribute Certificate (PAC).

TGT and Ticket Flags

In this section, we will analyze the Kerberos ticket flags. The ticket flags and their meaning are explained in Table 6.9.

To check the flags of the tickets that are cached in your personal Windows ticket cache you can use the kerbtray resource kit utility, which is illustrated in Figure 6.40. Kerbtray will reveal the following:

- Every ticket has the forwardable flag set. This flag can be reversed by setting the "Account is sensitive and cannot be delegated" property of the user's AD account object.

- Every ticket has the renewable flag set. When a user's TGT expires, Windows automatically requests a new one. This automatic TGT renewal is possible thanks to the LSA that keeps a secured copy of a user's hashed password (master key). TGT renewal is limited by the "Maximum lifetime for user ticket renewal" GPO setting—which is explained in more detail in Section 6.5.1 of this chapter.

- Every ticket has the preauthenticated flag set. Kerberos preauthentication is the default in Windows Kerberos.

- Every TGT has the initial flag set. This means that all TGTs in the cache were issued following a Kerberos authentication exchange.

- A ticket has the "OK as delegate" flag set if the service or user account for which the ticket was issued has the "Account is trusted for delegation" property set, or, in the case of a computer account, if the computer object has the "Trust computer for delegation" property set.

A single ticket can contain multiple flags. The flags are added to a ticket's properties as a hexadecimal 8-bit number, of which only the first 4

Table 6.9 *Kerberos Ticket Flags*

Flags	Meaning
Forwardable	Indicates to the ticket-granting server that it can issue a new TGT with a different network address based on the presented TGT.
Forwarded	The ticket has either been forwarded or was issued following an authentication that involved a forwarded TGT.
Proxiable	Indicates to the ticket-granting server that only non-TGTs (service tickets) may be issued with different network addresses.
Proxy	The ticket is a proxy ticket. The network address in this ticket is different from the one in the TGT that was used to obtain the ticket.
May be postdated	Indicates to the ticket-granting server that a postdated ticket may be issued based on this TGT. This flag was not supported in Windows 2000. It is supported in Windows Server 2003 and R2.
Postdated	Indicates that the ticket has been postdated. This flag was not supported in Windows 2000. It is supported in Windows Server 2003 and R2.
Invalid	The ticket is invalid and must be validated by a KDC before use. A postdated ticket is flagged as invalid until its start time.
Renewable	The ticket is renewable. If this flag is set, the time limit for renewing the ticket is set in the RenewTime ticket field.
Initial	The ticket was issued following a Kerberos AS protocol exchange and not based on an existing ticket granting ticket.
Preauthenticated	Indicates that, during initial authentication, the client was authenticated by the KDC before a ticket was issued.
Hardware preauthentication	Indicates that the protocol used for initial authentication required the use of hardware.
Target trusted for delegation (OK as delegate)	This flag means that the target of the ticket is trusted by the directory service for delegation.

bits are significant. One bit can refer to different flags. If flags refer to the same bit position, they are added hexadecimally. This hexadecimal number is displayed when you look at the TGTs in your Kerberos ticket cache using the klist resource kit tool. Kerbtray automatically displays the flag settings corresponding to the hexadecimal number. For more information on the klist and kerbtray tools, see the sidenote on "Using Klist and Kerbtray."

6.4.4 Kerberos Time Sensitivity

Time is a critical service in Windows 2000, Windows Server 2003, and R2. Timestamps are needed for Active Directory replication conflict resolution, but also for Kerberos authentication. Kerberos uses timestamps to protect against replay attacks. Computer clocks that are out of sync between systems can generate additional Kerberos authentication traffic or can—in the worst-case scenario—cause Kerberos authentication to fail.

To illustrate the importance of time for Kerberos authentication, the following steps explain what happens during a Windows KRB_AP_REQ and KRB_AP_REP Kerberos exchange from a time validation point of view:

1. A client uses the session key it received from the KDC to encrypt its authenticator. The authenticator is sent to the resource server together with a ticket.

2. The resource server compares the timestamp in the authenticator with its local time. If the time difference is within the allowed time skew (as configured in the Kerberos policy; see Section 6.5.1), the validation process on the resource server goes to step 4.

3. If step 2 failed, the resource server sends its local current timestamp to the client. The client then sends a new authenticator using the new timestamp: this brings the validation process back to step 1.

4. The resource server compares the timestamp it received from the client with the entries in its replay cache (this is a list of recently received authenticators). If it finds a match, the client's authentication request fails. If no match is found, client authentication succeeds and the resource server adds the authenticator to its replay cache.

The service responsible for time synchronization between Windows 2000, Windows XP, Windows Server 2003, and R2 computers is the Windows Time service (W32time.exe).

Using Klist and Kerbtray

The Windows Server 2003 Resource Kit contains two utilities you can use to look at the content of the Kerberos ticket cache: kerbtray.exe (illustrated in Figures 6.40 and 6.41) and klist.exe (illustrated in Figure 6.42). Kerbtray.exe is a GUI tool, and klist.exe is a command-line tool. Both tools can be used to display and/or purge the content of the Kerberos ticket cache.

To bring up the kerbtray dialog box and look at your logon session's Kerberos ticket cache, double-click the kerbtray icon in the status area of your Windows taskbar. The kerbtray icon is only displayed if you started the kerbtray program—it looks like a green ticket. The upper pane of the kerbtray dialog box shows all Kerberos tickets (both service tickets and TGTs) that are cached in your logon session's Kerberos ticket cache. The lower part of the dialog box has four tabs: Names, Times, Flags, and Encryption Types. The content of these tabs differs depending on the ticket that is selected in the upper pane.

- The Names tab shows the name of the service for which the ticket was issued.

- The Times tab shows the validity period of the ticket: its start and end time, and renew-until timestamp. For both TGTs and tickets, the default validity period is 10 hours. The default renewal period is 7 days.

- The Flags tab shows the ticket flags that have been set in the ticket. For a more detailed explanation of the Kerberos ticket flags, refer to Section 6.4.3.

- Finally, the Encryption Types tab shows the names of the encryption algorithms that were used by the Kerberos software to encrypt the tickets' content.

To purge the tickets in the Kerberos ticket cache, right-click the kerbtray icon in your desktop's taskbar and select Purge Tickets. This option deletes all tickets in your ticket cache. Use this option with extreme caution: Deleting tickets may stop you from authenticating to other Windows services during your logon session.

To display the content of the Kerberos ticket cache using the klist command-line utility, type the following at the command prompt:

```
Klist tickets
```

or

```
Klist tgt
```

The first command will bring up the service tickets in the cache, and the second command will bring up the TGTs in the cache. To purge the cache from the command line, type (use this command with extreme caution):

```
Klist purge
```

The kerbtray utility displays more ticket information than klist does. It also displays the information in a much more readable format. For example, the klist utility displays the hexadecimal string that is used for the Kerberos ticket flags, but it doesn't explain its meaning.

Figure 6.40
*Looking at the
Kerberos ticket flags
using the Kerbtray
utility.*

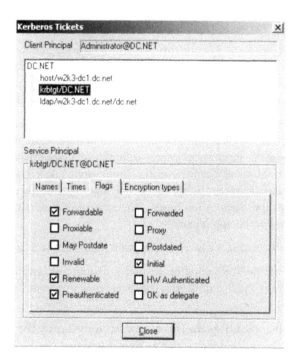

Figure 6.41
*Looking at the
Kerberos ticket
cache using the
Kerbtray utility.*

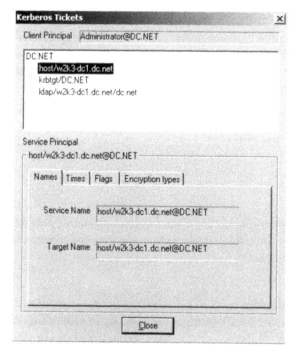

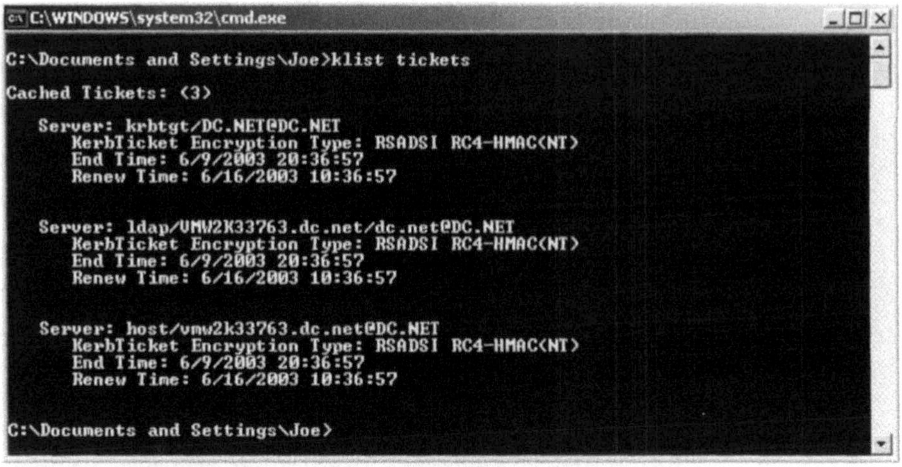

Figure 6.42   *Looking at the Kerberos ticket cache using the Klist utility.*

For more information on the Windows time service and how to configure it in an AD environment, read the following Microsoft documentation:

- Windows time service white paper: www.microsoft.com/windows2000/docs/wintimeserv.doc.

- "Using Windows Time Service in a Managed Environment," www.microsoft.com/technet/prodtechnol/windowsserver2003/technologies/security/ws03mngd/26_s3wts.mspx.

6.4.5   Kerberized Applications

Kerberized applications use the Kerberos authentication protocol to authenticate their users. Windows 2000, Windows Server 2003, and R2 include the following Kerberized applications:

- LDAP-based access to AD

- Print spooler services

- CIFS/SMB remote file access (Common Internet File System (CIFS) is the new name of Microsoft's Server Message Block (SMB) protocol, which is mainly used for file and print sharing)

- Distributed File System (DFS) management and referrals

- IPsec host-to-host authentication

- IIS Integrated Windows Authentication

- Certificate requests for domain users and computers to a Windows 2000 or later certification authority (CA)

- Windows logon—including smart card logon, which is explained in more detail in the next section

Smart Card Logon

Windows 2000, Windows XP, Windows Server 2003, and R2 include extensions to Kerberos version 5 to support public key–based authentication. These extensions are known as PKINIT—which stands for use of Public Key cryptography for INITial authentication. They are defined in an IETF Internet draft that can be found at www.ietf.org. PKINIT enables smart card logon to a Windows 2000 or later domain. In a PKINIT-based Kerberos authentication sequence,[31] all occurrences of a user's master key are replaced by the user's public key credentials. This is illustrated in Table 6.10.

PKINIT introduces a new trust model, illustrated on the right side of Figure 6.43. When using PKINIT, the KDC is not the first entity that authenticates the users—as is the case for classical Kerberos. In PKINIT, users have already authenticated to the certification authority when they request their smart card logon certificate. In the PKINIT trust model, both the users and the KDC must trust the same CA. In other words, in the PKINIT model, the CA is the most important security authority.

The CA you use for Windows smart card logon should preferably be a Windows 2000, Windows Server 2003, or R2 enterprise CA. See also the following Microsoft Knowledge Base article for more information on the

Table 6.10 *Mapping the Standard Kerberos Master Key to the PKINIT Public-Private Key Pair*

Standard Kerberos Usage of User's Master Key	PKINIT Replacement for User's Master Key
Client-side encryption of the preauthentication data	User's private key
KDC-side decryption of the preauthentication data	User's public key
KDC-side encryption of the session key	User's private key
Client-side decryption of the session key	User's public key

---

31.   These are the Kerberos Authentication Request (KRB_AS_REQ) and Reply (KRB_AS_REP) messages.

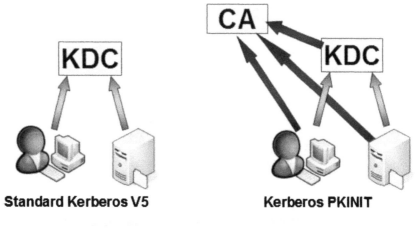

Standard Kerberos V5   **Kerberos PKINIT**

Figure 6.43   *Smart card logon trust model.*

Windows smart card logon certificate and CA requirements: Q281245. Windows PKI will also be discussed in more detail in the second book of this two-book series.

Figure 6.44 shows how the Kerberos smart card logon process works. In the outline of the different PKINIT steps below, you will note that the cryptic names of the Kerberos messages have changed:

- Alice starts the logon process by introducing her smart card and by authenticating to the card using her PIN code. The smart card contains Alice's public key credentials: her private key and certificate.

- A TGT request is sent to the KDC (AS). This request contains the following data (this is the PA-PK-AS-REQ message):

  — Alice's principal name and a timestamp, both signed using Alice's private key
  — A copy of Alice's certificate

- To validate the request and the digital signature, the KDC first validates Alice's certificate. The KDC then queries the Active Directory (AD) for a mapping between Alice's certificate and a Windows user account. If the KDC finds a mapping, it generates a new session key and issues a TGT for the corresponding user account.

- The KDC sends the TGT to Alice, together with a secured copy of the session key. Alice's copy of the session key is encrypted using her public key (this is the PA-PK-AS-REP message).

- To retrieve her copy of the session key, Alice uses her private key.

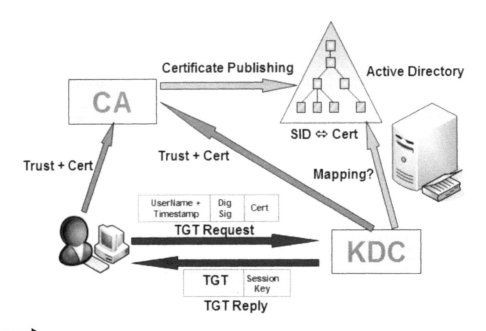

Figure 6.44   *Smart card logon.*

We will examine smart card logon in more detail in Chapter 10 in *Advanced Microsoft Windows Security Services* (part 2 of this series).

6.5   Kerberos Configuration

This section discusses Windows Kerberos-related configuration settings.

6.5.1   Kerberos GPO Settings

The Windows 2000, Windows Server 2003, and R2 Account Policies include a special subfolder for Kerberos-related policy settings (as illustrated in Figure 6.45). The settings are explained in Table 6.11.

These Kerberos policy GPO configuration settings can only be set on a per-domain basis (the same is true for account lockout policies and password policies—see Chapter 2 for more information). You cannot define, for example, different Kerberos settings for individual organizational units (OU).

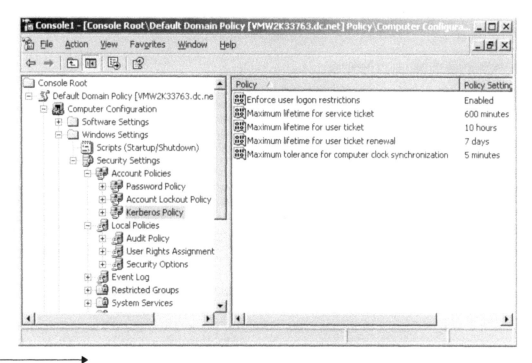

Figure 6.45 *Kerberos-related GPO settings.*

Another Kerberos-related GPO entry is located in the Local Policies\User Rights Assignment container: "Enable computer and user accounts to be trusted for delegation." Enabling this setting will set the "trusted for delegation" property of user and computer objects in a particular domain, site, or organizational unit.

Table 6.11 *Kerberos Policy GPO Settings*

Kerberos Policy Setting	Meaning
Enforce user logon restrictions	This setting determines whether the KDC will validate a user service ticket request against the user rights on the resource computer. If a user does not have the right to log on locally or access this computer from the network on the resource computer, the ticket request will fail. By default, the setting is enabled.
Maximum lifetime for service ticket	This setting determines the service ticket lifetime in minutes. The default lifetime is 10 hours (600 minutes). If the value is 0, the tickets will never expire.
Maximum lifetime for user ticket	This setting determines the ticket granting ticket (TGT) lifetime in hours. The default lifetime is 10 hours.

Table 6.11   *Kerberos Policy GPO Settings (continued)*

Kerberos Policy Setting	Meaning
Maximum lifetime for user ticket renewal	This setting determines how long a TGT can be renewed (in days). By default, the same TGT can be renewed up until seven days after its issuance. After seven days, a brand-new TGT must be issued. Note that during TGT renewal, the KDC checks whether the user account hasn't been disabled. It also refreshes the PAC content using a brand-new group expansion.
Maximum tolerance for computer clock synchronization	This setting determines the maximum time skew (in minutes) that can be tolerated between a client's and a server's clock in a Windows Kerberos environment. Kerberos uses timestamps to protect against replay attacks. When a resource server receives a Kerberos authenticator, it compares the timestamp in the authenticator with its local time. Setting the time skew too high creates a higher risk for replay attacks. The default setting is five minutes.

6.5.2   Kerberos-Related Account Properties

Every Windows 2000, Windows Server 2003, and R2 user, computer, or service AD account has a set of Kerberos-related properties. Most of them are related to Kerberos delegation. All properties are listed and explained in Table 6.12.

6.5.3   Kerberos Transport Protocols and Ports

RFC 4120 defines that a Kerberos client should connect to a KDC over port 88, using the connectionless UDP protocol. By default, Microsoft Kerberos uses UDP. Microsoft Kerberos can also use TCP to take advantage of TCP's bigger Maximum Transmission Unit (MTU) capacity. Microsoft Kerberos switches to TCP if the ticket size is bigger than 2 Kilobytes (Kb). A Windows Kerberos ticket can easily grow beyond 2 Kb if it is carrying a large PAC field. This can, for example, occur when a user is a member of a large number of groups.

The default 2-Kb limit can be decreased to an even lower value using the following registry setting. Setting this value to 1 will force Kerberos to use TCP all the time.

```
HKEY_LOCAL_MACHINE\SYSTEM\CurrentControlSet\Control\Lsa\
Kerberos\Parameters
Value Name: MaxPacketSize
Data Type: REG_DWORD Value: 1–2000 (in bytes)
```

Kerberos uses port 88 on the KDC side and a variable port on the client side for the Kerberos authentication exchanges. If your Kerberos clients communicate only with Kerberos V5 KDCs (this is the Kerberos version used in Windows 2000, Windows Server 2003, and R2), it is sufficient to keep port 88 open on your firewall. If they also communicate with Kerberos V4 KDCs, you must also open port 750. Table 6.13 gives an overview

Table 6.12 *Kerberos-Related AD Account Properties*

Kerberos-Related AD Account Property	Meaning
Computer accounts	
Trust computer for delegation	Used to trust/not trust the computer for delegation. Setting appears only in Windows 2000 and Windows Server 2003 domains that are not at the Windows Server 2003 functional level. Domain controllers are by default trusted for delegation.
Delegation tab	Used to trust/not trust the computer for delegation and to configure constrained delegation and protocol transition (as explained in Section 6.4.1). The delegation tab appears only if the domain is at the Windows Server 2003 functional level. Domain controllers are by default trusted for delegation to any service.
User and service accounts	
Account is trusted for delegation	Enables the account for delegation. Means that a service that uses this account can act on another user's behalf using Kerberos delegation. See also Section 6.4.1.
Account is sensitive and cannot be delegated	Means that no service will ever be allowed to act on behalf of the user that has this property set. See also Section 6.4.1.
Use DES encryption types for this account	Switches Kerberos ticket encryption from RC4-HMAC to DES-CBC-MD5 for the account that has this property set. This may be needed for interoperability with other non-Windows Kerberos implementations. See also Section 6.4.3.
Do not require Kerberos preauthentication	Switches off Kerberos preauthentication (which is enabled by default). This may be needed for interoperability with other non-Windows Kerberos implementations. See also Section 6.4.3.
Delegation tab	Used to trust/not trust the account for delegation and to configure constrained delegation and protocol transition (as explained in Section 6.4.1). The delegation tab appears only if the domain is at the Windows Server 2003 functional level and if the account has an SPN registered in AD.

Table 6.13   *Kerberos-Related Ports*

Port	Protocol	Function Description
53	UDP TCP	DNS
88	UDP TCP	Kerberos V5 ticket service
123	UDP	SNTP, NTP time service
749	TCP	Kerberos V5 password changing service
750	UDP TCP	Kerberos V4 Authentication
751	UDP TCP	Kerberos V4 Authentication
761	TCP	Kerberos V4 password changing service

of all Kerberos-related ports. The only ports you should care for in a Windows-centric Kerberos environment are ports 53 (DNS), 88 (Kerberos), and 123 (SNTP, NTP).

6.6   **Kerberos Troubleshooting**

In the following two sections, we will explore some basic Kerberos troubleshooting tools.

6.6.1   **The Event Viewer**

An indispensable troubleshooting tool for every administrator is the Windows Event Viewer. You can enable advanced Kerberos event logging using the following Windows registry change: set the Loglevel registry key (REG_DWORD) to value 1. Loglevel is located in the following registry container:

Table 6.14   *Kerberos-Specific Event IDs*

Event ID	Meaning
672	Event (success or failure) related to a Kerberos authentication service (AS) request.
673	Event (success or failure) related to a Kerberos ticket granting service (TGS) request.
675	Kerberos preauthentication failed.

HKEY_LOCAL_MACHINE\SYSTEM\CurrentControlSet\Control\Lsa\ Kerberos\Parameters.

In Windows Server 2003, Microsoft included some Kerberos-specific event IDs. They are listed and explained in Table 6.14. Table 6.15 shows the Kerberos-related error codes as they appear in the Windows Event Viewer and their meaning. Both tables can give interesting hints when troubleshooting Kerberos authentication problems.

Table 6.15 *Kerberos Error Codes and Their Meaning*

Code	Meaning
0x3	Requested protocol version number not supported
0x6	Client principal unknown in Kerberos database
0x7	Server principal unknown in Kerberos database
0x8	Multiple principal entries in Kerberos database
0x9	Null key error
0xA	Ticket not eligible for postdating
0xB	Requested start time is later than end time
0xC	KDC policy rejects request
0xD	KDC cannot accommodate requested option
0xE	KDC does not support encryption type
0xF	KDC does not support checksum type
0x10	KDC does not support preauthentication data type
0x12	Client's credentials revoked
0x17	Password has expired
0x18	Preauthentication failed
0x1A	Requested server and ticket do not match
0x1B	Server principal valid for user-to-user only
0x1C	KDC policy rejects transited path
0x1D	A service is not available
0x1F	Integrity check on decrypted field failed
0x19	Preauthentication error

Table 6.15   *Kerberos Error Codes and Their Meaning (continued)*

Code	Meaning
0x20	Ticket has expired
0x21	Ticket not yet valid
0x22	Session request is a replay
0x23	Ticket isn't for us
0x24	Ticket and authenticator do not match
0x25	Clock skew too great
0x26	Bad address in Kerberos session tickets
0x28	Invalid message type
0x29	Message stream modified
0x34	Response too big for UDP, retry with TCP
0x3C	Generic error
0x44	User-to-user TGT issued different KDC

6.6.2   Troubleshooting Tools

Microsoft offers several tools to troubleshoot Kerberos-related authentication problems—they are listed in Table 6.16. Most of them are command prompt tools. A great source of information is also the "Troubleshooting Kerberos Errors" white paper, which can be downloaded from www.microsoft.com/technet/prodtechnol/windowsserver2003/technologies/security/tkerberr.mspx. If you must troubleshoot Kerberos delegation-related problems, We advise you to look at the "Troubleshooting Kerberos delegation" paper available from www.microsoft.com/technet/prodtechnol/windowsserver2003/technologies/security/tkerbdel.mspx.

6.7   Kerberos Interoperability

Kerberos is an open standard that is implemented on different platforms. Because of this Kerberos can be used as a single-sign-on (SSO) solution between Windows and other platforms.

This section focuses on using Kerberos for multiplatform SSO. It does not cover using Kerberos for application SSO. Organizations rarely use

Table 6.16 *Kerberos Troubleshooting Tools*

Tool	Comments
Klist (Resource Kit)	Command prompt tool to look at the local Kerberos ticket cache. Klist can also be used to purge tickets from the cache.
Kerbtray (Resource Kit)	GUI tool that displays the content of the local Kerberos ticket cache. Kerbtray can also be used to purge tickets from the cache.
Netdiag (Support tools)	Netdiag helps isolate networking and connectivity problems by providing a series of tests to determine the state of your network client. One of the netdiag tests is the Kerberos test. To run the Kerberos test, type "netdiag /test:Kerberos" at the command prompt.
Replication monitor (Support tools)	Using replication monitor (replmon.exe), an administrator can check not only the AD replication traffic but also the number of AS and TGS requests and the DC Operations Master roles.
Network monitor (Limited version on server CD/Full version in Microsoft SMS)	Network monitor enables you to capture network traces and analyze them.
Setspn (Resource Kit)	Tool allowing you to manage (view, reset, delete, add) service principal names (SPNs).
Tokensz (Download)	Tokensz is a command-line tool to view the maximum Kerberos token size for an account. It can be downloaded from http://go.microsoft.com/fwlink/?LinkId=42933.

Kerberos-based application SSO because of the lack of out-of-the-box Kerberized applications on the UNIX and Linux side. The few organizations that are using Kerberos for application SSO today have Kerberized their applications using custom in-house developments. Examples of Kerberized UNIX/Linux applications and protocols are Telnet, POP, and Samba. Examples of common UNIX/Linux applications that are typically not Kerberized are Linux desktop applications (Gnome, KDE), and custom-built and home-grown UNIX/Linux applications.

6.7.1 Non-Microsoft Kerberos Implementations

Table 6.17 lists other non-Microsoft Kerberos implementations and the platforms for which they are available—this is a nonexhaustive list. The

Table 6.17   *Non-Microsoft Kerberos Implementations (Nonexhaustive List)*

Kerberos Implementation	Platform
MIT Kerberos	Windows, Mac, Linux, UNIX
Heimdal Kerberos	DEC-UNIX, Linux, Mac, Solaris
CyberSafe TrustBroker	Solaris, Tru64, Windows, AIX, HP-UX, Redhat Linux, SuSE Linux
HP-UX Kerberos	HP-UX
Sun SEAM	Solaris
Kerberos PAM	Linux, HP-UX

most popular non-Microsoft Kerberos implementations are MIT Kerberos and Heimdal Kerberos.

6.7.2 Comparing Windows Kerberos to Other Implementations

Before going into the details of Windows Kerberos interoperability scenarios, it is worthwhile to look at what makes the Windows Kerberos implementation different from other Kerberos implementations.

- Windows Kerberos is tightly integrated with the Windows 2000, Windows XP, Windows Server 2003, and R2 operating systems. Each Windows 2000, Windows XP, Windows Server 2003, and R2 system runs the Kerberos Security Support Provider (SSP). Each Windows 2000, Windows Server 2003, and R2 domain controller (DC) has a KDC service.

- Kerberos principals locate the KDC using DNS. Windows 2000, Windows Server 2003, and R2 DNS include special SRV records that point to Kerberos KDC providers.

- Microsoft implemented the RC4-HMAC encryption algorithm (with 56- or 128-bit keys) as the preferred Kerberos encryption type. Microsoft still supports DES-CBC-CRC and DES-CBC-MD5 (with 56-bit keys) for interoperability reasons. See also Section 6.4.3 for more information.

- Windows Kerberos caches a user's master key on the Kerberos client to allow automatic TGT renewal.

- Windows Kerberos KDCs require Kerberos clients to perform preauthentication by default. See also Section 6.4.3 for more information.

- Microsoft uses its SSPI Application Programming Interface (API) (see Chapter 4) to access Kerberos services. Microsoft Kerberos does not support the raw krb5 API or the GSS-API (as defined in RFC 2078).

- Microsoft uses the authorization data (authdata) field in the ticket to transport Windows authorization data. Microsoft refers to this field as the Privilege Attribute Certificate (PAC). See also Section 6.4.3 for more information.

- Microsoft Windows caches a user's Kerberos master key for the duration of a user logon session, because they need it to perform NTLM authentication to downlevel clients and to automatically renew the user's Kerberos TGT.

- Microsoft does not support multipart principal names, which are supported on most UNIX Kerberos implementations. An example of a multipart principal name is host/unixbox.dc.net.

6.7.3 Interoperability Scenarios

In this section, we will focus on setting up Kerberos interoperability between Windows 2000, Windows XP, Windows Server 2003, or R2 Kerberos and a non-Microsoft Kerberos implementation: for example, a UNIX Kerberos implementation.

We will only discuss interoperability scenarios that leverage built-in OS functions or features, or OS plug-ins that can be added without additional costs. In Chapter 8, on UNIX-Windows authentication integration, we will discuss some of the commercial software packages providing Kerberos-based authentication interoperability between Windows and UNIX (for example: Quest Vintela, Centrify, Cybersafe).

Kerberos authentication interoperability can be set up in three different ways:

- Scenario 1: The Windows KDC is the KDC for both Windows and UNIX security principals. This means that all principals are administered from the Windows KDC.

- Scenario 2: The UNIX KDC is the KDC for both Windows and UNIX security principals. This means that all principals are administered from the UNIX KDC.

- Scenario 3: A cross-realm trust relationship is defined between a Windows domain and a UNIX Kerberos realm. This means that part of the principals is administered from the Windows KDC, and another part is administered from the UNIX KDC. In this scenario, there are at least two KDCs—one KDC on each side of the trust relationship.

These three scenarios are explained in more detail in the following sections. A lot of valuable information on how to set up interoperability can be found in the following white papers:

- "Step-by-Step Guide to Kerberos 5 Interoperability," available from www.microsoft.com/technet/prodtechnol/windows2000serv/howto/ kerbstep.mspx.

- "Solution Guide for Windows Security and Directory Services for UNIX," available from www.microsoft.com/technet/itsolutions/cits/ interopmigration/unix/usecdirw/00wsdsu.mspx.

- "Windows 2000 Kerberos Interoperability," by Christopher Nebergall, available from www.sans.org/rr/paper.php?id=973.

Principals Defined on a Windows KDC

This scenario allows for Kerberos principals on both Windows and non-Windows platforms to log on to a Windows KDC using Windows credentials.

To enable a user to log on to Windows from a UNIX workstation, the UNIX Kerberos configuration file (typically named krb5.conf) must be edited to point to the Windows KDC. On the AD side, a user account must be defined for the UNIX user. The UNIX user's AD account must have the "Use DES encryption types for this account" property set. This property can be set from the Account Options on the Account tab of the AD user object properties in the AD Users and Computers (ADUC) MMC snap-in. When you have completed these configuration steps successfully, the UNIX user can log on using his or her Windows account and the UNIX kinit command, which is the logon command in most UNIX Kerberos implementations.

The setup is a bit more complicated for enabling a UNIX service or machine to log on to a Windows KDC using Windows credentials. In this case, the Windows administrator must complete the following configuration steps:

- Edit the krb5.conf file on the UNIX machine to point to the Windows KDC.

- Create a user account for the UNIX service or machine in the Active Directory, and make sure the account has the "Password never expires" and "User cannot change password" properties set. If you prefer for security reasons not to enable the "Password never expires" property, make sure that you have a routine in place to change the password at regular intervals.

- Use the ktpass.exe command-line tool to:

  — Create a keytab file, which contains the password that will be used by the UNIX service or machine to log on to the Windows domain.

  — Create an AD account mapping for the UNIX service or machine.

- Set the AD account's "Use DES encryption types for this account" property.

  The ktpass command-line tool can perform all the above actions in a single run. Ktpass comes with the Windows Server 2003 and R2 Support Tools.

  For example, the following ktpass command generates a keytab file for a UNIX machine named unixbox that is mapped to the unixbox AD account in the windows.dc.net domain—you must run this command on your Windows DC:

  ```
  ktpass -out unixbox.keytab -princ host/
  unixbox@WINDOWS.DC.NET -pass * -mapuser unixbox
  ```

  In this command the -pass * switch makes ktpass prompt for the unixbox AD account's password. Instead of using the *, you can also spell out the password in the command line. Also make sure that in the ktpass command you spell the realm portion of the UNIX principal name (the part following the @) in uppercase. Kerberos realm names are traditionally written in uppercase.

- Copy the keytab file to the UNIX platform and merge it with the service's or machines existing keytab file; this is typically done using the UNIX ktutil utility.

Principals Defined on a Non-Windows KDC

This scenario allows Kerberos principals on both Windows and non-Windows platforms to log on using UNIX credentials to a UNIX KDC. For a standalone Windows workstation or member server to use a UNIX KDC, you must complete the following configuration steps:

- Create a security principal and password for both the Windows workstation and the Windows user on the UNIX KDC. In most non-Microsoft Kerberos implementations, you can use the kadmin command line to add security principals to the KDC database and set their passwords.

- Configure the Windows workstation using ksetup.exe. The goal of this step is to point the Windows workstation to the UNIX KDC and to inform the machine about its password (as it was set in the previous step in the UNIX KDC database). The ksetup tool also comes with the Windows Server 2003 and R2 Support Tools.

- For example, to point a Windows workstation to a UNIX Kerberos realm named test.net with a KDC named unixkdc.test.net, and to teach the workstation about its password "windowspassword", you must use the following ksetup commands on the Windows workstation—all commands make local registry changes:[32]

To point the Windows workstation to the UNIX Kerberos realm:

```
ksetup /setrealm TEST.NET
```

To point the Windows workstation to a KDC in the UNIX Kerberos realm:

```
ksetup /addkdc TEST.NET unixkdc.test.net
```

To point the Windows workstation to the KDC in the UNIX Kerberos realm that can change user passwords:

```
ksetup /addkpasswd TEST.NET unixkdc.test.net
```

To teach the Windows workstation about its password in the UNIX Kerberos realm:

```
ksetup /setcomputerpassword windowspassword
```

- Create a mapping on the Windows workstation between a user's principal in the UNIX realm and the user's local account on the Windows workstation. This mapping is needed for Windows authorization purposes: a UNIX principal doesn't mean anything to a Windows security authority. Windows needs a Security Identifier (SID), which can be provided if you map the UNIX principal to a local Windows account. This will allow a principal defined on the UNIX KDC to

---

32.   These registry changes are stored in HKEY_LOCAL_MACHINE\CurrentControlSet\Control\LSA\Kerberos\Domains.

log on to the UNIX realm from a Windows workstation.[33] These mappings can be defined using the ksetup command-line tool.

For example, to create a mapping between the windows-user@TEST.NET UNIX user principal and the local declercqj Windows account, you must type the following ksetup command on the Windows workstation:

```
ksetup /mapuser windowsuser@TEST.NET declercqj
```

- Restart the Windows workstation.

Cross-Realm Trust

This is probably the most flexible Windows-UNIX Kerberos interoperability scenario. It can enable non-Windows Kerberos principals to log on to their UNIX KDC and to access resources in a Windows domain and, vice versa, for Windows principals to log on to their Windows KDC and to access resources in a UNIX realm.

To define a cross-realm trust between a Windows domain and a UNIX realm, you must do the following:

- Define a trust relationship for the UNIX realm in the Windows domain. This can be done using the AD Domains and Trusts MMC snap-in, as follows:[34]

    Select the Windows domain and open its properties. Select the Trusts tab. Click the New Trust... pushbutton (illustrated in Figure 6.46) to start the New Trust Wizard. In the New Trust Wizard you must provide the following data:

    — The name of the UNIX realm, for example: UNIX.TEST.NET
    — The trust type; in this example: a realm trust
    — Whether the trust must be made transitive; in this example: the trust can be non-transitive
    — The direction of the trust; in this example: One-way: outgoing (as illustrated in Figure 6.47)
    — The trust password: in Windows Server 2003 and R2, you must make sure you honor the password complexity requirements when entering the trust password

---

33. The name of the UNIX realm will appear in the "Log on to" drop-down list of the Windows logon dialog box.
34. See Chapter 3 for more information on Windows trust relationships and how to configure them.

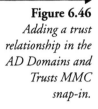

Figure 6.46
Adding a trust relationship in the AD Domains and Trusts MMC snap-in.

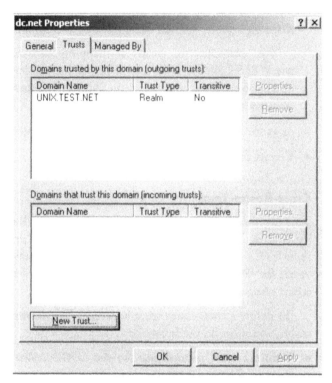

Figure 6.47
New Trust Wizard: direction of the trust.

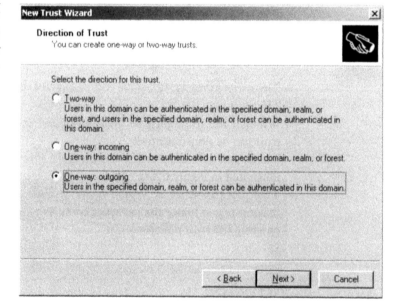

When you complete the trust wizard successfully, the UNIX.TEST.NET UNIX realm should be listed in the "Domains trusted by this domain (outgoing trust)" section (as illustrated in Figure 6.46).

The steps outlined above allow principals defined in the UNIX realm to log on using Kerberos to the Window domain. In other words, these steps created a one-way trust relationship from the Windows domain to the UNIX realm.

If you also want your Windows accounts to log on using Kerberos to the UNIX realm (in other words, if you want a two-way trust relationship), you must repeat the above steps. This time you must add the UNIX.TEST.NET UNIX realm to the "Domains that trust this domain (incoming trust)" section and you must make sure that you select "One-way: incoming" as the trust direction in the New Trust Wizard (see Figure 6.47).

- Define a trust relationship security principal for the Windows domain in the UNIX realm. In most UNIX Kerberos implementations you can use the kadmin tool to add any kind of security principal to the KDC database.

    For example: for the trust relationship between the WINDOWS.TEST.NET windows domain and the UNIX.TEST.NET UNIX realm—in which the Windows domain trusts the accounts of the UNIX realm—you must add the krbtgt/WINDOWS.TEST.NET@UNIX.TEST.NET[35] principal to the UNIX KDC database. Make sure that you enter the correct password for this principal: this password must match the one you entered in the AD Domains and Trusts MMC snap-in in the previous configuration step.

    Again, the previous paragraph defines a one-way trust relationship. If you also want the principals defined in the UNIX realm to log on using Kerberos to the Window domain, you must also add the krbtgt/UNIX.TEST.NET@WINDOWS.TEST.NET principal to the UNIX KDC database. This will make the trust a two-way trust relationship. Remember that you must enter the correct password for the principal.

- Define entries for the UNIX realm in the system registry of the machines in the Windows domain. This applies to all machines: Windows workstations, member servers, and also domain controllers.

---

35. The krbtgt account was explained in Section 6.3.2.

To add a realm mapping, use the ksetup tool that comes with the Windows Server 2003 and R2 Support Tools. For example, to add the KDC named unixkdc in the UNIX.TEST.NET realm to the system registry of your Windows boxes,[36] use the following ksetup command line:

```
ksetup /addkdc UNIX.TEST.NET unixkdc.unix.test.net
```

To apply the ksetup configuration changes, each Windows machine must be rebooted.

- Define proxy accounts for the UNIX security principals in Active Directory. This configuration step maps UNIX security principals in the UNIX realm to Windows accounts in the Windows domain.

  This step is needed because Windows and UNIX use different authorization logic. Whereas UNIX relies on principal names for authorization, Windows relies on security identities (SIDs). This means that—despite the trust relationship between the UNIX realm and the Windows domain—if we did not explicitly define proxy accounts, UNIX users would never be able to access resources in the Windows domain or log on to their UNIX realm from a machine in the Windows domain. Proxy accounts resolve these issues because they provide a mechanism to map a Windows SID to a SIDless UNIX account.

Figure 6.48
Defining Kerberos account mappings.

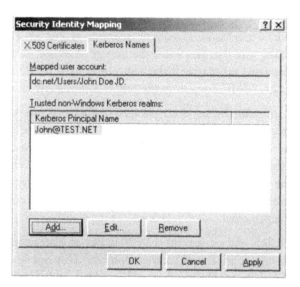

---

36.   These registry changes are stored in HKEY_LOCAL_MACHINE\CurrentControlSet\Control\LSA\Kerberos\Domains.

Proxy accounts are stored in the altSecurityIdentities attribute of a Windows AD account. They can be defined from the AD Users and Computers (ADUC) MMC snap-in, as follows:

- In the ADUC MMC snap-in's View menu option, select Advanced Features...

- Right-click the user account for which you want to define the proxy account and select Name Mappings... This brings up the Security Identity Mapping dialog box, illustrated in Figure 6.48.

- Select the Kerberos Names tab, and then click the Add... pushbutton to add the UNIX Kerberos Principal Name. In the example shown in Figure 6.48, the principal is named John@TEST.NET.

Let us have a look now at what will happen when a UNIX principal wants to access a resource hosted on a machine in the Windows domain (as illustrated in Figure 6.49).

- Step 1: The UNIX principal logs on to the UNIX domain. At the end of step 1, the UNIX principal will have a TGT for the UNIX domain.

- Step 2: The UNIX principal wants to access a resource hosted in the Windows domain. The local UNIX KDC refers the UNIX principal to the Windows KDC.

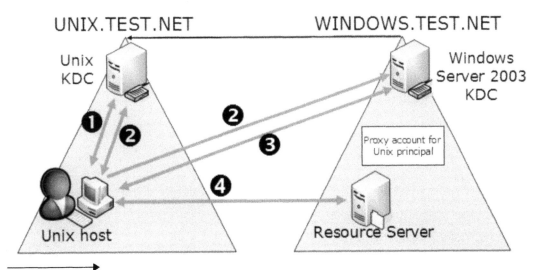

Figure 6.49 *UNIX-Windows Kerberos interoperability using a cross-realm trust.*

- Step 3: The Windows KDC attempts to create a service ticket for the UNIX principal. To create the ticket, the Windows KDC must know a SID. The KDC then queries the Active Directory for an account mapping between the UNIX principal and a Windows SID. If a SID is found, the Windows KDC generates the ticket and populates its authorization data in the PAC. The service ticket is then forwarded to the UNIX principal.

- Step 4: Using the service ticket, the UNIX principal authenticates to the Windows resource.

Note that the setup in Figure 6.49 also allows a principal defined in the UNIX realm to log on to his/her UNIX realm from a workstation in the Windows domain. In this scenario, the UNIX realm appears in the "Log on to" drop-down list of the Windows logon dialog box.

When the Windows domain also contains NT4 servers or workstations that can only authenticate using NTLM, the scenario illustrated in Figure 6.49 also requires password synchronization between the UNIX realm (where the accounts and their passwords are defined) and the Windows domain (where the proxy accounts are defined). NTLM authentication will only work if the Windows proxy account has the same password as the UNIX principal. One of the tools you can use here is the password synchronization tool available in CyberSafe's Trustbroker product.

IIS Authentication

This chapter focuses on the authentication methods supported in Internet Information Services (IIS) 6.0. Microsoft has made radical changes to its Web server in Windows Server 2003. Some of these changes and their impact on the overall security quality of the IIS Web server are explored in Section 7.1.

7.1   Secure by Default in IIS 6.0

Windows Server 2003 is Microsoft's first enterprise operating system (OS) that shipped with the label "secure by default." One of the most visible effects of this is that IIS is now an optional service and is not installed by default on a Windows Server 2003 installation.[1] This really makes sense if you remember the numerous IIS security exploits that have occurred over the past years. In a Windows Server 2003 domain, administrators can even prevent the installation of IIS 6.0 using the GPO setting "Prevent IIS installation," which is located in the Computer Configuration\Administrative Templates\Windows Components\Internet Information Server GPO container. Note that this setting will not prevent an administrator from installing an IIS 5.0 or earlier Web server.

Like the Windows Server 2003 OS, when IIS 6.0 is installed, it will be in a locked-down state. By default, IIS 6.0 is only capable of providing static Web page support (static meaning plain HTML files). The dynamic content (for example, active server pages) that can be served by IIS is controlled using a new administration feature called Web Service Extensions in the IIS Internet Services Manager (ISM) MMC snap-in.

---

1.   This not true for Windows Server 2003 Web Edition, as it is specifically targeting Web servers.

Another feature illustrating IIS 6.0's secure by default configuration is that URLscan-like functionality has been implemented as an integral part of the Web server. Also, stronger access control settings are set on the IIS log files and cache directories. URLscan is a tool that restricts the types of HTTP requests IIS processes. For example, if URLscan spots suspicious URLs, it blocks the HTTP request. Many Web server hacks consist of sending a URL to the Web server that contains a string that can be interpreted by the Web server as an instruction to execute a particular command. For IIS 4.0 and 5.0, URLscan is available as an add-on tool.

Even though IIS 6.0 includes URLscan-like functionality, we still recommend that you install the URLscan tool on IIS 6.0 servers. URLscan supports security features (for example, the ability to remove the server header information from the server HTTP response) that are not included in the IIS 6.0 URLscan-like functionality. You can download the latest URLscan version (2.5) from this URL: www.microsoft.com/downloads/details.aspx?FamilyID=23d18937-dd7e-4613-9928-7f94ef1c902a&DisplayLang=en. See also the following Microsoft TechNet article for more information on the URLscan tool: www.microsoft.com/technet/security/tools/urlscan.mspx.

Perhaps the most fundamental change that makes IIS 6.0 more secure by default is its brand-new architecture. Microsoft completely reengineered the HTTP engine of the Web server.[2] The key characteristic of this architecture is isolation. IIS 6.0 supports an operation mode that is known as worker process isolation mode (WPIM), which enables different Web sites (and their worker processes) that are running on the same physical server to operate completely independent of one another—as though a logical firewall has been set up between them. This isolation enables a per–Web site configuration of security parameters (for example, the security identity used by a Web site) and performance parameters (for example, the amount of system resources that can be consumed by a Web site). This architecture also provides better protection against denial-of-service (DOS) attacks. An attack on one Web site can never bring down the complete Web server and all the other Web sites running on it.

Figure 7.1 illustrates the IIS 6.0 architecture. The entities providing application and Web site isolation are the application pools. As Figure 7.1 shows, an application pool can host several Web applications and sites. Each application pool can be assigned different security and performance parameters—application pools are logically separated from one another.

---

2.   This new architecture does not apply to the SMTP, NNTP, and FTP portions of the IIS 6.0 Web server.

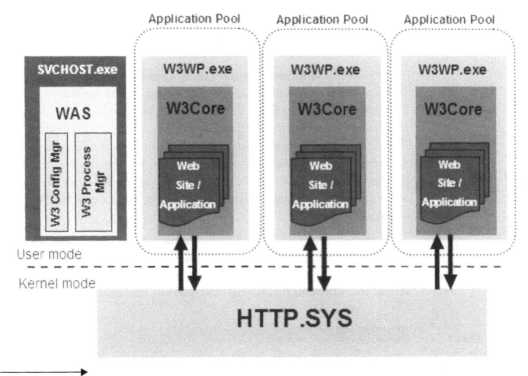

Figure 7.1   *IIS 6.0 architecture.*

Each application pool shows up in the Windows task manager as a separate instance of the w3wp.exe process. In IIS 6.0, Microsoft also provides separate processes for the administration and housekeeping of the Web server (the Web Administration Service (WAS) or the svchost.exe process) and the treatment of incoming and outgoing HTTP messages (the kernel-mode HTTP.sys driver).

7.2   **Introducing IIS Authentication**

Microsoft's Web server supports the classical HTTP authentication methods—basic and digest authentication—and certificate-based authentication based on the secure sockets layer (SSL) and transport layer security (TLS) protocols. These three authentication methods are discussed extensively in this chapter. Besides these three, IIS also includes support for the typical Windows authentication methods—NTLM and Kerberos authentication—and Microsoft's Internet Single Sign-On authentication protocol—Passport. NTLM and Kerberos authentication were explained in Chapters 5 and 6. In this chapter, we will explain how the Kerberos and NTLM protocols fit into the IIS authentication exchange and configuration. The built-in support for MS Passport authentication is new to IIS 6.0 and will be discussed in Section 7.5.

The IIS authentication options can be set from the properties of an IIS Web site, directory, or file (as Figure 7.2 shows). Select the ISM: Go to the Directory Security tab, then click the Edit... pushbutton in the "Authentication and access control" section. To set SSL authentication options for a Web site, directory, or file, click one of the buttons in the "Secure communications" section of the Directory Security tab. You can also set the authentication options globally for the complete Web server using the master Web site properties. The latter are accessible from the properties of the Web Sites container in the ISM.

By default, every IIS Web resource has both anonymous access and integrated Windows authentication enabled. This means that IIS will always first attempt to give a user access using anonymous (or unauthenticated) access. If anonymous access does not succeed, IIS will try to give the user

Figure 7.2
Configuring IIS
authentication
options.

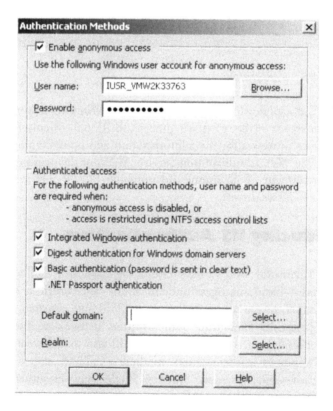

access using integrated Windows authentication and the user's Windows credentials.

This default configuration also means that in order to enable the authentication of a user to IIS you must in the first place uncheck the "Enable anonymous access" option in the ISM Authentication Methods configuration screen, and then select one or more authentication methods in the "Authenticated access" section.

If you have enabled the integrated Windows, digest, and basic authentication options, IIS will first try to give users access using the integrated Windows and digest authentication protocols—only after trying these two methods and failing will IIS try with the basic authentication protocol. This authentication option ranking is also reflected in the WWW-authenticate HTTP headers returned by IIS Web servers.

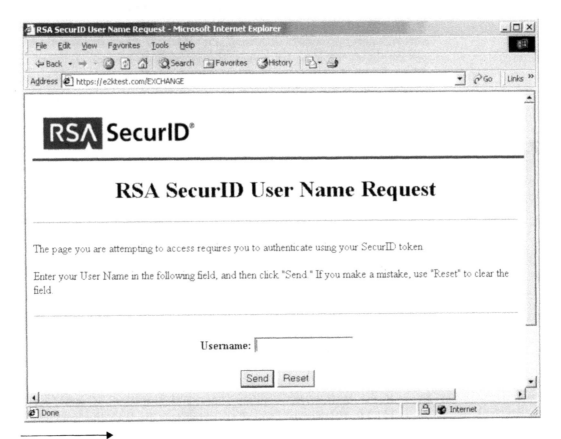

Figure 7.3   *SecurID authentication agent-based IIS authentication.*

The above authentication options are not the only ones that can be made available to an IIS user. Web site administrators and application developers can also build their custom authentication methods or rely on authentication solutions provided by other software vendors.

An example of an IIS authentication solution from another vendor is the SecurID Authentication Agent plug-in from RSA Security (illustrated in Figure 7.3—more information can be found at www.rsasecurity.com/ node.asp?id=2807).

Forms-based authentication is an example of a custom authentication method. In a forms-based authentication scenario, a user enters his or her authentication credentials on a Web page and then the Web page's code logic validates the credentials against a credential database. The credential database can be any kind of repository (an LDAP-accessible directory, an SQL database, or so forth). Some of these custom authentication methods do not rely on the built-in Windows security mechanisms and services, such as security principals, accounts, and credential databases (like the AD and the SAM). Custom IIS authentication methods are not explained in this book. The IIS 6.0 Resource Kit contains a good custom authentication example named CustomAuth version 1.0. Another example is Exchange Outlook Web Access (OWA) forms-based authentication.

7.3   HTTP Authentication

The HTTP protocol specification includes a set of specific HTTP headers to deal with authentication in a Web environment. The HTTP specification also defines Web authentication methods: basic authentication, which is a part of the HTTP version 1.0 specification, and digest authentication, which is a part of the HTTP version 1.1 specification. Both authentication protocols are explained next. HTTP also allows anonymous or unauthenticated access to Web resource.

Figure 7.4 shows the different messages exchanged between a Web browser and server during an HTTP-based authentication exchange:

1.   The browser requests data from the Web server using an HTTP GET command.

2.   If the Web server requires client authentication, it sends an HTTP 401 Access Denied error message back to the browser, along with:

   ▪ A list of the authentication schemes the Web server supports.

■ A challenge. Not all Web authentication protocols use this challenge. When using digest authentication, for example, the browser uses the challenge to calculate the authentication reply that is sent back to the server. The challenge is sent as one or more WWW-Authenticate headers in the server's response.

3. The browser chooses one of the Web authentication protocols that it supports and constructs an authentication response. The response is based on the user's credentials and—depending on the authentication protocol used—also on the challenge that was sent by the server. To obtain the user's credentials, the browser will prompt the user.[3] The response is sent back to the server as part of an authorization header.

4. The server authenticates the data it got from the browser and, assuming everything is okay, sends the response and the requested resource back to the user. The response message includes an HTTP 200 status code, which is a "no errors" message.

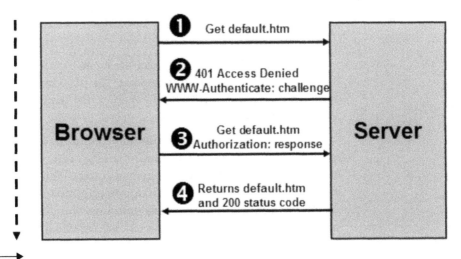

Figure 7.4 *Typical HTTP authentication exchange.*

---

3. This credential prompt will not occur if the user has previously cached his credentials in the user profile (using the "Remember my password" option; see also the sidenote on "Caching Credentials in Internet Explorer" later in this chapter) or if the URL that was used to access the Web site contains the username and password (see the Section 7.3.2 on Basic Authentication).

7.3.1   **Anonymous Access**

Step 2 of the authentication exchange in Figure 7.4 begins with "If the Web server requires client authentication." Authentication is indeed an option. Many Web sites do not care about the identity of a user. Good examples are Web sites containing public information that should be available to everyone. For such sites, authentication is just overhead, slowing down the information exchange. That is why most Web servers (including IIS) also provide an anonymous access method. If a Web site is configured to use anonymous access, anyone is allowed to access the site, even without providing credentials.

Even though—from an end-user point of view—anonymous access appears as "no identification at all," there will be an authentication process at the Web server level. IIS always authenticates every anonymous session against the Windows security infrastructure using a preconfigured anonymous account. By default, this account is the IUSR_<computername> account (which is also known as the Internet guest account). This account is created automatically in the Windows Security database (SAM or AD) when an IIS Web server is installed. As part of the IIS 6.0 installation process, the Internet guest account is also assigned to the Guests and Domain Users built-in groups.

Figure 7.5 shows an anonymous access message exchange between a Web browser and server. In this instance, the Web server has been enabled for anonymous access, and thus any request that does not contain credentials is a valid request.

The advantage of the back-end anonymous authentication process is that regular Windows authorization settings can be applied to Web resources that are accessed by anonymous users. This also means that if a Web resource has specific authorization settings that do not give access to the Internet guest account, an anonymous user who tries to access this more locked-down resource will be prompted for credentials.

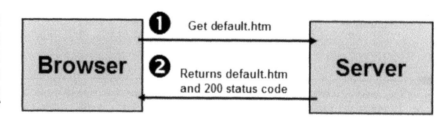

Figure 7.5   *Anonymous access exchange.*

The Internet guest account can be changed for each individual Web server, virtual directory, directory, and file. This can be done by clicking the Browse button in the anonymous access section of the ISM Authentication Methods configuration screen (see also Figure 7.2). Changing the Internet guest account on a particular virtual directory allows you to set different authorization settings on that directory. For example you may not want everyone to have access to every directory on every server using the same anonymous access account.

An IIS 6.0 change worth pointing out is that the password of the anonymous account in the IIS metabase is not automatically synchronized with the password of the Internet guest account, as it is set in AD or the SAM. Microsoft refers to this anonymous account password synchronization feature as subauthentication. The IIS metabase anonymous account password is the one you can set from the ISM Authentication Methods configuration screen (as illustrated in Figure 7.2). The IIS 6.0 default is that the administrator must manually change the password in the ISM when the Internet guest account's password is changed. When he/she fails to do so, anonymous access to the Web server will fail.

In IIS 6.0, you can enable the automatic anonymous password synchronization as it is available in earlier IIS versions by making the following changes on your IIS 6.0 Web server:

- The IIS worker process of the applications on which you grant anonymous access must run as LocalSystem.

- The AnonymousPasswordSync IIS metabase property must be set to true.

- The subauthentication DLL "iissuba.dll" must be registered. You can do so from the command line, as follows:

```
regsvr32 iissuba.dll
```

Even though it is a pain to keep the anonymous passwords in sync manually, for security reasons, we recommend that you not enable subauthentication on IIS 6.0. It is a bad idea to run applications in the security context of the LocalSystem account, as it is a very highly privileged account on a Windows computer. This also explains why Microsoft has disabled subauthentication in IIS 6.0.

By default, IIS 6.0 performs a network cleartext logon when an authentication occurs using the Internet guest account. In IIS 6.0 the Internet guest account is also automatically assigned the network logon user right (this is the "Access this computer from the network" user right). In IIS 5.0

Examining Web Authentication Exchanges

A great tool for testing and troubleshooting Web servers is the IIS 6.0 Resource Kit tool WebFetch (wfetch) (illustrated in Figure 7.6). WebFetch does not render the HTTP content that it receives from the Web server—which makes it an interesting tool for analyzing HTTP messages. Note the WWW-Authenticate headers that are sent back by the Web server in the example shown in Figure 7.6.

The IIS 6.0 Resource Kit tools can be downloaded from www.microsoft.com/downloads.

Another great tool for troubleshooting IIS authentication (and access control) problems is the Authentication and Access Control Diagnostics tool. This tool is not in the IIS Resource Kit, but is available as a separate download from www.microsoft.com/downloads.

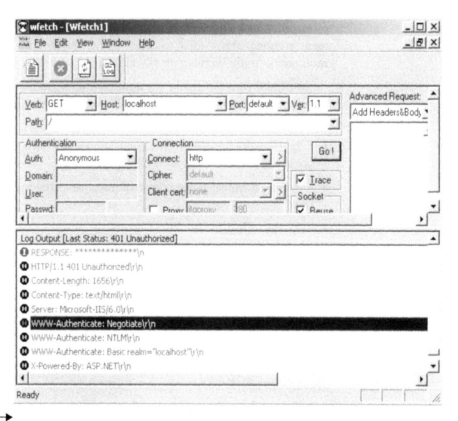

Figure 7.6   *Using the IIS Resource Kit WebFetch (WFetch) tool.*

and earlier versions the default logon type was interactive. Interactive logon requires the interactive logon user right. The latter imposes a security risk because of the high amount of system privileges associated with an interactive logon. For more information on the differences between interactive logon and network logon, see Chapter 5.

7.3.2   Basic Authentication

The basic authentication protocol is part of the HTTP 1.0 protocol specification and is commonly supported by Web browsers and servers. Basic authentication provides a simple mechanism to transmit user credentials (a user ID and password) to a Web server.

Figure 7.7 shows the different messages that are exchanged between a Web browser and server during a basic authentication exchange. The first two steps of this exchange are, with the exception of the authentication schemes supported by the server, identical to the example that was given in Figure 7.4:

1.   The browser requests data from the server using an HTTP GET command.

2.   If the Web server requires the client to authenticate himself, it sends an HTTP 401 Access Denied error message back to the browser, along with:

      ▪ A list of the authentication schemes supported by the Web server. When using basic authentication, this list includes the "basic" verb.

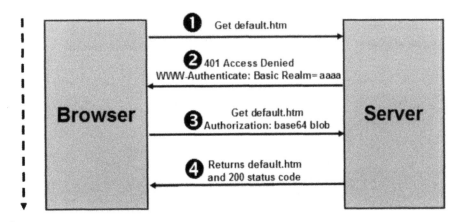

Figure 7.7   *Basic authentication exchange.*

- The name of the basic authentication realm. The concept of a realm will be explained below.

3. Before replying to the challenge, the browser prompts the user for his username and password (as illustrated in Figure 7.8). This credential prompt will not occur if the user has previously cached his credentials in the user profile (using the "Remember my password" option—see also the sidenote on "Caching Credentials in Internet Explorer") or if the URL that was used to access the Web site contains the username and password. The browser then responds to the authentication request by base64 encoding its username, password, and the authentication realm and sending the encoded blob back to the Web server as an authorization host header.

4. The server authenticates the browser's response and, if everything is okay, sends the response and the requested resource back to the user. The response message includes an HTTP 200 status code. If the credentials the user provides are not okay, the Microsoft Internet Explorer (IE) browser gives the user two more basic authentication attempts.

You can shortcut the basic authentication exchange by including the user credentials in the URL that is passed to the Web server. To do so, use the following URL format:

```
http://username:password@yourwebsite.com
```

Figure 7.8
*Basic
authentication
credential prompt.*

You must be aware of a potential security hole when you use basic authentication: the credential information sent between a Web browser and server is not secured. The credentials are just base64 encoded, which means they are relatively easy to decode. Base64 encoding stores every three 8-bit characters as four 6-bit characters.

The easiest way to decode base64 is to use one of the online base64-decoder tools, such as the tool at http://base64-encoder-online.waraxe.us/. Try, for example, to decode the following basic authentication string at the above URL:

ZG9tYWluXHVzZXJuYW1lOnBhc3N3b3Jk

What is the result of the decoding? Just by copying this string into the box, you should receive the decoded results, domain\username:password.

Because decoding a base64 encoding is relatively easy, you must secure the basic authentication HTTP traffic using the SSL/TLS protocols. When you enable basic authentication on a Web resource, IIS warns you about this potential security hole (as Figure 7.9 shows).

When setting basic authentication (or digest authentication, as will be explained later) for a Web resource, you can also configure the default domain and realm at the bottom of the ISM authentication methods configuration screen (see also Figure 7.2).

The default domain allows you to set the domain to which a user should be authenticated when no domain is provided during the authentication process. In the example of Figure 7.8, the user provided an authentication domain called "dc" by preceding his username with dc\. This means that in this particular example, the default domain specified in the IIS authentica-

Figure 7.9
Basic authentication warning.

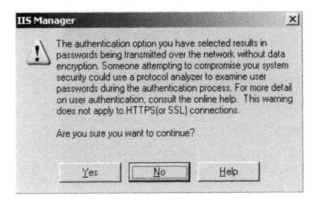

tion properties will be ignored. To enable user principal name (UPN)-based logon in a Windows 2000 or later domain environment, you must specify "\" in the default domain field.

The realm is a level within the IIS metabase hierarchy that a user is allowed to access when using basic authentication. By default, it is the IIS computer name—which provides access to all levels in the IIS metabase hierarchy (as illustrated in Figure 7.8 for machine vmw2k33763). The realm always appears in the left top corner of the basic authentication dialog box. Figure 7.10 shows how the custom realm /LM/W3SVC/1/Root/ MyVirtualDir is displayed in the basic authentication dialog box. A Web resource's realm property can be set from the bottom of the Authentication Methods dialog box or in the IIS metabase. The way to specify custom realms is explained in the IIS documentation. Both digest and advanced digest authentication (explained below) also use the realm concept.

Other interesting basic authentication options that cannot be set from the ISM GUI but only by editing the IIS metabase or the system registry are the following:

- The logon type (LogonMethod metabase property) specifies the logon type that IIS performs when a basic authentication Web logon session occurs. As for anonymous access, by default, IIS performs a network cleartext logon (LogonMethod value 3). Other possible LogonMethod values are:

  — 0 for interactive logon
  — 1 for batch logon
  — 2 for network logon

Figure 7.10
Basic authentication credential prompt with custom realm.

Caching Credentials in Internet Explorer

User credentials (user IDs and passwords) can be cached in the IE Temporary Internet Files folder by checking the "Remember my password" or "Save this password in your password list" options in the IE credential prompt dialog boxes.

We advise you not to use IE credential caching. Tools are available on the Internet that can reveal your cached IE passwords. An example of such a tool is the Protected Storage PassView tool (pspv.exe), which can be downloaded from www.nirsoft.net/utils/pspv.html.

This IE credential caching should not be confused with the more secure OS-based credential caching of domain credentials explained in Chapter 5, nor with the credential manager-based credential caching that will be explained in Chapter 9.

■ The token cache time (UserTokenTTL system registry entry) specifies the amount of time a user's IIS-level access token is cached and remains valid on the Web server. The default is 15 minutes. If you do not want to cache access tokens on the Web server, set the User-TokenTTL to 0. The UserTokenTTL (REG_DWORD) property must be set in the following system registry container: HKEY_LOCAL_MACHINE\SYSTEM\CurrentControlSet\Services\InetInfo\Parameters. The UserTokenTTL value is expressed in seconds.

7.3.3 Digest Authentication

Digest authentication was originally specified as part of the HTTP 1.0 protocol specification—an enhanced version is defined in the HTTP 1.1 protocol specification. Both digest authentication versions are defined in RFC 2617. Like the NTLM authentication protocol, digest authentication uses a challenge-response–based authentication method.

HTTP 1.1 and enhanced digest authentication are not supported by all browser and Web server types and versions. On the Microsoft side, they are supported by IE 5.0 and IIS 5.0 and later versions.

Key advantages of digest authentication are that it does not transmit the user credentials in the clear over the network (like basic authentication does) and that it does not require the use of the SSL or TLS protocols. Similar to basic authentication, digest authentication uses the realm notion to partition a Web server's resources.

A major disadvantage of digest authentication is that it requires Active Directory user accounts (IIS warns you about this when enabling digest authentication, as Figure 7.11 shows) and, more importantly, less secure

Figure 7.11
*Digest
authentication
warning.*

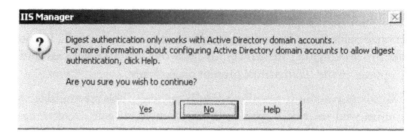

storage of the user password in AD. To deal with the latter issue, Windows Server 2003 supports "advanced" digest authentication—which will be explained in more detail at the end of this section.

In AD, you can set clear-text password storage for a user account using the "Store Password using Reversible Encryption" user account property. This property can be configured from the account tab in the user properties, that can be accessed from the AD Users and Computers (ADUC) MMC snap-in. You can also enforce clear-text password storage using the "Store Passwords using Reversible Encryption" Group Policy Object (GPO) setting (located in the Security Settings\Account Policies\Password Policy container). After enabling reversible encryption, the user or administrator must set a new password to activate the clear-text storage of the password. For obvious security reasons, we recommend that you not enable reversible encryption for AD-based password hashes and instead use the more secure advanced digest authentication.

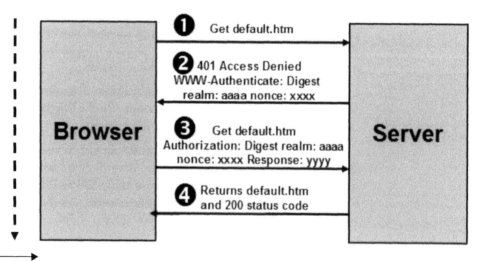

Figure 7.12   *Digest authentication exchange.*

Figure 7.12 shows how digest authentication works:

1. The user's browser requests access to the default.htm Web page.

2. The Web site replies with a 401 Access Denied message. The server's reply also tells the browser that the Web page requires digest authentication (the WWW-authenticate contains the word "digest") and lists the digest authentication realm to which the Web page belongs (in the example, realm "aaaa"). Most important, the reply also contains a digest challenge—which is usually referred to as the nonce (in the example, "xxxx").

3. Before replying to the challenge, the browser prompts the user for his username and password. The browser generates an MD5 hash using the challenge, the username, the user password, and realm. The resulting hash (in the example, response "yyyy") is then sent back to the Web server together with the nonce (in the example, "xxxx") and the realm (in the example, "aaaa").

4. The Web server forwards the hash and the nonce to a domain controller for validation. The DC calculates a response using the AD copy of the user's password and the nonce, and compares it to the response forwarded by the Web server. The DC informs the Web server about the outcome of the response validation process. If everything is okay, the Web server sends the requested resource back to the user. The response message includes an HTTP 200 status code.

The use of digest authentication will generate a typical authentication dialog box on the browser side. This dialog box is illustrated in Figure 7.13. The dialog box explicitly refers to the name of the resource the user tries to access and the use of the digest authentication protocol.

Two important digest authentication architectural changes in Windows Server 2003 and IIS 6.0 are the inclusion of a digest security support provider (SSP) and the support for advanced digest authentication.

In Windows Server 2003, Microsoft has implemented digest authentication and advanced digest authentication (which is explained next) in the operating system using an SSP authentication plug-in (SSPs were explained in Chapter 5).

Advanced digest authentication is an enhanced version of the digest authentication protocol. The enhancements lie primarily in the way the digest response is verified on a domain controller. The key advantages of

Figure 7.13
Digest
authentication
dialog box.

advanced digest authentication are that it does not require clear-text storage of users' passwords (even though it requires the use of an AD account), and that it leverages the Windows Server 2003 digest SSP.

Advanced digest authentication is only available for Web authentication on an IIS 6.0 Web server if the browser used on the client side is IE 5.0 or a later version, if the user account used for authentication is defined in a Windows Server 2003 domain that is at functional level 2 (this means that the domain contains only Windows Server 2003 domain controllers), and if the UseDigestSSP IIS metabase property is set to 1 (true). On brand-new Windows Server 2003 IIS 6.0 installations, the UseDigestSSP metabase property defaults to true. If one of the above conditions is not met, simple digest authentication will be used.

7.4   Integrated Windows Authentication

The IIS Integrated Windows Authentication option really consists of two authentication protocols: the NTLM and the Kerberos authentication protocols. Remember from Chapter 5 some of the key advantages of using Kerberos over NTLM:

- Kerberos is faster than NTLM.

- Kerberos is more secure than NTLM.

- Kerberos supports mutual authentication.

- Kerberos supports credential forwarding.

- Kerberos is an open standard.

Windows Integrated Authentication calls on three different Security Support Providers (SSPs): the Kerberos, NTLM, and Negotiate SSP. The Negotiate SSP allows a client to select the most appropriate authentication protocol (Kerberos or NTLM). These three SSPs were also explained in Chapter 5.

As with digest authentication, Integrated Windows Authentication never transmits the password in the clear, and thus does not require the use of SSL or TLS. From all Web authentication protocols listed so far in this chapter, Integrated Windows Authentication also requires the least configuration and user intervention. It will automatically retrieve the user's credentials from the user logon session's credential cache, unless Integrated Windows Authentication has been disabled in the Internet Explorer (IE) configuration settings. In IE, Integrated Windows Authentication support can be enabled or disabled using the "Enable Integrated Windows Authentication" setting in the advanced configuration options. Changing this setting requires an IE restart. Unfortunately, both NTLM and Kerberos authentication support are specific to Microsoft browsers.

NTLM authentication does not work across most HTTP proxies, because it requires persistent point-to-point connections between the Web browser and server. Web servers typically close an HTTP authentication connection after they send out a 401 Access Denied HTTP error message. When using NTLM, the IIS Web server keeps the HTTP connection open for the duration of the NTLM challenge/response sequence. Most HTTP proxies do not support this. Notable exceptions are the Squid proxy[4] and Microsoft's ISA Server running in proxy (cache-only) mode: they can deal with NTLM authentication traffic. A possible workaround for this issue is to tunnel the HTTP traffic using, for example, the IPsec or L2TP tunneling protocols—but then again, few organizations allow the creation of tunnels that bypass their proxies and/or firewalls.

Kerberos authentication is only available on IE 5.0 or later browsers and IIS 5.0 or later Web servers. For Kerberos authentication to work, the browser user and the Web server must also be in the same or a trusted Windows 2000 or later domain, the browser must have permanent access to a Windows domain controller (which means that you must open Kerberos port TCP/88 on your firewalls), and the Web server must have a valid service principal name (SPN) that is registered in the Active Directory.

---

4. More information on the Squid proxy and its NTLM support can be found at www.squid-cache.org/, http://devel.squid-cache.org/ntlm/, and www.squid-cache.org/Doc/FAQ/FAQ-11.html#ss11.14.

Figure 7.14
*Integrated
Windows
authentication
dialog box.*

From the above, it is clear that Integrated Windows Authentication is best suited for intranet Web authentication and is not a good option for authentication in an extranet or Internet environment where the Web browsers and servers are separated by proxies and firewalls.

Unless the user's current logon credentials can be used to authenticate to the Web server, the use of Integrated Windows Authentication will generate a typical authentication dialog box on the browser side. This dialog box is illustrated in Figure 7.14. In the top left side of the dialog box, it always shows "Connecting to" followed by the name of the resource the user tries to connect to.

7.5   Passport-Based Authentication

.NET Passport, or "Passport" for short, is Microsoft's single identity and sign-on solution for the Web. This section explores the security and privacy features of Passport and explains the Passport authentication exchanges. Throughout the text, we will particularly focus on how Microsoft has integrated Passport with its latest operating system platforms: Windows XP, Windows Server 2003, and R2.

Even though at the time of writing IIS 6.0 only supported Passport authentication, we will also introduce the key concepts behind Windows Live ID, the next version of the Passport system. Windows Live ID is the next evolution of Passport, so quite a few things we say about Passport also apply to Windows Live ID. Where it is applicable, we will point out the ways that Windows Live ID is different from Passport.

To learn more about how to set up Passport for authenticating users of your Web site, refer to the following Microsoft documentation: the Passport 2.5 Service Guide Kit (SGK) available from http://msdn.microsoft.com/archive/en-us/passport25/start_full.asp. A high-level introduction to Windows Live ID is available from http://msdn.microsoft.com/library/default.asp?url=/library/en-us/dnlive/html/winliveidserv.asp.

This section is primarily based on Passport version 2.5. Compared to earlier versions, Passport 2.5 includes the following security enhancements:

- New installations of Passport Manager support HTTP-only cookies, which protect against cross-site scripting attacks that can expose sensitive information about the users of a particular Web site. The support for HTTP-only cookies was introduced in IE 6. New installations of the Passport Manager (explained below) version 2.5 turn on the HTTP-only property in all Passport cookies.

- In new installations of Passport Manager version 2.5 the Passport logon page is always transmitted using HTTP over SSL. This protects against Passport credential dictionary and replay attacks.

- Passport version 2.5 requires e-mail validation when a new user signs up for Passport. The user's Passport account will not be activated until the user has clicked the URL in the validation e-mail message. This protects against the creation of Passport accounts that are associated with other people's e-mail addresses.

7.5.1 Passport and Windows Live ID

Microsoft announced Windows Live ID as the next Passport version while we were writing this book (April 2006). Microsoft will upgrade all current Passport users automatically to the new system. Windows Live ID is part of a Microsoft rebranding campaign for MSN services: Hotmail is being rebranded as Windows Live Mail, and MSN Messenger is being rebranded as Windows Live Messenger.

There are a couple of ways in which Windows Live ID will differ from Passport:

- Microsoft is not positioning Windows Live ID as a universal Web authentication and SSO service, as it initially did with Passport. Windows Live ID is intended as a Microsoft-only service that facilitates users' access to Microsoft Live services.

- Windows Live ID will support Windows CardSpace (formerly known as InfoCard). CardSpace is a client-side identity management system that will be built into Windows Vista (the next version of the Windows client OS) and that will also be available for Windows XP as part of the WinFX Runtime Components.

  CardSpace will store users' personal information on their PCs in the form of identity cards they can submit to Web sites and services. This will save users the trouble of retyping this information into forms manually. As with Passport, users will have to enter a valid e-mail address and password to receive a CardSpace identity (or Info-Card) that works with Windows Live ID. The combination of Windows Live ID and CardSpace will eliminate the requirement for users to enter a username and password to access Windows Live sites. More information on CardSpace is available from http://msdn.microsoft.com/winfx/reference/infocard/default.aspx.

- Windows Live ID will support the emerging WS-* identity federation standards for exchanging identity information and credentials over the Web. The WS-* standards are also a fundamental building block for Microsoft's "Identity Metasystem" vision. An introduction to the Identity Metasystem is available from http://msdn.microsoft.com/library/default.asp?url=/library/en-us/dnwebsrv/html/identitymetasystem.asp.

  The link between Windows Live ID, the WS-* standards, and the Identity Metasystem will allow organizations to federate their internal identity management systems with Windows Live ID. This can enable them for example to accept Windows Live IDs as logon credentials to their local network, or to let employees access external Windows Live ID-enabled Web sites using their internal identities.

Microsoft CardSpace and the Identity Metasystem will also be covered in more detail in Chapter 3 of *Advanced Microsoft Windows Security Services* (part 2 of this series).

7.5.2 Passport-Enabling Web Technologies

Passport uses common Web technologies supported by all browsers. These technologies are the Hypertext Transport Protocol (HTTP) and cookies; Dynamic Web Pages with embedded JavaScript code; and the Secure Sockets Layer (SSL) protocol.

Passport uses HTTP to:

- Retrieve Web pages from Passport-enabled Web servers

- Transport Passport-related user information
- Create Passport client-side cookies and retrieve information from Passport client-side cookies
- Redirect browsers from one Passport-enabled Web site to another

Passport makes extensive use of HTTP redirect messages, which enable Web sites to communicate with one another without setting up a direct communication between the Web sites' Web servers. All communications take place via the user's browser.

The Passport infrastructure servers use cookies to store Passport-related information on the user desktop. To store personal user information, Passport uses encrypted cookies.

JavaScript code embedded in Web server pages enables Passport to deliver dynamic Web content, such as personalized Web pages, to the user's browser. The reason Microsoft has selected JavaScript over typical MS scripting technologies like VBScript is because JavaScript is supported on all browsers (and not just on Microsoft browsers).

Passport uses SSL to create secure tunnels for the transport of user data between browsers and Web servers. The SSL tunnel provides data authentication, confidentiality and integrity protection, and server-side authentication. The SSL protocol will be explained later in this chapter.

7.5.3 Passport Infrastructure

Before diving into the nuts and bolts of how Passport authentication works, we need a clear view of the Passport infrastructure. The Passport infrastructure components can be classified in three categories (as illustrated in Figure 7.15):

- The Microsoft Passport Nexus servers
- The Passport (and Windows Live ID) domain authority servers
- The Web servers of the participating Web sites

The infrastructure servers that a Passport user deals with are the domain authorities and participating Web sites.

- A participating Web site is a site that provides its users with the possibility to authenticate using Passport SSO. The owners of the site have installed some Passport-specific code on the Web server (including the Passport Manager COM object) and have signed an agreement with Microsoft or one of the Passport domain authorities to join the

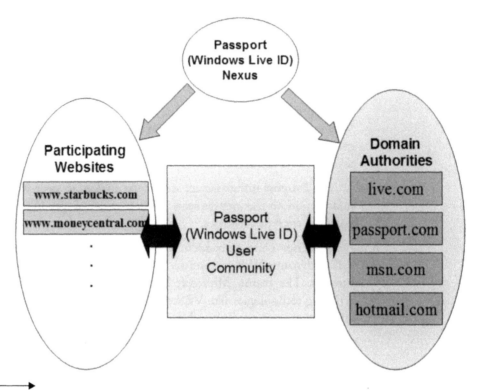

Figure 7.15   *Passport infrastructure.*

Passport SSO network. Examples of participating Passport sites are MoneyCentral and Starbucks.

- A domain authority server is a trusted third party that owns a Passport domain and acts as a Passport authentication authority for that domain. Examples are the domain authority servers for the live.com, msn.com, hotmail.com, and passport.com domains. Until now, all domain authorities were run by Microsoft or by business entities that are very closely related to Microsoft. Every domain authority manages a domain authority database that contains a secured copy of the users' Passport credentials and profile information.

- The Microsoft Passport Nexus servers make up the core of the Passport system. They provide configuration information to all other servers in the Passport Infrastructure. This configuration information includes things like the Passport user profile schema and the cryptographic keys used to secure certain Passport cookies.

7.5.4   Basic Passport Authentication Exchange

In this section, we will explain the Passport authentication exchange. In our sample scenario, the user is working from a Windows XP machine, has previously registered to create a set of Passport credentials, but is not logged on to Passport. The scenario starts when the user enters the www.starbucks.com URL in his browser. Let us look at what happens next from a Passport message exchange point-of-view (the exchanges are illustrated in Figure 7.16):

1.   To authenticate to Passport and the Starbucks Web site, the user clicks the Passport "Sign In" icon (illustrated in Figure 7.17) on the Starbucks sign-in Web page (note that a user can also choose to authenticate using a local Starbucks account).

2.   Clicking the "Sign In" icon causes an HTTP redirect to the Passport domain authority server's login page.

3.   The Passport domain authority server presents the user with a Passport login page.

4.   The user enters his or her Passport credentials in the Passport login page (https://login.passport.com[5]). The credentials are sent

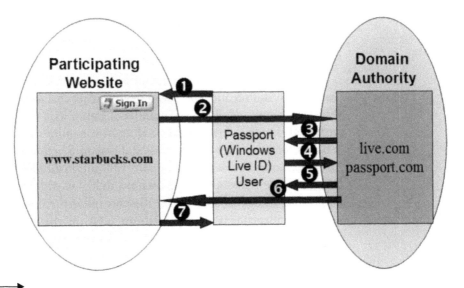

Figure 7.16   *Passport authentication sequence.*

---

5.   For Windows Live ID this is https://login.live.com.

to the Passport domain authority server over an SSL connection. The domain authority server validates the user credentials.

5.   If the user's Passport credentials are okay, the Passport domain authority server writes a set of domain- and user-specific Passport data to the user's machine.

6.   If the user's Passport credentials are okay, the Passport domain authority server generates an HTTP redirect back to the Starbucks server.

7.   The Starbucks Web server sends a new copy of the Starbucks homepage to the user's browser. On this new copy, the Passport "Sign In" icon has changed to a "Sign Out" icon (illustrated in Figure 7.17). The Starbucks Web server also writes a set of site- and user-specific Passport data to the user's machine.

If the user did not have a set of Passport credentials before clicking the "Sign In" icon in step 1 of the exchange, the scenario would look slightly different. In that case, Passport would first redirect the user to a registration Web page to create a set of Passport credentials.

An important feature of the basic Passport authentication sequence explained above is that the user's Passport credentials are never sent to the participating Web site. The participating Web site relies on a Passport-specific mechanism to authenticate the user. This mechanism is explained in the section on Passport Cookies below.

The credentials the user uses to authenticate to Passport in step 4 are the user's e-mail address and a password of at least six characters. From Passport version 2.0 onwards, Passport supports a feature that is known as "strong credential sign-in." Strong credential sign-in requires the user to enter, in addition to his or her e-mail address and password, a four-digit security key to authenticate to Passport. Passport will automatically block the user's Passport account key after three attempts to log on with the wrong security key. Strong-credential sign in is a Passport infrastructure feature: its availability is independent of the platform used on the Passport user side. Strong-credential sign in significantly enhances the security of the Passport authentication protocol.

Figure 7.17   *Passport Sign In and Sign Out icons.*

Another initiative that IT administrators can take to enhance the Passport security quality is to make Passport users aware of the risks for Passport spoofing. A simple trick you can teach your users is to check the authenticity of the name attributes of a Passport server's SSL certificate (for example, making sure that the certificate was issued to the "passport.com" Web site and not "pasport.com"—to check the content of a Web site's certificate, double-click the lock icon in the IE browser tray) or a Passport Web site's URL (for example, making sure the URL shows http://login.passport.com, and not http://login.pasport.com; or, in the case of Windows Live ID, http://login.live.com and not http://login.life.com). In earlier Passport versions, these spoofing attacks were also known as "Bogus Merchant" attacks. For an overview of these spoofing attacks, take a look at David Kormann and Aviel Rubin's paper, available at: http://avirubin.com/passport.html.

7.5.5 XP and Windows Server 2003 Passport User Changes

In Windows XP, Windows Server 2003, and R2, Passport registration works differently: instead of redirecting the user to a Passport registration page, Windows XP and Windows Server 2003 start the .NET Passport wizard (illustrated in Figure 7.18). The .NET Passport wizard guides users through the Passport registration process.

Figure 7.18
.NET Passport wizard.

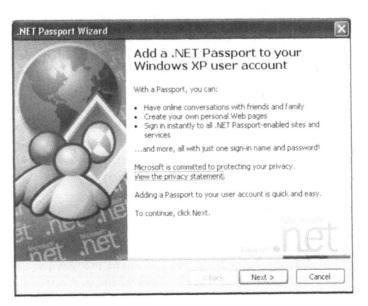

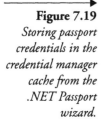

Figure 7.19
Storing passport credentials in the credential manager cache from the .NET Passport wizard.

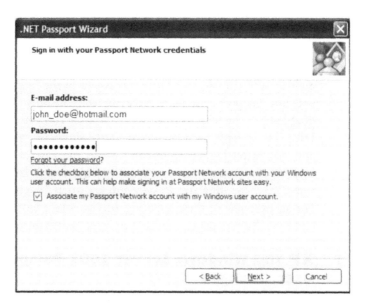

In Windows XP, the .NET Passport wizard can be started from the User Accounts Control Panel applet by clicking the "Set up my account to use a .NET Passport" option in the account properties. In Windows Server 2003 and R2, the wizard can be started from the Advanced tab in the User Accounts configuration screen. The User Accounts configuration screen can be started by typing "control userpasswords2" at the command line.

In XP and Windows Server 2003, Microsoft implemented a security feature called the credential manager. Credential manager is a single-sign-on solution that leverages a secure client-side credential cache. Credential manager will be explained in greater detail in Chapter 9 of this book. Passport credentials can also be cached in the credential manager. To store your Passport credentials in the credential manager cache, check the "Associate my Passport Network account with my Windows user account" check box in the .NET Passport wizard (as illustrated in Figure 7.19).

7.5.6   Passport Cookies

To better understand how Passport works, it is worthwhile to look at the different Passport cookies exchanged between the Passport user's browser, the participating Web sites, and the Passport domain authorities.

The easiest way to see the content of the cookies sent to the user browser during a Passport authentication sequence is to disable automatic cookie

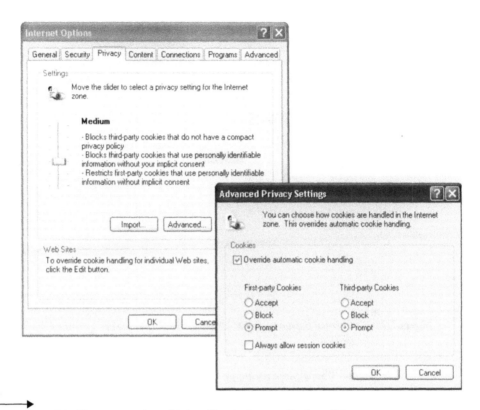

Figure 7.20   *Disabling automatic cookie handling in Internet Explorer 6.0.*

handling and set the cookie "Prompt" option in the properties of your Internet Explorer browser. This will make your browser prompt you each time it receives a cookie. To set this up in Internet Explorer 6.0, select Internet Options from the Tools menu option, and go to the Privacy tab. Click the "Advanced" button (as illustrated in Figure 7.20) and check the "Override automatic cookie handling" box; then select "Prompt" for both first-party and third-party cookies.

Next time a Passport authentication sequence occurs, your browser will generate a Privacy Alert warning dialog box (like the one illustrated in Figure 7.21) each time the Web site you are accessing tries to write a cookie to your machine. If you click "More Info" in the warning dialog box, the dialog box is expanded and shows all the cookie properties. Interesting cookie properties to look at are:

- The cookie name

- The cookie domain, which is the domain that's attempting to write a cookie to your machine

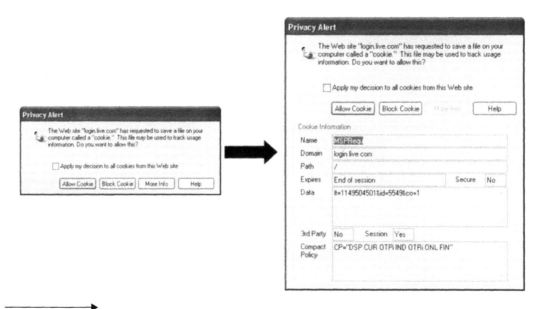

Figure 7.21 *Internet Explorer cookie "Privacy Alert" (for cookies generated by Windows Live ID servers).*

- The expires property, which holds the cookie expiration time

- The secure property, which tells whether the cookie's content is encrypted

- The session property, which tells whether the cookie is persistent or deleted when the browser session ends

Table 7.1 lists important cookies types the Passport system uses (this list is not complete). Most Passport cookies are session cookies (also known as nonpersistent cookies) that are deleted from the cookie cache (for IE, this is the Temporary Internet Files folder in the user profile) at the end of the browser session. An exception to this is when the user selects "Save my e-mail address and password" when signing in to Passport (as illustrated in Figure 7.22); in that case, Passport cookies survive the end of a browser session. Passport cookies can also expire at the end of the time period that is specified in the cookie by the Passport domain authority or a participating Web site. Cookies are also deleted when the user signs out of Passport. The last column of the table shows whether the cookie is set by the Web server of a Passport domain authority or a participating site.

Passport uses a set of symmetric encryption keys to provide data confidentiality protection of the Passport cookie content. Every domain authority has an encryption key, and every participating Web site has an

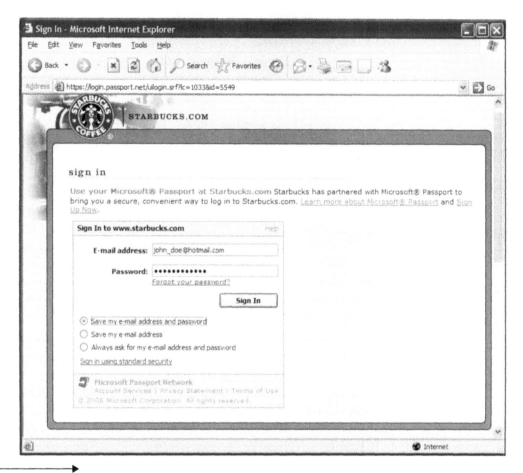

Figure 7.22 *Sign in to Passport using the "Save my e-mail address and password" option.*

Table 7.1 *Important Passport Cookie Types (Nonexhaustive List)*

Cookie Name	Cookie Short Name	Cookie Properties	Written by Domain Authority and/or Participating Site?
Ticket-Granting Cookie	MSPSec	Session	Domain Authority
Ticket Cookie	MSPAuth	Session	Domain Authority
Profile Cookie	MSPProf	Session	Domain Authority Participating Site
Visited Sites Cookie	MSPVis	Session	Domain Authority

encryption key. The latter key is known by both the domain authority and the participating Web site.

Passport uses two types of ticket cookies: ticket-granting cookies and "plain" ticket cookies. This system is very much inspired by the Kerberos authentication protocol.

- The **Passport ticket-granting cookie** is the cookie generated at the beginning of a Passport logon session. A Passport logon session begins when the user signs in to Passport using the Sign In icon. It ends when the user closes his browser or when he signs out from Passport by clicking the Sign Out icon. The ticket-granting cookie is used to silently request a new ticket cookie for a participating Web site to the Passport domain authority. Thanks to the ticket-granting cookie, the user does not have to re-enter his Passport credentials when he needs a new ticket cookie. The ticket-granting cookie contains a user's Passport unique identifier (PUID) and a hash of the user's credential information. The cookie's content is encrypted using the domain authority's encryption key.

- A **Passport ticket cookie** is used to authenticate a user to the domain authority or to a participating Web site during a Passport logon session. It contains the user's PUID and a set of encrypted timestamps. The latter protect against replay attacks. A ticket cookie's content is encrypted using the domain authority's encryption key (in the case of the ticket cookie for the domain authority) or using the participating Web site's encryption key (in case of a ticket for a participating Web site).

The visited sites cookie contains a list of the participating Web sites a user has visited from his or her computer since last Sign Out. This site list is used to clear all Passport-related cookies when a Passport user clicks the Sign Out icon to sign out of his or her Passport account.

A profile cookie contains a Passport user's profile data and provides personalization services. Like ticket cookies, profile cookies provide ease-of-use to a Passport user: the user doesn't have to retype personal data every time he or she accesses another Web site. Passport deals with two different profile cookie types.

- General profile cookies contain a user's general profile information. Its content is encrypted using the domain authority's encryption key.

- Additional profile cookies contain a user's general profile information and additional profile information that is specific to a participating

Web site. Its content is encrypted using the participating Web site's encryption key.

The user's general profile cookie always contains the user's e-mail address and may optionally contain the user's first and last name, country/region, postal code, state, time zone, preferred language, gender, accessibility, occupation, and full birth date. The option to include or not include the latter data in the user's profile is entirely up to the user. Passport stores the user data into the Passport core profile at registration time. From Passport 2.0 on, a user can, at any time after the initial registration, change the content of the profile and decide which profile data to share with Passport participating Web sites. This will be explained in the section on "Passport and Personally Identifiable Information."

Table 7.2 gives an overview of the Passport user data we discussed so far. It shows the required and optional data for Passport registration and whether the data are by default shared with participating Passport sites during a Passport logon session.

An important component in the Passport cookie exchanges is the Passport Manager COM object. It is a server-side automation object installed on all participating Web sites. The Passport Manager object provides encryption services to protect Passport user data and handles the Passport

Table 7.2   *Passport User Data*

Passport User Data Type	Content		Required during Passport Registration?	Shared with Other Participating Sites?
PUID	Passport Unique Identifier		Yes	Yes
Passport Credentials	Standard	E-mail address	Yes	If the user agrees (user opt-in)
		Password	Yes	No
		Secret Q&A	No	No
	Strong-credential sign-in	Four-digit key	No	No
User General Profile	First Name, Last Name		No	If the user agrees (user opt-in)
	Country/Region, Postal Code, State, Time Zone, Preferred Language, Gender, Occupation,			
	Birth Date			

cookie setting, parsing, and expiration logic. The Passport Manager also silently communicates with the Passport Nexus servers to determine the current configuration of the Passport network.

Besides cookies, Passport Manager also uses HTTP query strings as an intermediary for querying the central user store at the Passport domain authority. The advantage of using cookies over the HTTP query string as a data storage intermediary is that the URL display in the user's browser (the IE "Address Bar") doesn't become cluttered with cryptic information.

7.5.7 Passport and Personally Identifiable Information

Tightly entangled with the ubiquity of the World Wide Web is the problem of distribution of personally identifiable information (PII). Several government and industry privacy regulations attempt to control the exchange of PII.

Microsoft understands the importance of addressing privacy issues effectively in order to win universal acceptance for its Passport Single Sign-On technology. Among the Microsoft privacy-related initiatives are support for the TRUSTe privacy label initiative (www.truste.org) and the W3C's P3P initiative, as well as the inclusion of privacy-related features in Microsoft's latest Internet-focused software products (including IE and the latest Passport versions). To read Microsoft's general privacy statement, go to www.microsoft.com/info/privacy.htm. To read the Passport-specific privacy statement, go to https://accountservices.passport.net/PPPrivacyStatement.srf.

From Passport version 2.0 onwards, a Passport user can easily modify the content of his or her Passport user profile. This can be done from the Passport Account Services Web pages. These Web pages can be accessed from https://accountservices.passport.net[6] or by clicking the Change Passport Attributes pushbutton in the properties of your user account. This pushbutton can be accessed from the Change my .NET Passport option in the account properties of the User Accounts Control Panel applet.

Another important privacy-related technology you can use when you're worried about how a Passport-enabled Web site deals with your personal information is IE 6.0's built-in P3P support. The Platform for Privacy Preferences (P3P) is a combined protocol and architecture designed to inform World Wide Web users about the data-collection practices of Web sites. P3P is driven by the World Wide Web Consortium (W3C). In IE, P3P

---

6.   For Windows Live ID, this is https://login.live.com.

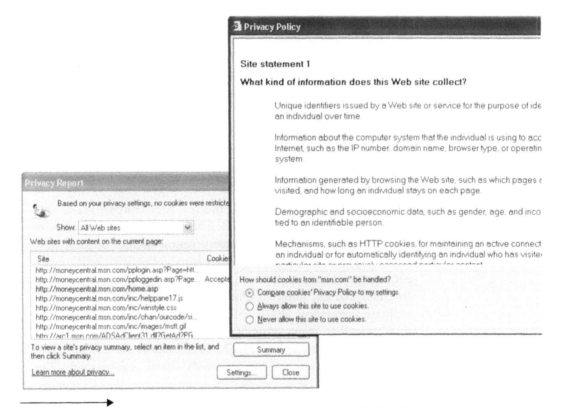

Figure 7.23   *Checking out a site's Privacy Report in Internet Explorer 6.0.*

provides an easy way to block cookies based on a user's privacy preferences. Figure 7.20 showed how cookie handling can be configured in IE 6.0. More info about P3P is available from www.w3.org/P3P.

To check a Web site's P3P privacy report in Internet Explorer 6.0, select View\Privacy Report... from the menu, then select a Web site's URL and click Summary (as illustrated in Figure 7.23 for the MoneyCentral home-page).

7.5.8   Passport Integration in Windows Server 2003

In Windows Server 2003, Microsoft included the following Passport integration features:

- The ability for users to authenticate to a Windows Server 2003 IIS Web server using Passport credentials. ".NET Passport Authentication" is now listed in the "Authentication Methods" configuration dialog box in the ISM (refer back to Figure 7.2). To use Passport for authentication, your IIS Web site must be joined to the Passport infrastructure as a participating Web site. Microsoft does not support the creation of enterprise Passport infrastructures, where an organization would be its own domain authority and not linked in any way to the Microsoft Web Passport infrastructure.

- At the time of writing, Microsoft was planning to allow organizations to federate (link) their internal identity management systems with the Windows Live ID infrastructure using the combination of Windows Live ID, the WS-* standards, and Microsoft's Identity Metasystem (see also the section on Windows Live ID above).

- The ability to define a mapping between a user's Passport PUID and a Windows security identifier (SID). Thanks to this, an administrator can apply Windows SID-based access control settings to users who have authenticated using Passport credentials. The PUID-SID mapping can be defined in the altSecurityIdentities property of an Active Directory account object. Unlike Alternate Kerberos identities and certificate mappings, PUID-SID mappings currently cannot be added using the "Name Mappings…" option in the advanced view of the Users and Computers (ADUC) MMC snap-in. To define PUID-SID mappings you can use an LDAP-based editing tool (like LDIFDE or ADSIEdit), or you can script the creation of the mappings using ADSI.

- If no PUID-SID mappings are defined in AD, IIS automatically creates an anonymous authentication session with the anonymous user account credentials (by default this is the IUSR_<*ComputerName*> account). In that case IIS also creates an authentication token for the anonymous account that contains a reference to the user's PUID.

🔟 HTTP/1.1 302 Object moved\r\n
🔟 Date: Tue, 05 Aug 2003 19:48:32 GMT\r\n
🔟 Server: Microsoft-IIS/6.0\r\n
🔟 X-Powered-By: ASP.NET\r\n
🔟 Content-Type: text/html\r\n
🔟 Location: https://current-login.passporttest.com/ppsecure/secure.srf?lc=1033&id=1&ru=https://localhost/&tw=1800&fs=1&kv=1&ct=1060112912&cb=
🔟 er=2.1.6000.1&tpf=cc452f8f5e2b24da57210747a281216a\r\n
🔟 Content-Length: 0\r\n
🔟 WWW-Authenticate: Passport1.4 lc=1033,id=1,tw=1800,fs=1,ru=https://localhost/,ct=1060112912,kv=1,ver=2.1.6000.1,seclog=10,tpf=57859df77e
🔟 b2b4429\r\n
🔟 \r\n

Figure 7.24   *WFetch HTTP Passport authentication trace.*

> **Recognizing IIS Passport Authentication Messages**
>
> To recognize and troubleshoot IIS Passport authentication exchanges, you can use the webfetch (wfetch) tool, included with the IIS 6.0 Resource Kit. An IIS 6.0 Web site with Passport authentication enabled will send out a WWW-authenticate message containing the Passport verb (see the example in Figure 7.24).

Even though Windows Server 2003 includes advanced Passport support, it does not include a Passport-specific security support provider (SSP). Passport support in IIS is enabled using an ISAPI dynamic link library (DDL) called "passport.dll."

7.6   Certificate-Based Authentication

Today, online shopping is about as popular as driving to the mall was a few years ago, and registering for a class or seminar is much easier to do online instead of by telephone. But honestly, don't you always hesitate for a second before you enter your credit card number and personal information? So what's behind that secure HTTP (HTTPs) Internet connection between your browser and the online site's server? Most likely, the online site is using either the Secure Sockets Layer (SSL) protocol or Transport Layer Security (TLS) protocol. SSL and TLS are security protocols that sit between the application and the transport layers of the TCP/IP networking stack (as illustrated in Figure 7.25). Both protocols support Certificate-based authentication of Web clients and servers. Microsoft includes SSL/TLS support in the Internet Explorer (IE) browser and the IIS Web server.

SSL was initially developed by Netscape. The latest SSL specification (3.0) can be downloaded from http://wp.netscape.com/eng/ssl3. In 1999, SSL was standardized by the IETF in RFC2246 and named Transport Layer Security (TLS) protocol (more information is available at www.ietf.org/rfc/rfc2246.txt). TLS 1.0 is also referred to as SSL version 3.1. Other than a new SSL version number, TLS also doubles the number of SSL error messages and includes some cryptographic optimizations. RFC 3546 (for more information, see www.ietf.org/rfc/rfc3546.txt) defines a set of interesting TLS 1.0 extensions. A great book that reveals all the nuts and bolts of both protocols is Eric Rescorla's *SSL and TLS: Designing and Building Secure Systems* (Addison-Wesley, 2001).

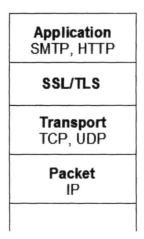

SSL can provide the following security services:

- **Server authentication**: SSL-enabled applications use an X.509 server certificate to authenticate a server.

- **Data confidentiality and integrity services**: SSL provides channel encryption services—also referred to as secure channel services—that secure traffic exchanged between an SSL-enabled client and server.

- **Client authentication**: SSL uses an X.509 client certificate to authenticate a client. Client authentication is an optional SSL service.

SSL and TLS can provide these security services to a wide range of application-level protocols, such as HTTP for secure Web communications, SMTP for secure mail transfer operations, and Network News Transfer Protocol (NNTP) for secure news operations. Because of its position in the TCP/IP stack, SSL can provide these secure channel services to application layer protocols in a transparent way—in other words, without modifying the application layer data.

Client authentication is the most interesting SSL security service in the context of this chapter on IIS authentication methods. Contrary to the methods discussed earlier, certificate-based client authentication does not use the HTTP AUTH headers.

The SSL/TLS protocols are built on symmetric and asymmetric cryptographic protocols (also known as public key crypto) and X.509 certificates. For more information on X.509 certificates, see Chapter 6 in *Advanced Microsoft Windows Security Services* (part 2 of this series), which discusses public key infrastructures (PKIs).

Figure 7.26 *Internet Explorer SSL/TLS lock symbol.*

When users connect to Web pages secured using SSL/TLS, they must use a secure URL that begins with https://. The use of https tells the browser it should try to establish a secure SSL connection with the Web server. By default, these secure connections are made over port 443. In IE, a small lock symbol shows up at the bottom of the screen to show the user that he or she are connected over a secure SSL/TLS connection (illustrated in Figure 7.26). If you move over the lock symbol with your mouse pointer, you can see the SSL encryption strength[7] that has been used. If you double-click the lock symbol, you will see the properties of the Web server's SSL/TLS certificate. If something is wrong with the Web server's certificate (for example, the certificate has expired or is not trusted), the lock symbol will be covered with an exclamation mark.

From an operation point of view, SSL/TLS is a client/server handshake protocol. Setting up an SSL/TLS connection between a browser and a Web server involves the following steps:

1. A client browser connects to a Web server by using a secure URL (i.e., https://).

2. The Web server sends a server certificate (containing the Web server's public key) to the browser for server authentication. The browser logic checks the server name in the certificate against the name that was provided in the URL.

3. Optionally, the browser sends the Web server the client certificate (containing the client's public key) for client authentication.

4. The browser and Web server negotiate the cryptographic ciphers to be used for authentication, integrity, and confidentiality protection during the SSL/TLS exchange.

5. The browser and Web server establish a set of cryptographic keys that will be used for SSL channel encryption. The cryptographic mechanisms that establish these keys are based on a cryptographic

---

7.   In most cases, SSL/TLS uses 128-bit DES encryption; upcoming browser versions (e.g., IE 7.0) will support 256-bit AES encryption.

key agreement protocol, such as the RSA cipher or the Diffie-Hellman protocol.

6.   The browser and Web server exchange HTTPS data by using the previously established keys (i.e., server's public key, client's public key, and the cryptographic keys).

For a more detailed explanation of the SSL/TLS protocol exchanges, see the sidenote entitled "SSL/TLS Operation."

SSL/TLS Operation

Figure 7.27 illustrates the SSL/TLS protocol. The SSL/TLS exchange can be split into eight steps, as follows:

1. The SSL client informs the SSL server about the cryptographic ciphers it supports and forwards a random number (that was generated on the client side).

2. The SSL server selects a cryptographic cipher, forwards a random number (generated on the server side), forwards its SSL server certificate, and (optionally) requests the client SSL certificate.

3. The SSL client optionally authenticates to the SSL server a digital signature. Attached to the digital signature is the SSL client certificate. The SSL server validates the client's digital signature.

4. The SSL client generates a secret key (based on the previously exchanged random numbers) and securely sends it to the SSL server. The secure channel is created by encrypting the secret key with the SSL server's public key.

5. Both the SSL client and the SSL server derive the SSL key from the secret key. The SSL key will be used in step 8 to provide secure channel services for the application layer data transmitted using SSL/TLS.

6. The SSL client calculates a hash value of the handshake messages previously exchanged. This hash provides a mechanism to check the integrity of the handshake messages.

7. The SSL server calculates a hash value of the handshake messages (for the same reason as step 6).

8. The application layer data are securely transmitted using the previously generated SSL key.

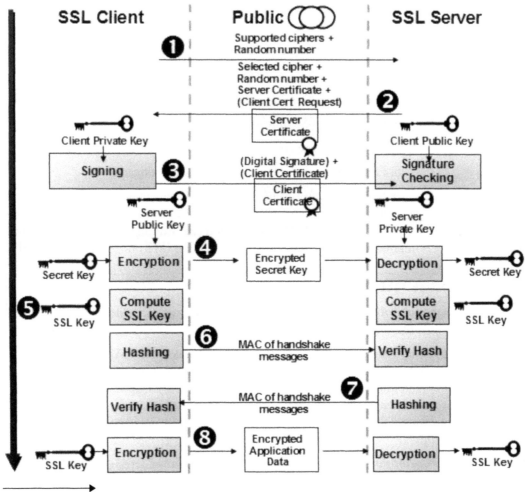

Figure 7.27 *SSL/TLS operation.*

7.6.1 SSL Setup

The use of SSL/TLS requires X.509 certificates. You always need a server certificate, and if you also want client certificate-based strong authentication, you will also need client certificates. To illustrate the SSL/TLS Web server setup, we will use the example of Internet Information Services 6.0— this is the Web server that comes with the Microsoft Windows Server 2003 operating system.

Setting up SSL/TLS on an IIS 6.0 Web server typically includes the following steps:

1. Generating a server certificate request file

2. Generating a server certificate

3. Installing a server certificate on the Web server

4. Configuring SSL on a Web server

5. Optionally generating, acquiring, and installing client certificates

6. Ensuring that SSL clients trust the CA certificate

Before you begin setting up SSL/TLS, you might want to familiarize yourself with the process of requesting and generating an SSL/TLS server certificate for your IIS Web server. You can issue a test certificate from your internal Windows Public Key Infrastructure (PKI) or request a test certifi-

---

SSL Diagnostics Tool Version 1.0

The SSL Diagnostics tool (SSLDiag) can help IIS administrators in different ways when troubleshooting SSL:

- SSLDiag provides a single GUI that displays all the relevant IIS SSL configuration information. Most of this information is spread across the IIS metabase, and part of it is not displayed in the Internet Services Manager (ISM) MMC snap-in. The tool also displays useful reference information about the selected configuration setting (in the example of Figure 7.28, the "ServerCacheEntries" setting) in the bottom part of the SSLDiag GUI.

- SSLDiag checks for the correct configuration of SSL objects and settings and informs the administrator if something is wrong. These objects and settings include SSL client and server certificates, SSL ports, and private keys.

- SSLDiag allows IIS administrators to easily test whether their current SSL server certificate is working properly. IIS administrators can temporarily replace their current SSL server certificate with a self-signed certificate from the SSLDiag GUI. Installing a self-signed certificate is as simple as right-clicking a Web site level (for example, in Figure 7.28, [W3SVC/1]) and selecting "Create New Cert."

- SSLDiag allows IIS administrators to simulate an SSL connection between their Web server and a browser. This is very helpful for determining where exactly in the SSL handshake process the SSL connection breaks down. To simulate an SSL handshake, right-click a Web site level and select "Simulate SSL Handshake…": this will bring up the "SSL Diagnostics—Probe SSL" dialog box.

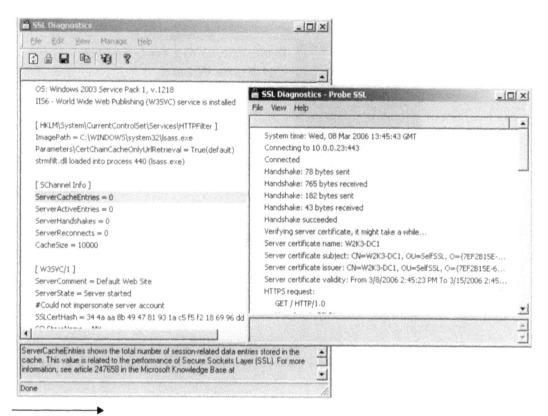

Figure 7.28   *SSL Diagnostics tool interface.*

cate from Thawte or Verisign—two popular commercial certificate providers. To request a test certificate from Thawte, go to: www.thawte.com/ucgi/
gothawte.cgi?a=w46840165357049000.

The SSL Diagnostics tool is great for troubleshooting an IIS SSL setup.
Version 1 of the SSL Diagnostics tool for x86 platforms can be downloaded
from www.microsoft.com/downloads. ia64 and AMD64 platform versions
of the tool are available from the same URL. See also the sidenote on "SSL
Diagnostics Tool Version 1.0" for more information.

Generating an SSL Server Certificate Request

The easiest way to generate an SSL server certificate request is to use the IIS
Web Server Certificate Wizard (illustrated in Figure 7.29). This wizard
guides you through the certificate request file generation process.

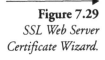

Figure 7.29
SSL Web Server
Certificate Wizard.

You can start the wizard from the IIS Internet Services Manager (ISM) MMC snap-in: right-click the Web site on which you want to set up SSL, select properties, then in the directory security tab—in the secure communications section—select Server Certificate (as illustrated in Figure 7.30).

Figure 7.31 shows two options available on the wizard's Delayed or Immediate Request window that you can use to generate a server certificate request file offline or online: "Prepare the request now, but send it later" or "Send the request immediately to an online certification authority." The online certificate request method is typically used when requesting SSL certificates for protecting intranet resources; the offline request method is typically used when requesting SSL certificates from commercial certification authorities or for protecting extranet resources.

Use the offline option if you want to request an SSL/TLS server certificate from a commercial certification authority (CA)—e.g., Verisign or Thawte—or from a non–Active Directory (AD) integrated internal CA (this Windows CA type is also known as a standalone CA). An offline certificate request is not automated, which means you must save the request to a file (by default, this file is named certreq.txt), submit the request file to a CA, then install the resulting certificate on your Web server. If you open the certificate request file, you will find text that is formatted similarly to the text below—this is the base64-encoded certificate request.

```
-----BEGIN CERTIFICATE REQUEST-----
MIIB2TCCAUICAQAwgZgxCzAJBgNVBAYTAlVTMRAwDgYDVQQIEwdHZW9yZ2lhMREwDwYDVQQ
HEwhDb2x1bWJ1czEbMBkGB1UEChMSQUZMQUMgSW5jb3Jwb3JhdGVkMQswCQYDVQQLEwJJV
DEYMBYGA1UEAxMPd3d3LmFmbGFjbnkuY29tMSAwHgYJKoZIhvcNAQkBFhFKR2FybW9uQGFmb
GFjLmNvbTCBnzANBgkqhkiG9w0BAQEFAAOBjqAWgYkCgYEAsRqHZCLIrlxqqh8qs6hCC0KR9qEPX
2buwmA6GxegICKpOi/IYY5+Fx3KZWXmta794nTPShh2lmRdn3iwxwQRKyqYKmP7wHCwtNm2taCRV
oboCQOuyZjS+DG9mj+bOrMK9rLME+9wz1f810FuArWhedDBnI2smOKQID45mWwB0hkCAwEAAaAA
MA0GCSqGSIb3DQEBBAUAA4GBAJNlxhOiv9P8cDjMsqyM0WXxXWgagdRaGoa8tv8R/UOuBOS8/H
qu73umaB9vj6VHY7d9RKqDElFc/xlXeDwoXNiF8quTm43pmY0WcqnL1JZDGHMQkzzGtg502CLTHM
ElUGTdKpAK6rJCkucP0DKKEJKcmTySSnvgUu7m
-----END CERTIFICATE REQUEST-----
```

Use the online option if you want to send the request immediately to an online CA. After you select the online option, the wizard generates and sends the certificate request file and automatically installs the certificate. This option works only if you have an operational Windows enterprise CA in your IIS environment. A Windows enterprise CA is an AD–integrated CA published in AD.

Figure 7.30
Starting the Web Server Certificate Wizard.

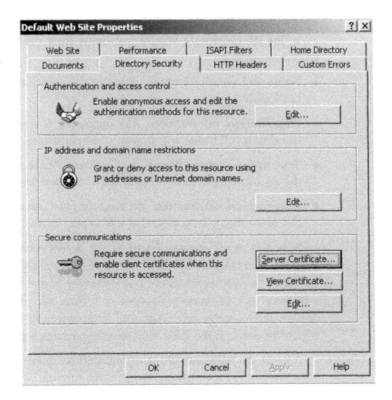

Figure 7.31
*Server Certificate
Wizard: Delayed
or Immediate
Request options.*

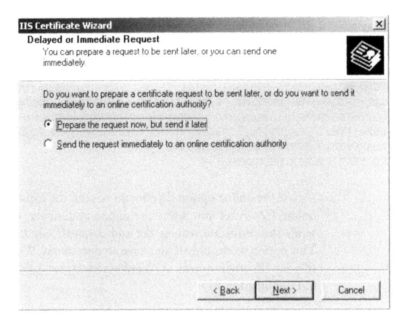

In the IIS Certificate Wizard, you must enter the following certificate-related information:

- **Name and security settings**: name of the certificate and encryption key length

- **Organization information**: AD organization name and organizational unit (OU) that will appear in the certificate

- **Your site's Common Name**: the Common Name that will appear in the certificate (this term is explained in the next paragraph)

- **Geographical information**: the country code, state or province, and city or locality information that will appear in the certificate

A certificate's Common Name is the X.509 term for the name that uniquely identifies an SSL/TLS server certificate and links the requested certificate to your organization. The Common Name must match the name a browser uses to securely connect to a Web site. The Common Name appears in the server certificate, and if the name in the certificate doesn't match the name in the URL, the browser generates an SSL error message.

You can use wildcards in the certificate's Common Name, which lets you reuse the SSL/TLS certificate for different physical Web sites: for example, w*.*mydomain*.com or *w.*mydomain*.com. Using a Common Name with wildcards is an interesting option for Web farms in which the only differences between farm members are the machines. However, you should never use wildcards in your organization's domain name (in the above example: mydomain.com) because this would compromise SSL/TLS server authentication. For more information about how Microsoft uses wildcards, see the article "Accepted Wildcards Used by Server Certificates for Server Authentication" at http://support.microsoft.com/default.aspx?scid=kb;en-us;258858.

Generating the SSL Server Certificate

After you've generated an SSL/TLS server certificate request file by using the offline certificate request option in the IIS Certificate Wizard, you can use the file to request a Web server certificate from an internal Windows CA (i.e., either a standalone, an enterprise Windows 2000, or a Windows Server 2003 CA) or an external commercial CA (e.g., Thawte or Verisign).

If you use an internal Windows CA, the easiest way to submit your SSL server certificate request file is to use the CA's Web interface. To do so, connect to the CA's Web site from your browser using the URL http://<server-name>/certsrv. On the CA's Web site, select the following:

- On the CA's Welcome page, select *Request a certificate*.

- On the resulting certificate request page, select *Submit an advanced certificate request*.

- On the resulting page, select *Submit a certificate request by using a base64-encoded CMC or PKCS#10 file, or submit a renewal request by using a base64-encoded PKCS#7 file*.

- On the resulting page (illustrated in Figure 7.32), paste the base64-encoded content of your certificate request into the *Saved Request* field by selecting and pasting the text that starts with --BEGIN NEW CERTIFICATE REQUEST-- and ends with --END NEW CERTIFICATE REQUEST-- from the SSL/TLS server certificate request file. You can also use the *Browse for a file to insert* function on the Submit a Certificate Request or Renewal Request page to search for a certificate request and insert the certificate request content.

To manually submit your SSL/TLS server certificate request file to a commercial CA, you must follow the enrollment instructions the commercial CA provides. Most commercial CAs publish their enrollment instructions on their Web site. Enrollment instructions vary among commercial CAs and different SSL server certificate types. For an overview of the Thawte enrollment instructions, for example, consult the following Thawte document: www.thawte.com/guides/pdf/enroll_sum_eng.pdf.

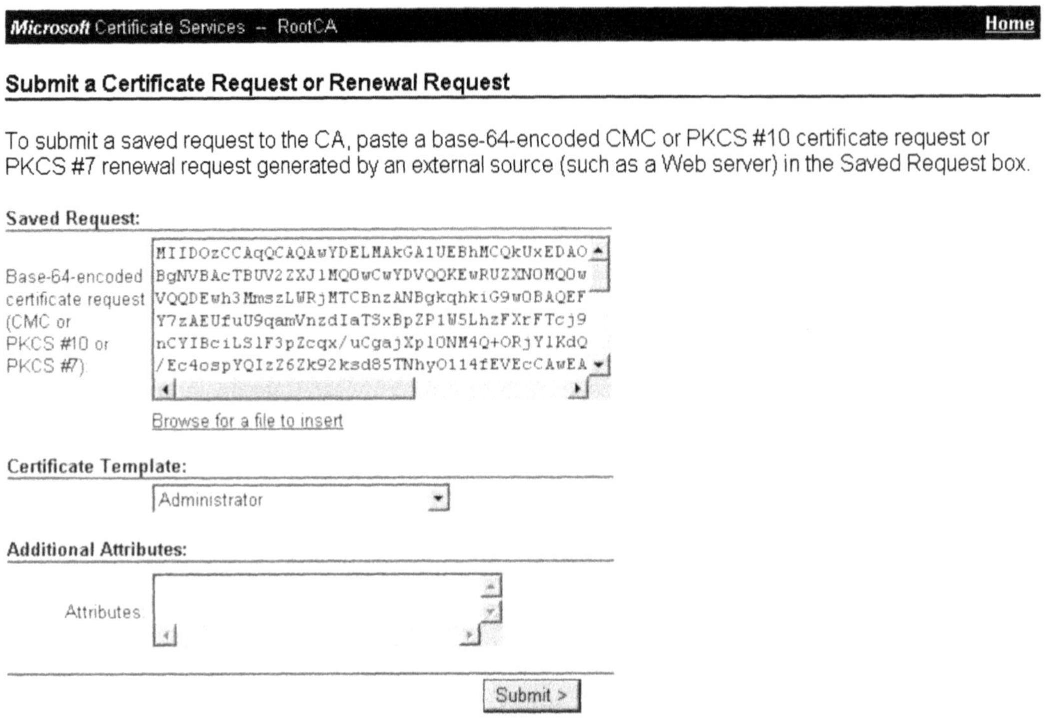

Microsoft Certificate Services -- RootCA   Home

Submit a Certificate Request or Renewal Request

To submit a saved request to the CA, paste a base-64-encoded CMC or PKCS #10 certificate request or PKCS #7 renewal request generated by an external source (such as a Web server) in the Saved Request box.

Saved Request:

Base-64-encoded
certificate request
(CMC or
PKCS #10 or
PKCS #7)

MIIDOzCCAqQCAQAwYDELMAkGA1UEBhMCQkUxEDAO
BgNVBAcTBUV2ZXJlMQOwCwYDVQQKEwRUZXNOMQOw
VQQDEwh3MmszLWRjMTCBnzANBgkqhkiG9w0BAQEF
Y7zAEUfuU9qamVnzdIaTSxBpZP1W5LhzFXrFTcj9
nCYIBciLSlF3pZcqx/uCgajXp1ONM4Q+ORjYlKdQ
/Ec4ospYQIzZ6Zk92ksd85TNhyO114fEVEcCAwEA

Browse for a file to insert

Certificate Template:

Administrator

Additional Attributes:

Attributes

Submit >

Figure 7.32   *CA Web interface: inserting the SSL Certificate Request content.*

Thawte can provide three types of SSL Web server certificates:

- *Standard SSL Web server certificates.*

  These are the standard Thawte SSL Web server certificates. Their prime characteristic is that they offer a very high level of authentication. This is why they are more expensive then the SSL123 SSL Web server certificates (explained below) and why their enrollment procedure is more complex and takes more time. The way to enroll for a standard SSL Web server certificate is detailed in the following Thawte document: www.thawte.com/guides/pdf/enroll_ssl_eng.pdf.

- *SSL123 SSL Web server certificates.*

  SSL123 SSL Web server certificates offer a lower level of authentication than the standard SSL Web server certificates: they only validate that your domain is registered and that you have authorized the purchase of the certificate. That is why they are cheaper and why it takes less time to enroll for an SSL123 certificate. The way to enroll for an

SSL123 SSL Web server certificate is detailed in the following Thawte document: www.thawte.com/guides/pdf/enroll_ssl123_eng.pdf.

- *Thawte Server Gated Crypto (SGC) SuperCert SSL Web server certificates.*

This SSL server certificate allows Windows clients to automatically step up to 128-bit SSL encryption.[8] A Thawte SGC SuperCert allows SSL-secured Web sites to extend 128-bit encryption to all their clients, even if these use browsers (IE 4.X or Netscape 4.06 and later) that are limited to 40-bit or 56-bit encryption capabilities. SGC is a mechanism that automatically turns 40-bit and 56-bit browsers into 128-bit strong browsers while users are visiting a Web site. How to enroll for a SGC SuperCert SSL Web server certificate is detailed in the following Thawte document: www.thawte.com/guides/pdf/enroll_ssl_eng.pdf.

Another option for obtaining an SSL server certificate is to use the Self-SSL Internet Information Server Resource Kit command-line tool. SelfSSL generates self-signed certificates, so you don't need a CA or PKI to generate a certificate. Also, SelfSSL doesn't require the Web server to generate a certificate request file; rather, the tool generates and installs the certificate right away. Use self-signed SSL certificates only for test purposes or for protecting Web resources that are for internal use. We recommend that you always run SelfSSL with the /T switch. This switch directs SelfSSL to add the self-signed certificate to the list of trusted certificates in the local machine's certificate store.

Installing the SSL Server Certificate on Your Web Server

To install an SSL/TLS Web server certificate on your Web server, you can use the IIS Certificate Wizard, the IIScertdeploy.vbs script from the IIS 6.0 Resource Kit, or the certreq.exe command-line utility. The certreq utility is automatically installed to your server when you install the Windows 2000 or Windows Sever 2003 Certificate Services.

If you use the IIS Certificate Wizard to install a Web server certificate, select "*Process the pending request and install the certificate*" in the Pending Certificate Request window (illustrated in Figure 7.33). After you select this option, the wizard will prompt you for the location of the certificate file.

---

8.   Users using a Windows 2000 server OS that does not have Microsoft's High Encryption pack or Service Pack 2 installed cannot receive 128-bit encryption irrespective of the version of Internet Explorer used on the client side.

Figure 7.33
*Server Certificate
Wizard: "Process
Request" option.*

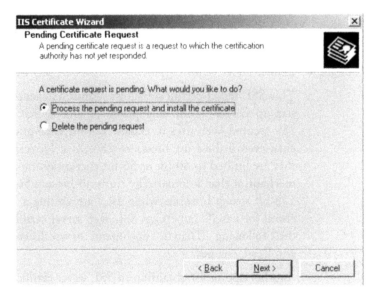

To accept a newly generated Web server certificate (for example, ssl.cer) and install it on your Web server by using certreq.exe, type the following certreq command at the command line:

```
Certreq -accept ssl.cer
```

Configuring SSL on Your Web Server

You can configure SSL/TLS in the Microsoft IIS ISM MMC snap-in. From the Directory Security tab, go to the Secure Communications section (as Figure 7.30 shows) and click the Edit button. Note that the Edit button is only enabled if you have successfully installed a server certificate on the server.

Figure 7.34 shows the Secure Communications window. Use this window to select the following SSL/TLS security attributes for your Web site:

- **Require secure channel.** Click this check box to enable SSL/TLS for a Web site.

- **Require 128-bit encryption.** Click this check box to provide extra protection for Web sites that have sensitive personal and financial information.

- **Client Certificates section.** Use the radio buttons in this section to select the appropriate client certificate-based authentication options. Select *Ignore client certificates* if you don't want to use the client certificate-based authentication. Both the "Accept client certificates" and "Require client certificates" options require the deployment of certificates to your browser clients. "Require client certificates" means that users can only access your Web site if they have an SSL client certificate installed. "Accept client certificates" means that users can also access your Web site if they don't have an SSL client certificate installed; in that case, they can authenticate to the Web server using another HTTP authentication method (basic, digest authentication, etc.). As with SSL/TLS server certificates, you can acquire SSL/TLS client certificates from an internal CA or from an external commercial CA.

- **Enable client certificate mapping.** Click this check box if you want to map a client certificate to a Windows user account during authentication. Client certificate mapping is explained in more detail below.

- **Enable certificate trust lists (CTLs).** Click this check box if you want to use CTLs. Web server administrators use CTLs to define a set of CAs that must be trusted by all of its SSL users. For more information about CTLs, see the Microsoft article "HOW TO: Configure Certificate Trust Lists in Internet Information Services 5.0" at http://support.microsoft.com/default.aspx?scid=kb;en-us;313071.

Figure 7.34
Configuring
SSL/TLS.

If you want to configure the port used for SSL communications, you can do so from the Web Site tab in your Web site's Properties dialog box (as illustrated in Figure 7.35). The default port used for SSL is 443. The SSL port field is only enabled if you have installed an SSL server certificate on your Web server. Note that different Web sites that are hosted on the same Web server can use the same SSL port provided that they have different IP addresses.

To facilitate Web server access control enforcement, you can map IIS certificates to Windows security identities; this is known as certificate mapping. Use certificate mapping if you want to apply authorization settings defined for Windows security identities to users that used a certificate to authenticate to IIS.

You can define certificate-mapping attributes in AD or in the IIS metabase (i.e., the IIS configuration database). To use IIS metabase-based mapping, you must select the *Enable client certificate mapping* check box on the Secure Communications window and define the mappings from the ISM

Figure 7.35
Configuring
SSL/TLS: SSL
Port.

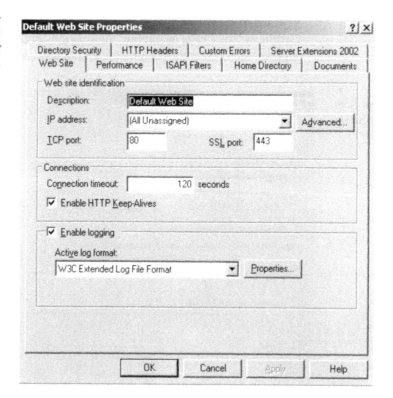

Account Mappings window (as Figure 7.36 shows). You can set up certificate mappings that are defined in the metabase in two different modes:

- **One-to-one mapping** means that IIS looks at the complete content of the SSL client certificate to map the certificate to a Windows security identity.

- **Many-to-one certificate mapping** is based on rules. In this case, IIS looks at particular attributes of the SSL client certificate (as defined in the rules) to map the certificate to a Windows security identity. This is the least secure certificate-mapping mode and shouldn't be used in environments requiring a high level of security.

When certificate mappings are defined in the AD, IIS uses a service known as the "Windows directory service mapper." AD-based mapping is an interesting option if you have multiple Web servers that require certificate mappings to be defined. Instead of defining the mappings on individ-

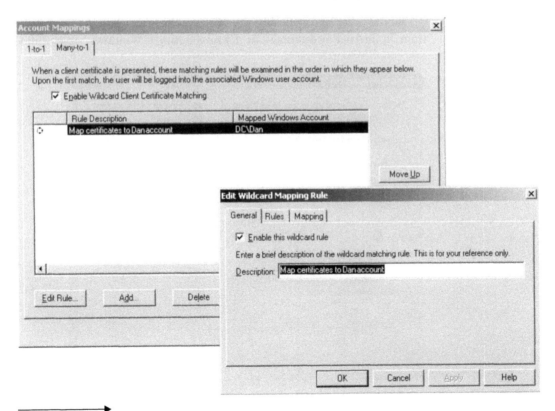

Figure 7.36 *Setting up a many-to-one certificate mapping rule in the IIS Internet Service Manager (ISM).*

ual Web servers, you can define the certificate-mapping attributes once in the central AD repository. Use the AD Users and Computers (ADUC) MMC snap-in to define the AD-based mapping. Select the *Name mappings* option on the account object's context menu. This option is only available if the snap-in is in Advanced Features viewing mode. AD-based mapping only allows one-to-one mapping. AD-based mapping, or the Windows directory service mapper, is enabled from the properties of the *Web Sites* container in the Internet Service Manager (ISM) (as Figure 7.37 shows).

Getting Client SSL Certificates

If you also want to strongly authenticate your SSL/TLS clients by using certificates on the browser side, you should deploy SSL/TLS client certificates to your users' browsers. This step is optional, because not all organizations want to do this. A typical scenario requiring SSL/TLS client certificates is a secure extranet Web site.

Similar to server certificates, you can request a client SSL/TLS certificate from an internal or external CA. If you are using a Windows Server 2003–

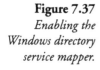

Figure 7.37
Enabling the Windows directory service mapper.

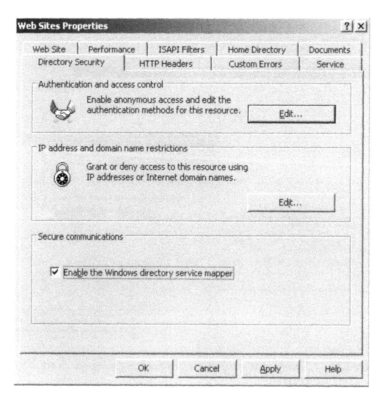

rooted PKI, users can request certificates using their MMC Certificates snap-in or the CA's Web interface (this is using the http://<servername>/certsrv URL). Administrators can also automatically enroll users for SSL/TLS certificates by using the Autoenrollment Group Policy Object (GPO) settings.

Ensuring That SSL Clients Trust the CA Certificate

An important but often forgotten last step is to make sure that your clients trust the CA that issued the client and server SSL/TLS certificates. In Windows, this means making sure that the CA's certificate is stored in the client's trusted root certificate store. To look at the contents of a certificate store, open the MMC Certificates snap-in. Trust is not a real concern when you're using certificates issued by a commercial CA. Many commercial CAs certificates come with the Windows OS software and are trusted by default. CA trust is an issue if you're using certificates generated by an internal PKI that is run by your company or a partner organization. In this case, you can use different methods to add the certificate of the CA to your users' trusted root certificate stores:

- Use the Internet Explorer Administration Kit (IEAK) to create an IE installation kit that adds the CA certificate to the trusted root certificate store

- Put the CA's certificate on a publicly accessible Web site where users can download it

- Distribute the CA's certificate by using the Trusted Root Certification Authorities GPO setting

7.6.2 Web Browser SSL Support

Today, all Web browsers come with built-in support for the SSL/TLS protocols. Most commonly used Web browsers are Microsoft Internet Explorer (IE), Netscape Navigator, Mozilla Firefox, and Opera.

Web browsers differ in the SSL/TLS configuration options they offer. These options include:

- The capability to switch SSL 2.0/SSL 3.0/TLS 1.0 support on or off

- The capability to configure Certificate Revocation List (CRL)-based certificate revocation checking. Revocation checking is explained in the next section on certificate validation

Table 7.3   *Comparison of Browser's SSL/TLS Configuration Options*

	Internet Explorer 6.0	Netscape Navigator 8.0	Mozilla Firefox 1.0	Opera 8.0
SSL 2.0 support	Yes	Yes	Yes	Yes
SSL 3.0 support	Yes	Yes	Yes	Yes
TLS 1.0 support	Yes	Yes	Yes	Yes
CRL support	Yes	Yes	Yes	Yes
OCSP support	No*	Yes	Yes	No

* Microsoft will embed OCSP support in the IE 7.0 release.

- The capability to configure Online Certificate Status Protocol (OCSP)-based certificate revocation checking

Table 7.3 gives an overview of the most important SSL/TLS configuration options of today's commonly used Web browsers.

Figure 7.38 shows the IE 6.0 SSL/TLS configuration interface on a Windows XP Service Pack 2 (SP2) installation. This configuration interface can be accessed from the Advanced tab in IE's Internet Options. On a Windows XP SP2 platform, IE 6.0 has by default only support for the SSL 2.0 and SSL 3.0 protocols enabled. This will change in the next IE release, where SSL 3.0 and TLS 1.0 will be enabled by default.

An interesting property of the SSL implementation in IE 6.0 and later is that users can clear the SSL cache manually from the IE GUI. This means that the client-side SSL authentication certificates can be removed from the browser cache. Normally, certificates remain in the cache until the computer is restarted. This can be an interesting option when a user has multiple client SSL certificates. To clear the SSL cache, use the "Clear SSL State" pushbutton in the IE Internet Options\Content tab.

7.6.3 Certificate Validation

During the SSL/TLS protocol exchanges, both the browser and the Web server must validate each other's certificates. For the server side, this is only true if client-side certificate authentication has also been enabled. SSL/TLS certificate validation includes the following checks (illustrated in Figure 7.39): an X.509 digital signature check, a trust check, a time check, a revocation check, and a formatting check. The certificate validation process is

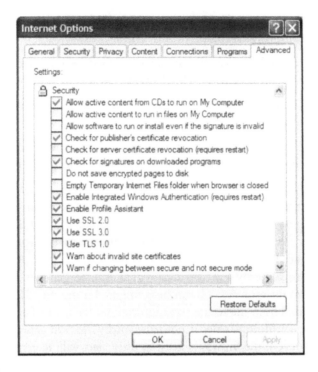

Figure 7.38 *Windows XP SP2 IE SSL/TLS configuration interface.*

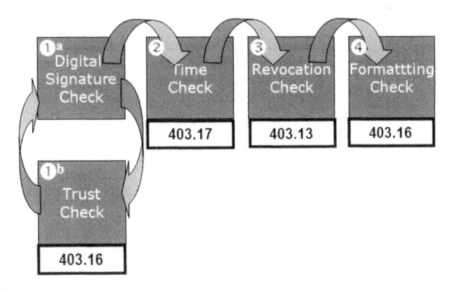

Figure 7.39 *Certificate validation process.*

explained in greater detail in Chapter 8 of *Advanced Microsoft Windows Security Services* (part 2 of this series).

Every X.509 certificate includes a digital signature that is validated when the certificate is used. The digital signature check includes:

- An **integrity check** to determine whether the certificate has been tampered with

- An **authentication check** to verify that the Web site owns the private key associated with the public key stored in the certificate

The trust check validates whether the issuer of the Web site's certificate is trusted. Chapter 8 (in part 2 of this series) explains in greater detail how Windows and its users and services (including IIS) determine whether or not a certificate is trustworthy. One feature that is worth pointing out here is the IIS support for Certificate Trust Lists (CTLs). A CTL is a signed list of trustworthy CA certificates that can be generated by the Web server administrator. A CTL can be configured using the CTL wizard that can be started from the secure communications dialog box (see also Figure 7.34). If the certificate's issuer is not trustworthy, IIS will generate a 403.16 HTTP error. On the browser side, a security alert will be generated, stating, "The security certificate was issued by a company you have not chosen to trust. View the certificate to determine whether you want to trust the certifying authority" (see Figure 7.40(a)).

The time check validates whether the certificate has expired. Every X.509 certificate has a limited lifetime. If the certificate has expired, IIS will generate a 403.17 HTTP error. On the browser side a security alert will be generated, stating, "The security certificate has expired or is not yet valid" (see Figure 7.40(b)).

The revocation check validates whether the certificate has been revoked. In a Public Key Infrastructure (PKI), a Certification Authority (CA) administrator must revoke a certificate if the associated private key is compromised—for example, if a user loses the smart card holding his private key. By default, Internet Explorer 6.0 does not perform a certificate revocation check, and IIS 6.0 does.

Both IE and IIS leverage Certificate Revocation Lists (CRLs) for certificate revocation checking.[9] In IIS, revocation checking can be controlled

---

9.   In future releases, Microsoft will also include support for the Online Certificate Status Protocol (OCSP) in its software: for example, IE 7.0 will include OCSP support. The differences between CRLs and OCSP will be discussed in Chapter 8 of part 2 of this series. Both are mechanisms a CA administrator can use to distribute certificate revocation information to certificate users.

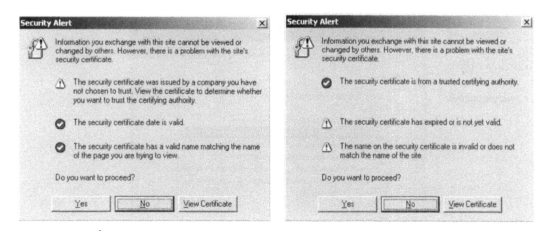

Figure 7.40 *Security alerts: Browser-side certificate trust error (left); Browser-side certificate time and name error (right).*

using the certcheckmode metabase parameter (value 1 means revocation checking is disabled/value 0 means revocation checking is enabled). If the certificate has been revoked, or if the CRL is not available, IIS generates a 403.13 HTTP error. On the IE browser side, a security alert like the one shown in Figure 7.41 will be generated if the CRL is not available. On the browser side, revocation checking can be controlled using the "Check for server certificate revocation" entry in the browser's Internet options (illustrated in Figure 7.42).

The formatting check validates whether the content of an X.509 certificate conforms to the X.509 certificate format specification. The check also validates whether the Common Name in the certificate matches the name of the Web site as it was entered in the URL. If the certificate is ill formed or if the Common Names do not match, IIS will generate a 403.16 HTTP error. On the browser side, a security alert will be generated stating that "The name of the security certificate is invalid or does not match the name of the site" (illustrated in Figure 7.40(b)).

Figure 7.41
Browser-side
SSL/TLS
revocation
check error.

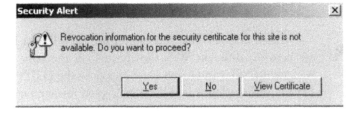

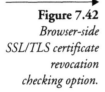

Figure 7.42
*Browser-side
SSL/TLS certificate
revocation
checking option.*

7.6.4 Deployment Considerations

In most enterprise environments, you must consider the following deployment issues when setting up SSL/TLS for securing Web resources:

- SSL/TLS cannot be used in combination with HTTP host headers

- SSL/TLS can have a performance impact on the Web server side

- SSL/TLS and HTTP load balancing can be combined

- SSL/TLS and HTTP proxy and/or firewall operation can be combined

The last three issues are discussed in greater detail in the following sections.

When using HTTPs, you cannot use HTTP host headers to differentiate between different Web sites hosted on the same Web server. This is because the SSL connection is set up before the HTTP connection, and the HTTP information is sent in an encrypted format over the wire.

Optimizing SSL Server-Side Performance

The asymmetric cryptographic operations behind the certificate-based authentication in SSL/TLS can impact the Web server performance. To deal with this performance issue, you can do three things:

- **Use hardware crypto accelerators devices.** These devices offload the main system processor by using a dedicated processor for the cryptographic operations. Table 7.4 is a nonexhaustive list of these devices.

- **Limit the Web page size.** Limiting the Web page size reduces the amount of data that need to be cryptographically processed.

- **Reuse cached SSL sessions to limit the number of SSL negotiations.** On the Microsoft IIS Web server, for example, you can fine-tune the SSL caching behavior by using the registry parameters in Table 7.5. They are located in the HKEY_LOCAL_MACHINE\system\currentcontrolset\control\securityproviders\schannel registry key. See also the following Microsoft Knowledge Base article for more information: http://support.microsoft.com/?kbid=247658.

SSL and Load Balancing

When using SSL in a Web load balancing environment (for example, in a Web farm setup), you must make sure that your load balancing solution

Table 7.4 *SSL Acceleration Device Products and Vendors*

Vendor	Device	More Information at:
Broadcom	CryptoNetX BCM800 CryptoNetX BCM1600 CryptoNetX BCM4000	www.broadcom.com
F5	Big IP SSL Accelerator	www.f5.com/products/bigip/modules/index.html
HP	Atalla AXL 300 Atalla AXL 600L	http://h18000.www1.hp.com/products/servers/security/axl300 http://h18000.www1.hp.com/products/servers/security/axl600l
Intel	Netstructure	www.intel.com/support/netstructure/index.htm
nCipher	nFast Ultra nFast 800 nFast 300	www.ncipher.com/cryptographic_hardware/ssl_acceleration/
SafeNet	Rainbow Cryptoswift	www.safenet-inc.com/products/accCards/index.asp

Table 7.5 *Microsoft IIS SSL Session Cache Tuning Parameters*

Registry Parameter	Data Type	Meaning
MaximumCacheSize	REG_DWORD	Maximum number of SSL sessions to maintain the cache
ClientCacheTime	REG_DWORD	Time in milliseconds required to expire a client-side cache element
ServerCacheTime	REG_DWORD	Time in milliseconds required to expire a server-side cache element

supports sticky sessions. Sticky sessions ensure that the HTTP connection always returns to the same Web server in a server farm during a load-balanced SSL-secured HTTP connection.

This problem surrounding SSL and load balancing is also referred to as SSL persistence. The electronic shopping cart example clearly illustrates this problem. A shopping cart is a logical repository for the items a customer selects while shopping online. The selected items are typically maintained on the Web server to which the customer first connected. If at any point during the session the client is switched to another server, the customer's shopping cart data will be lost.

To understand the challenge with SSL persistence, let us first quickly look at how persistence can be ensured for unsecured HTTP connections. HTTP load-balancing devices can use two mechanisms to ensure unsecured HTTP connection persistence: the source IP address, or HTTP cookies.

When using Source IP persistence, load balancers identify users by their source IP address, and they use this identifier to link users to the appropriate server. This method cannot be used when the HTTP connection travels across proxy servers and network-address translation (NAT) devices. Proxies represent different users by a single IP address, NAT devices can change IP addresses throughout the life of a session.

Cookie persistence uses a browser cookie to uniquely identify users. In this case, either the Web application or the load balancer itself hands out cookies to users at the start of a session. The user's browser then automatically returns the cookie during each Web server hit. By tracking the cookie information, load balancers are able to determine which Web server should receive the subsequent traffic. Cookie persistence does not work with SSL: SSL encrypts all data, including cookies, and as a consequence, load balancers are unable to inspect the cookie.

SSLv3 introduced a solution specifically for SSL persistence called SSL session ID-based persistence. SSLv3 moves the SSL session ID, a unique 32-byte session identifier, out of the encrypted portion of the data into a clear portion. Load-balancing and content-switch vendors are able to read this unique identifier and can use it to balance the traffic to the appropriate server.

SSL session-ID–based persistence works with all Microsoft IE browsers up to version 5 (not included). In IE5, Microsoft changed the behavior of their SSL libraries to force a renegotiation of a new SSL session every two minutes. This breaks the SSL session ID-based persistence mechanism.

Given the above issue with IE 5.0 and later browsers, the only viable solution to provide SSL persistence is to use the combination of a load balancer and SSL accelerator device. In this scenario, when SSL-secured HTTP traffic arrives at the load balancer, it is redirected to an SSL accelerator. The SSL accelerator decrypts the content, including cookies, and sends it back to the load balancer. The content switch can then inspect cookies and other URL data and use them to provide SSL persistence similar to that of unsecured connections. This solution also allows load balancers to set persistence cookies for outgoing HTTP traffic. Note that this solution terminates the secured SSL tunnel at the load balancer–SSL accelerator level. This mechanism is commonly supported by today's load balancing networking devices from vendors such as Cisco, Sonicwall, F5, and so on.

SSL in Proxy and Firewall Environments

SSL can be configured in different ways when dealing with HTTP proxies; the different approaches can be categorized as either SSL tunneling or SSL bridging. Today, HTTP proxies are used in almost every perimeter security solution that includes application proxy-based firewalls.

An SSL tunneling setup provides true end-to-end SSL: the SSL tunnel starts on the browser and ends on the Web server, as illustrated in Figure 7.43. It requires an SSL authentication certificate on the Web server and, optionally, an SSL client certificate on the client side.

The problem with SSL tunneling is that it breaks the role of an HTTP proxy. An HTTP proxy typically inspects the content of an HTTP request before it lets the request through. When using SSL the HTTP request cannot be inspected, because the HTTP content is encrypted by the SSL tunnel. This is because an SSL tunnel is always set up before the HTTP application-level traffic reaches the destination host. SSL operates on the

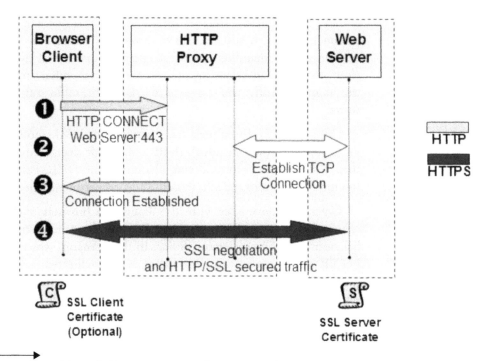

Figure 7.43   *SSL and HTTP proxy approaches: SSL tunneling.*

session level of the TCP/IP networking stack, while HTTP operates on the application level.

Does this mean that it is impossible to let an SSL tunnel flow through a firewall or HTTP proxy? No. To enable SSL tunnels to flow through HTTP proxies, SSL-enabled applications can use the HTTP CONNECT method. This method tells the proxy to ignore the content of an SSL session and to simply forward the SSL packets to the destination host (in this case a Web server). The HTTP CONNECT method is defined in RFC 2817 (available from the IETF Web site, at http://www.ietf.org). It is important to stress that from a pure security point of view, SSL tunneling is not the best approach; it basically punches holes in your firewalls.

The alternative to SSL tunneling is SSL bridging. Using SSL bridging takes away the security concern expressed earlier for SSL tunneling. SSL bridging basically means that the SSL tunnel is started or terminated on the HTTP proxy. As a consequence, there is no more end-to-end SSL tunnel setup. SSL bridging can be set up in different ways:

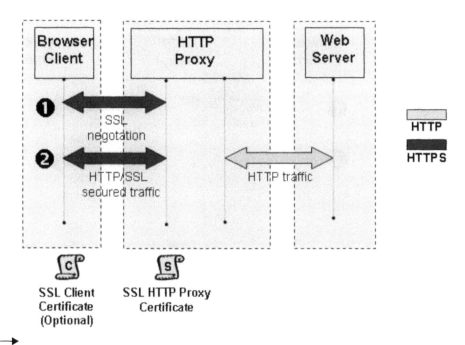

Figure 7.44 *SSL and HTTP proxy approaches: SSL bridging (single tunnel terminated on proxy).*

- **Using a single SSL tunnel that starts on the client side and terminates on the HTTP proxy.** This approach is illustrated in Figure 7.44. It requires an SSL certificate for the HTTP proxy and, optionally, an SSL certificate on the client side (if strong client-side authentication is required).

- **Using a single SSL tunnel that starts on the HTTP proxy and terminates on the Web server.** This approach is illustrated in Figure 7.45. It requires an SSL certificate for the Web server and, optionally, an SSL certificate for the HTTP proxy (if strong client-side authentication is required).

- **Using two SSL tunnels:** This approach, illustrated in Figure 7.46, has one tunnel starting on the client and terminating on the HTTP proxy, and another tunnel starting on the HTTP proxy and terminating on the Web server. It requires an SSL certificate on the HTTP proxy and Web server and, optionally, an SSL certificate on the client side (if strong client-side authentication is required).

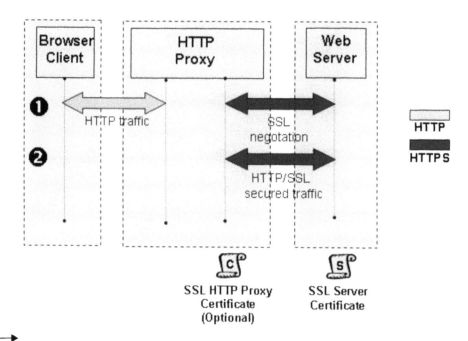

Figure 7.45   *SSL and HTTP proxy approaches: SSL bridging (single tunnel terminated on Web server).*

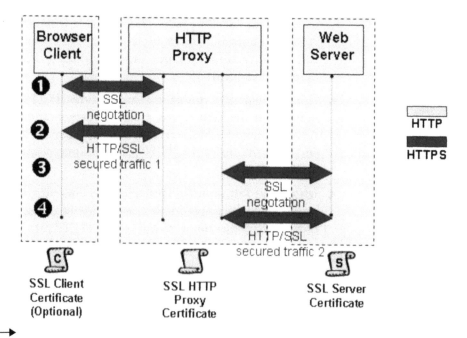

Figure 7.46   *SSL and HTTP proxy approaches: SSL bridging (two tunnels).*

Table 7.6 *SSL and HTTP Proxy Approaches: Comparison*

SSL Approach	Pros	Cons
SSL Tunneling	End-to-end SSL	Security hole on HTTP proxy and firewall level: the proxy cannot screen for malicious content any more
SSL Bridging—Option 1: Single SSL tunnel, started on client and terminated on proxy	HTTP content inspection on HTTP proxy and firewall level (no security hole) Offloads SSL processing from Web server	No end-to-end SSL HTTP traffic goes in the clear between proxy and Web server
SSL Bridging—Option 2: Single SSL tunnel, started on proxy and terminated on Web server	HTTP content inspection on HTTP proxy and firewall level (no security hole) HTTP traffic is encrypted between proxy and Web server	No end-to-end SSL HTTP traffic goes in the clear between browser and HTTP proxy
SSL Bridging—Option 3: Two SSL tunnels	HTTP content inspection on HTTP proxy and firewall level (no security hole) HTTP traffic is encrypted both between browser and proxy and between proxy and Web server	

Table 7.6 shows the different SSL approaches and their advantages and disadvantages.

7.7 IIS Authentication Method Comparison

Table 7.7 contains a comparison of the different IIS authentication protocols based on some key features.

Table 7.7 *IIS Authentication Method Comparison*

	Basic Auth	Digest Auth	NTLM	Kerberos	Certificate Based (SSL/TLS)	Passport
Protocol based on Open Standard	Yes	Yes	No	Yes	Yes	No
Relies on Windows accounts	Yes	Yes	Yes	Yes	No	No
Delegation support (credential forwarding)	Yes	No	No	Yes	Yes	Yes

Table 7.7   *IIS Authentication Method Comparison (continued)*

	Basic Auth	Digest Auth	NTLM	Kerberos	Certificate Based (SSL/TLS)	Passport
Supports non-IE browsers	Yes	No	No	No	Yes	Yes
Requires SSL	Yes	No	No	No	Yes	No
Requires Windows 2000 or later clients and servers	No	Yes	No	Yes	No	No
Supports authentication through firewalls and proxies	Yes	Yes	Only on selected proxies	Only if Kerberos traffic is allowed	Yes	Yes
Overall Security Quality	Weak—base64 encoded, requires SSL	Strong—because, based on a challenge-response mechanism; advanced digest auth is the recommended version	Strong—based on a challenge-response mechanism; NTLMv2 is the recommended version	Strong—based on an open standard; even stronger if combined with smart cards (Kerberos PKINIT)	Strong—based on asymmetric cryptographic mechanism	Strong—if combined with SSL

8

UNIX/Linux and Windows Authentication Integration

Many organizations have an IT infrastructure made up of a mix of Windows, UNIX, Linux, and mainframe computers. Although we surely should not neglect the importance of the mainframe and its applications, we must also admit that more and more organizations are moving critical applications to the UNIX platform and, lately, to even the Windows and Linux platforms. Also, CIOs usually do not want to bet on a single horse: they prefer not to stick to a single platform and vendor.

All of these arguments have placed a growing focus on the integration of Windows, UNIX, and Linux platforms and their applications. Platform and application integration inevitably includes integration of core security services such as account management and authentication. Account management deals with the management of security principal identities and their attributes (and possibly also user privileges). An authentication service deals with the verification of a security principal's identity.

The goal of this chapter is to give an overview of the different Windows and UNIX/Linux authentication integration solutions currently available on the IT market.

Regarding Windows, this chapter focuses on the Windows 2000, Windows XP, and Windows Server 2003 and R2 platforms, all of which are running in an AD-centric environment. As we will explain in this chapter, Microsoft included important UNIX/Linux integration changes in the Windows Server 2003 R2 OS.

Regarding UNIX/Linux, we will try to cover the most common UNIX and Linux flavors in use today: HP-UX, Sun Solaris, IBM AIX, and Redhat and Novell Suse Linux.

8.1   Comparing Windows and UNIX/Linux Authentication

Table 8.1 provides an overview of different authentication characteristics and how they are typically implemented on the Windows and the UNIX platforms. This table shows some clear differences between Windows and UNIX/Linux authentication that we will have to live with when looking at Windows and UNIX/Linux integration. For example, Windows uses secu-

Table 8.1   *Windows and UNIX/Linux Authentication Characteristics*

Authentication Characteristic	Windows	UNIX/Linux
Authentication Mechanisms	■ Native support for UserID: password and smart card (only Windows 2000 and later) ■ Other mechanisms available through third-party extensions	■ Native support for UserID: Password ■ On some UNIX/Linux platforms: Smart card (through special PAM modules) ■ Other mechanisms available through third-party extensions
Authentication Authorities	■ Local Authority ■ Domain Authority	■ Local Authority ■ Domain Authority (NIS, NIS+ domain, Samba domain)
Authentication Protocol	■ Plain UserID: password ■ NTLM ■ Kerberos V5 (Windows 2000 and later)	■ Plain UserID: password ■ Protocol based on crypt(3) or MD5 hash function ■ Other protocols using special PAM or other modules (Kerberos, etc.)
Credential Database	■ Local (SAM) or Centralized (SAM or AD) ■ SAM (Security Database): Any NT4 machine (local or domain authority) and Windows 2000 and later standalone machines and member servers ■ AD (Active Directory): Windows 2000, Windows Server 2003, and R2 domain authorities (domain controllers (DCs))	■ Local (/etc/passwd/ and /etc/shadow) or Centralized (NIS, NIS+, LDAP, or Samba (smbpasswd))
Security Principal Identifiers	■ SIDs (security identifiers) for users, groups, machines	■ UIDs (user identifiers) for users ■ GIDs (group identifiers) for groups
User Principal Names	■ Maximum 20 characters ■ Case insensitive ■ Cannot be identical to group names	■ Typically maximum eight characters ■ Case sensitive ■ Can be identical to group names

rity identifiers (SIDs) for uniquely identifying security principals; UNIX/ Linux typically uses user identifiers (UIDs) and group identifiers (GIDs).

8.2   Interoperability Enabling Technologies

The key Windows enablers for account management and authentication interoperability in a mixed UNIX/Linux and AD-centric Windows environment are AD's support for the LDAP directory access protocol and for the Kerberos distributed authentication protocol. Microsoft includes support for both protocols in Windows 2000 and later operating system versions. Microsoft's adoption is driven by the fact that both protocols are based on open standards.

8.2.1   LDAP

The Lightweight Directory Integration Protocol (LDAP) defines a set of protocols to access the data stored in X.500-based directories. LDAP also defines an information model providing structure and naming standards for directory data. LDAP version 3 is the latest LDAP version. LDAP v3 was standardized by the IETF in RFC 2251.

Microsoft LDAP Support

In Windows 2000 and later server OS versions, Microsoft adopted the LDAP v3 standard as the default protocol to access the information stored in Active Directory. Also, the AD information model is based on LDAP v3.

On the Windows client side, Microsoft includes LDAP v3 support in Windows 2000, Windows XP, Windows Server 2003, and R2. Below is a summary of how the LDAP v3 standard has been implemented in the Microsoft AD LDAP implementation. For a more detailed overview of the Microsoft AD LDAP implementation, we refer to the book *Active Directory Forestry*, by John Craddock and Sally Storey.

- LDAP clients can query, create, update, and delete information stored in AD using LDAP. LDAP is the only network protocol that can be used to access AD directory data. The default LDAP connection ports are TCP/389 for plain LDAP and TCP/636 for LDAP over SSL (LDAPs).

- The AD LDAP information model is based on entries that contain information about objects referencing users, computers, groups, etc.

Objects are composed of attributes, which have a type and one or more values. Each attribute has a predefined syntax that determines the values allowed in the attribute. Objects and their attributes are linked together in object classes. For example, AD has a user and contact object class. New AD objects are created as instances of these object classes; this means that a new object instance inherits all attributes and properties of its object class.

- AD object classes, their attributes, and possible values are defined in the AD schema. AD comes with a predefined schema. The AD schema can also be extended to include custom objects and attributes that are proper to a particular organization, for example.

- An AD LDAP infrastructure can consist of one or more AD servers that contain the data making up the global AD LDAP directory tree. In other words: the AD directory information can be spread across different AD LDAP servers. When an LDAP client connects to an AD server and requests information, the server performs an LDAP query and provides the information, or it refers the client to another AD server that might be capable of providing the information.

- AD provides a global LDAP directory service. It does not matter what AD server a client connects to: the object name used on one AD server references the same object that it would reference on another AD server. AD objects and their attributes are kept synchronized between different AD servers using a multimaster replication model. This means that an object can be updated on different AD servers;[1] the change is automatically replicated to the other AD servers.

Microsoft LDAP Particularities

Next is a short list of some of the particularities of the Microsoft AD LDAP implementation that may be important when discussing LDAP interoperability between Windows and other platforms.

1.   AD uses some Microsoft-specific schema extensions.[2] The most important is that AD stores user account information in objects of the class user, which is derived from the object class organiza-

---

1.   There are some exceptions to this rule; for example, AD schema extensions can only be created on a single DC in the AD forest (this is the Schema Master DC—see Chapter 2 for more information on DC Operations Master roles).
2.   The storage of the AD LDAP schema itself inside the same LDAP directory (AD) is also special to the Microsoft implementation of an LDAP server. LDAP server implementations from other vendors typically define the schema in a separate file.

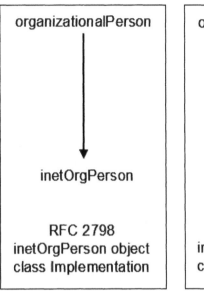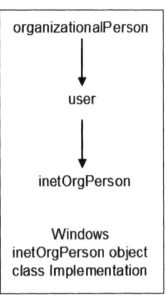

Figure 8.1
*inetOrgPerson
object class
implementation.*

tionalPerson (this is illustrated in Figure 8.1). Microsoft added
the user class to store the attributes required for a user in an AD
domain. The user class extends the organizationalPerson class
with additional attributes that are defined in two auxiliary classes:
securityPrincipal and mailRecipient.

- The auxiliary class securityPrincipal contains Windows-spe-
  cific security information about the user, such as the user's
  SID.

- The auxiliary class mailRecipient contains information related
  to the user's e-mail account. These attributes are used by
  Microsoft's messaging server Exchange Server.

2. When Windows 2000 was released, AD could not be deployed as
    a standalone LDAP directory. Organizations that wanted to use
    AD as a plain LDAP repository had to deploy a complete Win-
    dows 2000 infrastructure, including all the Windows security
    services. This has changed since the release of ADAM (AD Appli-
    cation Mode) in 2003. ADAM provides a standalone LDAP
    repository. It is available as an add-on for Windows 2000, Win-
    dows XP, and Windows Server 2003, and is included out of the
    box in the Windows Server 2003 R2 release. ADAM for Win-
    dows 2000, Windows XP, and Windows Server 2003 can be

downloaded from www.microsoft.com/downloads (search for the "ADAM" keyword). ADAM will be covered in more detail in Chapter 4 in *Advanced Microsoft Windows Security Services* (part 2 of this series).

3. In the Windows 2000 release, the AD schema does not support the inetOrgPerson object class. Microsoft has, however, provided an add-on software kit that adds support for the inetOrgPerson class to the Windows 2000 AD schema. This kit can be downloaded from www.microsoft.com/downloads (search for the "inetOrgPerson" keyword). The inetOrgPerson class is included by default in the Windows Server 2003 and R2 AD schema.

    The inetOrgPerson object class is defined in RFC 2798 and is used by other LDAP directories (such as Novell eDirectory and Sun iPlanet) to store user information. Also, many third-party non-Microsoft applications use inetOrgPerson to store user information. For interoperability between AD and these other directories and applications, it is very important that AD also supports the inetOrgPerson class.

The Microsoft AD implementation of inetOrgPerson differs from RFC 2798 in the following ways:

-   The inetOrgPerson object class is derived from the user object class, instead of the organizationalPerson object class. This is illustrated in Figure 8.1.

-   The inetOrgPerson object class inherits the following two mandatory attributes from the user class: the cn and samAccountName attributes. Mandatory attributes are attributes that must be set when a new instance of an object of a particular class is created.

-   The objectCategory for the inetOrgPerson object class is set to person. The user and contact AD object classes have the same objectCategory. The objectCategory attribute simplifies LDAP searches in AD.

8.2.2   **Kerberos**

Over the years, the Kerberos authentication protocol for distributed client-server environments has proven itself to be secure and efficient. Kerberos version 5 (the version used in Windows 2000 and later OS versions) has been standardized in RFC4120 (which updates and replaces RFC

1510). The Kerberos protocol and how it is implemented in Windows 2000, Windows XP, Windows Server 2003, and R2 were explained in detail in Chapter 6.

The following is a short list of some of the particularities of the Microsoft Kerberos implementation that may be important when discussing Kerberos interoperability with other platforms:

- Windows Kerberos is tightly integrated with the Windows 2000, Windows XP, Windows Server 2003, and R2 operating systems. Each of these systems runs the Kerberos Security Support Provider (SSP, explained in Chapter 5). Each Windows 2000, Windows Server 2003, and R2 domain controller (DC) has a KDC service.

- Kerberos principals locate the KDC using DNS. Windows 2000, Windows Server 2003, and R2 DNS include special SRV records that point to Kerberos KDC providers.

- Microsoft implemented the RC4-HMAC encryption algorithm (with 56- or 128-bit keys) as the preferred Kerberos encryption type. Microsoft still supports DES-CBC-CRC and DES-CBC-MD5 (with 56-bit keys) for interoperability reasons.

- Windows Kerberos caches a user's master key on the Kerberos client to allow automatic TGT renewal.

- Windows Kerberos KDCs require Kerberos clients to perform preauthentication by default.

- Microsoft uses its SSPI application programming interface (API) (see Chapter 4 of this book) to access Kerberos services. Microsoft Kerberos does not support the raw krb5 API or the GSS-API (as defined in RFC 2078).

- Microsoft uses the authorization data (authdata) field in the ticket to transport Windows authorization data. Microsoft refers to this field as the Privilege Attribute Certificate (PAC).

- Microsoft Windows caches a user's Kerberos master key for the duration of a user logon session, because the key is needed perform NTLM authentication to down-level clients and to automatically renew the user's Kerberos TGT.

- Microsoft does not support multipart principal names, which are supported on most UNIX Kerberos implementations. An example of a multipart principal name is host/unixbox.dc.net.

8.3   UNIX/Linux Security-Related Concepts

The next sections introduce some typical UNIX/Linux security-related concepts that will be referred to throughout this chapter. We will discuss PAM, UNIX/Linux naming services (local files, NIS, NIS+, and NSS), and Samba.

8.3.1   PAM

The pluggable authentication module (PAM) architecture provides a framework to make different authentication technologies available for UNIX/Linux platforms. For a great introduction to PAM, read the Sun white paper, "Making Login Services Independent of Authentication Services," available at http://wwws.sun.com/software/solaris/pam/pam.external.pdf. The PAM architecture is supported on most Linux platforms (Redhat, Suse) and on the HP-UX (from version 11.0 onwards), Solaris, and AIX platforms.

UNIX and Linux users typically log on by providing a username and password. To authenticate the user, the username and password are compared to those stored in the local /etc/passwd and /etc/shadow files. PAM allows the username and password information to be stored in other places—for example, in an LDAP directory.

Thanks to PAM, UNIX and Linux system administrators can also plug different authentication protocols and methods into UNIX and Linux operating systems. For example, besides the classical username- and password-based authentication, PAM can also provide support for token- or biometrics-based authentication methods.

The authentication protocols and methods that are available through PAM can be leveraged by UNIX and Linux system entry applications such as login, ftp, telnet, su, and rlogin.

The following is a nonexhaustive list of authentication methods and protocols that PAM can make available to applications:

- UNIX file–based authentication (using the /etc/passwd or /etc/shadow files)

- LDAP-based authentication

- NIS- or NIS+-based authentication

- Kerberos-based authentication

- S/Key-based authentication

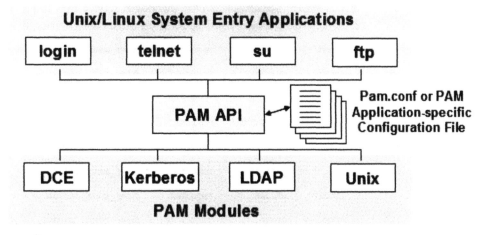

Figure 8.2   *The PAM architecture.*

- SecurID-based authentication

- NTLM-based authentication

Figure 8.2 shows the PAM architecture. A key element in this architecture is the PAM configuration file: it allows you to configure different PAM authentication behavior for each PAM-enabled service. This can be done for all services together in the /etc/pam.conf file or per individual service using the service's proper PAM configuration file (located in the /etc/pam.d directory).

Among the configuration parameters specified in a PAM configuration file are the authentication modules that must be loaded for a particular system entry application's authentication process to complete.

PAM modules are stackable, which means that during the authentication process a service may be configured to call on different PAM modules to verify the user credentials. For example, for user authentication, several password entries can be stacked so that a valid user password could be the password that is found in the /etc/passwd file, the /etc/shadow file, a Network Information System (NIS, explained below) database, or an LDAP database.[3] Below is an example of a PAM configuration file that holds the PAM authentication configuration for the login, ftp, and telnet services. In

---

3. This does not mean that authentication would succeed even if the same user has a different password in different authentication databases. PAM uses a well-defined logic to determine the outcome of a stacked authentication process: this logic takes into account the order in which the different modules are listed in the PAM configuration file and the value of the control flags for the different PAM modules (in the above example: required, sufficient, and requisite). Detailed examples of how this works can be found at http://docs.sun.com/app/docs/doc/816-4863/6mb20lvfj?a=view#pam-15.

this example, authentication for the rlogin service uses different "stacked" PAM modules ("rlogin auth" appears on three configuration lines).

login	*auth*	*required*	*pam_unix_auth.so*
login	*session*	*required*	*pam_unix_session.so*
login	*account*	*required*	*pam_unix_account.so*
login	*password*	*required*	*pam_unix_passwd.so*
ftp	*auth*	*required*	*pam_skey_auth.so*
ftp	*session*	*required*	*pam_unix_session.so*
telnet	*session*	*required*	*pam_unix_session.so*
rlogin	*auth*	*sufficient*	*pam_rhosts_auth.so*
rlogin	*auth*	*requisite*	*pam_authtok_get.so*
rlogin	*auth*	*required*	*pam_dhkeys.so*

In the above configuration file, you may have noticed that PAM provides more than just authentication services. It also provides the following services that are closely related to authentication: account, password, and session management services.

- Account management modules allow system entry applications to retrieve account-related information (such as logon hours, account expiration date, and so forth) from a local or central repository.

- Password management modules allow system entry applications to change users' passwords.

- Session management modules allow for the logging of session information to a local or central repository.

In the context of this discussion on UNIX and Windows authentication integration, the following PAM modules are of particular interest:

- **pam_unix:** a PAM module supporting authentication, account, and password and session management. The pam_unix supports UNIX crypt(3) password hashing.

- **pam_ldap:** a PAM module used in conjunction with the pam_unix module for authentication and password management with an LDAP server.

- **pam_kerberos (pam_krb5):** a PAM module that adds support for the Kerberos authentication protocol (as defined in RFCs 1510 and 4120).

- **pam_mkhomedir:** although this PAM module does not implement an authentication method or protocol, it can be critical for letting a logon to a UNIX or Linux system succeed. On many UNIX and Linux systems, user logon fails if the user's home directory does not exist. Thanks to this special PAM module, the home directory can be automatically created the first time the user logs on.

Another PAM module that could be used in the context of a Windows-UNIX/Linux security integration project is pam_smb. The pam_smb module supports the NT LAN Manager (NTLM) authentication protocols and can be used to authenticate UNIX hosts and users against a Windows server or domain controller (DC). We will not discuss the pam_smb in this chapter, because it does not leverage any of the key protocols for Windows-UNIX/Linux security integration in an AD-centric world: LDAP and Kerberos. Also, the NTLM authentication protocols are based on proprietary standards and are considered less secure than the Kerberos authentication protocol (see Chapter 5 for details). More information on pam_smb can be found at www.csn.ul.ie/~airlied/pam_smb. Later in this chapter, we will discuss Samba—even though the latest Samba version (3.0) still supports NTLM authentication, it also includes Kerberos authentication support.

The Windows equivalent of PAM is the security support provider interface (SSPI) and its security support provider (SSP) modules. Back in the 1990s, a team at the University of Michigan developed a PAM-like architecture for NT. More information on this interesting project can be found at www.citi.umich.edu/u/itoi/ni_pam_usenix.pdf.

8.3.2 Naming Services

A naming service is a repository that stores different types of information and that allows this information to be queried by user, machine, or application clients. Some naming services can also be configured to allow updates on certain types of information. The information stored in naming service repositories can include host-to-IP address mappings, user account names, credential information (hashed passwords), access permissions, access intermediaries (groups) and their memberships, and printer definitions.

Examples of typical Windows naming services are local files (the hosts and lmhosts files), the Windows Internet Name Service (WINS), the Domain Name System (DNS), and LDAP-based naming services offered by AD. Also, the Windows security database (SAM or AD) governed by the local or domain security authority can be designated as a naming service: one that is specifically focusing on security-related information.

Table 8.2 *Common UNIX Naming Services and Their Characteristics*

	Local Files	DNS	LDAP	NIS	NIS+
Namespace	Flat	Hierarchical	Hierarchical	Flat	Hierarchical
Data Storage	Files	Files	Directories	Two column binary maps	Multi-columned tables
Server Types	—	Primary/ Secondary	Master/replica/ multi-master	Master/slave	Root domain master/subdomain master/replica
Security	File permissions	Public key extensions	SSL (LDAPs)	None	DES/public-private key–based authentication

Over the years, the UNIX and Linux operating systems have supported a wide range of naming services. As for Windows, these include local files (stored in the /etc directory), DNS, and LDAP-based naming services. Most UNIX and Linux platforms also support two other naming services: the Network Information System (NIS) and the Network Information System Plus (NIS+) naming services. We will discuss these two naming services in more detail in the following sections.

In the context of this chapter, naming services are primarily used to enable different computers to share authentication-related information by storing them in a central repository that is governed by a naming service. In distributed client-server environments, centralized naming services offer an interesting alternative to the local naming services that are based on locally stored configuration files.

Table 8.2 summarizes the characteristics of the most commonly used UNIX/Linux local and centralized naming services. This list is not exhaustive; less common naming services such as the Federated Naming Service (FNS)[4] are not mentioned.

8.3.3 NSS

The previous section showed that UNIX and Linux clients, servers, and applications can call on many different naming services (Local files, DNS, LDAP, NIS, NIS+). To link clients and servers to these naming services and to allow them to switch easily from one naming service to another, Sun

---

4.   See also http://en.wikipedia.org/wiki/Federated_Naming_Service.

developed the concept of a universal naming service provider: the naming service switch (NSS). NSS is a client-side technology.

Thanks to NSS, UNIX and Linux clients and applications do not need to know which naming service stores which information. When the client or application wants to resolve a name, it simply calls on the NSS API. NSS then determines which naming services should be searched and in which order they should be searched. The NSS configuration is nailed down in the nsswitch.conf file stored in the /etc directory. Figure 8.3 shows the NSS architecture. Notice that PAM modules can also call on NSS for naming services.

Below is an example of the configuration data that can be found in an nsswitch.conf file. The configuration file contains one line for each type of information that needs to be resolved on a UNIX or Linux host. An information type is named after the database that stores the information of that particular type. For example, the passwd database contains user account information and the group database contains user group information. The different databases (and information types) supported by NSS are listed in Table 8.3.

passwd: files nisplus nis

shadow: files nisplus nis

group: files nisplus nis

hosts: files nisplus nis dns

services: nisplus files

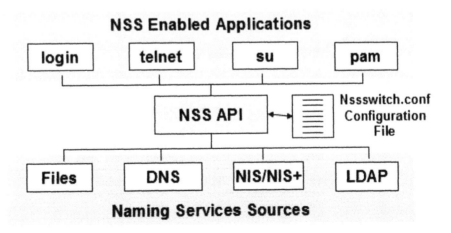

Figure 8.3   *The NSS architecture.*

Table 8.3   *NSS Supported Databases*

Database Name	Database Content
ethers	Ethernet MAC-to-IP address translations
group	User groups
hosts	Host name-to-IP address translations
netgroup	Network-wide list of hosts and users—used for access rules
network	Network names and numbers
passwd	User account information (see Section 8.3.4 for more info)
protocols	Network protocols
publickey	Public and private keys used by secure RPC
rpc	Remote Procedure Call (RPC) names and numbers
services	Network services
shadow	User password and account parameters (see Section 8.3.4 for more info)

For each information type, the nsswitch.conf file can specify different naming services and the order in which these must be tried. Table 8.4 gives an overview of the different naming services supported by NSS.

In the above example, NSS will first try the local configuration files in the /etc directory, then NIS+, then NIS, and finally DNS to resolve a hostname.

Table 8.4   *NSS Supported Naming Services*

Service Name	Meaning
db	Use local database files ending with the suffix .db
dns	Use the Domain Name System (DNS)
files	Use local configuration files under /etc
nis	Use the Network Information Service (NIS)
nisplus	Use NIS+
ldap	Use LDAP

To speed up name resolution, most UNIX/Linux NSS clients support a caching mechanism known as the name service caching daemon (nscd).

NSS is currently supported on Solaris, Linux, and HP-UX (from version 11.0 onward). AIX has a concept similar to NSS called the Information Retrieval System (IRS), which is rooted on Bind 8 code.

8.3.4   Local Files

On UNIX and Linux systems, local configuration files are typically stored in the local /etc directory. In the context of this chapter on Windows and UNIX/Linux authentication integration, the following UNIX/Linux local configuration files are particularly interesting: etc/passwd and etc/shadow.

The etc/passwd file contains a list of lines, one line for each user defined on the system. Each line can contain the following user information:

- The user's unique accountname on the local system

- The user's hashed password, which on most UNIX/Linux systems contains a "*" or "X," meaning that the actual hashed password is stored in the etc/shadow file (see below)

- The user identifier (UID)

- The user's primary group identifier (GID)

- The General Electric Comprehensive Operating System (GECOS) field, which is typically used to store the full name of the user or a comment

- The home directory of the user

- The user's login shell

The etc/shadow file contains hashed user passwords. This file can only be accessed by a user with root privileges. On a UNIX/Linux system, root privileges are the equivalent of Windows administrator-level access.

8.3.5   NIS

In 1985 SUN Microsystems released NIS: the Network Information Service, which Sun initially referred to as the Yellow Pages (yp). NIS was one of the first UNIX-based naming services. UNIX administrators wanted to get rid of the management overhead of local configuration files (/etc/passwd, /etc/hosts), and the primary goal of NIS was to make network management easier by providing a centralized naming service and repository.

NIS uses centralized files called NIS maps that make up the NIS namespace and that can replace or augment the local files available on all UNIX/Linux systems, such as passwd, group, hosts, etc.

- NIS can replace local files with the NIS copy.

- Local files can be augmented with the content of the NIS copy. In this case, the local files maintain their content, but if no match is found in the local file during a search, the search will be redirected to the appropriate NIS map.

Whether a local file is replaced or augmented depends on the naming services switch (NSS) configuration on the local UNIX/Linux host; this is illustrated in the example below:

- If the local passwd file is replaced with the NIS data, the nsswitch.conf file would contain the following passwd entry:

  passwd: nis

- If the local passwd file is augmented with the NIS data, the nsswitch.conf file would contain the following passwd entry:

  passwd: files nis

Like NT, NIS uses the notion of a domain to provide an administrative grouping of machines. A UNIX or Linux host's NIS domain basically determines which NIS server the host will query. Within an NIS domain, NIS uses a single-master information replication model made up of a master and multiple slave NIS servers. Figure 8.4 shows the NIS architecture. Figure 8.4 also shows some typical NIS commands: ypbind to connect to an NIS server, and yppush to push changes from NIS master to slave servers (the yp in these commands stands for Yellow Pages).

One of the biggest deficiencies of NIS is its complete lack of security: NIS does not authenticate users, NIS data are transmitted in the clear, NIS has major difficulties working through a firewall (it uses RPCs), and so forth. NIS also lacks a hierarchical namespace (it uses a flat namespace), an easily extensible data structure, and an efficient information replication model.

Even though Sun still officially supports NIS, Sun encourages customers to migrate to LDAP. Sun also provides tools that can facilitate the migration of NIS data to an LDAP repository; a good example is the NIS to LDAP Transition Tool (N2L: more info at www.sun.com/bigadmin/content/n2l/). All this does not change the importance of considering NIS as a building block for Windows and UNIX/Linux authentication integration.

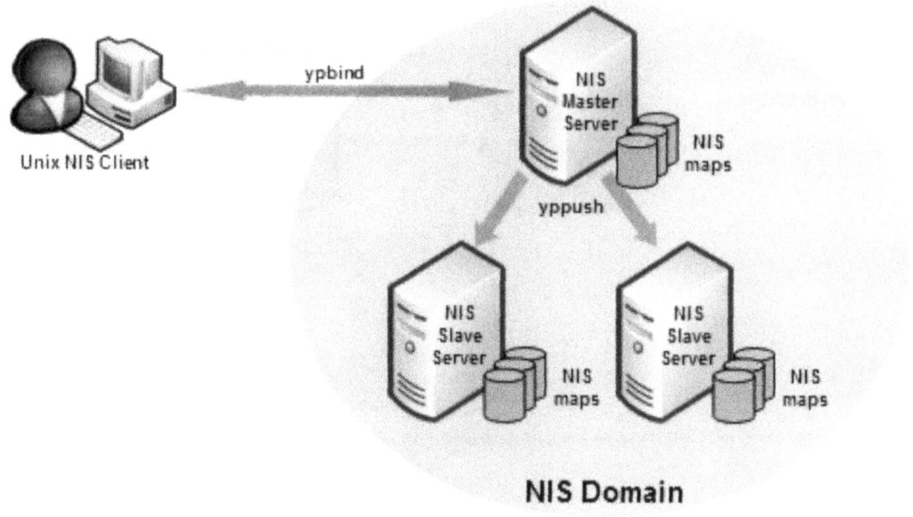

Figure 8.4 *The NIS architecture.*

8.3.6 **NIS+**

NIS+ was introduced by Sun as part of the Solaris 2 OS as an enhanced naming service for NIS. Similar to NIS, the primary focus of NIS+ was to make network management easier by providing a centralized naming service and repository.

The most important enhancements in NIS+, as compared to NIS, are the support for a hierarchical namespace, client authentication (both for users and hosts), secured data transmission (using DES encryption), object access control lists (ACLs), incremental updates between master and slave servers, and a better data storage model. Instead of using binary files, NIS+ stores information in database-like tables.

The NIS+ architecture can be made up of several hierarchical layers of master and replica NIS+ servers. At the top of the hierarchy sits a root master server, and below it can be one or more subdomain master servers. Each of the master servers can have one or more replica servers. Figure 8.5 illustrates the NIS+ architecture.

Many NIS+ concepts are similar to the concepts used by LDAP-rooted naming services, so it will come as no surprise that in Solaris version 9, Sun adopted LDAP as the default naming service. Sun considers NIS+ an end-of-feature (EOF) naming service. EOF means that Sun will provide no

Figure 8.5
*The NIS+
architecture.*

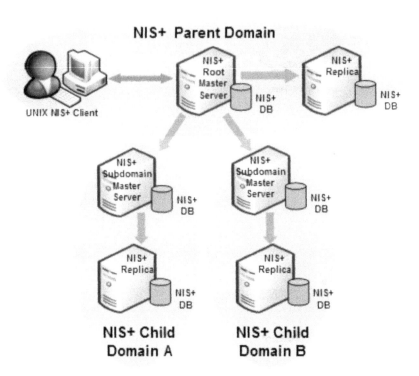

more feature enhancements to NIS+ and that the NIS+ functionality may be removed in a future Sun Solaris update. For more information, see the Sun NIS+ statement at www.sun.com/software/solaris/9/faqs/nisplus.xml.

8.3.7   NIS and LDAP Integration

IT environments looking for integrated Windows and UNIX/Linux account management and authentication and that still require NIS naming services on the UNIX/Linux side of the house, can benefit from an NIS and LDAP integration solution.

Two common NIS and LDAP integration approaches are the following:

- Extend the LDAP schema to enable the storage of NIS data. In this approach, UNIX and Linux clients must talk the LDAP language with their naming service. This approach is described in RFC 2307, "An Approach for Using LDAP as a Network Information Service" (an IETF Internet draft) and RFC 2307bis (a revised version of RFC 2307). Both RFCs describe an LDAP directory schema for storing NIS data in an LDAP directory. We will discuss this solution in more detail below.

- Extend the LDAP schema to enable the storage of NIS data in an LDAP repository and, in addition, provide an NIS-to-LDAP gateway service. In this approach, NIS queries are translated into LDAP queries, and the NIS data are stored in an LDAP repository. This solution allows UNIX and Linux clients to continue talking the NIS language with their naming service. We will discuss NIS-to-LDAP gateway solutions in more detail later in this chapter.

The default AD schema that Microsoft provides in Windows 2000 and Windows Server 2003 does not contain NIS-specific extensions allowing for the storage of NIS data in AD. However, Microsoft provides two solutions that can enable AD to store NIS data:

- **Microsoft Services for UNIX (SFU) version 3.5.** SFU is a software package that Microsoft provides to Windows 2000 and Windows Server 2003 customers at no additional cost. It includes tools and services for integrating Windows and UNIX platforms, as well as AD schema extensions that enable AD to store NIS data. The SFU 3.5 schema extensions are not RFC 2307-compliant. For example, the names of quite a few SFU 3.5 attributes start with "msSFU30" (msSFU30GidNumber, msSFU30LoginShell, msSFU30HomeDirectory, etc.), which is not compliant with the attribute names defined in RFC 2307.

  For a detailed overview of the SFU schema extensions, read the document titled "Schema Changes for Server for NIS," which can be downloaded from www.microsoft.com/downloads (search for the "Server for NIS" keyword). The SFU 3.5 software can be downloaded from the same URL (search for the "SFU" keyword).

- **Windows Server 2003 R2.** The schema of the Windows Server 2003 R2 AD automatically includes the schema extensions to store NIS data in AD. Contrary to the SFU 3.5 extensions, these schema extensions are RFC 2307-compliant. You can identify the R2 AD schema as follows:

  — By checking the schema.ini file that accompanies the Windows Server 2003 R2 distribution: the schema class object should be listed with an objectversion=31
  — By checking the AD attributes and object classes from the AD Schema Management MMC snap-in: they should include the NIS-specific attributes and object classes listed in Table 8.5 (as defined in RFC 2307)

Table 8.5   *Object Classes and Attributes Defined in RFC 2307*

Object Classes	posixAccount, shadowAccount, posixGroup, ipService, ipProtocol, oncRpc, ipHost, ipNetwork, nisNetgroup, nisMap, nisObject, ieee802Device, bootableDevice
Attributes	uidNumber, gidNumber, gecos, homeDirectory, loginShell, shadowLastChange, shadowMin, shadowMax, shadowWarning, shadowInactive, shadowExpire, shadowFlag, memberUid, memberNisNetgroup, nisNetgroupTriple, ipServicePort, ipServiceProtocol, ipProtocolNumber, oncRpcNumber, ipHostNumber, ipNetworkNumber, ipNetmaskNumber, macAddress, bootParameter, bootFile, nisMapName, nisMapEntry

8.3.8 Samba

Samba is a collection of software that provides services to UNIX and Linux platforms:

- Samba allows UNIX and Linux clients to access file and print services using the Server Message Block (SMB) and Common Internet File System (CIFS) network protocols.

- Samba allows the UNIX and Linux server to provide file and print services using the SMB and CIFS network protocols.

- Samba allows users to log on to UNIX or Linux using credentials defined in the NT SAM or in Windows 2000/Windows Server 2003 AD.

SMB is the default Microsoft file- and print-sharing protocol. CIFS is the name Microsoft uses to designate the SMB flavor that can run without requiring NetBIOS over TCP (NBT).

The two first services make Samba the ideal gateway for sharing file and print services between a Windows and a UNIX/Linux environment "the Microsoft way"—that is, using the SMB protocol. As part of the SFU 3.5 suite and the Windows Server 2003 R2 operating system, Microsoft provides the following solutions that can be used for file service sharing between Windows and UNIX "the UNIX way"—that is, using the Network File System (NFS) protocol: the NFS server, NFS client, and User Name Mapping Service. In R2, these NFS services are referred to as Microsoft Services for NFS.

This chapter will not discuss the SMB-based file- and print-sharing capabilities in mixed Windows and UNIX/Linux environments. In the context of this chapter, we are primarily interested in Samba's third capability, which allows users to log on to a UNIX or Linux host using SAM- or AD-based credentials. This Samba functionality is provided by the Samba Winbind service.

At the time of writing, the latest Samba version was 3.x, and Samba 4 was in the making (in January 2006, a Technology Preview 1 version of Samba 4 was released). More information on Samba and its different versions can be found at www.samba.org. Samba runs on a variety of server platforms, many of which are UNIX and Linux flavors (AIX, Redhat Linux, etc.) but also on VMS, Netware, and OS/2. Samba is freeware software, available under the GNU public license (more information on this license is available at http://ftp.easynet.be/samba/docs/GPL.html).

From a security point of view, Samba 3.x comes with the following features and functionality:

- Can act as a Windows primary domain controller (PDC) server in an NT 4.0-like domain

- Can be configured as a backup domain controller (BDC) server to a Samba PDC server (a Samba server cannot be a BDC to an NT 4.0 PDC)

- Can be a member server in a Windows NT 4.0, Windows 2000, or Windows Server 2003 domain—for Windows 2000, this is independent of the domain mode (mixed or native); for Windows Server 2003 and R2, this is independent of the functional level

- Supports NTLM authentication and NTLM pass-through authentication

- Supports Kerberos authentication on the Samba client side (Samba cannot provide Kerberos KDC services; client-side Kerberos support is not available in older Samba versions, i.e., before 3.x)

- Supports Windows NT 4.0-style nontransitive interdomain trust relationships—NT 4.0-style trust relationships can be set up between Samba and NT4.0, Windows 2000, Windows Server 2003, or R2 domains, but this feature is not available in older Samba versions (before 3.x)

- Supports NetBIOS name resolution services; a Samba server can even act as a WINS server

- Allows users to log on to a UNIX or Linux host using Windows credentials defined in the Windows NT SAM, Windows 2000, or Windows Server 2003 AD, thanks to the Samba Winbind service

At the time of writing, it was not possible for a Samba (version 3.x) server to operate as a domain controller (DC) in a Windows 2000 or later environment. This will change in Samba 4, in which a Samba server can be configured as an Active Directory (AD) DC.

If you want to learn more about Samba 3.x technical details, we advise you to read the "Official Samba-3 HOWTO and Reference Guide," available from http://us4.samba.org/samba/docs/man/Samba-HOWTO-Collection/. For more information on Samba Winbind, read http://us4.samba.org/samba/docs/man/Samba-HOWTO-Collection/winbind.html.

8.4   Windows and UNIX/Linux Account Management and Authentication Integration Approaches

The account management and authentication integration approaches for the Windows and UNIX/Linux platforms that are discussed in this chapter can be categorized as follows:

- **Coexistence solutions:** In these solutions, the NIS and AD/LDAP infrastructures coexist. Usually, these solutions do not provide a single point of administration, nor do they provide SSO; however, they do provide integrated authentication. In this context, integrated authentication means using the same authentication credentials and/or protocols in the UNIX/Linux and the Windows environment. A well-known set of solutions in this category are credential synchronization services, which can synchronize credentials between the UNIX/Linux and Windows security authentication authorities and their repositories.

- **Centralized user management solutions:** These solutions provide a single point of administration for both UNIX/Linux and Windows accounts and credentials. This approach is also referred to as single-source sign-on. In an AD-centric Windows environment, it is quite obvious to use AD as the central repository. Some solutions in this category provide a special front end to AD, so users can keep using their legacy communication protocol (for example, NIS) and do not need to change to LDAP to communicate with AD.

- **Single Sign-On (SSO) solutions:** Whereas the two previous approaches still require users to enter a set of credentials each time they access another environment, true SSO only requires users to enter their credentials once: to the primary authentication authority (for example, a Windows DC). Afterward, authentication to secondary authentication authorities (for example, a UNIX resource server) happens transparently. There are quite a few different SSO architectures available. For a high-level outline of the different SSO architectures and examples of commercial software supporting them, see Chapter 9.

Many organizations consider coexistence solutions such as an AD and NIS infrastructure to be intermediary solutions. The coexistence solution is then used as a stepping-stone for a future centralized user management or SSO solution.

The solutions for integrated account management and authentication discussed in this chapter are listed in Table 8.6. Note that this is a nonexhaustive overview of Windows and UNIX/Linux integration solutions.

In our overview of coexistence solutions, we focus on the integration solutions that Microsoft offers with its Windows Server 2003 R2 platform and as part of the Services for UNIX 3.5 (SFU 3.5) UNIX/Windows integration suite.

Table 8.6   *Solution Overview*

Coexistence Solutions (Mixed NIS and AD Infrastructure) Using SFU 3.5 or Windows Server 2003 R2
■ Server for NIS (AD-Integrated NIS)   ■ Password Synchronization
Centralized User Management Using AD/LDAP Repository
■ PADL NIS/LDAP gateway   ■ Pam_unix-centric   ■ Pam_ldap-centric   ■ Pam_kerberos-centric   ■ Samba WinBind   ■ Quest Software Vintela Authentication Services (VAS)   ■ Centrify DirectControl

8.4.1   Coexistence Solutions between an NIS and an AD Infrastructure

This section focuses on the following Windows and UNIX/Linux coexistence solutions coming with the Microsoft Services for UNIX 3.5 (SFU 3.5) integration suite and Windows Server 2003 R2: Server for NIS and the Password Synchronization Service.

In Windows Server 2003 R2, Server for NIS and the Password Synchronization Service can be installed from the Add/Remove Programs control panel applet. In the Windows Components dialog box, select "Identity Management for UNIX," as illustrated in Figure 8.6.

Server for NIS

Server for NIS is an SFU 3.5 and Windows Server 2003 R2 service that allows Windows AD-based domain controllers (DCs) to act as NIS master servers for one or more NIS domains. The overall architecture of the Server for NIS solution is illustrated in Figure 8.7.

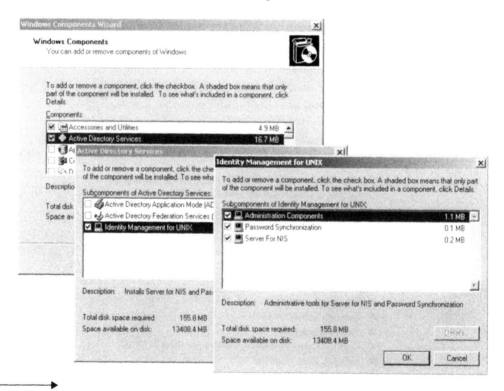

Figure 8.6   *Installing Identity Management for UNIX components in Windows Server 2003 R2.*

When using Server for NIS, you do not need to add LDAP logic on the client side. Server for NIS understands NIS remote procedure calls (RPCs), which means that UNIX and Linux clients can keep on talking NIS RPCs to the AD-based NIS servers. A Server for NIS-enabled Windows DC can translate the NIS queries it receives from UNIX and Linux NIS clients into AD LDAP queries, and return the data to the NIS clients in an NIS format and using NIS RPCs. The only required change on the client side is that you must point them to the correct AD NIS server.

Server for NIS can replicate NIS data to both Windows and UNIX NIS slave servers (as Figure 8.7 shows):

- The Windows servers with which Server for NIS replicates are also Windows DCs that have Server for NIS installed. In this case, the NIS data are replicated using the AD replication model and protocols.

- The UNIX servers with which Server for NIS replicates are NIS slave servers. In this case, NIS data are replicated using the NIS yppush protocol.

For users to authenticate against a UNIX or Linux host using credentials stored in an AD-based NIS server, the UNIX or Linux host must have the appropriate PAM and NSS modules installed to talk to an NIS server (typically pam_unix and nss_nis). Also, the PAM and NSS configuration files

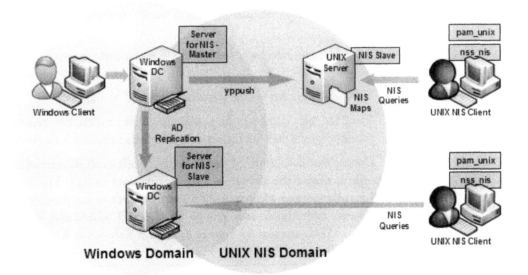

Figure 8.7 *SFU Server for NIS architecture.*

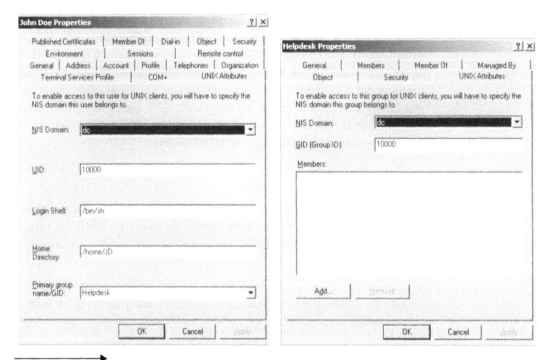

Figure 8.8   *User and Group Object "UNIX Attributes" tab in the AD Users and Computers MMC snap-in.*

must point to the NIS service. In an NIS-based authentication scenario, the actual verification of the user credentials occurs on the UNIX or Linux host as follows:

- The PAM and NSS logic retrieve the user's hashed password from the NIS server.

- The PAM logic hashes the password provided by the user.

- The PAM logic compares the two hashes. If they match, the credentials provided by the user are correct, and user authentication is successful.

During the installation of Server for NIS, SFU and R2 extend the AD schema to enable the storage of NIS-specific data in AD. The Server for NIS installation also adds the UNIX Attributes tab in the properties of the AD users, computers, and groups in the AD Users and Computers (ADUC) MMC snap-in (as Figures 8.8 and 8.9 show for R2[5]). This addi-

---

5.   In R2, the UNIX attributes tab for the ADUC can also be installed separately on a DC or an administration machine (without installing Server for NIS) by selecting the "Administration Components" underneath "Identity Management for UNIX" in the Windows Components Wizard.

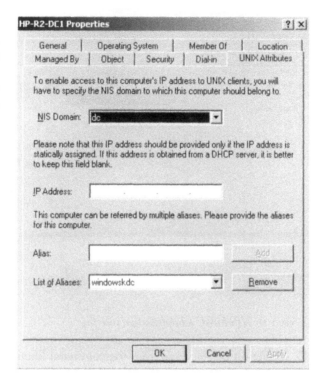

Figure 8.9
Computer Object "UNIX Attributes" tab in the AD Users and Computers MMC snap-in.

tional ADUC tab can provide a single point of administration for both the Windows and UNIX/Linux authentication and authorization data. Also, thanks to Server for NIS, organizations can leverage a single repository (AD) for storing both Windows- and UNIX/Linux-specific naming information.

Besides the ADUC MMC snap-in UNIX Attributes tab, you can also manage the AD objects' NIS attributes from the command line, using the nismap utility. For more information on the nismap syntax see the R2 Server for NIS help files.

Figure 8.10 shows the Server for NIS MMC-based administration interface included with Windows Server 2003 R2. From this interface, you can view NIS master and slave servers, define slave servers, start the NIS Migration Wizard (explained below), set NIS configuration parameters (e.g., frequency of map updates, password hash algorithm), and force NIS replication. Most of these administrative actions can also be performed from the command line using the nisadmin utility.

Server for NIS comes with two migration tools that administrators can use to migrate the content of the NIS maps defined on an NIS server to

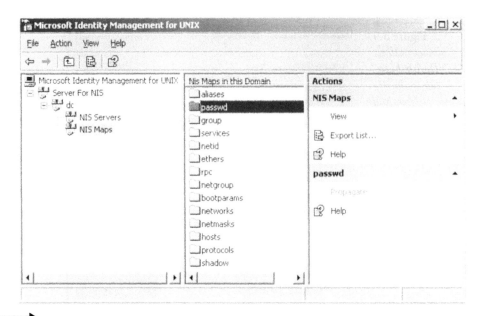

Figure 8.10   *R2 Server for NIS MMC administration interface.*

AD. Migration can be done from the command line using the nis2ad executable or using the NIS Migration Wizard. The NIS migration wizard (illustrated in Figure 8.11) can be started from the context menu of the Server for NIS container in the Microsoft Identity Management for UNIX MMC snap-in (see Figure 8.10) by selecting NIS Data Migration Wizard.

It is a bit misleading to call these tools "migration tools": they do not actually transform the NIS data to LDAP data, but rather preserve NIS data in an AD LDAP store. Both tools can move NIS domain data into an AD NIS domain with the same or a brand-new name, or they can merge different NIS domains into a single AD NIS domain.

A security feature that is definitely worth mentioning is the following: if you also have the SFU or R2 Password Synchronization Service installed on your Windows DCs, unidirectional password updates of the AD Windows password property can be provided to the AD UNIX password property. This means that if a user's Windows password is changed in AD, the Password Synchronization Service will automatically change the corresponding UNIX password property of the same AD user object. Server for NIS then automatically replicates the password change to the other Windows NIS servers and the UNIX NIS slave servers.

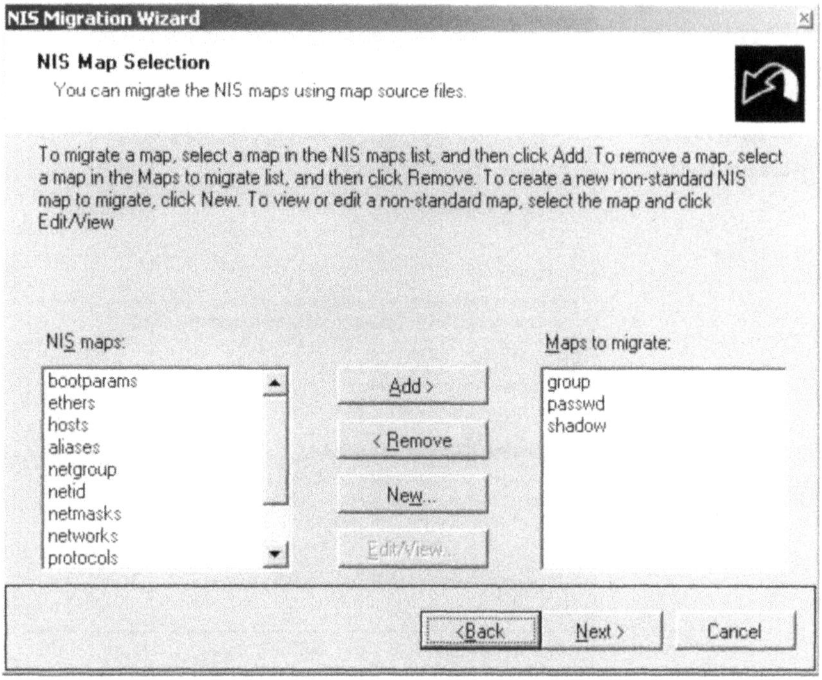

Figure 8.11 *NIS Migration Wizard.*

To enable the unidirectional password update from the AD Windows password property to the UNIX password property, open the properties of the Password Synchronization container in the Microsoft Identity Management for UNIX MMC snap-in, select the Configuration tab, and check the "Enable Windows to UNIX (NIS) Password Sync" box (as illustrated in Figure 8.12). This feature can only be enabled if all domain controllers in the domain run Windows Server 2003 SP1 or Windows Server 2003 R2.

The use of this password synchronization feature mandates that in a Windows domain that is made up of multiple DCs, Server for NIS and the Password Synchronization Service are installed on all DCs. This is because in a multi-master directory replication model like the one AD uses, a user's original password change can occur on any of the DCs in the user's domain. There can also be situations where you do NOT want to install the Server for NIS and the Password Synchronization Service on all the DCs of your AD domain. For example, in an AD setup consisting of many different sites and branches, it would be acceptable to install these services only on the DCs of the AD site that leverages them. In a hub and spoke environment

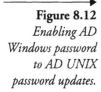

Figure 8.12
Enabling AD Windows password to AD UNIX password updates.

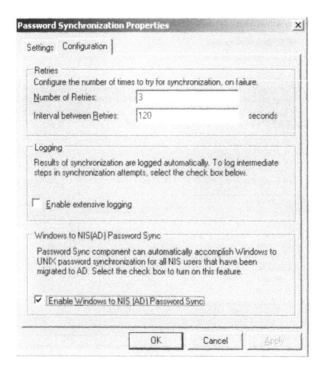

with many branch offices, it is not uncommon that the branches do not access UNIX resources. More often, you see the UNIX access limited to IT and development departments, etc.

If you want bidirectional password synchronization to also replicate the password changes originating on machines in the UNIX environment, you must explicitly configure the Password Synchronization Service between these UNIX machines and the Server for NIS DCs. For more information on this, read Section 8.4.1 on the SFU and R2 Password Synchronization Service.

Password Synchronization Solutions

Another alternative for setting up security coexistence between a Windows and a UNIX/Linux environment is to keep user passwords synchronized between the two worlds. Synchronizing passwords eases the life of both administrators and users: users must remember only a single password, and administrators will receive fewer password-reset calls. Password synchronization does not provide SSO: users must still provide their password credentials to the Windows and UNIX/Linux systems. In this section, we will focus on the password synchronization solution, called the "Password Synchronization Service," that Microsoft provides as part of SFU 3.5 and the Windows Server 2003 R2 operating system.

As opposed to the Server for NIS password synchronization discussed above, which synchronizes the password between two different password attributes of a single AD account, the password synchronization solutions discussed in this section are used between two different accounts that are stored on different systems (for example, in a NIS database on a UNIX host and an AD database on a Windows box).

Because both Windows and UNIX/Linux use specific hashing algorithms to securely store user passwords, true password synchronization between the two credential databases is impossible. Hashing algorithms are one-way functions: given the password hash, it is not possible to derive the original password. This explains why password synchronization can only occur when a user password is set or reset—in other words, before the OS hashes the password.

A critical item you must always check when setting up password synchronization between different systems is the compatibility of the systems' password policies. The password policy of the system in which the password is changed should be at least as restrictive as the password policy of the system to which the change is synchronized. If this is not the case, password synchronization will fail.

SFU and R2 Password Synchronization Service

The SFU 3.5 and R2 Password Synchronization Service allows for password synchronization between the Windows NT4 Server and Workstation, Windows 2000 Professional and Server, Windows XP, and Windows Server 2003 and R2 platforms on the Windows side, and the HP-UX 11, AIX 4.3.3, Redhat Linux 7.0, and Solaris 7 platforms on the UNIX side. For all the above-mentioned UNIX platforms—with the exception of AIX—password synchronization works in both directions: from Windows to UNIX and from UNIX to Windows. AIX password synchronization only works from Windows to UNIX.

The Password Synchronization Service triggers a password synchronization action each time a user updates his password on a Windows machine (for Windows-to-UNIX synchronization) or on a UNIX/Linux host (for UNIX-to-Windows synchronization).

The Password Synchronization Service can be administered using the Password Synchronization MMC snap-in and from the command line using the psadmin utility. Both tools allow you to define UNIX password synchronization target computers, and to configure Password Synchronization Service parameters (e.g., synchronization direction, port number, secret key, retry and logging parameters, etc.).

The Password Synchronization Service provides secure password synchronization. The passwords are encrypted using the 3DES algorithm and a secret key that is shared between the UNIX/Linux and Windows platforms. The secret key can be set from the properties of a UNIX synchronization target computer object in the Password Synchronization Service MMC snap-in, as illustrated in Figure 8.13; it can be set differently for each password synchronization connection. The secret key must be at least 16 characters long and adhere to a set of complexity requirements outlined in the Password Synchronization Service help files.

If passwords are to be synchronized between a Windows domain and UNIX/Linux, the SFU and R2 password synchronization service must be installed on all Windows domain controllers (a password update can occur on any server in a multimaster model). The service must also be installed on a Windows standalone machine if passwords are to be synchronized between the standalone machine and UNIX/Linux.

Figure 8.13
Setting the secret key for password synchronization connections.

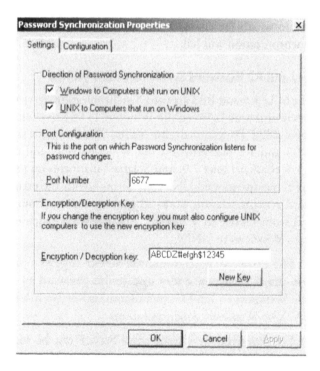

The password synchronization service is even required on Windows DCs if passwords are to be synchronized the other way around, from UNIX to Windows. As we will explain below (see Figure 8.15), when a UNIX user updates his password, he will perform the update on a Windows DC, which will then synchronize the password change to the UNIX NIS server using the password synchronization service. Microsoft preferred this approach because installing the password synchronization service on the Windows DCs should be much less of a challenge than doing so on all UNIX/Linux clients and servers.

SFU and R2 password synchronization also comes with two other modules that are required for password synchronization to work on the UNIX side:

- Windows-to-UNIX password synchronization requires the ssod daemon on the UNIX platform. This UNIX platform can be either a UNIX NIS server or a UNIX standalone machine.

- UNIX-to-Windows password synchronization requires the pam_sso module on the UNIX side. This UNIX platform can be either a UNIX machine using NIS or a standalone machine.

At the time of writing, the pam_sso and ssod modules were not included on the R2 CDs; they are, however, available in the SFU 3.5 installation package. See the following Microsoft Knowledge Base article for more information on this: https://premier.microsoft.com/default.aspx?scid=kb;en-us;324542.

Windows administrators can control which user passwords are synchronized by creating two local user groups: PasswordPropAllow and PasswordPropDeny. The PasswordPropAllow group contains the users for which passwords should be synchronized. The PasswordPropDeny group contains users for which passwords should not be synchronized.

A similar feature is available on the UNIX/Linux side: UNIX administrators can ensure that the passwords of certain accounts are never synchronized. They must edit the sso.conf password synchronization configuration file on the UNIX/Linux host and add accountname preceded by a minus sign (–) to the SYNC_USERS= line. For example, to ensure that the password of the root account is never synchronized with a Windows account of the same name, you must make sure the following line appears in sso.conf:

```
SYNC_USERS=-root
```

Figure 8.14 shows how password synchronization works from Windows to UNIX. The figure shows the following password synchronization scenarios:

- Windows-to-UNIX password synchronization in a Windows domain environment:

    — Scenario 1: to a UNIX NIS database
    — Scenario 2: to a standalone UNIX/Linux machine

- Windows-to-UNIX password synchronization from a Windows standalone machine.

    — Scenario 3: to a UNIX NIS database
    — Scenario 4: to a standalone UNIX/Linux machine

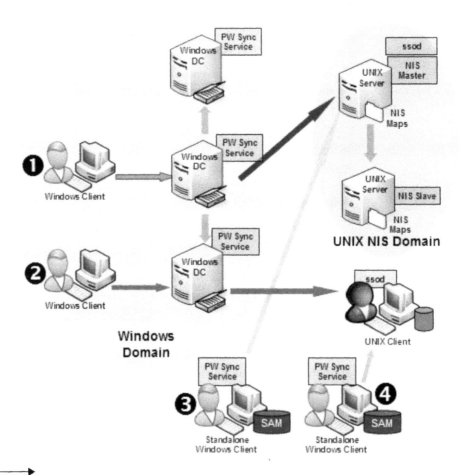

Figure 8.14   *SFU password synchronization architecture: Windows to UNIX.*

Figure 8.15 shows how password synchronization works from UNIX to Windows. The figure shows the following password synchronization scenarios:

■ UNIX-to-Windows password synchronization in a UNIX NIS environment:

— Scenario 1: to a Windows AD database
— Scenario 2: to a standalone Windows machine

■ UNIX-to-Windows password synchronization from a UNIX/Linux standalone machine:

— Scenario 3: to a Windows AD database
— Scenario 4: to a standalone Windows machine

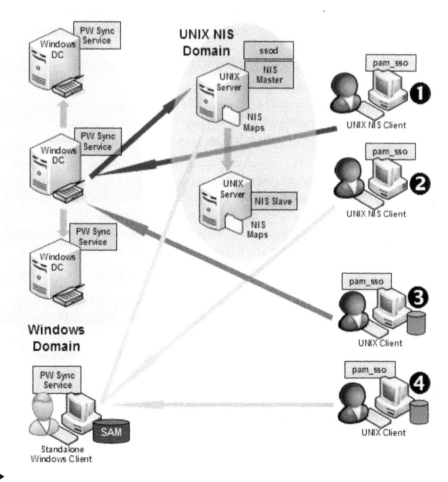

Figure 8.15   *SFU password synchronization architecture: UNIX to Windows.*

Table 8.7   *Password Synchronization Solutions*

Vendor/Product	URL
Passgo InSync	www.passgo.com
Proginet SecurPass-Sync	www.proginet.com
M-Tech P-Synch	www.psynch.com

Note in Figure 8.15 that if password synchronization is set up between a UNIX NIS domain and a Windows AD domain or standalone machine, the pam_sso module installed on the UNIX/Linux client will propagate the password change first to the Windows side (DC or standalone machine). Only after this is done will the Windows password synchronization service synchronize the password change with the UNIX NIS database.

Other Password Synchronization Solutions

Quite a few software vendors provide password synchronization solutions for mixed Windows and UNIX/Linux environments. Table 8.7 provides a nonexhaustive list of password synchronization solutions. A detailed discussion of these solutions is beyond the scope of this book.

An interesting open source solution for password synchronization between Windows and UNIX/Linux is the solution proposed in the OpenLDAP directory-based "LDAP Account Synchronization Project." This solution uses a password-filtering DLL that intercepts password changes on the Windows DC and then synchronizes them with the OpenLDAP server. More information is available from http://acctsync.sourceforge.net.

8.4.2 Solutions Providing Centralized User Management Using an AD/LDAP Repository

The following sections discuss solutions providing centralized user management for Windows 2000 (and later) and UNIX/Linux platforms using a central AD/LDAP repository.

NIS/LDAP Gateway

NIS-to-LDAP gateway functionality can be provided on UNIX servers by a daemon called ypldapd—a solution from PADL software (www.padl.com). ypldapd provides an NIS server interface to NIS clients. Contrary to a normal

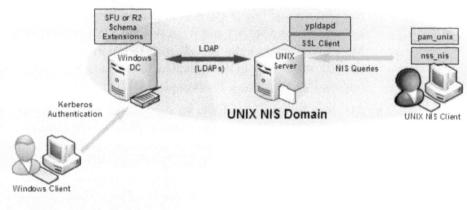

Figure 8.16 *NIS/LDAP gateway architecture.*

NIS server, the ypldapd NIS server stores its NIS data in an LDAP directory and not in NIS maps. The intent of ypldapd is to allow an organization to leverage the scalability and distributed nature of LDAP directory services, while maintaining an existing NIS infrastructure. A key ypldapd feature is that no special services need to be installed on the LDAP servers (Windows DCs): the NIS-to-LDAP translation happens on the UNIX server that acts as an NIS server to clients, instead of the AD DC that actually holds the NIS data. The ypldapd architecture is illustrated in Figure 8.16.

ypldapd allows organizations to get rid of their older NIS servers without reconfiguring the NIS clients. ypldapd acts as a broker between UNIX NIS clients and the LDAP server, and classic NIS client utilities such as ypcat, ypmatch, and login will work unmodified. ypldapd converts NIS RPC requests into LDAP operations and then converts the answers back into NIS replies. The only exception is the NIS password-changing utility (yppasswd). Because passwords are stored in LDAP, the classic NIS password-change utility will not work. To deal with this issue, ypldapd provides a special password-changing utility called ldappasswd that addresses the LDAP server directly when a user wishes to change his password.

Before ypldapd can access NIS data in the AD LDAP repository, you must complete the following steps:

- The AD schema must be extended to make it RFC 2307 compliant—the way to do this was explained in Section 8.3.7.

- The NIS data must be migrated to AD.[6] This can be done using the nis2ad command line or the NIS Migration Wizard, which are both included in the SFU 3.5 and R2 Server for NIS (see Section 8.4.1). Most UNIX vendors also provide tools to export the NIS data from the NIS maps into LDIF-formatted files. These files can then be imported into AD using, for example, LDIFDE.

- AD must be made searchable by the ypldapd service. An easy and secure way to set this up is to create a special search account in AD for the ypldapd service. A solution we do not recommend is to allow anonymous AD access (removing anonymous AD access restrictions is explained in the Microsoft KB article 326690).

- For better security, we also advise you to set up an SSL tunnel for the LDAP traffic between the NIS/LDAP gateway and AD. Provided it has an SSL server certificate,[7] AD supports LDAPs out of the box. To add SSL capabilities to your UNIX NIS/LDAP gateway, you can use the stunnel software; more information on this is available at www.stunnel.org.

The binary distribution of ypldapd is available for Solaris 2.6, 7, and 8, Linux, and AIX 4.3.3 (on PowerPC). Source licensees may build ypldapd for other platforms, except for HP-UX. The ypldapd for HP-UX is available directly from HP as part of the LDAP-UX integration for HP-UX software package: more information is available at http://h20293.www2.hp.com/portal/swdepot/displayProductInfo.do?productNumber=J4269AA. More information on the ypldapd daemon is available from the following URL: www.padl.com/Products/NISLDAPGateway.html.

nss_ldap

Contrary to the NIS-to-LDAP gateway solution we discussed in the previous section, all the following solutions allow UNIX/Linux clients to access the AD/LDAP repository directly. In these solutions, there is no more need for a gateway that translates NIS requests to LDAP queries.

The basic enabler behind these solutions is the nss_ldap NSS module, which allows UNIX and Linux clients to communicate directly with an

---

6.   You can also manually enter the NIS data in the UNIX attributes tab of AD users and groups from the AD Users and Computers (ADUC) MMC snap-in. However, depending on the size of your UNIX population, this may be a time-consuming task.

7.   How to set up LDAPs on an AD domain controller will be explained in Chapter 10 in *Advanced Microsoft Windows Security Services* (part 2 of this series).

LDAP repository. The nss_ldap is available from the PADL Web site and is distributed under the terms of the GNU Lesser General Public License (www.padl.com/OSS/nss_ldap.html). nss_ldap supports AIX 4.3.3, HP-UX 11i, Linux, and Solaris 2.6 and above.

To enable a UNIX or Linux host to call on nss_ldap for naming information, you must include the ldap naming service in the nsswitch.conf NSS configuration file. For example, the following nsswitch configuration lines augment the content of the local configuration files with the content of an LDAP repository for querying the passwd, shadow, and group databases:

passwd: files ldap

shadow: files ldap

group: files ldap

Linked to the nss_ldap file is a special configuration file (ldap.conf) that must be modified to contain the following configuration data:

- **The AD search account and its associated password.** As was the case for the ypldapd-based solution, AD must be made searchable when using nss_ldap. The recommended way to make AD searchable is to set up a special AD search account. Below are a set of a sample ldap.conf configuration lines for specifying an AD search account named "adsearchaccount" and its password (instead of a DN, you can also use a UPN):

  binddn cn=adsearchaccount,cn=Users,dc=domain,dc=net

  bindpw Password1!

- **The AD attribute where the username can be found.** This allows a user to log on to a UNIX/Linux box using the same name he would use on a Windows machine. Below is the ldap.conf configuration line for specifying this:

  pam_login_attribute sAMAccountName

- **Where to start searching in AD.** Below are a set of sample ldap.conf configuration lines for specifying this:

  nss_base_passwd cn=users,dc=domain,dc=net

  nss_base_shadow cn=users, dc=domain,dc=net

  nss_base_group cn=users,dc=domain,dc=net

- **Attribute and object class mappings.** Below are the mapping definitions needed when using the SFU 3.5 and when using the R2 AD schema extensions (notice the attribute naming differences between SFU 3.5 and R2):

— for SFU 3.5

nss_map_attribute uid sAMAccountName

nss_map_attribute uidNumber msSFU30UidNumber

nss_map_attribute gidNumber msSFU30GidNumber

nss_map_attribute loginShell msSFU30LoginShell

nss_map_attribute gecos name

nss_map_attribute homeDirectory msSFU30HomeDirectory

nss_map_attribute uniqueMember member

nss_map_attribute cn sAMAccountName

nss_map_objectclass posixGroup Group

nss_map_objectclass posixAccount user

nss_map_objectclass shadowAccount user

— for R2

nss_map_attribute uid sAMAccountName

nss_map_attribute uidNumber uidNumber

nss_map_attribute gidNumber gidNumber

nss_map_attribute loginShell loginShell

nss_map_attribute gecos name

nss_map_attribute homeDirectory unixHomeDirectory

nss_map_attribute uniqueMember member

nss_map_attribute cn sAMAccountName

nss_map_objectclass posixGroup Group

nss_map_objectclass posixAccount user

nss_map_objectclass shadowAccount user

You should also not forget to add the UNIX/Linux-specific user attributes in the UNIX attributes tab of the AD user accounts—this can be done from the AD users and computers (ADUC) MMC snap-in.

Two of the four solutions outlined next not only rely on nss_ldap to retrieve user profile information (home directory, login shell, and so forth) from an LDAP repository, but also to help with the user authentication process.

pam_unix-centric Approach

The pam_unix PAM module supports the classic UNIX authentication protocol that is based on the crypt(3) hash function. pam_unix has the capability to calculate a crypt(3) hash given a user password, to compare this hash to another hash stored in some repository, and—based on the outcome of the comparison—to decide whether the user's identity is authentic or not. The pam_unix module also provides password management and is supported on all UNIX and Linux flavors discussed in this chapter: Linux, HP-UX, Solaris, and AIX.

To leverage pam_unix in an AD environment (as illustrated in Figure 8.17), the AD schema must be extended to make it RFC 2307-compliant; the way to do this was explained in Section 8.3.7. This will enable storing the UNIX user password in a UNIX crypt(3) hash format in AD.

To secure the LDAP network traffic between the UNIX client and AD, it is advisable to use LDAP over SSL (LDAPs). SSL support is available out

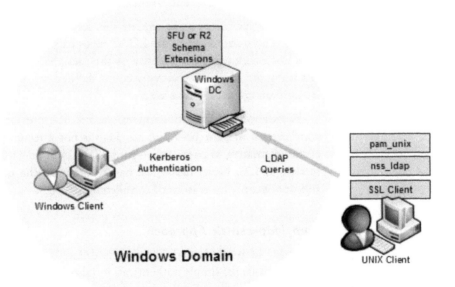

Figure 8.17   *pam_unix-centric architecture.*

of the box on an AD domain controller. To support it on the UNIX and Linux side, you can use the stunnel software www.stunnel.org).

When UNIX and Linux clients rely on the pam_unix PAM module, user authentication occurs as follows:

- pam_unix first retrieves the user's password hash from the LDAP repository. To connect to the LDAP repository, pam_unix calls on nss_ldap.

- The hash nss_ldap retrieved is then validated on the UNIX host by pam_unix. This means that pam_unix will compare it to the local password hash. The latter is the outcome of the application of a hash function on the password entered by the user.

- If the validation process by the pam_unix module is okay, the user is given access to the UNIX client.

- After the initial authentication, the UNIX login program usually calls on nss_ldap for a second time to retrieve additional user profile information from the LDAP repository.

In this scenario, the LDAP repository is not the true authentication authority—this is the role of the local pam_unix module. The LDAP repository only provides authentication data to the pam_unix module.

Security specialists argue against this solution, because it typically uses the same account to access the LDAP repository. Access to the LDAP data does not occur using the identity of the user that must be authenticated, but using the identity of proxy account defined on the UNIX host. Some setups even use anonymous access.

Because of the limitations mentioned in the previous paragraphs, the combination of pam_unix and nss_ldap is not a recommended option. A better alternative to pam_unix—pam_ldap—will be explained in the next section (8.4.2). Nevertheless, we had to mention the pam_unix/nss_ldap solution, mainly for reasons of completeness.

pam_ldap-centric Approach

The pam_ldap PAM module supports different LDAP-based authentication mechanisms: simple authentication (also known as plaintext authentication or a simple LDAP bind), CRAM-MD5-based authentication, or digest authentication (the last two are used in conjunction with the SASL negotiation protocol). pam_ldap also provides password management. It does not provide account and session management services. That is why, once a user is authenticated using pam_ldap, applications must call on other modules to retrieve user profile information. Just like pam_unix, pam_ldap calls on nss_ldap to retrieve user profile information from the LDAP repository.

A pam_ldap module for AIX 5L, HP-UX 11i, Linux, and Solaris 2.6 and above is available from PADL software (www.padl.com). More information on pam_ldap is also available from www.padl.com/OSS/pam_ldap.html.

The pam_ldap-centric solution is illustrated in Figure 8.18. To leverage pam_ldap in an AD environment, the AD schema must be extended to make it RFC 2307-compliant; the way to do this was explained in Section 8.3.7. To secure the LDAP traffic between the UNIX/Linux client and the LDAP server, it is once more advisable to use LDAP over SSL.

The pam_ldap solution has several security advantages over the pam_unix solution:

- Contrary to the pam_unix-centric approach, the LDAP repository acts as a true authentication authority. In this solution, the LDAP server will decide whether the user authentication is successful and then return the result to the UNIX/Linux host.

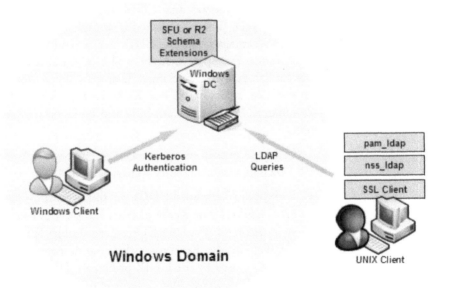

Figure 8.18   *pam_ldap-centric architecture.*

- Access to the LDAP repository does not occur in the security context of a proxy account. pam_ldap authenticates to the LDAP server using the user credentials.

- All authentication attempts can be subjected to a central security policy that is stored in the LDAP repository.

Excellent guidance on how to leverage pam_ldap and nss_ldap in an AD-centric environment is also available from Microsoft at www.microsoft.com/technet/itsolutions/cits/interopmigration/unix/usecdirw/08wsdsu.mspx.

pam_kerberos-centric Approach

The pam_kerberos PAM module enables a UNIX or Linux host to authenticate against a Kerberos key distribution center (KDC). As is the case with pam_ldap, in this solution a centralized service (the KDC) is the authentication authority and not the UNIX client (remember pam_UNIX). pam_kerberos also typically provides account, password, and session management capabilities. On most UNIX and Linux platforms, Kerberos PAM modules are known as pam_krb5, where krb5 refers to version 5 of the Kerberos authentication protocol.

A nice thing about using the Kerberos authentication protocol for UNIX/Linux and Windows integration is that it can also be used as a SSO solution for Windows and UNIX applications that understand the Kerberos protocol. These applications are referred to as Kerberized applications. Unfortunately, in the UNIX/Linux world, there are few Kerberized applications. Examples of Kerberized UNIX/Linux applications and protocols are Telnet, POP, and Samba. Examples of common UNIX/Linux applications that typically are not Kerberized are Linux desktop applications (Gnome, KDE), and custom-built and home-grown UNIX/Linux applications.

In an AD-centric environment there are two Kerberos-based Windows-UNIX/Linux interoperability scenarios:

- **Using only Windows KDCs.** In this scenario, illustrated in Figure 8.19, UNIX/Linux Kerberos users and services receive Kerberos tickets issued by a Windows KDC. Even though Windows embeds profile data in the Kerberos tickets (authorization data), these data cannot be used by the UNIX principals. UNIX principals can, however, fall back to nss_ldap to retrieve their UID, GIDs, and other profile data from the LDAP repository.

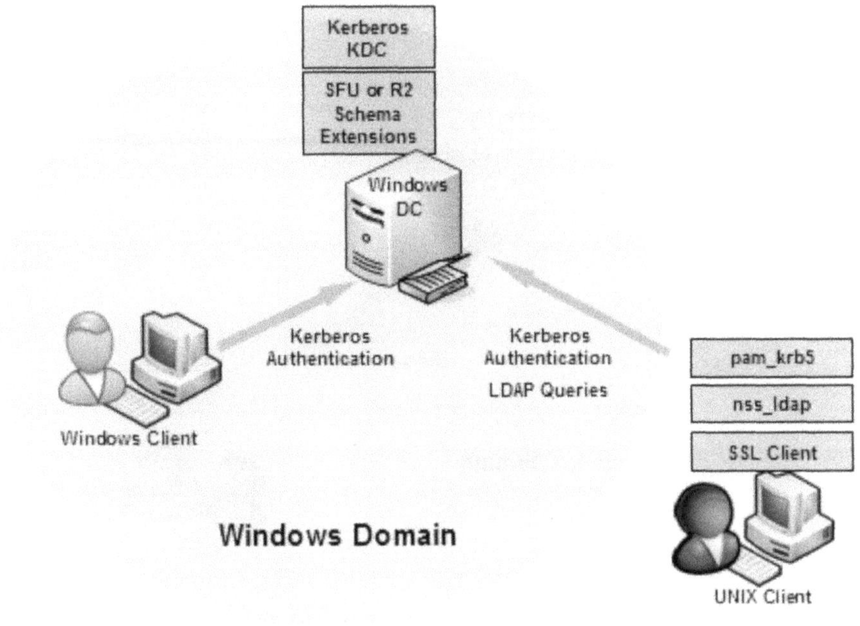

Figure 8.19 *Kerberos-centric architecture: Windows KDCs.*

■ **Using both Windows and UNIX/Linux KDCs and a cross-realm trust relationship between the UNIX/Linux and Windows KDCs.** In this scenario, illustrated in Figure 8.20, UNIX/Linux Kerberos users and services receive Kerberos tickets issued by a UNIX/Linux KDC and trusted by the Windows KDC. In this scenario, UNIX/Linux hosts also need nss_ldap to retrieve their UID, GIDs, and other profile data from the LDAP repository.

For more information on Windows and UNIX/Linux Kerberos interoperability, refer to Chapter 6.

Samba Winbind

Samba winbind can provide a unified logon experience between UNIX/Linux and Windows systems: it allows users to log on to a UNIX/Linux host using Windows domain credentials. Winbind comes bundled with the Samba software (Samba was discussed in Section 8.3.8). winbind can provide the unified logon experience independently of whether the UNIX/Linux host is acting as a Samba SMB file and print-sharing server.

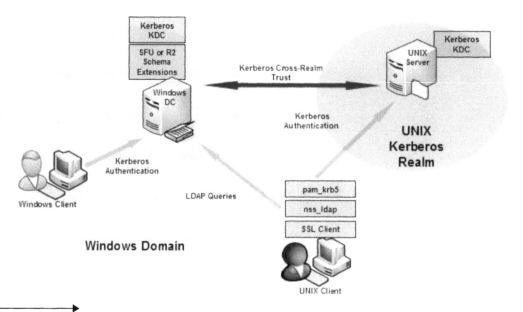

Figure 8.20   *Kerberos-centric architecture: UNIX and Windows KDCs, and cross-realm relationship.*

A great thing about winbind is that it does not require changes on the Windows domain controller side: all changes are UNIX or Linux client-related. However, it must be said that on the UNIX/Linux client side, winbind configuration is relatively complex; we will give some examples of winbind configuration difficulties you may face below.

The winbind architecture is illustrated in Figure 8.21. Note in the figure that winbind not only allows a UNIX/Linux user to use a Windows domain for authentication, it also allows for the UNIX/Linux host to be joined and to authenticate to the Windows domain. winbind can work with NT4, Windows 2000, Windows Server 2003, and R2 domain controllers and domains.

The winbind solution is built on the winbind daemon (winbindd), a pluggable authentication module (PAM) called pam_winbind, a name service switch (NSS) module called libnss_winbind, and a database file called winbind_idmap.tdb.

The winbindd code includes a UNIX implementation of Microsoft Remote Procedure Calls (RPCs). winbindd uses RPCs to authenticate users against a Windows domain, to obtain Windows domain user and group details from a Windows domain controller, and to change the passwords of Windows accounts.

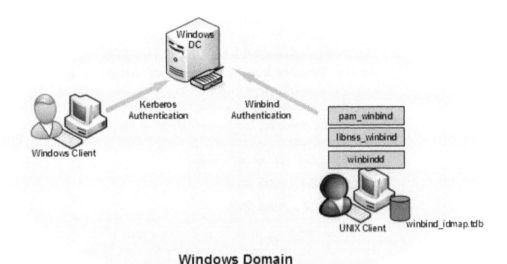

Windows Domain

Figure 8.21   *Samba winbind architecture.*

The pam_winbind PAM module enables users to log on to a UNIX/ Linux host using Windows credentials. The following is an excerpt of a sample PAM configuration file that enables the UNIX/Linux logon process to call on winbind for authenticating a user—in this particular example, pam_unix would reuse the credentials provided by the user if winbind authentication failed:

login   auth   sufficient   pam_winbind.so

login   auth   required   pam_unix.so nullok try_first_pass

The libnss_winbind NSS module enables a UNIX/Linux host and the services running on these hosts to call on a Windows domain controller for user password and group naming information. To use the winbind NSS module, you must edit the nsswitch.conf NSS configuration file as follows:

passwd: files winbind

group: files winbind

The winbind_idmap.tdb database contains mappings between a Windows user and group names and their corresponding UNIX/Linux UIDs and GIDs. When a user logs on to a UNIX/Linux host using a Windows account, the UNIX/Linux host does not understand the Windows account format. Also, Windows accounts cannot be used to set permissions on UNIX/Linux resources: UNIX/Linux access control settings require UIDs and GIDs. That is why winbind automatically creates a Windows user account-to-UNIX/Linux UID mapping for each new Windows user that logs on to a winbind-enabled UNIX/Linux host. The UIDs winbind uses for the Windows account mappings are defined in the Samba smb.conf configuration file. Administrators can set aside a range of UIDs and GIDs to be used by winbind on a UNIX/Linux host by setting the idmap parameters in the smb.conf Samba configuration file. For example, the following smb.conf entries set aside the UID range 2,000 to 3,000 and the GID range 2,000 to 3,000 for use by winbind:

idmap uid = 2000-3000

idmap gid = 2000-3000

These mappings must be defined on each UNIX/Linux host to which users will log on using Windows credentials. When defining the idmap UID and GID ranges for a host you must make sure the idmap UID and GID ranges do not overlap with locally defined UNIX/Linux users or groups. Also, standard winbind does not include a feature to ensure that the same Windows user is assigned the same UID on different UNIX/Linux hosts. This explains why idmap can lead to inconsistencies if Windows users are logging on from different UNIX/Linux hosts and accessing shared resources, for example, NFS file servers. Since different UNIX/Linux hosts can map different UIDs, whether a user is allowed to access a particular NFS resource may depend on what UID he uses or, in other words, which UNIX/Linux host he uses to accesses the resource. Some winbind implementations provide a solution to this problem based on the idmap_rid smb.conf configuration setting. The idmap_rid setting enables winbind daemons to generate unique UIDs and GIDs across a Windows domain;[8] the uniqueness is based on mapping the RID portion of a Windows SID[9] to a UNIX/Linux UID or GID.

The above UID/GID issue and its configuration complexity make winbind a less attractive solution than the nss_ldap solutions discussed previously (even though these require changes on both the server and the client side). When using an nss_ldap-based solution, the UID/GID problem does not exist; in these solutions, AD is the sole authoritative source for managing UIDs and GIDs.

More information on how to set up winbind and its different components can be found in the Samba-HOWTO Collection documentation,

---

8.   An example of a Samba version supporting this is the HP-UX SMB server: see also http://docs.hp.com/en/B8725-90093/ch07s04.html.

9.   See Chapter 2 for more details on Windows SIDs and GIDs.

available from http://us4.samba.org/samba/docs/man/Samba-HOWTO-Collection/winbind.html#id2619422.

Quest Vintela Authentication Services

Vintela Authentication Services (VAS) is a commercial software offering from Quest Software that provides centralized AD-based user and machine account management for Windows and UNIX/Linux clients. More information on VAS can also be found at www.quest.com/Vintela_Authentication_Services.

Key VAS features are its ability to integrate UNIX/Linux hosts in a Windows domain environment and its ability to secure the LDAP traffic between the UNIX/Linux hosts and AD using the Kerberos protocol. VAS can leverage the UNIX/Linux machine's Kerberos session key to secure LDAP exchanges. This explains why VAS—as opposed to the previous solutions—does not require an SSL-secured connection between the UNIX/Linux client and the AD domain controller. This also eliminates the setup of dummy user accounts or anonymous access to query AD data.

Similar to the solutions discussed above, VAS enables users to use the same credentials on Windows and UNIX/Linux without installing special credential synchronization software; all credential data are centralized in AD. VAS version 2.6 supports the following UNIX and Linux platforms: RedHat Linux 7.3 and 9.0; SuSE Linux 8.0 and 9.0; Solaris 8, 9, and 10; HP-UX 11.0 and 11i; and AIX 4.3, 5.2, and 5.3.

The VAS integration solution is easy to set up and administer, especially when compared to some of the free alternatives we discussed above, such as winbind, nss_ldap, etc. Ease of setup and administration always has a price, though. The same is true for the commercial solution discussed in the next section: Centrify DirectControl.

The VAS architecture is illustrated in Figure 8.22. The architecture includes components on the Windows DC and the UNIX/Linux host side. For Windows DCs, VAS includes a set of RFC 2307-compliant AD schema extensions—these extensions are not required on a Windows Server 2003 R2 AD platform—and an extension for the AD Users and Computers (ADUC) MMC snap-in, which adds the "UNIX Account" tab in the properties of AD users, groups, and computers (as illustrated in Figure 8.23).

For UNIX or Linux hosts, VAS includes special PAM (pam_vas) and NSS (nss_vas) modules, and a special daemon called the vascd daemon (the VAS caching daemon).

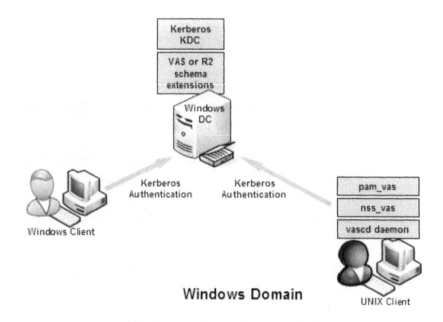

Figure 8.22   *Vintela Authentication Services (VAS).*

Besides LDAP, Kerberos, PAM, and NSS, VAS also builds on the following open standards: SASL, GSS-API, and SPNEGO:

- The Simple Authentication and Security Layer (SASL) protocol provides a method for adding authentication support to connection-based protocols (for example, LDAP). SASL includes a negotiation phase before the actual authentication takes place. More information on SASL can be found at http://asg.web.cmu.edu/sasl.

- The Generic Security Services API (GSS-API) is an API for authentication in a distributed client-server environment. It is basically an abstraction layer that enables applications to call on different authentication methods and protocols. GSS-API can be compared to the Windows SSPI (explained in Chapter 5). Most UNIX/Linux Kerberos implementations have a Kerberos authentication GSS-API plug-in. More information on GSS-API can be found at www.faqs.org/faqs/kerberos-faq/general/section-84.html. GSS-API is also documented in RFC 2743 (available from www.ietf.org).

The Simple and Protected GSS-API Negotiation Mechanism (SPNEGO) is closely related to the GSS-API. It allows applications to

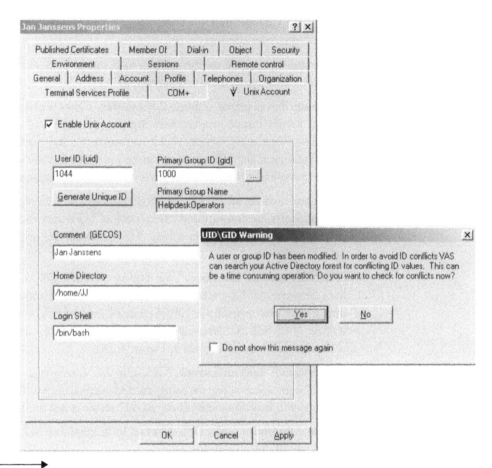

Figure 8.23   *VAS AD Users and Computers MMC snap-in extensions for user objects.*

negotiate which authentication mechanism to use. SPNEGO is documented in RFC 2478 (available from www.ietf.org).

Other important VAS features are the following:

- **Automatic keytab maintenance.** By joining UNIX/Linux workstations and servers to the domain, VAS eliminates the traditional Microsoft-UNIX/Linux-Kerberos interoperability steps of exporting and importing the keytab files, explained in Chapter 6. VAS automatically handles the creation of keytab files for both UNIX/Linux computer and UNIX/Linux service accounts.

- **Support for Microsoft AD-based password policies.** VAS fully supports AD password policies, including the password age, complexity, history, and length settings. VAS users with expired passwords are prompted to change their password when logging on to VAS-enabled UNIX/Linux workstations.

- **Command-line–based configuration**. VAS comes with a command-line administration tool called vastool.exe.

- **Computer-based access control**. This feature allows individual control of UNIX/Linux workstation log on access based on local users.allow/users.deny files. VAS introduces the concept of users.allow/users.deny files, which can be configured to allow or deny log on access based on Active Directory username, group, or domain.

- **Intelligent caching of LDAP data**. VAS uses special caching technology that limits the amount and complexity of NSS- and PAM-driven LDAP traffic and LDAP server load. This enhances the scalability of the VAS solution.

- **UID/GID conflict checking**. This feature prevents UID/GID conflicts between UNIX-enabled user and group AD accounts. Each time a new user or group is UNIX-enabled from the ADUC MMC snap-in, VAS will ask whether you want it to check for conflicting UIDs and GIDs (as illustrated in Figure 8.23).

- **Disconnected authentication**. VAS can be configured to allow UNIX/Linux users to log on using cached credentials when they are disconnected from the network or the AD server is not available.

- **NIS data migration tools**. NIS data can be migrated to AD using the vastool command-line utility.

- **Simplified time synchronization**. VAS includes time synchronization functionality that allows UNIX/Linux hosts to synchronize time with Windows domain controllers. Remember from Chapter 6 that time is a critical service for Kerberos authentication.

Centrify DirectControl

Centrify DirectControl is another commercial software offering that provides centralized AD-based user and machine account management for Windows and UNIX/Linux clients. DirectControl appeared later on the market than the VAS solution but has some interesting differentiators. More information on DirectControl can be found at www.centrify.com/directcontrol/overview.asp.

The most important Centrify DirectControl differentiators are:

- **DirectControl requires no changes to the AD schema**. It leverages the existing Windows 2000, Windows Server 2003, and R2 schema to store UNIX/Linux data. VAS requires schema extensions for a Windows 2000 and Windows Server 2003 AD.

- **DirectControl comes with built-in group policy object (GPO) functionality**. The GPO functionality (an administrative template) centrally manages the security settings of UNIX/Linux hosts from AD. VAS does not include GPO functionality; Quest Software offers GPO support in a separate product called Vintela Group Policy (VGP).

- **DirectControl uses the concept of zones to map UIDs or GIDs from different UNIX/Linux hosts to a single AD user or group account**. The zone concept is illustrated in Figures 8.25 and 8.26. Figure 8.25 shows how the AD account John Doe maps to UID 30000 in a zone named "AdvancedTechnologyGroup" and UID 40000 in a zone named "SecurityOffice"—these Centrify Profile properties can be viewed from the AD Users and Computers (ADUC) MMC snap-in. Figure 8.26 shows how zones can be defined from the DirectControl configuration utility. In VAS, only a single UID or GID can be mapped to an AD user or group. DirectControl zones offer an interesting solution to the Samba winbind idmap problem we outlined in Section 8.4.2, allowing an easier integration of multiple UNIX naming services with a central AD.

- **DirectControl supports delegated administration out of the box**. VAS requires extra software to obtain the same level of functionality. In VAS AD administrative delegation capabilities can, for example, be added by installing Quest's ActiveRoles software.

- **DirectControl has built-in reporting capabilities**. These reporting capabilities include a set of predefined reports. VAS does not include reporting tools.

- **DirectControl includes tools to migrate NIS, etc/passwd, and etc/group data to AD**. The migration wizard is integrated with the DirectControl configuration utility (illustrated in Figure 8.26). In VAS, NIS-to-AD data migration can be done using the vastool command-line utility.

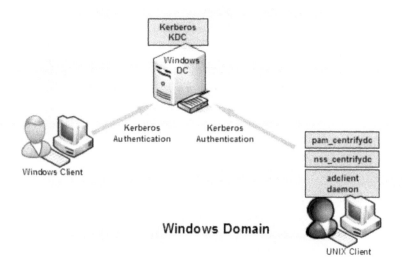

Figure 8.24   *Centrify DirectControl.*

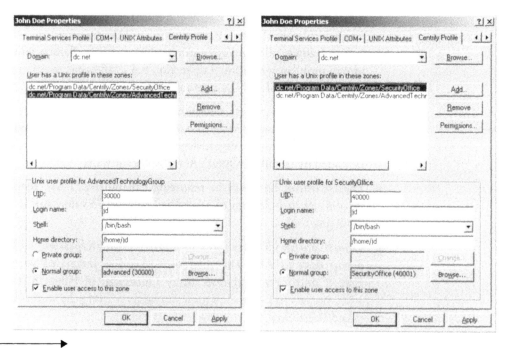

Figure 8.25   *Centrify DirectControl AD Users and Computers MMC snap-in extensions for user objects.*

Centrify DirectControl version 2.1.2 supports the following UNIX and Linux platforms: RedHat Linux 7.3 and 9.0; Debian Linux 3.0 and 3.1; SuSE Linux 8.0 and 9.0; Solaris 8, 9, and 10; HP-UX 11.0 and 11i; and AIX 4.3, 5.2, and 5.3. DirectControl also supports Apple Mac OS X.

The DirectControl architecture is illustrated in Figure 8.24. The architecture includes components on the Windows DC and the UNIX/Linux host side. For Windows DCs DirectControl includes an extension for the AD Users and Computers (ADUC) MMC snap-in; this extension adds the "Centrify Profile" tab in the properties of AD users, groups, and computers (as illustrated in Figure 8.25 for an AD user) and a special DirectControl configuration utility (as illustrated in Figure 8.26).

For UNIX/Linux hosts, VAS includes a special PAM (pam_centrifydc) and NSS (nss_centrifydc) module, and a special daemon called the adclient daemon.

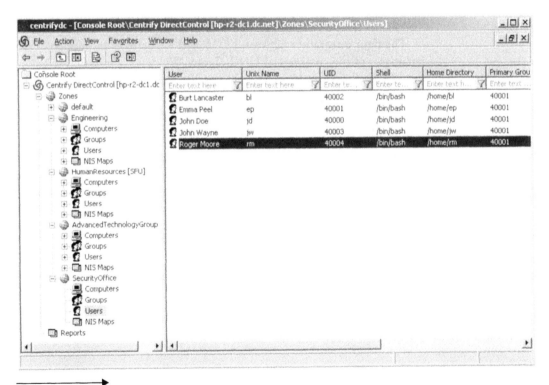

Figure 8.26   *Centrify DirectControl configuration utility.*

8.5   Summary

This chapter provided an introduction to different UNIX/Linux and Windows authentication integration approaches. The list of solutions in this chapter is certainly not complete. The primary goal was to illustrate the different integration mechanisms that can be put in place and the ways that Microsoft supports them in SFU 3.5 and Windows Server 2003 R2.

The combination of the Kerberos authentication protocol and an LDAP repository is definitely the most promising integration approach. Both LDAP and Kerberos are available on every Windows 2000 and later domain controller. Every DC hosts a Kerberos authentication authority (the KDC) and an LDAP-accessible repository (Active Directory, or AD). Both protocols nicely complement each other: LDAP is an efficient protocol for querying authentication and authorization data in a central repository, but lacks important security features like secure channel and single-sign on services—two key features of the Kerberos authentication protocol.

The tight integration between LDAP and Kerberos is an important differentiator of the commercial UNIX/Linux-Windows integration solutions from Quest Software (Vintela) and Centrify. Also, these solutions offer ease of deployment and configuration—something that cannot be said of the competing "free" solutions: pam_ldap combined with nss_ldap, pam_krb5 combined with nss_ldap, and Samba winbind.

Finally, to complement the information we provided in this chapter: In June 2006, Microsoft published a very helpful resource for facilitating UNIX/Linux and Windows security integration; it is called the "Windows Security and Directory Services for UNIX Guide v1.0" and can be downloaded from http://go.microsoft.com/fwlink/?LinkId=36975.

9

Single Sign-On

A major driver behind the creation of authentication infrastructures is Single Sign-On (SSO). In short, SSO is the ability for a user to authenticate once to a single authentication authority and then access other protected resources without re-authenticating. The Open Group defines SSO[1] as the mechanism whereby a single action of user authentication and authorization can permit a user to access all computers and systems where that user has access permission, without the need to enter multiple passwords.

This chapter focuses on the architectural approaches you can take when designing an SSO solution for a large IT infrastructure and on the security technology building blocks that can be used to construct such an SSO infrastructure. This chapter does not address the architecture of every SSO solution currently available on the software market. At the end of the chapter, we will pay special attention to the SSO solutions that Microsoft makes available to its customers.

9.1   SSO: Pros and Cons

The Network Applications Consortium (www.netapps.org) conducted a study of large enterprises that showed users spend an average of up to 44 hours per year performing logon tasks to access a set of four applications. The same study measured the content of the calls to companies' helpdesk: 70% of the calls were password reset requests.

SSO is advantageous for both users and administrators. There is no need to point out that users' and administrators' lives become much easier if they have to deal only with a single set of credentials—one for every user. An average user will have to provide his or her logon credentials only once

---

1.   See www.opengroup.org/security/l2-sso.htm for more details.

every day, and he or she will need to change only a single set of credentials at regular intervals. Indirectly, this will increase a user's productivity. The authentication infrastructure, its administrators, and helpdesk operators will only need to keep track of the changes to a single entry for every user in the credential database. A key advantage is also that all authentication data are centralized and can be accessed and manipulated using the same tools and procedures. The latter may also be a weakness: if a malicious person gets to the database and can bypass its security system, he or she gets access to all of the data at once.

The advantages of SSO are not only related to the ease of administration and use; SSO also brings important security advantages. Centralization eases the enforcement of a consistent authentication policy throughout the enterprise. Obviously, it is also much easier to secure a centralized than a distributed infrastructure. The lack of SSO services increases the risk for compromise of an authentication service's security. For example, if users need to keep track of different password credentials, they typically start writing them down and sticking them to their monitors or the backs of their keyboards. Indirectly, the absence of SSO can also affect the availability of an authentication service. The more passwords users have to remember or keep track of, the greater the chances that they forget or lose them.

A good SSO solution is platform- and/or application-neutral: it can hide the authentication implementation details on different operating system platforms from the SSO user and can provide support to outsource the application-level authentication logic to a centralized SSO authentication authority.

An often-heard argument against SSO is that SSO credentials are the "key to the kingdom." If one obtains the SSO credentials, one obtains access to all resources secured by them. This risk may be reduced when choosing SSO credentials that are not knowledge-based (a classic example of knowledge-based credentials is the password) but rather biometrics-based (e.g., fingerprints) or possession-based (e.g., cryptographic tokens or smart cards). The use of multifactor authentication solutions for SSO will further reduce this risk.

9.2   Web versus Enterprise SSO

Many of today's SSO product classifications differentiate between Web and enterprise SSO solutions. In this chapter we will cover both SSO solution categories.

Web SSO solutions provide a Web-based single sign-on experience, meaning: a transparent logon experience for users who access applications using a Web interface and the HTTP protocol. When you want to join an application to a Web SSO infrastructure, your application must be Web-enabled. In many cases, this comes down to having a multitiered Web front-ended application architecture. This is not possible for all applications; simply think about the many legacy mainframe-based applications that are still in use today, which are using terminal emulation front-ends. Web SSO is the focus area of Web Access Management Systems (WAMS) and the emerging federation solution market. Both solutions were discussed briefly in Chapter 1. Federation, and how Microsoft addresses this space with Active Directory Federation Services (ADFS), will be discussed in more detail in Chapter 5 of *Advanced Microsoft Windows Security Services* (part 2 of this series).

Enterprise SSO solutions can provide a much broader SSO experience. Enterprise SSO solutions not only cover SSO to Web-enabled applications, but also to applications that use terminal emulator-based user front-ends, terminal service-based applications that are accessed from thin clients, and all kinds of other non-Web enabled applications (e.g., mainframe, legacy client-server applications, etc.). As Section 9.3.2 on "Complex SSO Architectures" will explain, enterprise SSO solutions are more difficult to set up and maintain. This is mainly due to the fact that they are dealing with SSO in much more heterogeneous environments than Web SSO solutions do.

9.3　SSO Architectures

9.3.1　Simple SSO Architectures

SSO is relatively easy to implement in authentication infrastructures that are using a single authentication authority. Such an environment is illustrated in Figure 9.1. In this environment, users have a single set of credentials. The concept of users must be interpreted in a large sense: it covers all security principals accessing the resources under the control of the authentication authority. Figure 9.1 shows a user and a resource server security principal trusting the same authentication authority. Linked to the authentication server is a credential database, which is the primary source for account and credential management.

Operating system vendors such as Novell and Microsoft have proven that SSO can easily be implemented in homogeneous LAN and intranet environments, where all machines are running the same operating system and trusting the same authentication authority. Web Access Management

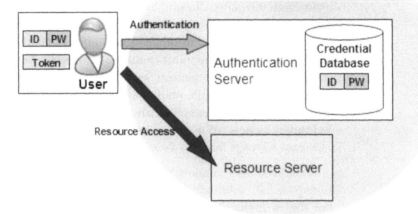

Figure 9.1   *SSO in an environment with a single authentication authority.*

System (WAMS) software vendors such as CA (Netegrity), RSA (Securant), HP (Baltimore Select Access), Entrust, and many others have proven the same thing for homogeneous Web portal environments.

Finally, remote-access authentication infrastructures using RADIUS, TACACS, or TACACS+ showed that setting up SSO is relatively straight-forward in environments using a centralized authority that communicates with a set of authentication proxies using a single well-defined authentication protocol. A nonexhaustive list of software products supporting simple SSO is given in Table 9.1.

Things get much more complex if the SSO scope is extended to cover different platforms and different organizations that are using different authentication credentials and protocols and are governed by many different authorities. Usually, this also means that the infrastructure has to deal with multiple credentials per user.

Having a single authentication authority doesn't necessarily mean that only one authentication server and a single credential database are available. For scalability, performance, and high availability reasons, a single authentication authority may consist of multiple authentication servers and a set of replicated credentials databases. Figure 9.2 illustrates SSO in an environment with a single Authentication Authority and multiple

Table 9.1   *Simple SSO Solutions (Nonexhaustive List)*

SSO Solutions Bundled with Operating System Software	SSO Bundled with Web Access Management System (WAMS) Software
Microsoft Windows NT, Windows 2000, Windows Server 2003, R2	CA eTrust SiteMinder (formerly Netegrity)
Novell Netware	RSA ClearTrust (formerly Securant)
SSO Using Centralized Network Access Security Software	HP OpenView Select Access (formerly Baltimore)
Cisco (TACACS, TACACS+ solutions)	Oracle CoreID Access and Identity (formerly Oblix Netpoint)
Microsoft (Internet Authentication Services [IAS] RADIUS solution)	IBM Tivoli Access Manager for e-business

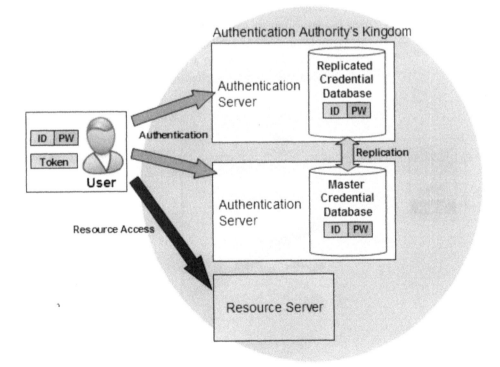

Figure 9.2   *SSO in an environment with a single authentication authority and multiple authentication servers.*

Authentication Servers. Note that the credential database is replicated to all authentication servers.

9.3.2 Complex SSO Architectures

A big challenge in today's authentication infrastructures is to extend the SSO scope to cover many different authentication authorities. "Different" in this context means implemented on different platforms and governed by different organizations. In most scenarios, these infrastructures also have to deal with multiple credentials per user and many different authentication protocols.

To ease the explanation of the different SSO architectures used in complex SSO setups, let us first look at how authentication works in an environment with multiple authentication authorities but without SSO support (as illustrated in Figure 9.3).

In the setup illustrated in Figure 9.3, the domain that the user uses most often is called the user's primary authentication domain. Domains that users use less often are called secondary authentication domains. Because in the example no SSO is available between the primary and the secondary authentication domains, when a user wants to access resources in the secondary domains, he has to authenticate to the trusted third parties (TTPs)

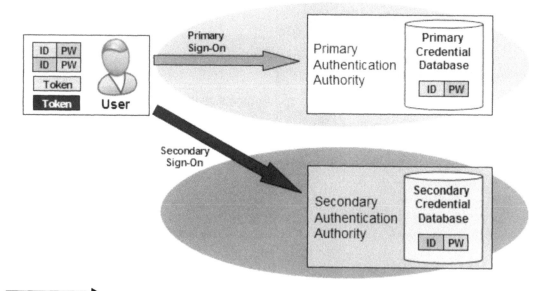

Figure 9.3   *Authentication in an environment with multiple authentication authorities.*

of those domains, using credentials as defined in that particular secondary authentication domain. Every secondary authentication domain also has its proper credential database. There is no need to explain that this setup creates an enormous credential-safeguarding burden for the end users when the number of secondary authentication domains increases. Note, too, that in this setup the user uses different authentication tokens, one for each authentication domain.

SSO Architectures Dealing with a Single Set of Credentials

The simplest complex SSO architectures are the ones that use a single set of credentials recognized by many different authentication authorities. In a pure Microsoft-based infrastructure with multiple forests and domains, this is typically achieved by implementing trust relationships between the domains or forests, as explained in Chapter 3. Obtaining the same result with heterogeneous authentication authorities is quite a bit more challenging. There are two important flavors of complex SSO architectures dealing with a single set of credentials: token-based and public key infrastructure (PKI)–based SSO systems.

Both SSO architectures provide SSO in a rather homogeneous environment. Homogeneous in this context means using a single account naming format and authentication protocol that are supported by each entity, application, and service participating in the SSO environment.

Token-Based SSO Systems

A classic example of an authentication protocol used for token-based SSO is the Kerberos authentication protocol. Kerberos is an open standard defined by the IETF that has been implemented on many different platforms.

In a token-based SSO architecture, users get a temporary software token when they have been successfully authenticated to the TTP (as illustrated in Figure 9.4). This token can be cached on the user's machine and reused to prove the user's identity to other secondary authentication domain TTPs. To validate the user token, the TTPs use cryptographic methods based on secret keys set up between the secondary authentication domain TTPs and the primary authentication domain TTP. This cryptographic key material represents a trust relationship between primary and secondary authentication domains.

Contrary to the tokens we will discuss in other SSO architectures, the tokens used in token-based SSO systems are valid for more than a single authentication authority. While it is true that in some token-based setups

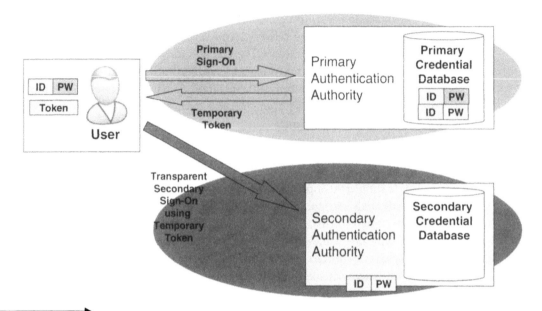

Figure 9.4   *Authentication in a token-based SSO environment.*

(for example, Kerberos) users do have more than a single token, in that case the authentication protocols support the automatic and transparent exchange of the token of one authentication authority for a token issued by another authentication authority.

When using a Kerberos token-based SSO solution, users authenticate to a central authentication service, called the Kerberos key distribution center (KDC) (the authentication TTP). If their authentication credentials are valid, they receive a ticket (the software token), which enables the user to request other tickets from the KDC in order to access other resources in the primary and secondary authentication domains. The tickets prove to the resource servers that the user has been authenticated before by a trusted authentication service—the Kerberos KDC.

Microsoft has implemented Kerberos as the default authentication protocol of Windows 2000 and later versions of its enterprise OS. CyberSafe sells plug-ins that can be used to enable an operating system platform to generate, understand, and validate Kerberos credentials (a process known as Kerberizing).

The Kerberos token-based SSO typically uses remote procedure calls (RPCs) to transport authentication tickets. In HTTP-based environments, token-based SSO can be provided using HTTP cookies. The latter mechanism is used by many Web Access Management Systems (WAMS),

Table 9.2   *Token-Based SSO Solutions (Nonexhaustive List)*

Kerberos Based
Microsoft Windows 2000, Windows Server 2003, R2
Cybersafe ActiveTrust
Cookie Based
CA eTrust SiteMinder
Oracle CoreID Access and Identity
RSA ClearTrust

such as CA's eTrust SiteMinder or Oracle's CoreID, when dealing with multiple authentication authorities. Microsoft uses a similar cookie-based token system to extend the SSO functionality of its Windows Live ID (previously known as Microsoft Passport) Web authentication solution across different Web sites.

Token-based SSO software comes out of the box with many of today's most popular operating system platforms (Windows Server 2003, Netware, and so forth). Table 9.2 gives some examples of software products providing token-based SSO support.

Public Key Infrastructure-Based SSO

In a public key infrastructure–based (PKI-based) SSO architecture (illustrated in Figure 9.5), users first register themselves at a trusted authentication authority—in this case called a certification authority (CA)—or at one of the authentication authority's registration agents, called registration authorities (RAs). During this registration process, different things occur: users identify themselves using a set of credentials; a piece of client-side software generates an asymmetric key pair; and the public key of this key pair is offered to the CA (or RA) for certification. Upon receipt of the user's credentials and the public key, the CA (or RA) will verify the user's credentials. If the credentials are valid, it will generate a public key certificate and send it back to the user. The user's public key certificate and the user's private key are cached on the user's machine (or on a smart card or cryptographic token). They both are used to generate a kind of software token similar to the ones used in token-based SSO systems. These tokens are used to prove the user's identity to other secondary authentication authorities in subsequent authentication requests.

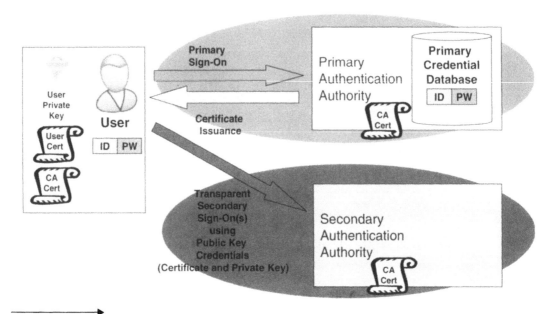

Figure 9.5   *Authentication in a PKI-based SSO environment.*

A major difference between a token-based and a PKI-based SSO architecture is that in the PKI case, the cryptographic methods used to validate the user token are asymmetric cryptography-based (using public and private keys). The outcome of this validation process also largely depends on the trust relationship between the secondary authentication authorities and the primary authentication authority. In the case of a PKI-based SSO architecture, the trust relationship between primary and secondary authentication authorities is represented by a secondary authentication authority's certificate (issued by the primary authentication authority). Similar to the tokens discussed in token-based SSO architectures, the tokens used in PKI-based SSO systems are valid for more than a single authentication authority.

Contrary to token-based SSO systems, PKI-based SSO systems are a relatively new technology. Early implementers of the technology experienced lots of interoperability problems. The latter were mainly related to immature PKI standards. Over the last few years, the security software industry and standardization organizations such as the IETF have made important efforts to make the PKI-based SSO systems enterprise-ready. Another early adopter problem was that few applications were PKI-enabled. Although the latter problem has not been fully resolved, most application software vendors have modified their application (for example, simply by Web-enabling them, which allows for SSL/TLS-based certificate authentication) to let

Table 9.3 *PKI-Based SSO Solutions (Nonexhaustive List)*

Inhouse PKI Products	External PKI Products
Entrust Authority PKI	Verisign
Microsoft PKI (Windows 2000, Windows Server 2003, R2)	Thawte

them understand PKI-based credentials. Table 9.3 gives some popular examples of PKI software solutions.

SSO Architectures Dealing with Different Sets of Credentials

There are three different flavors of SSO architectures that can deal with different sets of credentials: architectures that use credential synchronization, architectures using a secure client-side cache, and architectures using a secure server-side cache.

Contrary to token-based SSO, these three SSO architectures can provide SSO in a more heterogeneous environment. Besides different credential types, they can also support different account formats and multiple authentication protocols.

Credential Synchronization

Figure 9.6 shows an SSO architecture using a credential synchronization system. A classic example is a system that synchronizes user passwords between the credential databases of different authentication authorities. Although this architecture supports multiple credentials for every user, they are kept identical using the credential synchronization mechanism. Credential synchronization systems typically use a single master credential database, which can be used by administrators to update the user credentials.

Because in this setup the user is still prompted to enter his or her credentials by every single authentication authority, these systems are not considered true SSO systems.

Many security experts also consider it a very dangerous practice to synchronize credentials between the databases of different authentication authorities. Their objections are based on the "key to the kingdom" argument mentioned earlier. Another reason that credential synchronization solutions are considered less secure is the requirement to use the least common denominator with respect to, for example, password policies that the

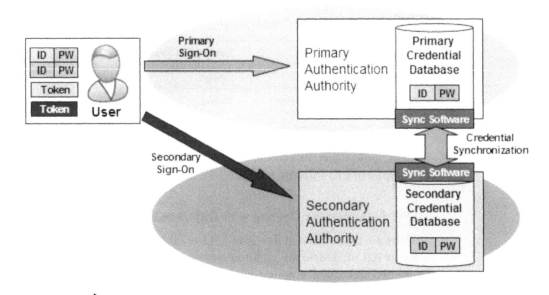

Figure 9.6   *Password synchronization-based SSO (logical).*

different systems support (length, complexity, …). Usually the same applies for the account names that are typically replicated as well.

The technology behind credential synchronization software is not as simple as Figure 9.6 may make you think. A key problem is the credential storage format in the credential databases of the different authentication providers. Credentials are typically stored in a hashed format, which means that it is impossible to derive the original password from the hash. Because most providers also use a different hash format, you cannot just synchronize the credentials between databases. That is why credential synchronization can only occur when the credentials are created or updated (e.g., when a user updates his or her password). This is illustrated in Figure 9.7.

Table 9.4 gives some examples of credential synchronization software products. The first category of products listed in Table 9.4 can be categorized as advanced enterprise password management products. Besides password synchronization, they also offer advanced self-service and delegated password management features. For example, these products allow users to reset their passwords using an intelligent Question and Answer (Q&A) system that users can start from a Web, Windows logon, or phone (voice) interface.

Password synchronization functionality is also included in provisioning and platform integration solutions. Examples of provisioning solutions

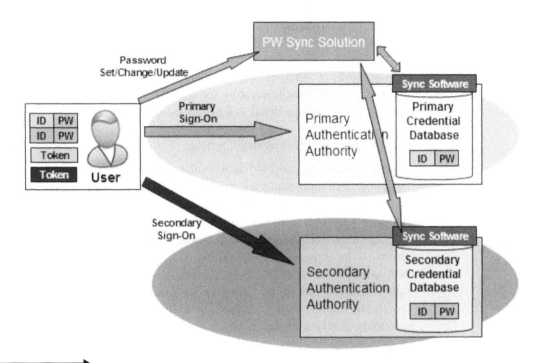

Figure 9.7   *Password synchronization-based SSO (physical).*

Table 9.4   *Credential Synchronization-Based SSO Products (Nonexhaustive List)*

Advanced Enterprise Password Management Solutions
Passgo InSync
Proginet SecurPass
Courion PasswordCourier
M-Tech P-Synch
Provisioning Solutions Offering Password Synchronization
HP OpenView Select Identity
Sun Java System Identity Manager
Microsoft Identity Integration Server
Platform Integration Solutions Offering Password Synchronization
Microsoft Services for Unix 3.5 (SFU) and Windows Server 2003 R2

offering password synchronization functionality are HP OpenView's Select Identity, Sun's Java System Identity Manager, and Microsoft's Identity Integration Server (MIIS). Finally, Microsoft Services for Unix 3.5 (SFU) and Windows Server 2003 R2 are examples of platform integration solutions offering password synchronization (SFU and R2 password synchronization were discussed in more detail in Chapter 8).

Secure Client-Side Credential Caching

Figure 9.8 illustrates an SSO architecture that is using a secure client-side credential caching mechanism. In this setup, a set of primary credentials is used to unlock a user's credential cache. Later, when the user wants to access resources requiring different authentication credentials, the other credentials are automatically retrieved from the local credential cache and presented to the authentication authority. If the credentials are valid, the user will be logged on transparently to the other resource servers. Because in this setup authentication to the secondary authentication domains relies on the credentials for the primary domain to unlock access to the credentials of secondary domains, the secondary domains must trust the primary domain.

In the early days of secure client-side credential caching, it was combined with client-side scripting to automate the SSO process. This created a lot of administrative overhead. Nowadays, credential caching is combined

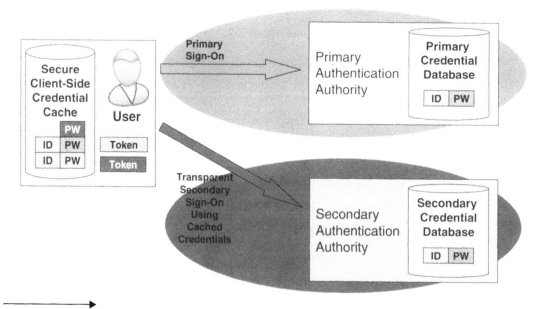

Figure 9.8   *Authentication in an SSO environment using a client-side secure cache.*

Table 9.5   *Secure Client-Side Cache SSO Products (Nonexhaustive List)*

Bundled with OS Software
Microsoft Windows XP, Windows Server 2003, R2 (Credential Manager)
Bundled with Other Software Products
Entrust Entelligence (PKI client)
Identix BioLogon (Client-side biometrics software using fingerprint identification)

with more intelligent and adaptive client-side software that can automatically retrieve and provide the correct credentials to the destination server. Table 9.5 gives some examples of secure client-side cache-based SSO software products.

In the context of this SSO architecture, secure storage of the cached credentials is absolutely vital. This is certainly the case if the cached credentials are used to give access to business-critical applications or data. In the latter case, it is not recommended to use this SSO architecture on portable client devices (such as laptops or PDAs) or on operating system platforms that are not sufficiently secure(d).

SSO based on a secure client-side cache can be implemented without the use of an integrated authentication infrastructure. In this case, the primary credentials unlocking the cache would be local credentials—"local" meaning defined in the local machine's security database and only valid for accessing local machine resources. In the context of an authentication infrastructure, the user's primary credentials are generally not local credentials but domain credentials.

Secure Server-Side Credential Caching

Figure 9.9 illustrates a secure server-side credential caching SSO architecture. Contrary to the use of a secure client-side cache, secure server-side credential caching SSO architectures store credentials in a central repository on a server. Contrary to a credential synchronization-based SSO architecture, the credentials used in a secure server-side credential caching SSO architecture are not necessarily the same for every authentication authority.

In a secure server-side credential caching SSO architecture, the master credential database contains (besides the user's primary credentials) the mappings between a user's primary and secondary credentials. That is why the primary authentication authority in this architecture is sometimes

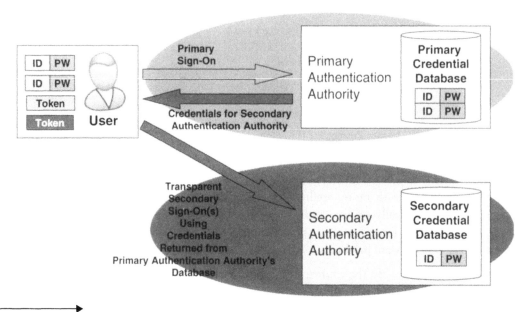

Figure 9.9   *Authentication in a secure server-side credential caching SSO environment.*

referred to as the authentication gateway. Another copy of the secondary credentials is kept in the secondary authentication domain databases.

In a secure server-side credential caching SSO setup, a user always first logs on to the primary authentication authority using his or her primary credentials and a predefined authentication protocol. If logon to the primary authentication authority is successful, the SSO software (depending on the product) either provides the user a list of available applications or transfers a secure wallet containing the user's secondary credentials to the user's workstation.

- In the latter case, the secure credential wallet is cached on the client for the duration of the logon session, and the specific application credentials are automatically retrieved on an as-needed basis.

- In the first case, the client-side SSO software will first communicate with the primary authentication authority to retrieve the appropriate user credentials. These are then forwarded to the user in a secure way.

- Finally, the user-side SSO software will use the secondary domain credentials to transparently log the user on to the secondary domains.

Server-side caching generally provides better security because the credentials are not permanently stored on the client side. The credentials may be temporarily downloaded to the client, but they will be deleted from the

Table 9.6 *Secure Server-Side Credential Caching SSO (Nonexhaustive List)*

IBM Tivoli Access Manager for Enterprise Single Sign-On
Computer Associates eTrust SSO Single Sign-On
Citrix Password Manager

client when the user logon session ends. Also, access to the server-side credential cache is only allowed after a successful logon to the central authentication authority.

An important challenge in these architectures is how to keep the copies of the credentials in the primary credential database and the ones in the secondary credential databases synchronized. Different products use different approaches to resolve this problem:

- Some products contain password synchronization services.

- Some products rely on the password synchronization services of specific software products (Passgo, Proginet, and so forth) or the password synchronization services built into the systems management software (BMC Patrol, CA Unicenter, IBM Tivoli).

- Some products do not use any password synchronization and rely on administrators or users (self-administration) to perform the credential updates.

Examples of secure server-side credential caching SSO systems are IBM's Tivoli Access Manager for Enterprise Single Sign-On and Computer Associates eTrust Single Sign-On (as listed in Table 9.6).

9.3.3 SSO Architectures: Summary

Table 9.7 gives an overview of the advantages and disadvantages of the different SSO architectures discussed in the previous sections.

Table 9.7 *Advantages and Disadvantages of Different SSO Architectures*

	Pros	Cons
Token-based	<ul><li>Single set of credentials simplifies life of user and administrator</li><li>Software usually comes bundled with OS software</li></ul>	<ul><li>Requires a homogeneous authentication infrastructure environment</li><li>Relies on symmetric cryptography</li></ul>

Table 9.7   *Advantages and Disadvantages of Different SSO Architectures (continued)*

	Pros	Cons
PKI based	■ Single set of credentials simplifies life of user and administrator ■ Software usually comes bundled with OS software (a good example is the Windows OS) ■ Relies on asymmetric cryptography	■ Can only deal with a single set of credentials ■ Complex certificate validation logic; requires a lot of processing on the client side ■ Requires a homogeneous authentication infrastructure environment (all services and applications must be PKI enabled)
Credential synchronization	■ Can deal with many different credentials ■ Does not require a homogeneous authentication infrastructure environment ■ Does not impact the client-side (no extra software needed)	■ Credentials are kept identical on different platforms ■ Does not provide true SSO ■ "Key to the kingdom" argument ■ Requirement to use the least common denominator with respect to credential policies that the different systems support (for example, password length, complexity, etc.) ■ Multiple sets of credentials complicate life of user and administrator ■ Requires extra software on server infrastructure side
Secure client-side credential caching	■ Can deal with many different credentials ■ Does not require a homogeneous authentication infrastructure environment ■ Has impact on client side (requires extra software or special OS version)	■ Requires a secure client-side credential cache—it is not recommended to use it from portable client devices or OSs that are less secure(d) ■ Multiple sets of credentials complicate life of user and administrator
Secure server-side credential caching	■ Can deal with many different credentials ■ Does not require a homogeneous authentication infrastructure environment ■ Has impact on client side (requires extra software)	■ Requires a credential synchronization mechanism (may be part of the SSO product) ■ Multiple sets of credentials complicate life of user and administrator ■ Requires extra software on server infrastructure side

9.4   Extending SSO

Big challenges for today's SSO products are to extend their scope to cover authentication authorities governed by different institutions and companies and to integrate them as an authentication provider with a wide range of applications. The following sections discuss possible approaches to overcome these challenges.

9.4.1 Extending SSO to Cover Different Organizations

One of the driving factors behind extending SSO to cover different organizations is companies' e-business requirement to easily authenticate users defined in other organizations and transaction requests initiated by business partners. The demand for SSO scope extension is very high in the world of Internet portals. SSO clearly benefits the Internet experience of any portal user from an ease-of-use point of view.

A major technology thread in today's efforts to provide Web SSO between different organizations is identity federation, which was introduced in Chapter 1. In a federated authentication infrastructure, foreign credentials have been validated by a foreign TTP and are also accepted by an organization's proper authentication authority. The reason they are accepted is because there is an agreement, trust, or federation between the foreign authentication authority and a company's proper authentication authority. This setup does not require a copy of the foreign organization's credential database. Also, in a federated setup users only have to take care of a single set of credentials.

As long as the SSO solution behind federated authentication infrastructures supports a mechanism to set up federation or trust relationships between different authentication infrastructures, it can use any of the architectures discussed earlier in this chapter.

PKIs use the concept of CA hierarchies, cross-certification, bridge CAs, or any other CA-to-CA interoperability solution to set up federations. Kerberos-based infrastructures support federations through cross-realm trust relationships. The following are some examples of commercial authentication infrastructure products and how they support trust or federation:

- Novell NDS eDirectory (version 8.5 and later) uses the concept of NDS tree federations.

- Microsoft Windows NT, 2000, and 2003 domains use interdomain trust relationships (see Chapter 3). In Windows 2000 and 2003, these trust relationships are built on Kerberos cross-realm authentication.

An important federation language is the Security Assertion Markup Language (SAML). SAML uses XML to encode authentication and authorization information. Because SAML leverages XML, it is platform-inde-

Table 9.8   *Federation Mechanism Comparison*

	Kerberos-Based Federation	PKI-Based Federation	SAML-Based Federation
Authentication technology	Kerberos	PKI	Any
Platform support	Many	Many	Many
Support for entity authentication	Yes	Yes	Yes
Support for data authentication	No	Yes	Yes
Authorization federation support	Yes, but not standardized	Yes, but very few products support it	Yes
Granularity of trust relationship and security policy support	Very monolithic, no policy support	Support for granular trust and security policies in some products	Supported
Status	Standardized	Standardized, though standardization is not complete	Emerging standards

pendent. SAML is authentication method–neutral: for example, it could be used to set up federations between PKI- and Kerberos-based authentication infrastructures. The development of SAML is driven by OASIS (the Organization for the Advancement of Structured Information Standards), a nonprofit international consortium that creates interoperable industry specifications based on public standards such as XML and SGML.

At the time of writing, the standardization efforts in the federation space were progressing in a very competitive way. Whereas Microsoft, IBM, and Verisign are pushing the Web services security standardization initiative (WS-Security) and the associated WS-Federation thread, most other major software vendors stick to the Liberty Alliance standards as the building blocks for a Web-based SSO infrastructure and federated Web services.

Table 9.8 compares Kerberos-, PKI-, and SAML-based authentication infrastructure federations.

9.4.2   **Extending SSO to Cover Different Applications**

Other important authentication infrastructure features that can help extend the SSO scope to cover different applications are the supported authentication application programming interfaces (APIs). Although this is not always

Table 9.9 *Authentication APIs*

Authentication API Name	Comments
Generic Security Service API (GSS-API)	Security services API providing authentication, confidentiality, and integrity services. Defined in RFC 2078.
Security Support Provider Interface (SSPI)	Microsoft's Authentication API; has been inspired by the GSS-API.
Pluggable Authentication Modules (PAMs)	Sun's pluggable authentication architecture; widely adopted by UNIX and Linux platforms (see also Chapter 8).
Java Authentication and Authorization Service (JAAS)	The Java Authentication and Authorization API. Includes a JAVA implementation of Sun's PAM. Obviously, the JAAS development is driven by SUN.
Common Data Security Architecture (CDSA)	Security services API for authentication, confidentiality and integrity services driven by the Open Group.
Novell Modular Authentication Service (NMAS)	Novell's pluggable authentication architecture.

an architect's primary concern, we found it useful to provide a list of popular authentication APIs. Any architect should at least know about them.

Table 9.9 lists a set of well known authentication APIs. APIs such as GSSAPI, JAAS, and CDSA provide vendor-neutral APIs—they also provide more than just authentication APIs. SSPI, PAM, and NMAS are driven by software vendors and only provide authentication services.

9.5 Microsoft SSO Technologies

Table 9.10 provides an overview of the specific SSO technologies currently provided by Microsoft. Some of them (as mentioned in Table 9.10) are covered in more detail in this book.

9.5.1 The Credential Manager

The requirement that Windows users re-enter the same credentials whenever they access resources on the same Internet or intranet server can be frustrating. Administrators often must cope with the same frustration when they have to switch to alternative credentials to perform administrative tasks.

The Windows XP Professional, Windows Server 2003, and R2 "Credential Manager" resolves these issues. Windows XP Home Edition only includes a limited version of Credential Manager: it can only cache Remote

Table 9.10   *Microsoft SSO Technologies*

SSO Technology	SSO Focus	Covered in:
Credential Manager	Enterprise and Web SSO	This chapter
Windows Live ID (previously known as Microsoft Passport)	Web SSO	Chapter 7
Windows Server 2003 R2 Active Directory Federation Services (ADFS)	Web SSO	Briefly covered in this chapter; covered in more detail in Ch. 5 of *Advanced Microsoft Windows Security Services* (Part 2 of this series)
Microsoft Host Integration Server (HIS) and Biztalk Enterprise SSO service	Enterprise SSO Extends Windows SSO to IBM RACF, Mainframe, PeopleSoft, SAP environments	This chapter
Microsoft SharePoint Portal Server 2003 Single Sign-On	Web SSO	This chapter
Microsoft Services for UNIX 3.5 and Windows Server 2003 R2	Enterprise SSO Extends Windows SSO to UNIX / Linux environments	Chapter 8
Microsoft Internet Authentication Service (IAS)	Network SSO	Briefly covered in this chapter

Access Services (RAS)/Virtual Private Networking (VPN) and Microsoft Passport credentials. The Credential Manager is a client-based SSO solution that uses an intelligent credential-caching mechanism.[2] Microsoft provides similar application-specific solutions, such as the Microsoft Internet Explorer's (IE's) credential-caching mechanism.

Architecture

Credential Manager consists of three components: the credential store, the key ring, and the credential collection component.

The Credential Manager keeps user credentials in a secure client-side credential store. Windows 2003 and XP use the Data Protection API (DPAPI) to secure access to the credential store content. Because the credential store is part of a user's profile, the store supports roaming. The store is unlocked using the user's primary credentials (these are also referred to as

---

2.   See "Secure Client-Side Credential Caching" on page 546 for a generic description of this SSO type.

the default credentials). When users log on locally to a machine or domain, they use their primary credentials.

The credential store contains credential-target maps.

1. A set of credentials can take one of three forms: a user ID and password, a user ID and a certificate/private key, or a set of Microsoft Passport credentials. Certificate/private key–based credentials can be stored on hard disk or on a smart card.

2. A target is the resource the user accesses. To specify a target, you can use a DNS name or NetBIOS name. A target name can contain wildcards. For example, entering *.hp.com as the target name makes the associated credentials available to all targets whose DNS name ends in hp.com. A target name is independent of the communication protocol used to access it—in other words, Credential Manager can deal with HTTP-, HTTPs-, FTP-, and SMB-based resource access.

Similar to a ring that holds the keys for your house, office, and car, the Credential Manager key ring holds sets of credentials for different targets (resources). The key ring component lets you manage the credential store's credential-target mappings and their properties. You view and modify the mappings and properties through the Stored User Names and Passwords dialog box, shown in Figure 9.10. The dialog box shows a list of all credential sets stored in the key ring. You can modify a credential set by selecting it and clicking the Properties button. This action brings up the Logon Information Properties dialog box, as illustrated in Figure 9.10 for the jdchome credential set.

How you access the Stored User Names and Passwords dialog box depends on the OS and the OS's user interface (UI):

■ **Windows Server 2003 and R2**—Open the Control Panel Stored User Names and Passwords applet.

■ **Windows XP's classic UI**—Open the Control Panel User Accounts applet. Click the Advanced tab, and then select the Manage Passwords option.

■ **Windows XP's user-friendly UI**—Open the Control Panel User Accounts applet and open the properties of the account with which you're currently logged on. In the Related Tasks list, select Manage my network passwords.

If you try to change a domain password that is stored in the Credential Manager store, the Credential Manager will first try to change it in the

Figure 9.10
Credential Manager key ring user interface.

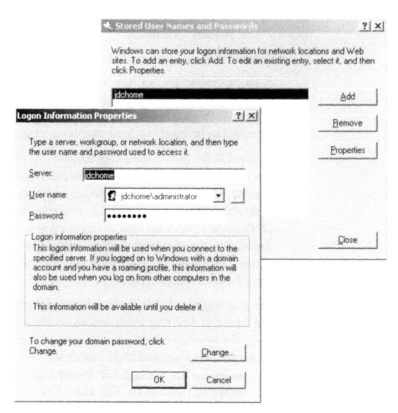

domain before actually writing the new domain password to the store. You cannot modify all the credentials from the key ring UI. For example, Passport credentials can only be modified from the Passport Web site.

When Credential Manager detects that it cannot use the primary credentials (or the credentials with which the user is currently logged on) to access a target, its credential collection component displays the Connect to dialog box, which Figure 9.11 shows. This dialog box prompts the user for alternative credentials. When the user selects the Remember my password check box, Credential Manager adds the credentials to the credential store. Then, the next time the user accesses the same target, Credential Manager automatically uses these credentials without prompting the user.

When a user uses RAS to remotely log on to a Windows domain, Credential Manager automatically adds a wildcard target for the user's logon domain (e.g., *.hp.net) and corresponding credentials to the credential store. Credential Manager uses these credentials as the user's primary credentials during the RAS logon session. This entry represents a permanent

Figure 9.11
Credential collection component.

credential cache addition—it remains in the cache after the RAS session has ended.

The Credential Manager included in Windows XP, Windows Server 2003, and R2 does not include a tool to easily export/import the credentials cached by Credential Manager from one machine to another. This will change in the next release of the Windows client OS: Windows Vista.

Operation

To explain how Credential Manager operates, we will use the example of a user named Bob who is working with his local account from his workstation, which is called bobws. Bob wants to access a share resource that's on a server called devserv. As Figure 9.12 shows, the following events occur:

1. Bob logs on as "bob", which is a local account defined on his bobws workstation.

2. Bob uses a Credential Manager-aware application (for example, Windows Explorer) or API to access a file share on a server named devserv. Bob accesses the share using the following universal naming convention (UNC) name: \\devserv\share.

3. The application asks the local security authority (LSA) to authenticate to \\devserv. The LSA calls on an authentication package (for example, the Kerberos authentication package). Authentication packages were explained in Chapter 5.

4. The authentication package queries Credential Manager for a set of credentials to use to access \\devserv. Credential Manager

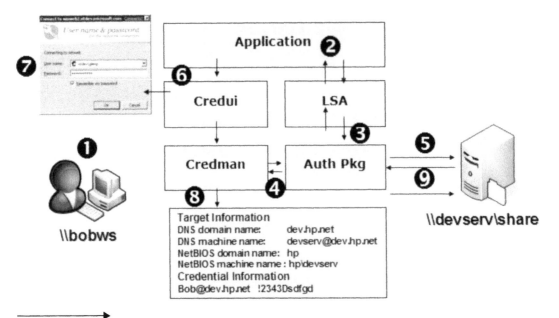

Figure 9.12 *Credential Manager operation.*

doesn't find a specific set of credentials, so it returns Bob's primary credentials (bob + password), which are the credentials with which Bob logged on.

5.   The authentication package tries to use Bob's primary credentials (bob + password) to authenticate to \\devserv\share, but fails.

6.   The LSA communicates this failure to the application, which calls on the credential collection component. This component brings up the Connect to dialog box.

7.   Bob enters appropriate credentials in the Connect to dialog box and selects the Remember my password check box to save the credentials.

8.   Credential Manager stores the credentials in the credential store.

9.   The application and authentication package use the new credentials to authenticate to \\devserv\share. This time the authentication succeeds.

Credential Manager provides a great deal of automation. However, it does not automate all credential-related management tasks. For example, suppose that the Credential Manager on your PC stores the credentials necessary to access a remote share on a file server. If the administrator for that

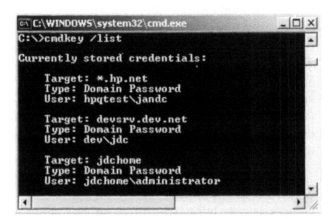

Figure 9.13
cmdkey operation.

file server changes the password to access the share, the password will not automatically be changed in your PC's Credential Manager cache, which might lead to an account lockout.

Administrators that do not want client-side credential storage on their Windows clients can disable Credential Manager with the "Network Access: Do not allow storage of credentials" or .NET Passports for network authentication group policy object (GPO) setting. You can find this setting in the Windows Settings\Security Settings\Local Policies\Security Options directory. When configuring this setting, the change will not take effect until you restart Windows. This setting can be used for both domain and standalone Windows Server 2003, R2, and Windows XP installations. In a domain environment, an administrator can use a GPO to enforce the setting. In a local setup, you would use the local security policy settings to configure it. When Credential Manager is disabled, the Stored User Names and Passwords dialog box will show up empty and with disabled push buttons, and the Credential Collection Component dialog box (illustrated in Figure 9.11) will lack the "Remember my password" checkbox.

Windows Server 2003 and R2 include the cmdkey tool, which lets you manage the credential store from the command line. You can use cmdkey to add, delete, and list credentials from the command line (as illustrated in Figure 9.13 for a list operation).

9.5.2 Biztalk Server and Host Integration Server Enterprise SSO

Microsoft BizTalk Server and Host Integration Server (HIS) include a service called Enterprise Single Sign-On (ENTSSO) that can provide SSO services. ENTSSO extends the Windows platform's built-in SSO functionality to cover other platforms (for example, Linux and UNIX), mainframe applications, and legacy enterprise applications such as employee relationship management software (for example, PeopleSoft and SAP). Architecturally, ENTSSO is an excellent example of a server-side credential caching-based SSO solution. The ENTSSO service is of great importance for enterprises with heterogeneous IT infrastructures that want to streamline and integrate the Windows-rooted portion of their IT infrastructure and applications with other legacy systems and applications.

Microsoft BizTalk Server 2006 (www.microsoft.com/biztalk) is the most recent version of Microsoft's enterprise applications integration (EAI) and business process integration server software. BizTalk Server 2006 helps enterprises integrate systems, employees, and partners through manageable business processes, enabling them to automate and orchestrate interactions in a highly flexible and highly automated manner.

Host Integration Server 2004 (HIS 2004; www.microsoft.com/hiserver) is the most recent version of Microsoft's mainframe gateway server software. Microsoft called earlier HIS versions SNA Server. HIS 2004 helps enterprises integrate their mission-critical host-based applications, data sources, messaging, and security systems within a Microsoft .NET Oriented Architecture, enabling the reuse of IBM mainframe and midrange data and applications across distributed environments.

ENTSSO is an optional component that can be selected during the Biztalk and HIS installation. The ENTSSO service shows up as the "Enterprise Single Sign-On Service" on machines that have ENTSSO installed.

Besides for server-side credential caching-based SSO, ENTSSO can also be used for bidirectional password synchronization between Windows and non-Windows environments. ENTSSO includes password synchronization interfaces and the password synchronization notification service (PCNS), a password synchronization Windows domain controller (DC) component.

ENTSSO is a not a universal SSO solution, like the products that were discussed in the intro section of this chapter. It specifically targets the facilitation of SSO in HIS and Biztalk application environments.

Microsoft Biztalk Server 2006 includes an updated version (version 2) of the ENTSSO service. The previous Biztalk version, Microsoft Biztalk Server 2004, and HIS 2004 both include version 1 of the ENTSSO service. In this section we will focus on version 2 of the ENTSSO service.

Architecture

The ENTSSO architecture, shown in Figure 9.14, is built on a service that maps a user's Windows account to one or more non-Windows accounts and their corresponding credentials. These credentials are needed for providing an SSO experience when Biztalk- or HIS-rooted applications access mainframe- or other non-Windows–rooted applications or platforms (called affiliate applications) that require non-Windows credentials.

The ENTSSO credential mappings are securely stored in a Microsoft SQL Server database—the default name of the ESSO database is SSODB. You can use the ssomanage.exe (on the server side) or ssoclient.exe (on the client side) command-line administration utilities, or the ENTSSO client-side GUI configuration utility (illustrated in Figure 9.17), to configure ENTSSO credential mappings.

As Figure 9.14 shows, ENTSSO credential-mapping lookups can be triggered by either BizTalk application adapters or HIS data providers. The first scenario is linked to a Windows-initiated SSO sequence. The second

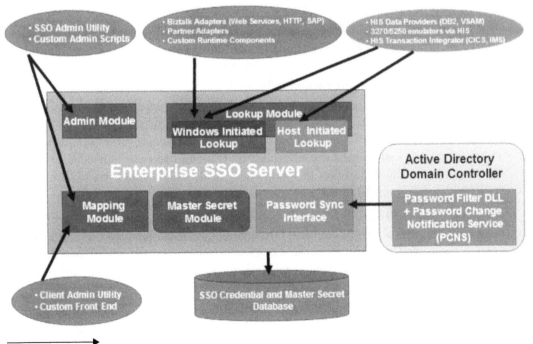

Figure 9.14   *ENTSSO architectural overview.*

scenario can be linked to either a Windows- or host-initiated SSO sequence.

- **Windows-initiated SSO** means that users who log on to a Windows environment can use SSO when they access non-Windows resources.

- **Host-initiated SSO** means that users who log on to a non-Windows environment (e.g., a mainframe application) can use SSO when they access Windows resources.

ENTSSO supports four account-mapping mechanisms:

- **A Windows individual mapping** defines a one-to-one relationship between Windows and non-Windows accounts. A user or administrator can manage this mapping.

- **A Windows group mapping** defines a many-to-one relationship between Windows and non-Windows accounts. All Windows users use the same non-Windows account to access the backend system. Only administrators can manage this mapping. Note that this option makes it impossible to trace individual Windows users' access on the target systems (since all Windows users use the same account).

- **A host individual mapping** is an HIS-specific mapping that is available only for host-initiated SSO and defines a one-to-one relationship between non-Windows and Windows accounts. A user or administrator can manage this mapping.

- **A host group mapping** is an HIS-specific mapping that is available only for host-initiated SSO and defines a many-to-one relationship between non-Windows and Windows accounts. Only administrators can manage this mapping. This option makes it impossible to trace individual non-Windows users' access on the target systems (since all non-Windows users use the same account).

To securely store the credentials in the SQL Server database, ENTSSO uses a 128-bit symmetric encryption key called the master secret to encrypt and decrypt passwords. The master secret is securely stored on a dedicated master secret server, which is a special ENTSSO server that multiple ENTSSO servers can share.

The ENTSSO service installation program creates the SSODB database in the SQL Server database. Among the 11 ENTSSO-specific tables the SSODB database holds are the following:

- The **SSOX_IndividualMapping** table stores the Windows domain name, Windows account name, external application name, and external account name.

- The **SSOX_ExternalCredentials** table stores the external application name, external account name, and encrypted external credentials. These credentials are encrypted using the master key.

In version 1 of the ENTSSO service, you must perform all ENTSSO administration and configuration tasks from the command line, as Figure 9.15 shows, because Microsoft doesn't include an administration GUI. In ENTSSO version 2 (the version that comes with Biztalk 2006), Microsoft included (in addition the ssomanage.exe and ssoclient.exe command line utilities) a client- and server-side GUI-based ENTSSO configuration utility, illustrated in Figures 9.16 and 9.17.

A typical ENTSSO setup consists of multiple ENTSSO servers (one for each application server that hosts a BizTalk adapter or HIS data provider), one ENTSSO master secret server, and one SQL Server machine that hosts the ENTSSO database. Every time an ENTSSO server decrypts or encrypts SSO data from the ENTSSO database, the server retrieves the master secret from the master secret server via secure remote procedure call (RPC). For fault tolerance reasons, you can cluster the SQL Server machine and the ENTSSO master secret server.

The ENTSSO server and client software is included in BizTalk 2004 (version 1), Biztalk 2006 (version 2), and HIS 2004 (version 1). You can install and configure the ENTSSO server as part of the BizTalk installation program or the HIS installation program. (Figure 9.18 shows the configuration for BizTalk 2006.) To install the client-side software, you can use the

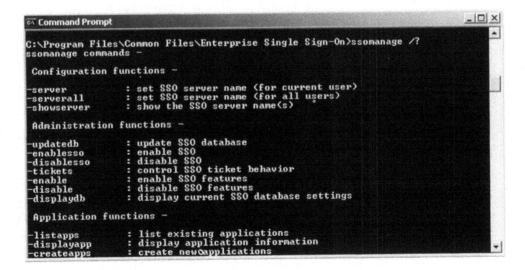

Figure 9.15 *ENTSSO command line administration.*

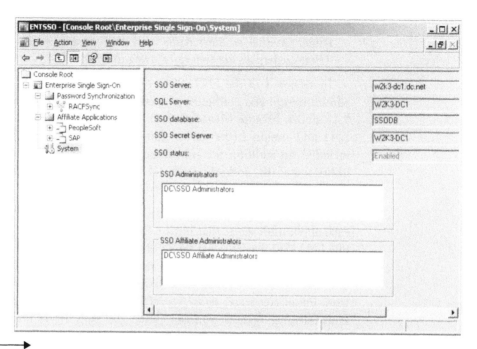

Figure 9.16   *ENTSSO server-side GUI administration.*

ssoclientinstall.exe program for BizTalk or the ssoclient.msi program for HIS 2004.

Both BizTalk and HIS have a long list of preinstallation requirements. You can find the detailed installation requirements at the following URLs:

- Biztalk 2004:
  www.microsoft.com/BizTalk/evaluation/sysreqs/default_2004.asp.

- Biztalk 2006:
  www.microsoft.com/biztalk/evaluation/sysreqs/default.mspx.

- HIS 2004:
  www.microsoft.com/hiserver/evaluation/sysreqs/default_2004.asp.

Operation

In the following sections, we will illustrate two ENTSSO use cases: a Windows-initiated SSO sequence and a host-initiated SSO sequence. The first use case uses BizTalk 2006 ENTSSO, and the second example uses HIS 2003 ENTSSO. After that, we will also explain how a user's SSO experience can be enhanced using password synchronization.

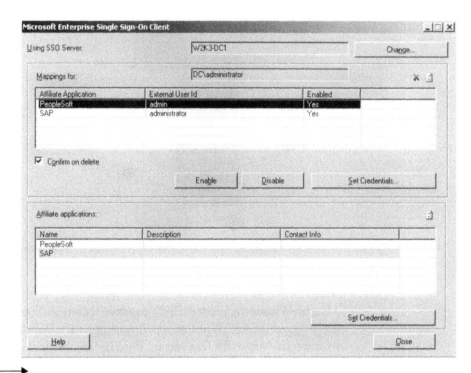

Figure 9.17 *ENTSSO client-side GUI administration.*

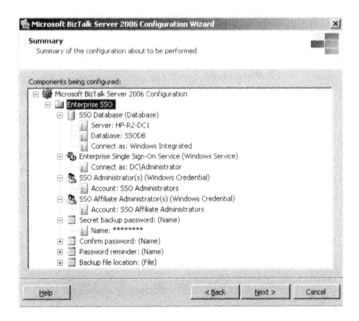

Figure 9.18 *Biztalk installation program and ENTSSO options.*

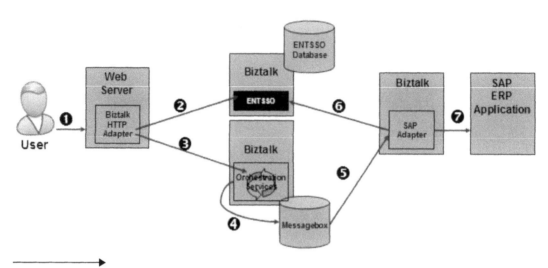

Figure 9.19   *Windows-initiated SSO using ENTSSO.*

In the Windows-initiated SSO sequence shown in Figure 9.19, a user who is logged on to a Windows environment uses a Web front-end server that interacts with a BizTalk server. The BizTalk server then accesses SAP data that are hosted by an SAP ERP application. In this example, the following messages are exchanged between the user, the Web front-end server, the Biztalk server, and the SAP server:

1.   The user accesses the Web application, which includes code that uses a BizTalk HTTP adapter to drop a data request into the Biz-Talk MessageBox. The MessageBox is a key part of BizTalk Orchestration Services, an advanced application messaging and workflow solution.

2.   The BizTalk HTTP adapter impersonates the user and requests an ENTSSO ticket to the ENTSSO server. Tickets are an ENTSSO concept (not to be confused with Kerberos or other tickets) that lets BizTalk components exchange user identities and request user credentials from the ENTSSO server. The BizTalk HTTP adapter on the Web server drops the data request and the ENTSSO ticket into the BizTalk MessageBox.

3.   While the request is in the MessageBox, BizTalk orchestration services transform the request into an SAP data request.

4.   The BizTalk SAP adapter, a specialized BizTalk adapter that understands the SAP messaging protocols, retrieves the SAP data request and the ENTSSO ticket from the BizTalk MessageBox.

5.   The BizTalk SAP adapter uses the ENTSSO ticket to request the user's SAP credentials from ENTSSO. These credentials are encrypted; to decrypt them, the ENTSSO service must first talk to the ENTSSO master secret server.

6.   The BizTalk SAP adapter uses the user's SAP credentials to access the SAP ERP application.

In the host-initiated SSO sequence that Figure 9.20 shows, a user who is logged on to a mainframe uses a mainframe application that interacts with a Windows-rooted SQL Server database. In this example, the user, mainframe, mainframe application, SQL Server, and HIS server exchange the following messages:

1.   The user logs on to the mainframe and uses the mainframe application.

2.   To access the SQL Server database, the mainframe application calls on the HIS Transaction Integrator.

3.   The HIS Transaction Integrator calls on ENTSSO to obtain the user's Windows account name.

4.   ENTSSO calls on a Windows domain controller (DC) to obtain a Windows access token for the user via the Kerberos delegation and protocol transition feature that Microsoft introduced in Windows

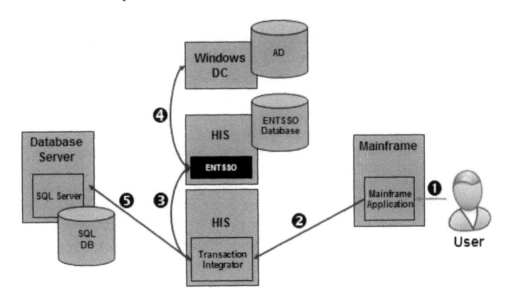

Figure 9.20   *Host-initiated SSO using ENTSSO.*

Server 2003. The ENTSSO service forwards the access token to the HIS Transaction Integrator.

5.   The HIS Transaction Integrator uses Integrated Windows authentication and the user's access token to access the SQL Server database on the user's behalf.

Password synchronization is a valuable feature that can enrich users' SSO experiences in a BizTalk or HIS ENTSSO environment. It ensures that user passwords on different platforms are in sync by automating the distribution of user- or administrator-initiated password updates. In environments where no automatic password synchronization is in place, it is also possible to use the same password on every platform, but then administrators or users would need to update the ENTSSO and non-Windows credential databases manually when a password is changed in AD—or the other way around when a password is changed in a non-Windows credential database. To avoid inconsistencies caused by users updating the passwords on a single system, administrators often choose to configure password policies with long-lasting or nonexpiring passwords, which is less than ideal from a security perspective. It also means administrators must be trusted to update all credential databases that are used in the context of the ENTSSO system. Additionally, updates must be reflected in the databases as soon as possible—which may put some time stress on the administrator performing the updates.

ENTSSO can work without password synchronization and with different user passwords on the different platforms. This again requires disciplined users and administrators; each time a user's non-Windows password is updated he or she must make sure this change is reflected in the ENTSSO database in a timely fashion.

Remember from the introduction of this chapter that security-minded people often argue against password synchronization because of the "key to the kingdom" problem: If the passwords on all platforms are identical, breaking the password on one platform gives an attacker access to all the other platforms. Synchronizing passwords also means that you need the same password policies on all platforms, which might also represent a compromise of security if one platform supports stronger password policies than the other platform does.

Password Synchronization

ENTSSO does not include all the building blocks necessary for bidirectional password synchronization between Windows and non-Windows environments. ENTSSO includes a set of password-synchronization interfaces and comes with the Password Change Notification Service (PCNS). Additional password-synchronization software is available from Proginet (http://eps.proginet.com), which supplies a range of ENTSSO password-synchronization software called Enterprise SSO Password Synchronization (ePS). So far, Proginet is the only password-synchronization software vendor to provide an adapter—the ePS Controller, which uses the ENTSSO password synchronization interfaces. For bidirectional password synchronization to work, non-Windows platforms require other Proginet ePS adapters. Proginet offers ENTSSO password-synchronization adapters for IBM's z/OS (includes adapters for IBM Resource Access Control Facility—RACF and Computer Associates' eTrust CA-ACF2 Security and eTrust CA-Top Secret Security), OS/400 (includes an adapter for IBM AS/400), IBM AIX, HP-UX, Sun Microsystems Solaris, and Linux. Figure 9.21 illustrates the ENTSSO password synchronization building blocks and flow.

PCNS is an add-on for Windows domain controllers (DCs) that you can use to notify other servers of AD password updates. Possible PCNS targets are ENTSSO servers or Microsoft Identity Integration Servers (MIIS). PCNS is also included in MIIS Service Pack 1 (SP1) and the Identity Inte-

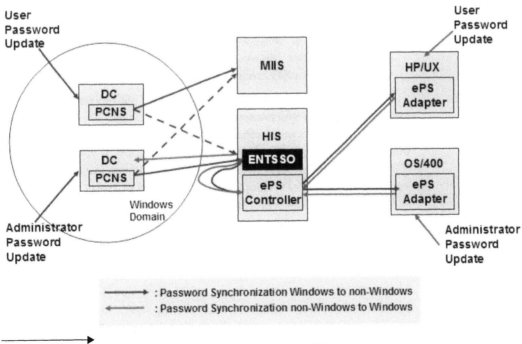

Figure 9.21 *Password synchronization components and flow.*

gration Feature Pack (IIFP). You can configure one PCNS service to serve multiple targets, but you must install PCNS on every domain controller (DC) in a Windows domain.

PCNS consists of three pieces of software:

- **A password filter dynamic link library (dll)** that obtains a cleartext copy of the updated or newly created password from a domain controller's Local Security Authority (LSA—lsass.exe)

- **The PCNS service** that receives the password-change notifications from the local password filter, queues them, and sends them to the target system

- **The PCNS configuration utility** that can update the PCNS configuration data stored in AD

You can configure ENTSSO password synchronization three ways:

- **Windows to non-Windows full synchronization**, which captures the AD password changes and synchronizes both the non-Windows and the ENTSSO credential databases

- **Non-Windows to Windows partial synchronization**, which captures the non-Windows password changes and synchronizes only the ENTSSO credential database

- **Non-Windows to Windows full synchronization**, which captures the non-Windows password changes and synchronizes both the ENTSSO and the AD credential databases

You must install the ePS Controller on an ENTSSO server. If you need to configure password synchronization between multiple Windows domains and a non-Windows environment, you have to deploy ENTSSO/ePS Controller servers in every Windows domain. In addition, if you have multiple ENTSSO servers that serve the same domain, you must install ePS Controllers on every server. ePS Controller uses a system of replay files to provide fault tolerance for connection failures. The ePS Controller can also be clustered and includes intelligence to protect against password-update loops.

9.5.3 SharePoint Portal Server SSO

Microsoft SharePoint Portal Server 2003 (SPS 2003), Microsoft's Web portal, collaboration, and information-sharing server, includes a SSO service. The SPS 2003 SSO service allows SharePoint-based Web applications to transparently retrieve information from back-end applications, even if these applications require special credentials—"special" meaning different from the credentials users use to authenticate to the SharePoint portal. This SSO functionality can be useful for integrating the data from back-end applications like SAP, PeopleSoft, Siebel, etc. into a single SharePoint Web portal.

The SPS 2003 SSO service logic is available on all SPS 2003 installations; no special options are required during the SPS installation. Enabling the SSO service does require special configuration steps after installation. The SPS SSO service shows up as the "Microsoft Single Sign-on Service" on machines that have SPS installed.

Architecture

Like the BizTalk and HIS ENTSSO service, SPS 2003 SSO is a secure server-side credential caching–based SSO service that stores the credential mappings in a SQL Server database. The SPS SSO credentials are stored in an encrypted format in the SQL server database.

SPS SSO includes fewer SSO features than Biztalk and HIS ENTSSO: SPS SSO does not support user password updates or password synchronization. SPS SSO only caches user credentials for use by the SPS Web logic (or Web parts as this logic is referred to in SPS documentation). Also, to let the Web logic leverage the credentials cached by the SPS SSO service and to let it automatically authenticate to and retrieve data from the back-end applications, custom coding is required.

SPS 2003 SSO can deal with one-to-one and many-to-one mappings between the SharePoint credentials and the credentials that are used for access to back-end applications. In the first case, back-end credentials are stored for each individual portal user; in the latter case, different portal users (a group of users) use the same credential set for accessing the back-end application.

The main administration interface for configuring SharePoint Portal Server's SSO service is SharePoint's Web administration interface, which is illustrated in Figure 9.22.

More information on SPS 2003 SSO is also available from www.microsoft.com/technet/prodtechnol/sppt/reskit/c2661881x.mspx.

Operation

Figure 9.23 illustrates a typical SharePoint SSO message exchange:

1. A user accesses a Web portal that can be used to query data maintained by a back-end application. This is the first time the user

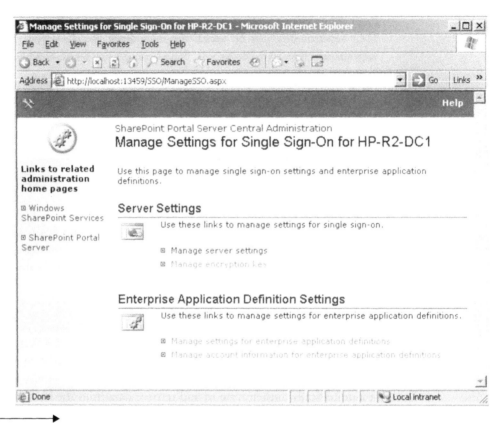

Figure 9.22   *SharePoint SSO administration interface.*

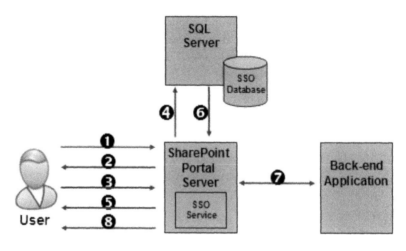

Figure 9.23   *SharePoint SSO flow.*

visits the portal. The Web portal's logic checks whether the user credentials required for the back-end application are stored in the SharePoint Portal Server SSO database. If the SSO database has a copy of the credentials, the process continues from step 6 in this list.

2. If there are no user credentials for the back-end application in the SSO database, the user's browser is redirected to the logon page for the back-end application.

3. The user supplies a set of credentials for the back-end application.

4. The user credentials are mapped to the user's Windows account and stored in the SSO database.

5. The user's browser is redirected to the original Web portal.

6. The Web portal retrieves the credentials from the SSO database.

7. The Web portal submits the credentials to the back-end application and retrieves the data.

8. The data are displayed to the user on the Web portal.

9.5.4 Active Directory Federation Services

Identity Federation, or federated identity management, is surely one of the trendiest topics in the IT industry; federation was introduced in Chapter 1 of this book. Identity federation is also a concept that software giant Microsoft could not leave untouched. In Windows Server 2003 R2, Microsoft includes an identity federation solution called Active Directory Federation Services (ADFS). The development codename Microsoft used for ADFS was "TrustBridge." In the Windows Server 2003 R2 release, ADFS is, in the first place, a Web SSO solution allowing enterprises to extend the reach of their AD and Web-based applications to other organizations.

Windows 2003 users looking for a Web SSO solution must have a look at ADFS. ADFS does not come with some of the advanced features of pure-play Web SSO solutions, such as CA's eTrust SiteMinder or HP's Open-View Select Access. It may also require more development and integration time on the Web application side, but it comes for free with the OS platform and integrates well with Microsoft's IIS Web server and SharePoint Portal Server.

Interoperability is key to making ADFS successful. That is why Microsoft is leading important efforts to extend the reach of ADFS. Several software vendors have already jumped on the ADFS bandwagon and brought out or promised to bring out ADFS-compliant solutions that extend the reach of ADFS to non-Microsoft-centric environments. Good examples are the solutions from Centrify and Quest Software, which can be used to extend ADFS Web SSO to non-IIS–based Web servers, such as Apache Tomcat and IBM WebSphere. Also, at the TechED 2005 conference Microsoft illustrated ADFS interoperability with identity management products from IBM, Netegrity, Oblix, OpenNetwork, Ping Identity, and RSA.

In this section, we will briefly introduce the ADFS architecture and operation. In Chapter 5 of *Advanced Microsoft Windows Security Services* (Part 2 of this series), we will provide more details on the different ADFS components and how to set them up. Another good start for learning more about ADFS is Microsoft's ADFS overview white paper, which you can download from http://www.microsoft.com/windowsserver2003/r2/identity_management/adfswhitepaper.mspx.

Architecture

ADFS leverages other Microsoft identity management building blocks like AD and ADAM and integrates tightly with Microsoft's application server, Internet Information Services (IIS). The core components in an ADFS deployment, such as the one illustrated in Figure 9.24, are the Federation Services (FS), ADFS Web Agents, and Active Directory (AD) or AD Application Mode (ADAM) repositories.

In Figure 9.24, the ADFS infrastructure enables a user Web SSO experience between different organizations. The browser users from one organization (the identity provider) can access a Web application that is located in another organization (the resource provider) while leveraging their AD account as it is defined by their proper identity provider. The Web application on the resource provider side runs on an IIS application server.

ADFS provides X.509 certificate-based tools to establish trust relationships between the identity provider and resource provider and to securely exchange data between them. ADFS trust relationships are one way. In our example in Figure 9.24, the resource provider trusts the identity provider.

The most important component of an ADFS setup is the Federation Service (FS). There is one FS at each organization participating in the federation.

- The FS on the identity provider side uses AD or ADAM to authenticate users and to populate ADFS security tokens. If user authentication is successful, the identity provider FS generates authentication cookies and security tokens. These security tokens contain claims, or statements about a user. Typical claim examples are a user's name, group memberships, e-mail address, etc. The identity provider FS signs the security tokens to protect them from tampering.

- The FS on the resource provider side verifies the authentication cookies and security tokens it receives from users that attempt to access its resources. It also translates them to a format that can be understood by its resources and forwards them to the resources.

How authentication cookies and security tokens are exchanged between the identity and resource provider FS is explained in the next section.

ADFS Web Agents enable IIS-hosted Web applications to participate in an ADFS federation. They know how to interact with the ADFS and how to deal with the ADFS authentication cookies and security tokens.

On the Web application side, application code changes may be required to ADFS-enable the application. ADFS-enabling basically means that you must enable the application to consume the claims in the ADFS security tokens and use them for user authorization decisions. Different integration

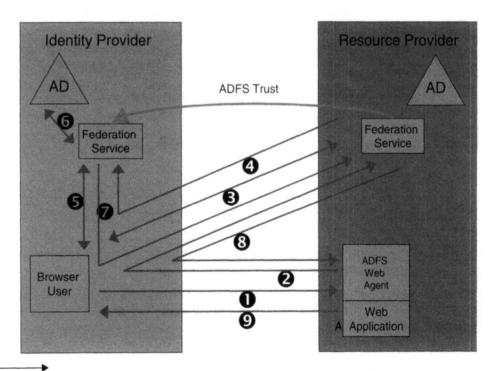

Figure 9.24 *ADFS components and operation.*

mechanisms can be used here: you can use the Authorization Manager (AzMan) authorization engine or one of the ASP.NET APIs (IsInRole or raw claims). For an introduction to AzMan, see Chapter 10 of this book. An application ADFS can integrate without making application coding changes is Microsoft's SharePoint Portal Server.

Operation

Figure 9.24 also shows a simple ADFS operation example—it illustrates the ADFS messages exchanged between the key ADFS entities. Remember that in this example ADFS enables Web SSO for a browser user defined at the identity provider while he accesses a Web application located at a resource provider. The following ADFS-related messages will be exchanged:

- Step 1: A browser user defined at the identity provider attempts to access a Web server application hosted at the resource provider.

- Step 2: The ADFS Web service agent detects the user has not been authenticated by ADFS and refers him to the resource provider's FS.

- Step 3: During this step, known as home realm discovery, the browser user provides his home domain information to the resource provider's FS. The home domain is the place where the user's identity is defined and maintained—in other words, the user's identity provider. Knowledge of the user's home domain enables the resource provider's FS to redirect the user to the correct identity provider FS for authentication. The first time, the user provides information such as the name of his/her identity provider or his/her e-mail address to tell the resource provider FS the identity provider he/she belongs to. In subsequent requests the resource provider's FS will find this information in a cookie that is forwarded by the user.

- Step 4: Based on the information provided during home realm discovery, the resource provider FS redirects the browser user to the user's identity provider FS.

- Step 5: The browser user authenticates to his/her identity provider FS using his/her AD account and associated credentials.

- Step 6: The identity provider FS validates the user credentials against AD. If authentication is successful, the identity provider federation server generates an authentication cookie and ADFS security token.

- Step 7: The identity provider FS redirects the browser user together with the security token and authentication cookie to the resource provider federation server.

- Step 8: The resource provider FS transforms the claims in the security token into a set of claims that can be understood by the Web application hosted at the resource provider and embeds them in a new security token. This process is known as claim transformation. The FS also generates a new authentication cookie and then redirects the browser user (together with the new security token and authentication cookie) to the Web application's ADFS Web Agent. The ADFS Web Agent then validates the authentication cookie and extracts the claims from the security token and passes them to the Web application.

- Step 9: The Web application interprets the claims for authorization purposes and returns the appropriate Web content to the browser user.

9.5.5   Internet Authentication Service

The Internet Authentication Service (IAS) is Microsoft's implementation of a Remote Authentication Dial-in User Service (RADIUS) server and proxy.[3] RADIUS is an IETF standard defined in RFCs 2865 and 2866. The IAS software comes with all Windows Server 2003 versions, with the exception of the Web server edition. The RADIUS proxy function is new to Windows Server 2003. It allows the forwarding of RADIUS requests to other IAS or RADIUS servers.

In a Windows environment, IAS is often used in conjunction with Microsoft's Routing and Remote Access Server (RRAS) to provide access control functions to dial-up users.

The meaning of the word RADIUS is confusing because it does not reveal the full capabilities of a RADIUS server:

- A RADIUS server not only deals with the authentication, but it also provides authorization and accounting services. As such, RADIUS is a good example of a triple-A service.

- A RADIUS server not only serves dial-in (remote access) users, but it can also handle the access control requests of wireless users and users connecting over a virtual private network (VPN) connection. This is illustrated in Figure 9.25.

The main reason IAS is discussed in this chapter is because it can provide an integrated SSO solution for Windows domain and network

---

3.   In the Longhorn Windows Server release IAS and its RADIUS functionality will be integrated in the Network Access Protection (NAP) Network Policy Server (NPS).

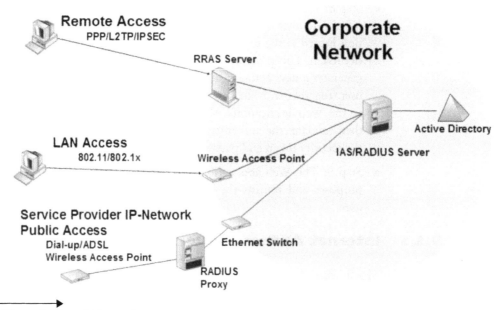

Figure 9.25   *IAS scenarios.*

access—independently of whether the user connects over a dial-up, wireless, or VPN connection. IAS can provide this functionality because it can
be integrated with Active Directory. This integration basically means that
IAS uses the AD credential database to authenticate users.

IAS SSO also works across multiple Windows domains that are in the
same or in different forests:

- To make SSO work across different domains, add the IAS and RRAS
  (used for remote access) servers to the built-in RAS and IAS Servers
  group in every domain of the forest.

- To make SSO work across different forests, use an IAS RADIUS
  proxy in every forest that is pointing to a central RADIUS server.

Table 9.11   *IAS Authentication Methods*

Authentication Method	Meaning
Password Authentication Protocol (PAP)	A very trivial authentication protocol for dial-up users. Transmits user password in the clear.
Shiva PAP (SPAP)	Special version of PAP developed by Shiva. Transmits user password in a reversibly encrypted format.

Table 9.11 *IAS Authentication Methods (continued)*

Authentication Method	Meaning
Challenge Handshake Authentication Protocol (CHAP)	Challenge-response–based authentication protocol.
Microsoft CHAP (MS-CHAP)	Microsoft proprietary version of the CHAP protocol.
Microsoft CHAP v2 (MS-CHAP v2)	Enhanced version of MS CHAP. Supports mutual authentication and other security enhancements.
Extensible Authentication Protocol (EAP)	Not an authentication protocol but a negotiation protocol to determine the authentication method to be used between a client and a server. Allows for the use of smart cards, tokens, and certificates as authentication mechanisms. Windows Server 2003 supports the MD5-CHAP and certificate/smart card EAP authentication packages.
Protected Extensible Authentication Protocol (PEAP)	Negotiation protocol based on EAP that uses TLS to provide a secure communication channel. Only used for authentication of wireless 802.11 clients.

IAS supports different authentication methods, which are listed in Table 9.11.

9.6   Conclusion

This chapter illustrated the complexity behind setting up an SSO infrastructure. As for any security solution, it is recommended to keep an SSO solution simple and to build it on open standards.

- For many organizations it may be more realistic and feasible to plan for a reduced sign-on solution instead of a universal SSO solution.

- Also, open standards (like the Kerberos and PKI SSO mechanisms) provide better security quality and more flexible interoperability options. If you choose a vendor-specific SSO solution (like the password synchronization and client-side and server-side credential caching mechanisms), you make your IT infrastructure very dependent on a single software vendor.

A critical new concept in the Web SSO space is federation. Federation solutions may revolutionize the use of SSO in Web authentication infrastructures.

Part VI

Authorization

Windows Server 2003 Authorization

Once an entity has been authenticated, we need some way to restrict its access to the resources available on a computer or in a domain. In most environments, not just anyone can access every computer or domain resource. This is the goal of an authorization service: it protects against unauthorized use and provides an answer to the questions "What can an entity do with a resource?" and "How can an entity interact with the resource?"

10.1 Authorization Basics

Authorization always deals with two entities (illustrated in Figure 10.1): a subject and an object, which the subject wants to access. In Active Directory, a subject can be a security principal such as a user, computer or an application. The object can be file resources hosted on a file server, eMails on a mailbox server, Active Directory objects on a Domain Controller or any other type of object accessible in an IT infrastructure. Authorization between the subject and the object is typically executed and enforced by a third entity that is generally referred to as the reference monitor. In a Windows environment, this third entity is known as the Security Reference Monitor (SRM). The

Figure 10.1
Generic access control model.

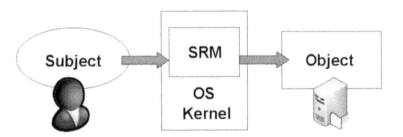

SRM runs in the highly privileged OS kernel mode. It checks all access to resources as requested by code that is running in user mode.

Authorization not only deals with access to visible Windows objects, such as files, printers, registry keys, and AD objects; it also deals with access to less visible objects, such as system processes and threads. Authorization also controls the ability to perform system-related tasks, such as changing the system time or shutting down the system. Microsoft calls these system-related tasks user rights.

10.2   The Windows Authorization Model

The authorization model in Windows Server 2003, SP1, R2, and even SP2 is basically the same as the one that was used in Windows 2000 and NT4. It includes quite a few new features, but is still based on the following key concepts: access token, access mask, security descriptor, and impersonation.

Figure 10.2 brings the different Windows authorization concepts together. It shows how, upon every object access, the security reference monitor (SRM) checks the access token and the access mask against an object's security descriptor. The access token and access mask are both linked to a process that impersonates a user. Let's have a closer look at these key authorization concepts.

- Impersonation means that a process acts on behalf of a user.

- The access token contains a user's access control data (such as group memberships and user rights).

- The access mask tells the SRM what the process wants to do with the resource (for example: read a file? write to a file?).

- The security descriptor of an object tells the SRM who can do what with this particular object.

Based on the outcome of the authorization comparison process, the SRM decides whether the process can access the resource. To inform the process of what it can do with the resource, the SRM will return another access mask, the granted access mask. In the following section, we will examine these key concepts more in detail and link them to the subject and object we introduced in Section 10.1.

To allow the operating system to associate a user's authorization data (the user's rights and group memberships, explained next) with every process started by the user, Windows uses an object called the access token. Access

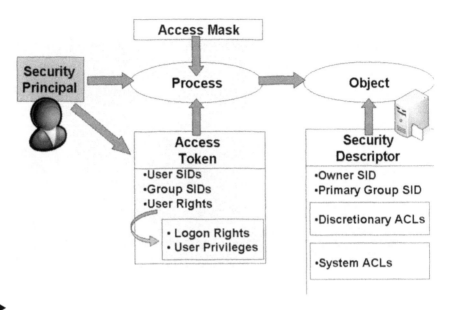

Figure 10.2 *Windows access control model.*

tokens are linked to a user's logon session. They are generated on every machine to which the user logs on, independent of the logon type (interactive, network, and so forth). An access token is always local and never travels across the network. The operating system component that generates access tokens is the Local Security Authority (LSA). Besides the user's domain authorization data, an access token also contains the user's local authorization data. The latter are the authorization data that are stored in a system's local security database (the SAM): they include a user's local group memberships and local user rights. A complete overview of all fields in the access token can be found in the Windows Server 2003 resource kit or the Microsoft Windows platform SDK. To look at the content of your Windows access token (including group memberships and user rights), use the resource kit tool whoami with the /all switch (as illustrated in Figure 10.3).

The main authorization attribute on the object side is called a security descriptor. A security descriptor tells the authorization system who can do what with the object. Every object that has a security descriptor linked to it is called a securable object. Securable objects can be shared between different users—and every user can have different authorization settings. Examples of securable objects are a file, a folder, a file system share, a printer, a registry key, an AD object, and a service. The security descriptor of a file system object is stored in the NTFS file system. The security descriptor of

Figure 10.3   *Using whoami /all to look at the access token content.*

an AD object is stored in the object's nTSecurityDescriptor attribute. Note that the nTSecurityDescriptor attribute is also replicated to the Global Catalog, which ensures that access to AD objects will be secured even if the object is replicated outside its domain boundary to GCs in other domains.

Every object's security descriptor contains a set of Access Control Lists (ACLs), illustrated in Figure 10.4. An ACL is composed of multiple Access Control Entries (ACEs). An ACE is also referred to as a permission. An ACE links a security identity (SID) to an access right (for example, read,

Figure 10.4
*Access Control List
(ACL) content.*

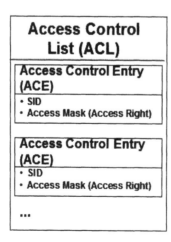

Table 10.1 *Typical Windows Access Masks and Their Meanings*

Access Mask Values	Meaning (Associated Access Right)
0x80000000	GENERIC_READ
0x40000000	GENERIC_WRITE
0x20000000	GENERIC_EXECUTE
0x10000000	GENERIC_ALL
0x1000000	SYSTEM_SECURITY
0x100000	SYNCHRONIZE
0x80000	WRITE_OWNER
0x40000	WRITE_DAC
0x20000	READ_CONTROL
0x10000	DELETE
0x100	DS_CONTROL_ACCESS
0x80	DS_LIST_OBJECT
0x40	DS_DELETE_TREE
0x20	DS_WRITE_PROP
0x10	DS_READ_PROP
0x8	DS_SELF
0x4	ACTRL_DS_LIST
0x2	DS_DELETE_CHILD
0x1	DS_CREATE_CHILD
-1	FULL_CONTROL

write, delete, execute). Typical examples of permissions are "Joe can read the monthly expense claim report," or "Alice can print on the human resource department printer."

In a security descriptor, an access right is represented using a hexadecimal value called the access mask. Table 10.1 shows some access mask values and their meaning. If an access right is made up of multiple access rights, then the associated access mask value will be the sum of the individual access rights. For example, an access right holding the READ_CONTROL and WRITE_DAC access right will have an access mask of 0x60000.

Every security descriptor contains two types of ACLs: discretionary and system ACLs.

■ Discretionary ACLs (DACLs) contain ACEs that are set by the owner of an object. They are called discretionary because their content is set at the object owner's discretion.

Ownership is a key concept in the Windows security model. It is a very powerful concept because the owner of an object is always granted the right to manage the object's permissions. By default, the object owner is the Windows user account that created the object. In the case in which a domain administrator or a member of the local administrators group creates an object, by default the Domain Admins or Administrators groups become the object owner.

This behavior can be changed in Windows Server 2003 thanks to the following GPO setting (part of the Security Options): "System objects: default owner for objects created by members of Administrators group." This GPO setting can be set to use either the administrator group or the object creator as the owner. It affects the nodefaultadminowner (REG_DWORD) registry value located in the HKEY_LOCAL_MACHINE\System\CurrentControlSet\Control\Lsa registry key.

An account can take ownership of an object if it has the "modify owner" permission on the object or if it has the "take ownership of files or other user objects" user right—by default, this right is given to members of the Administrators group. In an object's security descriptor, the owner is represented by its SID in the Owner SID field.

To look at an object's discretionary ACLs from the Windows GUI, you will typically use the ACL editor (explained in more detail below). To look at the DACLs of a file system object from the command prompt, you can use the cacls, xcacls, or showacls tools. SP2 of Windows Server 2003 adds an upgrade to the cacls tool, called icacls, that also allows you to backup and reset file and folder ACLs from the command line, even within the Recovery Console. For an AD object, you can use dsacls. We will return to these tools at the end of this chapter.

■ System ACLs (SACLs) contain an object's auditing settings and are set by an administrator. They are nondiscretionary: they are not related in any way to the owner of an object. SACLs are not the only thing needed in order to enable auditing on the object level. You also must enable "Audit object access" in a machine's audit policy. We will come back to Windows auditing in Chapter 12 of *Advanced Microsoft Windows Security Services* (part 2 of this series).

To look at an object's system ACL from the Windows GUI, you will also use the ACL editor. However, Windows does not include a native command-line utility to do this.

Beside the discretionary and system ACLs, an object's security descriptor also contains two other fields:

- The Owner SID field, which holds the SID of the owner of the object

- The Primary group SID field, which holds the SID of the object owner's primary group (the concept of a primary group is used for Posix and Macintosh compatibility reasons)

Note that the owner SID and the primary group SID of a Windows user are also special in the way that they can be used to assign permissions for new objects—for example, a new file created on a file server, or a new object in the Active Directory database. Windows offers specific "placeholders" for ownership permissions: CREATOR OWNER and CREATOR GROUP. How to handle these permissions and other general challenges for handling permissions for owners are described in more detail in a later section, "Managing Ownership Permissions," (page 618).

In the Windows authorization model, a user never accesses a resource directly: There is always a server process that acts on behalf of a user. This process is known in Windows terminology as impersonation. When a process impersonates a user, it means that it runs in the security context of the user and that it uses the user's authorization attributes.

The degree to which a process can act on behalf of a user can be controlled using impersonation levels, which are set in a user's access token.

Table 10.2 *Windows Impersonation Levels*

Impersonation Level	Meaning
Anonymous	The process impersonates an anonymous user (this means unidentified user). The access token will not contain any access control information.
Identify	The process can use the identity of the user for its own security processes. It cannot impersonate the user.
Impersonate	The process can act on behalf of a user to access resources on the local machine. The access token will contain the user's access control information.
Delegate	A service can act on behalf of a user to access resources on the local machine and also on remote machines. The access token will contain the user's access control information.

Windows Server 2003 uses the following impersonation levels: anonymous, identify, impersonate, and delegate. They are explained in Table 10.2. The anonymous and delegate impersonation levels were introduced in Windows 2000. The delegate level is the only impersonation level that can be controlled from the administration interface. Chapter 6 contains more information on the delegate impersonation level (or, in short, delegation) and the way it differs from the impersonate impersonation level.

10.3 Authorization Intermediaries

In large distributed computing environments consisting of many subjects and even much more objects, such as a Windows domain, the management of authorization data may become a very tedious and time-consuming task. With the exception of the full control permission that is automatically given to the owner of the object, all other permissions must be set manually by an administrator or by the object's owner. To ease access control management, Windows includes the following authorization intermediaries: groups and user rights.

- **Groups** provide a way to group entities with similar capabilities. They facilitate the access control management of object permissions. Administrators typically add all authenticated Windows entities (users, machines) with similar resource permissions or user rights to the same group.

- **User rights** define the capabilities of subjects to manage system resources and to perform system-related tasks. For instance: who can log on locally to a domain controller? Who can change the system time? Who can load device drivers? User rights facilitate the access control management for system resources and system-related tasks. User rights should not be confused with access rights or permissions; user rights apply to a computer system, access rights apply to an object.

Group intermediaries can be used to ease the administration of user rights intermediaries. For example, you can give all the members of the helpdesk department (i.e., members of a group such as GRP-All-Helpdesk-Administrators) the right to add workstations to your domain.

10.3.1 Groups

Windows has always supported groups. Compared to the group model used by Windows 2000 and Windows Server 2003, the model used by NT4 and earlier Windows versions can be called simple. The main differences between the two group models are:

- Windows 2000 and Windows Server 2003 support two group types: security groups and distribution groups. NT4 only supports security groups.

- Windows 2000 and Windows Server 2003 support three group scopes: universal, global, and local. Windows 2000 and Windows Server 2003 also support two flavors of the local group scope: domain local and system local. Groups with a domain local scope can be leveraged on any machine in a domain. Groups with a system local scope can only be leveraged on machines where the group is defined and stored. NT4 only supports the global and system local group scopes.

    When you define groups in a Windows 2000 or Windows Server 2003 domain database (AD), you can use the universal, global, and domain local scopes. The system local scope can only be used for groups defined on Windows 2000 or Windows Server 2003 member servers or standalone machines, or on domain controllers (DCs) that are part of a domain that includes NT4 DCs.

    When you define groups in an NT4 domain database (the SAM), you can use the global and system local scopes. On NT4 standalone machines or member servers, you can only define groups with a system local scope.

    The introduction of the universal group scope in Windows 2000 and Windows Server 2003 is a direct consequence of the Active Directory Global Catalog (GC): a domain controller (DC) feature that makes the AD objects and a subset of their attributes in a domain available to the DCs of the other domains in a Windows 2000 or Windows Server 2003 forest. Universal groups are the only groups that replicate their memberships to all GCs in a multidomain AD forest.

- In Windows 2000 and Windows Server 2003, a group's type and scope can be changed after the group is created. This is not possible in NT4.

- In Windows 2000 and Windows Server 2003, groups of the same scope and type can be nested. NT4 only supports nesting of global groups into system local groups.

Active Directory Group Types

Windows 2000 and Windows Server 2003 support two group types: distribution groups and security groups. Distribution groups can be used as e-mail distribution lists in AD-based e-mail servers like Exchange 2000 and Exchange 2003. Distribution groups demonstrate the tight integration of the Microsoft Exchange 2000 and later mail servers and the Windows 2000 and later operating systems.

Similar to distribution groups, security groups can be used as e-mail distribution lists. In addition, security groups can also be used for security-related administration tasks, such as setting permissions on resources or administrative delegation.

The reason distribution groups cannot be used for security-related administration is that—contrary to a security group—a distribution group's security identifier (SID) is not added to a Windows user's access token during the authentication process. Note that when you use the Exchange System Manager to add a normal distribution group in order to secure an Exchange object, such as a public folder, the Recipient Update Service (RUS) of Exchange will convert the group to a mail-enabled security group in AD.

Provided your domains are at the correct domain functional level (native Windows 2000 or Windows Server 2003), a security group can be converted to a distribution group and the other way around. Domain functional levels and their impact on group features will be explained in the section on "Active Directory Group Feature Availability," (page 595).

You can change the group type from the group properties in the AD Users and Computers (ADUC) MMC snap-in. To change the type of multiple groups, you can use the Windows Server 2003's DSMOD.exe command-line utility with the –secgrp [yes/no] option.

Before a security group is converted to a distribution group, Windows warns you about the possible authorization consequences of doing so: if a security group is converted to a distribution group and the security group was used to set permissions on resources, the users that are members of the security group will lose access to the resources.

In the following sections, we will focus on the features of security groups and how to best take advantage of them.

Active Directory Group Scopes

Windows 2000 and Windows Server 2003 AD support three group scopes: universal, global, and domain local. Similarly to how you select the group type when defining a new group from the ADUC MMC snap-in, you can select the group scope. A group with a universal scope is referred to as a universal group (UG); a global group (GG) is a group with a global scope and a domain local group (DLG) is a group with a domain local scope.

A group's scope defines the ways the group can be used in multidomain environments. For example, the group scope determines whether a group can contain users and/or groups defined in another domain and whether it can be used for setting permissions on a resource in another domain.

Table 10.3 shows which security principals (users, computers, or groups) can be a member of a UG, GG, and DLG. The table also shows whether the security principals must be located in the same domain as the one where the group is defined (SD) or if they can be in another domain that is part of the same forest (OD-INT) or in another trusted external domain (OD-EXT). Table 10.3 also shows that the availability of some of the group characteristics, which is again dependent on the domain functional level.

Now that we know what security principals can be a member of what kind of group, it is time to examine where we can use these groups to set permissions on resources. Table 10.4 shows whether a group can be used for setting permissions on resources in the group's proper definition domain only or if it can also be used to set resource permissions in another domain. It becomes obvious that domain local groups are the only groups that cannot be used to set permissions on resources beyond their proper definition domain.

Table 10.3 *Group Membership Restrictions*

… Can Contain …	Users/Computers			Domain Local Groups			Global Groups			Universal Groups		
	SD	OD-INT	OD-EXT	SD	OD-INT	OD-EXT	SD	OD-INT	OD-EXT	SD	OD-INT	OD-EXT
Universal groups (UG)	Y	Y	N	N	N	N	Y	Y	N	Y	Y	N
Global groups (GG)	Y	N	N	N	N	N	Y*	N	N	N	N	N
Domain Local groups (DLG)	Y	Y	Y	Y*	N	N	Y	Y	Y	Y	Y	Y

*Only in Windows 2000 native or Windows Server 2003 domain functional level.

Legend: Same domain (SD)/Other domain in the same forest (OD-INT)/Other external domain or domain in other forest (OD-EXT).

Table 10.4   *Group Use Restrictions (Proper Definition Domain/Other Domain)*

	Setting Permissions on a Resource in Proper Definition Domain	Setting Permissions on a Resource in Another Domain
Universal groups (UG)	Yes	Yes
Global groups (GG)	Yes	Yes
Domain Local groups (DLG)	Yes	No

The group scope also determines which group can be a member of another group. This is referred to as group nesting. In Windows 2000 and Windows Server 2003, the following group nesting rules apply:

- A **global group** can be a member of another global group in the same domain, of a universal group in any domain of the forest, or of a domain local group in any domain either within the forest or in externally trusted domains or forests.

- A **universal group** can be a member of another universal group in any domain of the forest or of a domain local group in any domain either within the forest or in externally trusted domains or forests, but not of a global group.

- A **domain local group** can only be nested inside another domain local group in the same domain.

The group nesting rules for the three group scopes are illustrated in Figure 10.5. The AD group nesting rules are dictated by the mechanism

Figure 10.5
AD group nesting rules.

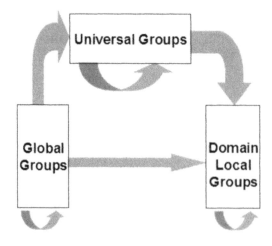

Figure 10.6
*AD group scope
conversion rules.*

Windows uses to find out about a user's group membership when a user logs on to a domain. This process is also known as group expansion and is explained in more detail in Chapter 6 in Section 6.4.2, "From Authentication to Authorization."

If your domain is at the native Windows 2000 or Windows Server 2003 functional level, the group scope of domain local, global, and universal security and distribution groups can be changed as illustrated in Figure 10.6. Group scope conversion is bound to the following limitations:

- A **domain local group** can only be converted to a universal group if the domain local group has no other domain local group members (a domain local group cannot be a member of a universal group).

- A **global group** can only be converted to a universal group if the global group is not a member of another global group (a universal group cannot be a member of a global group).

- In a multi-domain environment, a **universal group** can only be converted to a global group if all the members of the universal group are defined in the universal group's definition domain (global groups can only contain objects defined in their proper domain).

As with changing the group type, the group scope can be changed from the group's properties in the ADUC MMC snap-in. To change the scope of multiple groups you can use the Windows Server 2003 DSMOD.exe command-line utility with the -scope [l/g/u] option. You will only be able to change the scope of the group if its members and the group's own memberships adhere to the rules of the target group-scope.

Active Directory Group Feature Availability

In the previous sections, we mentioned that the availability of some group features depends on the domain functional level. Functional levels are a version management system that Microsoft introduced in Windows Server 2003. The functional level of a domain depends on the OS versions of its

Table 10.5 *Windows Server 2003 Domain Functional Levels*

Functional Level	Supported Domain Controller OS
Windows 2000 Mixed	Windows NT 4.0
	Windows 2000
	Windows Server 2003
Windows 2000 Native	Windows 2000
	Windows Server 2003
Windows Server 2003 Interim	Windows NT 4.0
	Windows Server 2003
Windows Server 2003	Windows Server 2003

domain controllers and impacts the AD features (including group features) that are available in the domain.

As a reminder, Table 10.5 shows the different Windows Server 2003 domain functional levels and the operating system versions they support on domain controllers (DCs). Table 10.6 gives an overview of the Windows group features available for the different domain functional levels.

Table 10.6 *Effect of the Domain Functional Level on Windows Group Features*

Windows 2000 Mixed or Windows Server 2003 Interim Functional Level	Windows 2000 Native or Windows Server 2003 Functional Level
Two group types: security and distribution	Two group types: security and distribution
Two group scopes for security groups: global and domain local	Three group scopes for security groups: global, domain local, and universal
Only domain controllers share domain local groups	All computers in domain share domain local groups
■ Only global groups can be nested in domain local groups ■ No other group nesting supported	■ A global group can be a member of another global group, a universal group, or a domain local group ■ A universal group can also be a member of another universal group or a domain local group ■ A domain local group can be a member of another domain local group
Group scope and type cannot be changed	Group scope and type can be changed

Built-in Security Groups

The goal of this section is not to provide a complete overview of the built-in Windows Server 2000 and Windows Server 2003 security groups. Table 10.7 lists the Windows 2000 built-in security groups, while Table 10.8 lists the ones that have additionally been made available with Windows Server 2003.

Table 10.7 *Built-In Windows 2000 Groups*

Built-In Group Name	Group Scope	Meaning
Account Operators	Domain Local	Members can administer domain user and group accounts.
Administrators	Domain Local	Administrators have complete and unrestricted access to the computer/domain.
Backup Operators	Domain Local	Backup Operators can override security restrictions for the sole purpose of backing up or restoring files.
Cert Publishers	Domain Local	Members of this group are permitted to publish certificates to the Active Directory.
DnsAdmins	Domain Local	Members of this group can administer the Windows 2000 DNS service.
DNSUpdateProxy	Global	DNS clients who are permitted to perform dynamic updates on behalf of some other clients (such as DHCP servers).
Domain Computers	Global	This group includes all computers that joined the domain, including domain controllers.
Domain Controllers	Global	This group includes all domain controllers of the domain.
Enterprise Admins	Universal	The Enterprise Admins group exists only in the root domain of an AD forest. The members of this group can make forest-wide changes and change the AD configuration naming context.
Group Policy Creator Owners	Global	Members of this group are authorized to create new Group Policy Objects in the AD.
Guests	Domain Local	Guests have the same access as members of the Users group by default, except for the Guest account, which is further restricted.
Pre-Windows 2000 Compatible Access	Domain Local	Members of this group have read access to all attributes on user and group AD objects.
Print Operators	Domain Local	Members can administer domain printers.

Table 10.7   *Built-In Windows 2000 Groups (continued)*

Built-In Group Name	Group Scope	Meaning
RAS and IAS Servers	Domain Local	Servers in this group can access remote access properties of users.
Replicator	Domain Local	Supports file replication in a domain.
Schema Admins	Universal	The Schema Admins group exists only in the root domain of an AD forest. The members of this group can change the AD schema naming context.
Server Operators	Domain Local	Members can administer domain servers.

No new built-in groups have been added with the Windows Server 2003 SP1 or R2 versions.

The pre–Windows 2000 compatible access group deserves some more explanation. It enables applications that cannot run using the AD authorization settings as they are enforced by a Windows 2000 Domain Controller, to run in a Windows 2000 or Windows Server 2003 environment. If the application's security identity is a member of this group, the application will be capable of reading AD user and group objects.

Well-Known Security Principals

This section focuses on a special category of security principals that deserves some extra attention: well-known security principals. They represent special entities that are predefined and controlled by the Windows security subsystem. Popular examples are the Everyone, Authenticated Users, Local System, Self, and Creator Owner security principals.

Unlike normal security principals, well-known security principals cannot be renamed or deleted. You cannot create your own well-known security principals; they are the same on every Windows system, although the list of available well-known security principals slightly varies by OS version. A well-known security principal also has the same security identifier (SID) on every Windows system. For example, SID S-1-5-10 always represents the Self well-known security principal and SID S-1-3-0 represents the Creator Owner principal.

Table 10.9 lists the well-known security principals available in Windows 2000, Windows Server 2003, and Windows XP Service Pack 2 (SP2). Table 10.10 shows the new well-known security principals introduced in Windows Server 2003—the ones that are also supported in Windows XP SP2

Table 10.8 *New Built-In Windows Server 2003 Groups*

Built-In Group Name	Group Scope	Meaning
HelpServicesGroup	Domain Local	This group is specifically for the Help and Support Center.
IIS_WPG	Domain Local	This is the IIS Worker Process group.
Incoming Forest Trust Builders	Domain Local	Members of this group can create incoming, one-way trusts to the forest.
Network Configuration Operators	Domain Local	Members in this group can have some administrative privileges to manage configuration of networking features.
Performance Log Users	Domain Local	Members of this group have remote access to schedule logging of performance counters on this computer.
Performance Monitor Users	Domain Local	Members of this group have remote access to monitor this computer.
Remote Desktop Users	Domain Local	Members in this group are granted the right to log on remotely.
TelnetClients	Domain Local	Members of this group have access to Telnet Server on this system.
Terminal Server License Servers	Domain Local	Terminal Server License Servers.
Windows Authorization Access Group	Domain Local	Members of this group have access to the computed tokenGroupsGlobalAndUniversal attribute on User objects.

are marked with a star. For each well-known security principal, the table also shows the corresponding SID. A listing of all well-known Windows SIDs is also available from the Microsoft Knowledge Base article KB243330. Most of them will be explained in more detail below.

In Windows Server 2003, Microsoft added the following well-known security principals: Local Service, Network Service, Digest Authentication, NTLM Authentication, Remote Interactive Logon, SChannel Authentication, Restricted Code, Other Organization, and This Organization. These new well-known security principals will only show up in AD if the domain controller (DC) holding the PDC emulator operations master role is running Windows Server 2003. In a domain that contains both Windows 2000 and Windows Server 2003 DCs you must first transfer this operations master role to a Windows Server 2003 DC. This issue should have little impact on your AD infrastructure, because many of the new features (some of which are explained below) that use the new Windows Server 2003 well-known security principals require Windows Server 2003 functional level.

Most of the well-known security principals listed in Tables 10.9 and 10.10—like Everyone and Authenticated Users—can be looked at as well-known security principal "groups." Unlike normal groups, the operating system, as opposed to an administrator, automatically controls their membership. Their membership depends on certain conditions. In Windows 2000 and Windows XP, the OS automatically assigns a user to the Interactive group if the user is logged on using the console at the computer where the resource resides or if the user is logged on to that computer using a Remote Desktop (RDP) connection. In Windows Server 2003, the user

Table 10.9 *Well-Known Security Principals Available in Windows 2000, Windows Server 2003, and Windows XP Service Pack 2 (SP2)*

Well-Known Security Principals (Corresponding SID)	Membership—Meaning
Everyone (S-1-1-0)	Included in the access token for all users, including the Guest account.
	Included in the access token for anonymous users if the "Network Access: Let Everyone permissions apply to anonymous users" policy setting has been enabled.
Creator Owner (S-1-3-0)	Placeholder used for permission inheritance between parent and child objects. On child objects, creator owner permissions are replaced by permissions for the actual owner of the object.
Creator Group (S-1-3-1)	Placeholder used for permission inheritance between parent and child objects. On child objects, creator group permissions are replaced by permissions for the primary group of the actual owner of the object.
Dial-up (S-1-5-1)	Included in the access token for all users logged on through a dial-up or VPN connection.
Network (S-1-5-2)	Included in the access token for all users logged on through a network connection.
Batch (S-1-5-3)	Included in the access token for all users logged on through a batch scheduler connection.
Interactive (S-1-5-4)	Included in the access token for all users logged on interactively.
Service (S-1-5-6)	Included in the access token for all principals that logged on as a service.

Table 10.9 *Well-Known Security Principals Available in Windows 2000, Windows Server 2003, and Windows XP Service Pack 2 (SP2) (continued)*

Well-Known Security Principals (Corresponding SID)	Membership—Meaning
Anonymous (S-1-5-7)	Included in the access token for all users that have logged on anonymously.
Enterprise Domain Controllers (S-1-5-9)	Included in the access token for all domain controllers in a Windows AD forest.
Self (S-1-5-10)	Placeholder for the object itself. Can be very useful for permission inheritance between parent and child objects.
Authenticated Users (S-1-5-11)	Included in the access token for all users who have authenticated to the operating system. Included in the access token for the Guest account in Windows 2000 and Windows XP, but not included in the access token for the Guest account in Windows Server 2003 and Windows XP SP2.
Terminal Server User (S-1-5-13)	Included in the access token for all users who have logged on using terminal services version 4.0 application compatibility mode.
System (S-1-5-18)	Represents the local system.

would be added to the Remote Interactive group. You could also refer to these well-known security principal groups as dynamic groups, because the OS determines their membership in a dynamic way. They should not be confused with the dynamic LDAP Query-based groups Microsoft introduced in the Windows Server 2003 Authorization Manager (AzMan), which will be explained later in this chapter.

An interesting characteristic of well-known security principals is the way they are replicated between AD instances. Even though they may apply to thousands of AD objects, only their name is replicated, not their membership. As a consequence you cannot query for their membership using the classical AD query and administration tools. If you consider how well-known security principals are used, you will realize there is no real need to store their membership. Well-known security principals' primary role is to provide a security identifier (SID) that can be added to the access token of a user when a user logs on to a system or accesses a resource. The presence of a particular well-known security principal in the access token gives the user certain privileges on the system or resource.

Table 10.10   *Well-Known Security Principals Added in Windows Server 2003*

Well-Known Security Principals (Corresponding SID)	Membership—Meaning
Restricted Code * (S-1-5-12)	Added to user's access token when running RunAs with the "Run this program with restricted access" option in Windows Server 2003 or the "Protect my computer and data from unauthorized program activity" option in Windows XP.
Remote Interactive Logon* (S-1-5-14)	Added to user's access token when the user is logged on using Terminal Services or Remote Desktop. Allows assigning permissions for users logged on via Terminal Services/Remote Desktop.
This Organization (S-1-5-15)	Used for forest trust and external trust selective authentication. Selective authentication allows an administrator to distinguish users from the trusted forest/domain and users from the trusting forest/domain when dealing with access control settings. This Organization is added to the access tokens in the trusting forest/domain of users that are defined in the trusting forest/domain. See also Other Organization.
Local Service* (S-1-5-19)	Least-privilege service account for services that only need access to local data and don't need access to other computers on the network.
Network Service* (S-1-5-20)	Least-privilege service account for services that do need access to other computers on the network.
NTLM Authentication (S-1-5-64-10)	Allows setting special permissions for down-level clients authenticating by the less secure NTLM protocol. Whenever a user logs on to a DC using NTLM, this SID is added to his access token. Access to resources can thus be restricted by using this well-known security principal in a deny ACE.
SChannel Authentication (S-1-5-64-14)	Allows setting special permissions for clients authenticating via an SSL/TLS secure channel. Examples are HTTPs authentication to an IIS Web server or LDAPs authentication to a Windows domain controller.
Digest Authentication (S-1-5-64-21)	Digest is another authentication packet that enables HTTP digest authentication on an IIS Web server. This security principal allows you to specify who can log on using digest and who cannot.
Other Organization (S-1-5-1000)	Used for forest trust and external trust selective authentication. Selective authentication allows an administrator to distinguish users from the trusted forest/domain and users from the trusting forest/domain when dealing with access control settings. Other Organization is added to the access tokens in the trusting forest/domain of users that are defined in the trusted forest/domain. See also This Organization.

* Also supported in Windows XP Service Pack 2 (SP2).

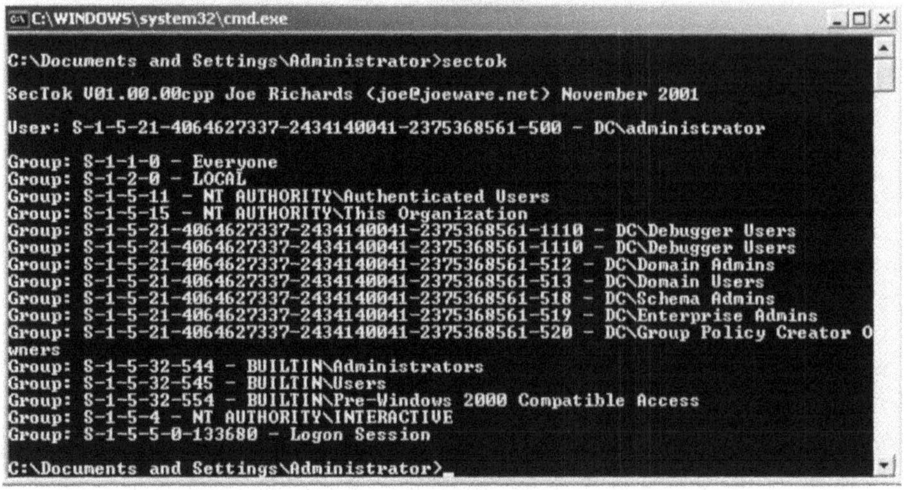

Figure 10.7   *Checking well-known security principal membership using sectok.exe.*

To look at the content of your access token, use the whoami.exe tool with the /all switch (whoami comes with Windows Server 2003 and the Windows 2000 Resource Kit) or a freeware tool like sectok.exe (downloadable from www.joeware.net), as illustrated in Figure 10.7.

Administering Well-Known Security Principals

Well-known security principals are available on all Windows OSs: it does not matter whether they are installed in domain or standalone mode. However, not ALL well-known security principals are added to standalone machines. Also, as was explained above, the list of available well-known security principals slightly varies by OS version.

In a Windows domain environment, Active Directory objects representing the well-known security principals are stored in the WellKnown Security Principals container beneath the Configuration container. To look at the content of this container, you can use the ADSIEdit tool, as illustrated in Figure 10.8. On a standalone machine, well-known security principals are stored in the local security database (or SAM).

You can add well-known security principals to other groups and to the access control list (ACL) of Windows objects. In AD, you can even delegate permissions to well-known security principals. A confusing detail is that the first time you try to add a well-known security principal to another group, you will not find them in the AD Users and Computers (ADUC). You must know the correct name of the well-known security principal; you can-

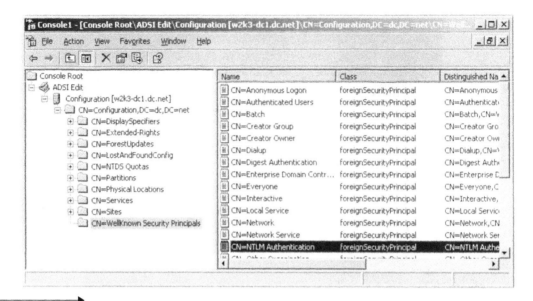

Figure 10.8　*Well-known security principals in AD (using ADSIEdit).*

not simply browse for the object using one of above administration tools. Even the advanced query options in the object picker will not help you if you don't know the correct name. This is because the ADUC administration tool focuses on managing the data in the AD domain naming context, and well-known security principals are stored in the AD configuration naming context. The same issue occurs when using the Local Users and Groups (LUG) MMC snap-in; in this case, well-known security principals are not visible to hide complexity from the nonprofessional Windows user.

In the ADUC, a well-known security principal will show up in the ForeignSecurityPrincipals container from the moment you use it. For example, when you add the Authenticated Users well-known security principal to the Print Operators group, an entry for Authenticated Users will be added to the ForeignSecurityPrincipals container. The content of the ForeignSecurityPrincipals container is illustrated in Figure 10.9. Note that most well-known security principals have a reference to NT Authority in their Readable Name. NT Authority is name of the security authority of the built-in Windows security domain existing on every Windows machine, which partially explains why the well-known security principals show up in the "foreign" security principal container.

You can also add well-known security principals to other groups or add them to the ACL of a resource from the command line. To add them to a group, you can use the "net group" and "net localgroup" commands.

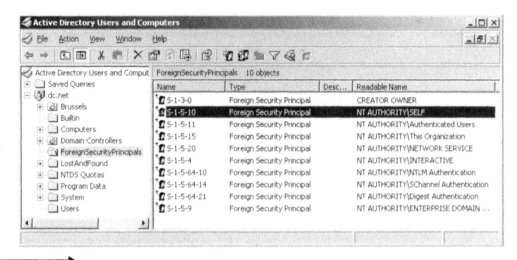

Figure 10.9   *Well-known security principals in ADUC.*

The following command, for example, adds the interactive well-known security principal to the Backup Operators domain local group.

```
net localgroup "Backup Operators" Interactive /add
```

To add well-known security principals to the ACL of a resource from the command line, you can use the subinacl.exe Resource Kit utility. For example, to give the local service principal read access to the MyApplication registry key, type the following at the command line:

```
subinacl /keyreg MyApplication /grant="local service"=r
```

Everyone and Authenticated Users

The Authenticated Users well-known security principal covers all users who are authenticated to Windows using a valid set of user credentials. This not only includes all users with valid credentials in the forest and its domains, but also users from other forests that access resources in the local forest using valid credentials and using a forest or external inter-forest trust relationship.

The Everyone well-known security principal is a superset of the Authenticated Users well-known security principal; it includes the Authenticated Users well-known security principal and the Guest account.

An important difference between the Everyone and Authenticated Users well-known security principals lies in their Guest and Anonymous accounts' membership (as summarized in Table 10.11).

Table 10.11   *Default Memberships of Everyone and Authenticated Users Well-Known Security Principals*

	Everyone	Authenticated Users
All users in domain	Yes	Yes
All users in forest	Yes	Yes
All users in trusted domains and forests	Yes	Yes
Guest	Yes	No
Anonymous	Only in a Windows 2000 AD and on Windows XP Not in Windows Server 2003 AD or on Windows XP SP2	No

- In a Windows 2000 AD and on Windows XP, the Guest account is automatically a member of both the Everyone and Authenticated Users well-known security principals. In Windows Server 2003 AD and on Windows XP SP2, this is only true for the Everyone well-known security principal.

- In a Windows 2000 AD and on Windows XP, the Anonymous account is automatically a member of the Everyone well-known security principal, but not the Authenticated Users well-known security principal. In a Windows Server 2003 AD and on Windows XP SP2, the Anonymous account is neither a member of the Authenticated Users well-known security principal nor by default a member of the Everyone well-known security principal. It is only a member if the following security policy setting is enabled: "Network Access: Let Everyone permissions apply to anonymous users." This setting can also be controlled using the following registry key: HKLM\System\CurrentControlSet\Control\LSA\EveryoneIncludesAnonymous (REG_DWORD). If this key is set to 1, the Anonymous account will be a member of the Everyone well-known security principal.

System, Local Services and Network Service

In Windows 2000 and earlier versions, Windows services and third-party applications typically ran in the security context of the system well-known security principal. This principal is also referred to as the local system account or LSA; in AD it shows up as Well-Known-Security-ID-System.

The System principal acts as the host computer account on the network. It appears as <Domainname>\<machine name>$. The actual name of the account is NT AUTHORITY\System; it does not have a password that an administrator needs to manage, and has SID S-1-5-18.

Running a service or application in the security context of the System principal gives it almost unlimited privileges on a Windows system. The System principal's powers are comparable to those of the root account on UNIX systems. If a service logs on using the System principal on a domain controller, for example, it has local system access on the domain controller itself. This could, if the service was compromised, allow malicious users to change anything they wanted in the AD database. Using it is definitely a bad practice when you are trying to honor the principle of least privilege.

To better deal with this when configuring application service accounts, Microsoft provided two new principals in Windows Server 2003 and Windows XP SP2: the Local Service (S-1-5-19) and the Network Service (S-1-5-20) well-known security principals. Both principals have significantly fewer privileges than the System principal.

A service that runs as Local Service accesses network resources as a null session; this means it uses anonymous credentials. The actual name of the Local Service principal is NT AUTHORITY\LocalService and—like the local system account—it does not have a password that an administrator needs to manage. The Local Service principal is tailored to services that only access local resources and do not need access to other network resources.

The Network Service account, on the other hand, is tailored to services or applications that do need access to network resources. A service that runs as the Network Service principal accesses network resources using the credentials of the computer account just as a Local System service does. The actual name of the account is NT AUTHORITY\NetworkService, and it does not have a password that an administrator needs to manage.

Examples of Windows Server 2003 and Windows XP SP2 services that are using the Local Service account by default are the Smart Card, Remote Registry, and Telnet services. Examples of services using the Network Service account by default are the DNS Client and the Remote Procedure Call (RPC) services.

When you want to configure a service to use one of these new accounts, you must enter the service accounts manually—you cannot simply select them from a list. To configure the local service account, type NT Authority\LocalService (as illustrated in Figure 10.10). To configure the network

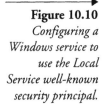

Figure 10.10
Configuring a
Windows service to
use the Local
Service well-known
security principal.

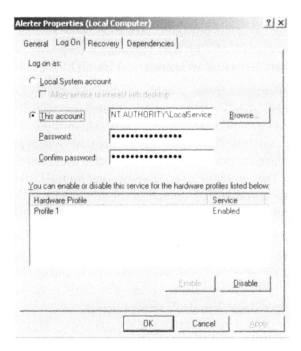

service account, type NT Authority\NetworkService. You do not need to provide a password.

This Organization and Other Organization

The This Organization and Other Organization well-known security principals were introduced in Windows Server 2003 and are related to a new interforest trust security feature called selective authentication (sometimes referred to as authentication firewall). Selective authentication allows administrators to define an additional layer of access control checks for making interforest resource access control decisions: it can be used to restrict initial logon to a computer and then to grant/deny access to objects within that computer. See Chapter 3 for more details on selective authentication and how to leverage these related well-known security principals.

Restricted Code

The Restricted Code well-known security principal is added to a user's access token when running RunAs with the "Run this program with restricted access" option in Windows Server 2003 (as illustrated in Figure 10.11) or the "Protect my computer and data from unauthorized program activity" option in Windows XP. RunAs offers high-privilege accounts (like

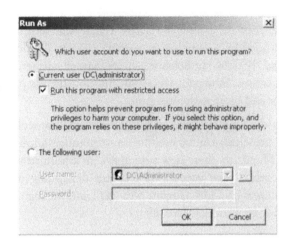

Figure 10.11
*Using RunAs with
the "Run this
program with
restricted access"
option.*

administrators) a convenient way to switch to the security context of
another least-privileged user to execute a program and thus limit the mal-
ware exposure of their high-privilege security context.

The presence of the Restricted Code well-known security principal in
the user's access token eliminates all user's rights held by the user (except for
Bypass Traverse Checking), prevents the application from accessing the
user's profile, and allows only Read access to the HKEY_LOCAL_
MACHINE and HKEY_CURRENT_USER registry hives.

The Restricted Code well-known security principal offers users a convenient way to honor least privilege without having to remember two user
accounts and two passwords. Instead of using RunAs to switch to the security context of another "least privilege" account, they can use RunAs to
switch to a locked-down version of their current security context—without
entering the credentials of a second account.

Logon and Authentication Type-Related Well-Known Security Principals

Windows XP, Windows 2000, and Windows Server 2003 all include well-
known security principals that are added to security principals' access
tokens based on the way they logged on to a Windows system—or, in Windows speak, based on the principal's logon type. These well-known security
principals are called batch, dialup, interactive, network, service, and terminal service user (for terminal services version 4.0 application compatibility
mode users). In Windows Server 2003 and Windows XP SP2, Microsoft
added the Remote Interactive Logon well-known security principal to identify users logging on using the Windows XP and Windows Server 2003 versions of terminal services or a remote desktop connection (RDP).

In Windows Server 2003 Microsoft also added a well-known security principal into the principal's access token that reflects the authentication protocol used by a principal to authenticate to Windows. These principals are called NTLM authentication, SChannel authentication, and Digest authentication. Strangely, Microsoft did not include principals to represent Kerberos and basic authentication.

Both the Logon Type and Authentication Protocol Related well-known security principals can be used for more granular administration of authorization. Thanks to these new principals, an administrator can now give different levels of user access to a resource depending on the authentication protocol used (NTLM, Digest, SSL, etc.) and the logon type (from the console, using terminal services, etc.).

Self, Creator Owner, and Creator Group

Windows includes several hierarchical object structures that support permission inheritance. Inheritance is the capability to define permissions on a parent object and let these permissions automatically apply to the parent object's child objects. These hierarchical object structures include the Active Directory, the registry, the file system, and so on. To facilitate permission administration in these hierarchical structures, Microsoft defined the Self, Creator Owner, and Creator Group well-known security principals.

All three principals are typically added to the ACL of a parent object and are inherited by child objects in a particular way. For example, the Self well-known security principal is a placeholder for the object itself. An AD administrator can add a permission, such as write the postalAddress user object attribute, for the Self principal to the ACL of an AD OU. If a user object called Jan is located in this OU, the user Jan will have write permissions for his postalAddress attribute. In other words, Jan will be allowed to maintain his proper postalAddress data in his AD user object. However, the same Self permissions on another user object in the same OU will not allow Jan to edit the other user's postalAddress, since that Self permission is in no way related to Jan's user account.

Another example of how the Self well-known security principal is used is that, by default, Self is granted read permissions on the member-attribute of a group. This means that all members of a group are able to see who else is a member of the group they are in. Nonmembers do not have this capability.

The use and application of the Creator Owner and Creator Group principals is further described in a later section, "Managing Ownership Permissions," (page 618).

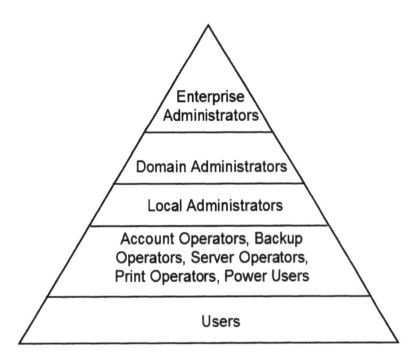

Figure 10.12
Windows administrator pyramid.

Administrator Groups

The pyramid shown in Figure 10.12 shows the level of administrative privileges Windows 2000 and Windows Server 2003 give to their default security groups. Table 10.12 shows the default memberships of these groups on a Windows 2000 workstation or member server and on domain controllers. Notice that some groups are not available on all Windows computer types (NA) and that some groups by default don't have members.

Let's look a little bit more in detail at the power of the Windows Enterprise Admins, Domain Admins, and Administrators groups. It is worth comparing these groups to the administrator groups that were available in NT4.

NT4 had two administrator groups: Domain Admins and Administrators:

- The Administrators group on domain controllers was one and the same group, shared between all domain controllers of a domain. A member of this group had the right to manage all domain resources, including users, groups, rights, account policy, audit policy, trusts, shares, and the services on all domain controllers.

- The Administrators group on a member server or a workstation had the right to manage all resources on the local workstation or member server system.

- The Domain Admins group itself didn't have proper rights. Members of the Domain Admins group receive administrative right over every system in a domain because, by default, when a system joined the domain, the Domain Admins group was added to the local Administrators group.

A key problem of NT4 is its inflexible character on the level of granular administration. Even if you wanted to give an administrator permission to manage only a subset of your domain accounts, you added him either to the Account Operators or even the Domain Admins group. This gave him administrative control not just over the subset but over every account in your domain. In case you used the Account Operators group, your domain admins were protected from changes through members of the Account Operators group.

Table 10.12   *Windows Administrator Groups*

Group	Default Members on Workstations, Member Servers	Default Members on Domain Controllers
Enterprise Admins	NA	Administrator of forest root domain
Domain Admins	NA	Administrator of the domain
Administrators	Administrator, Domain Admins*	Administrator, Domain Admins, Enterprise Admins
Users	Authenticated Users, Domain Users	Authenticated Users, Domain Users, Interactive
Power Users	Interactive Users	NA
Account Operators	NA	—
Server Operators	NA	—
Backup Operators	NA	—
Print Operators	NA	—

* The Domain Admins group is added to the local Administrators group when the machine joins a domain. The Domain Users is also added to the system's local Users group when the machine joins a domain.

Windows 2000 and Windows Server 2003 have three administrator groups: Enterprise Admins, Domain Admins, and Administrators:

- The Enterprise Admins group is created in the first domain that's created in the forest. The Enterprise Admins group is added automatically to every Administrators group of the domain controllers in every domain that joins the forest. This means that, by default, a member of the Enterprise Admins can manage the configuration of a forest and also every domain controller in the forest. Table 10.13 lists some Windows administrative tasks that require enterprise administrator rights and permissions by default, although many of these (such as Authorization of a DHCP server) can be delegated to other groups in your forest.

Table 10.13   *Administrator Tasks That Require Enterprise Administrator Permissions*

Task	Reason
Create new domain in forest	Creates crossRef objects in CN=Partitions, CN=Configuration subtree
Manage Sites and Subnets	Creates and modifies objects in CN=Sites, CN=Configuration subtree
Install Enterprise Certification Authority	Creates CA object in CN=Public Key Services, CN=Services, CN=Configuration subtree
Install Certification Authority for a child domain	Creates objects in CN=Public Key Services, CN=Services, CN=Configuration subtree
Create Admission Control Service (ACS) policies	Creates subnet objects in CN=Subnets, CN=Sites, CN=Configuration
	Creates CN=ACS, CN=Subnets, CN=Sites, CN=Configuration, and objects in this subtree
Install first Exchange server in forest	Extends schema configuration naming context
	Creates objects in CN=DisplaySpecifiers, CN=Configuration subtree
	Creates CN=MS Exchange, CN=Services, CN=Configuration, and objects in this subtree
Authorize a DHCP server	Creates CN=DHCPRoot, CN=NetServices, CN=Services, CN=Configuration, and objects in this subtree
Set up printer location tracking	Sets location attribute on subnet or site objects in CN=Sites, CN=Configuration subtree
	Sets location attribute on computer object in any domain
Set up Simple Certificate Enrollment Protocol (SCEP	Changes ACL on objects in CN=Public Key Services, CN=Services, CN=Configuration subtree

The Enterprise Admins group is not added to the Administrators group on member servers and workstations. However, since a member of the Enterprise Admins can manage the group membership of every group in a domain and is capable of modifying all Group Policies, he can configure appropriate rights for any server or workstation in the forest. This will give him administrative access to every domain controller, member server, and workstation in any domain of the forest. As such, both the Enterprise Administrators and the Domain Administrators must be highly trusted people in your organization.

- The same rules as in NT4 apply to the Domain Admins and the Administrators group on member servers and workstations (i.e., by default the Domain Admins group is made a member of the local administrators group for every server or workstation that joins the domain).

Both Windows 2000 and Windows Sever 2003 include major enhancements on the level of granular administration. In both OSs, it is also possible to grant an administrator the permission to manage only a subset of the domain accounts. We will come back to this in Chapter 11, on administrative delegation.

Group Usage Guidelines

One of the main challenges Windows administrators face is managing the access to resources as efficiently as possible. A golden rule is to use groups instead of individual accounts for assigning permissions to resources. Groups create an abstraction layer in your authorization model that makes the assignment of permissions independent of account level changes. This rule applies both to Windows domain and standalone environments.

For example, in many organizations, users regularly switch between organizational roles. Each role typically requires specific permissions to Windows resources. In AD you can create groups for organizational roles—for example, "helpdesk operators" or "developers"—and assign resource permissions to these groups. If someone switches roles, you must simply make his account a member of the associated group. This is much more efficient than resetting the permissions for the user's account on the resources the user needs to access in his new role.

Below are some more recommendations and best practices for efficient AD authorization group usage:

- Use global groups to group users, use domain local groups to set the permissions on resources, and put global groups into domain local groups to apply authorization settings. This rule is illustrated in Figure 10.13. Even though this is an NT4 rule that provides a workaround for missing NT4 delegation capabilities and NT4 domain database size limitations, it still applies to multidomain Windows 2000 and Windows Server 2003 forest environments. Group nesting and the choice of group scopes is less important in single domain Windows 2000 or Windows Server 2003 forest setups; in those cases, you must simply ensure that you do not assign permissions to users directly but, rather, use a group intermediary.

Your group nesting choices may also be influenced by the following two factors:

— The ownership and sensitivity of the data you protect using groups. For example, if data is very sensitive, the administrator responsible for the data requires complete control over who is granted access to the data. This is best done not by nesting any group, but instead by using a single group to control membership and using the same group to grant permissions to the resource. If, however, many users should have access to a specific resource and the resource owner does not want to or cannot control every single user's membership to the respective group, it makes sense to nest them so that other administrators can self-manage their users in their specific groups, and then nest these groups in another group that grants the permission on the resource.

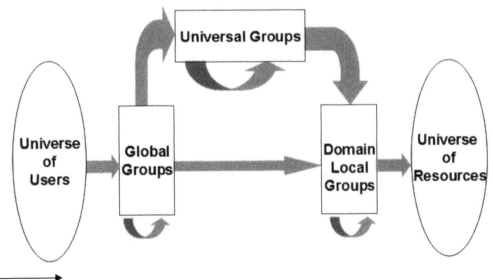

Figure 10.13   *AD group usage rules.*

— Recoverability of AD group memberships after the accidental deletion of AD objects. Memberships to domain local groups are the most difficult to recover when their members reside in a different domain. More information on this issue will be covered in part 2 of this series.

■ In general, for domain environments we recommend using domain local groups rather than system local groups. When you use system local groups, you lose the benefits of using a Windows domain: central control and accountability. System local groups cannot be controlled through AD and do not show up in a user account's group membership list in the AD Users and Computers (ADUC) snap-in. Also, system local group membership changes are logged to a local machine's security event log, and not to the domain controller's event log.

One notable exception to this guideline, in which you may want to use system local groups instead of domain local groups, is a large AD environment that requires a lot of local groups. Unlike AD groups, users' system local group memberships are not expanded at logon and do not impact the user Kerberos ticket size.

■ Use universal groups to give users access to resources that are spread across multiple domains. In other words, put global groups into universal groups, put the universal groups into domain local groups, and then use these domain local groups to set the permissions on resources.

■ Use universal groups when the group's membership is close to static. If you have frequently changing memberships, use global group intermediaries: add your users to global groups and then add the global groups to universal groups. Universal groups cause more network traffic in multidomain environments if their membership changes frequently. This is not true for domain local and global groups. The reason for this is that the membership of a universal group is stored in the Global Catalog (GC), which is replicated forest-wide.

This guideline only applies to Windows 2000 Active Directories (ADs) and Windows Server 2003 ADs that are not at the native Windows Server 2003 forest functional level. An AD in a native Windows Server 2003 forest supports a new feature called link-value-replication (LVR), which ensures that only group membership changes and not the entire group membership list are replicated between DCs when a group's membership is modified.

This guideline also does not apply to multidomain environments that include Exchange messaging servers, which need to use universal distribution groups. In that case, it is not recommended to use global group intermediaries, because Exchange servers cannot expand the membership of global groups defined in foreign domains.

Finally, we recommend that you create as few groups as possible, limit the number of group nesting levels, and implement a solid group-naming convention. Fewer groups and group nesting levels keep authorization management simple and easier to troubleshoot. Using fixed group-naming conventions allows you to deduce from the name how a group is used and the group type, both of which enhance management effectiveness and ease troubleshooting authorization issues.

AdminSDHolder and Permissions on Administrator Accounts

To protect against unauthorized modification of the permissions set on accounts that are members of one of the built-in Windows administrator groups, Microsoft provides a mechanism that automatically resets the permissions on these accounts at regular intervals.

In Windows 2000, this feature applies to members of the Enterprise Admins, Schema Admins, Domain Admins, and Administrators groups. In Windows Server 2003, it also applies to members of the Account Operators, Server Operators, Print Operators, Backup Operators, and Cert Publishers groups.[1]

This mechanism is based on a special AD container object called AdminSDHolder (Administrator Security Descriptor Holder object). Every hour, the holder of the PDC Emulator FSMO role compares the permissions on the administrator accounts against the permissions on the CN=AdminSDHolder, CN=System, DC=<*DomainName*>,DC=<*Domain-Extension*> container. If the permissions are different, the security descriptor on the administrator object is changed to reflect the permissions on the AdminSDHolder container.

To change the permissions the PDC emulator automatically applies to the administrator accounts, you must change the permissions on the AdminSDHolder container. Because AdminSDHolder is a container object,

---

1. The same is true on Windows 2000 with Service Pack 4 or if you have installed the hotfix mentioned in Microsoft KB article Q327825.

not all permissions applicable to a user account object can be set from the Windows GUI. For example, you cannot set the change password permission from the GUI. To do so, you can use the dsacls command line utility as shown in the example below.

```
dsacls cn=adminsdholder,cn=system,dc=<domainname> /G
"Everyone:CA;Change Password"
```

Managing Ownership Permissions

As described at the beginning of this chapter, the DACL model also assigns owner SIDs to every object created on a Windows resource or in Active Directory. By default, the owner of an object has the right to change the permissions on any object he or she creates, even though the default rights on the object may be minimal for the owner him- or herself.

However, the owner SID and the primary group SID of a Windows user are also special in the way that they can be used to assign permissions for new objects—for example, a new file created on a file-server. Windows offers specific well-known security principals (which we will explain in more detail later on in this chapter) that act as a placeholder for ownership permissions for new objects in an ACL of a container object, such as a folder on the file server:

- **Creator Owner**: Permissions in the ACL of a container object that are granted to Creator Owner will be replaced with the owner SID of the user who creates a new object. This type of permissioning is typically leveraged for folders containing public information, where all users are allowed to read existing objects and to add new ones, but only the originating user should be able to edit or delete their own objects. This can be achieved by granting Domain Users the read and create files permissions and granting Creator Owner the modify permission. If John and Mary both have normal user access to the Public folder, John could read files created by Mary, but only Mary could edit and delete them.

- **Creator Group**: Permissions in the ACL of a container object that are granted to Creator Group will be replaced with the Primary group SID of the user who created the object. This type of permissioning is typically leveraged for folders containing information from multiple departments, where all users are allowed to read existing files and to add new objects, but only users from the same department should be able to edit or delete the object. If you want to leverage this feature,

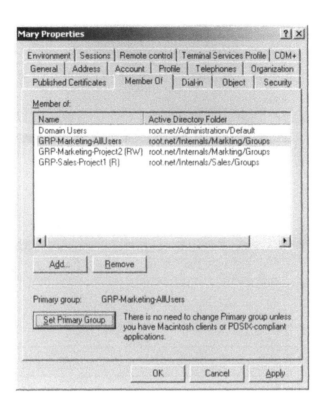

Figure 10.14
Setting the Primary Group of a user account.

you have to ensure that you first create appropriate groups for every department in your company. You then need to assign the respective group to all users of the department as their primary group. This can be done in the Active Directory Users and Computers MMC snap-in: first open your user's properties window, then select the Member Of tab. If the user is not already a member of the respective departmental group, you will need to add the group, then select it from the list of groups and click the Set Primary Group button. See Figure 10.14, where GRP-Marketing-AllUsers is set as the primary group for Mary. On the folder of your file-server, you would again grant Domain Users the read and create files permissions and now grant Creator Group the modify permission, as shown in Figure 10.15. Whenever Mary creates a new file in such a shared folder, the permissions for the Creator Owner group will be replaced with the GRP-Marketing-AllUsers group, granting all users from the Marketing department modify permissions on the file, but restricting other domain users to normal read permissions.

Figure 10.15
*Granting special
permissions to
Creator Group for
new objects.*

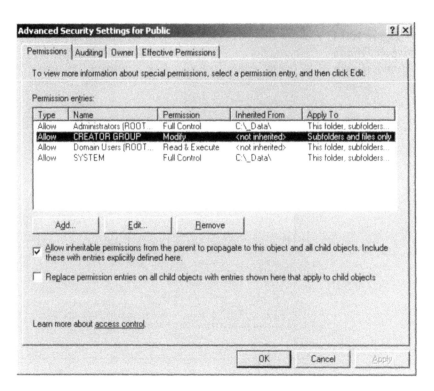

Warning: If you have more than 5,000 users in your AD domain, you should not change the primary group of your users unless your forest is using Windows Server 2003 and is either running in the Interims or the Windows Server 2003 Forest Functional Level. These functional levels ensure that Link Value Replication (LVR) is enabled for storing group memberships in AD—see Section 10.5.4 for more details on LVR. By default, all users' primary group is set to Domain Users—when changing the primary group of the users, they would typically become *explicit* members of the Domain Users group. In a large AD forest without LVR, changing the primary group of many users could thus overpopulate the Domain Users group with more than the suggested maximum of 5,000 users per group, potentially causing replication issues.

The DACLs Ownership Issue and Upcoming Changes in Vista and Longhorn Server

As this chapter describes, the Discretionary ACLs (DACLs) model allows the owner of an object to set its permissions (ACL) at the owner's discretion. Since the owner can change the permissions of his or her objects, the owner has full control of the object, including the rights to delete it. The DACL model is not only used for file server resources, but is also applied to objects within the Active Directory database.

Although originally designed as the solution to the problem of managing permissions for distributed resources in a mesh of trusted NT domains, the DACL model has various challenges in a more centrally managed AD-based infrastructure. While it is a basic requirement for users to create new files on file servers or Web-based document management systems, it is also quite common to delegate permissions for the creation of specific objects within an AD domain, such as user and computer accounts.

The increased need for IT departments to ensure availability of company data to meet regulatory compliance policies makes the current DACL model inapt, as it does not allow a controlled lifecycle for objects created by different users. There is no efficient way today to hinder users from deleting objects that they have created themselves.

This will change with the Owner Access Restriction (OAR) feature, which will be introduced with Windows Vista and Longhorn Server. OAR will allow the traditional discretionary access control model of Windows to be overridden for specific ACLed resources, such as folders on a file-system or OUs in Active Directory. This feature will give administrators the option of removing the owner of an object's ability to manage that object's permissions. It is achieved by introducing a new well-known security principal called Owner Rights, which is not the same as Creator Owner. When Owner Rights permissions are set on a container object (for example the read permission), these will replace the default write DACL permission that owners would usually have on objects they create, granting them the rights to fully control the object. (See Figure 10.16.)

As such, this extension to the DACL model will allow the implementation of special roles for creation and removal of objects, without the fear of the originator of an object deleting the data prior to its approval.

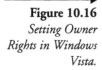

Figure 10.16
Setting Owner Rights in Windows Vista.

10.3.2 User Rights

User rights can be split in two categories: logon rights and user privileges. Logon rights control who can log on to a computer system and how he or she can do the logon. Logon rights are also discussed in Chapter 5. User privileges are used to control access to system resources and system-related operations.

User rights are machine-specific and are enforced by the LSA. As in NT4, user rights in Windows 2000 and Windows Server 2003 can be set on the machine level. To set them you can use the Local GPO editor (LGPO) or the command prompt utility ntrights.exe (part of the resource kit). From Windows 2000 onwards, user rights can also be set and enforced globally using GPO settings.

New Windows 2000 User Rights

Table 10.14 lists user rights that are new to Windows 2000 compared to NT4.

Table 10.14 *New Windows 2000 User Rights*

User Right	Meaning
■ Deny access to this computer from network ■ Deny logon as a batch job ■ Deny local logon ■ Deny logon as a service	Prohibits an entity from connecting to the computer from the network, from logging on as a batch job, from logging on locally, or from logging on as a service. These four rights all have a corresponding grant right. If both the grant and deny rights are set, the deny right will overrule the grant right.
■ Enable computer and user accounts to be trusted for delegation	Allows the user to change the Trusted for Delegation property on a user or computer object. Besides this right, the user must also have write access to the object's account control flags.
■ Remove computer from docking station	Allows the user of a portable computer to undock the computer by clicking Eject PC on the Start menu. This feature protects against theft on docking stations that have special security options to anchor the portable.
■ Synchronize directory service data	Allows a process to synchronize AD data. Obviously, this right is relevant only on domain controllers.

New Windows Server 2003 User Rights

Table 10.15 lists user rights that are new to Windows Server 2003 (compared to Windows 2000).

User Rights versus User Permissions

User rights are very different from user permissions (defined in an object's ACL). User rights ease authorization management for system resources and system-related tasks. Permissions are not authorization intermediaries. They control the access to any securable object. Also, permissions affect only a particular object or a group of objects on a computer system. User rights affect the entire computer. Finally, user rights are set by a GPO administrator. Permissions are set by the owner of an object or by the local administrator of a computer system.

If user rights conflict with permissions, user rights have precedence. For example, if an administrator has the right to back up files and directories on a system, and the owner of some files stored on the system has explicitly

Table 10.15   *New Windows Server 2003 User Rights*

User Right	Meaning
■ Impersonate a client* after authentication	When you assign this right to a user, you permit programs that run on behalf of that user to impersonate a client.
■ Allow log on through Terminal Services	Allows a user to log on to a machine using terminal services. When you grant this user right, you no longer have to grant the user the Log on locally right (which was a requirement in Windows 2000).
■ Create global objects	This user right is required for a user account to create global objects in a Terminal Services session.
■ Deny log on through Terminal Services	Denies a user to log on to a machine using terminal services. When you grant this user right, you no longer have to grant the user the Log on locally right (which was a requirement in Windows 2000).
■ Adjust memory quotas for a process	Determines who can change the maximum memory that can be consumed by a process.
■ Perform volume maintenance tasks	Determines which users and groups can run maintenance tasks on a volume, such as remote defragmentation.

* Both the "Impersonate a client after authentication" and "create global objects" user rights were introduced in Service Pack 4 (SP4) for Windows 2000.

denied the administrator access to these files, the administrator will still be able to back up the files.

10.4 Windows 2000 Authorization Changes

Windows 2000 introduced quite a few fundamental authorization changes. Because these are so important, we will also discuss them in the context of this book on Windows Server 2003 security. Most of the authorization changes applicable to Windows 2000 are still valid for Windows Server 2003, SP1 and R2. If this is not the case it will be explicitly mentioned.

Microsoft included the following major authorization changes in Windows 2000:

- Inclusion of a new ACL editor
- Fine-grain control over inheritance
- Support for object-type ACEs
- Support for property- and property set-based ACEs
- Support for extended rights
- New ACL evaluation rules

In the following, objects can refer to any securable object. These can be file system, share, printer, registry, Active Directory (AD), or service objects. As mentioned before, a securable object can also be a less tangible object, such as a process or a Windows station.

Some securable objects can contain other securable objects: they are called container objects. A container object can be a file system container (a folder), a registry container (a key), a printer container (a printer contains documents), or an AD container (an Organizational Unit).

Table 10.16 shows a subset of the securable objects available in Windows 2000 and Windows Server 2003 up to R2 and indicates which new authorization feature is or can be applied to their ACLs. This table does not

Table 10.16 *New Windows 2000 Authorization Features*

Securable Object Authorization Feature	AD Object Permissions	NTFS Object Permissions	Registry Object Permissions	Share Object Permissions	Printer Object Permissions
New ACL editor	Yes	Yes	Yes	Yes	Yes
Fine-grain inheritance control	Yes	Yes	Yes	No	No
Object-type ACEs (*)	Yes	No	No	No	No
Property-based ACEs (*)	Yes	No	No	No	No
Extended rights and property sets (*)	Yes	No	No	No	
New ACL evaluation rules	Yes	Yes	Yes	Yes	Yes
ACL version	4	2	2	2	2

list all Windows objects on which authorization settings can be set. For example, service and Windows station objects are not listed.

Some of the new features—the ones marked with (*) in Table 10.16—are part of a new ACL structure version (version 4). In Windows 2000 and Windows Server 2003, this new ACL structure has been implemented only for AD objects. The main change in version 4 ACLs is the support for object-type ACEs, which enable property-based ACEs, extended rights, and property sets. The main reason Microsoft incorporated this new ACL version change was to enable the definition of authorization data on AD objects in a more granular way. These ACL changes, for example, enable fine-grain administrative delegation on AD objects.

10.4.1   New ACL Editor

To enable a proper display of the ACE changes mentioned earlier, Microsoft provided a new ACL editor, which was shipped for the first time with NT4 SP4. In NT4 you can install it as part of the Security Configuration Editor (SCE) installation.

The most important characteristic of this ACL editor is its object independency: the same editor is used to set authorization settings on different types of securable objects. The new ACL editor also supports deny ACEs and the new ACL evaluation rules.

Although NT4 supported deny ACEs, the ACL editor could not display them properly. In NT4, you set "deny ACEs" programmatically. An error message was displayed when opening an ACL that was holding a deny ACE using the NT4 ACL editor. NT4 can display deny ACEs properly in the ACL editor on systems that have the Security Configuration Tool Set (SCTS) installed.

The new ACL editor also has a brand-new graphical user interface (GUI), consisting of a basic view and an advanced view. Figure 10.17 shows the basic view of the new ACL editor. Clicking the Advanced... button brings you to the advanced view. The advanced view is used to set more granular access permissions, control inheritance, change ownership, see the effective permissions for a particular account (a new feature in Windows Server 2003), and set auditing settings.

The permissions displayed in the basic view of the ACL editor are, in fact, groups of permissions. To see what permissions are contained in a group of permissions, go to the advanced view of the ACL editor. The use of groups of permissions in the basic view can lead to situations such as the one

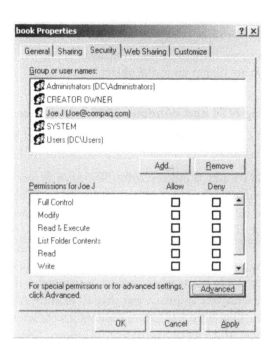

Figure 10.17
*Windows 2003
ACL editor GUI.*

illustrated in Figure 10.17. In this example, the administrator denied access to user Joe to read the attributes of the book file system folder. Because permissions on attributes are individual permissions rather than a group of permissions, they will not be displayed in the ACL editor's basic view.

Windows Server 2003 R2 leverages the same ACL editors as the original Windows Server 2003 version for normal resource and AD permissioning. However, it also includes a new ACL editor for even more fine-grained and detailed permission settings, which we will describe in more detail when we discuss leveraging the confidential bit for hiding sensitive data in Active Directory in this and the following chapter.

10.4.2   Fine-Grain Control over Inheritance

ACL inheritance is a mechanism that lets container objects pass access control information to their child objects. A container's child objects can be noncontainer objects as well as other container objects. From an administrator point of view, ACL inheritance simplifies access control management. An administrator can set the ACL on a parent object and, if inheritance is enabled, he shouldn't need to bother about setting ACLs on each individual child object. From a software logic point of view, ACL inheritance makes access control evaluation much more complex. The software needs to consider multiple ACLs: not just an object's proper ACLs (also known as explicit ACLs), but also all its inherited ACLs. Inherited ACLs can come from an object's immediate parent, but also from parent objects that are higher up in the object hierarchy.

Comparing NT4 and Windows 2003 Inheritance

Table 10.17 compares ACL inheritance in NT4 and Windows 2000. NT4 clearly offers no or very limited means to control ACL inheritance.

As in NT4 and Windows 2000, Windows Server 2003 still uses static ACL inheritance. Static inheritance means that an object inherits permissions from its parent object when the object is created and when the permissions on the parent object are changed. In NT4, the administrator had to select "Replace Permissions on Subdirectories and Replace Permissions on Existing Files" in the NT4 Folder Permissions dialog box to apply permissions to child objects when they were changed at the parent object. The main issue with this approach was that all existing ACLs on subfolder and files, which may have had customized ACLs themselves, were overridden with the new ACLs set on the parent. Windows 2000 and Windows Server 2003 will automatically update the child's ACLs when an administrator changes a parent object's ACLs and clicks apply in the ACL editor.

Static inheritance obviously takes some storage space and processor power while the permissions are copied to all child objects. But the impact of this is almost negligible when compared to the impact of dynamic inheritance. With dynamic inheritance (which is, for example, used in Novell

Table 10.17   *Comparing NT4 and Windows 2003 Inheritance*

NT4	Windows 2000/Windows Server 2003
Static inheritance	Static inheritance
ACL inheritance can be configured on file system objects	ACL inheritance can be configured on file system, registry, and AD objects
ACL inheritance can be enforced	ACL inheritance can be blocked and enforced
Inherited ACLs overwrite existing ACLs	Inherited ACLs do not overwrite existing ACLs
No way to remove inherited ACLs	Inherited ACLs can be removed from child objects
Inherited ACLs are not recognizable	Inherited ACLs are recognizable: they are displayed differently in the ACL editor

NDS), each opening of an object requires not only checking of the explicit permissions on the object itself but also of the permissions of all its parent objects.

Another important difference is that Windows 2000/2003 does not overwrite the child's proper explicit ACEs with the inherited parent ACEs. The OS simply adds inherited ACEs to the child's ACLs and tags them with a special inherited flag. You can observe the presence of this flag in the advanced view of the ACL editor (as illustrated in Figure 10.18); inherited permissions cannot be viewed from the ACL editor's basic view.

To stress the fact that inherited ACLs cannot be edited in the ACL editor of a child object, Microsoft grays out the key icons in the type column. Also, Microsoft added an explanatory text in the dialog box telling the user "this permission is inherited" and "you can edit the permission only at the parent object…". The latter two features are only used in Windows 2000 (as shown in Figure 10.18). In Windows Server 2003, these were replaced with an "Inherited From" column (as seen in Figure 10.19), showing from which parent object a child object inherits a particular permission.

In NT4, inherited permissions could be edited on the child object, because both the child object's proper ACLs and the inherited ACLs were merged, making the inherited ACLs unrecognizable.

Figure 10.18
Inheritance in the ACL editor's advanced view (Windows 2000).

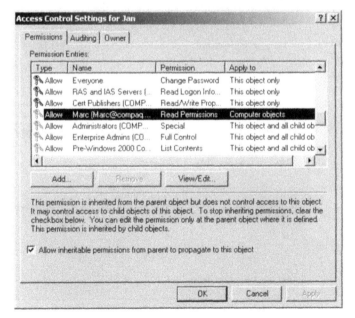

An interesting detail, from both an ACL inheritance and an AD replication point of view, is the way ACL changes on AD container objects are replicated in the Active Directory. Since AD is a multimaster database, ACL changes made on one instance of AD also need to be replicated to every other instance of the AD database. To limit the bandwidth impact, Microsoft only replicates the explicit permissions—and not the inherited permissions—between AD instances. This feature, combined with the static inheritance, means that when the permissions are evaluated on an AD child object, it should always have the latest ACL information—unless some permission change on another AD instance hasn't yet replicated to the child object's AD instance.

An important change in the way inherited ACEs are stored in AD is that Windows Server 2003 introduced Single-Instance storage for ACEs. This feature significantly reduces the space required in the AD database for ACE storage. The internal HP AD, for example, shrank from 12 GB down to 7 GB when upgrading from Windows 2000 to Windows Server 2003 domain controllers, because of this feature. You will not be able to regain this disk space from an upgraded Windows 2000 domain controller until you perform an offline database defragmentation (which requires booting each DC to Directory Services Restore Mode and starting the offline defrag

Figure 10.19
Inheritance in the ACL editor's advanced view (Windows Server 2003).

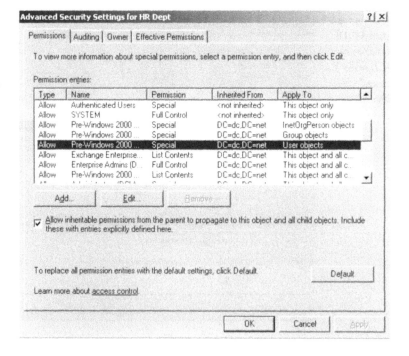

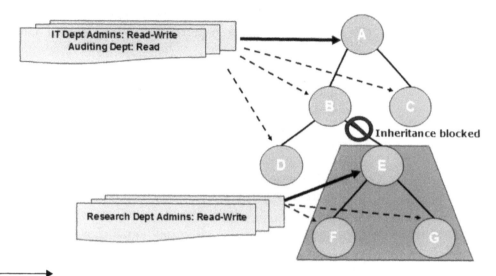

Figure 10.20 *Controlling ACL inheritance using blocking.*

using the NTDSUTIL tool). Single-instance storage for ACEs basically means that child objects just contain a pointer to the inherited ACEs that are stored in the parent object's explicit ACEs—the actual inherited ACEs are not copied to every single child object.

Controlling Inheritance

By default, Windows 2000/2003 ACL inheritance automatically flows down from container objects to all child objects. If desired, this default behavior can be modified by blocking ACL inheritance on a child object, by enforcing inheritance,[2] or by limiting the inheritance scope on a container object. Thanks to these features, both entire subtrees and leaf objects can be excluded from ACL inheritance in an object hierarchy (as illustrated in Figure 10.20). What these features really mean is that ACEs marked as inheritable are or are not written to the ACLs of all or specific child containers or objects.

You may want to use inheritance control to apply special access control rules to the file system folder or AD organizational unit of your organization's very special departments. Realize that blocking inheritance adds additional complexity to understanding the permissions set for your Active Directory or any resources on servers. Ideally, you should avoid

2.   Enforcement of inherited permissions is not possible for AD permission inheritance.

using blocked inheritance and, instead, design an OU or folder structure that allows granting the required rights using normal inherited and explicit permissions.

To illustrate the impact of blocking inheritance, Figure 10.20 shows the inheritance of the permissions that are explicitly set on the AD Organizational Unit A with inheritance for child OUs and objects. But at the level of E, OU permission inheritance has been blocked. As a consequence, the OU A permissions are only inherited to OU B, C, and D, but not to E or any of its sub-OUs (F and G). On OU E, an explicit permission is set that only gives read-write access to the research department admins. As this permission was also configured to apply to all child objects, it is also inherited to OU F and G.

To block inheritance on the child object-level, uncheck the "Allow inheritable permissions from the parent to propagate to this object and all child objects" option (available only in the advanced view of the ACL editor[3]), as illustrated in Figure 10.21. If you uncheck this box, Windows will bring up a dialog box (illustrated in Figure 10.22) that gives you the option to "Copy the previously inherited permissions to the object," to "Remove the inherited permissions and keep only the permissions explicitly specified on this object," or to cancel the action. The first choice removes the inherited flag from inherited ACEs and makes them explicit ACEs. The second choice effectively removes inherited ACEs.

When you recheck the "Allow inheritable permissions from the parent to propagate to this object and all child objects" checkbox (after you first unchecked it and removed the inherited permissions), you can reapply all inherited permissions.

File system and registry permission inheritance have another option that is not available for AD permission inheritance: to get around the inheritance blocking settings mentioned in the previous paragraph, the administrator of a child's parent folder can enforce the writing of the inheritable ACEs to the child object's ACEs. This is also done in the Advanced view of the ACL editor, using the "Replace permission entries on all child objects with entries shown here that apply to child objects" checkbox.

Another way to control inheritance on the parent container level is by using ACL inheritance scoping. ACL inheritance scoping is based on special inheritance flags added to a parent object's ACEs. The flags are listed in

---

3.   In Windows 2000, this option was also available in the basic view of the ACL editor.

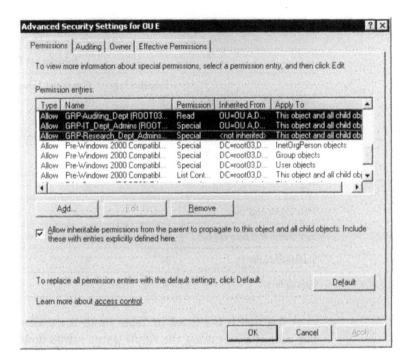

Figure 10.21
Setting inheritance in the ACL editor.

the top row of Table 10.18. The ones listed in this table apply to file system ACEs only; AD permissions are even more granular, as described further below.

The flags can be set from the advanced view of the ACL editor, using the View/Edit... pushbutton (as illustrated in Figure 10.23). In the Apply onto... listbox, different scopes can be selected: "This folder only", "files only", etc. Table 10.18 shows the inheritance flags corresponding to the setting chosen from the Apply onto... listbox. A noncontainer object obviously doesn't have these settings. In this case, the Apply onto... box just shows "this object only".

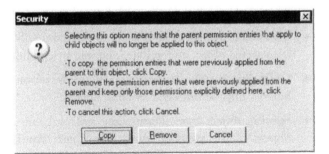

Figure 10.22
ACL Editor warning message.

Table 10.18 *Inheritance Flags Corresponding to the File System ACL Apply onto… Setting*

	Inheritance Flag		
"Apply onto …" Setting	**Inherit Only (IO)**	**Container Inherit (CI)**	**Object Inherit (OI)**
This folder only			
This folder, subfolders, and files		X	X
This folder and subfolders		X	
This folder and files			X
Subfolders and files only	X	X	X
Subfolders only	X	X	
Files only	X		X

A flag that is not listed in Table 10.18 is the non-propagate flag. This flag cannot be set using the Apply onto… drop down box; it must be set using the "Apply these permissions to objects and/or containers within this container only" checkbox (this checkbox is available from the advanced view only using the View/Edit… pushbutton), as illustrated in Figure 10.23. The non-propagate flag and the corresponding checkbox control the recursion depth of permission inheritance. If you check the checkbox, the parent's permissions will only be propagated one level down the hierarchy (only to child objects, not to grand-child objects and so forth). If you uncheck it, permission inheritance will be applied recursively all the way down the object tree.

AD permissions have a much richer set of inheritance scoping flags. In short, the AD permission inheritance scopes can be classified as follows:

- **This object only**: Permissions will only be set explicitly on the selected object and will not be inherited by child objects.
- **This object and all child objects**: Permissions will be set explicitly on the selected object and will be inherited by child objects.
- **Child objects only**: Permissions will not be set on the selected object but will only be inherited by child objects.
- **Specific object type**: Permissions will only be inherited by child objects of the specified type. The object type can be any object available in the Active Directory, including object types created by

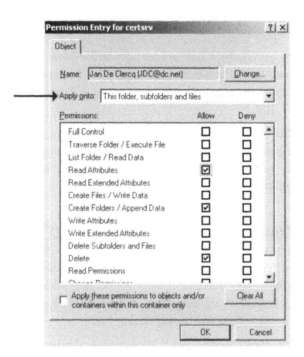

Figure 10.23
Setting inheritance in the ACL editor (file system).

extending the AD schema. Inheritance based on the object-type will be covered in more detail in the section on object type-based ACEs.

There is another important difference between the handling of permission inheritance on file system resources and permission inheritance for Active Directory objects: the default for inheritance scoping for new ACLs on file system resources is to enable full inheritance, that is, to inherit the new permission to "This folder, subfolders and files." This is not the case in Active Directory, and often causes confusion; the administrator must explicitly configure inheritance for the permissions added to objects so that they are inherited down to the child objects, if that is desired.

10.4.3 Object Type-Based ACEs

Object type-based ACEs are a new feature of version 4 ACLs. Microsoft implemented them in Windows 2000 and Windows Server 2003 for AD objects. Object-type based ACEs include two new ACE fields: an object type field and an inherited object type field. Using these two fields, an administrator can create fine-grain authorization settings for AD objects:

- He can define which object types an ACE applies to. The object type field of an ACE refers to an object GUID, which can be linked to an object type, an object property, a set of object properties, or an extended right.

- He can define which object types will inherit the authorization information defined in an ACE. The ACE field used for this feature is the inherited object type field. Like the object type field, it contains a GUID.

The following sections explain how you can set access control based on the object type, a property, a property set, or an extended right. We will also come back to the effect of object type-based ACEs on AD object ACL inheritance.

Setting Access Control Based on the Object Type

Object type-based ACEs can be used to set permissions based on the AD object type. Let's illustrate this with an example. As mentioned earlier in this book, AD objects can be grouped in containers called Organizational Units. Figure 10.24 shows how access control could be set on the "Brussels" OU using object-type based ACEs:

- Jan cannot create user child objects in the Brussels OU.
- Wim cannot create computer child objects in the Brussels OU.
- Marc can create group child objects in the Brussels OU.
- Paul can create computer child objects in the Brussels OU.

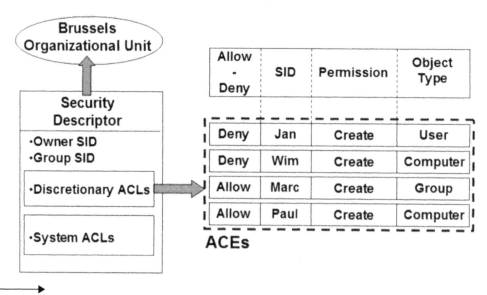

Figure 10.24   *Object type-based ACEs.*

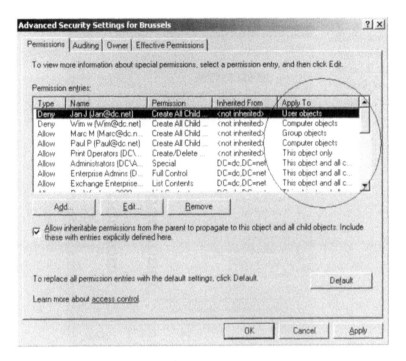

Figure 10.25 *Object type-based ACLs in the Advanced Security editor.*

Figure 10.25 shows how these "object type-based" ACEs are displayed in the ACL editor. You get this view from the Advanced View of the ACL editor. Notice that the ACEs are ordered in canonical order. Figure 10.26 shows how one of the ACEs (the one that allows Marc to create group objects) is set in the advanced view.

Setting Access Control Based on a Property or a Property Set

Object type-based ACEs can further be refined to set access control based on a property or a set of properties (called permission property sets) of an object. Examples of user object properties are a user's first name, Home directory, city, department, and associated manager. An example of a permission property set is Personal Information: it includes a user's address, telephone number, and many other attributes.

How to create custom property sets for your organization is explained in the Windows platform SDK. However, as understanding how permission property sets work is critical to correctly managing AD delegation, we will cover them in more detail later in this section. But first, let's explain how you would more generally set permissions for properties or property sets.

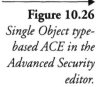

Figure 10.26
Single Object type-based ACE in the Advanced Security editor.

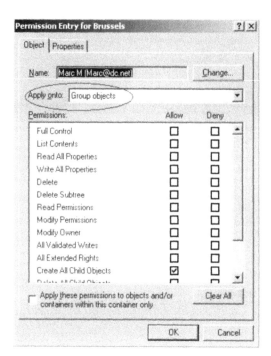

Modifying the AD Authorization Info Displayed in the ACL Editor

Because the number of different object classes and properties that are stored in AD is relatively big, by default the Advanced View of the ACL editor only displays a subset of the object classes and properties. To change the items displayed in the ACL editor, you can edit the dssec.dat file (illustrated in Figure 10.27), which is located in the %systemroot%\System32 directory of every domain controller and other machines, where the AD Users and Computers MMC snap-in is installed.

The dssec.dat file contains a bracketed entry for every object class. If an object class's @ value is set to 7, the type is not displayed in the ACL editor; if it's set to 0, it is displayed. The same is true for the different object properties. If a property's value is set to 7, it is not displayed; 6 means that only the read permission is included; 5 means that only the write permission is included; and 0 means that both the read and write permission are included for the property.

To reflect the changes made to dssec.dat, close and restart the AD Users and Computers MMC snap-in.

Another solution is to simply edit the AD object permissions using the ADSIEdit tool. This tool bypasses the display restrictions set in the dssec.dat file and displays all object types, attributes, and permissions.

Figure 10.27
Dssec.dat content.

Figure 10.28 shows how access control can be set on an AD user object Jan, based on its properties and the available property sets.

- Jan cannot change the name of his manager.

- Wim can change all properties of Jan's user object.

- Jan can change his personal information.

- Marc can read all information contained in Jan's Home Address property set.

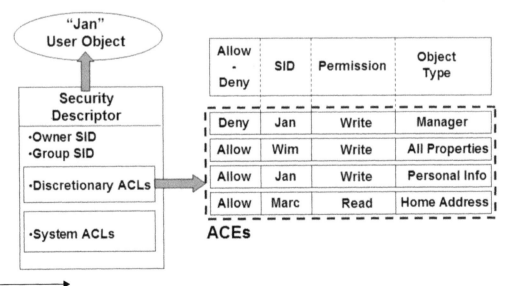

Figure 10.28 *Property-based ACEs.*

Figure 10.29
*Property-based
ACLs in the
Advanced Security
editor.*

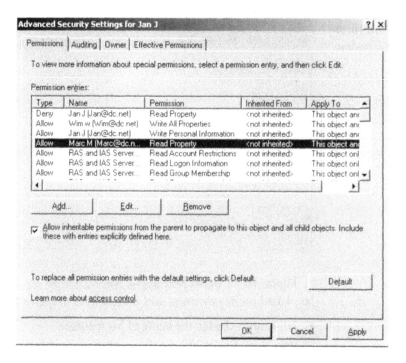

Figure 10.30
*Single property set–
based ACE in the
Advanced Security
editor.*

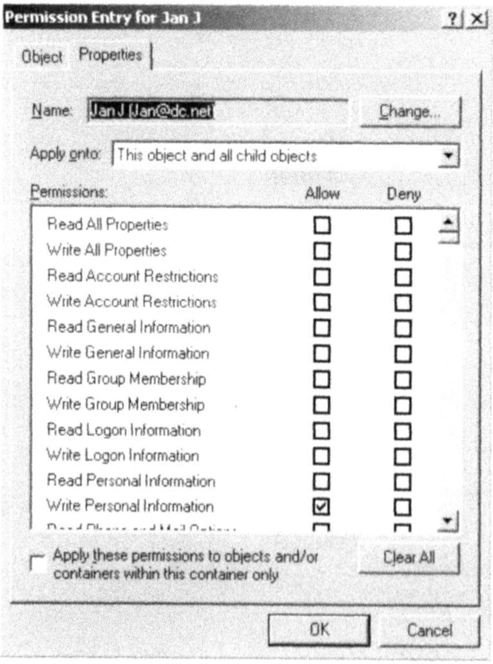

Figure 10.29 shows how these property-based ACEs are displayed in the ACL editor. Figure 10.30 shows how one of the ACEs (the one that allows Jan to change his personal information) is set in the advanced view of the ACL editor.

Permission property sets were implemented in Windows 2000/2003 to allow more efficient access control over multiple attributes in the directory. Although each attribute (or property) of an object can be treated completely separately, many attributes are grouped into so-called property sets to allow a single ACE to grant or deny permissions on an AD object for this collection of attributes all at once, rather than applying many separate ACEs for each attribute in this collection. As previously mentioned, a good example of a property set is "Personal Information," which contains a total of 41 attributes, including a user's address and telephone attributes.

An attribute is defined to belong to a property set by its *attributeSecurityGUID*, which matches the *rightsGUID* of the property set. Figure 10.31 shows how permissions of a property set are viewed in the security editor in AD, applied to, and evaluated for multiple attributes of a user object.

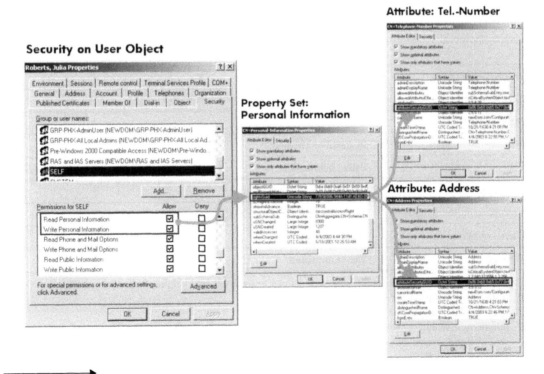

Figure 10.31 *AD permissions can apply to multiple attributes using property sets.*

Property sets were introduced for convenience: to simplify administration and to preserve storage space in AD. The latter should not be underestimated, since every ACE applied to an object needs to be stored in the directory, and a permission to a property set is not only displayed but also stored as a single ACE. Realize that any attribute in AD can only belong to a single property set, which is quite a restriction when it comes to customizing AD security.

The definition of all default property sets can most easily be retrieved from MSDN: http://msdn.microsoft.com/library/default.asp?url=/library/en-us/adschema/adschema/property_sets.asp?frame=true. (See Table 10.19.)

Table 10.19   *List of Default Property Sets in AD*

Property Set Name		Number of Attributes in Property Set in ...	
Common Name	**Display Name**	**Windows 2000**	**Windows Server 2003/R2**
DNS-Host-Name-Attributes	DNS Host Name Attributes	N/A	2
Domain-Other-Parameters	Other Domain Parameters (for use by SAM)	N/A	7
Domain-Password	Domain Password & Lockout Policies	8	8
Email-Information*	Phone and Mail Options	0	0
General-Information†	General Information	12	13
Membership‡	Group Membership	1	2
Personal-Information	Personal Information	41	41
Public-Information**	Public Information	34 (154 with E2k3)	37 (157 with E2k3)
RAS-Information	Remote Access Information	9	9
User-Account Restrictions††	Account Restrictions	4	5
User-Logon‡‡	Logon Information	9	12
Web-Information	Web Information	2	2

*   The Email-Information property set has been defined since Windows 2000, but without any attributes.
†   Additions in Windows Server 2003: *uid*.
‡   Additions in Windows Server 2003: *Is-Member-Of-DL*.
**   Additions in Windows Server 2003: *ms-DS-Allowed-To-Delegate-To, ms-DS-Auxiliary-Classes, ms-DS-Approx-Immed-Subordinates (and another 120 additions when extending AD Schema for Exchange Server 2003)*.
††   Additions in Windows Server 2003: *ms-DS-User-Account-Control-Computed*.
‡‡   Additions in Windows Server 2003: *Last-Logon-Timestamp, Script-Path, User-Workstations*.

Although the majority of the property sets are the same between Windows 2000 and Windows Server 2003, an important feature related to the default property sets was missing from Windows 2000 and has been made available in Windows Server 2003: the default property sets can now be edited. There are some restrictions to this feature, which we will cover when we discuss how to hide data in Active Directory in Chapter 11.

Note that Exchange 200x also extends the schema with various attributes, some of which are also added to the default property sets, but no new property sets are created by the Exchange installation. It is actually rather curious that Exchange does not leverage the *Phone and Mail Options* property set, which seems to have been designed for a mail system. Instead, Exchange adds all relevant attributes to a single property set: 120 attributes are added to *Public Information*. This includes all of the extensionAttributes. Note that Authenticated Users have read access to this property set by default. The Personal Information property set, on the other hand, is left untouched by an Exchange installation.

Note that the Personal Information property set should be of special interest to administrators, since it contains potentially sensitive data, such as the home phone number and home address of an employee. While companies may not add these data to AD automatically, by default every user has the capability to do so on his own through the permissions granted to the SELF security principal.

Table 10.20 lists the 41 attributes belonging to the Personal Information set.

Property sets are defined as a *controlAccessRight* in AD, with a *validAccess*[4] property equal to 48, and are stored in the Extended-Rights container of the Configuration NC:

```
CN=Extended-Rights,CN=Configuration,DC=root,DC=net
```

As such, they can be listed by executing the following LDAP filter, using the Extended-Rights container as the base for the search:

```
(&(objectcategory=controlAccessRight)(validAccesses=48))
```

This can be achieved with a variety of tools, including ADSIedit.msc and LDP.exe, which are part of the support tools of Windows 2000 and Windows Server 2003. To do so with ADSIedit, navigate to the Configuration container and add a new query (right-click on the Configuration

---

4.   Other controlAccessRights can be determined by the following value of their validAccess property:
      Extended Right = 256 / Validated Write = 8.

Table 10.20   *List of Attributes That Belong to the Personal Information Property Set*

assistant	c	facsimileTelephoneNumber
homePhone	homePostalAddress	Info
internationalISDNNumber	ipPhone	L
mobile	mSMQDigests	mSMQSignCertificates
otherFacsimileTelephoneNumber	otherHomePhone	otherIpPhone
otherMobile	otherPager	otherTelephone
pager	personalTitle	physicalDeliveryOfficeName
postalAddress	postalCode	postOfficeBox
preferredDeliveryMethod	primaryInternationalISDNNumber	primaryTelexNumber
registeredAddress	st	Street
streetAddress	telephoneNumber	teletexTerminalIdentifier
telexNumber	thumbnailPhoto	userCert
userCertificate	userSharedFolder	userSharedFolderOther
userSMIMECertificate	x121Address	

node ⇨ New ⇨ Query…). Then enter a name for the query, choose the Extended-Rights container as the root of your search, and type the above-mentioned LDAP filter into the query string field. (See Figure 10.32.)

If no other Property Sets have been defined in an AD forest, the list would be identical to those defined by default, as shown in Figure 10.33.

Both the property set and the AD attributes that belong to a property set have a specific property that is used to link both together: the rightsGUID property of the property set needs to be equal to the attributeSecurity-GUID of the attributes that are to belong to the property set.

For the Personal Information property set, the rightsGUID is:

```
77B5B886-944A-11d1-AEBD-0000F80367C1
```

If we use ADSIedit to look at the attributeSecurityGUID of a known member attribute of this property set in the Schema NC—Address (ldap-DisplayName = streetAddress), for example—we see that the GUID here is:

```
86 B8 B5 77 4A 94 D1 11 AE BD 00 00 F8 03 67 C1
```

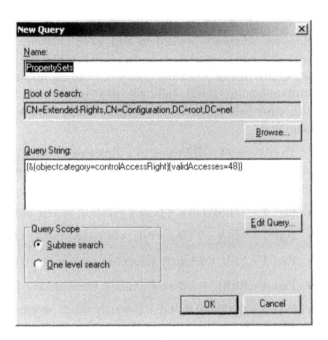

Figure 10.32   *LDAP query in ADSIedit to list all property sets in an AD forest.*

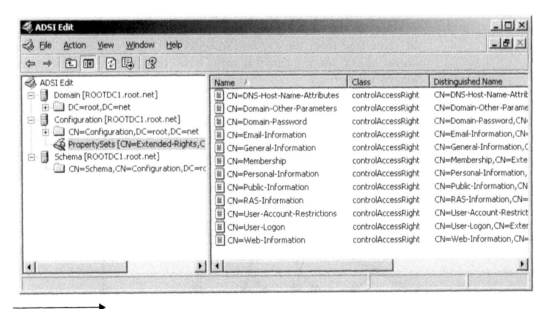

Figure 10.33   *Result of query for all property sets in an AD forest using ADSIedit.*

Although they look different, they actually represent the same value. However, Microsoft wanted to add some challenge to programmers by using different formats to store the GUID in AD: the rightsGUID is stored as a GUID string, while the binary octet string format is used to store the attributeSecurityGUID. Naturally, there is a formula for converting one to each other (which you can even figure out by looking closely at the above examples).

To convert a GUID string to a binary octet string, treat each of the five parts of a GUID string (delimited by the dash) separately from left to right and process as follows:

- **Part 1** = 77B5B886 = 4 binary values in reverse order: 86 B8 B5 77

- **Part 2** = 944A = 2 binary values in reverse order: 4A 94

- **Part 3** = 11d1 = 2 binary values in reverse order: d1 11

- **Part 4** = AEBD = 2 binary values in same order: AE BD

- **Part 5** = 0000F80367C1 = 6 binary values in same order: 00 00 F8 03 67 C1

Put all binary values together in a single string, beginning with Part 1 and ending with Part 5, to create the binary octet string (reverse the process to create a GUID string from a binary octet string).

Voila—as shown in Figure 10.34, the binary octet string is the same as the value read from the attributeSecurityGUID property of the Address schema object, proving that this string binds the attribute to the Personal Security property set.

There is an easier way to compare the GUIDs; if you use LDP.exe to look at the attributeSecurityGUID of the Address schema object, LDP will automatically convert the binary octet string to a GUID string. To make LDP show the binary octet version of a GUID, you can set the Value Parsing option in LDP to binary (Options ⇨ General). As we will explain below, the octet string can be rather useful.

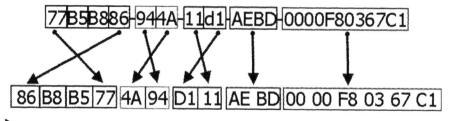

Figure 10.34 *Converting a GUID string to binary octet format.*

After ensuring we have the right value for the attributeSecurityGUID of a member attribute of the Personal Information property set, it would be nice to list the other member attributes in the schema as well. This can again be achieved with ADSIedit or LDP; however, to use a binary octet string like the attributeSecurityGUID as a search criteria in LDAP, some minor changes to the GUID value are required. Each byte of the GUID needs to be preceded by a backslash (\) escape character.

The following LDAP filter string can be used to find all attributes belonging to the Personal Information Property Set in the AD schema:

```
(&(objectcategory=attributeSchema)(attributeSecurityGUID
=\86\B8\B5\77\4A\94\D1\11\AE\BD\00\00\F8\03\67\C1))
```

And Figure 10.35 shows the result of this filter as applied with LDP.exe, after choosing to view the Schema NC (View ⇨ Tree ⇨ BaseDN: CN=Schema,…), setting the search options to dump the lDAPDisplayName and attributeSecurityGUID attributes (Options ⇨ Search ⇨ Attributes), and executing the search with the filter above (Browse ⇨ Search ⇨ Filter).

Now that we know how to determine property sets and their attributes, we can be certain that we understand which permissions we are truly granting to an AD user or group. At the same time, this knowledge is useful for documenting changes to the property sets, which can be handy when a change causes unexpected results with AD or applications leveraging it. If you think all of this GUID stuff is too cumbersome just to figure out which attributes belong to a property set, read the sidenote

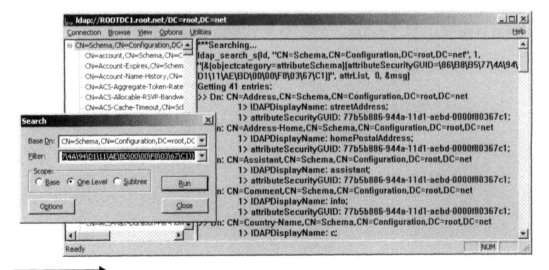

Figure 10.35 *Determining schema attributes of a property set using LDP.*

on "Using the Windows Server 2003 R2 Active Directory Schema Analyzer to View Property Sets."

Setting Access Control Using Extended Rights

Extended rights are special AD-object-related actions or operations that are not covered by any of the standard Windows access rights (read, write, exe-

---

Using the Windows Server 2003 R2 Active Directory Schema Analyzer to View Property Sets

Windows Server 2003 R2 includes an updated version of Active Directory Application Mode LDAP repository, better known as ADAM. When you install ADAM on an R2 server (available via Add or Remove Programs ⇨ Windows Components ⇨ Active Directory Services), it will install an ADAM instance along with various tools to manage it.

One of these tools is ADSchemaAnalyzer.exe, which is not only useful to compare and populate an ADAM instance with the same schema as you have in a production AD, but also can be used to connect to your production AD, simply to browse and view its classes and attributes. As a special feature, it also allows you to view permission property sets, classes the property sets can be applied to, and the attributes that belong to the property set as shown for the Personal Information property set in Figure 10.36.

Figure 10.36
Viewing Property Sets with the AD Schema Analyzer.

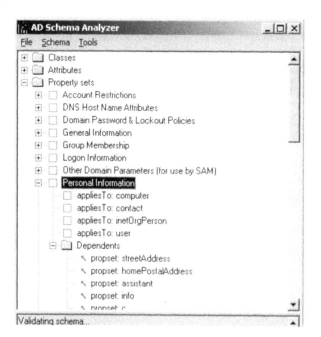

cute, delete, etc.). Good examples are the mailbox-specific send as and receive as extended rights. Although they are not linked to object properties, extended rights are displayed together with the standard object permissions in the ACL editor (as Figure 10.26 shows).

Extended rights can be classified in three types:

- Extended rights enforced by AD. They grant or deny a read or write operation to an Active Directory property set (see Table 10.21).

- Extended rights enforced by applications such as Exchange or Outlook (see Table 10.21).

Table 10.21   *New Windows Server 2003 Extended Rights*

Extended Right	Meaning
Allowed-To-Authenticate	Used for cross-forest selective authentication (feature of forest trust)
Create-Inbound-Forest-Trust	Allows the creation of inbound forest trust relationships.
DS-Execute-Intentions-Script	Should be granted to the partitions container. Allows the Rendom.exe or prepare operation to be used in a domain rename.
DS-Query-Self-Quota	Allows a user to query the user's own AD quotas (quotas are explained later in this chapter).
DS-Replication-Get-Changes-All	Allows the replication of secret domain data.
DS-Replication-Monitor-Topology	Allows the reading of replication monitoring data, such as replication status and object metadata.
Enable-Per-User-Reversibly-Encrypted-Password	Allows users to enable or disable the "reversible encrypted password" setting for user and computer objects.
Generate-RSoP-Logging	Enables the user who has the rights on an OU/Domain to generate logging mode RSoP data for the users/computers within the OU.
Generate-RSoP-Planning	Enables the user who has the rights on an OU/Domain to generate planning mode RSoP data for the users/computers within the OU.
Migrate-SID-History	Enables a user to migrate the SID-History without administrator privileges.
Reanimate-Tombstones	Allows deleted schema elements to be restored.

Table 10.21   *New Windows Server 2003 Extended Rights (continued)*

Extended Right	Meaning
Refresh-Group-Cache	Used for GC-less logon. GC-less logon relies on caching group memberships, and this control access right is used to permission administrators and operators with rights to cause an immediate refresh of the cache, contacting an available GC.
SAM-Enumerate-Entire-Domain	Allows usage of NetAPI calls that read whole domain.
Unexpire-Password	Allows a user to restore an expired password for a user object.
Update-Password-Not-Required-Bit	Allows a user to enable or disable the "password not required" setting for user objects.

- Extended rights enforced by the system. These are rights for specific operations that require validation prior to modification. They are also referred to as Validated Writes (see Table 10.22).

    Figure 10.37 shows an example of each of the three extended right types.

- The Send As extended right is enforced by an application.

- The Read Personal Information extended right is enforced by the AD.

- The Add/Remove self as member right which is enforced by the system itself.

    To get an overview of the extended rights, look at the Extended-rights container in the AD configuration naming context. As with property sets,

Table 10.22   *Windows Server 2003 Validated Writes*

Validated Write	Meaning
Add/Remove self as member (Self-Membership)	Enables updating membership of a group in terms of adding or removing one's own account.
Validated write to DNS host name (Validated-DNS-Host-Name)	Enables setting of a DNS host name attribute that is compliant with the computer name and domain name.
Validated write to service principal name (Validated-SPN)	Enables setting of the SPN attribute, which is compliant to the DNS host name of the computer.

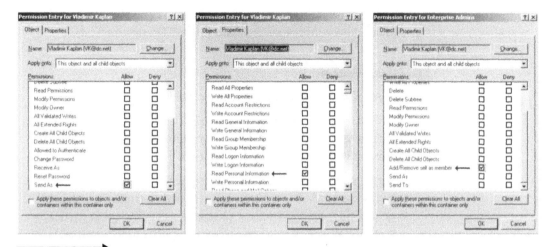

Figure 10.37   *Extended rights types.*

an organization can create additional custom extended rights; the way to set these up is explained in the Windows platform SDK. Table 10.21 gives an overview of the new extended rights coming with Windows Server 2003. Table 10.22 gives an overview of the validated writes coming with Windows Server 2003 (which are also available in Windows 2000).

Object Type-Based ACEs and Inheritance

An object type-based ACE also contains a special field that can be used to define which child objects will inherit the ACE. This feature can be controlled from the ACL editor GUI using the permission entry dialog box (see Figure 10.30). To set which object types will inherit the permission you set, select the object type from the Apply onto... dropdown box. Then check the "Apply these permissions to objects and/or containers within this container only" property to limit permission inheritance to direct child objects only. Unchecking this property will apply the permissions to all objects of that particular type all the way down the object tree.

10.4.4   ACL Evaluation Process

In Section 10.2, "Windows Authorization Model," we introduced the entities that are involved in the access control evaluation process: the subject (using an access token and an access mask), the object (having a security descriptor), and of course the SRM (Security Reference Monitor). In this section, we will examine how the SRM decides to allow a process access to a resource or to keep a process from accessing a resource. We will explain how the SRM generates the granted access mask based upon the access token, the access mask, the security descriptor, and the ACL Evaluation Rules.

The Basic Process

The basic ACL evaluation process can be summarized as follows:

- The SRM receives an access token and an access mask from some server process. Remember that the access mask tells the SRM what the process wants to do on behalf of a user.

- For every access right contained in the access mask, the SRM will then check the DACL of the object's security descriptor. It will check every ACE for an allow or deny permission matching that particular access right, as well as the user SID or one of the user's group's SIDs. Remember that user and group SIDs are contained in the access token.

- This ACL evaluation process will end when one of the following conditions occurs:

   — The SRM reaches the end of the object's security descriptor without finding a match for every requested access right. The granted access mask will be cleared and access will be denied. This is very important: if no matching entry is found for every single requested access right, access is denied.
   — The SRM finds matching allow permissions for all the access rights that were requested in the access mask. The granted access mask will be complete and access will be granted.
   — The SRM finds a deny permission for one of the access rights that was requested in the access mask. The granted access mask will be empty and access will be denied.

Evaluation Rules and Order

All the access control changes listed in the previous sections forced Microsoft to review the Discretionary ACL evaluation rules and order. The new DACL evaluation order is illustrated in Figure 10.38. Microsoft calls the new evaluation order the canonical order.

This canonical evaluation order contains three fundamental rules:

- Explicitly defined access control settings always have precedence over inherited access control settings. This is a direct consequence of the Windows discretionary access control model.

- Parent object access control settings defined at a lower level in the object hierarchy have precedence over parent object access control settings defined at a higher level of the object hierarchy.

- Deny permissions have precedence over allow permissions. If this was not the case, a user with a deny access right could still be allowed to access a resource based on, for example, an allow ACE for one of the user's groups. In this case, the evaluation order would be: Allow for the group/Deny for the user. Since ACL processing stops when all access rights in the access mask are granted, the evaluation process wouldn't even get to the deny ACE for the user object.

A very important side effect of the new canonical evaluation order is the following: although deny permissions generally do take precedence over allow permission set at the same level in a folder or OU hierarchy, an *explicit allow permission will override an inherited deny.* Due to the various permissions granted by default to new objects in an Active Directory domain, this is more of a challenge for handling AD permissions than it is for handling permissions on file servers or other resources. For example, authenticated users—that is, any user who has authenticated to AD either directly or from a trusted domain—are by default granted read permissions to the Personal Information property set of any new account in AD. As shown in Table 10.20, this property set includes the phone-number attribute of the users. More about the default permissions of object in AD is covered in Section 11.4, "Hiding Objects in AD," in Chapter 11.

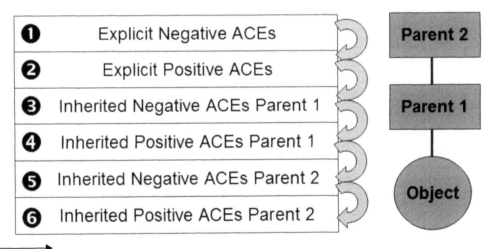

Figure 10.38 *Canonical evaluation order.*

So even if an administrator were to deny access to the phone-number user-attribute for a specific group of users (e.g., all external employees) at the top of the domain node in AD, these permissions would generally be overridden by the default permissions granted to all authenticated users in the forest, which also include the external employees who have an account in a company's AD.

Figure 10.39 illustrates the situation: although the ExtUsers group is denied read permissions at a top-level OU, or even at the domain node, some of the sub-OUs still apply the default permissions or have created objects with the default permissions that grant read access to all kinds of attributes to authenticated users. Naturally, the top-level deny will not be able to traverse far down the tree if it comes across an OU that has blocked inheritance of permissions from its parent OU.

Figure 10.40 and Figure 10.41 give some more concrete ACL evaluation examples. In both examples, a process impersonating a user, Jan, is requesting read and delete access to a resource. The user Jan is a member of two groups: consultants and AMTG.

- In the first example (Figure 10.40) access is denied based on a deny delete permission for the consultants group (this is an inherited ACE). Note that even though Jan was granted read access, the granted access mask is empty. Also note that Jan would have been granted read access had he not invoked a process that also requested the delete permission (such as trying to delete the object).

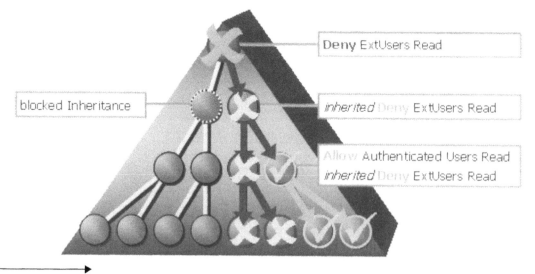

Figure 10.39   *Sample explicit Allow permission overriding top-level Deny.*

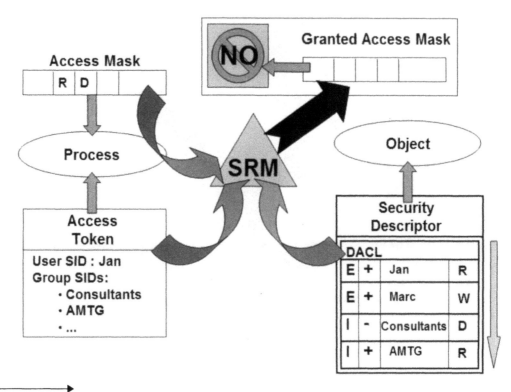

Figure 10.40   *ACL evaluation example 1.*

- In the second example (Figure 10.41) access is allowed based on an allow read permission for Jan (explicit permission) and an allow delete permission for AMTG (inherited permission). The granted access mask has both the read and delete access rights set.

An interesting property of the new ACL editor is that it displays the ACLs in canonical order in the advanced view (as illustrated in various previous figures), unless you sort them by clicking on one of the columns in the header row. However, whenever you save any changes in an ACL, the ACL editor will put the ACL back to canonical order. In fact, the Windows 2000/2003 ACL editor does not open any ACLs that are not stored in canonical order.

Putting ACLs in noncanonical order can be interesting for certain applications. For example, in Exchange, noncanonical order enables hiding the distribution list member objects from the global address list (GAL) for everyone (deny read members for everyone ACE), while still allowing Exchange servers to manage and replicate the objects (allow read/write members for Exchange Servers). In noncanonical order, the allow ACE for

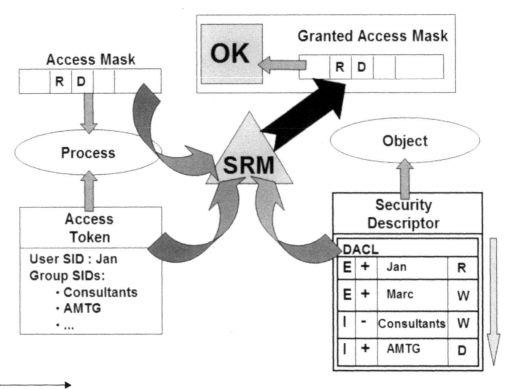

Figure 10.41   *ACL evaluation example 2.*

Exchange Servers precedes the deny ACE for everyone on objects to be hidden in the GAL. And since the SRM will always analyze the ACL from top to bottom, the Exchange Servers will be granted the read/write members of the distribution list, while all other users cannot view it—not even administrators, if they use the "normal" AD Users and Computers interface.

As such, it is possible to set ACLs in a noncanonical order; however, when you want to do this, you cannot use the ACL editor, and you'll have to do it programmatically. When you try to edit noncanonical ACLs in the AD Users and Computers MMC snap-in, the ACL Editor will return the following error: "Windows can not edit the permissions on <object_name> because they have been written in a non-standard format by another application. To enable editing, you must use the application to restore the permissions to a standard format." Alternatively, the ACL editor offers you to reorder the ACL into canonical format.

In the ACL evaluation process, special care must be taken of empty and missing DACLs. A missing DACL is also known as a null DACL. An empty DACL doesn't grant access to anyone. A null DACL gives access to everyone. In the case of a null DACL the SRM simply copies the requested access mask to the granted access mask.

10.4.5 SID History

SID history is an AD user account attribute[5] used to facilitate the authorization process in Windows domain migration scenarios. It was introduced in Windows 2000 and is still used in Windows Server 2003 and R2. SID History helps in migration scenarios where a new domain infrastructure is created in parallel with the old domain infrastructure. In other words, there's a period of coexistence where the old and the new domains are both operational. In such scenarios, it is typically required that the migrated user accounts in the new infrastructure still be able to access resources in the old infrastructure. The key problem here is that the resources in the old infrastructure are secured using ACLs that refer to the old security identities (SIDs) of the user accounts defined in the old infrastructure, which can either be an NT4 domain or an AD domain in another forest. However, it is not possible to re-create the objects in the new domain with the same SID as the object in the old domain, as the domain controllers automatically assign a SID at the time of object creation. And since all permissions for resources are based on the SIDs of the objects, a migrated account will fail to access resources that still use the old SIDs for assigning permissions.

To resolve this problem, Microsoft allows the SID of an account in a trusted domain (typically the one being migrated away from, i.e., the source) to be added to that of an account in an Active Directory domain (typically the domain being migrated to, i.e., the target). The same can be done for security groups. When a migrated AD user now authenticates against the AD domain, not only will he have the SIDs of his own account and the groups he is a member of in his access token, any SID in the SID history attribute of the account or groups will also be added to the access token, just like any other group SID. If the user now accesses the old resources, the access that the corresponding account or group from the source domain was granted will now be granted transparently to the user due to the SIDs from the SID history in his access token.

Naturally, it is not that easy to add a SID to the SID history attribute of any object in AD, even if an administrator has full control over the account or group. This would otherwise be cause for concern, since any SID of another trusted domain's group or user could be added to an AD user or group, potentially granting a lot of permissions in the trusted domain. To

---

5. The exact name of the attribute is SidHistory.

protect from such misuse, Microsoft has added various restrictions to write to the SID history attribute:

- It is system owned, so only the DC can write to the attribute.

- The source account or group must still exist in the source domain (i.e., you can't add the SID of a deleted object to the SID history of an AD object)

- The account used to read the SID from the source account or group must have

  — Administrative rights in the source domain
  — Administrative rights in the target AD domain (Windows 2000)

  OR

  — The Migrate-SID-History extended rights in the target AD domain plus administrative rights on the target account or group (Windows 2003)

These rules are validated by a special API called the cloneprincipal API, which must be used to add SIDs to the SID history attribute to objects in AD. The cloneprincipal API is used by Microsoft's Active Directory Migration Tool (ADMT—currently, version 3). ADMT is a freeware migration tool downloadable from the Microsoft Web site.

SID history is not available in a Windows 2000 mixed mode domain. It is available in Windows 2000 native mode and all higher Windows Server 2003 domain functionality levels (Windows Server 2003 interim and Windows Server 2003).

Although SID history eases the migration process, it also represents some problems:

- The fact that a migrated user can use different security identifiers can be regarded as a security breach. Because there's no one-to-one mapping between a user's account and its security identifier, security auditing becomes a difficult task.

- Another problem is token bloat, a direct result of augmenting the number of entries in access tokens. It may make you end up with decreasing network performance or access tokens that grow beyond the access token limit. Token bloat can even occur if a user belongs to too large a number of groups. Token bloat was also explained in Chapter 6.

- Maliciously adding SIDs to the SID history attribute of AD accounts potentially allows elevation of privilege attacks against trusted domains. SID history filtering can be enabled to reduce this thread. This is described in detail in the "Restricting Trusts" section in Chapter 3 on trust relationships.

■ Some tools, such as the MS Quota management, will report objects with the legacy domain SID and the new user SID as different users (i.e., they do not leverage SID history).

10.5 Windows Server 2003 Authorization Changes

In this section, we will discuss the Windows Server 2003, SP1, and R2 Authorization changes. We will cover the effective permissions tab, the changes to the default AD object security descriptor, the notion of quotas for AD objects, Access-Based Enumeration (ABE), and the Authorization Manager (AzMan).

10.5.1 More Restrictive Authorization Settings

A direct consequence of Microsoft's security push is that Windows Server 2003 includes much more restrictive default authorization settings. Here are some examples:

■ The NTFS root directory permissions have been tightened such that non-administrators cannot write into the root directory, nor can non-administrators modify files created by other users off of the root. In Windows 2000, everyone had Full Control permission. The permissions in Windows Server 2003 are:

— Administrator, System Account, Creator Owner: Full Control
— Everyone: Read/Execute
— Users:
  Read/Execute
  Create Folders/Append Data (this and subfolders)
  Create Files/Write Data (subfolders)

■ More restrictive default share permissions: now everyone has read-only permission. In Windows 2000, everyone had Full Control permission.

■ More restrictive permissions on critical console applications, such as cmd.exe. Cmd.exe now has the following default ACL:

— Administrators: Full Control
— System: Full Control
— Interactive: Read and Execute
— Services: Read and Execute

- The Anonymous account is no longer a member of the Everyone group.

- Security on Windows event logs has been tightened.

  — For the application and custom logs:
  Interactive users can read and write to it locally
  Administrators can access it remotely
  — For the system log:
  Interactive users can read it locally
  Localsystem, localservice, and networkservice can write to it locally
  Only administrators can read it remotely

  Also, the default security settings on the event logs can be customized in Windows Server 2003 using the registry changes outlined below. The permissions in these registry keys are defined in the SDDL format (explained in the sidenote below).

  HKEY_LOCAL_MACHINE\System\CurrentControlSet\Services\Eventlog\Application\CustomSD

  HKEY_LOCAL_MACHINE\System\CurrentControlSet\Services\Eventlog\System\CustomSD

- Windows Server 2003, SP1, and R2 have further tightened the permission on the Service Control Manager. Nonadministrators are no longer able to remotely access the service control manager. This prevents computer administration tools from connecting to a machine without administrator credentials to discover the running services.

10.5.2   Effective Permissions

The advanced view of the Windows Server 2003 ACL Editor contains a new tab called Effective Permissions (illustrated in Figure 10.42). This tab allows you to let the system calculate the effective permissions that will be applicable for a particular user account or group. The effective permissions logic takes both the explicit and inherited permissions into account when calculating the effective permissions for an account. The resulting effective permissions need to be considered as a "best effort" result, since the routine does not necessarily take all group memberships of a user or nested groups into consideration, especially if the user is a member of groups in another domain.

Figure 10.42
*Effective
Permissions tab.*

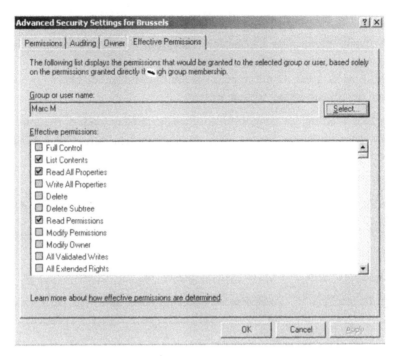

10.5.3   Default AD Security Descriptor Changes

Windows Server 2003 includes some interesting changes related to the management of the default security descriptor for AD objects. For every AD object class (user, group…) Microsoft has defined a default security descriptor that describes the default permissions that are set when an AD object instance of a particular object class is created. Windows Server 2003 includes changes to the way you define the content of this security descriptor and the way that you can apply and reapply it to a particular object instance.

The default security descriptor can be set from the properties of an AD object class. The easiest way to do this is by using the Active Directory Schema MMC snap-in. Before you can use this snap-in, you must register the schmmgmt.dll. To do so type the following at the command line:

```
Regsvr32 schmmgmt.dll
```

For example, to set the default security descriptor for the user object class, open the Active Directory Schema MMC snap-in, locate the user object in the classes container, then open up the class properties. To change

---

Introducing the Security Descriptor Definition Language (SDDL)

The Security Descriptor Definition Language is a text format defined by Microsoft for storing and transporting information in a security descriptor. The SDDL syntax is explained in great detail at http://msdn.microsoft.com/library/en-us/security/security/security_descriptor_string_format.asp.

An SDDL string can contain four tokens to indicate each of the four main components of a security descriptor: owner (O:), primary group (G:), DACL (D:), and SACL (S:). Below is an SDDL string example, followed by its meaning.

O:BA G:SY D: (D;;0xf0007;;;BG) (A;;0x3;;;SU)

O:BA	Object owner is the built-in administrator (BA)
G:SY	Primary group is the system (SY)
D:	Start of the DACL portion
(D;;0xf0007;;;BG)	Deny built-in guests (BG) all access
(A;;0x3;;;SU)	Allow service accounts read and write permission

---

the default security descriptor, go to the default security tab (as illustrated in Figure 10.43). In Windows 2000, this tab was simply named Security—which was a bit confusing. Reasons for adjusting the default security of objects and how best to do so are further described in Section 11.4, "Hiding Objects in AD," in Chapter 11.

You can also retrieve the content of the default security descriptor attribute of an AD object class using other tools. You can, for example, use ldp.exe or the adsiedit MMC snap-in; look for the defaultSecurityDescriptor attribute of the AD object class. In both cases, you'll have to decipher the content of the attribute. Both tools display the content of the attribute in a Security Descriptor Definition Language (SDDL) format (see SDDL sidenote). SDDL is the native format Windows uses to store security descriptor information in AD. Below is another sidenote on how to use ldp.exe to retrieve the defaultSecurityDescriptor attribute in SDDL format.

To retrieve all default security descriptors stored in the AD schema, you could also use the following ldifde command:

```
Ldifde - f ADdefaults.txt -d
cn=schema,cn=configuration,dc=<domainname> -r
(objectCategory=classSchema) -l
defaultsecuritydescriptor
```

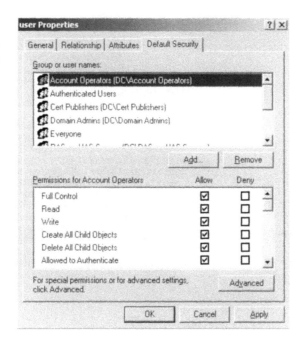

Figure 10.43
Modifying the default AD security descriptor.

Using ldp.exe to Retrieve the defaultSecurityDescriptor AD Attribute

After installing the support tools from your Windows Sever CD (or from the download from the Microsoft Web site), you can start Ldp by typing ldp at the command line or in the Run… menu option. Then complete the following steps:

- From the Connection menu option select Connect... Enter the name of the AD server in the Connect dialog box.

- From the Connection menu option select Bind… Enter a set of valid credentials in the bind dialog box.

- From the View menu option select Tree. Enter the following base DN to retrieve, for example, the defaultSecurityDescriptor attribute of the user object class:

  cn=user,cn=schema,cn=configuration,DC=<root-domain>

- Locate the content of the defaultSecurityDescriptor attribute in the right pane (as illustrated in Figure 10.44)

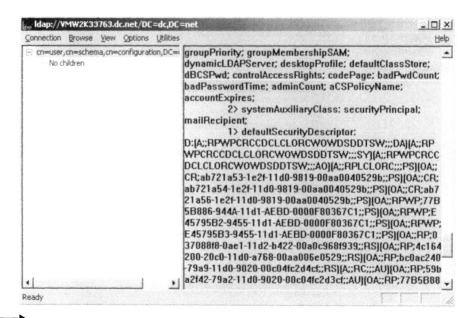

Figure 10.44　　*Using LDP to view the defaultSecurityDescriptor.*

10.5.4　AD Link Value Replication and Group Membership Updates

An important deficiency of the way that groups are implemented in Windows 2000 AD is that a group's membership attribute is completely replicated between DCs every time a group membership change occurs—even a change as small as adding or removing a single user to/from the group. This is because group membership is implemented as a normal multivalue AD attribute, and multivalue attributes are replicated a single data blob.

Besides transferring more data over the wire than really required, the key problem with this implementation is that when administrators are updating group membership almost simultaneously on different DCs, one of the administrator's changes will be overwritten by the other administrator's changes, as these are replicated between the two DCs. In Windows 2000 AD, the last writer wins and the first writer's changes are lost.

Windows Server 2003 AD replication introduces a new feature known as Link Value Replication (LVR) that resolves the above problem. Thanks to LVR, individual values of a multivalue attribute can be replicated separately between AD instances. Besides reducing AD replication traffic, network bandwidth usage, and processor and memory usage, LVR also helps AD get rid of the group membership limit (5,000) that exists in Windows 2000. Realize that this recommended maximum number of group members is related to a size limit in the database engine used with Active Directory—more precisely, the AD version store. This problem still exists in Windows Server 2003, SP1, and R2; however, as with LVR, only changes are replicated in a group's member attribute; there is basically no limit as to how many members a group can contain in Windows Server 2003 (this has been tested with millions of members). Yet the limit still applies to how many changes can be performed to the membership list of a group at once; you should still avoid adding or removing more than 5,000 members to any group at once. Instead, update the group in chunks of less than 5,000 members.

LVR is only available if the Windows Server 2003 forest is in the Windows 2003 interim or native Windows 2003 functionality level (meaning that the forest does not include Windows 2000 DCs).

10.5.5 Quotas for AD Objects

AD object quotas determine the number of objects that can be owned in a given AD naming context or partition by a particular security principal. Quotas can help prevent denial-of-service (DOS) attacks on AD domain controllers. Without them (which is the case for Windows 2000) a security principal could, for example, create AD objects until a domain controller runs out of storage space.

AD object quotas are specified and administered for each individual AD naming context and partition. You cannot define them for the schema naming context. You can define a default quota for every AD naming context and partition. If you do not explicitly set a default quota on a partition, the default quota of the partition is unlimited.

Tombstone objects owned by a security principal are also counted as part of the AD object quota consumption of the principal. For each naming context and partition, you can specify a tombstone quota factor that determines the weight that is given to a tombstone object in quota accounting. For example, if the tombstone quota factor for a given naming context or partition is set to 25, then a tombstone object in the partition is counted as 25% of a normal AD object. The default tombstone quota factor for each partition is set to 100, which means that by default, normal and tombstones objects are weighted equally.

You can assign quotas to every security principal: this includes users, computers, groups, and iNetOrgPerson objects. When a security principal is covered by multiple quotas, the effective quota is the maximum of the quotas assigned to the security principal. A user could, for example, be assigned an individual quota and also belong to a security group that has quotas assigned to it. Members of the Domain and Enterprise Administrator groups are exempt from quotas.

AD object quotas are stored in the NTDS Quotas container of the AD naming context or partition as objects of the msDS-QuotaControl class. There is no UI available to manage the AD quotas; they are managed via the new DS* command line tools:

- Adding Quotas: DSADD QUOTA
- Changing Quotas: DSMOD QUOTA or DSMOD PARTITION
- Deleting Quotas: DSRM QUOTA
- Viewing Quotas: DSQUERY QUOTA

See the sidenote on "Setting and Testing AD Quotas" for examples and the DS* syntax for adding and modifying Active Directory quotas.

Setting and Testing AD Object Quotas

To set an AD object quota of 10 for user Joe in the Accounting domain naming context, type the following dsadd command:

```
Dsadd quota -part DC=Accounting,DC=COM -acct Accounting\Joe -qlimit
10 -desc "Quota for Joe"
```

If user Joe tries to create more than 10 AD objects in the Accounting domain, an error similar to the one shown in Figure 10.45 will be generated.

To modify the tombstone quota factor for the Accounting domain naming context, use the following dsmod command:

```
Dsmod partition DC=Accounting,DC=COM -qtmbstnwt 25
```

To modify the default object quota setting to 0 for the Acounting domain naming context, use the following dsmod command:

```
Dsmod partition DC=Accounting,DC=COM -qdefault 0
```

Figure 10.45
AD object quota error.

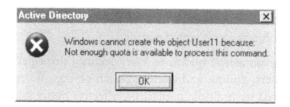

Only domain controllers running Windows Server 2003 can enforce quotas. Quotas are enforced only on originating directory operations; they are not enforced on replicated operations. To effectively use AD object quotas in an AD domain directory partition, all domain controllers in that domain should be running Windows Server 2003. To use AD object quotas in an AD configuration partition, all domain controllers in the forest should be running Windows Server 2003. However, the AD quota functionality is not bound to any domain or forest functionality level—the mere fact that downlevel DCs such as Windows 2000 would ignore any quota restrictions should keep you from using them in a mixed environment.

Windows 2000 includes a very limited version of the AD quota system coming with Windows Server 2003: you can restrict how many computer accounts can be created by an authenticated user in the default computer's OU of the domain. To do so, use the ms-DS-MachineAccountQuota attribute of the AD domain object. As with the object quotas described above, the restriction does not apply to members of the Domain Admins and Account Operators groups. The ms-DS-MachineAccountQuota attribute is still supported in Windows Server 2003 (default value is 10). This allows any user who is authenticated against the Active Directory domain to add up to 10 computers to the domain. While this may be useful for smaller companies, it is typically an undesirable feature for larger companies, as they must control more tightly who can add any computer to their domain.

To disable the addition of computer accounts by any authenticated user to the default computer's OU, you can set the ms-DS-MachineAccount-Quota attribute to 0. A similar effect can be obtained by taking away the "Add workstations to domain" user right from the Authenticated Users group from the Default Domain Controllers Group Policy. In both Windows 2000 and Windows Server 2003 this right is given by default to the Authenticated Users group.

10.5.6 The Confidential Bit for AD Attributes

Another important authorization change introduced in Windows Server 2003 SP1 is the Confidential Bit, which can be applied to AD attibutes. The goal of this feature is to support hiding specific attributes from users who only have generic read permissions to the attribute. One of the reasons for adding this feature to AD was to support another new security-related feature in SP1: the new Credential Roaming feature, officially called the Digital Identity Management Service (DIMS). DIMS is a Windows PKI feature that will be covered in more detail in Chapter 8 of part 2 of this series.

As will be further discussed in Section 11.4, "Hiding Objects in AD," it is important to know that every AD user has read permission to all of the attributes of his proper user object, since the self well-known security principal is granted the Read All Properties permission to a user object. Furthermore, it is not an uncommon practice in many companies to grant a special group the Read All Properties permission to a whole tree of objects (if not the whole domain or forest)—for example, to allow certain service accounts to read any data from AD without requiring domain admin privileges.

So how do you prevent access to sensitive data for accounts that have been granted read access to certain attributes either directly, through property sets, or through the all-encompassing Read All Properties permission? These could be the attributes holding the Social Security number of employees or even the employee ID, if this is considered sensitive data in a company. This is where the Confidential Attribute Bit comes in. As the name implies, it configures specific attributes in AD to be confidential, which translates to "not accessible without special permissions above read."

We will cover the details on how to mark an attribute as confidential and how to grant access to read a confidential attribute in Chapter 11, but the basic idea is to do the following:

1.   The new confidential bit is set as bit 7 (=128 decimal) in the searchFlags property of the respective attributeSchema object in the AD schema. So adding 128 to any existing value designates the attribute as confidential.

2.   Granting access to a confidential attribute to users or groups who need to read the confidential data in the attribute requires the granting of CONTROL_ACCESS on the attribute for the respective objects.

There is an important limitation to be aware of when trying to use the confidential bit: Microsoft does not let you apply the bit to the base schema attributes. The inability to do this basically rules out leveraging the confidential bit for 90% of the default attributes that come with AD.

The base schema attributes are category 1 attributeSchema objects and are identified via their systemFlags attribute, as bit 4 (=16 decimal). But not all default attributes are category 1 attributes: the AD schema comes out of the box with 863 attributes in Windows 2000 and 1070 in Windows Server 2003. R2 adds another 81 attributes (mostly for SFU and DFSR). As Windows 2000 doesn't support the confidential bit anyways, we won't analyze its attributes for this feature.

To figure out which attributes are category 1 attributes we will search for all attributeSchema objects with bit 4 enabled. You could simply dump all attributeSchema objects along with their systemFlags property with a filter such as (objectCategory=attributeSchema) and do the analysis in some other tool like Excel. However, it is much nicer to run an LDAP query that gives you the final result right away. We cannot run a query checking for a simple decimal value in the systemFlags property, since an attribute could have other bits set in the systemFlags as well. Therefore, we need to run an LDAP query with a bitwise test, which is done by adding the RuleOID 1.2.840.113556.1.4.803[6] into the searchfilter:

```
(&(objectCategory=attributeSchema)(systemFlags:1.2.840.1
13556.1.4.803:=16))
```

As we expect a value above 1,000, we need to enable a paged query in LDP, which is done through the search options dialog, and setting the Search Call Type to *Paged* as shown in Figure 10.46. Entering the OID 1.1 in the Attributes field tells LDP to only return DNs and no attributes.

The results of the paged query against the Schema NC of a Windows Server 2003 AD with the filter above, returns **1,007** attributes that belong

Figure 10.46
Options for running a paged query with LDP.

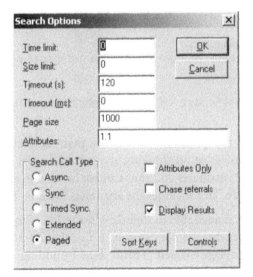

---

6.   There are two RuleOIDs for bitwise operations (Matching Rules):
      1.) 1.2.840.113556.1.4.803 is an AND condition (only true if all bits of the decimal value are matched)
      2.) 1.2.840.113556.1.4.804 is an OR condition (true if any bit of the decimal value is matched)

to category 1 (R2 does not add any category 1 attributes to AD). The query results below have been shortened for easier readability:

```
***Searching...
ldap_search_init_page(ld,
"CN=Schema,CN=Configuration,DC=root,DC=net", 2,
"(&(objectCategory=attributeSchema)(systemFlags:1.2.840.113
556.1.4.803:=16))", attrList,  0, svrCtrls, ClntCtrls, 0, 0
,SortKeys)
0x0 = ldap_get_next_page_s(ld, hPage, 1000, &timeout, 0,
0xC05750);
Result <0>:
Matched DNs:
Getting 1000 entries:
>> Dn: CN=Account-Expires,CN=Schema,CN=Configuration,DC=…
>> Dn: CN=…
>> Dn: CN=…
>> Dn: CN=Well-Known-
Objects,CN=Schema,CN=Configuration,DC=…
-----------


   -=>> 'Run' for more, 'Close' to abandon <<=-
0x0 = ldap_get_next_page_s(ld, hPage, 1000, &timeout, 0,
0x9549D8);
Result <0>:
Matched DNs:
Getting 7 entries:
>> Dn: CN=When-Changed,CN=Schema,CN=Configuration,DC=…
>> Dn: CN=…
>> Dn: CN=…
>> Dn: CN=X509-Cert,CN=Schema,CN=Configuration,DC=…
-----------
```

If you run the query, you will notice that many of the potential candidates that come to mind thinking about confidential data in AD are actually category 1 attributes and thus can *not* be used in combination with the confidential bit. This includes the attributes listed in Table 10.23.

As such, it is advisable to slightly edit the LDAP query to show us only those attributes that are not category 1, i.e., that do not have the fourth bit of their systemFlags enabled. This is done by adding a NOT expression to the filter:

```
(&(objectCategory=attributeSchema)
     (!(systemFlags:1.2.840.113556.1.4.803:=16)))
```

The result is obviously 63 attributes for Windows Server 2003 and 144 for the R2 edition of Windows Server 2003, all of which can potentially be

Table 10.23 *Excerpt of the List Attributes That CANNOT Be Used with the Confidential Bit*

CN	lDAPDisplayName	WinOS 2003	WinOS 2000
Comment	info	TRUE	TRUE
Description	description	TRUE	TRUE
Employee-ID	employeeID	TRUE	TRUE
Phone-Home-Primary	homePhone	TRUE	TRUE
Phone-Home-Other	otherHomePhone	TRUE	TRUE

used with the confidential bit. To put this into perspective, the following list is reduced to only those attributes that are allowed to be used with user class object—this brings it down to the 25 attributes listed in Table 10.24 (most of which were not even available with Windows 2000).

Table 10.24 *Default User Attributes That Can Be Used with the Confidential Bit*

CN	lDAPDisplayName	WinOS 2003	WinOS 2000
Address-Home	homePostalAddress	TRUE	TRUE
attributeCertificateAttribute	attributeCertificateAttribute	TRUE	FALSE
Audio	Audio	TRUE	FALSE
carLicense	carLicense	TRUE	FALSE
departmentNumber	departmentNumber	TRUE	FALSE
Employee-Number	employeeNumber	TRUE	TRUE
Employee-Type	employeeType	TRUE	TRUE
houseIdentifier	houseIdentifier	TRUE	FALSE
jpegPhoto	jpegPhoto	TRUE	FALSE
labeledURI	labeledURI	TRUE	FALSE
ms-DS-Object-Reference-BL	msDS-ObjectReferenceBL	TRUE	FALSE
ms-Exch-Assistant-Name	msExchAssistantName	TRUE	FALSE
ms-Exch-House-Identifier	msExchHouseIdentifier	TRUE	FALSE
ms-Exch-LabeledURI	msExchLabeledURI	TRUE	FALSE
Network-Address	networkAddress	TRUE	TRUE

Table 10.24   *Default User Attributes That Can Be Used with the Confidential Bit (continued)*

CN	lDAPDisplayName	WinOS 2003	WinOS 2000
Other-Mailbox	otherMailbox	TRUE	TRUE
photo	Photo	TRUE	FALSE
preferredLanguage	preferredLanguage	TRUE	FALSE
Registered-Address	registeredAddress	TRUE	TRUE
roomNumber	roomNumber	TRUE	FALSE
secretary	Secretary	TRUE	FALSE
Text-Encoded-OR-Address	textEncodedORAddress	TRUE	TRUE
userPKCS12	userPKCS12	TRUE	FALSE
User-SMIME-Certificate	userSMIMECertificate	TRUE	TRUE
x500uniqueIdentifier	x500uniqueIdentifier	TRUE	FALSE

There is not much sense in questioning why Microsoft chose specific attributes to be base schema attributes and why other of the same nature are not, and vice versa. Basically, Microsoft wanted to limit using the confidential data feature to custom extensions to AD, such as an attribute containing the Social Security Number of a user, which is not part of the default schema. We will cover in more detail how to set the confidential attribute and associated permissions to grant read access to such an attribute in Section 11.4, "Hiding Objects in AD."

10.5.7   Hiding Data in the File System and Shares

Have you ever wanted to hide file server data from your users—for example, the content of a shared folder—and found that the Windows permission system was not sufficient to respond to your needs? Or have you ever been digging to find out where an application stores data—for example: where a text file stores file summary data—and came to the conclusion that neither the Windows Explorer nor the registry editor could give you the right answer? If you are in any of these cases, read on! The following paragraphs discuss two little-known data hiding features of the Windows operating system: NTFS file streams and access-based enumeration (ABE).

NTFS file streams is a feature of the Windows NTFS file system, which is also referred to as alternate data streams (ADSs). The NT File System

(NTFS) is the default file system of Windows NT, Windows 2000, Windows XP, and Windows Server 2003. ADSs are leveraged by Windows applications such as the Encrypting File System (EFS) and Windows Explorer to attach file-specific data to files stored on an NTFS-formatted drive. If you know how to use an ADS, you can also use it to hide data in the NTFS file system. In what follows, we will explain how you can set up an ADS and how ADSs are used by common Windows applications.

ABE is a Windows share-level feature that Microsoft introduced in Windows Server 2003 Service Pack 1 (SP1). ABE can be used on any Windows file share hosted on any volume of a file server. ABE allows administrators to suppress the visibility of folders and files in a share from users who do not have permissions to access them. Even though Novell Netware has had a feature similar to ABE for many years, it was still missing in Windows. In what follows, we will explain how you can set up and leverage ABE.

Both ADS and ABE are welcome additions to the Windows access control toolset. ADS can be a dangerous feature when it is used by the wrong people or processes and when there are no tools in place to control its use. To protect against data hiding misuse, your administrators must have complete control over the access control settings of shared resources, as well as the appropriate tools in place to monitor access control changes and to recover from disaster. And even more importantly, you must make sure you have trustworthy administrators!

Introducing NTFS Alternate Data Streams

A file stored on the NTFS file system always includes a default data stream called the $DATA stream that includes the file's content. This is the file stream most of us deal with unnoticed in our day-to-day work. Every NTFS file can also have one or more alternate data streams (ADS). Users and applications can use ADS to attach additional data to a file. Windows, for example, uses ADS to store the file summary data of non-Microsoft Office documents, such as simple text files (*.txt). A text file's summary data can be entered on the Summary tab of the file's properties and include data like title, subject, and author information. The summary data are stored in an ADS named SummaryInformation.

The main reason that Microsoft included ADS was to enable a Windows NT system to act as a file server for Macintosh clients. The Mac OS uses a similar feature, called resource forks, to store file metadata (which is why the Apple OSes do not "care" about file extensions).

What makes ADS both interesting and dangerous at the same time is that neither a file's ADS names nor its ADS content show up in Windows Explorer. Also, a user or application can select any name for an ADS. There are no predefined ADS naming standards. As a result, only the person that created an ADS knows how to access the ADS content.

This makes ADS a very attractive tool for attackers. They can use ADS to hide information or malicious code on a system. A good example of how ADS was leveraged by malicious mobile code is the VBS.Potok@mm worm. This worm added several Visual Basic scripts (VBS) in ADS that were attached to the ODBC.ini file. When the worm executed, it created an account with administrative privileges and replicated itself using the addresses found in the Outlook address book. More insights on the VBS.Potok@mm worm operation can be found at www.symantec.com/avcenter/venc/data/vbs.potok@mm.html.

Another dangerous characteristic is that the space allocated to ADS does not show up in the Windows Explorer size and free space data. A malicious user could use ADS to fill up a file server's disk space and leave the administrator clueless. Also, the dir command line utility does not take ADS in account during its size calculations. At the time of writing, the only tool that does consider ADS in its size calculations is chkdsk.

But ADS can also provide very useful services. One use of ADS (showing the great value of ADS) is the way ADSs are leveraged by the Windows Encrypting File System (EFS). EFS uses ADSs to attach encryption and recovery data to encrypted files. Thanks to this use of ADSs, EFS can provide decentralized file encryption and recovery services.

Another example is Internet Explorer (IE) in XP SP2. IE leverages ADS to safeguard the IE security zone classification of files stored on the NTFS file system; the ADS used by IE is called Security.Zone. This way, IE can block elevation-of-privilege attacks that could occur when a user downloads a piece of malicious code from the untrusted Internet security zone and saves it to the local disk. IE classifies locally saved content in the Local Machine security zone, which has a higher set of privileges than the Internet Security zone. In XP SP2, Windows will always first check the Security.Zone information before allowing the code to do anything on the local system.

Using NTFS Alternate Data Streams

Now that we know what ADS can be used for, let us look at how you can set them up. Anyone that has write permission to an NTFS file can attach an ADS to the file using common operating system commands. For example, to set up an alternate data stream called mystream, attach it to an existing file named file.txt, store some "top secret" data in it, and type the following at the command prompt:

```
echo top secret > file.txt:mystream
```

To display mystream's content, type the following at the command prompt:

```
more < file.txt:mystream
```

An even more powerful example that clearly shows the ADS data hiding capabilities is the example in which ADS is used to store an executable. For example, to add a hidden copy of the built-in Windows calculator (calc.exe) to a file "file.txt" in an ADS called calc.exe, you must type the following command:

```
type calc.exe > file.txt:calc.exe
```

To execute the hidden calculator, type the following:

```
start .\file.txt:calc.exe
```

To prove our earlier point that ADSs and their content don't show up in Windows Explorer, check the properties of the above file.txt file in Explorer after adding the ADS. If there is no data in the default $DATA file stream, Explorer will report 0 KB as the file size, even though there is a 112 KB file embedded in the calc.exe ADS.

From the above, it should be clear that there are quite a few risks associated with the NTFS ADS feature. This is certainly the case if your NTFS resources are not properly permissioned and if access to your Windows servers is not accurately controlled. The first level of protection you must leverage to protect against malicious ADS use is the NTFS access control system. If attackers do not have the permission to write to a file, they also cannot create an ADS that is attached to it.

If a malicious person manages to bypass the permissions you set, you can use special tools to detect the existence of ADS. System integrity–checking software, such as the Tripwire integrity checker, can detect all NTFS file system changes that occur on a Windows system, including addition of or changes to ADSs. More information about the Tripwire software is available from www.tripwiresecurity.com.

To find out the names of a file's ADS, you can use the freeware Streams or Streamwriter utilities. Streams is a command line utility that

Figure 10.47
*Listing ADS using
the Streams
command line
utility.*

can be downloaded from the Sysinternals Web site, at www.sysinternals.com/utilities/streams.html. Figure 10.47 shows how you can use the streams utility to reveal the name of the calc.exe ADS that is attached to the file.txt file. Streamwriter is a GUI tool. Besides detecting ADS, streamwriter can also read and write to ADS. The streamwriter source code can be downloaded from www.planet-source-code.com/vb/scripts/ShowCode.asp?txtCodeId=47299&lngWId=1.

Note that streams are only supported on NTFS file systems, so that copying files to a different file system can potentially lead to the loss of stream data. When you attempt to use the Windows Explorer to copy a file with an attached ADS to a non-NTFS file system (for example, a FAT or FAT32 drive), NTFS will generate an error similar to the one illustrated in Figure 10.48. If you do the same thing using the command line copy command, copy will not complain; it simply copies the file to the non-NTFS file system and removes the ADS.

Introducing Access-Based Enumeration

Access-Based Enumeration (ABE) is a Windows share level feature that Microsoft introduced in Windows Server 2003 Service Pack 1 (SP1). ABE allows administrators to suppress the visibility of folders and files in a share from users who do not have the appropriate NTFS-level permissions to access them. To do this, administrators must set a special property on the Windows shared folder.

Without ABE, a user who connects to a shared folder will see all file and folders in the share, even those for which he doesn't have any read permissions or to which he is denied access. It is only when the user tries to open a file or folder in the share that he will receive an access denied error. Users may be confused by these errors, and may even call your helpdesk. Ever since the Windows file system began supporting long names, merely the name of a file or folder in a share could disclose information to the wrong

Figure 10.48
*Confirm Stream
Loss dialog box.*

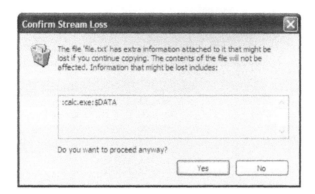

users, without even having access to read the file or folder content. By lever-aging ABE, a fileserver will only return those files or folders to the user accessing a share to which the user has at least read permissions.

Figures 10.48 and 10.49 illustrate the effect of enabling ABE on a shared folder. In both figures, the user has connected to the same shared folder ("shareddocs") using the \\10.0.0.25\shareddocs share name. Figure 10.49 shows the content of the share when ABE is not enabled—even though the user is not granted read access to the AMD, Apple, Dell, and IBM folders, they are visible as existing folders in the share. Figure 10.50 shows the content of the share when ABE is enabled. Note that when ABE is enabled (Figure 10.50), Windows only shows the folders for which the user has the appropriate access permissions. The simple fact that users only see what they are allowed to access greatly benefits the ease of use of your file servers. Indirectly, enabling ABE can also positively impact your help-desk load and increase the overall security of the information stored on the file servers. Realize that this function does come at a cost for the server; prior to returning the list of objects in a folder back to the client connecting

Figure 10.49
*Share content (no
ABE enabled).*

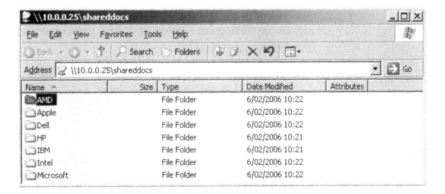

Figure 10.50
*Share content
(ABE enabled).*

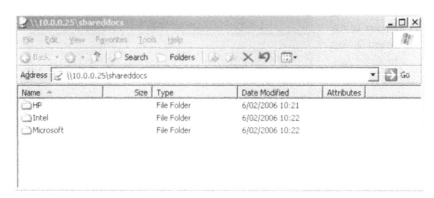

to the respective share, the server has to evaluate every ACL of the contained objects before it knows what to return. Especially for shares containing many objects, this process can have a noticeable performance impact.

ABE is a great solution for setting up for example users' home directory shares: instead of creating a hidden share for each user's home directory, administrators can now create a single share on the root home directory folder (containing all users' home directories), let users connect to this root directory, and control the visibility of other users' home directories using ABE and permissions.

Using Access-Based Enumeration

ABE uses a new share-level flag called "SHI1005_FLAGS_ENFORCE_ NAMESPACE_ACCESS". At the time of writing, this flag is only supported in Windows Server 2003 SP1 and R2. To set the flag, you can use the Windows Explorer folder properties extensions or the abecmd.exe command line tool.

Microsoft provides both the ABE Explorer extension and the command line tool in the ABE installation package. This package can be installed as an add-on for Windows Server 2003 SP1 platforms and can be downloaded from the following URL:

www.microsoft.com/downloads/details.aspx?FamilyId=04A563D9- 78D9-4342-A485-B030AC442084&displaylang=en.

Because ABE is a server-side extension that is enforced on the server side, it can be used independently of the Windows client operating system version used.

On systems that have the ABE bits installed, ABE can be enabled from the access-based enumeration tab in the properties of the shared folder (as

Figure 10.51
Enabling ABE from the folder properties.

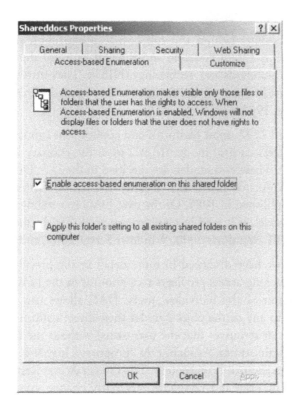

illustrated in Figure 10.51). To turn on ABE for the selected folder only, check the "Enable access-based enumeration on this shared folder" box. To turn ABE on for all shares on that particular system, check the "Apply this folder's setting to all existing shared folders on this computer" box. To turn on ABE for a share named shareddocs from the command line, type the following abecmd command:

```
abecmd /enable shareddocs
```

10.5.8 Authorization Manager

In Windows Server 2003, Microsoft explores some interesting new paths in the area of access control enforcement. One of them is enterprise rights management using the Rights Management Services (RMS, which will be explained in Chapter 2 of part 2 of this series). Another one is the support for role-based access control (RBAC) management using a technology called the Authorization Manager (AzMan) and its associated API—the Authorization API (Authz API). Both technologies can be used to role-enable Line-of-Business (LOB) applications that run on top of the Windows platform.

Introducing RBAC

The concepts behind the role-based authorization model (RBAC) were defined by David Ferraiolo and Richard Kuhn of the U.S. National Institute of Standards and Technology (NIST). They introduced the concept of role-based access control in their paper entitled "Role-Based Access Controls" in 1992.

Until 1992, most platforms and applications supported either a mandatory access control model (MAC) or a discretionary access control model (DAC). These two models are specified in the U.S. Department of Defense (DoD) Trusted Computer Security Evaluation Criteria (TCSEC), which were published in 1985. Of the two, DAC is certainly the more commonly used model. It is used in many commercial OSs, including Microsoft Windows NT, Windows 2000, Windows Server 2003, and R2.

As we have discussed in more detail in the previous sections, granting and revoking access privileges to a resource in the DAC model is left to the discretion of the individual users. DAC allows users to grant or revoke access to any of the objects under their direct control (in Windows terms, objects or resources that the user owns) without the intervention of a system administrator. As such, DAC proposes a highly decentralized approach to access control management. The Owner Access Restriction feature introduced in Vista and Longhorn server will change some of the behaviors of this model, as described in the sidebar "The DACLs Ownership Issue and Upcoming Changes in Vista and Longhorn Server."

On the other end of the spectrum is the MAC model. MAC proposes a highly centralized access control model where a central authority grants or denies user access to resources. In the MAC model, a central authority typically performs the following two key tasks:

1.   It gives users a clearance level (a process that is also known as granting membership or clearing users).

2.   It labels the resources with an access level for the different clearance levels (a process that is also known as associating operational sensitivities to resources).

In the RBAC model, access to resources is based on the role users have in an organization. This is quite different from the normal DAC model, where access control management and enforcement is very object- and resource-centric. From an administrative point of view, it is more natural to manage access control in a role-based fashion, which is why the DAC model creates the overhead for an administrator to translate the organizational model—based on users' organizational roles—into the object-centric model—based on access rights to resources.

The role concept in the RBAC model can be thought of as a special type of access control group. A role is basically a special group linked to a set of tasks that a user or a set of users can perform in the context of a particular organization and the applications that are defined in that organization.

A role is nonetheless fundamentally different from a normal security group. The key difference between a role and a group is that groups, as we know them from the DAC model, are only used to facilitate access control management on the resource level. They group users and take away the administrative burden to define and maintain access control for every individual user. A role, on the contrary, directly implies a set of resource access permissions. These permissions are based on the role definition or the role-to-task/operation mappings stored in the RBAC access control policy database. To know what tasks or operations a user is allowed to perform, it is sufficient to know the user's role and to query the policy database.

The RBAC model can also be better aligned to the administrative model that most organizations use for resource and application access control management:

- The security administrator is responsible for enforcing the access control policy in a centralized way. Contrary to the DAC model, in the RBAC model a user cannot simply assign permissions for a resource to other users at his discretion.

- The administrators managing people are responsible for adding users to roles. To facilitate role management, they can create user groups. In RBAC, groups are not used to facilitate ACL management (as in the DAC model), but to facilitate role management.

- Resource and application administrators define what a given role can do in terms of application and resource operations and tasks. They pass this information to the security administrator. The security administrator then makes sure the appropriate role-to-operation/task mappings are stored in the access control policy database. As opposed to the DAC model, resource and application administrators should not bother about setting the appropriate ACLs on individual resources.

Table 10.25 summarizes the major differences between the DAC and RBAC models. Figure 10.52 illustrates the differences between the two models.

Table 10.25   *DAC-RBAC Comparison*

	Discretionary AC (DAC)	Role-Based AC (RBAC)
Focus Area	Object- and resource-centric	Organizational role-centric
Access Control Policy Storage	Decentralized access control policy storage	Centralized access control policy storage
Administrative Model Mapping	Difficult to map to administrative model used for access control management	Relatively easy to map to administrative model used for access control management

Role-based access control is not entirely new to Microsoft operating systems and applications:

- The concept of user and resource groups, which have been around since the early days of Windows NT, provides role-like functionality. Nevertheless, as explained earlier, NT groups are fundamentally different from RBAC roles.

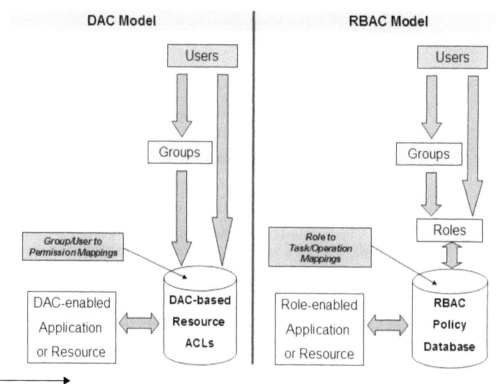

Figure 10.52   *RBAC versus DAC models.*

- The COM development framework also has the notion of an application-specific role. This role is very similar to the one used in the Windows Server 2003 AzMan RBAC model. The key difference with RBAC roles is that COM roles can only be used in applications written using the COM and COM+ development frameworks. The Windows Server 2003 AzMan RBAC model is independent of the development framework used.

Architecture

Figure 10.53 shows the Windows Server 2003 RBAC architecture and its major components. At the center of the RBAC architecture sits the Authorization Manager (AzMan), the management and decision-making engine of the RBAC system.

The Authorization Manager ensures RBAC information is properly stored in the policy database. It also provides a policy database access point for applications (to query the authorization policy) and for administrators (to manage the authorization policy).

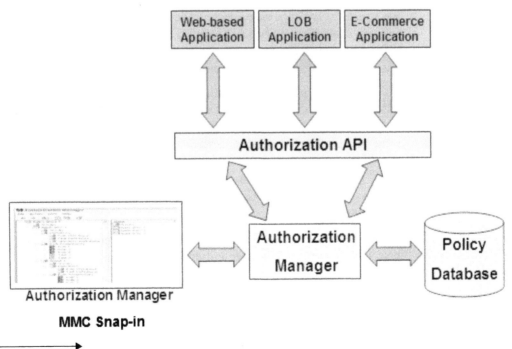

Figure 10.53 *AzMan architecture.*

RBAC-enabled applications can query the Authorization Manager to find out whether a particular user is allowed to perform certain application-level operations. The Authorization Manager gives a go/no-go based on the role membership of the user and the application operation/task-to-role mapping information stored in the policy database. RBAC-enabled applications access the Authorization Manager and its functions through a set of COM-based runtime interfaces. These are commonly referred to as the Authorization API (Authz API).

The Authorization Manager's access policy database can be kept either in Active Directory (AD), Active Directory Application Mode (ADAM), or in an XML file.

To use AD as the access control policy store, your AD domain should be at the native Windows Server 2003 functional level. The advantage of using AD rather than an XML file for storage is that you can delegate the administration of subcomponents of your access control policy to different administrators.

AD-based Authorization Stores are by default stored in the "Program Data" container in the AD domain naming context. As a consequence, they are replicated to every domain controller (DC) in a domain. If you want you can also select another AD location for the AzMan store. ADAM is a good AD alternative if you cannot upgrade your Windows DCs to the native Windows Server 2003 functional level.

The primary administration interface to the authorization manager is an MMC snap-in called azman.msc, which is illustrated in Figure 10.54. The snap-in supports two modes: developer mode and administrator mode. The most restricted mode is administrator mode; in this mode users can do everything except create new authorization stores, applications, or operations. Also, they cannot change operations, application names, or version information (these concepts are explained later). To switch between modes, use the Action\Options... menu options.

A key feature of the Windows Server 2003 Authorization Manager is that it allows for highly flexible and dynamic access control decisions.

- The access control policy can be easily applied to application-specific objects or operations (e.g., "send a mail," "approve an expense"). This is a key AzMan differentiator with Microsoft's implementation of the DAC model which is tailored to be applied to specific objects, such as file system objects, registry objects, and database object

Figure 10.54
AzMan MMC snap-in.

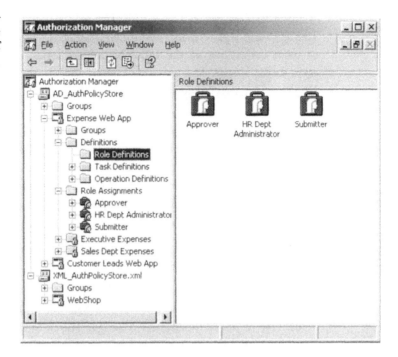

- Thanks to the following Authorization Manager features, the access control decision-making behavior can easily be changed at runtime:
  — Authorization Manager supports dynamic groups whose membership can change depending on the outcome of an LDAP query launched at runtime.
  — Authorization Manager supports authorization scripts that are executed at runtime and can be used to link access control decisions to real-time data, such as the time of day, currency, and stock values.

All this makes the Authorization Manager's access control model very well suited for line-of-business (LOB) applications. In such applications, access control decisions often depend on specific business logic. The latter may involve special operations or even the execution of a piece of workflow logic. Examples are querying a directory, waiting for a mail approval to come back from a manager, or querying a Web service for a currency or stock value. This richness is very distinct from the limited access control decision logic available in Microsoft's classic DAC model. In this model, access control decisions are simply based on the static group memberships and user rights that are contained in users' access tokens.

Concepts

The Authorization Manager's Authorization Policy Store is made up of one or more collections of the following object types: applications, groups, roles, tasks, scopes, and bizrules. These concepts are illustrated in Figure 10.55 and explained below.

The policy store can contain the access control policies of multiple applications. In the example in Figure 10.55, it contains the access control policy for a Web-based expense application and a Web-based customer lead application. In the following examples, we will look in more detail at the access control policy elements of the Web-based expense application.

To assign users to role definitions, Authorization Manager can use Windows users and groups or Authorization Manager–specific groups.

- Windows users and groups have a Security Identity (SID) and exist in the Windows security database (AD).

- Authorization Manager–specific groups (these are also referred to as "application groups") do not have an SID and only exist within the context of an Authorization Manager Policy Store, application, or application scope.

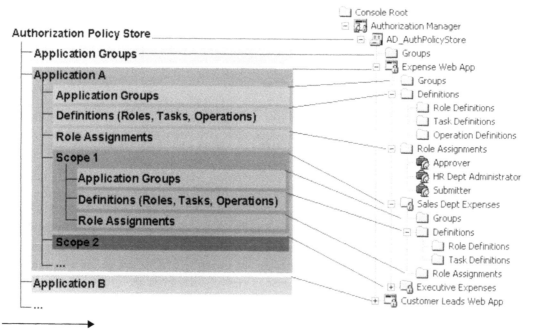

Figure 10.55   *AzMan concepts.*

As Figure 10.55 shows, the Groups container appears on the policy store, application container, and scope levels.

There are two types of Authorization Manager–specific application groups:

1. **Static application groups.** These are regular groups as we know them from AD, with the unique property that they carry both a members attribute and a nonmembers attribute. The latter allows for exceptions similar to the deny ACEs used on AD and file system objects. Both attributes can contain Windows users and groups and other Authorization Manager application groups.

2. **Dynamic application groups.** These groups have the unique property that they can provide dynamic group membership based on LDAP queries launched against AD at runtime. Dynamic groups cannot be defined when you use an XML file-based AzMan access policy store.

An Authorization Manager role is defined in terms of tasks and operations:

- An operation is a low-level operation that usually only makes sense to the manager of a resource. Examples are "read user expense quotum" or "write user password." Operations can only be defined at the application level and are always identified by an operation number (which is an integer).

- Tasks are collections of operations that do make sense to the administrator of an application. Examples are "Approve Expense" or "Submit Expense." Tasks can be defined at both the application and the scope levels.

Authorization Manager supports the creation of a hierarchical role model and role inheritance. During the definition of a role, Authorization Manager allows for the specification of a lower-level role from which the newly created role will inherit all associated tasks and operations.

As mentioned earlier, to make the authorization process more dynamic, Authorization Manager allows for administrators to link authorization scripts (or Bizrules, as Microsoft calls them) to tasks. Just like the LDAP queries behind dynamic application groups, Bizrules are evaluated at runtime to qualify real-time information such as the time of day, currency, or stock values. They can be written in either VBscript or Jscript and are stored in the policy store along with all the other policy information.

An application access control policy can also be fine-tuned using Authorization Manager scopes. A scope is a subcollection of objects within an application's access control policy. A scope can be as simple as a file system path (for a file system–based application), an AD container (for an AD-based application), or a URL (for a Web-based application). In the example of Figure 10.55, we defined two additional scopes within the Expense Web application: one for the treatment of the sales department expenses and another for executive expenses.

Deployment Scenarios

Authorization Manager supports interesting new application deployment scenarios. In what follows, we look at how Authorization Manager can enhance the security quality of multitier applications that are using the trusted application architectural model.

Two commonly used architectural models for multitier applications are the impersonation/delegation and trusted application models. The differences between the two models are summarized below. Windows Server 2003 comes with enhancements for both models. An interesting change that enhances the impersonation/delegation model is the new Kerberos extensions included in Windows Server 2003: constrained delegation and protocol transition (as explained in Chapter 6).

In the impersonation/delegation model, the middle-tier application (typically a Web server application) can do one of the following:

- Generate an impersonation token that reflects the user's access control data and use this token to access back-end resources on the user's behalf.

- Forward the user's authentication token to the back-end resource. The latter is called delegation and only works when the Kerberos authentication protocol is used. The use of the Kerberos authentication protocol also enables multitier delegation.

The basic idea behind the impersonation/delegation model is that the user identity survives beyond the middle tier. Doing so, access control settings on back-end resources can be set using the user identity.

In the trusted application model, the user's identity does not survive beyond the middle tier. In the trusted application model, all access to back-end resources is done using the Web server or the Web application's service account. The difference between the two models is illustrated in Figure 10.56.

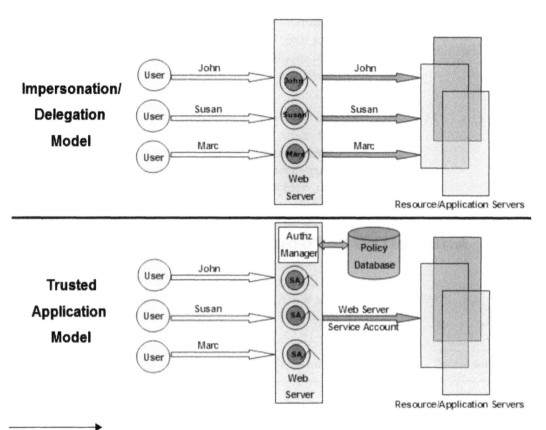

Figure 10.56   *Impersonation/delegation versus trusted application deployment scenarios.*

Integrating Authorization Manager into the trusted application model has the following advantages:

- It adds the capability to perform very granular role-based access control enforcement at the Web application level.

- It provides fine-grain run-time auditing capabilities at the Web application level.

In addition to these two key advantages brought by Authorization Manager, the trusted application model obviously keeps its classic advantages:

- Access control management on the back-end resource/application servers is easier. All access control settings can be set using a single account: the Web server or Web application's service account.

- Support for connection pooling provides a higher level of scalability. Connection pooling only makes sense if all connections to the back-end infrastructure run in the same user security context. Connection pooling does not add a lot of value when the impersonation/delegation model is used, because every connection runs in another user's security context (the context of the impersonated or delegated user).

- A controlled access point is provided. In the trusted application model, all user access to back-end resources occurs using the Web front end. There is no way for users to access the back-end resources using some other channel bypassing the Web front end (on the condition that the appropriate ACLs are in place on the back-end resources).

10.6   Authorization Tools

Table 10.26 lists the access control troubleshooting and administration tools shipped with Windows Server 2003, as part of the Windows Server 2003 resource kit, or with the Windows Server 2003 support tools.

Table 10.26   *Authorization Administration and Troubleshooting Tools*

Tool	Explanation
Windows Server 2003	
cacls	A command-line tool to view and update file system ACLs.
whoami	A tool that can be used to look at the content of a user's access token (use the /all switch).
Resource Kit Tools	
Showpriv	A command-line tool that displays the privileges granted to users and groups.
ntrights	A command-line tool that can be used to grant or revoke Windows 2000 rights for a user or group.
permcopy	A command-line tool that copies share permissions and file ACLs from one share to another.
showacls	A command-line tool that enumerates access rights for files, folders, and trees.
subinacl	A command-line tool to transfer security information from user to user, from local or global group to group, and from domain to domain.
showmbrs	A command-line tool that shows the user names of members of a given group.

Table 10.26   *Authorization Administration and Troubleshooting Tools (continued)*

Tool	Explanation
icacls	New with Windows Server 2003 SP2; icacls is a powerful command-line tool upgrade of the cacls.exe tool. It can be used to view, set, and backup the account control lists (ACLs) from files and folders of NTFS volumes and reset them—even from within the Recovery Console. Unlike Cacls.exe, Icacles.exe correctly propagates changes to and creation of inherited ACLs on files and folders.
Support Tools	
Acldiag	A command-line tool that helps diagnose and troubleshoot problems with permissions on Active Directory objects.
ADSIEdit	Very useful tool to administer the permissions on AD objects.
Dsacls	A command-line tool to manage the ACLs of AD objects.
Ldp	A GUI-based tool that can either display the raw content of an AD object's security descriptor (in the SDDL format), or—using the new version from the R2 ADAM—display and edit all attributes of a given ACE in a new security editor.
Sidwalker	Sidwalker consists of three separate programs. Two of these, Showaccs and Sidwalk, are command-line tools for examining and changing ACEs. The third, Security Migration Editor, is an MMC snap-in for editing mapping between old and new SIDs.
Sdcheck	A command-line tool that displays the security descriptor for any AD object.
xcacls	A command-line tool that can be used to set all file-system security options accessible in Windows Explorer from the command line.

More Information on Managing Windows Authorization Settings Using Scripting and WMI

It is possible to automate the Windows security descriptor configuration with scripts instead of using the ACL Editor. Alain Lissoir's book, *Leveraging WMI Scripting* (ISBN 1555582990) demonstrates how this can be achieved for the registry, the file system (files and folders), the WMI CIM repository, Active Directory, and Exchange 200x mailboxes. 210 pages of WMI and ADSI security scripting techniques are dedicated to help administrators to understand and automate this complex configuration. More information can be found at www.lissware.net.

Active Directory Delegation

Active Directory enables administrators to assign permissions to all directory objects at a very granular level in order to delegate Windows AD infrastructure-related administrative tasks to a particular administrator account or group. When planning and designing an AD delegation model, administrators need to leverage this capability carefully to differentiate who can see or do what in which part of a directory, as the granularity of permissions in Active Directory can be hugely overwhelming. This chapter describes the challenges and best practices for planning an AD delegation model.

I I.I Introduction

Most companies that implement a Microsoft Active Directory–based network infrastructure today try to gain more central control over management of their users, computers, and related AD objects. Compliancy regulations have forced stricter control over changes in most parts of a company's IT infrastructure, which cannot be guaranteed by granting high administrative privileges such as Enterprise Admins, Domain Admins, or Account Operators to too many IT employees. At the same time, a company must reduce the cost of operating a large enterprise-wide AD deployment, often spread over many geographically dispersed locations in different time zones. Usually, decentralized IT operators in these locations require daily repetitive administrative tasks, such as adding computers to the domain, resetting a user's password, or managing group memberships.

Both goals can be reached by implementing an efficient AD delegation model, which will ensure increased overall security and the ability to audit changes of a company's IT infrastructure. At the same time, it will allow controlled changes of specific parts of the Active Directory by dedicated operators with different roles and in different locations of the company.

If an AD forest has been implemented as multiple domains, there are special things to consider with respect to planning a delegation model. Most administrative tasks in Active Directory do not require Domain Administrator privileges or higher; this is true for single- and multidomain models alike. Clearly, the main tools for a solid delegation model are permissions granted at the Organizational Unit (OU) level. As such, the OU hierarchy plays a critical role for any Active Directory delegation model.

11.1.1   Level-of-Privilege Considerations

The goal of any AD delegation model is to ensure that the delegated administrators do not gain sufficient rights to elevate their own privileges to those of a full administrator, such as a domain or enterprise administrator. Instead, delegated administrators should only be granted the fewest privileges they require to perform the administrative tasks they have been delegated to do—no more, no less. If the role of a helpdesk operator is to reset users' passwords, there is no need to give this group full control of an OU containing all user accounts, since this would allow the helpdesk operator to perform many other changes to user accounts and other objects in the same OU as well.

The permissions to implement most administrative roles can be set in such a fashion that does not allow elevation of privileges in AD, but there are certain roles where this cannot be guaranteed, due to the security model used for Active Directory and the Window Operating system as a whole. Enterprise Admins, Schema Admins, Domain Admins, and Administrators are highly privileged groups, whose members have complete control over the forest or the domain in which they reside. While this is obvious, there are other default groups in Active Directory that give their members the capabilities for an elevation-of-privilege attack against a DC. Although this would have to be performed via a malicious act, either intentionally or not (e.g., via a virus), members of a group such as Server Operators can elevate their privileges fairly easily to become Administrators of a DC, the whole domain, or the whole forest.

Members of the server operators group can, for example, log on locally to domain controllers (physical access) and perform critical tasks such as backup and restore of the DC. More importantly, they have sufficient privileges to change and install new binaries on a DC, which allows them to inject code to the DC that is executed with higher privileges than the Server Operator group has itself. Such code could add the user to a more highly privileged group. And since members of the Account Operators group control the membership of the Server Operators group, the same risk applies for these users.

As a result, it is a best practice to differentiate between two types of administrators for any Active Directory delegation model:

- Service Administrators

  — Members of groups that grant sufficient rights to allow physical access to domain controllers, perform configuration changes to the AD (e.g., security, replication), have administrative rights over any DC, or can manage any Group Policy that affects domain controllers (e.g., domain- or site-level GPOs) are considered service administrators

  — Members of the Active Directory groups listed in Table 11.1 are considered service administrators by default

  — Members of custom groups that grant similar permissions to those named above (e.g., full control of an AD site, which allows site-level group policy management), must also be considered service administrators

- Data Administrators

  — Members of custom-defined groups are only granted permissions to control objects within OUs and have no permission to directly administer a domain controller

  — Groups typically include those created for computer and user administration within an OU, group-membership management, or management of specific member servers

Any service administrator in an AD forest must be highly trusted by the company that owns the forest. The company must consciously accept the risk for the potential of an elevation-of-privilege attack and should implement appropriate means to audit the activity of service administrators. Furthermore, the groups that grant service administration privileges should be tightly controlled and monitored so that changes do not go unnoticed. Ideally, AD service administration is completely controlled by only using the following default administration groups:

- Enterprise Admins

- Schema Admins

- Domain Admins

- Administrators

Table 11.1   *Default Service Administrator Groups*

Active Directory Group Name	Default Administrative Scope
Enterprise Admins	Forest
Schema Admins	Forest
Administrators	Domain
Domain Admins	Domain
Server Operators	Domain
Account Operators	Domain
Backup Operators	Domain
Printer Operators	Domain
Administrator (DS Restore Mode)	Domain Controller

Some tasks that by default require the user to be a member of these groups can also be delegated to non-service admin groups without additional risk—for example, the authorization of a DHCP server, which will be described in more detail later in this chapter. However, the usage of service-level groups such as Account Operators should be avoided and instead implemented at the OU level via separate data administration groups. As listed in Table 11.1, even the local Administrator account of every Windows Server 2003 DC—which is the account used to logon to the DC when booted to the Directory Services Restore Mode—should be treated with sufficient caution. Basically, it is not possible with Windows 2000 or Windows Server 2003 DCs to implement complete separation of the administrator role on a single server. The sidenote "Separating the Administrator Role on Domain Controllers" explains this dilemma in more detail: how it can be mitigated for Windows Server 2003 DCs and how the next version of the Windows Server OS, currently code-named Longhorn Server, will alleviate this challenge.

However, for the most common delegation requirements, custom groups should be created to allow implementation of a solid data administration model. This will be the main focus for the remainder of this chapter.

Separating the Administrator Role on Domain Controllers

If we disregard the special Flexible Single Master Operation (FSMO) roles such as the Schema Master and the PDC Emulator, all Domain Controllers are basically equal. Administrators of any Windows 2000 or Windows Server 2003 DCs are able to write changes to the AD database and are able to replicate these changes to other DCs in their AD domain or forest. As such, changes performed on a single DC can impact the whole domain or even the whole forest—how an elevation of privilege attack can be used to negatively impact a company's AD infrastructure is described in the next section.

This equality is what makes the separation of the administrator role for Windows 2000 or Windows Server 2003 DCs basically impossible—any administrator rights (or any of the service-level roles) granted to a user on a DC is valid for all DCs in the domain. The DC role should thus not to be hosted on a server along with other roles such as a file server, which may need to be administered by non-domain admins. This can be particularly difficult and costly when deploying DCs in small branch offices where ideally a single server would serve all roles.

However, thanks to the decreasing costs for powerful server hardware and the grown acceptance of virtualization technologies such as VMware Server or Microsoft Virtual Server 2005, it is possible and supported to host Windows Server 2003 DCs with SP1 as a Virtual Machine. This does allow the DC role to run in a separate server instance on a multi-role branch-office server, allowing to implement administrative separation of the DC role and other roles hosted on the branch-office server. For more information on how to host DCs as a Virtual Machine and the implications involved around this, read the Microsoft whitepaper on how to run Domain Controllers in Virtual Server 2005 (http://go.microsoft.com/fwlink/?LinkId=38330).

Note that the next server OS, currently code-named Longhorn Server, will introduce a new DC type called the Read-Only Domain Controller (RODC). As the name implies, this DC type does not have the capabilities to write changes to the AD database and then replicate these out to other DCs. An RODC is merely capable to replicate changes coming from other writeable DCs; it also does not store the password of any admin account in the domain—both of these features strongly reduce the potential for an attack against a company's complete AD infrastructure in case a single RODC should be compromised (for example if a hacker has physical access to the server). This major reduction in attack surface allowed Microsoft to implement a real Administrator Role Separation feature for RODCs: companies will for example be able to deploy the RODC role on a file-server in a branch office and grant the local staff of the respective branch administrative rights on their RODC (this is done using the NTDSUTIL tool on the respective DC). The local branch admin will only be able to administer that one RODC, for example to create file-shares or add printer queues, and will not have any administrative rights in AD. Realize that this won't hinder the local branch admin to perform offline attacks against the AD database on the server, however, as the RODC will not replicate any changes out to any other DCs the damage done will be local to the one server. As to be expected, writeable Longhorn DCs will not have the Administrator Role Separation function.

11.1.2   Multidomain Considerations

The domain and forest concepts were discussed in detail in Chapter 2 of this book. One of the key statements in that chapter was that the introduction of the forest concept in Windows 2000 changed the Windows security boundaries as they existed in earlier Windows versions. From Windows 2000 on, the notion of referring to a domain as a security boundary was no longer valid: now, the true security boundary is the forest. All DCs from any domain in a forest store both domainwide and enterprise wide data. And because any domain administrator has access to the complete AD database on their DCs, they also have the potential power to add, delete, or change any object anywhere in the AD forest.

Elevation of Privilege

Figure 11.1 shows a multidomain AD forest, implemented with a separate root domain and two child domains. A domain model using an empty root-domain and separate child domains per region of the globe, such as Americas, EMEA, and Asia Pacific, is not uncommon for many large companies; it has in fact also been implemented this way internally at HP. While the replication of the fully writable copy of each child's domain partition is restricted only to DCs of the same domain, we know from Chapter 2 that all DCs in an Active Directory forest replicate the same configuration and

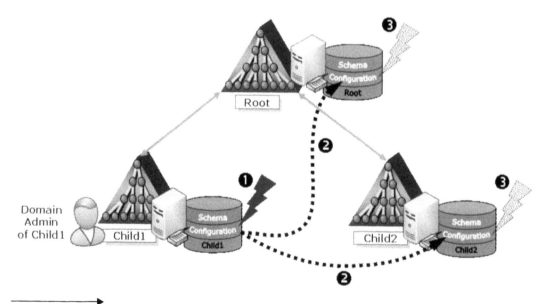

Figure 11.1   *Child1 domain admin affecting all other domains in AD forest.*

schema partition between themselves. This means that a malicious domain admin from one child domain can potentially leverage his own DCs to impact DCs in any other domain of the forest. As an administrator of his own DCs, the domain admin can easily elevate his privileges by making code run with the credentials of his domain controller. While only members of the Enterprise Admins group have explicit permissions to change the configuration partition, the DCs themselves also have this privilege. Figure 1.1 shows how this can be leveraged by the Child1 domain administrator to have a negative impact on the DC in the Child2 domain and all other DCs in the AD forest, including the root domain:

- Step 1: The domain administrator of the Child1 domain logs onto a DC of Child1. As administrator of the DC, he can execute code with the credentials of the DC, for example, by launching any executable via the AT command:

```
at 15:00 /interactive "mmc.exe"
```

   This AT command will trigger the execution of an empty MMC console at 3:00 p.m.; it will be launched by the task scheduler service that runs on the DC in the security context of the Local System account. Child processes started by the task scheduler service will inherit this security context. The /interactive switch will make the MMC console visible and active in the user session of the Child1 domain admin, who can then add any MMC snap-in to the console. Simply adding the AD Sites and Services MMC snap-in allows the editing of critical data, such as AD replication settings stored in the configuration partition. However, this includes potentially malicious changes, such as editing the permissions on data stored in the configuration partition in order to make the data inaccessible to other DCs in the forest.

- Step 2: Changes performed by Child1's domain admin to the configuration partition on a DC in the Child1 domain are replicated to all other DCs in the forest via the normal AD replication mechanisms.

- Step 3: All DCs in the forest update their configuration partition with the changes they received through replication from a Child1 DC. Depending on the changes performed by the Child1 domain admin, there could be a negative impact on the functionality of the whole AD forest and any application relying on it.

As such, domain administrators in any domain of the forest must be trusted as much as forest enterprise administrators. While it is sometimes difficult to avoid implementing a multidomain AD forest for political reasons, some environments may actually technically benefit from a multido-main model—for example, they could use it to reduce the replication of many objects to specific regions around the globe.

In any case, the service administration of all domains in a forest should be controlled centrally by a trusted group of administrators within the company. Domains should not be used as a means to delegate administration to specific regions or business units. If there is no way to get around the implementation of multiple domains, a dedicated team should be implemented in the IT organization, which is responsible for the service administration of the complete AD forest. This includes setting up the delegation model for managing everyday AD operational tasks solely based on the use of data administration privileges in any of the domains of the forest. To achieve this, an appropriate OU hierarchy should be implemented.

The sample above showed very clearly that if you do need complete security isolation in different domains, you should set up multiple separate AD forests instead of multiple domains in the same AD forest.

Group Scopes

Administrators who manage permissions for Active Directory objects in a multidomain environment must also be very aware of the scope of the different security groups available in AD. These were explained in detail in Chapter 10. A multidomain forest adds the challenge that most of the domain data are replicated to all global catalogs (GC) in the forest. The GCs replicate a partial attribute set of all objects in a domain (i.e., they copy all objects of a domain, including all of their security settings), but only a specific (partial) set of attributes from these objects. This means that certain permissions that are valid in one domain will not work when the data are read from a GC of another domain.

Let us clarify this with an example using the domain structure shown in Figure 11.1. A domain admin of the Child1 domain wants to deny all temporary users in the forest read access to the OU that contains all permanent employees in the Child1 domain. To do so, he creates a domain local group that contains all temporary users in the forest and uses this group to deny generic read permissions to his permanent employee OU. Let us suppose for now that he has also set this deny permission explicitly on all users objects in this OU (we will discuss this topic in more detail in Section 11.4). The administrator thinks his permissions work fine, as no temporary user can now see any of the permanent employee accounts when connected to a Child1 DC and browsing the AD or searching for objects by performing LDAP queries.

However, if the same temporary users connect to a GC in the Child2 domain and search for users from the Child1 domain, they will be able to see all users from the Child1's permanent employee OU, including most of their attributes. The problem here is that the domain local group of the Child1 domain is not available in the security token of the temporary user accounts when they connect to the Child2 GC. As such, the deny permission for the domain local group does not have any relevance, and instead the default read permission granted to all authenticated users prevails. If the Child1 domain administrator had chosen to use a universal security group instead, the permission would also have been valid on replicated copies of the domain in the global catalog. The security token expansion process and the implications of the different group types on this process are covered in detail in Chapter 6, on Kerberos.

11.1.3   Organizational Units

An important enabler for the administrative delegation of AD objects is the inclusion of a container object in AD, called an organizational unit (OU). You can use an OU to delegate the administrative control over the objects contained in it.

When dealing with OUs, we must always keep the following in mind:

- An OU is an AD container object that's primarily used to organize AD objects in a hierarchical way and to delegate control over these objects to different administrators.

- OUs are also the primary way to apply group policy settings to a dedicated set of objects in AD. Often, the implementation of special OUs is required for applying Group Policies that do not have special permissions for delegated administration, and vice versa. For example, there could be two OUs for computer accounts—one for laptops and one for desktops—that are both managed by the same staff. The laptop OUs allow the staff to set specific mobility settings, via GPO, that are unwanted on desktop computers.

- OUs are not security principals. They don't have a security identity (SID). This is why they cannot be used in ACLs. Instead, administrators must leverage AD security groups to grant authorization settings for delegation of data administration on OUs.

- An object can only be contained in a single OU, although from a hierarchical point of view, an object often has multiple parent OUs.

- An OU is bound to a single domain. It cannot span multiple domains.

There is no single correct way of implementing a solid Organizational Unit structure for a company. The good thing is that the OU structure is fairly flexible and can be adjusted without too much effort if there should be a requirement to do so. This is quite different from domains, which cannot be easily restructured.

An OU structure should follow your need for delegating administration in the AD infrastructure; it should not necessarily follow the structure of a company's business unit, unless the IT organization is also set up this way. More typically, we find that business units are spread across different geographical regions and tend to change more frequently than the physical locations where a company may have located its different offices. Most often these offices or factories have some local IT support and require some level of independence from the central IT department to react quickly to the needs of their local users—for example, to add a new computer to the domain. Consequently, a geographically based model suits many large companies.

Once you have decided on the general path forward for your OU model (e.g., based on geography or based on business units), you have to make a decision regarding the general format of your OU structure:

- Should the top-level OUs represent your object types (users, computers, groups)—for example, to ease application of GPO settings for all computers of a specific type? In this case, the lower-level leaf OUs that contain the actual objects would represent your different locations.

- Or should the top-level OUs better represent your locations and the leaf OUs the object types? Typically, this arrangement would facilitate easier handling for delegated permissions for objects in a specific location, as shown in Figure 11.2.

Both approaches are valid, and there is no general rule of thumb to come up with the only correct OU structure for any AD deployment. However, Table 11.2 should help you decide which structure is suitable for you:

The example in Figure 11.3 illustrates the use of Organizational Units more concretely: it shows the OU structure of an AD infrastructure spanning

Figure 11.2
Structural OUs by location, with leaf OUs containing objects.

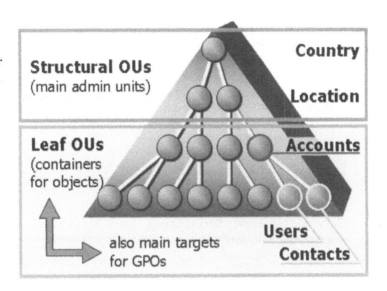

Table 11.2   *Options for OU Structure*

Option for OU Structure	Choose if...
Business Unit–based	... your IT department is split up into different entities that represent your business units, and each business unit needs to control its own accounts and clients.
Geography-based	... your company is split up across multiple locations and typically has local IT staff that supports your users in the various locations.
Object types as top-level OUs (and BU- or Geography-based structure as Leaf OUs)	... you plan to strongly leverage Group Policies to enforce settings equally on all users and clients of the same type in your infrastructure and plan to strongly differentiate delegated administration by the types of objects that are stored in AD.
Object types as leaf OUs (and BU- or Geography-based structure as top-level OUs)	... you plan to grant permissions for delegation of administration for a whole location, including the various object types a location may need to administer. You also want the ability to easily grant permissions to handle group policy administration for clients and accounts in the respective locations.

Figure 11.3
Organizational Unit hierarchy example.

several geographical locations. The top-level OUs reflect the geographical locations (Country and City) of the infrastructure: US is the top OU, and underneath there are OUs for Atlanta (ATL) and Phoenix (PHX). Per location, the OUs are then split in subOUs based on the object types that must be administered: there's an OU for the local administrators, OUs for non-admin accounts, computers, groups, printers, and servers, and an OU for shares. You should create a separate OU for each object type that you wish to be delegated for administration; this facilitates the process of setting the required permissions for the respective delegation tasks, which will be explained later on in this chapter. Some of the object-type OUs, such as for Computers, have other subOUs that are not necessarily created to set different delegated admin permissions. Instead, these OUs enable different Group Policy settings for deviations of the object type—in this case, Desktop and Mobile computers.

The nesting of OUs is reflected in an AD object's Distinguished name, as illustrated in the following example of the PHXPC007 mobile computer object from Phoenix (shown as part of the OU structure in Figure 11.3):

```
CN=PHXPC007,OU=Mobile,OU=Computer,OU=PHX,
    OU=US,DC=<domain>
```

While designing your OU structure, you should implement a naming convention and define a standardized path and depth for your OU structure, as it should be used throughout your forest. Standardization is key to simplifying the overall management of your AD forest, especially to reduce cost if specific roles should be managed centrally. A central helpdesk operator should know immediately where to look for a user account that works in any of your locations. Using the sample hierarchy shown in Figure 11.3, he would find a user working in Phoenix by the following OU path: US ⇨ PHX ⇨ Accounts ⇨ Users. A user from Atlanta would be found here: US ⇨ ATL ⇨ Accounts ⇨ Users.

Depending on your chosen OU model and the number of physical locations or business units within company, you may very well not require a country-level OU as used in the example above, and either remove the country information completely or add it to the location-level OU name.

Standardization of your OU structure also allows you to better automate tasks for managing your AD. This includes setting the permissions for delegated administration, as explained in more detail in the following chapters, but also other automation tasks, such as provisioning of user accounts and groups. The work involved to prepare any tasks that perform changes in AD in an automated fashion heavily depends on the structure of your OU hierarchy.

11.2   General AD Delegation Guidelines

Organizational Units should be the only entities that are used to configure delegated administration permissions for your forest. It is not recommended to use delegation on the level of AD domains and sites.

Delegating administration tasks on the site level is not recommended, because sites are bound to the physical layout of the network used for your AD infrastructure. Sites are based on IP addresses and subnets. The fact that a single site can span different domains and OUs may make the ACL evaluation process too complex.

Delegation on the domain level cannot fully isolate the administrative authority of a particular administrator. As described in detail in Section 11.1.2, you should either use OUs that are delegated as administrative entities or, for complete security isolation, set up multiple AD forests. This does not mean that you cannot delegate data-administration permissions for all normal users, computers, groups, and other AD objects in a whole domain all at once. To do so, it is a good practice to create a separate top-level OU at the root of your domain node—which, for example, could be called "Delegated Management"—to be a parent OU for all other OUs that are used to delegate data administration tasks (see Figure 11.4). This arrangement keeps the root of your domain less cluttered with OUs and facilitates granting permissions for data administration of all delegated OUs without the need to set these permissions at the domain-level.

11.2.1 Honoring Least Privilege for AD Administration

Service Administration accounts for your domain should not be contained within the Delegated Management OU. Instead, create a separate OU that holds all your service management accounts and groups, including those used as highly privileged service accounts for special applications, such as backup software. This could, for example, be called "Domain Management," as shown in Figure 11.4. By following this simple guideline, you reduce the risk of accidentally granting sufficient rights to your data administrators that allow them to edit the account or groups of a service administrator in order to elevate their own privileges.

The Domain Management OU should not contain any normal user accounts; in fact, none of the accounts that are members of groups granted permissions for AD service or data administration should be used for everyday logon to the respective users' workstations. Instead, these users should be given two accounts: one low-privileged normal user account used to log

Figure 11.4
Sample top-level OU structure for delegated AD management.

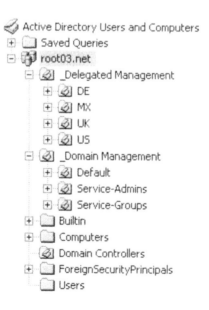

on to computers and perform everyday office tasks such as e-mailing, normal file or printing tasks, and Internet access, and a second account that grants the respective service or data administration privileges. This setup would allow the user to perform required administration tasks while at the same time honoring the principle of least privilege: give a user or a piece of code only the privileges it needs to do the job—no less and no more. Windows 2000 and XP clients, as well as Windows Server 2003, provide the RunAs functionality to enable logging onto the computer with a low-privileged account and specifically elevate the user's privileges by running dedicated applications—such as the Active Directory Users and Computer MMC snap-in—with different credentials. More tips for better honoring least privilege are given in Chapter 4.

Another option that is particularly useful for delegated administration of Active Directory is to set up a terminal server instance, in which all the required tools, such as the AD Users and Computers MMC snap-in and the Group Policy Management Console, are installed. By using a terminal server, these tools would not have to be installed on all the computers used by the delegated administrators. Users can log on to their computers with their normal account and open up a terminal server session using their higher-privileged service or data administration account to perform any administrative tasks in AD.

11.2.2 Controlling Password Management

To further enhance the principle of least privilege for delegation of AD administration as well as the overall security of your AD domain, Windows Server 2003 provides three new extended rights to control who can change critical password attributes on user accounts that they manage:[1]

- Enable-Per-User-Reversibly-Encrypted-Password

- Unexpire-Password

- Update-Password-Not-Required-Bit

These extended rights allow more granular control over settings that are stored together with 20 other settings in a single binary attribute called userAccountControl.[2] Due to this fact, these settings cannot be easily controlled by granting or denying access to a normal attribute of a user account for which you want to control delegation of specific password

---

1. For a list of all 15 new extended rights, see Table 10.21 in Chapter 10.
2. For a list of all settings stored in the userAccountControl attribute, go to http://msdn.microsoft.com/library/en-us/adschema/adschema/a_useraccountcontrol.asp.

management features. By default, any data admin that is delegated the right to fully manage a user object is granted the permission to read and write almost all attributes of the user account, including any password-related setting such as "Password not required." However, as explained next, it should be the goal of domain administrators to hinder data administrators from applying these sensitive settings to their accounts. The availability of the new extended rights in Windows Server 2003 makes this task much easier.

The "Enable-Per-User-Reversibly-Encrypted-Password" right controls access to the "Store Password using reversible encryption" option in the account tab of a User object in the AD Users and Computers MMC snap-in (see Figure 11.5). Choosing this option stores a simple hash of the password, which can be easily converted back to a plain-text password and thus significantly reduces the security level of password storage in your domain. Similarly, the "Unexpire-Password" right controls access to the "Password never expires" option in the same UI, also shown in Figure 11.5. Allowing

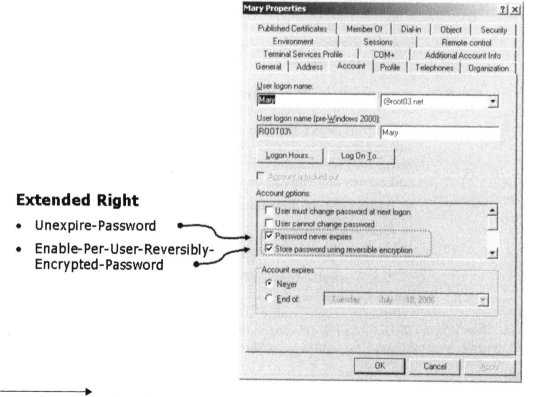

Extended Right

- Unexpire-Password
- Enable-Per-User-Reversibly-Encrypted-Password

Figure 11.5   *Critical password account options in Account tab.*

data administrators to choose this option for accounts that they manage often leads to surprising results; delegated administrators who are not very security aware commonly configure a high percentage of their users with the "Password never expires" option simply to avoid issues with the users when they change their password (finding 30% of all accounts in a domain configured with a password that does not expire is not uncommon). Naturally, such a practice undermines any password age policy set at the domain level.

The "Update-Password-Not-Required-Bit" right controls access to a password setting that is not available in the native UIs of the OS but can be set programmatically or via the command line using the NET USER command:

```
net user smithbob /passwordreq:no
```

As with the "Password never expires" option, disabling the requirement for a password on a user account effectively undermines a domain- or corporate-wide password policy and can cause serious security holes in a company's AD forest.

In contrast to many other extended rights that need to be set directly for user objects, such as the Reset-Password right, the three new extended rights have been implemented to apply at the domain level. As shown in Figure 11.6, by default the Authenticated Users group has been granted these rights at the root of the domain (the "Enable Per User Reversibly Encrypted Password" option is not visible in the screenshot).

Along with either "Allow – Full Control" or "Allow – Write AccountRe-strictions" for a user object, these default rights allow any data administrator, for example, to set the "Password never expires" option for accounts that he or she manages. If you remove the Unexpire-Password right for Authenticated Users at the root of the domain, this will not be possible. Granting the rights to Authenticated Users by default has been done for compatibility reasons so that the initial permissions for these new security options in a Windows Server 2003 domain behave the same way as they did in Windows 2000, where these extended rights did not exist.

To allow better control over the password management options in your Windows Server 2003 AD, you should remove all default extended rights for managing passwords (Update-Password-Not-Required-Bit, Unexpire-Password, Enable-Per-User-Reversibly-Encrypted-Password) from the Authenticated Users ACE at the root of your domain(s). You now have the flexibility to create your own security group for each of the rights and restrict their use to members of the group (as domain admins have also been

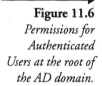

Figure 11.6
Permissions for Authenticated Users at the root of the AD domain.

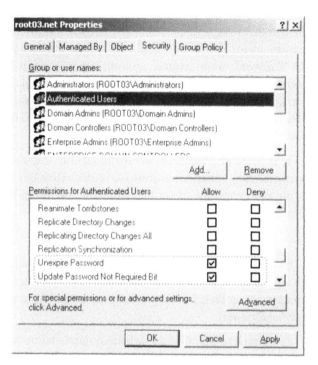

granted these rights by default, they will be exempt from this restriction). Other password management options, such as the Reset-Password right or setting the "User must change password at next logon" option, should be configured for user objects at the OU level, which we will describe in the Helpdesk Scenario further below.

11.2.3   Designing Roles for AD delegation

Along with designing your OU structure, you need to plan the actual roles that you wish to delegate to your AD data administrators. Typical roles include

- User Administration

- User Password Reset

- Computer Administration

- Group Administration

A role itself does not define the scope of its application—it merely describes an administrative task or tasks that will be performed by a specific group of delegated administrators in your company. The scope for applying a role will be determined later by the group of data administrators whom you wish to perform the role. For example, you may want to grant your central helpdesk the User Password Reset role for all users in your Delegated Administration OU, while the local IT support staff in the Phoenix location will only be granted this right for users in the Phoenix Accounts OU.

The description of your role should contain a list of the "real" management tasks (an example is given in Table 11.3) that you expect your delegated administrators to perform. This information will help you to derive the required permissions that you need to set for the administrative role in AD. The list of tasks should include specific information as to how often you expect the tasks to be performed and the associated risk of performing

Table 11.3   *Sample Task List for User Administration Role*

User Administration Role (Tasks)

Task	Account	Subtasks	Usage	Risk
User Administration	Data Admin Account	Creating users in local OU	often	medium
User Administration	Data Admin Account	Deleting users in local OU	rare	high
User Administration	Data Admin Account	Renaming users in local OU	often	low
User Management	Data Admin Account	Moving users to *Transfer* OU*	rare	medium
User Administration	Data Admin Account	Moving users in local OU	rare	medium
User Administration	Data Admin Account	Enabling/disabling users in local OU	often	low
User Administration	Data Admin Account	Resetting user passwords in local OU	often	low
User Administration	Data Admin Account	Modifying user properties in local OU	often	low
Group Management	Data Admin Account	Adding users to groups in local OU	often	low
Group Management	Data Admin Account	Removing users from groups in local OU	often	low
Group Management	Data Admin Account	Viewing group members in local OU	often	low
Mailbox Management	Data Admin Account	Enable and disable Instant Messaging	often	low
Mailbox Management	Data Admin Account	Create and delete Mailbox on local Exchange servers	often	medium
Contact Management	Data Admin Account	Managing contacts	often	low

* A Transfer OU is often used to grant two data administrators of different OUs, who each only have rights to manage users in their own OU, the ability to relocate a user account to the other location's OU without requiring the intervention of a service-level administrator, such as a domain admin account.

the task. The latter allows the managers held responsible for the security in your company to better judge the level of required personal trust associated with a specific task or role prior to assigning it to a person.

Sample User Administration Role

A sample task list for a User Administration role is described in Table 11.3. Some of the upcoming examples describe tasks or permissions that relate to Microsoft Exchange. Since the main focus of this book is on Windows Security, we will not go into too much detail on describing the Exchange security model. The sidenote "Delegating Microsoft Exchange Tasks in AD" gives a short introduction to this topic.

Once the tasks have been defined, it is time to identify the minimal permissions required to perform the tasks, which are the sum of the AD permissions that would need to be granted to an AD security group to allow its members to perform the respective data admin roles.

The AD permissions for each role typically need to be applied to different OUs to limit the scope of where the specific data administrators are allowed to perform the tasks described in the role.

Establishing a good naming convention for the administrative groups you use to delegate permissions helps in automating and, later, in managing your AD delegation permissions. A proven naming convention for AD delegation implementations is one that contains the scope of where it should be applied and the role that it represents, such as

Group-Name: ADM-<LocationCodeOrScope>-<DataAdminRole>

Using the naming convention above, it is clear that the security group called "ADM-PHX-UserAdmins" will be used to grant the permissions of the User Administration role for the PHOENIX OU, while the "ADM-CORP-UserAdmins" would grant the same permission to manage all users in your AD forest. The role- and scope-specific security groups that you create for this purpose should not be under control of your data administrators, which could otherwise again lead to an elevation of privilege attack. Instead, they should be located either in a child OU of your Domain Management OU or in a special admin OU in each of your location OUs that is exempt from applying inherited permissions from parent OUs.

The following rules help to understand the required permissions that must be applied to perform the user administration role:

- Allowing Full Control for any object does not include the permission to create new or delete existing objects of the object type (user objects in this case). These permissions have to be granted separately as create and delete permissions for the respective object type. Depending on your user administration model, you may not need or want to grant full control to the data administrators for managing user accounts. However, if you want to grant them the permissions to create users, then they will have the ability to change the security of users they

---

Delegating Microsoft Exchange Tasks in AD

Many of the everyday user management tasks can be combined very well with tasks required to perform Exchange mailbox management. The administration of the Exchange Servers themselves should be treated as a service-level role, similar to administering an AD domain, as Exchange Servers are granted very powerful rights for managing most user and group objects in your AD forest. A delegated admin who is granted administrative rights on an Exchange Server should thus be treated with the same level of trust as a domain administrator or any other AD service-level administrator.

In general, you should decide on your user administration model prior to implementing Exchange in your Active Directory forest. As an Exchange Organization is tightly integrated with AD, a clear separation for administration of a user's mailbox attributes versus other user attributes and management tasks requires very complex and error-prone delegation settings. If the goal is to strictly separate Exchange Administration from AD user administration, a dedicated Exchange resource forest would be the preferred way to implement Exchange. Note that Exchange 2007 will simplify the delegation of Exchange-related write permissions on user objects in the same forest, as it introduces a new permission property set that contains all the relevant Exchange attributes and thus no longer conflicts with other permissions on the user object from the base OS.

On the other hand, if you embrace the possibility of handing off the everyday mailbox and distribution list management tasks to your user administrators—which can be done quite elegantly with the AD User and Computers MMC snap-in in combination with the extensions from the Exchange System Manager—you will clearly see value in implementing Exchange in the same AD forest. The following two examples show how this can be achieved:

- **Exchange Mailbox management:** Requires permissions to manage the user account in combination with the "Exchange View Only Administrator" permissions assigned via the Exchange System Manager to the appropriate Exchange AdminGroup. You can further restrict the mailbox stores that are accessible by your delegated user administrators by denying read permissions to individual mailbox stores on the Exchange Servers for the User Admins group. This tactic will hinder them from choosing these stores when mail-enabling users in their OU.

- **Exchange Instant Messaging:** Managing IM for a mailbox-enabled user object requires the "View Information Store Status" permission on your Exchange Servers hosting the Instant Messaging role.

created anyway. You will have more options once the next version of Windows Server—currently codenamed Longhorn—is released; it will allow you to restrict the permissions an owner has on the objects he or she created. See the sidenote on "The DACLs Ownership Issue and Upcoming Changes in Vista and Longhorn Server" in Chapter 10. If you wish to isolate the possibility to set permissions on user objects from normal management of the user object in Windows Server 2003, you need to separate the roles for the creation of user objects to a different role, which would then need to be performed by a different user or an automated account provisioning process.

■ When managing group memberships for a user object, no special write permissions are required on the user object itself; instead the membership attribute of the group object is edited during this process. The "Member Of" tab of a user object may look like you are editing the user; however, this tab only shows the so-called "backlinks" of the group memberships as they are stored with the group object. As such, it is particularly challenging if you do not want to grant a delegated administrator the permissions to add specific users to the groups that he controls—the method of doing this will be covered in more detail in Section 11.4.

■ Delegating specific Exchange tasks to your user admins requires special permissions in your Exchange Organization configured via the Exchange System Manager, as is explained in the sidenote "Delegating Microsoft Exchange Tasks in AD."

In summary, Table 11.4 describes the definition of the User Admin role scope and permissions as they would need to be applied to our sample AD OU structure.

Sample Computer Administration Role

Some of your roles will require a combination of permissions that are not only granted to objects within AD, but also to other resources in your AD domain. If this is the case, you should clearly describe this requirement as part of your role definition. The Exchange permissions for the User Administration role may seem like it falls into this category; however, all the required permissions for the Exchange management are actually set in the configuration container of your AD forest. Rights granted by the Exchange ESM apply to Exchange objects in the following location:

```
CN=Microsoft Exchange,CN=Services,CN=Configuration,
    DC=<ForestRootDomain>
```

Table 11.4 *Sample User Administration Role Description, Including Permissions*

User Administration Role (AD Permissions)

	Description	Example
AD AdminGroup	ADM-<LocationCode>-UserAdmins	ADM-PHX-UsersAdmins
Purpose	UserAdmins are granted full control on user objects on the appropriate leaf-level in the location's OU. As part of this task, they are granted the necessary rights to manage the group memberships of the users (for the groups in the location's OU). User admins do not have the rights to manage administrative user accounts or groups.	
Scope – AD	Leaf-Level OU "Users" and "Groups" with scope "This object and all child objects," allowing management of all user and group objects.	US\PHX\Accounts US\PHX\Groups
Inheritance	Yes, "Allow inheritable permissions from parent to propagate to this object" is true for both leaf OUs	Inherits permissions from US\PHX OU
Rights in AD	*Object*	*Permissions*
	Organizational Unit	Allow – List Contents Allow – Read All
	Group	Allow – Write Members
	User	Allow – Full Control Allow – Create Allow – Delete
Rights in Exchange	*Object*	*Exchange Permission*
	Administration Group	Exchange View Only Administrator
	IM Servers	View Information Store Status

A role that requires permissions outside of AD is, for example, the computer administration role. The tasks performed by this role are listed in Table 11.5. Table 11.6 lists the permissions that are required in AD and on related resources. The administrators performing this role may not require many permissions in Active Directory itself, but they do require administrative rights on the clients they manage, so that they can install or repair hardware components or deploy software, such as drivers, to the computers.

More sample roles are described later in this chapter. Realize that understanding the Windows and AD Authorization model is key to the success of

Table 11.5   *Sample Task List for Computer Administration Role*

Computer Administration Role (Tasks)

Task	Account	Subtasks	Usage	Risk
Computer Administration	Data Admin Account	Installing computers in location	often	low
Computer Administration	Data Admin Account	Creating computer accounts in local OU	often	medium
Computer Administration	Data Admin Account	Joining local computers to domain	often	medium
Computer Administration	Data Admin Account	Removing local computers from domain	often	medium
Computer Administration	Data Admin Account	Resetting passwords of computer accounts in local OU	often	medium
Computer Administration	Data Admin Account	Administering all computers in location	often	medium

Table 11.6   *Sample Computer Administration Role Description, Including Permissions*

Computer Administration Role (AD Permissions)

	Description	Example
AD AdminGroup	ADM-<LocationCode>-ComputerAdmins	ADM-PHX-ComputerAdmins
Purpose	Computer Admins manage all computers in the location, including joining them to the location's OU.	
Scope	Leaf-Level OU "Computers" with scope "This object and all child objects," allowing management of all computer objects (e.g., desktops and mobiles).	US\PHX\Computers
Inheritance	Yes, "Allow inheritable permissions from parent to propagate to this object" is true.	Inherits permissions from US\PHX OU
Rights in AD	**Object**	**Permissions**
	Computer	Allow – Full Control Allow – Create Allow – Delete
Rights on Physical Computers	**Member of Group**	**Scope**
	Administrators	All computers of location (can be set via GPO at OU level, using the restricted groups feature)

defining AD delegation roles, as described in detail in Chapter 10. Specific challenges regarding handling permissions in Active Directory are described in Section 11.4, which will also help you further understand AD permissions that you may consider for defining your normal AD delegation roles.

Planning the Application of Your Roles to AD

A final part of your preparation work for delegating AD administration is to create an overview of all the roles and the AD security groups that you will use to implement them. The overview, along with a graphical representation of a sample administrative unit in your OU structure, helps exemplify your overall delegation model—this is critical to managing it correctly. Figure 11.7 shows what an overview of the security groups used for AD delegation, along with their role descriptions, could look like for our sample OU structure. The figure also clearly shows that these security groups are not stored in the normal groups OU, but in a separate Admin Groups OU created for this location. This protects the delegation groups from changes performed by the UserAdmins role, as this role will be granted permissions for managing the other groups used in this location.

Figure 11.8 shows an overview of the AD delegation groups used for the Phoenix location, along with the permissions that must be granted at different levels of the OU structure. The lines connecting the rows of the table with the different OUs allow you to more easily comprehend the scope of the permissions for the various parts of the OU hierarchy. Note that only the ADM-PHX-OUAdmins group is granted rights at the top level of the

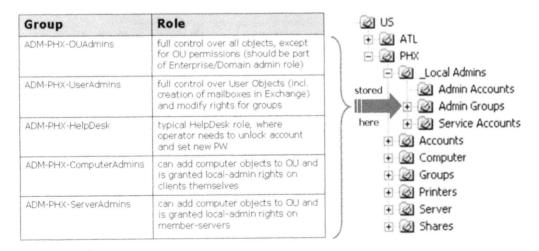

Figure 11.7   *Overview of sample AD delegation groups and role descriptions.*

location's OU tree. Members of this group are granted permissions to manage all required object types for their location; however, they only have read permission for the OUs themselves. This way, users performing this role cannot change the security settings on their own OUs and cannot create other subOUs, which is a best practice to ensure that your company wide delegation model and OU structure remains standardized and under central control of the domain administrators. Naturally, there will always be requirements for exceptions to your model. However, these exceptions—such as additional subOUs or security groups to implement other delegation roles, or a structure to apply group policy objects—should remain within central control and implemented by your domain admins.

The OU admins role, as implemented in Figure 11.8 is a very powerful role that could be compared to the capabilities of a domain admins role for a complete NT4 domain: in addition to the management of all objects (other than OUs), this role also manages the AD delegation groups for its own location, and thus fully controls administrative access to all AD objects for the location. If even more central control over the memberships of the AD delegation groups is desired, these groups should be stored outside of the location's OU structure, for example, in the Domain Management OU we've previously defined.

In the following sections, we will describe how you can best configure the actual security settings on your OU structure to implement your designed roles for AD delegation.

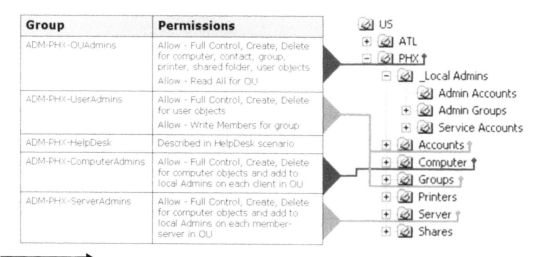

Figure 11.8   *Overview of sample AD delegation groups, permissions, and scope.*

As a final recommendation regarding your role design, keep in mind that it is typically not recommended to delegate any administrative tasks to data admins who are involved with AD infrastructure-related activities. The following are examples of tasks that should only be performed by service admins:

- Management of AD security settings

- Management of the Default Domain and Domain Controller Group Policies

- Backup and Restore of AD

- Promotion and Demotion of AD Domain Controllers

However, a few of the tasks that require service administrator privileges by default, such as the authorization of DHCP servers, can nonetheless be delegated at very low risk to data-level admins. Section 11.3.2, "Advanced Service Management Delegation Scenarios," describes these scenarios.

11.3   Setting up Administrative Delegation

To support setting up the permissions for administrative delegation in AD, Microsoft provides a couple of options:

- The ACL Editor

- The AD delegation wizard (GUI tool)

- The DSACLs commandline tool

- APIs that can be used to fully script security settings

The ACL editor and the delegation wizard are used to manually set permissions, while DSACLs and the APIs allow you to fully automate the configuration of permissions on AD objects. Setting up the required OU permissions manually may be sufficient for smaller companies, but if you need to consider many administrative units in your AD delegation model, you should think about automating the process. While automating using the APIs is highly complex, the use of DSACLs and the application of a properly standardized OU structure make the automation of security settings in AD quite doable for nonprogrammers.

The preferred way to set permissions in any larger Active Directory infrastructure is to use an automated routine to replace the error-prone manual tasks for setting the different permissions at the various levels of your OU structure. DSACLS.EXE is a utility that comes with the OS and is part of the Windows 2000 and Windows Server 2003 support tools. Several examples of how to use DSACLs are part of Section 11.4.

In this section, we will describe how to use and configure the AD delegation wizard to ease the manual setting of permissions. We will also describe some advanced AD delegation scenarios.

11.3.1 The AD Delegation Wizard

The delegation wizard (illustrated in Figure 11.9) is accessible from the Windows GUI on the level of sites, domains, and OUs. The delegation wizard allows an administrator to choose among a set of predefined delegation tasks (listed in Table 11.7). You can also create custom tasks to better reflect the organizational needs—for example, to more exactly match the AD delegation roles you have previously defined, as will be described further below.

The main challenge with using the delegation wizard is that it is only a tool to set additional permissions to those that already exist in AD. It does

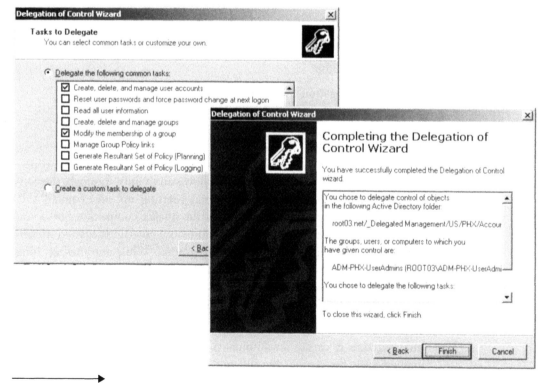

Figure 11.9   *Delegation wizard.*

Table 11.7   *Predefined Windows Server 2003 Delegation Tasks*

Domain
Join a computer to the domain
Manage group policy links

Site
Manage group policy links

OU
Create, delete, and manage user accounts
Reset user passwords and force password change at next logon
Read all user information
Create, delete, and manage groups
Modify the membership of a group
Manage group policy links
Generate Resultant Set of Policy (Planning)
Generate Resultant Set of Policy (Logging)
Create, delete, and manage inetOrgPerson accounts
Reset inetOrgPerson passwords and change password change at next logon
Read all inetOrgPerson information

not support you to remove or change existing permissions that are set for any OU in your delegated OU structure. This is true for any of the default permissions, as well as any permission that has been granted by the delegation wizard itself.

Undelegating administrative permissions is not supported by the delegation wizard and instead needs to be done directly from the ACL editor (if you want to do so using a GUI). This provides a special challenge for administrators if they need to remove all the permissions that are set for an account or a group of objects in the domain, as there is no easy way to search for ACLs using the existing GUI tools. But Microsoft has provided a free download called dsrevoke.exe to ease the reporting of permissions granted to your security principals in AD and to automate the removal of these permissions on hierarchical object structures. You can find the tool at www.microsoft.com/downloads.

Figure 11.10
*Delegwiz.inf
configuration file.*

```
delegwiz.inf - Notepad                                    _ | □ | x |
File  Edit  Format  View  Help
[version]                                                        ▲
signature="$CHICAGO$"

[DelegationTemplates]

Templates = template1, template2, template3, template4, template

;-------------------------------------------------------------
[template1]
AppliesToClasses=domainDns,organizationalunit,container

Description = "Create, delete, and manage user accounts"

ObjectTypes = SCOPE, user

[template1.SCOPE]
user=CC,DC

[template1.user]
@=GA
;-------------------------------------------------------------
                                                                ▼
◄ |                                                      ► | //.
```

In addition to the need to manually walk down your OU structure and apply the various delegated permissions at the OU level of your choice, another challenge of using the delegation wizard is the fact that often the existing roles in the wizard may not match your requirements. The process of selecting all the appropriate subroles while you click through the wizard is also fairly error-prone, especially if you have to do it multiple times in a row.

To slightly ease this pain, you can define custom tasks and add them as predefined tasks to the wizard. This is done be modifying the delegwiz.inf configuration file (illustrated in Figure 11.10), located in the %Windir%/inf directory of the machine where you have installed the Active Directory Users and Computers MMC snap-in (ADUC). This file is a simple text file that can be edited while the ADUC is running—ADUC will read the template file each time you start the delegation wizard.

The following sample template grants rights to unlock (`lockout-Time=RP,WP`) a user account (`ObjectTypes = user`) that has been locked due to too many attempts to log on to the domain with the wrong password. It applies to domain and OU container objects (`AppliesTo-Classes=domainDns,organizationalUnit,container`), so it will appear in the delegation wizard when it is run from the properties of Domain or OU objects:

```
; ---------------------------------------------------------
[template14]
AppliesToClasses=domainDns,organizationalUnit,container
Description = "Unlock locked user accounts"
ObjectTypes = user
[template14.user]
lockoutTime=RP,WP
; ---------------------------------------------------------
```

After adding your template to the delegwiz.inf file, be sure to add it to the list of available templates, which is stored as a comma-separated string in the Templates variable directly underneath the [DelegationTemplates] identifier.

The syntax of the templates in the delegwiz.inf file allows you to combine multiple permissions for different object types in a single template, so that you can create most of the roles that you may have defined for your AD delegation model as templates for the AD delegation wizard. You will still have to apply them manually to the different OUs in your hierarchy, but at least the process will be less prone to error. The syntax is explained in detail in the Microsoft Knowledge Base article Q308404, available from http://support.microsoft.com/default.aspx?scid=kb;en-us;308404.

Naturally, administrators who are familiar with the new ACL editor and the changes on the level of the ACL model in Windows 2000 and Windows Server 2003 can do without the delegation wizard and set delegation through the ACL editor of a site, an OU, or any other object directly via the ACL editor.

Another management tool that is fairly convenient to delegate administrative control over group policy objects, OUs, and domains is the Group Policy Management Console (GPMC). The GPMC GUI contains a delegation tab for every GPO (as illustrated in Figure 11.11). GPMC is a free add-on tool that can also be downloaded from the Microsoft Web site.

11.3.2   Administrative Delegation Examples

In addition to the user administration and computer administration roles, which were previously described in detail in Section 11.2, the following examples illustrate how you could use administrative delegation in a Windows Server 2003 domain for a typical helpdesk role and for some administrative tasks related to networking. We refer to Section 11.4 for some more challenging aspects of AD delegation.

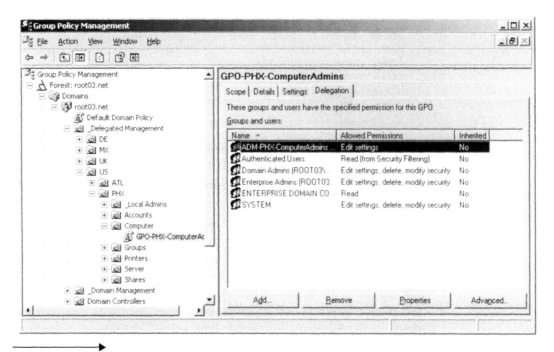

Figure 11.11   *Delegation tab in GPMC.*

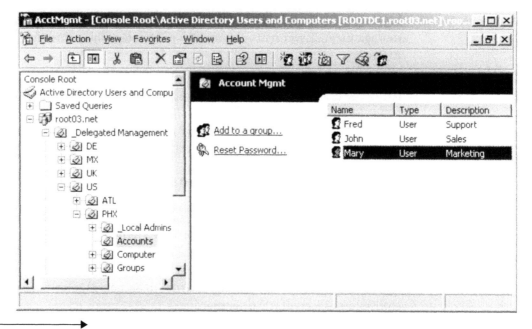

Figure 11.12   *MMC Taskpad for AD account management.*

Using Taskpads to Manage AD Objects

Once you have delegated the desired permissions in your AD infrastructure, you may want to reflect the administrative delegation on the level of the administrative interfaces used by the respective operators. To do so, Windows 2000 and Windows Server 2003 allow you to develop customized administration interfaces called taskpads, as illustrated in Figure 11.12.

To create a taskpad, use the Taskpad View Wizard: open a new MMC console and add a snap-in, such as Active Directory Users and Computers. Right-click the snap-in container and select New Taskpad View. Customized MMC consoles and taskpads can be saved as regular files. You can, for example, send them by mail to the administrators who need them.

Helpdesk Scenario

A typical scenario in which AD administrative delegation is very helpful is a helpdesk scenario. From a Windows account management point of view, organizations typically want to give the following abilities to their helpdesk administrators:

- Reset an account's password

- Set the "User must change password at next logon" account property

- Unlock an account by unchecking the "Account is locked out" account property

As shown in Table 11.7, the template for unlocking an account is not available by default within the AD delegation wizard. If, however, a company has defined an account lockout policy for their AD domain that locks out a user after a specific number of unsuccessful logon attempts and requires an administrator to unlock it, it is a good practice to combine the tasks having to do with password reset with the tasks related to unlocking an account. After all, a user will usually not call for help to get his password reset until it is too late and the account is locked.

To delegate the above administrative tasks to your helpdesk administrators, you must set the following permissions on the OU for which you want to delegate permissions:

- Allow – Reset Password for user objects (grants permission to reset an account's password)

- Allow – Write lockoutTime for user objects (grants permission to unlock an account)

- Allow – Write pwdLastSet for user objects (grants permission to set "User must change password at next logon")

- Allow – Read AccountRestrictions for user objects (grants permission to read all account options, which is required to view important status information about the user—for example, the little red circle with a white "x" on a disabled user object when viewed via the AD Users and Computers MMC snap-in)

In line with our previous delegation samples, the permissions required for the helpdesk role are listed in Table 11.8. Figure 11.13 is an overview of where to apply the permissions in our sample OU structure.

Note that by default you cannot see all objects and properties that you could possibly set permissions on using the advanced view of ACL editor in the AD Users and Computers MMC. The visibility is controlled by the dssec.dat configuration file, located in your %WinDir%/System32 directory. The dssec.dat is a simple text file that must be edited on each system being used to run the Users and Computers snap-in and ACL Editor. It uses an INI data format to lists the properties of each class that should be filtered out of the list in the Properties section of the ACL Editor and contains about 12,000 lines of configuration data by default. This means that approximately 12,000 properties and various objects are not shown by default in the ACL editor when using AD Users and Computers MMC snap-in to manage ACLs of AD objects.

Table 11.8 *Helpdesk Role Description, Including Permissions*

HelpDesk Role (AD Permissions)

	Description	Example
AD AdminGroup	ADM-<LocationCode>-HelpDesk	ADM-PHX-HelpDesk
Purpose	Allow reset of passwords, unlock account, and set the "User must change password at next logon" account property.	
Scope – AD	Leaf-Level OU "Users" with scope "This object and all child objects," allowing management of all user objects.	US\PHX\Accounts
Inheritance	Yes, "Allow inheritable permissions from parent to propagate to this object" is true for both leaf OUs.	Inherits permissions from US\PHX OU

Rights in AD	**Object**	**Permissions**
	User	Allow – Reset Password
		Allow – Write lockoutTime
		Allow – Write pwdLastSet
		Allow – Read AccountRestrictions

Figure 11.13
Overview of HelpDesk scenario applied to sample OU structure.

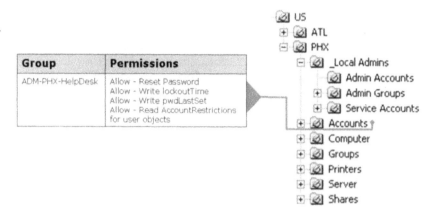

The format of the file content is:

```
[objectclass-name1]
@=value
property-name1=value
property-name2=value
.
.
property-nameX=value
[objectclass-name2]
@=value
property-name1=value
property-name2=value
.
.
property-nameX=value
```

where <objectclass-nameX> refers to the AD schema object class for which the visibility in the ACL editor should be controlled and <attribute-nameX> to the attribute. The "@" placeholder controls the visibility of the object itself. The actual values have the following meaning:

- Property=7: do not include property in dialog box

- Property=6: include "Read" property in dialog box

- Property=5: include "Write" property in dialog box

- Property=0: include both "Read" and "Write" property in dialog box (same as nonexisting entry in file)

The dssec.dat file is read when opening AD Users and Computers so that changes won't take effect until closing and reopening the respective MMC console. ADSIedit, on the other hand, ignores the dssec.dat file and

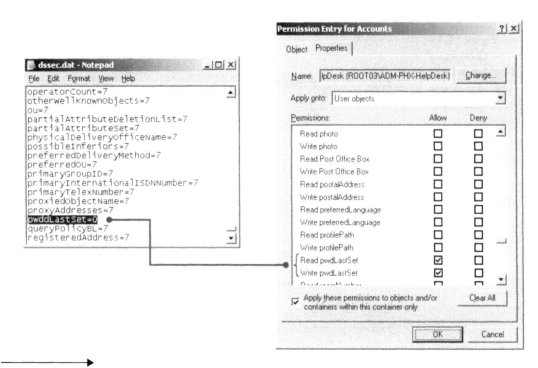

Figure 11.14   *Setting permissions for the pwdLastSet user account attribute.*

always shows the full list of available properties for permission management.

For the Windows 2000 versions of ADUC, you are required to adjust the dssec.dat file to display the pwdLastSet and lockoutTime user account properties. You must set the lockoutTime and pwdLastSet attributes to value 0 (default is 7). This process is illustrated in Figure 11.14. The dssec.dat file in the Windows Server 2003 version of ADUC has already been adjusted to show these properties by default.

Advanced Service Management Delegation Scenarios

Although the following tasks require service admin permissions by default, you may want to consider adding these tasks to your respective AD data admin roles:

- Authorize a DHCP server

- Create domain-based DFS Roots

- Stop, start DNS servers

They are fairly low-risk tasks that allow your data administrators greater independence from service administrators while at the same time reducing the workload you would have to put onto your AD service administrators. Tables 11.9, 11.10, and 11.11 describe the permissions that you would have to grant for delegating these three service management tasks, but let's also briefly explain why you may want to consider granting these permissions.

Authorize a DHCP server: Deployment and configuration of DHCP servers are typically performed by network administrators, who are not necessarily AD administrators. By default, the authorization of a DHCP server requires enterprise administrator privileges, as write privileges are required to the CN=DHCPRoot, CN=NetServices, CN=Services, CN=Configuration, and objects in this subtree.

Create domain-based DFS Roots: Distributed File System (DFS) management is typically a task performed by file server administrators. Even though domain-based DFS roots store their configuration data in AD, a file server administrator does not require domain administrative rights to manage a DFS root. He or she does, however, require administrative rights on the server that hosts the DFS root.

If this is a normal member server, then a file server administrator merely needs some write permissions to the DFS-Configuration container located

Table 11.9   *Delegation of DHCP Authorization*

DHCP Administration Role (AD Permissions)

	Description	Example
AD AdminGroup	ADM-<LocationCode>-DHCPAdmins	ADM-PHX-DHCPAdmins
Purpose	Grant permissions to DHCP administrators to authorize DHCP servers in their location	
Scope – AD	DHCPclass objects in CN=DHCPRoot, CN=NetServices, CN=Services, CN=Configuration, DC=<ADroot-Domain>	
Inheritance	Yes, "Allow inheritable permissions from parent to propagate to this object" is true	Inherits permissions from CN=NetServices

Rights in AD	**Object**	**Permissions**
	DHCPclass	Allow – Create Allow – Read Allow – Write Allow – All Validated Writes

Table 11.10　*Delegation of DFS Root Creation*

DHCP Administration Role (AD Permissions)

	Description	Example
AD AdminGroup	ADM-<LocationCode>-DFSAdmins	ADM-PHX-DFSAdmins
Purpose	Grant permissions to create domain based DFS roots	
Scope – AD	ftDfs object class in CN=Dfs-Configuration, CN=System, DC=<ADdomain>	
Inheritance	Yes, "Allow inheritable permissions from parent to propagate to this object" is true	Inherits permissions from CN=System
Rights in AD	**Object**	**Permissions**
	DHCPclass	Allow – Create Allow – Read Allow – Write Allow – All Validated Writes

in the System container of the domain partition. By default, only domain administrators can write to this area of the domain partition.

Stop, start DNS servers: If your DNS is installed as an AD integrated DNS infrastructure, the DNS services are hosted on your domain controllers and can only be stopped and started by an administrator of the DC—that is, a domain or enterprise admin. However, often the administration of DNS zones is delegated to the default DnsAdmins group in an AD domain.

Table 11.11　*Delegation of DNS Service Administration*

DNS Admin Role (Permissions)

	Description	Example
AD AdminGroup	DnsAdmins (default group)	DnsAdmins
Purpose	Grant permissions to DnsAdmins to stop and start the DNS server service on DCs	
Scope	DNS server service on all DCs in domain	
Inheritance	Not applicable	
Rights on DCs	**Object**	**Permissions**
	DNS server service (via Group Policy)	Allow – Read Allow – Start, stop, and pause

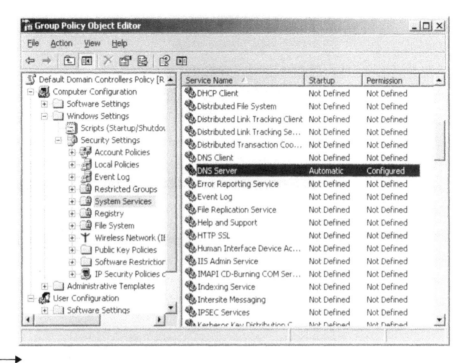

Figure 11.15   *Setting permissions for Services.*

This group does not have permissions to stop or start the DNS service, but it would be an appropriate task to delegate out to this group. Setting permissions for services is best done using the System Services feature from Group Policies, located in <GPO> / Computer Configuration / Windows Settings / Security Settings / System Services (see Figure 11.15). Note that due to AD's dependency on a functional and available DNS service, the delegation of DNS administration for an AD integrated DNS infrastructure is generally a riskier task to delegate than the other two examples above, and it should be treated with appropriate caution.

User Self-Management Scenario

User Self-Management is closely related to the challenge of managing permissions to hide data in AD, which is described in detail in Section 11.4.

By default, Active Directory allows specific user account attributes to be edited by the user. Examples include the user's phone number and office location. This feature can be leveraged to reduce workload on the helpdesk administrators for simple and recurring user account property changes.

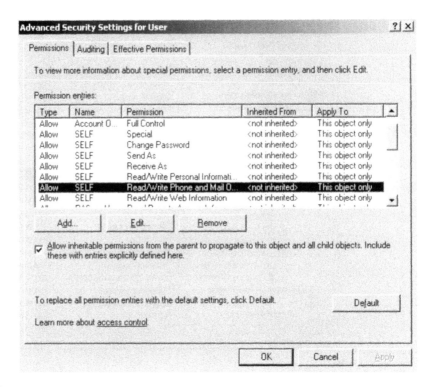

Figure 11.16   *Default permissions for SELF security principal.*

To enable user self-management, Microsoft provides a special security principal called SELF. By default, various permissions are set for the SELF security principal, enabling every user to edit attributes on his or her own user account in AD. To edit the attributes that can be self-managed, change the default authorization settings (default security descriptor) for the user class object in AD. Figure 11.16 shows the permissions given by default to the SELF security principal for the user object class. The default AD security descriptor and its properties will be discussed in the next section. Here we will also discuss how some of the default permissions granted to SELF make life difficult for administrators who need to make certain data inaccessible to unauthorized accounts, including the user accounts themselves.

11.4 Hiding Objects in AD

As described in Chapter 10 and the previous sections of this chapter, Active Directory has quite decent capabilities for setting permissions on objects in the directory to allow delegated administration of things like users, groups, or computers to nondomain admins. But when it comes to making specific data visible to only those users who need to view it, either because normal users should simply not see the objects or the data are truly confidential, the default permissions in AD quickly make this task rather complex.

11.4.1   Understanding the Challenge of Hiding Data in AD

This section discusses the options for hiding data by either leveraging the normal permissions available in AD or enabling a special AD permission feature (List Mode). It describes how to use the Confidentiality bit, a new option introduced with Windows Server 2003 Service Pack 1. It also describes some of the caveats administrators may run into when hiding specific objects.

The main reason that hiding data in Active Directory is somewhat of a challenge is the various permissions granted by default within an AD forest. These permissions will be covered in greater detail below.

Many companies are slowly becoming aware of the wealth of default read (and write) permissions that are granted to basically every employee with a user account in his or her corporate AD; they might very well want to differentiate between internal and external employees. Internals would be allowed to query for all other accounts in AD, while external users such as contractors should not be able to do so. Also, companies that wish to adopt Active Directory for more than just a NOS[3] directory, actually leveraging it as an LDAP directory for other applications requires more control over who can see what in AD. In companies where, for example, delegation of AD administration plays a greater role, access to and visibility of sensitive accounts is another critical aspect that needs to be planned for appropriately. Most obviously, this is the case for outsourcers that might host users from various companies within the same AD forest.

More Details on the Default Security of Objects in AD

During the design of Active Directory, instead of locking down the default permissions on objects created in AD and requiring administrators to grant appropriate read permissions that would suit their environment, Microsoft chose to grant numerous read permissions to all authenticated users for almost all new objects created in a forest. As always, there are pros and cons

---

3.   NOS stands for Network Operating System; the main purpose of an NOS directory is to authenticate users to the network.

Table 11.12   *Default Permissions for New OUs in AD*

Group	Object	Default Permissions (Explicit)
Account Operators	Users	Allow – Create/Delete object
	Groups	Allow – Create/Delete object
	Computers	Allow – Create/Delete object
	InetOrgPerson	Allow – Create/Delete object
Authenticated Users	This object only (the OU)	Allow – List Contents, Read All Properties, Read Permissions
Domain Admins	This object only (the OU)	Allow – Full Control
Print Operators	Printers	Allow – Create/Delete object
System	This object only (the OU)	Allow – Full Control
Enterprise Domain Controllers	This object only (the OU)	Allow – List Contents, Read All Properties, Read Permissions

to both approaches. One could even argue that the less restrictive default permissions in AD are in part a reason for the high success rate of AD deployments throughout the world, as less intervention was required by administrators to make things work. However, the default permissions are also a challenge for administrators who need to take care of the delegation of AD if certain data are to be hidden from normal users.

By default, all authenticated users in an AD forest are granted explicit read permissions on any organizational unit created by any administrator, due to the default permissions configured for OUs as shown in Table 11.12. As such, any logged on user can see all objects within any OU in an AD forest.

The situation doesn't improve if we look more closely at the default permissions for the different types of objects in AD: for example, see a user-Class object in Table 11.13.

Besides these explicit permissions for every new object, various permissions are inherited from parent OUs. Fairly critical default permissions are those granted to the "Pre-Windows 2000 Compatible Access" group, which includes "Read All Properties" for user objects.

So one of the main challenges is to limit the permissions for authenticated users in a way that does not allow them to see everything by default. It is critical to understand a very important detail when discussing permis-

Table 11.13   *Default Permissions for New User Objects in AD*

Security Principal	Default Permissions (Explicit)
Account Operators	Allow – Full Control
Authenticated Users	Allow – Read Permissions, Read General Information, Read Personal Information, Read Web Information, Read Public Information ·
Cert Publishers	Allow – Read/Write userCertificate
Domain Admins	Allow – Full Control
Everyone	Allow – Change Password
RAS and IAS Servers	Allow – Read Remote Access Information, Read Account Restrictions, Read Group Membership, Read Logon Information, Read Public Information
SELF	Allow – List Contents, Read All Properties, Read Permissions, Change Password, Send As, Receive As, Read/Write Personal Information, Read/Write Phone and Mail Options, Read/Write Web Information
System	Allow – Full Control

sions in an AD forest and potentially how to adjust them. Notice the term "explicit" permissions, which we used quite often above—explicit permissions are those set directly on objects, as opposed to inherited permissions, which are set on a container object above and are configured to apply to objects within that container (and subcontainers). Remember from Chapter 10 that explicit allow permissions have a higher priority than inherited deny permissions during the ACL evaluation process. This basically means that the various read permissions granted by default to the Authenticated Users group cannot be overruled simply by setting deny read permissions at the OU level and inheriting them down the tree.

When Is It Necessary to Hide Data in AD?

From the previous chapter, you should have a good understanding that the challenge of hiding data in AD is very closely related to three things:

1.   The default read permissions granted on new objects in AD

2.   The priority for inherited permissions during the evaluation of an ACL

3.   The grouping of attributes into Property Sets

This chapter would certainly have had a different focus if the default read permissions for authenticated users in AD were not as pervasive as they are. We would not even be talking about "hiding" information in AD— rather, we would be discussing how to make things "visible" or accessible within the directory.

Most often, companies' OU structures are designed to group objects of similar type or location into one OU, while objects of another type or location are grouped into another OU. We have previously worked with the sample OU structure illustrated in Figure 11.3, and will continue to use it for some further thoughts.

In this example, we created a special subOU called "Local Admins" that was meant to hold special account data for administrative users of that location to implement a dual account model. To protect these users from potential misuse or DOS attacks, it is a good idea to hide the "Local Admin" OUs from normal users (also see Section 4.2 in Chapter 4).

Another reason for hiding users or complete OUs is that you don't want other users to know of their existence in the directory. This can be the case for sensitive environments such as financial institutions or government agencies, but especially for outsourcing companies where each top-level OU could represent a different customer and each one of them should only be able to see objects from his own company.

But there are also technical reasons to hide data in AD. This is especially the case whenever it becomes important to limit delegated administrators in their capabilities to link objects in AD. When you add a user as a member to a group, you link that user to the group; however, you're not actually editing the user. Only the group's membership attribute (the forward link, or FL) is being edited. The information in the memberOf attribute of the user (the backlink, or BL) is not editable and is managed by the system. Figure 11.17 shows how users are groups that are linked together.

So using our sample OU structure, by default a delegated administrator who has all the required permissions to manage groups and users in Phoenix (OU PHX) but does not have any permissions to manage users in Atlanta (OU ATL) is still able to add users from the ATL OU or any other place in the AD forest to his groups. Usually, companies unknowingly

Figure 11.17
Linking users to groups.

accept this model, since it allows an easy way to establish cross-boundary access to shared resources such as file servers. However, in sensitive environments, it is often very important that administrators not be able to add users outside their scope of responsibility (i.e., users outside the OU they manage) to groups that they manage. In this case, a company will also need to hide users from delegated administrators outside of the OU they manage, so that these are unable to add the "foreign" users to their groups or to add them to any other linked attributes, such as to the manager attribute of a user or the managedBy attribute of objects like printers, groups, or OUs.

Finally, a company might very well have the need to hide data stored in specific attributes of different types of objects in AD, instead of hiding the complete object. The need to do so obviously depends on the sensitivity of the data stored in the attributes, which is judged differently by each company. If, for example, a company stores the employee numbers of their users in AD, the company may want to hide that information from all users who are not from HR. Similarly, the company may want to restrict access to the home phone number attribute. More often, companies have added their own attributes in the AD schema to store additional information for other applications. Common schema extensions include attributes for cost centers or special application-specific roles, but can go as far as an attribute to store token IDs in order to support other authentication methods using AD as an LDAP server. Many of these special attributes are not meant for the eyes of the end-user or lower-privileged administrators such as help desk operators, as the information contained therein could potentially pose a risk to the company if it fell into the wrong hands. As such, the company must hide the data within these sensitive attributes from all users who don't need explicit access to them.

In summary, the most common reasons for hiding objects in AD are:

1.   Protecting administrative accounts from misuse and DOS attacks

2.   Hiding existence of specific objects for legal reasons

3.   Honoring least privilege for special administrative tasks, such as ensuring that delegated group administrators can only change membership for users within their own administrative scope

4.   Ensuring that sensitive data within attributes is not disclosed to users

What are the options for hiding data in AD?

The general goal is to hide data from unauthorized users and only make it accessible to those who are specifically allowed to view it (for example, via a membership in an appropriate security group). With this goal in mind, it is generally preferable to limit the access to objects or attributes by ensuring that only specific security principals (e.g., security groups) are granted access to them, rather than first granting general access to an object (e.g., to all authenticated users) and then trying to *deny* access to all users who should not be allowed to access the data.

Table 11.14   *Options for Configuring Permissions in AD Used for Hiding Data*

Permission Option	Scope	OS Version	Short Description
Using "Normal" permissions on AD objects and attributes	Objects and Attributes	Windows 2000 Windows Server 2003	Sensibly restricting normal read permissions in AD already gives an administrator great control over the visibility of objects and attributes. Read permissions at the OU level will always make all child objects visible.
Enabling List Object Mode in Forest	Objects	Windows 2000 Windows Server 2003	Special mode that allows differentiation of the visibility of single objects within containers such as OUs.
Adjusting the default security of objects in AD	Objects and Attributes	Windows 2000 Windows Server 2003	Only valid for new objects. The permissions applied to objects at the time of their creation in AD can be adjusted.
Adjusting the built-in Property Sets	Attributes	Windows Server 2003	Not possible in Windows 2000. The set of attributes that belongs to the built-in property sets can be adjusted.
Using the Confidentiality Bit	Attributes	Windows Server 2003 with SP1	New option in SP1. Similar to List Mode, this option can hide specific attributes, even when general access to read all or a set of attributes of an object are granted.

We also need to differentiate *what* data are supposed to be hidden in the first place—the whole object, or just specific attributes of an object? Table 11.14 lists the main options available for hiding data in AD, including the scope (objects or attributes) and the operating system version which supports the respective option.

In reality, administrators often have to combine different permission configuration options to reach their AD security targets with respect to hiding data in Active Directory, as discussed in the following sections.

11.4.2 Hiding Data Using "Normal" Permissions on AD Objects and Attributes

It is possible to use the normal capabilities of Active Directory permissions to ensure that users can only view and access objects and attributes they are supposed to. The principles are pretty straightforward: if a user is not authorized to view an object or attribute, AD will not display the information to the user.

Managing Visibility of Objects

To view the objects within an OU, the minimal permission required by a user is "list contents" on the OU. As described in detail in the previous section, various security principals, including Authenticated Users, are granted the read permission on any newly created OU. They are also granted the list object permission on an OU; however, AD does not enforce this permission by default (this will be discussed further in the next section). Realize that the default read permission is a combination of different permissions, including list contents, as shown in the advanced view of the permissions in Figure 11.18.

By default, the list contents permission will grant sufficient rights to list *all* objects contained in an OU; an administrator does not have any control over *which* objects are displayed. As a result, any authenticated user is granted sufficient rights to list any objects in newly created OUs in an AD forest. If, however, the list contents permission for Authenticated Users is removed from an OU, a query for all user objects in the AD forest will not return objects stored in this OU. This includes listing the objects in the operating system's object picker, which is typically used to add users to groups or to select a security principal for granting permissions to resources. By default, the object picker will display all appropriate objects within containers for which the current user has list contents permission.

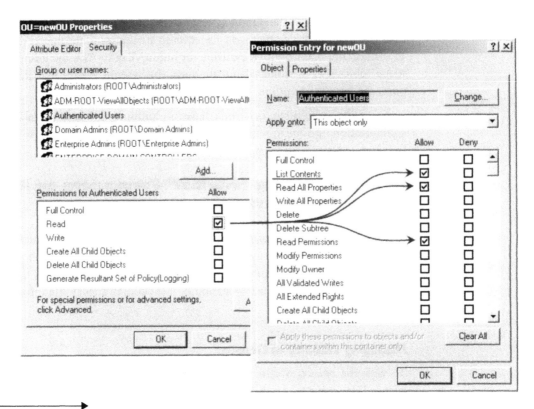

Figure 11.18   *Set of permissions granted with the read permission.*

Consequently, removing the list contents permission for Authenticated Users on OUs effectively hides the objects for all users in AD, unless the users are members of other groups that are specifically granted this permission. A similar goal can be reached by explicitly denying the list contents permission to a group, but it is generally preferable to work with positive permissions (allow, or the lack thereof) instead of negative permissions (deny) to keep things simple and comprehensible for any administrator of the system, unless there is a good reason to do otherwise.

Removing the permission for a single OU can be done most easily via the ADUC or ADSIedit GUI using the security editor. To do so from the command line, you can use the DSACLS.EXE utility that comes with the OS; however, this command is not able to remove single permissions directly—you first have to remove all permissions for the respective security principal and then assign new ones as described in the sidenote "DSACLS-Sample 1."

DSACLS-Sample 1 (Removing the List Contents Permission for OUs)

To remove the list contents permissions for Authenticated Users on a new OU, you would use the following command to remove all permissions for Authenticated Users:

```
DSACLS <DN of object> /R <security principal>
```

For example:

```
DSACLS "OU=newOU,DC=root,DC=net" /R "Authenticated Users"
```

Afterwards, reset all the default permissions on the object, except the one that was to be removed (read permissions, read all properties, list object):

```
DSACLS <DN of object> /G <security principal>:RCRPLO
```

For example:

```
DSACLS "OU=newOU,DC=root,DC=net" /G "Authenticated Users":RCRPLO
```

To combine both commands into one execution statement, you can leverage variables and the && command as follows:*

```
set DN="OU=newOU,DC=root,DC=net"&& set SP="Authenticated Users"&&
DSACLS %DN% /R %SP%&& DSACLS %DN% /G %SP%:RCRPLO
```

Note: Any character preceding the && command will be part of the previous command; this is especially tricky when using it after setting a variable via set (a trailing space would be added to the variable).

Naturally, removing all permissions for a security principal from the command line should not be taken too lightly if you don't know exactly which permissions the security principal had on the object. As such, you should first run a report on the ACLs of the object so that these can be reset if required. There are a couple of tools available to achieve this, and all of them have their pros and cons. Typically, the DSREVOKE.exe tool from Microsoft achieves good results, as it runs a report on ACLs for a specific security principal. However, it cannot do so for well-known security principals such as Authenticated Users, or built-in ones such as Administrators. DSACLS gets the job done (as Figure 11.19 shows), but it will always list the permissions for all security principals. However, this is better than not listing any.

Managing Visibility of Attributes

If a user has sufficient access to list an object, this does not mean that he or she will also automatically be able to view the attributes of all objects listed

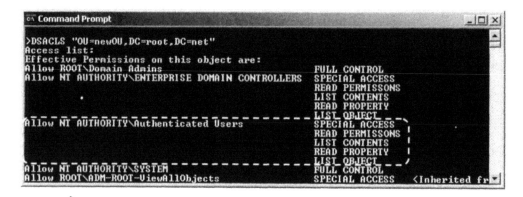

Figure 11.19   *(Partial) result of DSACLS listing ACLs on OU.*

in an OU. To do so, a user requires read permissions on the respective attributes of the objects within that OU.

If the requesting user does not have or is denied read access to an attribute, AD will not return any data stored within this attribute. The graphical user interfaces (GUIs) that come with AD will either display an empty field (AD Users and Computers) or will display "<Not Set>" for the attribute value (ADSIedit), as shown in Figure 11.20.

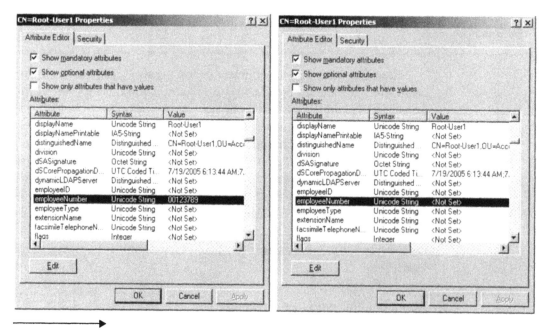

Figure 11.20   *Displaying content of attributes with read access (left) and without (right).*

The special challenge with controlling the READ access at the attribute level in AD stems from what was described in Section 10.4.3 and Section 11.4.1: the grouping of attributes in Permission Property Sets and the vast amount of explicit default permissions assigned to new objects in AD.

What does this mean if, for example, we want to restrict access to the homePhone attribute to members of the HR department? Well, if we review Table 10.20 in Chapter 10, which lists the 41 attributes that belong to the Personal Information property set, we know that the homePhone attribute also belongs to this property set. Also, we know from Table 11.13 that Authenticated Users are granted read permissions to this property set for any new user object in AD. This basically means that to remove the permission for Authenticated Users to read a user's homePhone attribute without using a deny permission, the read permission for the Personal Information Property Set would have to be replaced with 40 separate read permissions for all the other attributes in this Property Set.

In this case, it would be much more efficient to apply a deny read permission on the homePhone attribute to the respective user objects for a security group that contains all users except the HR department. Let's call this group "non-HR-users" for this example. Obviously, creating such a group and keeping it up to date is a challenge on its own, but the next challenge we meet is that we cannot just set the required deny permission at the OU level, let alone the domain level and inherit it down to the respective user objects. As described in Section 10.4.4 (Chapter 10) on the ACL evaluation process, it is clear that the allow permissions for the user object, which were explicitly granted to Authenticated Users, will override the inherited permission from any parent object. As a result, we now need to add an explicit deny read permission for the non-HR-users group to all user objects in the AD forest. While this is not pretty, and you would certainly not want to set the explicit deny permission to all objects by clicking through the GUI for hours, it can be achieved fairly efficiently using the DSACLS, as described in the sidenote "DSACLS-Sample 2."

So hiding objects and attributes with the normal permissions available in AD (as it is installed by default) all comes down to understanding these basic things:

1.   Understand the default and the current permissions granted to an object and its parent container—if a user is not granted the list contents permission on a container object, the objects within that container object will not be visible to that user.

2. Understand how attributes are granted permissions by property sets—an attribute is not visible if a user does not have or is denied read access to that property.

3. Understand that if a permission for an attribute that is to be denied is also part of a property set that is explicitly granted the respective permission, the deny permission on the attribute must be explicitly set on all objects to be affected.

DSACLS-Sample 2 (Setting Explicit Deny Read for an Attribute)

As we need to set explicit permissions on each user object to achieve our goal, we need to run separate DSACLS commands, each with the distinguished name of a user object for which the deny permission is to be set. There are various ways to retrieve this list of DNs—for example, we could use the DSQUERY command that comes with Windows Server 2003 (and also works for the most part against Windows 2000).

To set the permission of the homePhone attribute to deny read on a single user object, you can use this command:

```
DSACLS <DN of object> /D <security principal>:RP;homePhone
```

For example:

```
DSACLS "CN=Doe\, John,OU=newOU,DC=root,DC=net" /D root\non-HR-
users:RP;homePhone
```

For multiple objects, first create a list of DNs and save these to a file. Using DSQUERY, the command would be similar to this:

```
DSQUERY user <StartNode> > queryresult.txt
```

For example:

```
DSQUERY user OU=newOU,DC=root,DC=net > queryresult.txt
```

Then perform a FOR loop to execute the above DSACLS command against all objects in the file:*

```
for /f "delims=" %I in (queryresult.txt) do DSACLS "%~I" /D root\non-
HR-users:RP;homePhone
```

This will efficiently set the desired permission for all objects listed as DNs in the file called queryresult.txt.

*Note: To use the FOR command in a batch program, specify %%I instead of %I.

11.4.3 Enabling List Object Mode in Forest

As previously mentioned, for any newly created OU, Authenticated Users are granted the read and the list object permission. However, in its default configuration, AD does not enforce this permission, and the ACL editor in AD does not display it. Once the List Object mode has been enabled by an Enterprise Administrator (this is only possible for the whole forest), the list object permissions will be enforced.

Understanding the List Object Concept

The concept of the list object permission is quite simple: without it, when a user queries a container's contents in AD, AD does not evaluate the permissions of any objects underneath the container object, such as an OU. If the user has not been granted the list contents permission (which is a subset of the read permission; see Figure 11.18) on the OU, no child objects are returned to the user from AD. And once the user has been granted the list contents permission on the OU, AD will return *all* child objects of that OU to the user—no matter whether or not the user has read permission, even if the user is explicitly denied access to the child object. Realize that a GUI like the AD Users and Computers MMC cannot correctly display the type of object if the user does not have read access on the child object; instead it

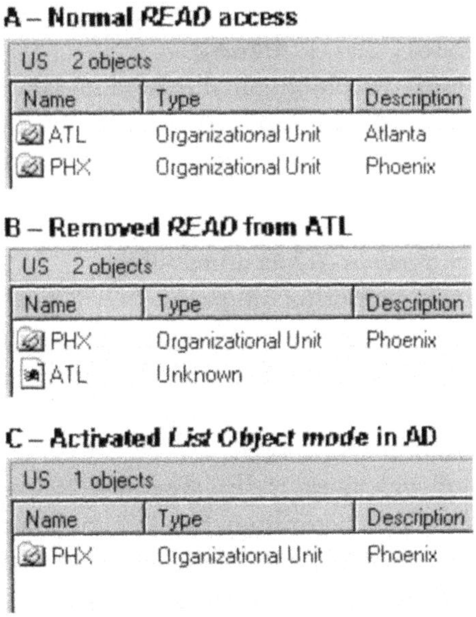

Figure 11.21
Displaying objects in list object mode.

A – Normal READ access

US	2 objects	
Name	Type	Description
ATL	Organizational Unit	Atlanta
PHX	Organizational Unit	Phoenix

B – Removed READ from ATL

US	2 objects	
Name	Type	Description
PHX	Organizational Unit	Phoenix
ATL	Unknown	

C – Activated List Object mode in AD

US	1 objects	
Name	Type	Description
PHX	Organizational Unit	Phoenix

will be displayed as type "unknown," as shown in Figure 11.21. With list object mode enabled, administrators can remove or deny the list contents permission on a parent container, and AD will still process the permissions on the child objects of the container to check if the user has been granted the list object permission on any child object. If so, AD will add the object to the result set; if not, the object will be omitted.

The three sample situations displayed in Figure 11.21 show the impact of using the list object mode versus using normal permissions to hide objects in AD from users:

- **Situation A**

  — List object mode in AD is turned **OFF**
  — User is granted list contents permission on parent OU "US" via normal read permissions granted to Authenticated Users
  — User also has read permission on child objects (OUs "ATL" and "PHX")
  — **Result:** two objects are displayed in ADUC, and both of them can be evaluated by the UI and displayed with the correct icon, etc.

- **Situation B**

  — List object mode in AD is turned **OFF**
  — User is granted list contents permission on parent OU "US" via normal read permissions granted to Authenticated Users.
  — User still has read permission on PHX, but read access to ATL for Authenticated Users is removed.
  — **Result:** again, two objects are displayed in ADUC, but only PHX can be evaluated and displayed correctly by the UI. ATL is displayed as unknown object, yet the user knows that it exists.

- **Situation C**

  — List object mode in AD is turned **ON**
  — List contents permission on parent OU "US" is **removed** for user by removing the permission for Authenticated users
  — User has the default read and list object permission on PHX. The user still has the default read permission on ATL, but the list object permission is removed
  — **Result:** only one object is displayed in ADUC—the one that the user has list object permissions for. Due to the additional read permissions to other attributes, the object is evaluated and displayed correctly by the UI; ATL is no longer displayed, so that the user does not know of its existence in AD.

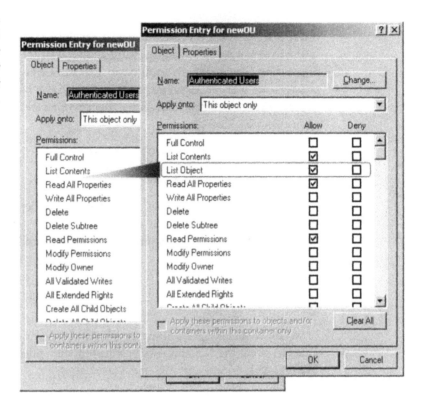

Figure 11.22
AD ACL editor before and after enabling list object mode in AD.

As you can see, the list object permissions are ideally suited for situations where users are not supposed to see certain objects in AD at all. This method is typically used on OUs to fully remove their visibility for all OU-administrators, except for the ones responsible for managing an OU. The list object permission is mostly helpful in outsourcing environments, where the outsourcer is hosting a directory for multiple companies (and users or OU administrators of company A should not even see the OU for company B).

Within an organization, the list object permission is often used to hide security-sensitive objects, such as admin accounts from unauthorized users, mainly to limit the potential for DOS attacks against these accounts. The list object permission is not active or visible in AD's ACL editor until the list object mode in the forest has been enabled. Once the feature is enabled, a new permission will appear in AD's ACL editor, as shown in Figure 11.22.

Configuring the List Object Mode

Enabling AD's list object mode involves editing a property of the Directory Services object in the configuration container of AD. This will replicate to all other domain controllers in the forest and notify them of the change. It is not possible to activate the mode on a per-domain basis. List object mode is activated simply by setting the third character of the **DSHeuristics** property on the Directory Service object to 1. If the **DSHeuristics** property has not been set with other values, set it to 001 (if the first two characters are already set to a nonzero value, leave them as they are). The Directory Services object is located here:

```
cn=Directory Service,cn=Windows
NT,cn=Services,cn=Configuration,
   dc=ForestRootDomain
```

Other DSHeuristics settings[4] on the Directory Service object are used to control Name-Resolution during AD searches. By default, Active Directory's search function is configured to expand the ambiguous name resolution (ANR) filter to evaluate a searchstring, which contains an embedded space. This is mainly meant to find matching user and contact objects in AD by the Lastname (sn) and Firstname (givenName) attributes, regardless of their order of entry in the search string.

When enabled, the list object permission has to be administered in conjunction with the list contents permission; the rules are summarized in Table 11.15.

Table 11.15   *Rules for Using List Object and List Contents Permissions*

Permissions on...

Organizational Unit	Child Objects	Result
List contents and list object	N/A	The list object permission on the OU makes the OU visible. As list contents is also granted to the OU, this will prevail over any missing list object permissions for child objects, and AD will automatically list all objects in the container.
		A delegated administrator can browse to the OU and all child objects with ADUC.
		An LDAP Query for all objects will return OU and ALL child objects.

---

4.   The three-character *DSHeuristics* attribute on the Directory Service object starts with a two-character value that determines the behavior of first/last and last/first search functionality. The default value of *DSHeuristics* is 00, with which both functions are enabled—i.e., when searching for "John Smith", AD will find a "John Smith" and a "Smith John". The first character determines the first/last, the second character the last/first functionality. The two characters can be modified to suppress either one or both functionalities (10x = suppress first/last; 01x = suppress last/first; 11x = suppress last/first and first/last functionality).

Table 11.15 *Rules for Using List Object and List Contents Permissions (continued)*

Permissions on...

Organizational Unit	Child Objects	Result
List object (List contents not granted or denied)	List object	The list object permission on the OU makes the OU visible. If list contents is not granted, or if it is denied AND if list object is granted to the container object (OU), AD will evaluate the list object permission for the child objects and only list those where the list object (or Read) permission has been granted. A delegated administrator can browse to the OU with ADUC and selected child objects. An LDAP Query for all objects will return OU and only those child objects, where list object permissions have been granted
List contents (List object not granted or denied)	N/A	The OU will NOT be visible. As list contents is granted to the OU, this will prevail over any missing list object permissions for child objects and AD will automatically list all objects in the container. A delegated administrator *cannot* browse to the OU or child objects in ADUC. An LDAP Query for all objects will NOT return the OU object, but ALL of its child objects.
Neither list contents nor list object is granted	N/A	The OU will NOT be visible. As neither list contents nor list object is granted to the container object (OU), AD will NOT evaluate any permissions of the child objects. A delegated administrator *cannot* browse to the OU or child objects in ADUC. An LDAP Query for all objects will NOT return the OU nor any of its child objects.

Hiding the Existence of Different Companies in AD

The goal of the next permission example is to use the list contents and list object permissions appropriately to set up OU permissions for a company that runs an outsourcing business for multiple clients. Here, it is important that only Authorized Users (members of the groups UserAdmins_CompanyX) are able to view their respective OU (CompanyA, CompanyB, CompanyC), including the contents underneath a parent OU called UserAccounts (see Figure 11.23).

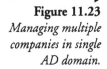

Figure 11.23
Managing multiple
companies in single
AD domain.

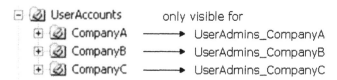

This involves the following steps:

1.   Remove the default list contents permission for Authenticated Users from the UserAccounts OU (so that permissions of child objects are evaluated).

2.   Remove the default list object permission for Authenticated Users from all Company OUs to hide visibility of the Company OUs themselves. In addition, list contents will be removed from the OU, to hide the objects within them (so that they are also not returned via an LDAP query).

3.   Grant the list object and list contents permission for each User-Admins group on the respective Company OU.

While the list contents and list object permissions can be set via the ACL editor in AD, they can be set more easily for multiple OUs using DSACLS, as shown in the sidenote "DSACLS-Sample 3." The result of this permission example would effectively hide all user accounts of any hosted company in AD from unauthorized users. Members of the respective UserAdmins_CompanyX group could only view accounts from their company. The permissions for a company's UserAdmins group can be further extended to allow appropriate delegated admin functions (such as PW reset, etc.).

To effectively hide all other objects in the AD domain, such as the Builtin, Computers, System, and Users containers or any other container object from nondomain admins, remove the list contents permission for Authenticated Users from the domain object itself (e.g., root.net). Then remove the list object permission for Authenticated Users for any container that should be hidden. Domain admins (as well as enterprise admins) will still have full access to all objects through other inherited or explicit permissions for their respective groups on the OUs. The results are shown in Figures 11.24 and 11.25.

It goes without saying that changing the visibility of objects in AD as configured above can also have an impact on other applications that leverage AD. These applications may themselves rely on permissions granted to Authenticated Users, so testing is required to evaluate the impact of hiding

---

DSACLS-Sample 3 (Leveraging the List Object Permission)

Removing the list contents permission on an OU, as required for step 1, was described previously in DSACLS-Sample 1 and can be applied equally to this scenario (the list object permission will remain on the UserAccounts OU):

```
set DN="OU=UserAccounts,DC=root,DC=net"&& set SP="Authenticated
Users"&& DSACLS %DN% /R %SP%&& DSACLS %DN% /G %SP%:RCRPLO
```

The goal in step 2 is to remove the default list object and list contents permission for Authenticated Users from all Company OUs. As with removing just the list contents permission, using DSACLS first involves removing all permissions for Authenticated Users and then resetting the permissions we want to keep (in this case, read and read all properties). For a single OU the command would be:

```
set DN="OU=CompanyA,OU=UserAccounts,DC=root,DC=net"&& set
SP="Authenticated Users"&& DSACLS %DN% /R %SP%&& DSACLS %DN% /G
%SP%:RCRP
```

Similar to DSACLS-Sample 2, for multiple OUs it would be easier to first create a list of DNs and save these to a file, for example, by using DSQUERY:

```
DSQUERY ou "OU=UserAccounts,DC=root,DC=net" -scope onelevel >
queryresult.txt
```

and then to perform a FOR loop to execute the above DSACLS command against all objects in the file, such as:*

```
for /f "delims=" %I in (queryresult.txt) do set SP="Authenticated
Users"&& DSACLS "%~I" /R %SP%&& DSACLS "%~I" /G %SP%:RCRP
```

Finally, in step 3, the actual permission to view the correct OU and its content needs to be granted to the respective UserAdmins group for each company by granting the list object permission to the correct group (list object, list content):

```
DSACLS <DN of object> /G <security principal>:LOLC
```

For example:

```
DSACLS "OU=CompanyA,OU=UserAccounts,DC=root,DC=net" /G "UserAdmins-
CompanyA":LOLC
```

Using a for-loop similar to the previous step, in combination with a naming convention in place that uses the name of the OU as part of the group that is to view it, this step can also be automated rather nicely as follows:*

```
for /f "delims=" %I in (companylist.txt) do DSACLS
 "OU=%~I,OU=UserAccounts,DC=root,DC=net" /G "UserAdmins_%~I":LOLC
```

where companylist.txt contains a flat list of the company names.

Note: To use the FOR command in a batch program, specify %%I instead of %I.

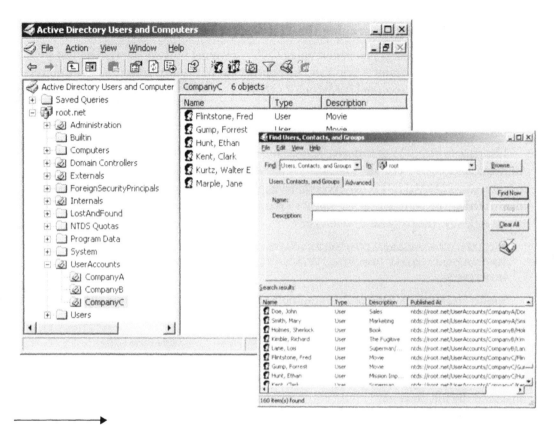

Figure 11.24   *Viewing "hidden" OUs as domain admin; all objects are visible.*

OUs in an AD domain. However, in a hosting environment with Exchange this actually works quite well, since the Exchange Servers are granted their own special rights on the objects that they are required to process. Nevertheless, further adjustments are required to appropriately display address lists to users of a company; the global address list would typically be disabled and company-specific, and an LDAP filter pointing only to the company OU would be used instead.

The list object mode in AD, which is available since Windows 2000, can actually be compared quite well with the new access-based enumeration (ABE) file-system feature introduced with SP1 for Windows Server 2003 (described in Chapter 10). By default, the normal NTFS file-system permissions on folders will also allow a user who has read or list permissions on the folder to see all files and subfolders, no matter whether he has permission to open the files to read them or not. When ABE is activated on a share, the file server will first evaluate the permissions of the user for every

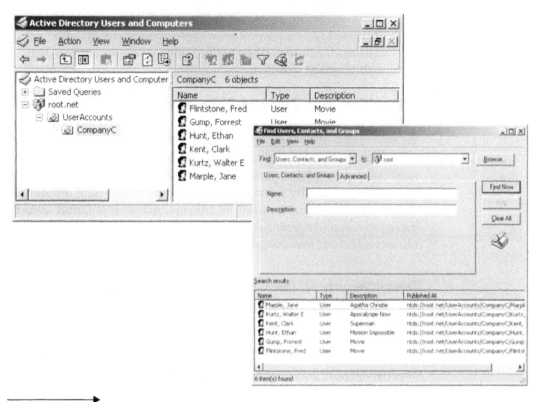

Figure 11.25 *Viewing "hidden" OUs as UserAdmin of CompanyC; only objects of CompanyC are visible and searchable.*

file or subfolder prior to returning the list of objects to the user. As there is no dedicated list object permission for files and folders in NTFS, a user requires at least read permissions to view a file or folder in an ABE-enabled share.

The most important things to remember when working with the list object mode in AD are:

1. The list object mode can only be enabled for a whole AD forest; it is not possible to enable it per domain.

2. To leverage the list object permission on child objects, the list contents permission for Authenticated Users should be removed from the respective parent container; if a user is granted the list contents permission on a container object, the objects herein will be visible no matter what the underlying list object permissions of the child objects are.

3.   Enabling the list object mode does not add any features to hide attributes; its sole purpose ·is to allow setting more granular permissions for listing objects within container objects only to users authorized to view them.

11.4.4 Adjusting the Default Security of Objects in AD

Any new object created in AD gets a security descriptor at the time of creation. This security descriptor can explicitly be passed to AD by the command creating the object, but more commonly, objects are created without passing along a security descriptor—for example, when using the ADUC GUI or the DSADD command. In this case, AD adds a default security descriptor as explicit permissions to the new object in addition to the permissions inherited from the parent container.

Default Security of User Objects

This default security descriptor is stored with the classSchema objects in the AD schema. For a user object, for example, it is stored here:

Object: CN=User,CN=Schema,CN=Configuration, DC=root,DC=net

Property: defaultSecurityDescriptor

As described in Chapter 10, the default security descriptor can be viewed and edited using the LDP.exe or ADSIedit.msc tools, which are part of the support tools for Windows 2000 and Windows Server 2003. However, it is much easier and far less prone to error to do so using the Schema Manager MMC snap-in. Figure 11.26 shows the default permissions of the user class object using the Schema Manager, which is displaying the permissions granted to Authenticated Users.

Realize that editing the default security of any object class does not directly impact the security on any existing object of that class. So if the read personal information permission for Authenticated Users is removed from the default security of the user classSchema object, the attributes defined in the personal information property set will still be accessible to Authenticated Users for all previously created user accounts. However, any newly created object will apply the security as defined in the schema, so that an early adjustment of the default security is most effective, for example, prior to migrating objects from an existing domain into a new AD forest.

If the adjusted default security should also be applied to existing objects, this can be performed via the DSACLS command, as shown in the sidenote "DSACLS-Sample 4." Alternatively, Windows Server 2003's version of the

Figure 11.26
*Viewing and
editing the default
security of user
objects using the
AD Schema
Manager.*

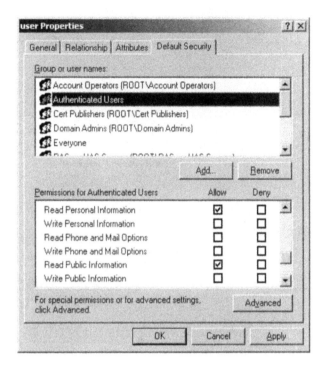

ACL editor offers a new option to reset a single object's permissions back to
the default permissions defined in the schema using the Advanced ACL editor options, as shown in Figure 11.27.

A word of caution: besides the fact that many security-related changes
described in this chapter must be well understood before applying any of
them in production, changing the default security of objects in the schema

---

DSACLS-Sample 4 (Resetting AD Object Permissions to Defaults)

DSACLS has two options to restore the permissions of objects in AD back to the default
security descriptor of the respective object class: it can perform the task either on a single
object (/S) or on a whole tree of objects (/S /T).

To reset the permission on the UserAccounts OU, including all subOUs and objects
within all of the OUs, execute this command:

```
DSACLS <DN of object> /S /T
```

For example:

```
DSACLS "OU=UserAccounts,DC=root,DC=net" /S /T
```

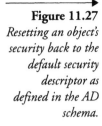
Figure 11.27
*Resetting an object's
security back to the
default security
descriptor as
defined in the AD
schema.*

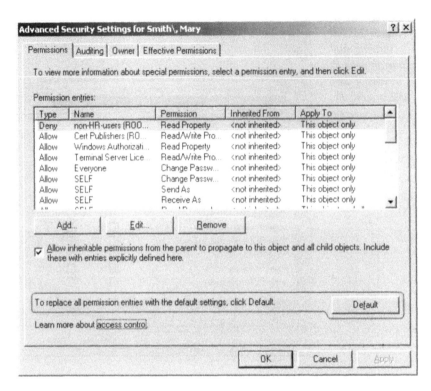

and then resetting the security of existing objects in AD to the default is especially risky and can cause unexpected results. To be totally clear: the risky part is not to change the default security descriptor in the schema; it is applying it to existing objects. This is actually a destructive task, as any existing explicit permissions on objects will be removed and replaced with the explicit permissions defined in the schema. While this could very well be desired, the removed permissions could also include permissions that existed on user objects that the administrator might not be aware of; this is especially true for AD forests that also host Microsoft Exchange, which applies a multitude of additional explicit permissions to any mailbox-enabled user account or group. The replacement of the permissions to the default cannot be undone without performing an authoritative restore of the objects in AD.

When Is It Appropriate to Change the Default Security?

As described in the two previous sections about hiding objects using the "normal" AD permission options and enabling the list object mode in AD, hiding objects and attributes involves removing certain permissions from objects so that AD either does not list the object at all for unauthorized users or so that it does not grant READ permissions to attributes storing sensitive data.

Rather than removing the unwanted permissions on all newly created objects after their creation, it could well be advisable to remove them from the default security descriptor of the respective objects class in the schema and take care of the correct permission on the objects after their creation. A good example is the Authenticated Users security principal on the user, group, and organizationalUnit objects. If hiding objects and specific attributes from unauthorized users in AD is the goal, then completely removing the Authenticated Users from in the default security of the user and group classSchema objects and removing the "List Content" and the "List Object" permissions for Authenticated Users from the default security of the organizationalUnit classSchema objects in the AD schema is a compelling option.

Administrators can then ensure that the appropriate permissions are afterwards inherited to the objects, for example only minimal permissions for Authenticated Users on user objects and extended permissions for all internal employees. If required, this also allows the flexibility to inherit a deny permission that has a higher priority than the inherited allow permissions for a security principal, eliminating the need to repermission all objects in a container with explicit permissions to set a deny ACE only to override an explicit permission granted to Authenticated Users. If insufficient permissions were granted to Authenticated Users, it would be easy to adjust them by editing the inheritable permissions on the parent container, for example, a top-level OU.

Once the list content and the list object permissions have been removed for Authenticated Users from the default security of the organizationalUnit object and the List Object mode has been enabled in AD, the creation of a new OU would no longer make this OU nor its contents automatically visible for unauthorized users. An administrator could then easily explicitly grant the List Object permissions to a respective security group, so as to make the OU only visible for certain delegated administrators or end users. Likewise, the List Content permission would be granted to appropriate security groups on the same OU to list all objects within the OU.

Remember the following points when you consider changing the default security descriptor for objects in the AD schema:

1.   Any object in AD has a default security descriptor that is defined and editable in the schema. The AD schema management MMC snap-in provides the easiest way to do so.

2.   Any change of the default security descriptor in the AD schema will have no direct impact on existing objects of the respective type; while the adjusted security descriptor can be reapplied to existing objects (e.g., using DSACLS), this is not recommended for AD environments that host other applications which change permissions of existing objects (such as Exchange 200X for mail-enabled users and groups).

3.   A valid option for adjusting the default security descriptor to hide objects and attributes from unauthorized users is removing the default permissions for Authenticated Users from the user, group, and organizationalUnit classSchema objects. The desired permissions on newly created objects can then be handled more easily by administrators through inheritance or by adding only specific explicit rights.

11.4.5   Adjusting the Built-In Property Sets

Understanding Property Sets is very important when discussing hiding data in AD. Why? Quite simple: if you go back to Table 11.13, which lists the default permissions granted to every new user object in AD, you'll see that four *explicit* allow read permissions for Authenticated Users are granted to property sets (General Information, Personal Information, Web Information, Public Information). While all of them are relevant, the Personal Information property set is the one that is usually of greatest interest to administrators when trying to hide access to specific account data for unauthorized users.

Understanding the Challenge of Property Set Permissions

Combining the knowledge about the default permissions with the understanding that explicit allow permissions have a higher priority than inherited deny permissions, it becomes apparent that you cannot hide the data of attributes which are part of a property set by setting a deny permission for an object's attribute on the OU level and inherit it to the respective objects. As a result, administrators require a good understanding of property sets and the attributes that belong to them to fully understand the effect of permissions granted or denied to specific attributes in AD.

Property Sets and the ways they can be analyzed are described in great detail in the previous chapter. With respect to hiding information in AD, the main challenge with Property Sets is their inflexibility. An attribute can only belong to a single Property Set, so it is not possible to create different sets of Property Sets with overlapping attributes. Hopefully, this will change in future versions of AD, but this is not the case for Windows 2000, Windows Server 2003 with or without SP1, and Windows Server 2003 R2.

Nonetheless, while it is not even possible to *edit* the built-in Property Sets, such as Personal Information, in Windows 2000, Microsoft at least added this capability in Windows Server 2003. There are limitations as to which attributes can be removed from or changed to a different Property Set: Property Set settings for the Security Accounts Manager (SAM) attributes, such as *samAccountName, samAccountType* (both in General-Information Property Set), and *members* (in the Membership Property Set), cannot be changed.

The Personal Information Property Set is one that can be edited quite well to suit the needs of a company. In the examples for hiding data with "normal" permissions in AD, we discussed the necessity of removing access to the homePhone attribute of user accounts for all users who were not from the HR department. The default rights for Authenticated Users grant read permissions to the Personal Information Property Set for any new user (and all of those that have already been created in AD using the default permissions). Our options to remove access to the homePhone attribute were either to remove the read permission on the whole Property Set and replace it with a separate read permission for each of the remaining 40 attributes that we still want to grant access to, or to add an explicit deny read permission to the homePhone attribute of all user objects for non-HR-users. In reality, neither of these options is very appealing to administrators.

So how could we reach our goal to hide the homePhone attribute, leveraging our knowledge about Property Sets? Well, we know that the homePhone is made a member of the Personal Information Property Set by its attributeSecurityGUID, which matches the rightsGUID of the Property Set. So if they no longer match, then the attribute will no longer be a member of the Property Set. This can be achieved by removing the attributeSecurityGUID from the homePhone attribute.

How does removing the attributeSecurityGUID of an attribute and thus editing the members of a Property Set affect AD and the existing objects? That's where the beauty of this solution is: while the previous solution to deny access to the attribute involved a resource- and time-consuming process of touching all existing objects to change their ACLs (and potentially overwriting existing ACLs in a destructive manner), the approach of changing a Property Set is nondestructive and has immediate impact on all objects where this permission is used. No objects need to be touched and no ACLs need to be adjusted. As the Property Set's attributes are evaluated when the SRM[5] of a DC analyzes the permissions to an object and its attributes, a change in the attribute membership of a Property Set will be active immediately.[6]

Removing an Attribute from a Property Set

Removing the attributeSecurityGUID from a schemaAttribute class object (such as homePhone) is a change in the AD schema, and like any other schema change, it requires membership in the schema admins security group. Before making any changes, it is important to document the existing attributeSecurityGUID of an attribute, so that the change can be undone in case of unexpected results (e.g., with applications that require access to this attribute and expect to get the access via the respective Property Set). The good news is that it can be undone without a problem.

Figure 11.28
Removing an attribute from a Property Set using LDP.

---

5.   SRM is the Security Reference Monitor, part of the Windows operating system kernel.

6.   The schema change needs to replicate to all DCs, and the DCs need to refresh the schema cache, which they do every five minutes by default. The SRM on the DC also caches the property sets and needs to refresh the cache before the change is active (within approximately ten minutes).

As the homePhone attribute belongs to the same Property Set as the streetAddress attribute that we analyzed above, it also has the same attribute-SecurityGUID (86 B8 B5 77 4A 94 D1 11 AE BD 00 00 F8 03 67 C1). The DN of the homePhone attribute is:

```
CN=Phone-Home-
Primary,CN=Schema,CN=Configuration,DC=root,DC=net
```

LDP.exe is an appropriate tool to use to remove the attributeSecurity-GUID. All you do is browse to the attribute in the Schema NC and choose to modify the schema object (either right-click the object and choose Modify, or via Menu: Browse ⇨ Modify). In the Modify dialog box, ensure that the correct DN is set, enter "attributeSecurityGUID" (the name, not the value) in the Attribute field, and choose Delete as the operation. Then click Enter and Run. (See Figure 11.28.)

The results of the above modify command performed with LDP should look like this in the output of LDP:

```
-----------
***Call Modify...
ldap_modify_
s(ld, 'CN=Phone-Home-Primary,CN=Schema,CN=Configuration,DC=
root,DC=net',[1] attrs);
Modified "CN=Phone-Home-Primary,CN=Schema,CN=Configuration,
DC=root,DC=net".
-----------
```

In Section 10.4.3, we explained how to query for all attributes of a Property Set using LDP, and found that 41 belonged to the Personal Information Property Set. Re-executing this query would show that (as expected) there's one less now:

```
-----------
***Searching...
ldap_search_s(ld,
"CN=Schema,CN=Configuration,DC=root,DC=net", 1,
"(&(objectcategory=attributeSchema)(attributeSecurityGUID=\
86\B8\B5\77\4A\94\D1\11\AE\BD\00\00\F8\03\67\C1))",
attrList,  0, &msg)
Getting 40 entries:
>> Dn:...
```

So without modifying any additional permission on objects in AD, let us compare the query results before (Figure 11.29) and after (Figure 11.30) of this change for a query against AD performed by a normal nonadmin user, John Doe. John Doe is allowed to list the contents of the CompanyC

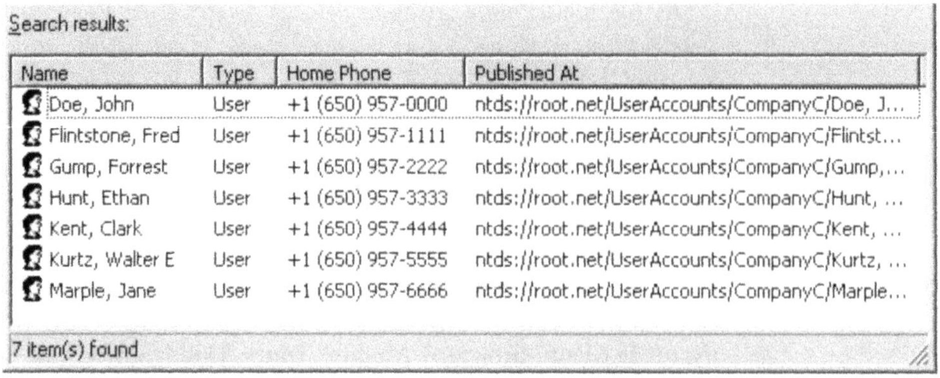

Search results:

Name	Type	Home Phone	Published At
Doe, John	User	+1 (650) 957-0000	ntds://root.net/UserAccounts/CompanyC/Doe, J...
Flintstone, Fred	User	+1 (650) 957-1111	ntds://root.net/UserAccounts/CompanyC/Flintst...
Gump, Forrest	User	+1 (650) 957-2222	ntds://root.net/UserAccounts/CompanyC/Gump,...
Hunt, Ethan	User	+1 (650) 957-3333	ntds://root.net/UserAccounts/CompanyC/Hunt, ...
Kent, Clark	User	+1 (650) 957-4444	ntds://root.net/UserAccounts/CompanyC/Kent, ...
Kurtz, Walter E	User	+1 (650) 957-5555	ntds://root.net/UserAccounts/CompanyC/Kurtz, ...
Marple, Jane	User	+1 (650) 957-6666	ntds://root.net/UserAccounts/CompanyC/Marple...

7 item(s) found

Figure 11.29 *List of users with home phone numbers PRIOR to editing Property Set.*

OU, but has no additional permissions other than the defaults on the user accounts.

The results are almost as expected: prior to editing the Personal Information Property Set, all home phone numbers of the users in the CompanyC OU were visible to John Doe; after removing the home phone number from the Personal Information Property Set, no home phone numbers are returned from AD in the search results except for his own number. Of course there is a simple reason why John is still able to see his own home phone number; if you again check out the default permissions for user objects as listed in Table 11.13, you will notice several explicit permissions granted to the SELF security principal. SELF is basically a representation of the object itself; thus, the permissions for SELF are granted to John for his own user object, which he authenticated with. Specifically, SELF, besides

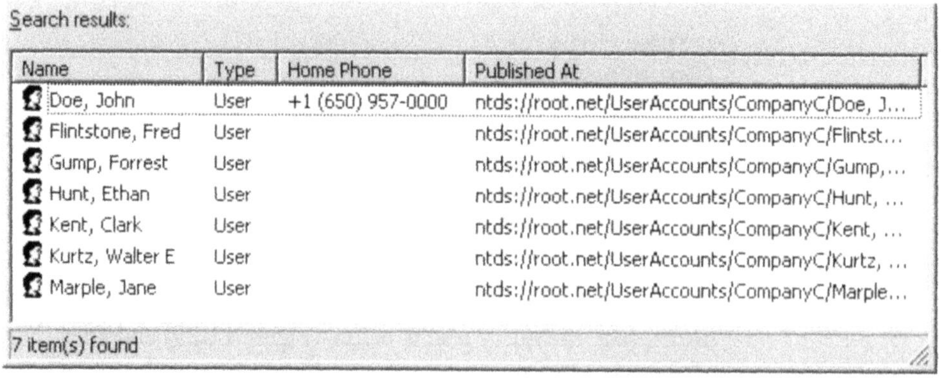

Search results:

Name	Type	Home Phone	Published At
Doe, John	User	+1 (650) 957-0000	ntds://root.net/UserAccounts/CompanyC/Doe, J...
Flintstone, Fred	User		ntds://root.net/UserAccounts/CompanyC/Flintst...
Gump, Forrest	User		ntds://root.net/UserAccounts/CompanyC/Gump,...
Hunt, Ethan	User		ntds://root.net/UserAccounts/CompanyC/Hunt, ...
Kent, Clark	User		ntds://root.net/UserAccounts/CompanyC/Kent, ...
Kurtz, Walter E	User		ntds://root.net/UserAccounts/CompanyC/Kurtz, ...
Marple, Jane	User		ntds://root.net/UserAccounts/CompanyC/Marple...

7 item(s) found

Figure 11.30 *List of users with home phone numbers AFTER editing Property Set.*

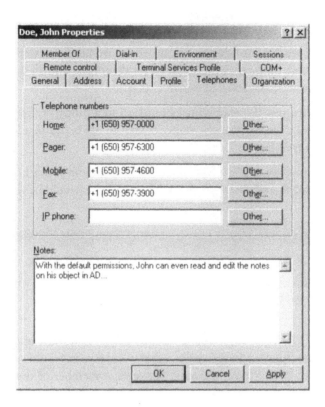

Figure 11.31
*Impact of editing a
Property Set on a
user's ability to
modify his own
attributes.*

being granted read and write (!) for the Personal Information Property Set, is also granted the read all properties permission to a user object.

But if we let John have a look at his own object properties in the AD Users and Computers MMC and move to the Telephone tab, you will also see the impact of removing the homePhone attribute from the Personal Information Property Set for this user, since he no longer has the write permissions on the homePhone attribute, as shown in Figure 11.31.

Setting Inherited Permissions for Specific Attributes

If our final goal was to grant all HR users the permissions to read and possibly to write the homePhone attribute, we would now be in a position to use inherited permissions to do so. As the explicit permissions for Authenticated Users to read the homePhone attribute are no longer applicable, there is no need for us to use a deny permission on the user objects. Instead, we can grant appropriate permissions at the container level (i.e., a parent OU) and inherit them to the user objects in that container. How to do this is explained in the "DSACLS-Sample 5" sidenote.

DSACLS-Sample 5 (Setting Permissions That Inherit to Child Objects)

As we now want to work with inherited permissions, we need to use the inheritance flags with DSACLS (/I) with an appropriate scope (*T* for this object and all subobjects, *S* for subobjects only, *P* to limit propagation to one level deep).

Since we want to apply the read/write permission to a property (homePhone) of a specific object type (user), the correct inheritance switch to use is /I:S in addition to supplying the inherited object type (user).

So to set the permission to grant read and write of the home phone attribute to a security group on all user objects underneath a container object, this would be the correct DSACLS command:

```
DSACLS <DN of container> /I:S /G <secprin>:RPWP;homePhone;user
```

For example:

```
DSACLS "OU=UserAccounts,DC=root,DC=net" /I:S /G root\HR-
users:RPWP;homePhone;user
```

Due to the removal of the homePhone attribute from the Personal Information Property Set, other normal users would still not be able to view the homePhone attribute. However, a member of the HR users group can now view and edit the homePhone attribute of any user underneath the UserAccounts OU, as shown in Figure 11.32.

Adding an Attribute to a Property Set

The examples above show the power of editing Property Sets, since not a single permission change was required on the objects themselves to change the effective permissions for Authenticated Users that were granted on the respective attributes. This power should not be underestimated, though, as leveraging it will always affect the complete forest and all applications that build upon being authorized to read or write attributes of objects via the respective Property Set. This is different from changing the security of objects by editing the ACLs on them, thus limiting the impact of a potential damage through false permissions to the objects whose permissions were changed. So any change needs to be well understood, tested in a lab environment, and documented prior to applying it in production. On the positive side, it is very easy to re-add an attribute back to a Property Set, in case this should be required; the risk of editing Property Sets should not be overestimated and should not keep you from changing them if you have a valid necessity.

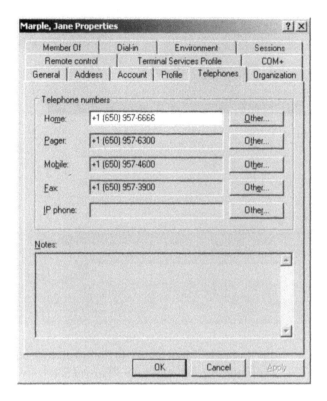

Figure 11.32
HR-user is allowed to view and edit the homePhone attribute after setting approriate inherited permissions.

Undoing the removal of an attribute from a Property Set or adding new attributes to the Property Set is basically as easy as removing it: the correct GUID needs to be written in to the attributeSecurityGUID property of the respective attributeSchema object. So to re-add the homePhone attribute to the Personal Information Property Set, the binary octet GUID value "86 B8 B5 77 4A 94 D1 11 AE BD 00 00 F8 03 67 C1" needs to be written back to the attribute. As this is not such an easy task using LDP.exe, you should use ADSIedit to do so instead. In ADSIedit you can take the GUID value, navigate to the object, and edit its attributeSecurityGUID as a hexadecimal value, as shown in Figure 11.33.

After applying the change and replicating it to other DCs, the home-Phone attribute would again be a member of the Personal Information Property Set.

Things to consider when editing Property Sets in AD:

1.   Property Sets are used for adding a single permission (ACE) to multiple attributes (properties) of an object. The rightsGUID of

Figure 11.33
*Adding an
attribute to a
Property Set using
ADSIedit.*

the Property Set is equal to the attributeSecurityGUID of the attributes that belong to the Property Set.

2. A change to a Property Set will always immediately impact all existing (and new) objects that have permissions assigned to the respective Property Set. While it is good that the objects do not need to be repermissioned, the impact on other applications, which rely on the permissions granted on an object's attributes through the property set, is an unknown factor until thorough testing has been performed.

3. A change to a Property Set is nondestructive and can easily be undone by re-adding a previously removed attributeSchema object back to the Property Set.

11.4.6   Using the Confidentiality Bit

The last of the five options we will discuss for hiding data in AD is the usage of the new confidentiality bit, introduced in Windows Server 2003 SP1. A detailed introduction of the confidentiality bit was given in Chapter 10. It is important for administrators to understand that this new feature is not applicable for most of the existing attributes in AD, since it cannot be used with category 1 attributes.

Setting the employeeNumber Attribute to Confidential

You may, for example, want to store the employeeID in AD, preferably in an attribute that can be set to be confidential so that only authorized users can read and edit it. If that is the case, you could choose not to store the data in the attribute called employeeID, but instead use the employeeNumber attribute or any custom attribute that you have extended your AD schema with. EmployeeNumber is not a category 1 attribute; therefore, it can be configured as a confidential attribute. As its searchFlag attribute is empty, it is sufficient to write the value 128 into the searchFlags property of the employeeNumber attribute in the schema (see Figure 11.34)—realize that if the searchFlag is not empty, you need to add the number. The searchFlag defines various other options for an attribute such as if it is indexed (bit 1) or if it remains in the tombstone object at deletion (bit 3).

If you accidentally do try to set the confidential bit on an attribute that is a category 1 attribute (base schema), you will receive a rather misleading error message, which is illustrated in Figure 11.35. Always keep in mind that base schema attributes cannot set the confidential bit for employeeNumber with ADSIedit.

Figure 11.34
Setting the confidential bit for employeeNumber with ADSIedit.

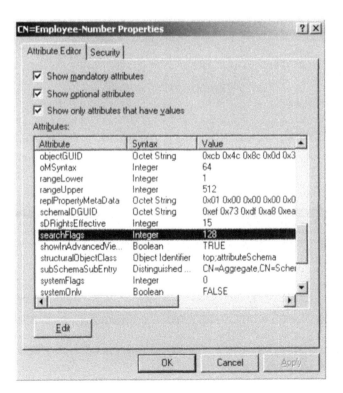

Figure 11.35   *Error when trying to set the confidential bit for a base schema attribute.*

As soon as this flag is set (and the schema cache is updated), a populated employeeNumber attribute will no longer be visible for the user himself, who is granted the read all attributes permission via SELF in the default permissions.

Granting Read Access to a Confidential Attribute

But the next challenge is already ahead of us. How do we set the control_ access permission for the hidden attribute? This should actually be an easy task, but Microsoft does not supply any tools with Windows Server 2003 SP1 that can set this access at the attribute level.

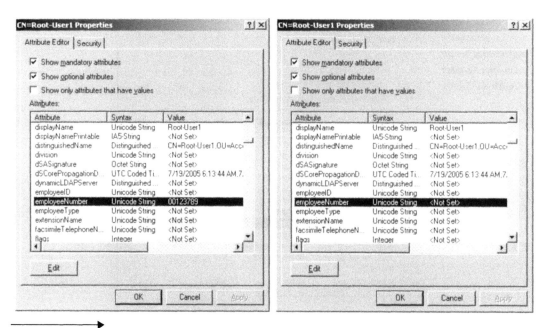

Figure 11.36   *Viewing the contents of employeeNumber as SELF prior (left) and after activating the confidential bit (right).*

The correct syntax to add the control_access permission via DSACLS would theoretically be as follows:

```
DSACLS <DN of container> /G <secprin>:CA;employeeNumber
```

For example:

```
DSACLS "CN=Root-User1,OU=UserAccounts,DC=root,DC=net"
    /G root\HR-users:CA;employeeNumber
```

But the current version of DSACLS does not yet support setting any permissions other than read or write property when you set ACEs for a property. This situation did not change with R2, however. There will be an update to DSACLS in the next version of the Windows server OS, currently code-named Longhorn Server, which is capable of setting these rights.

Other than setting the control_access permission via a script, there is one more option R2 offers to help us out: the new version of ADAM in R2 also includes a newer LDP version, which has a very powerful security editor as part of the tool. Although this security editor is not perfect either (for example, it does not show you where certain permissions have been inherited from, which is done by the built-in security editor), it does allow you to set the control_access flag on a specific attribute of a user.

Using LDP.exe from the R2 version of ADAM, you can browse to the object whose permissions you want to change, right-click the object, and choose Advanced ⇨ Security Descriptor. The new LDP will then pop up a dialog box to set the options for displaying the Security Descriptor; do not choose the text dump, which will dump the descriptor to the output window. Leaving it as is starts the new Security Editor (see Figure 11.37).

Choosing "Add ACE" grants the control access permission for the employeeNumber attribute (see Figure 11.38).

Managing the permissions for attributes on a list of separate objects in AD does not work very efficiently when using a UI. For now, it should be okay to use the new LDP Security Editor from R2 to manage the security at a parent OU for all given child objects. However, we strongly hope that we will soon see an out-of-band update of DSACLS that will support setting the control_access permission on properties.

Here are a couple of things you must remember when you consider using the confidential bit to hide attributes from general read access in AD:

1.   Like none of the other data-hiding options, the confidential bit will not hinder domain or OU admins from viewing the confidential attributes of an object in AD. However, it hinders users who are

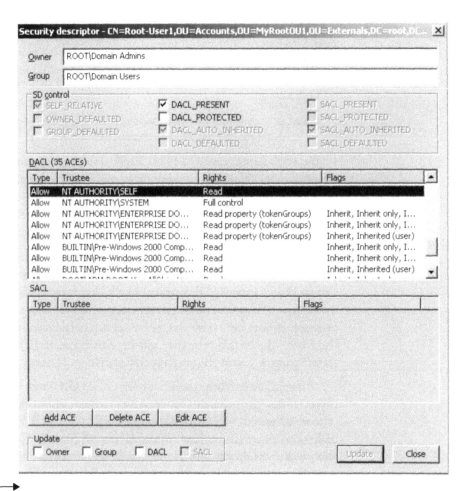

Figure 11.37   *Security Editor from LDP.EXE from Adam in R2.*

merely granted general read permissions on the whole object or
via a property set, keeping them from reading the data in an
attribute configured to be confidential.

2.   Marking an attribute confidential will immediately change the
permissions of the respective attribute for all objects in AD. Most
of the default attributes in AD (all of which are base-schema
attributes) cannot be marked confidential. As with the change of
Property Sets, no repermissioning of the objects in AD is required
to activate the change of permission in an AD forest. However,
granting read access to nonadministrators does require granting
the target group the control_access permission to the confidential
attribute.

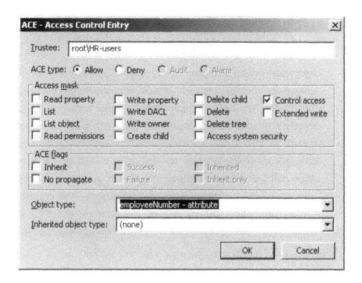

Figure 11.38
Setting Control
Access for a
property via
LDP.EXE in R2.

3.   There is currently a lack of tool support to manage the permissions for confidential attributes. The LDP Security Editor from R2 gets the job done, but Microsoft currently doesn't provide a command-line option to manage the control_access permission for attributes. Scripting a solution may require extra effort.

11.5 Third-Party AD Delegation Tools

Table 11.16 lists a set of third-party software products that can help facilitate AD administrative delegation. All of them provide a role-based abstraction layer that is implemented on top of AD. They all include logic that

Table 11.16   *Third-Party AD Delegation Tools*

Product	More Information at:
Quest ActiveRoles	www.quest.com/activeroles_direct
	www.quest.com/activeroles_server
NetPro AccessManager	http://www.netpro.com/products/accessmanager
Symantec (BindView) bv-Control for Active Directory	www.bindview.com/Products/bvControl/WinActiveDirectory.cfm
NetIQ Directory Security Administrator (part of the Security Administration Suite)	www.netiq.com/products/admin/default.asp

translates the roles and their associated AD administration tasks into native AD access permissions.

Note that no third-party software will actually take the burden away from any administrator to actually understand the Windows and Active Directory security model, which was discussed in great detail in this book. The tools can, however, lower the efforts required in implementing a sound security model (often requiring less scripting), in documenting the model (most of the tools include security reporting features), and in auditing changes to your security model. In a world of IT governance and compliance rules, the latter feature may be of particular interest for larger companies as otherwise manual security changes—for example, at the level of an Organizational Unit in Active Directory—may go unnoticed for a long time.

Index

AAA security services, 7
Access-based enumeration (ABE),
          676–79
  defined, 676
  enabling, 677, 679
  share content, 678
  using, 678–79
Access Control Entries (ACEs), 586
  object-based, 635–51
  property-based, 639
Access Control Lists (ACLs)
  adding well-known security
          principals to, 605
  content, 586
  defined, 586
  discretionary, 588
  inheritance, 627–35
  property-based, 640
  system, 588
  See also ACL editor
Access control management, 18, 31
Accinfo.dll, 105
Account lockouts, 100–108
  defined, 100
  disabling accounts versus, 101
  management tools, 105–8
  policy, 103–4
  policy settings, 104
  process, 101–3

process illustration, 102
  protection, 100
Account management, 69–73
  domain, 69
  local, 70–73
Accounts, 73–77
  administrator, 73, 74–75
  disabled, Kerberos and, 337
  disabling, 101
  guest, 75–77
  objects, 40
Acldiag, 691
ACL editor, 589, 626–27
  AD authorization info display, 638
  List Object mode and, 747
  setting inheritance in, 633, 635
  warning message, 633
  See also Access Control Lists (ACLs)
ACL evaluation process, 651–57
  basic, 652
  canonical evaluation order, 653
  examples, 655, 656
  rules and order, 652–57
  See also Access Control Lists (ACLs)
Active Directory (AD), 40
  account management, 724
  Application Mode (ADAM), 481–82
  authentication database, 314
  domain local group, 276

Active Directory (AD) *(cont'd.)*
   domains, 46
   Federation Services (ADFS), 573–77
   forests, 118, 119
   forest-wide replication, 45
   group feature availability, 595–96
   group nesting rules, 594
   group scopes, 592–95
   group types, 592
   hiding data in, 732–71
   infrastructures, trusts between, 140
   LDAP information model, 479–80
   namespace, 44
   Schema Analyzer, 648
   Trusted Domain Object (TDO), 133
   trust relationships, 113–14
   user/group objects, 276
   user logon time storage, 299
   well-known security principals, 604
   See also AD delegation; AD object quotas
Active Directory Federation Services (ADFS),
      121–22, 573–77
   architecture, 574–75
   components and operation, 575
   defined, 573
   interoperability, 573
   message exchange, 576–77
   operation, 576–77
   security tokens, 575
   setup, 574
   software vendors, 574
   "TrustBridge" codename, 573
   Web service agents, 575, 576
   X.509 certificate-based tools, 574
Active Directory Users and Computers MMC
      snap-in, 77
ActiveRoles, 771
AD delegation, 693–771
   administrative, 719–32
   administrator types, 695
   Computer Administration role, 710, 714–17

data administrators, 695
   delegation wizard, 720
   on domain level, 705
   Group Administration role, 710
   groups and role descriptions, 717
   guidelines, 705–19
   least privilege, 706–7
   level-of-privilege considerations, 694–97
   Microsoft Exchange tasks, 713
   multidomain considerations, 698–701
   organizational units (OUs), 701–5
   password management, 707–10
   roles, 710–19
   roles, planning application, 717–19
   service administrators, 695, 696
   third-party tools, 771
   User Administration role, 710, 711,
      712–14
   User Password Reset role, 710
AD Directory Services Restore Mode
      (DSRM), 96
Add-on manager, 187–89
   access, 187
   administrator control, 187–88
   defined, 187
   illustrated, 188
   See also Internet Explorer
Administrative delegation
   advanced service management delegation
      scenarios, 728–31
   DFS root creation, 730
   DHCP authorization, 729
   DNS service administration, 730
   examples, 723–32
   helpdesk scenario, 725–28
   predefined tasks, 721
   setting up, 719–32
   undelegating, 721
   See also AD delegation
Administrator account, 73, 74–75
   account lockout and, 100

authentication mechanism, 74–75
defined, 73
disabling, 75
renaming, 74, 75
securing, 74–75
See also Accounts
Administrator groups, 611–14
Administrators, 611–12
Domain Admins, 612
Enterprise Admins, 612, 613, 614
list, 612
See also Groups
AdminSDHolder object, 617–18
AD object quotas, 665–67
enforcement, 667
error, 666
setting, 666
storage, 666
testing, 666
AD objects
attribute visibility, managing,
741–44
default security, 733–35
default security, adjusting, 754–58
displaying in List Object mode, 745
viewing, 739
visibility, managing, 739–41
ADSIedit, 152, 154, 643, 644
defined, 691
query to list property sets, 645
AD Users and Computers (ADUC), 101, 277,
287, 353, 592
in domain account management, 69
UPN from, 56
user password reset, 95
well-known security principals, 605
Advanced Encryption Standard (AES), 17
Alockout.dll, 105
Aloinfo.exe, 82, 107
Alternate data streams (ADS), 673–76
defined, 673

listing, with Streams command line utility,
676
names, finding, 675
predefined naming standards, 674
using, 674–76
See also NTFS
Anonymous access, 271–77, 416–19
back-end, 416
defined, 271
exchange, 416
GPO security options, 272, 273–75
HTTP authentication, 416–19
See also Authentication
Anonymous passwords, 417
Anti-Spyware Enterprise, 214
Application programming interfaces (APIs),
552–53
Asymmetric ciphers, 17
Attachment Manager (AM), 185
Audit account logon events, 293
Auditing
logon events, 292–93
providers, 30
systems, 7
Authenticated Users well-known security
principal, 605–6, 757
Authentication, 233–301
anonymous access, 271–77
basics, 233–38
certificate-based, 445–75
client, 446
common protocols, 236
concurrent logon sessions and, 281–92
credential caching, 277–81
cross-forest, 146
delegation, 306–7, 345–60
digest, 423–26
host-to-host, 387
HTTP, 414–26
IAS methods, 578
IIS, 409–76

Authentication *(cont'd.)*
    integrated Windows, 426–28
    interactive, 243–47
    Kerberos, 121
    logon rights, 255
    machine, 252
    methods overview, 237
    multifactor, 236
    mutual, 305
    Netlogon logging and, 298–300
    noninteractive, 247–50
    NTLM-based, 261–71
    Passport-based, 428–45
    PKI-based SSO, 542
    policies, 18
    providers, 30
    qualifying, 235–38
    secure channel requestor, 155
    secure client-side credential caching, 546
    secure server-side credential caching, 548
    SecurID, 227
    selective, 127–32
    service accounts, 252
    terminology, 233–35
    tokens, 310
    troubleshooting, 292–300
    U2U, 324–26
    Windows, basics, 238–55
    Windows event logging, 292–98
Authentication authorities, 233
Authentication credentials, 234
Authentication infrastructures, 6, 9–11
    defined, 9, 233
    federation-based, 9–10
    integrated with network operating
        systems, 9
    integrated with WAMS, 9
    servers, 9
    software products, 9–10
    solutions, 10
    Web, 9

Authentication packages (APs), 243–44
Authentication Protocol Related well-known
    security principal, 610
Authentication servers, 233
Authentication Service Exchange, 322–23
Authentication to authorization, 361–69
    multiple domain environment, 364–67
    NTLM, 367–69
    single domain environment, 361–64
Authentication token, 235
Authenticator
    content, 381–82
    defined, 370
    ticket relationship, 369
Authorization, 583–691
    basics, 583–84
    centralization shift, 13
    data storage, 363
    decision making, 12
    groups, 590–622
    intermediaries, 590–624
    policies, 19
    policy management, 12
    providers, 30
    services, 11–13
    tools, 690–91
    troubleshooting, 690–91
    user rights, 622–24
    Windows 2000 changes, 624–59
    Windows model, 584–90
    Windows Server 2003 changes, 659–90
Authorization infrastructures, 6, 11–15
    defined, 11
    services, 11–13
    WAMS, 13–15
Authorization Manager, 679–90
    access control decisions, 684
    access policy database, 684
    application groups, 687
    architecture, 683–85
    architecture illustration, 683

Authorization Policy Store, 686
   concepts, 686–88
   defined, 679
   deployment scenarios, 688–90
   hierarchical role model support, 687
   impersonation/delegation model, 688, 689
   integrating, 689
   MMC snap-in, 685
   role, 687
   trusted application model, 689–90
Availability, 7

Backup domain controllers (BDCs), 49
Base64 encoding, 421
Basic authentication, 419–23
   credential prompt, 420
   exchange, 419
   logon type, 422
   method comparison, 475–76
   security hole, 421
   setting, 421
   shortcut, 420
   token cache time, 423
   warning, 421
   See also HTTP authentication
Batch User Manager, 94
BIOS administrator, 222
BizTalk Server, 559
   defined, 560
   HTTP adapter, 566
   installation program options, 565
   preinstallation requirements, 564
   SAP adapter, 566, 567
Browser security, 186–94
Built-in property sets. *See* Property sets
ByControl for Active Directory, 771

Cachedump tool, 278, 279
Cacls, 690
CardSpace, 430
CC EAL4+ certification, 31

Centrify DirectControl, 528–31
   ADUC MMC snap-in extension, 530
   architecture, 531
   built-in GPO functionality, 529
   configuration utility, 531
   defined, 528
   delegated administration support, 529
   differentiators, 529
   illustrated, 530
   NIS migration, 529
   reporting capabilities, 529
   zones, 529
Certificate-based authentication, 445–75
   certificate validation, 464–68
   client SSL certificates, 462–63
   deployment considerations, 468–75
   method comparison, 475–76
   SSL client trust, 463
   SSL configuration, 458–62
   SSL server certificate generation, 455–57
   SSL server certificate installation, 457–58
   SSL server certificate request generation,
      451–55
   Web browser SSL support, 463–64
   See also IIS authentication
Certificate revocation checking, 463–64
   CRL-based, 463
   OCSP-based, 464
Certificate Revocation Lists (CRLs)
   certificate revocation checking, 463
   leveraging, 466
Certificate trust lists (CTLs)
   defined, 466
   enabling, 459
   wizard, 466
Certificate validation, 464–68
   digital signatures, 466
   process, 464–66
   process illustration, 465
Certificate Wizard, 453–54
Certification authorities (CAs), 16, 456

Client authentication, 446
Client certificate mapping, 459, 460–61
Client security, 165–230
    aspects, 165, 166
    IE 7.0 client features, 228–30
    least privilege, 166–78
    malicious mobile code protection, 205–15
    overview, 165–66
    TPM security functions, 215–28
    Windows Vista features, 228–30
Client-Server Authentication Exchange,
        323–24
Cmdkey operation, 559
Common Internet File System (CIFS), 387,
        496
Companies
    hiding existence, 749–54
    multiple, managing, 750
Compliance management, 18
Computer Administration role, 710, 714–17
    description, 716
    permissions, 716
    sample, 714–17
    task list, 716
Concurrent logon sessions, limiting, 281–92
Confidential Bit, 667–72
    default user attributes used with, 671–72
    defined, 667
    list attributes not used with, 671
    using, 766–71
Constrained delegation, 351–55
    benefits, 351–52
    configuring, 353–55
    defined, 351
    exchanges in, 352
    See also Delegation
Cookies, 430
    automatic, disabling, 436–37
    content, viewing, 436
    content encryption, 438
    domain, 437

exchanges, 441
expiration time, 438
HTTP, 540
name, 437
Passport, 436–42
persistent, 438
profile, 440–41
properties, 437–38
ticket, 440
types, 439
CounterSpy Enterprise, 214
Creator Group well-known security principal,
        610
Creator Owner well-known security principal,
        610
Credential caching, 277–81
    alternative, 280
    defined, 277
    disabling interactive domain logon with,
        280
    domain logon using, 278
    dumping with cachedump, 279
    generation process, 279
    in Internet Explorer, 423
    security risk, 279
    user credential storage versus, 281
Credential database, 234
Credential Manager, 227, 553–59
    architecture, 554–57
    automation, 558
    components, 554
    credential collection, 554, 557
    credential store, 554–55
    defined, 554
    events, 557–58
    key ring, 555, 556
    operation, 557–59
    operation illustration, 558
Credential synchronization, 543–46
    password synchronization-based (logical),
        544

password synchronization-based (physical), 545
pros/cons, 550
software technology, 544
SSO products, 545
See also Single Sign-On (SSO)
Cross-forest trust, 119, 121
authentication, 146
between multiple forests, 120
See also Trusts
Cross-realm trust, 403–8
Cryptographic keys, 215–16
Cryptographic service providers (CSPs), 249
CTRL+ALT+DEL key sequence, 239, 243
CyberSafe, 540

Data encryption standard (DES), 249
Data Execution Protection (DEP), 186
Dcdiag, 160
DC PasswordChanger, 94
Dcpromo process, 113
Default security
adjusting, 754–58
change, when to, 756–58
change guidelines, 757–58
descriptor, 661–64
resetting back to, 756
user objects, 754–56
viewing, 755
See also AD objects
DefaultSecurityDescriptor attribute, 662–64
retrieving, 663
viewing, 664
Delegation, 306–7, 345–60
AD, 693–771
allowed for all services, 353–54
allowed for limited set of services, 354
component configuration, 360
configuring (Windows 2000), 355
configuring (Windows Server 2003), 354
constrained, 351–55

defined, 345
disadvantages, 346
disallowed, 353
exchange for forwarded tickets, 349
exchange for proxy tickets, 348
Kerberos support, 347
multitier benefits, 346
protocol transition, 357–58
protocol transition configuration, 358–59
security advantages, 345–46
test scenario, 359–60
ticket, flags, 347
in Windows 2000, 350–51
wizard, 720
Delegwiz.inf configuration file, 722, 723
Demilitarized zone (DMZ), 118
Denial-of-service attack, 375
DES-CBC-CRC, 372
DES-CBC-MD5, 372
Devserv, 557
Digest authentication, 423–26
advanced, 425–26
advantages, 423
architectural changes, 425
authentication dialog box, 425, 426
defined, 236
disadvantages, 423–24
exchange, 424
functioning, 425
method comparison, 475–76
specification, 423
warning, 424
See also IIS authentication
Digital Rights Management (DRM), 27
Digital signatures, 466
DirectControl, 528–31
Directories, 21–22
meta-directory, 22
solutions, 21
virtual, 22

Directory Information Tree (DIT), 313
Directory Services Recovery Mode (DSRM),
    379
Disabled accounts, Kerberos and, 337
Discretionary access control (DAC) model,
    680
    granting/revoking access privileges in,
        680
    RBAC comparison, 682
Discretionary ACLs (DACLs), 621
    defined, 588
    missing, 656
    model, 621
    null, 656–57
    See also Access control lists (ACLs)
Distinguished name (DN), name conversion,
    253
Distributed file system (DFS), 253, 387
Distribution groups, 591
DNS, 487
    configuration, 144, 145
    dynamic update, 253
    name resolution, 144–45
    query for domain controller, 252
    query for KDC service, 252
    query for LDAP service, 251
    servers, 145
    SMB dialect negotiation, 252
    suffixes, 134
DNS namespaces, 134, 135
    collisions, 136, 138
    collisions, avoiding, 138
    disabling, 136
    TLN restrictions excluding, 138
Domain controllers (DCs), 47–51
    authenticating, finding, 255
    backup (BDCs), 49
    in cross-forest authentication, 146
    defined, 38, 47
    Domain Naming Master, 51
    GC, 50, 51

Infrastructure Master, 52
LSA versus, 38–39
multiple, 48
operations master roles, 51–52
PDC, 49
PDC Emulator, 52
RID Master, 52
SA processes/subprocesses, 39
Schema Master, 51
separating administrator role form, 697
special-purpose, 50
Domain logons, disabling, 280
Domain Name System. *See* DNS
Domain Naming Master, 51
Domain-only replication, 45
Domains
    account management, 69
    concept, 44–46
    cookie, 437
    defined, 44
    direct trusts between, 143
    functional levels, 596
    function levels, 46–47, 48
    mixed-mode, 341
    multiple DCs, 48
    policy, default, 81
    trusted, 110
Domains and Trusts MMC snap-in, 147
Domain security authority. *See* Domain
        controllers (DCs)
DriveLock, 228
DropMyRights, 176
DSACLS, 741, 742, 744
DSHeuristics settings, 748
DSREVOKE.exe tool, 741
Dssec.dat file, 638, 639
Dumpsec, 83
Dynamic Host Configuration Protocol
        (DHCP), 250
Dynamic link library (DLL), 445
Dynamic service-port mappings, 162

Effective Permissions, 660–61
Elevation of privilege, 698–700
Emergency repair disk (ERD), 88
Encrypted session keys, 309
Encrypting File System (EFS), 83, 225, 227, 673
Encryption types, Kerberos, 372–74
  default, 373
  encryption keys, 372
  key lengths in bits, 373
  request, 373
Endorsement Key (EK), 223
Enterprise Admins group, 612, 613, 614
Enterprise Single Sign-On (ENTSSO), 559–70
  architecture, 561–64
  architecture overview illustration, 561
  client-side GUI administration, 565
  command line administration, 563
  credential mappings, 561
  defined, 559–60
  host-initiated SSO using, 567
  mapping mechanisms, 562
  operation, 564–68
  as optional component, 560
  options, 565
  password synchronization, 568–70
  server and client software, 563
  server-side GUI administration, 564
  service installation, 562
  setup, 563
  use cases, 564
  Windows-initiated SSO using, 566
  without password synchronization, 568
  See also Single Sign-On (SSO)
Enterprise SSO, 535
Error codes, Kerberos, 395–96
ETrust PestPatrol Anti-Spyware, 214
Event logging, authentication-related, 292–98
Exchange Servers, administration, 713

Extended rights
  access control with, 648–51
  new Windows Server 2003, 649–50
  types, 651
Extending SSO, 550–53
  to cover different applications, 552–53
  to cover different organizations, 551–52
  See also Single Sign-On (SSO)

Fast User Switching (FUS), 168, 173–75, 239
  defined, 173
  improper use, 175
  switching, 174
Federation, 23–26
  AD, services, 573–77
  defined, 24
  goal, 24
  identity, 25
  management, 18, 31, 573
  mechanism comparison, 552
  policies, 19
  solutions, 24
  standards, 25–26
  See also Active Directory Federation Services (ADFS)
Federation-based authentication infrastructures, 9–10
Findstr.exe, 299
Firewalls
  port configurations, 161–62
  SSL and, 471–75
  trusts and, 161–63
Flexible Single Master Operation (FSMO), 697
Forest function levels, 49
Forests
  AD, 118, 119
  interims, using, 140
  multidomain production, 141
  selective authentication between, 133
  SID filtering between, 123

Forest trust, 118–22
   attributes, 154
   authentication flow, 344
   cross, 119, 120, 121
   defined, 116
   features, 119–20
   SAM account name limitations and, 121
   SID filtering across, 124
   See also Trusts
Forest-wide replication, 45
Forwarded tickets, 347
   delegation exchange, 349
   in TGT request, 347
   See also Tickets
Fully Qualified Domain Name (FQDN),
      192, 200

General Electric Comprehensive Operating
      System (GECOS), 491
General profile cookie, 440, 441
Generic Security Services API (GSS-API), 526
GINA (Graphical Identification and
      Authentication), 173
Global address list (GAL), 655
Global catalog (GC)
   DCs, 50
   in object queries, 51
Global Catalog-less (GCless) logon, 366
   defined, 366
   enabling, 368
Global groups, 591
   nesting rules, 594
   scope conversion, 595
   See also Groups
Global LSA secrets, 41
Global unique identifiers (GUIDs), 68, 646
Group Administration role, 710
Group Policy Objects (GPOs), 79–80, 103
   to centrally administer security zones,
      203–5
   interactive logon related settings, 246–47

Kerberos settings, 390–92
   MMC snap-in, 259, 260
   processing of, 117
   WF configuration, 181
Groups, 590–622
   AD feature availability, 595–96
   administrator, 611–14
   AD nesting rules, 594
   AD scopes, 592–95
   AD types, 592
   AD usage rules, 615
   built-in, 599
   defined, 590
   defining, 591
   distribution, 591
   domain functional levels and, 596
   dynamic, 601
   global, 591, 594, 595
   linking users to, 737
   local, 591, 594, 595
   membership restrictions, 593
   nesting factors, 615–16
   primary, setting, 619
   recovery of memberships, 616
   scope, 700–701
   security, 591, 597–98
   support, 591
   universal, 591, 594, 595, 616
   usage guidelines, 614–17
   use restrictions, 594
   well-known security principal, 600
   See also Authorization
Guest account
   defined, 73
   disabling, 75–76
   password-protecting, 76
   renaming, 76
   securing, 75–77
   See also Accounts

Helpdesk scenario, 725–28

defined, 725
overview, 727
role description, 726
See also Administrative delegation
Hiding data, 732–71
built-in property sets, adjusting, 758–66
challenge, 733–39
companies, 749–54
Confidentiality Bit, 766–71
default security, adjusting, 754–58
necessity, 735–39
with "normal" permissions, 739–44
permission configuration options, 738
Host group mapping, 562
Host individual mapping, 562
Host-initiated SSO, 562
preinstallation requirements, 564
using ENTSSO, 567
Host Integration Server (HIS), 559
defined, 560
Transaction Integrator, 568
HP ProtectTools software, 219–26
HP TPM-enabled applications, 226–28
HTTP
cookies, 540
engine, 410
headers, 414
host headers, 468
proxies, 427
proxy approaches, 472–75
redirect messages, 431
secure (HTTPs), 445
specifications, 414
HTTP authentication, 414–26
anonymous access, 416–19
basic, 419–23
digest, 423–26
exchange, 414–15
exchange illustration, 415
See also Authentication
Hypertext Transport Protocol. *See* HTTP

Icacls, 691
Identities
defined, 27–28
digital, 27
selective authentication and, 132
Identity federation, 573
ADFS, 573–77
defined, 25
See also Federation
Identity management
consumable value components, 30
data repository components, 29
defined, 29
infrastructure components, 29–31
lifecycle components, 30
management components, 31
security components, 30
TSIs and, 27–31
Identity policies, 18
Idp.exe, 663
IIS
6.0 architecture, 411
anonymous account password, 417
Certificate Wizard, 453–54
Integrated Windows Authentication,
426–28
Internet Services Manager (ISM) MMC
snap-in, 409, 452
secure by default, 409–11
Web resources, 412
IIS authentication, 409–76
agent-based, 413
certificate-based, 445–75
configuring, 412
forms-based, 414
HTTP, 414–26
integrated Windows, 426–28
introduction to, 411–14
method comparison, 475–76
Passport-based, 428–45
See also Authentication

Incoming Forest Trust Builders, 145
INetOrgPerson object, 54, 481–82
Information technology (IT), 3, 4
Infrastructure Master, 52
Inheritance, 627–35
    ACL, 627–35
    ACL editor, 629, 630
    AD permission, 634
    blocking impact, 632
    controlling, 631–35
    file system, 632
    fine-grained control, 627–35
    flags, 634
    NT4 and Windows 2003 comparison,
        628–31
    object type-based ACEs and, 651
    permission, 635
    registry permission, 632
    setting, in ACL editor, 633, 635
Instant Messaging (IM), 175
Integrated Windows Authentication, 426–28
    advantages, 426
    authentication protocols, 426
    dialog box, 428
    Security Support Providers (SSPs), 427
    uses, 428
Interactive authentication, 243–47
Interactive logon, 258, 328–30
    multiple domain environment, 333–35
    in single domain environment, 328–30
    See also Logon
Internet Authentication Service (IAS), 577–79
    authentication methods, 578
    defined, 577
    multiple Windows domains, 579
    scenarios, 577
Internet Connection Firewall (ICF), 178–79
Internet Engineering Task Force (IETF), 306
Internet Explorer
    add-on management registry hacks, 189
    add-on manager, 187–90

caching credentials in, 423
cookie "Privacy Alert," 438
disabling automatic cookie handling, 437
hidden security changes, 192–94
Internet options security configuration
    interface, 203
pop-up blocking, 190–92
Privacy Report, 443
security features, 186, 229
security functionality, 187–94
security zones, 194–205
SSL/TLS lock symbol, 447
Internet Explorer Administration Kit (IEAK),
    463
    to centrally administer security zones,
        204–5
    IE Customization Wizard, 205
    Profile Manager, 205
    programs, 205
Internet Information Services. See IIS; IIS
    authentication
Internet security zone, 195
Internet Services Manager (ISM) MMC
    snap-in, 409, 452
Interoperability, 396–407
    cross-realm trust, 403–8
    principals defined on non-Windows KDC,
        401–3
    principals defined on Windows KDC,
        400–1
    scenarios, 399–408
Interoperability-enabling technologies,
    479–83
    Kerberos, 482–83
    LDAP, 479–82
IPsec host-to-host authentication, 387
ISAPI DLL, 445

John the Ripper (JtR), 91–92
    benchmarking test, 91–92
    brute-force password cracking process, 92

defined, 91
john.exe, 91
running, 92

Kerberized applications, 387–90
Kerberos, 235, 303–408
    account mappings, 406
    account properties, 392, 393
    advanced topics, 345–90
    advantages, 304–7
    authentication delegation support, 306–7
    authentication tokens, 310
    basic protocol, 307–27
    configuration, 390–94
    constrained delegation, 351–55
    data confidentiality, 324
    defined, 236, 303
    delegation, 345–60
    design assumptions, 309–10
    disabled accounts and, 337
    disabling in migration scenarios, 330–32
    encryption types, 372–74
    entries, 310
    error codes, 395–96
    event IDs, 394
    event logging, 394
    faster authentications, 305
    GPO settings, 390–92
    integrity services, 324
    interoperability, 396–408
    as interoperability-enabling technology,
        482–83
    KDC, 312–14
    key hierarchy, 315
    method comparison, 475–76
    multiple domain logon, 333–43
    mutual authentication, 305
    Names tab, 407
    NAT and, 371
    non-Microsoft implementations,
        397–98

NTLM comparison, 307, 308
as open standard, 305–6
passwords and, 310
ports, 394
preauthentication data, 378–81
Privilege Attribute Certificate (PAC), 361,
    374–78
protocol transition, 357–58
protocol transition configuration,
    358–59
security principal limit, 310
single domain logon, 328–33
smart card logon support, 307
symmetric key cryptography, 310–12
TGT, 319–22
three heads, 304
ticket delegation flags, 347
ticketing system, 305
time sensitivity, 384–87
timestamps, 310
token-based SSO solution, 540
transport protocols, 392–94
troubleshooting, 394–96
troubleshooting tools, 396–97
U2U authentication, 324–26
UNIX-Windows interoperability, 407
Windows implementation comparison,
    398–99
Windows logon with, 327–45
See also Key distribution centers (KDCs)
Kerbtray, 385, 386
    defined, 397
    ticket cache with, 386
    using, 385
Key distribution centers (KDCs), 16, 99, 304,
    312–14, 520
    list, 146
    scalability, 313
    session key distribution, 317–19
    as trusted third party, 313
    UNIX, 402

Key hierarchy, 315
    defined, 316–17
    illustrated, 316
Key management infrastructures, 7, 15–18
    CA-based, 17, 18
    function, 15
    solutions, 16
    symmetric key ciphers and, 15
Keytab file, 401
Klist, 385, 387, 397
Krb5.conf file, 400
Ksetup, 406
Ktpass.exe command, 401

LAPM, 94–95
LCP, 88–91
    combination of characters, 90–91
    cracking method support, 90
    defined, 88
    GUI, 89
    password hash sources, 88–89
Ldap.conf, 515–16
LDP.exe, 643, 691, 761
    Security Editor from, 769, 770
    setting control access via, 771
Least privilege, 166–78
    fast user switching, 173–75
    respect, 167
    RunAs, 167–73
    support in Windows Vista, 168
    third-party tools, 175–77
    See also Client security
Least Privileged User Account (LUA), 167,
        168
Liberty Identity Federation Framework, 26
Libnss_winbind, 523
Lightweight Directory Access Protocol
        (LDAP), 479–82
    AD access, 387
    AD information model, 479–80
    clients, 479

defined, 479
    engines, 21
    as interoperability-enabling technology,
        479–82
    Microsoft support, 479–80
    naming services, 487
    NIS integration, 494–96
    query for GPO links, 253
    query for PKI configuration, 253
LimitLogin
    AD application partition, 285
    AD setup, 286
    ADUC configuration options, 287
    application partition, 288
    architecture, 284
    client setup program, 286
    components, 284–85
    configuring, 287–92
    defined, 281
    delete/logoff behavior options, 290–91
    diagnostics, 291
    for enterprise-level AD deployments,
        282
    installation program, 285
    installing, 285–87
    logon script, 283
    operation, 282–83
    operation illustration, 283
    requirement, 282
    user object configuration dialog box, 288,
        289
    Web service, 283, 287
Link Value Replication (LVR), 620
    defined, 664
    uses, 664–65
List Object mode
    ACL editor and, 747
    concept, 745–47
    configuring, 747–48
    enabling, 745–54
    object display in, 745

permissions, use rules, 748–49
working with, 753–54
Llogincmd, 291
LMCompatibilityLevel settings, 266, 267
LM hash
ALT character codes not generating, 271
calculation, 270
NT hash versus, 269
LM hash storage
disabling, 268–71
location, 268
security best practice, 269
LMHosts file, 156
Load balancing, SSL and, 469–71
Local account management, 70–73
Local Computer security zone, 195
administering, 201–2
customizing, 201–2
Local configuration files, 491
Local groups, 591
nesting rules, 594
scope conversion, 595
See also Groups
Local Intranet security zone, 194
Local Machine security zone, 193
Local secrets, 41
Local security authority (LSA), 39–44, 585
database, 40–42
defined, 39
domain security authority versus, 38–39
global secrets, 41
local secrets, 41
machine secrets, 41
OS user mode, 39
private secrets, 41
secrets, 40–41
subprocesses, 40
system key, 42–44
Local Users and Groups (LUG) MMC
snap-in, 70–72, 77, 78, 604
Lockoutstatus.exe, 107–8

Logon
GCless, 366
interactive, 328–30
multiple domain environment, 333–43
multiple forest, 343–45
noninteractive, 330
process field values, 298
rights, 622
in single domain environment, 328–33
smart card, 307, 388–90
type field values, 297
Windows, with Kerberos, 327–45
Logon events
account, event IDs, 297
audit, 292–93
authentication-related, 292–98
event detail fields, 295
event IDs, 295, 296
failed, 294
logon account, 293
successful, 294
Logon names, 55–56
downlevel, 55
user principal, 55–56
Logon rights, 255–61
best practices, 261
default assignments, 261
defined, 255
deny, 256, 259
managing, 259, 260
uses, 255
Windows, 256
Logon Type well-known security principal,
610
Longevity, 30

Machine
authentication, 252
LSA secrets, 41
passwords, 98–100
startup, 250–53

Malicious mobile code (MMC) protection,
        205–15
    solution overview, 205
    spyware protection guidelines, 214–15
    Windows Defender, 206–14
Master keys
    concept, 315
    defined, 316
    generated, 314
Maximum Transmission Unit (MTU), 392
Message authentication code (MAC), 324
Message digest 4 (MD4), 249
Meta-directory, 22
Microsoft Baseline Security Analyzer (MBSA),
        86–87
Microsoft Identity Integration Server (MIIS),
        33, 546
Microsoft Management Console (MMC),
        starting, 168
Microsoft Operations Manager (MOM),
        33–34
    architecture, 34
    defined, 33
Microsoft Systems Management Server
        (SMS), 33, 34–35
Microsoft Update (MU), 185
Mixed-mode domains, 341
Multifactor authentication, 236
Multiple domain, authentication and
        authorization, 364–67
Multiple domain logon, 333–43
    illustrated, 342, 343
    interactive, 333–35
    noninteractive, 335–38
    shortcut trusts and, 338–39
Multiple forest logon, 343–45
Mutual authentication, 305

Name resolution, 143–45
    DNS, 144–45
    NetBIOS, 144

WINS, 144, 145
Name suffix routing, 132–39
Naming services, 487–88
    characteristics, 488
    NIS, 491–93
    NIS+, 493–94
    NSS, 488–91
    types, 487–88
Naming service switch (NSS), 488–91
    API, 489
    architecture, 489
    clients, 491
    defined, 489
    supported databases, 490
    supported naming services, 490
Negotiate package, 249
NetBIOS
    browser election, 253
    domain name, 142
    name resolution, 144
    name resolution services, 497
    over TCP (NBT), 496
Netdiag, 160, 397
Netdom.exe, 99, 159
NetIQ Directory Security Administrator, 771
Netlogon
    log files, 298
    logging, 298–300
    process, 39
.NET Passport wizard, 436
Network Access Protection (NAP) support,
        229
Network Address Translation (NAT), 371
Network File System (NFS), 496
Network Information System (NIS), 488,
        491–93
    administrative grouping, 492
    architecture, 493
    deficiencies, 492
    defined, 491
    LDAP integration, 494–96

maps, 492
   server for, 500–506
   SFU server, 501
Network interface initialization, 250
Network monitor, 397
Network Operating Systems (NOSs), 12
Network Password Age tool, 83
Newsid, 68
New Trust Wizard, 404
NIS+, 488, 493–94
   architecture, 493, 494
   defined, 493
   as EOF naming service, 493–94
   functionality, 494
NIS Data Migration Wizard, 503–5
   illustrated, 505
   starting, 504
NIS/LDAP gateway, 512–14
   architecture, 513
   functionality, 512
   ypldapd, 513, 514
Nlparse.exe, 108, 299
   defined, 299
   using, 300
Nltest.exe utility, 156, 160
Noninteractive authentication, 247–50
   architecture illustration, 248
   NTLMv2 for, 266
   SSPI, 247, 248
Noninteractive logon, 330
   in multiple domain environment, 335–38
   in single domain environment, 331
   See also Logon
Nss_ldap, 514–17
   defined, 514
   ldap.conf, 515–16
   UNIX/Linux host, enabling, 515
NTFS
   alternate data streams, 673–76
   defined, 672–73
   file streams, 672

NTLM, 90, 235, 236
   authentication, 261–71
   authentication and authorization, 367–69
   authentication flow, 262
   authentication steps, 262–63
   challenge-response mechanism, 305, 368,
      427
   as default authentication protocol, 249
   flavors, 264–65
   flavors, controlling, 265–68
   handshake, 368
   Kerberos comparison, 307, 308
   method comparison, 475–76
   for noninteractive authentication, 266
   pam_smb module support, 487
   protocol, 261–64
   security features, 265
   support, 264
   symmetric key cryptography, 311
   version 2 (NTLMv2), 264, 265
   weaknesses, 263–64
NtlmMinClientSec registry key, 266, 267,
   268
NtlmMinServerSec registry key, 266, 267,
   268
Ntrights, 690

OASIS (Organization for the Advancement of
      Structured Information Standards),
      552
Object-based ACEs, 635–51
   access control based on object type,
      636–37
   access control based on property/property
      set, 637–48
   ACE fields, 635
   in Advanced Security editor, 637
   illustrated, 636
   inheritance and, 651
   See also Access Control Entries (ACEs)
One-to-one mapping, 461

Online Certificate Status Protocol (OCSP), 464
OpenLDAP, 512
Organizational units (OUs), 376, 701–5
  bound to single domain, 702
  default permissions, 734
  defined, 701
  hidden, viewing, 752, 753
  hierarchy example, 704
  nesting, 704
  structure, 702, 703
  structure options, 703
  structure standardization, 705
  top-level, 702
Other Organization well-known security principal, 608
Outlook Express (OE), 185
Outlook Web Access (OWA), 345
Owner Access Restriction (OAR) feature, 621
Ownership permissions, 618–19
  Creator Group, 618–19
  Creator Owner, 618

Pam_kerberos, 486
  centric architecture, 521
  support, 520
Pam_ldap, 486
  centric architecture, 519
  security advantages, 519–20
  support, 518
Pam_mkhomedir, 487
Pam_unix, 486, 517–18
  centric architecture, 517
  leveraging, 517
  UNIX authentication protocol support, 517
  user authentication, 518
Partial attribute set (PAS), 50
Passport
  account key, 434
  cookies, 436–42

  credentials, storing, 436
  HTTP redirect messages, 431
  infrastructure, 431–32
  infrastructure illustration, 432
  integration, 443–45
  nexus servers, 432, 442
  PUID, 444
  security enhancements, 429
  Sign In/Sign Out icons, 434
  SSL, 431
  strong credential sign-in, 434
  symmetric encryption keys, 438
  ticket cookie, 440
  ticket-granting, 440
  user changes, 435–36
  user data, 441
  Windows Live ID and, 429–30
  wizard, 435
Passport-based authentication, 428–45
  defined, 428
  exchange, 433–35
  messages, 445
  method comparison, 475–76
  security, 434
  sequence, 433
  support, 428
  See also IIS authentication
Passport.dll, 445
Passport Manager, 429
  HTTP query strings, 442
  Nexus server communication, 442
  objects, 441
Password Change Notification Service (PCNS), 569–70
  configuration utility, 570
  defined, 569
  non-Windows to Windows full synchronization, 570
  non-Windows to Windows partial synchronization, 570
  password filter dll, 570

service, 570
targets, 569
Windows to non-Windows full
    synchronization, 570
Password configuration, 77–83
Password management
    controlling, 707–10
    options, 708–9
Password Reset Disk (PRD), 96–98
    defined, 96
    Forgotten Password Wizard, 97
    on standalone Windows XP machine, 97
Passwords
    account properties, 77–79
    administrator reset tools, 96
    anonymous, 417
    bulk change tools, 93–95
    caching, 84
    change permission, 86
    cracking on preauthentication data, 381
    credentials, 77–100
    generation, online, 85–86
    guidelines, 83–86
    Kerberos and, 310
    longer, 84
    machine, 98–100
    policy settings, 79–80
    quality, checking, 86–93
    quality enhancement, 83–95
    random, generation, 85
    reporting tools, 82–83
    reset permission, 86
    reset tools, 95–98
    saving, 83–84
    as secret key, 314
    stronger, 84–86
    time limit, 310
Password synchronization, 505
    bidirectional, 506
    ENTSSO, 568–70
    password filtering DLL, 512

secure, 508
SFU and R2, 507–12
solutions, 506–12
SSO and, 506
SSO (logical), 544
SSO (physical), 545
Password Synchronization Service, 507–12
    administration, 507
    architecture (UNIX to Windows), 511
    architecture (Windows to UNIX), 510
    parameters, 508
    secure password synchronization, 508
PDC Emulator, 52
Permcopy, 690
Permissions
    assigning, 148–50
    authenticated users, 710, 734
    default, for new OUs, 734
    default, for new user objects, 735
    default share, 659
    effective, 660–61
    inheritance, 634, 635
    NTFS root directory, 659
    OU, removing, 740
    ownership, 618–19
    property sets, 641
    read, 740
Personal Information property set, 643, 644,
    759
Personalization, 30
Personally identifiable information (PII), 210
Personal Secure Drive (PSD), 225, 227
PKI-based SSO, 541–43
    authentication, 542
    defined, 541
    list, 543
    as new technology, 542
    pros/cons, 550
    token-based SSO versus, 542
    See also Single Sign-On (SSO)
PKINIT, 388

Platform for Privacy Preferences (P3P), 442
Pluggable authentication module (PAM),
        484–87
    account management modules, 486
    architecture, 485
    authentication protocols/methods, 484
    configuration file, 485
    defined, 484
    logic hashes, 502
    password management modules, 486
    services, 486
    session management modules, 486
    stackable modules, 485
    Windows equivalent, 487
Policy Administration Points (PAPs), 12
Policy Decision Points (PDPs), 12
Policy Enforcement Points (PEPs), 12
Policy objects, 40
Pop-up blocking, 190–92
    behavior, 192
    configuration illustration, 191
    configuration options, 190–91
    default, 191–92
    detection, 191
Preauthentication, 378–81
    attack protection, 381
    benefits, 380
    data, 380
    data, password cracking based on, 381
    See also Kerberos
Primary domain controller (PDC), 49
Principal identifiers, 54–68
    logon names, 55–56
    security identifiers (SIDs), 60–68
    See also Security principals
Print spooler services, 387
Privacy
    management, 31
    protection policies, 19
Private data objects, 40
Private LSA secrets, 41

Privilege Attribute Certificate (PAC), 361,
        374–78, 483
    authorization data storage method,
        376–77
    defined, 374
    group-membership data, 376
    user account data stored in, 374
    See also Kerberos
Privilege Bar, 176–77
    defined, 176
    illustrated, 177
Profile cookies, 440–41
    additional, 440–41
    general, 440, 441
Property-based ACEs, 639
Property sets, 641, 642
    attributes, removing, 760–63, 764–66
    attributes, setting inherited permissions,
        763–64
    built-in, adjusting, 758–66
    default, 643
    default, list, 642
    definition, 643
    permission, 641
    permission challenge, 758
    Personal Information, 643, 644, 759
    schema attributes, determining, 647
Provisioning, 30
Provisioning systems, 22–23
    services/components, 23
    solutions, 22
Proxy-based WAMS, 14
Proxy tickets, 347, 351
    delegation exchange for, 348
    delegation setup, 348
Public key infrastructures (PKIs), 7,
        446, 450
PUID-SID, 444
Pwdump2 tool, 89

Quotas, AD objects, 665–67

RADIUS, 536, 577–79
  IAS proxy, 579
  proxy function, 577
  requests, 577
  servers, 578
RainbowCrack, 88, 93
Read-Only Domain Controller (RODC),
    697
Regedit, 171
Regedt32, 171
Registration authorities (RAs), 16
Relative Identifiers (RIDs), 377
Remote Desktop (RDP) connections, 177,
    609
Remote Interactive Logon well-known
    security principal, 609
Remote procedure calls (RPCs)
  automatically opening/closing, 183
  dynamic service-port mappings and, 162
  operation, 163
  variable ports use, 183
  WF and, 183
Replication
  domain-only, 45
  forest-wide, 45
  monitor, 397
  well-known security principals, 601
Restricted Code well-known security
    principal, 608–9
Restricted security zone, 195
RID Master, 52
Rights Management Services (RMS), 33, 230,
    679
Role-based access control (RBAC), 679
  applications, 684
  DAC comparison, 682
  introducing, 680–83
  role concept, 681
RunAs, 167–73
  as default action, 169, 170
  multiple nested commands, 173

Restricted Code well-known security
    principal and, 608–9
  switches, 172
  using from command line, 169
  using from Windows Explorer, 169, 170
  using to start Windows shell, 172
  See also Least privilege

Samba, 496–98
  defined, 496
  features/functionality, 497–98
  HOWTO Collection documentation,
    524–25
  resources, 498
  server platforms, 497
  versions, 497
  winbind, 521–28
Schema Analyzer, 648
Schema Master, 51
Sdcheck, 691
Secondary Logon Service (SLS) service, 169
Secret key, 312, 314
Secure Attention Sequence (SAS), 239
Secure channels, 154–60
  creation, 154
  defined, 155
  requestor, authentication, 155
  security registry settings, 157–58
  services, fine-tuning, 157–58
  setup, 155, 252
  setup, controlling, 156
  troubleshooting tools, 159–60
  trust and, 154–60
  validating, 156–57
  in Windows environment, 155
Secure client-side credential caching,
    546–47
  authentication, 546
  defined, 546
  implementation, 547
  products, 547

Secure client-side credential caching *(cont'd.)*
  pros/cons, 550
  See also Credential caching
Secure HTTP (HTTPs), 445
Secure server-side credential caching, 547–49
  authentication, 548
  challenges, 549
  defined, 547
  master credential database, 547
  products, 549
  pros/cons, 550
  See also Credential caching
Secure Sockets Layer (SSL), 199, 411
  bridging, 475
  channel encryption services, 446
  client authentication, 446
  clients, 448
  in firewall environments, 471–75
  load balancing and, 469–71
  negotiations, limiting number of, 469
  Passport use, 431
  in proxy environments, 471–75
  security services, 446
  servers, 448
  server-side performance, 469
  session-ID based persistence, 471
  setup, 449–63
  tunneling, 471, 473, 475
  Web browser support, 463–64
  X.509 certificates, 449
SecurID authentication, 227
Security Accounts Manager (SAM), 40
  files, 88–89
  security database, 89
Security Assertion Markup Language (SAML),
    26, 551
Security authorities, 37–52
  defined, 37
  kingdom, 37–38
  local, 39–44
  local versus domain, 38–39

security principals and, 53
  trust relationships and, 110
Security Center
  configuration interface, 184
  defined, 183
  dialogs, 183
  notification, 184
Security configuration
  defined, 18
  policies, 19
Security Configuration Tool Set (SCTS), 626
Security Descriptor Definition Language
    (SDDL), 662
Security descriptors
  of AD objects, 585–86
  default, 661–64
  defined, 585
Security groups, 591
  built-in, 597–98
  list, 597–98
  See also Groups
Security identifiers (SIDs), 60–68, 377
  creation, 60
  defined, 60
  filtering. *See* SID filtering
  history, 657–59
  layout, 60–63
  predefined layouts, 61–62
  structure, 61
  top-level authorities, 62–63
  utilities, 67–68
  well-known, 63–66
Security management infrastructures,
    6, 18–23
  access control management, 18
  compliance management, 18
  directories, 21–22
  federation management, 18
  policy controls, 18–19
  provisioning systems, 22–23
  security configuration, 18

solutions, 20
user management, 18
Security principals, 53–108
account lockouts, 100–108
account management, 69–73
concept, 53
defined, 47
identity, verifying, 54
Kerberos limit, 310
key Windows accounts, 73–77
password credentials, 77–100
principal identifiers, 54–68
security authority and, 53
SELF, 732
well-known, 598–610
Security Reference Monitor (SRM), 583–84,
651
access token retrieval, 652
checks, 584
null DACL and, 657
Security support provider interface (SSPI),
247, 487
defined, 248
SSP modules, 487
workbench, 249, 250
Security support providers (SSPs), 244, 247,
327–28, 427
Security zones, 194–205
central administration, 203–4
classification, 195
complexity, 194
configuration settings, controlling, 203–5
configuring, 195–96
default security levels, 197
defined, 194
defining, 194–99
explicitly adding URLs to, 200
illustrated, 196
Internet, 195
Local Computer, 195, 201–2
Local Intranet, 194

Local Machine, 193
machine-level-only configuration settings,
202–3
predefined, 194–95
Restricted Sites, 195
security option default values, 197–98
Trusted Sites, 195
Web site identification, 189–201
Selective authentication, 127–32
administrator benefit, 130
benefits, 130–32
defined, 127
enabling, 129
between forests, 133
security identity, 132
See also Authentication
SELF security principal, 732
Self service, 30
Self-SSL Internet Information Server Resource
Kit, 457
Self well-known security principal, 610
Server for NIS, 500–506
administration interface, 503, 504
installation, 502
Server Message Block (SMB), 387, 496
Service accounts authentication, 252
Service administrators, 695, 696
Service-for-User (S4U), 351
Service-for-User-to-Proxy (S4U2Proxy), 351,
358
Service-for-User-to-Self (S4U2Self), 351,
352, 355–57
combined S4UsProxy operation, 358
defined, 355
illustrated, 352, 357
operation steps, 357
use requirements, 356
Service Guide Kit (SGK), 429
Service principal names (SPNs), 57–60, 427
defined, 57
displaying, 59

Service principal names (SPNs) *(cont'd.)*
    format, 59–60
    role in logon, 332–33
    storage, 58
Services for UNIX (SFU), 495
Session keys, 309
    defined, 316
    distribution, 317–19
    encrypted, 309
    secure transport, 314–17
    U2U, 325
Setok.exe, 603
Setprfdc.exe, 158, 160
Setspn, 397
SharePoint Portal Server, 570–73
    architecture, 571
    message exchange, 571–73
    operation, 571–73
    SSO, 570–73
    SSO administration interface, 572
    SSO flow, 572
Shortcut trusts
    examples, 339
    multiple domain logon and, 338–39
Showacls, 690
Showmbrs, 690
Showpriv, 690
Sid2user, 67
SID filtering, 122–27
    defined, 123
    disabling, 125, 140
    between two forests, 123
SIDHistory attribute, 125, 127
SID&User (SAU), 67
Sidwalker, 691
Simple and Protected GSS-API Negotiation
        Mechanism (SPNEGO),
        526–27
Simple Authentication and Security Layer
        (SASL), 526
Simple network time protocol (SNTP), 253

Single domain, authentication and
        authorization, 361–64
Single domain logon
    interactive, 328–30
    noninteractive, 330, 331
    SPN role, 332–33
    See also Logon
Single Sign-On (SSO), 4
    AD federation services, 573–77
    architectures, 535–50
    architectures pros/cons, 549–50
    architectures summary, 549–50
    complex architectures, 538–49
    Credential Manager, 553–59
    credential synchronization, 543–46, 550
    defined, 30, 533
    enterprise, 534–35
    ENTSSO, 559–70
    extending, 550–53
    host-initiated, 562
    IAS, 577–79
    password synchronization and, 506
    PKI-based, 541–43, 550
    pros/cons, 533–34
    secure client-side credential caching,
        546–47, 550
    secure server-side credential caching,
        547–49, 550
    services, 24
    SharePoint Portal Server, 570–73
    simple architectures, 535–38
    technologies, 553–79
    technologies list, 554
    token-based, 539–41, 549
    Web, 534–35
    Windows-initiated, 562, 566
Smart card logon, 388–90
    illustrated, 390
    Kerberos support, 307
    trust model, 389
    See also Logon

Software Update Services (SUS), 35
SpyNet, 208–9
Spy Sweeper Enterprise, 214
Spyware
    defined, 206
    freeware tools, 214
    protection guidelines, 214–15
SSL client certificates, 462–63
    getting, 462–63
    trust, 463
SSL Diagnostics (SSLDiag) tool, 450
    Common Name, 454
    functions, 450
    interface, 451
    for troubleshooting IIS SSL setup, 451
SSL server certificates
    configuring on Web server, 458–62
    generating, 455–57
    information, 454
    installing on Web server, 457–58
    request file, 455
    request generation, 451–55
SSL/TLS
    certificate trust error, 467
    client/server handshake, 447
    configuration options comparison, 464
    defined, 236
    exchanges, 448
    IE lock symbol, 447
    operation, 448, 449
    positioning, 446
    revocation check error, 467
    revocation checking option, 468
    secure connection, 447
    server certificate, 452
    SSL port configuration, 460
    Web server certificates, installing,
        457–58
    Web site security attributes, 458–59
Start of authority (SOA), 253
Storage Root Key (SRK), 223

Stored User Names and Passwords dialog box,
    555
Strong credential sign-in, 434
Subinacl, 690
Symmetric key ciphers, 15, 17
Symmetric key cryptography, 310–12
    illustrated, 311
    Kerberos authentication, 311
    NTLM use, 311
System ACLs (SACLs), 588
System key, 42–44
    configuring, 43
    defined, 42
    levels, 44
    system data protection, 42
Systems Management Server (SMS),
        33, 34–35
    architecture, 35
    defined, 34
    Software Update Services (SUS), 35

TACACS, 536
TACACS+, 536
Taskpads, 725
This Organization well-known security
        principal, 608
Ticket Granting Service (TGS), 323, 340
Ticket-granting ticket (TGT), 319–22, 364
    defined, 320
    referral, 366
    reuse, 322
    role, 321
    ticket flags, 382–84
Ticketing
    distribution, 317, 318
    faster authentication, 305
    for session key transport, 315
    See also Kerberos
Tickets
    analyzing, 369–71
    authenticator relationship, 369

Tickets *(cont'd.)*
    cache, purging, 364
    client address field, 371
    content, 370
    cookies, 440
    delegation flags, 347
    flags, 382–84
    forwardable, 347
    PAC field, 377
    proxy, 347
    purpose, 369
Timestamps, 310
Token-based SSO systems
    authentication, 540
    defined, 539
    Kerberos, 540
    list, 541
    PKI-based SSO versus, 542
    pros/cons, 549
    See also Single Sign-On (SSO)
TokenBloat attacks, 379
Tokens, 310
Tokensz tool, 378, 397
Top Level Name (TLN)
    example, 136, 137
    filtering, 134
    restrictions, 135, 136, 154
TPM key hierarchy, 222–26
    application-specific keys, 225–26
    defined, 222–23
    Endorsement Key (EK), 223
    illustrated, 224
    resource, 223
    signing/storage keys, 225
    Storage Root Key (SRK), 223
    user storage keys (USKs), 223–25
    See also Trusted Platform Module (TPM)
Transitive trusts, 114
    in DC versions and, 341
    in mixed-mode domains, 341
    See also Trusts

Transport layer security (TLS) protocol,
    411, 445
Troubleshooting
    authentication, 292–300
    authorization, 690–91
    Kerberos, 394–96
    secure channels, 159–60
Trusted Computing Platform Alliance
    (TCPA), 216
Trusted domain, 110, 111
Trusted Domain Object (TDO), 133, 340
    account, 150, 151
    defined, 40
    object attributes, 152–53
    objects, checking, 152
    replication, 154
Trusted Platform Module (TPM)
    administrative concepts, 219–22
    administrative roles, 220
    applications, 226–28
    cryptographic key creation, 215
    defined, 215
    as embedded smart card, 216
    hardware requirements, 218–19
    key hierarchy. *See* TPM key hierarchy
    owner, 220–21
    recovery agent, 221–22
    security functions, 215–28
    software requirements, 218–19
    specifications, 216
    user(s), 221
    in Windows Vista, 217
Trusted security infrastructures (TSIs)
    auditing systems, 7
    authentication infrastructures, 6, 9–11
    authorization infrastructures, 6, 11–15
    building blocks, 31–35
    challenge, 3–35
    components, 6–7
    core security services, 4
    identity management and, 27–31

key management infrastructures, 7, 15–18
layer, 5
outsourcing and, 4
positioning, 5–7
roles, 8–23
security management infrastructures, 6,
    18–23
unified/universal security infrastructure, 6
Trusted security zone, 195
Trusted third-parties (TTPs), 3, 122, 539
    centralized environment, 4
    cryptographic methods, 539
TRUSTe privacy label initiative, 442
Trusting domain, 110
Trust relationships, 109–63
    AD, 113–14
    behind the scenes, 151
    classification properties, 111
    creating, 145–48
    defining, 109–11
    forest, 119–20
    granular definition, 116
    monitoring, with WMI, 159
    security authorities and, 110
    two-way, 113–14
Trusts
    creation methods, 147–48
    cross-realm, 403–8
    direct, between domains, 143
    features, 116–17
    firewalls and, 161–63
    forest, 116, 118–22
    fundamental role, 8
    manual creation, 147–48
    name resolution, 143–45
    name suffix routing, 132–39
    nontechnological solutions, 8
    number required, 115
    properties, 112, 114
    properties, setting from command line, 126
    restricting, 122–39

scope, minimizing, 141
scope of authenticated users across, 128
secure channels and, 154–60
selective authentication, 127–32
shortcut, 338–39
SID filtering, 122–27
smart card logon, 389
transitive, 114, 341
types, 112
types, selecting, 139–43
wizard, 116–17
working with, 139–50
Tunneling, SSL, 471

Unique identifiers, 28
Universal groups, 591
    group membership and, 616
    nesting rules, 594
    scope conversion, 595
    for user resource access, 616
    See also Groups
Universal naming Convention (UNC) names,
    201
UNIX KDC, 402
UNIX/Linux
    account management and authentication
        integration, 498–532
    authentication comparison, 478–79
    local files, 491
    naming services, 487–88
    NIS, 491–93
    NIS+, 493–94
    NIS/LDAP integration, 494–96
    NSS, 488–91
    PAM, 484–87
    Samba, 496–98
    security concepts, 484–98
URLscan, 410
User
    linking to groups, 737
    logon, 254–55

User *(cont'd.)*
  management, 18, 31
  permissions, 623
  privileges, 255, 622
User2sid, 67
User Account Control (UAC), 168
User Account Protection (UAP), 167, 229
User Accounts control panel applet, 72–73
User Accounts dialog box, 72
User Administration role, 710, 711, 712–14
  description, 715
  permissions, 715
  required permissions, 712–14
  sample, 712–14
  sample task list, 711
User Password Reset role, 710
User Principal Names (UPNs), 55–56, 332
  format, 55
  suffixes, 56, 134
  suffixes, defining, 56–60
User rights, 255, 622–24
  assigning, 261
  categories, 622
  defined, 590
  logon rights, 622
  user permission versus, 624
  user privileges, 622
  Windows 2000, 622–23
  Windows Server 2003, 623, 624
User Self Management, 731–32
User storage keys (USKs), 223–25
UserTokenTTL system registry entry, 423
User-to-user authentication, 324–26
  defined, 324–25
  illustrated, 326
  session key, 325
  uses, 325
  See also Authentication

Vintela Authentication Services (VAS),
    525–28

AD-based password policy support,
    527–28
automatic keytab maintenance, 527
command line-based configuration,
    528
computer-based access control, 528
defined, 525
disconnected authentication, 528
features, 525
GSS-API, 526
illustrated, 526
intelligent caching of LDAP data, 528
NIS data migration tools, 528
NSS module, 525
PAM module, 525
SASL, 526
simplified time synchronization, 528
UID/GID conflict checking, 528
UNIX/Linux platform support, 525
Virtual directories, 22
Virtual private networking (VPN)
  connectors, 16
  tunnel endpoints, 5
VMWare, 68

Web access management systems (WAMS),
    9, 10, 13–15, 536
  centralize authorization decision making,
    13
  central policy engine, 14
  organizations, building, 24
  proxy-based, 14
  software products, 14
  vendors, 15
Web authentication infrastructures, 9
WebFetch (WFetch) tool, 418, 444
Web sites, SSL/TLS security attributes,
    458–59
Web SSO, 535
Welcome screen, 241

Well-known security principals,
        598–610
    in AD, 604
    adding to ACL, 605
    administering, 603–5
    in ADUC, 605
    Authenticated Users, 604–6
    Authentication Protocol Related, 610
    checking, 603
    Creator Group, 610
    Creator Owner, 610
    defined, 598
    groups, 600
    list, 601, 602
    Logon Type, 610
    Other Organization, 608
    primary role, 601
    Remote Interactive Logon, 609
    replication, 601
    Restricted Code, 608–9
    Self, 610
    SID, 598
    This Organization, 608
    See also Security principals
Well-known SIDs, 63–66
    defined, 63
    list, 63–66
Whoami tool, 68, 690
Winbind, 521–28
    architecture, 522
    architecture illustration, 523
    daemon, 522
    defined, 521
Winbind_idmap.tdb, 523
Windows
    access control model, 585
    administrator, 222
    group mapping, 562
    impersonation levels, 589
    individual mapping, 562

Windows 2000
    ACL editor, 626–27
    ACL evaluation process, 651–57
    authorization changes, 624–59
    delegation in, 350–51, 355
    fine-grained control over inheritance,
        627–35
    object type-based ACEs, 635–51
    SID history, 657–59
    user rights, 622–23
Windows accounts, 73–77
    administrator, 73, 74–75
    guest, 75–77
Windows and UNIX/Linux integration,
        498–531
    centralized user management solutions,
        498, 512–32
    coexistence solutions, 498, 500–512
    solution overview, 499
    SSO solutions, 499, 533–79
Windows authentication
    architecture, 242–50
    basics, 238–55
    concepts, 238–42
    interactive, architecture, 243–47
    in machine startup, 250–53
    noninteractive, architecture, 247–50
    UNIX/Linux authentication comparison,
        478–79
    user logon, 254–55
    See also Authentication
Windows Defender, 206–14
    alerts, 212
    changes, 206–7
    configuration settings, 208
    defined, 206
    extra tools, 213–14
    getting started, 210–12
    history log, 213
    installation, 207–10

overview, 207–10
real-time protection, 208
real-time protection configuration,
    212–13
run as a service, 207
scan results, 210
scan results screen, 211
software explorer, 213
SpyNet participation levels, 209
summary screen, 211
Windows Firewall (WF), 178–83
    boot-time policy, 179–80
    configuration profile support, 182
    configured as Windows XP unattended
        setup, 182
    dialog box, 181
    enabling, 181–82
    global configuration interface, 180
    GPO configuration, 181
    RPCs and, 183
    startup detection, 181
    unattended setup configuration, 182
Windows-initiated SSO, 562, 566
Windows Internet Name Service (WINS),
    144, 145, 487
Windows Live ID, 428, 429–30
Windows Management Instrumentation
    (WMI)
    CIM repository, 691
    monitoring trust relationships with, 159
Windows Server 2003
    ACL editor, 627
    AD domains, 46
    authorization, 583–691
    authorization changes, 659–90
    Authorization Manager, 679–90
    authorization settings, 659–60
    Common Criteria Configuration Guide,
        32, 33
    Confidential Bit, 667–72

default AD security descriptor changes,
    661–64
domain functional levels, 596
effective permissions, 660–61
extended rights, 649–50
forest trust attributes, 154
hiding data in file system and shares,
    672–79
Identity Management for UNIX
    components, 500
Link Value Replication (LVR), 664–65
Passport integration, 443–45
Passport user changes, 435–36
password policy GPO settings, 79–80
predefined delegation tasks, 721
principal identifiers, 54–68
quotas for AD objects, 665–67
SP1, 32
trust wizard, 116–17
as TSI building block, 31–33
user rights, 623, 624
validated writes, 650
Windows Update Service (WUS), 185
Windows Update (WU), 185
Windows Vista
    least privilege support, 168
    owner rights in, 622
    TPM in, 217
Windows XP SP2 security, 178–86
    changes, 185–86
    easier management, 183–85
    Internet Explorer, 187–205
    Windows Firewall (WF), 178–83
Worker process isolation mode (WPIM),
    410
World Wide Web Consortium (W3C), 442
WS-Federation, 26

X.509 certificates, 449
Xcacls, 691

Ypldapd, 513
    binary distribution, 514
    required steps, 513–14
    See also NIS/LDAP gateway

Zone elevation blocking, 193

Lightning Source UK Ltd.
Milton Keynes UK
UKHW021606260922
409461UK00007B/1689